Generative AI with␣ TensorFlow 2

Create images, text, and music with VAEs, GANs, LSTMs, GPT models and more

Joseph Babcock

Raghav Bali

Packt>

BIRMINGHAM - MUMBAI

Generative AI with Python and TensorFlow 2

Copyright © 2021 Packt Publishing

All rights reserved. No part of this book may be reproduced, stored in a retrieval system, or transmitted in any form or by any means, without the prior written permission of the publisher, except in the case of brief quotations embedded in critical articles or reviews.

Every effort has been made in the preparation of this book to ensure the accuracy of the information presented. However, the information contained in this book is sold without warranty, either express or implied. Neither the authors, nor Packt Publishing or its dealers and distributors, will be held liable for any damages caused or alleged to have been caused directly or indirectly by this book.

Packt Publishing has endeavored to provide trademark information about all of the companies and products mentioned in this book by the appropriate use of capitals. However, Packt Publishing cannot guarantee the accuracy of this information.

Producer: Tushar Gupta

Acquisition Editor – Peer Reviews: Suresh Jain, Saby D'silva

Content Development Editors: Lucy Wan, Joanne Lovell

Technical Editor: Gaurav Gavas

Project Editor: Janice Gonsalves

Copy Editor: Safis Editing

Proofreader: Safis Editing

Indexer: Pratik Shirodkar

Presentation Designer: Pranit Padwal

First published: April 2021

Production reference: 2190521

Published by Packt Publishing Ltd.
Livery Place
35 Livery Street
Birmingham B3 2PB, UK.

ISBN 978-1-80020-088-3

www.packt.com

Contributors

About the authors

Joseph Babcock has over a decade of experience in machine learning and developing big data solutions. He applied predictive modeling to drug discovery and genomics during his doctoral studies in neurosciences, and has since worked and led data science teams in the streaming media, e-commerce, and financial services industries. He previously authored *Mastering Predictive Analytics with Python* and *Python: Advanced Predictive Analytics* with Packt.

> *I would like to acknowledge my family for their support during the composition of this book.*

Raghav Bali is a data scientist and a published author. He has led advanced analytics initiatives working with several Fortune 500 companies like Optum (UHG), Intel, and American Express. His work involves research and development of enterprise solutions leveraging machine learning and deep learning. He holds a Master of Technology degree (gold medalist) from IIIT Bangalore, with specializations in machine learning and software engineering. Raghav has authored several books on R, Python, machine learning, and deep learning, including *Hands-On Transfer Learning with Python*.

> *To my wife, parents, and brother, without whom this would not have been possible. To all the researchers whose work continues to inspire me to learn. And to my co-author, reviewers, and the Packt team (especially Tushar, Janice, and Lucy) for their hard work in transforming our work into this amazing book.*

About the reviewers

Hao-Wen Dong is currently a PhD student in Computer Science and Engineering at the University of California, San Diego, working with Prof. Julian McAuley and Prof. Taylor Berg-Kirkpatrick. His research interests lie at the intersection of music and machine learning, with a recent focus on music generation. He is interested in building tools that could lower the barrier of entry for music composition and potentially lead to the democratization of music creation. Previously, he did a research internship in the R&D Division at Yamaha Corporation. Before that, he was a research assistant in the Music and AI Lab directed by Dr. Yi-Hsuan Yang at Academia Sinica. He received his bachelor's degree in Electrical Engineering from National Taiwan University.

Gokula Krishnan Santhanam is a Python developer who lives in Zurich, Switzerland. He has been working with deep learning techniques for more than 5 years. He has worked on problems in generative modeling, adversarial attacks, interpretability, and predictive maintenance while working at IBM Research and interning at Google. He finished his master's in Computer Science at ETH Zurich and his bachelor's at BITS Pilani. When he's not working, you can find him enjoying board games with his wife or hiking in the beautiful Alps.

I would like to thank my wife, Sadhana, for her continuous help and support and for always being there when I need her.

Table of Contents

Preface	**ix**
Chapter 1: An Introduction to Generative AI: "Drawing" Data from Models	**1**
Applications of AI	**2**
Discriminative and generative models	3
Implementing generative models	6
The rules of probability	**7**
Discriminative and generative modeling and Bayes' theorem	10
Why use generative models?	**12**
The promise of deep learning	12
Building a better digit classifier	13
Generating images	13
Style transfer and image transformation	**14**
Fake news and chatbots	17
Sound composition	17
The rules of the game	17
Unique challenges of generative models	**18**
Summary	**18**
References	**19**
Chapter 2: Setting Up a TensorFlow Lab	**23**
Deep neural network development and TensorFlow	**24**
TensorFlow 2.0	28
VSCode	**31**
Docker: A lightweight virtualization solution	**32**
Important Docker commands and syntax	33
Connecting Docker containers with docker-compose	35

Kubernetes: Robust management of multi-container applications	**36**
Important Kubernetes commands	38
Kustomize for configuration management	39
Kubeflow: an end-to-end machine learning lab	**42**
Running Kubeflow locally with MiniKF	43
Installing Kubeflow in AWS	44
Installing Kubeflow in GCP	46
Installing Kubeflow on Azure	48
Installing Kubeflow using Terraform	50
A brief tour of Kubeflow's components	**53**
Kubeflow notebook servers	54
Kubeflow pipelines	**55**
Using Kubeflow Katib to optimize model hyperparameters	**60**
Summary	**64**
References	**65**
Chapter 3: Building Blocks of Deep Neural Networks	**67**
Perceptrons – a brain in a function	**68**
From tissues to TLUs	69
From TLUs to tuning perceptrons	73
Multi-layer perceptrons and backpropagation	**75**
Backpropagation in practice	79
The shortfalls of backpropagation	82
Varieties of networks: Convolution and recursive	**84**
Networks for seeing: Convolutional architectures	84
Early CNNs	85
AlexNet and other CNN innovations	87
AlexNet architecture	89
Networks for sequence data	**91**
RNNs and LSTMs	91
Building a better optimizer	**93**
Gradient descent to ADAM	94
Xavier initialization	96
Summary	**97**
References	**97**
Chapter 4: Teaching Networks to Generate Digits	**103**
The MNIST database	**104**
Retrieving and loading the MNIST dataset in TensorFlow	105
Restricted Boltzmann Machines: generating pixels with statistical mechanics	**109**
Hopfield networks and energy equations for neural networks	109

Modeling data with uncertainty with Restricted Boltzmann Machines	111
Contrastive divergence: Approximating a gradient	113

Stacking Restricted Boltzmann Machines to generate images: the Deep Belief Network — 117
Creating an RBM using the TensorFlow Keras layers API — 120
Creating a DBN with the Keras Model API — 127
Summary — 133
References — 133

Chapter 5: Painting Pictures with Neural Networks Using VAEs — 137

Creating separable encodings of images — 138
The variational objective — 143
   The reparameterization trick — 147
Inverse Autoregressive Flow — 148
Importing CIFAR — 150
Creating the network from TensorFlow 2 — 153
Summary — 164
References — 165

Chapter 6: Image Generation with GANs — 167

The taxonomy of generative models — 168
Generative adversarial networks — 170
   The discriminator model — 170
   The generator model — 171
   Training GANs — 172
      Non-saturating generator cost — 174
      Maximum likelihood game — 174
Vanilla GAN — 175
Improved GANs — 181
   Deep Convolutional GAN — 181
      Vector arithmetic — 184
   Conditional GAN — 184
   Wasserstein GAN — 190
Progressive GAN — 196
   The overall method — 196
   Progressive growth-smooth fade-in — 198
   Minibatch standard deviation — 199
   Equalized learning rate — 199
   Pixelwise normalization — 200
   TensorFlow Hub implementation — 200
Challenges — 203
   Training instability — 204
   Mode collapse — 204

Table of Contents

Uninformative loss and evaluation metrics	206
Summary	**206**
References	**207**
Chapter 7: Style Transfer with GANs	**209**
Paired style transfer using pix2pix GAN	**210**
The U-Net generator	211
The Patch-GAN discriminator	216
Loss	219
Training pix2pix	219
Use cases	223
Unpaired style transfer using CycleGAN	**224**
Overall setup for CycleGAN	225
Adversarial loss	227
Cycle loss	228
Identity loss	228
Overall loss	229
Hands-on: Unpaired style transfer with CycleGAN	229
Generator setup	229
Discriminator setup	231
GAN setup	232
The training loop	234
Related works	**238**
DiscoGAN	239
DualGAN	243
Summary	**245**
References	**246**
Chapter 8: Deepfakes with GANs	**247**
Deepfakes overview	**249**
Modes of operation	**251**
Replacement	252
Re-enactment	253
Editing	254
Key feature set	**255**
Facial Action Coding System (FACS)	255
3D Morphable Model	256
Facial landmarks	257
Facial landmark detection using OpenCV	257
Facial landmark detection using dlib	258
Facial landmark detection using MTCNN	260
High-level workflow	**263**
Common architectures	264

[iv]

Table of Contents

Encoder-Decoder (ED)	265
Generative Adversarial Networks (GANs)	265
Replacement using autoencoders	**266**
Task definition	267
Dataset preparation	267
Autoencoder architecture	274
Training our own face swapper	278
Results and limitations	280
Re-enactment using pix2pix	**286**
Dataset preparation	286
Pix2pix GAN setup and training	287
Results and limitations	293
Challenges	**297**
Ethical issues	297
Technical challenges	298
Generalization	298
Occlusions	298
Temporal issues	299
Off-the-shelf implementations	**299**
Summary	**300**
References	**301**
Chapter 9: The Rise of Methods for Text Generation	**305**
Representing text	**306**
Bag of Words	306
Distributed representation	310
Word2vec	311
GloVe	317
FastText	319
Text generation and the magic of LSTMs	**320**
Language modeling	322
Hands-on: Character-level language model	324
Decoding strategies	329
Greedy decoding	329
Beam search	330
Sampling	331
Hands-on: Decoding strategies	333
LSTM variants and convolutions for text	**335**
Stacked LSTMs	336
Bidirectional LSTMs	338
Convolutions and text	340
Summary	**344**
References	**344**

Chapter 10: NLP 2.0: Using Transformers to Generate Text — 347
    Attention — 348
    Contextual embeddings — 350
    Self-attention — 352
    Transformers — 353
        Overall architecture — 353
        Multi-head self-attention — 356
        Positional encodings — 357
    BERT-ology — 358
GPT 1, 2, 3… — 359
    Generative pre-training: GPT — 359
    GPT-2 — 360
        Hands-on with GPT-2 — 363
    Mammoth GPT-3 — 367
Summary — 369
References — 370

Chapter 11: Composing Music with Generative Models — 373
Getting started with music generation — 374
    Representing music — 376
Music generation using LSTMs — 378
    Dataset preparation — 379
    LSTM model for music generation — 383
Music generation using GANs — 385
    Generator network — 386
    Discriminator network — 387
    Training and results — 388
MuseGAN – polyphonic music generation — 391
    Jamming model — 392
    Composer model — 393
    Hybrid model — 393
    Temporal model — 394
    MuseGAN — 395
        Generators — 396
        Critic — 399
        Training and results — 401
Summary — 402
References — 403

Chapter 12: Play Video Games with Generative AI: GAIL — 405
Reinforcement learning: Actions, agents, spaces, policies, and rewards — 406
    Deep Q-learning — 411

Inverse reinforcement learning: Learning from experts	413
Adversarial learning and imitation	417
Running GAIL on PyBullet Gym	**420**
The agent: Actor-Critic network	424
The discriminator	430
Training and results	432
Summary	**438**
References	**438**
Chapter 13: Emerging Applications in Generative AI	**441**
Introduction	441
Finding new drugs with generative models	**442**
Searching chemical space with generative molecular graph networks	442
Folding proteins with generative models	446
Solving partial differential equations with generative modeling	**449**
Few shot learning for creating videos from images	**452**
Generating recipes with deep learning	**453**
Summary	**454**
References	**456**
Other Books You May Enjoy	**461**
Index	**463**

Preface

"Imagination is more important than knowledge."

– Albert Einstein, Einstein on Cosmic Religion and Other Opinions and Aphorisms (2009)

In this book we will explore *generative AI*, a cutting-edge technology for generating synthetic (yet strikingly realistic) data using advanced machine learning algorithms. Generative models have been intriguing researchers across domains for quite some time now. With recent improvements in the fields of machine learning and more specifically deep learning, generative modeling has seen a tremendous uptick in the number of research works and their applications across different areas. From artwork and music composition to synthetic medical datasets, generative modeling is pushing the boundaries of imagination and intelligence alike. The amount of thought and effort required to understand, implement, and utilize such methods is simply amazing. Some of the newer methods (such as GANs) are very powerful, yet difficult to control, making the overall learning process both exciting and frustrating.

Generative AI with Python and TensorFlow 2 is the result of numerous hours of hard work by us authors and the talented team at *Packt Publishing* to help you understand this *deep*, *wide*, and *wild* space of generative modeling. The aim of this book is to be a kaleidoscope of the generative modeling space and cover a wide range of topics. This book takes you on a journey where you don't just read the theory and learn about the fundamentals, but you also discover the potential and impact of these models through worked examples. We will implement these models using a variety of open-source technologies – the Python programming language, the TensorFlow 2 library for deep neural network development, and cloud computing resources such as Google Colab and the Kubeflow project.

Having an understanding of the various topics, models, architectures, and examples in this book will help you explore more complex topics and cutting-edge research with ease.

Who this book is for

Generative AI with Python and TensorFlow 2 is for data scientists, ML engineers, researchers, and developers with an interest in generative modeling and the application of state-of-the-art architectures on real world datasets. This book is also suitable for TensorFlow beginners with intermediate-level deep learning-related skills who are looking to expand their knowledge base.

Basic proficiency in Python and deep learning is all that is required to get started with this book.

What this book covers

Chapter 1, An Introduction to Generative AI: "Drawing" Data from Models, introduces the field of generative AI, from the underlying probability theory to recent examples of applied products of these methods.

Chapter 2, Setting Up a TensorFlow Lab, describes how to set up a computing environment for developing generative AI models with TensorFlow using open source tools – Python, Docker, Kubernetes, and Kubeflow – in order to run a scalable code laboratory in the cloud.

Chapter 3, Building Blocks of Deep Neural Networks, introduces foundational concepts for deep neural networks that will be utilized in the rest of the volume – how they were inspired by biological research, what challenges researchers overcame in developing ever larger and more sophisticated models, and the various building blocks of network architectures, optimizers, and regularizers utilized by generative AI examples in the rest of the book.

Chapter 4, Teaching Networks to Generate Digits, demonstrates how to implement a deep belief network, a breakthrough neural network architecture that achieved state-of-the-art results in classifying images of handwritten digits through a generative AI approach, which teaches the network to generate images before learning to classify them.

Chapter 5, Painting Pictures with Neural Networks Using VAEs, describes variational autoencoders (VAEs), an advancement from deep belief networks which create sharper images of complex objects through clever use of an objective function grounded in Bayesian statistics. The reader will implement both a basic and advanced VAE which utilizes inverse autoregressive flow (IAF), a recursive transformation that can map random numbers to complex data distributions to create striking synthetic images.

Chapter 6, Image Generation with GANs, introduces generative adversarial networks, or GANs, as powerful deep learning architectures for generative modeling. Starting with the building blocks of GANs and other fundamental concepts, this chapter covers a number of GAN architectures and how they are used to generate high resolution images from random noise.

Chapter 7, Style Transfer with GANs, focuses on a creative application of generative modeling, particularly GANs, called style transfer. Applications such as transforming black and white images to colored ones, aerial maps to Google Maps-like outputs, and background removal are all made possible using style transfer. We cover a number of paired and unpaired architectures like pix2pix and CycleGAN.

Chapter 8, Deepfakes with GANs, introduces an interesting and controversial application of GANs called deepfakes. The chapter discusses the basic building blocks for deepfakes, such as features and different modes of operations, along with a number of key architectures. It also includes a number of hands-on examples to generate fake photos and videos based on key concepts covered, so readers can create their own deepfake pipelines.

Chapter 9, The Rise of Methods for Text Generation, introduces concepts and techniques relating to text generation tasks. We first cover the very basics of language generation using deep learning models, starting from different ways of representing text in vector space. We progress to different architectural choices and decoding mechanisms to achieve high quality outputs. This chapter lays the foundation for more complex text generation methods covered in the subsequent chapter.

Chapter 10, NLP 2.0: Using Transformers to Generate Text, covers the latest and greatest in the NLP domain, with a primary focus on the text generation capabilities of some of the state-of-the-art architectures (like GPT-x) based on transformers and the like, and how they have revolutionized the language generation and NLP domain in general.

Chapter 11, Composing Music with Generative Models, covers music generation using generative models. This is an interesting yet challenging application of generative models and involves understanding a number of nuances and concepts associated with music. This chapter covers a number of different methods to generate music, from basic LSTMs to simple GANs and eventually MuseGAN for polyphonic music generation.

Preface

Chapter 12, *Play Video Games with Generative AI: GAIL*, describes the connection between generative AI and reinforcement learning, a branch of machine learning that teaches "agents" to navigate real or virtual "environments" while performing specified tasks. Through a connection between GANs and reinforcement learning, the reader will teach a hopping figure to navigate a 3D environment by imitating an expert example of this movement.

Chapter 13, *Emerging Applications in Generative AI*, describes recent research in generative AI, spanning biotechnology, fluid mechanics, video, and text synthesis.

To get the most out of this book

To be able to follow along with this book's code, the following requirements are recommended:

- Hardware (for local computation):
    - 128GB HDD
    - 8GB RAM
    - Intel Core i5 processor or better
    - NVIDIA 8GB graphics card or better (GTX1070 or better)
- Software:
    - Python 3.6 and above
    - TensorFlow 2.x
    - Chrome/Safari/Firefox browser for directly executing code through Google Colab or Kubeflow (if training in the cloud)

Download the example code files

The code bundle for the book is hosted on GitHub at https://github.com/PacktPublishing/Hands-On-Generative-AI-with-Python-and-TensorFlow-2. We also have other code bundles from our rich catalog of books and videos available at https://github.com/PacktPublishing/. Check them out!

Download the color images

We also provide a PDF file that has color images of the screenshots/diagrams used in this book. You can download it here: https://static.packt-cdn.com/downloads/9781800200883_ColorImages.pdf.

Conventions used

There are a number of text conventions used throughout this book.

`CodeInText`: Indicates code words in text, database table names, folder names, filenames, file extensions, pathnames, dummy URLs, user input, and Twitter handles. For example: "We can visually plot some examples using the `show_examples()` function."

A block of code is set as follows:

```
def cd_update(self, x):
    with tf.GradientTape(watch_accessed_variables=False) as g:
        h_sample = self.sample_h(x)
        for step in range(self.cd_steps):
            v_sample = tf.constant(self.sample_v(h_sample))
            h_sample = self.sample_h(v_sample)
```

When we wish to draw your attention to a particular part of a code block, the relevant lines or items are set in bold:

```
def cd_update(self, x):
    with tf.GradientTape(watch_accessed_variables=False) as g:
        h_sample = self.sample_h(x)
        for step in range(self.cd_steps):
            v_sample = tf.constant(self.sample_v(h_sample))
            h_sample = self.sample_h(v_sample)
```

Any command-line input or output is written as follows:

```
pip install tensorflow-datasets
```

Bold: Indicates a new term, an important word, or words that you see on the screen, for example, in menus or dialog boxes, also appear in the text like this. For example: "Select **System info** from the **Administration** panel."

> Warnings or important notes appear like this.

> Tips and tricks appear like this.

Get in touch

Feedback from our readers is always welcome.

General feedback: If you have questions about any aspect of this book, mention the book title in the subject of your message and email Packt at customercare@packtpub.com.

Errata: Although we have taken every care to ensure the accuracy of our content, mistakes do happen. If you have found a mistake in this book, we would be grateful if you could report this to us. Please visit www.packtpub.com/support/errata, select your book, click on the **Errata Submission Form** link, and enter the details.

Piracy: If you come across any illegal copies of our works in any form on the Internet, we would be grateful if you would provide us with the location address or website name. Please contact us at copyright@packtpub.com with a link to the material.

If you are interested in becoming an author: If there is a topic that you have expertise in and you are interested in either writing or contributing to a book, please visit http://authors.packtpub.com.

Reviews

Please leave a review. Once you have read and used this book, why not leave a review on the site that you purchased it from? Potential readers can then see and use your unbiased opinion to make purchase decisions, we at Packt can understand what you think about our products, and our authors can see your feedback on their book. Thank you!

For more information about Packt, please visit packtpub.com.

1
An Introduction to Generative AI: "Drawing" Data from Models

In this chapter, we will dive into the various applications of generative models. Before that, we will take a step back and examine how exactly generative models are different from other types of machine learning. The difference lies with the basic units of any machine learning algorithm: probability and the various ways we use mathematics to quantify the shape and distribution of data we encounter in the world.

In the rest of this chapter, we will cover:

- Applications of AI
- Discriminative and generative models
- Implementing generative models
- The rules of probability
- Why use generative models?
- Unique challenges of generative models

Applications of AI

In New York City in October 2018, the international auction house Christie's sold the **Portrait of Edmond Belamy** (*Figure 1.1*) during the show **Prints & Multiples** for $432,500.00. This sale was remarkable both because the sale price was 45 times higher than the initial estimates for the piece, and due to the unusual origin of this portrait. Unlike the majority of other artworks sold by Christie's since the 18th century, the **Portrait of Edmond Belamy** is not painted using oil or watercolors, nor is its creator even human; rather, it is an entirely digital image produced by a sophisticated machine learning algorithm. The creators—a Paris-based collective named Obvious—used a collection of 15,000 portraits created between the 14th and 20th centuries to tune an artificial neural network model capable of generating aesthetically similar, albeit synthetic, images.

Figure 1.1: The Portrait of Edmond Belamy[1]

Portraiture is far from the only area in which machine learning has demonstrated astonishing results. Indeed, if you have paid attention to the news in the last few years, you have likely seen many stories about the ground-breaking results of modern AI systems applied to diverse problems, from the hard sciences to digital art. Deep neural network models, such as the one created by Obvious, can now classify X-ray images of human anatomy on the level of trained physicians,[2] beat human masters at both classic board games such as Go (an Asian game similar to chess)[3] and multiplayer computer games,[4] and translate French into English with amazing sensitivity to grammatical nuances.[5]

Discriminative and generative models

These other examples of AI differ in an important way from the model that generated **The Portrait of Edmond Belamy**. In all of these other applications, the model is presented with a set of inputs—data such as English text, images from X-rays, or the positions on a gameboard—that is paired with a target output, such as the next word in a translated sentence, the diagnostic classification of an X-ray, or the next move in a game. Indeed, this is probably the kind of AI model you are most familiar with from prior experiences of predictive modeling; they are broadly known as **discriminative** models, whose purpose is to create a mapping between a set of input variables and a target output. The target output could be a set of discrete classes (such as which word in the English language appears next in a translation), or a continuous outcome (such as the expected amount of money a customer will spend in an online store over the next 12 months).

It should be noted that this kind of model, in which data is **labeled** or **scored**, represents only half the capabilities of modern machine learning. Another class of algorithms, such as the one that generated the artificial portrait sold at Christie's, don't compute a score or label from input variables, but rather **generate new data**. Unlike discriminative models, the input variables are often vectors of numbers that aren't related to real-world values at all, and are often even randomly generated. This kind of model—known as a **generative model**—can produce complex outputs such as text, music, or images from random noise, and is the topic of this book.

Even if you didn't know it at the time, you have probably seen other instances of generative models in the news alongside the discriminative examples given earlier. A prominent example is deep fakes, which are videos in which one person's face has been systematically replaced with another's by using a neural network to remap the pixels.[6]

Figure 1.2: A deep fake image[7]

Maybe you have also seen stories about AI models that generate **fake news**, which scientists at the firm OpenAI were initially terrified to release to the public due to concerns they could be used to create propaganda and misinformation online.[8]

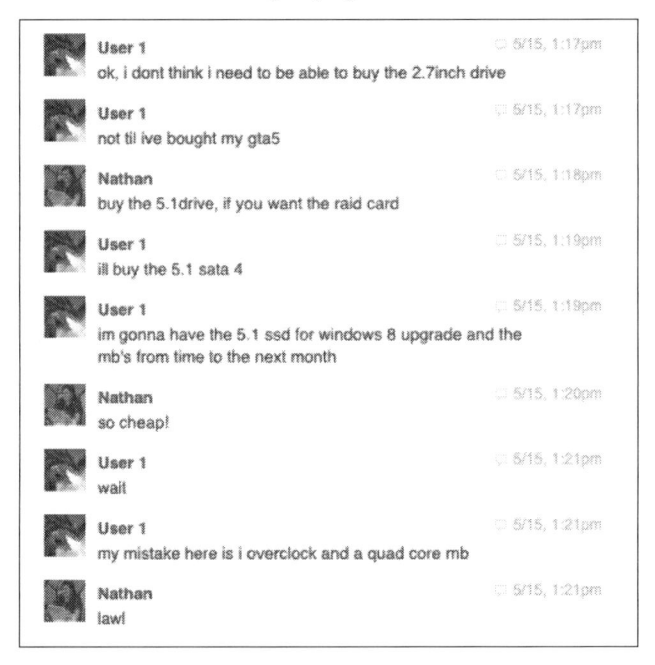

```
User 1                                           5/15, 1:17pm
ok, i dont think i need to be able to buy the 2.7inch drive

User 1                                           5/15, 1:17pm
not til ive bought my gta5

Nathan                                           5/15, 1:18pm
buy the 5.1drive, if you want the raid card

User 1                                           5/15, 1:19pm
ill buy the 5.1 sata 4

User 1                                           5/15, 1:19pm
im gonna have the 5.1 ssd for windows 8 upgrade and the
mb's from time to the next month

Nathan                                           5/15, 1:20pm
so cheap!

User 1                                           5/15, 1:21pm
wait

User 1                                           5/15, 1:21pm
my mistake here is i overclock and a quad core mb

Nathan                                           5/15, 1:21pm
lawl
```

Figure 1.3: A chatbot dialogue created using GPT-2[9]

In these and other applications, such as Google's voice assistant Duplex, which can make a restaurant reservation by dynamically creating a conversation with a human in real time,[10] or software that can generate original musical compositions,[11] we are surrounded by the outputs of generative AI algorithms.

Figure 1.4: Examples of style transfer using Generative Adversarial Networks (GANs)[12]

These models are able to handle complex information in a variety of domains: creating photorealistic images or stylistic **filters** on pictures (*Figure 1.4*), synthetic sound, conversational text, and even rules for optimally playing video games. You might ask, where did these models come from? How can I implement them myself? We will discuss more on that in the next section.

Implementing generative models

While generative models could theoretically be implemented using a wide variety of machine learning algorithms, in practice, they are usually built with deep neural networks, which are well suited to capturing complex variations in data such as images or language.

In this book, we will focus on implementing these deep generative models for many different applications using **TensorFlow 2.0**. TensorFlow is a C++ framework, with APIs in the Python programming language, used to develop and productionize deep learning models. It was open sourced by Google in 2013, and has become one of the most popular libraries for the research and deployment of neural network models.

With the 2.0 release, much of the boilerplate code that characterized development in earlier versions of the library was cleaned up with high-level abstractions, allowing us to focus on the model rather than the plumbing of the computations. The latest version also introduced the concept of **eager** execution, allowing network computations to be run on demand, which will be an important benefit of implementing some of our models.

In upcoming chapters, you will learn not only the underlying theory behind these models, but the practical skills needed to implement them in popular programming frameworks. In *Chapter 2, Setting up a TensorFlow Lab*, you will learn how to set up a cloud environment that will allow you to run TensorFlow in a distributed fashion, using the **Kubeflow** framework to catalog your experiments.

Indeed, as I will describe in more detail in *Chapter 3, Building Blocks of Deep Neural Networks*, since 2006 an explosion of research into **deep learning** using large neural network models has produced a wide variety of generative modeling applications. The first of these was the **restricted Boltzmann machine**, which is stacked in multiple layers to create a **deep belief network**. I will describe both of these models in *Chapter 4, Teaching Networks to Generate Digits*. Later innovations included **Variational Autoencoders** (**VAEs**), which can efficiently generate complex data samples from random numbers, using techniques that I will describe in *Chapter 5, Painting Pictures with Neural Networks Using VAEs*.

We will also cover the algorithm used to create **The Portrait of Edmond Belamy**, the GAN, in more detail in *Chapter 6, Image Generation with GANs*, of this book. Conceptually, the GAN model creates a competition between two neural networks. One (termed the **generator**) produces realistic (or, in the case of the experiments by Obvious, artistic) images starting from a set of random numbers and applying a mathematical transformation. In a sense, the generator is like an art student, producing new paintings from brushstrokes and creative inspiration.

The second network, known as the **discriminator**, attempts to classify whether a picture comes from a set of real-world images, or whether it was created by the generator. Thus, the discriminator acts like a teacher, grading whether the student has produced work comparable to the paintings they are attempting to mimic. As the generator becomes better at fooling the discriminator, its output becomes closer and closer to the historical examples it is designed to copy.

There are many classes of GAN models, with additional variants covered in *Chapter 7, Style Transfer with GANs*, and *Chapter 11, Composing Music with Generative Models*, in our discussion of advanced models. Another key innovation in generative models is in the domain of natural language data. By representing the complex interrelationship between words in a sentence in a computationally scalable way, the Transformer network and the **Bidirectional Encoder from Transformers** (BERT) model built on top of it present powerful building blocks to generate textual data in applications such as chatbots, which we'll cover in more detail in *Chapter 9, The Rise of Methods for Text Generation*, and *Chapter 10, NLP 2.0: Using Transformers to Generate Text*

In *Chapter 12, Play Video Games with Generative AI: GAIL*, you will also see how models such as GANs and VAEs can be used to generate not just images or text, but sets of rules that allow game-playing networks developed with reinforcement learning algorithms to process and navigate their environment more efficiently — in essence, learning to learn. Generative models are a huge field of research that is constantly growing, so unfortunately, we can't cover every topic in this book. For the interested reader, references to further topics will be provided in *Chapter 13, Emerging Applications in Generative AI*.

To get started with some background information, let's discuss the rules of probability.

The rules of probability

At the simplest level, a model, be it for machine learning or a more classical method such as linear regression, is a mathematical description of how various kinds of data relate to one another.

In the task of modeling, we usually think about separating the variables of our dataset into two broad classes:

1. **Independent data**, which primarily means **inputs** to a model, are denoted by X. These could be categorical features (such as a "0" or "1" in six columns indicating which of six schools a student attends), continuous (such as the heights or test scores of the same students), or ordinal (the rank of a student in the class).
2. **Dependent data**, conversely, are the outputs of our models, and are denoted by Y. (Note that in some cases Y is a **label** that can be used to condition a generative output, such as in a conditional GAN.) As with the independent variables, these can be continuous, categorical, or ordinal, and they can be an individual element or multidimensional matrix (tensor) for each element of the dataset.

So how can we describe the data in our model using statistics? In other words, how can we quantitatively describe what values we are likely to see, and how frequently, and which values are more likely to appear together? One way is by asking the likelihood of observing a particular value in the data, or the probability of that value. For example, if we were to ask what the probability is of observing a roll of 4 on a six-sided die, the answer is that, on average, we would observe a 4 once every six rolls. We write this as follows:

$$P(X=4) = 1/6 = 16.67\%$$

where P denotes *probability of*.

What defines the allowed probability values for a particular dataset? If we imagine the set of all possible values of a dataset, such as all values of a die, then a probability maps each value to a number between 0 and 1. The minimum is 0 because we can't have a negative chance of seeing a result; the most unlikely result is that we would never see a particular value, or 0% probability, such as rolling a 7 on a six-sided die. Similarly, we can't have greater than 100% probability of observing a result, represented by the value 1; an outcome with probability 1 is absolutely certain. This set of probability values associated with a dataset belong to discrete classes (such as the faces of a die) or an infinite set of potential values (such as variations in height or weight). In either case, however, these values have to follow certain rules, the **Probability Axioms** described by the mathematician Andrey Kolmogorov in 1933:[13]

1. The probability of an observation (a die role, a particular height, and so on) is a non-negative, finite number between 0 and 1.
2. The probability of *at least one* of the observations in the space of all possible observations occurring is 1.
3. The joint probability of distinct, mutually exclusive events is the sum of the probability of the individual events.

While these rules might seem abstract, you will see in *Chapter 3, Building Blocks of Deep Neural Networks*, that they have direct relevance to developing neural network models. For example, an application of rule 1 is to generate the probability between 1 and 0 for a particular outcome in a **softmax** function for predicting target classes. Rule 3 is used to normalize these outcomes into the range 0-1, under the guarantee that they are mutually distinct predictions of a deep neural network (in other words, a real-world image logically can't be classified as both a dog and a cat, but rather a dog or a cat, with the probability of these two outcomes additive). Finally, the second rule provides the theoretical guarantees that we can generate data at all using these models.

However, in the context of machine learning and modeling, we are not usually interested in just the probability of observing a piece of input data, X; we instead want to know the **conditional** probability of an outcome, Y, given the data, X. In other words, we want to know how likely a label is for a set of data, based on that data. We write this as *the probability of Y given X*, or *the probability of Y conditional on X*:

$$P(Y|X)$$

Another question we could ask about Y and X is how likely they are to occur together or their **joint probability**, which can be expressed using the preceding conditional probability expression as follows:

$$P(X, Y) = P(Y|X)P(X) = P(X|Y)(Y)$$

This formula expressed *the probability of X and Y*. In the case of X and Y being completely independent of one another, this is simply their product:

$$P(X|Y)P(Y) = P(Y|X)P(X) = P(X)P(Y)$$

You will see that these expressions become important in our discussion of **complementary priors** in *Chapter 4, Teaching Networks to Generate Digits*, and the ability of **restricted Boltzmann machines** to simulate independent data samples. They are also important as building blocks of Bayes' theorem, which we will discuss next.

Discriminative and generative modeling and Bayes' theorem

Now let's consider how these rules of conditional and joint probability relate to the kinds of predictive models that we build for various machine learning applications. In most cases—such as predicting whether an email is fraudulent or the dollar amount of the future lifetime value of a customer—we are interested in the conditional probability, $P(Y|X=x)$, where Y is the set of outcomes we are trying to model, X represents the input features, and x is a particular value of the input features. As discussed, this approach is known as **discriminative modeling**.[14] Discriminative modeling attempts to learn a direct mapping between the data, X, and the outcomes, Y.

Another way to understand discriminative modeling is in the context of Bayes' theorem,[15] which relates the conditional and joint probabilities of a dataset:

$$P(Y|X) = P(X|Y)P(Y)/P(X) = P(X, Y)/P(X)$$

In Bayes' formula, the expression $P(X|Y)/P(X)$ is known as the **likelihood** or the supporting evidence that the observation X gives to the likelihood of observing Y. $P(Y)$ is the **prior** or the plausibility of the outcome, and $P(Y|X)$ is the **posterior** or the probability of the outcome given all the independent data we have observed related to the outcome thus far. Conceptually, Bayes' theorem states that the probability of an outcome is the product of its baseline probability and the probability of the input data conditional on this outcome.

> The theorem was published two years after the author's death, and in a foreword Richard Price described it as a mathematical argument for the existence of God, which was perhaps appropriate given that Thomas Bayes served as a reverend during his life.

In the context of discriminative learning, we can thus see that a discriminative model directly computes the posterior; we could have a model of the likelihood or prior, but it is not required in this approach. Even though you may not have realized it, most of the models you have probably used in the machine learning toolkit are discriminative, such as the following:

- Linear regression
- Logistic regression
- Random forests
- Gradient-boosted decision trees (GBDT)
- Support vector machines (SVM)

The first two (linear and logistic regression) model the outcome, Y, conditional on the data, X, using a normal or Gaussian (linear regression) or sigmoidal (logistic regression) probability function. In contrast, the last three have no formal probability **model** — they compute a function (an ensemble of trees for random forests or GDBT, or an inner product distribution for SVM) that maps X to Y, using a loss or error function to tune those estimates. Given this nonparametric nature, some authors have argued that these constitute a separate class of **non-model** discriminative algorithms.[16]

In contrast, a **generative model** attempts to learn the joint distribution $P(Y, X)$ of the labels and the input data. Recall that using the definition of joint probability:

$$P(X, Y) = P(X|Y)P(Y)$$

We can rewrite Bayes' theorem as follows:

$$P(Y|X) = P(X, Y)/P(X)$$

Instead of learning a direct mapping of X to Y using $P(Y|X)$, as in the discriminative case, our goal is to model the joint probabilities of X and Y using $P(X, Y)$. While we can use the resulting joint distribution of X and Y to compute the posterior, $P(Y|X)$, and learn a **targeted** model, we can also use this distribution to sample new instances of the data by either jointly sampling new tuples (x, y), or samping new data inputs using a target label, Y, with the following expression:

$$P(X|Y=y) = P(X, Y)/P(Y)$$

Examples of generative models include the following:

- Naive Bayes classifiers
- Gaussian mixture models
- Latent Dirichlet Allocation (LDA)
- Hidden Markov models
- Deep Boltzmann machines
- VAEs
- GANs

Naive Bayes classifiers, though named as a discriminative model, utilize Bayes' theorem to learn the joint distribution of X and Y under the assumption that the X variables are independent. Similarly, Gaussian mixture models describe the likelihood of a data point belonging to one of a group of normal distributions using the joint probability of the label and these distributions.

LDA represents a document as the joint probability of a word and a set of underlying keyword lists (topics) that are used in a document. Hidden Markov models express the joint probability of a state and the next state of data, such as the weather on successive days of the week. As you will see in *Chapter 4*, *Teaching Networks to Generate Digits*, deep Boltzmann machines learn the joint probability of a label and the data vector it is associated with. The VAE and GAN models we will cover in *Chapters* 5, 6, 7, and 11 also utilize joint distributions to map between complex data types. This mapping allows us to generate data from random vectors or transform one kind of data into another.

As already mentioned, another view of generative models is that they allow us to generate samples of X if we know an outcome, Y. In the first four models in the previous list, this conditional probability is just a component of the model formula, with the posterior estimates still being the ultimate objective. However, in the last three examples, which are all deep neural network models, learning the conditional of X dependent upon a hidden, or **latent**, variable, Z, is actually the main objective, in order to generate new data samples. Using the rich structure allowed by multi-layered neural networks, these models can approximate the distribution of complex data types such as images, natural language, and sound. Also, instead of being a target value, Z is often a random number in these applications, serving merely as an input from which to generate a large space of hypothetical data points. To the extent we have a label (such as whether a generated image should be of a dog or dolphin, or the genre of a generated song), the model is $P(X | Y=y, Z=z)$, where the label Y controls the generation of data that is otherwise unrestricted by the random nature of Z.

Why use generative models?

Now that we have reviewed what generative models are and defined them more formally in the language of probability, why would we have a need for such models in the first place? What value do they provide in practical applications? To answer this question, let's take a brief tour of the topics that we will cover in more detail in the rest of this book.

The promise of deep learning

As noted already, many of the models we will survey in the book are deep, multi-level neural networks. The last 15 years have seen a renaissance in the development of deep learning models for image classification, natural language processing and understanding, and reinforcement learning. These advances were enabled by breakthroughs in traditional challenges in tuning and optimizing very complex models, combined with access to larger datasets, distributed computational power in the cloud, and frameworks such as TensorFlow that make it easier to prototype and reproduce research.

Chapter 1

Building a better digit classifier

A classic problem used to benchmark algorithms in machine learning and computer vision is the task of classifying which handwritten digit from 0-9 is represented in a pixelated image from the MNIST dataset.[17] A large breakthrough on this problem occurred in 2006, when researchers at the University of Toronto and the National University of Singapore discovered a way to train deep neural networks to perform this task.[18]

One of their critical observations was that instead of training a network to directly predict the most likely digit (*Y*) given an image (*X*), it was more effective to first train a network that could **generate images**, and then classify them as a second step. In *Chapter 4, Teaching Networks to Generate Digits*, I will describe how this model improved upon past attempts, and how to create your own **restricted Boltzmann machine** and **deep Boltzmann machine** models that can generate new MNIST digit images.

Generating images

A challenge to generating images such as the **Portrait of Edmond Belamy** with the approach used for the MNIST dataset is that frequently, images have no labels (such as a digit); rather, we want to map the space of random numbers into a set of artificial images using a latent vector, *Z*, as I described earlier in the chapter.

A further constraint is that we want to promote **diversity** of these images. If we input numbers within a certain range, we would like to know that they generate different outputs, and be able to tune the resulting image features. For this purpose, VAEs were developed to generate diverse and photorealistic images (*Figure 1.5*).

Figure 1.5: Sample images from a VAE[19]

[13]

In the context of image classification tasks, being able to generate new images can help us increase the number of examples in an existing dataset, or reduce the **bias** if our existing dataset is heavily skewed toward a particular kind of photograph. Applications could include generating alternative poses (angles, shades, or perspective shots) for product photographs on a fashion e-commerce website (*Figure 1.6*):

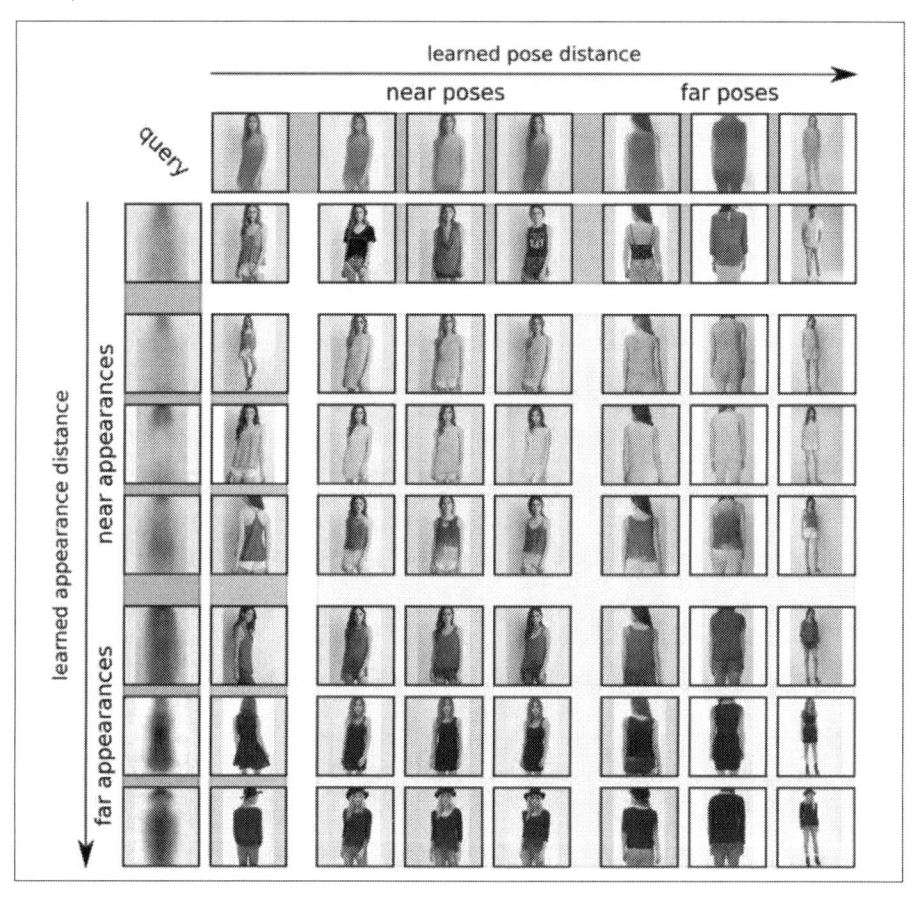

Figure 1.6: Simulating alternative poses with deep generative models[20]

Style transfer and image transformation

In addition to mapping artificial images to a space of random numbers, we can also use generative models to learn a mapping between one kind of image and a second. This kind of model can, for example, be used to convert an image of a horse into that of a zebra (*Figure 1.7*), create **deep fake videos** in which one actor's face has been replaced with another's, or transform a photo into a painting (*Figures 1.2* and *1.4*):[21]

Chapter 1

Figure 1.7: CycleGANs apply stripes to horses to generate zebras[22]

Another fascinating example of applying generative modeling is a study in which lost masterpieces of the artist Pablo Picasso were discovered to have been painted over with another image. After X-ray imaging of **The Old Guitarist** and **The Crouching Beggar** indicated that earlier images of a woman and a landscape lay underneath (*Figure 1.8*), researchers used the other paintings from **Picasso's blue period** or other color photographs (*Figure 1.8*) to train a **neural style transfer** model that transforms black-and-white images (the X-ray radiographs of the overlying paintings) to the coloration of the original artwork. Then, applying this transfer model to the **hidden** images allowed them to reconstruct **colored-in** versions of the lost paintings:

a) The Old Guitarist Picasso.
b) X-radiograph of The Old Guitarist.
c) Content images, constructed from b).
d) Style image, Picasso's La Vie.
e) Stylised image, *La femme perdue.*

a) The Crouching Beggar, Picasso.
b) X-radiograph of The Crouching Beggar Picasso.
c) Content images, constructed from b).
d) Style image, Terraced Garden in Mallorea, Santiago Rusinol.
e) Stylised image, *Pare del Laberint d' Horta.*

Figure 1.8: Deep learning was used to color in the X-ray images of the painted-over scenes (middle), with color patterns learned from examples (column d) generating colorized versions of the lost art (far right)[23]

An Introduction to Generative AI: "Drawing" Data from Models

All of these models use the previously mentioned GANs, a type of deep learning model proposed in 2014[24] In addition to changing the contents of an image (as in the preceding zebra example), these models can also be used to map one image into another, such as paired images (such as dogs and humans with similar facial features, as in *Figure 1.9*), or generate textual descriptions from images (*Figure 1.10*):

Figure 1.9: Sim-GAN for mapping human to animal or anime faces[25]

this flower is yellow and purple in color, with petals that are striped near the center.	this flower is yellow in color, and has petals that are rounded and curled around the center.	the large round center of this flower is covered with whitish pink anthers and the petals are white closest to the center and end in a red point.	this flower has a lot of pointed red petals in a ray-like shape around the many stamen.

Figure 1.10: Caption-GAN for generating descriptions from images[26]

We could also condition the properties of the generated images on some auxiliary information such as labels, an approach used in the GANGogh algorithm, which synthesizes images in the style of different artists by supplying the desired artist as an input to the generative model (*Figure 1.4*).[27] I will describe these applications in *Chapter 6, Image Generation with GANs*, and *Chapter 7, Style Transfer with GANs*.

Fake news and chatbots

Humans have always wanted to talk to machines; the first chatbot, ELIZA,[28] was written at MIT in the 1960s and used a simple program to transform a user's input and generate a response, in the mode of a **therapist** who frequently responds in the form of a question.

More sophisticated models can generate entirely novel text, such as Google's BERT and GPT-2,[29,30] which use a unit called a **transformer**. A transformer module in a neural network allows a network to propose a new word in the context of preceding words in a piece of text, emphasizing those that are more relevant in order to generate plausible stretches of language. The BERT model then combines transformer units into a powerful multi-dimensional encoding of natural language patterns and contextual significance. This approach can be used in document creation for **natural language processing** (**NLP**) tasks, or for chatbot dialogue systems (*Figure 1.3*).

Sound composition

Sound, like images or text, is a complex, high-dimensional kind of data. Music in particular has many complexities: it could involve one or several musicians, has a temporal structure, and can be divided into thematically related segments. All of these components are incorporated into models such as MuseGAN, as mentioned earlier, which uses GANs to generate these various components and synthesize them into realistic, yet synthetic, musical tracks. I will describe the implementation of MuseGAN and its variants in *Chapter 11, Composing Music with Generative Models*.

The rules of the game

The preceding applications concern data types we can see, hear, or read. However, generative models also have applications to generate rules. This is useful in a popular application of deep learning: using algorithms to play board games or Atari video games.[31]

While these applications have traditionally used **reinforcement learning** (RL) techniques to train networks to employ the optimal strategy in these games, new research has suggested using GANs to propose novel rules as part of the training process,[32] or to generate synthetic data to prime the overall learning process.[33] We will examine both applications in *Chapter 12*, *Play Video Games with Generative AI: GAIL*.

Unique challenges of generative models

Given the powerful applications that generative models have, what are the major challenges in implementing them? As described, most of these models utilize complex data, requiring us to fit large models to capture all the nuances of their features and distribution. This has implications both for the number of examples that we must collect to adequately represent the kind of data we are trying to generate, and the computational resources needed to build the model. We will discuss techniques in *Chapter 2*, *Setting up a TensorFlow Lab*, to parallelize the training of these models using cloud computing frameworks and **graphics processing units** (GPUs).

A more subtle problem that comes from having complex data, and the fact that we are trying to generate data rather than a numerical label or value, is that our notion of model **accuracy** is much more complicated: we cannot simply calculate the distance to a single label or scores.

We will discuss in *Chapter 5*, *Painting Pictures with Neural Networks Using VAEs*, and *Chapter 6*, *Image Generation with GANs*, how deep generative models such as VAE and GAN algorithms take different approaches to determine whether a generated image is comparable to a real-world image. Finally, as mentioned, our models need to allow us to generate both large and **diverse** samples, and the various methods we will discuss take different approaches to control the diversity of data.

Summary

In this chapter, we discussed what generative modeling is, and how it fits into the landscape of more familiar machine learning methods. I used probability theory and Bayes' theorem to describe how these models approach prediction in an opposite manner to generative learning.

We reviewed use cases for generative learning, both for specific kinds of data and general prediction tasks. Finally, we examined some of the specialized challenges that arise from building these models.

In the next chapter, we will begin our practical implementation of these models by exploring how to set up a development environment for TensorFlow 2.0 using Docker and Kubeflow.

References

1. https://www.christies.com/features/A-collaboration-between-two-artists-one-human-one-a-machine-9332-1.aspx

2. Baltruschat, I.M., Nickisch, H., Grass, M. et al. (2019). *Comparison of Deep Learning Approaches for Multi-Label Chest X-Ray Classification*. Sci Rep 9, 6381. https://doi.org/10.1038/s41598-019-42294-8

3. *AlphaGo* (n.d.). DeepMind. Retrieved April 20, 2021, from https://deepmind.com/research/case-studies/alphago-the-story-so-far

4. The AlphaStar team (2019, October). *AlphaStar: Grandmaster level in StarCraft II using multi-agent reinforcement learning*. DeepMind. https://deepmind.com/blog/article/AlphaStar-Grandmaster-level-in-StarCraft-II-using-multi-agent-reinforcement-learning

5. Devlin, J., Chang, M., Lee, K., Toutanova, K. (2019). *BERT: Pre-training of Deep Bidirectional Transformers for Language Understanding*. arXiv. https://arxiv.org/abs/1810.04805v2

6. Brandon, J. (2018, February 16). *Terrifying high-tech porn: Creepy 'deepfake' videos are on the rise*. Fox News. https://www.foxnews.com/tech/terrifying-high-tech-porn-creepy-deepfake-videos-are-on-the-rise

7. https://seanbmcgregor.com/DeepfakeDetectionGame.html

8. *Better Language Models and Their Implications*. (February 14, 2019). OpenAI. https://openai.com/blog/better-language-models/

9. https://devopstar.com/static/2293f764e1538f357dd1c63035ab25b0/d024a/fake-facebook-conversation-example-1.png

10. Leviathan Y., Matias Y. (2018, May 8). *Google Duplex: An AI System for Accomplishing Real-World Tasks Over the Phone*. Google AI Blog. https://ai.googleblog.com/2018/05/duplex-ai-system-for-natural-conversation.html

11. Hao-Wen Dong, Wen-Yi Hsiao, Li-Chia Yang and Yi-Hsuan Yang. MuseGAN. https://salu133445.github.io/musegan/

12. https://neurohive.io/wp-content/uploads/2018/06/neural-style-transfer-example-e1530287419338.jpg

13. Kolmogorov A. N., (1956). *Foundations of the Theory of Probability*. (2nd edition). Chelsea Publishing Company New York. https://www.york.ac.uk/depts/maths/histstat/kolmogorov_foundations

14. Jebara, Tony., (2004). *Machine Learning: Discriminative and Generative*. Kluwer Academic (Springer). https://www.springer.com/gp/book/9781402076473

15. Bayes Thomas, (1763) *LII. An essay towards solving a problem in the doctrine of chances. By the late Rev. Mr. Bayes, F. R. S. communicated by Mr. Price, in a letter to John Canton, A. M. F. R. S* Phil. Trans. R. Soc.53370–418. https://royalsocietypublishing.org/doi/10.1098/rstl.1763.0053

16. Jebara, Tony., (2004). *Machine Learning: Discriminative and Generative.* Kluwer Academic (Springer). https://www.springer.com/gp/book/9781402076473

17. http://yann.lecun.com/exdb/mnist/

18. G. Hinton, S. Osindero, & Y.-W. Teh. (2005). *A Fast Learning Algorithm for Deep Belief Nets.* www.cs.toronto.edu/~fritz/absps/ncfast.pdf

19. https://jaan.io/images/variational-autoencoder-faces.jpg and https://miro.medium.com/max/2880/1*jcCjbdnN4uEowuHfBoqITQ.jpeg

20. Esser, P., Haux, J., Ommer, B., (2019). *Unsupervised Robust Disentangling of Latent Characteristics for Image Synthesis.* arXiv. https://arxiv.org/abs/1910.10223

21. *CycleGAN.* TensorFlow Core. Retrieved April 26, 2021, from https://www.tensorflow.org/tutorials/generative/cyclegan

22. https://www.tensorflow.org/tutorials/generative/images/horse2zebra_2.png

23. Bourached, A., Cann, G. (2019). *Raiders of the Lost Art.* arXiv:1909.05677. https://arxiv.org/pdf/1909.05677.pdf

24. Goodfellow, I. J., Pouget-Abadie, J., Mirza, M., Xu, B., Warde-Farley, D., Ozair, S., Courville, A., Bengio, Y. (2014). *Generative Adversarial Networks.* arXiv. https://arxiv.org/abs/1406.2661

25. Goodfellow, I. J., Pouget-Abadie, J., Mirza, M., Xu, B., Warde-Farley, D., Ozair, S., Courville, A., Bengio, Y. (2014). *Generative Adversarial Networks.* arXiv. https://arxiv.org/abs/1406.2661

26. Gorti, S. K., Ma, Jeremy (2018). *Text-to-Image-to-Text Translation using Cycle Consistent Adversarial Networks.* arXiv. https://arxiv.org/abs/1808.04538

27. rkjones4, adam-hanna, erincr & rodrigobdz (2020). GANGogh. GitHub repository. https://github.com/rkjones4/GANGogh

28. Weizenbaum Joseph. (1976) *Computer and Human Reason.* W. H. Freeman and company. blogs.evergreen.edu/cpat/files/2013/05/Computer-Power-and-Human-Reason.pdf

29. Schwartz B., (2019, October 25). *Welcome BERT: Google's latest search algorithm to better understand natural language.* Search Engine Land. https://searchengineland.com/welcome-bert-google-artificial-intelligence-for-understanding-search-queries-323976

30. *Better Language Models and Their Implications.* (2019, February 14). OpenAI. https://openai.com/blog/better-language-models/

31. Mnih V., Kavukcuoglu K., Silver D., Graves A., Antonoglou I., Wierstra D., Riedmiller M. (2013, January 01). *Playing Atari with Deep Reinforcement Learning.* DeepMind. https://deepmind.com/research/publications/playing-atari-deep-reinforcement-learning

32. Liu, Yang; Zeng, Yifeng; Chen, Yingke; Tang, Jing; Pan, Yinghui (2019). *Self-Improving Generative Adversarial Reinforcement Learning.* AAMS 2019. http://www.ifaamas.org/Proceedings/aamas2019/pdfs/p52.pdf

33. Kasgari, A T Z, Saad, W., Mozaffari, M., Poor, H V (2020). *Experienced Deep Reinforcement Learning with Generative Adversarial Networks (GANs) for Model-Free Ultra Reliable Low Latency Communication.* arXiv. https://arxiv.org/abs/1911.03264

2
Setting Up a TensorFlow Lab

Now that you have seen all the amazing applications of generative models in *Chapter 1, An Introduction to Generative AI: "Drawing" Data from Models*, you might be wondering how to get started with implementing these projects that use these kinds of algorithms. In this chapter, we will walk through a number of tools that we will use throughout the rest of the book to implement the deep neural networks that are used in various generative AI models. Our primary tool is the *TensorFlow 2.0* framework, developed by Google[1][2]; however, we will also use a number of additional resources to make the implementation process easier (summarized in *Table 2.1*).

We can broadly categorize these tools:

- Resources for replicable dependency management (Docker, Anaconda)
- Exploratory tools for data munging and algorithm hacking (Jupyter)
- Utilities to deploy these resources to the cloud and manage their lifecycle (Kubernetes, Kubeflow, Terraform)

Tool	Project site	Use
Docker	https://www.docker.com/	Application runtime dependency encapsulation
Anaconda	https://www.anaconda.com/	Python language package management
Jupyter	https://jupyter.org/	Interactive Python runtime and plotting / data exploration tool

Kubernetes	`https://kubernetes.io/`	Docker container orchestration and resource management
Kubeflow	`https://www.kubeflow.org/`	Machine learning workflow engine developed on Kubernetes
Terraform	`https://www.terraform.io/`	Infrastructure scripting language for configurable and consistent deployments of Kubeflow and Kubernetes
VSCode	`https://code.visualstudio.com/`	Integrated development environment (IDE)

Table 2.1: Tech stack for generative adversarial model development

On our journey to bring our code from our laptops to the cloud in this chapter, we will first describe some background on how TensorFlow works when running locally. We will then describe a wide array of software tools that will make it easier to run an end-to-end TensorFlow lab locally or in the cloud, such as notebooks, containers, and cluster managers. Finally, we will walk through a simple practical example of setting up a reproducible research environment, running local and distributed training, and recording our results. We will also examine how we might parallelize TensorFlow across multiple CPU/GPU units within a machine (vertical scaling) and multiple machines in the cloud (horizontal scaling) to accelerate training. By the end of this chapter, we will be all ready to extend this laboratory framework to tackle implementing projects using various generative AI models.

First, let's start by diving more into the details of TensorFlow, the library we will use to develop models throughout the rest of this book. What problem does TensorFlow solve for neural network model development? What approaches does it use? How has it evolved over the years? To answer these questions, let us review some of the history behind deep neural network libraries that led to the development of TensorFlow.

Deep neural network development and TensorFlow

As we will see in *Chapter 3, Building Blocks of Deep Neural Networks*, a deep neural network in essence consists of matrix operations (addition, subtraction, multiplication), nonlinear transformations, and gradient-based updates computed by using the derivatives of these components.

In the world of academia, researchers have historically often used efficient prototyping tools such as MATLAB[3] to run models and prepare analyses. While this approach allows for rapid experimentation, it lacks elements of industrial software development, such as **object-oriented** (**OO**) development, that allow for reproducibility and clean software abstractions that allow tools to be adopted by large organizations. These tools also had difficulty scaling to large datasets and could carry heavy licensing fees for such industrial use cases. However, prior to 2006, this type of computational tooling was largely sufficient for most use cases. However, as the datasets being tackled with deep neural network algorithms grew, groundbreaking results were achieved such as:

- Image classification on the ImageNet dataset[4]
- Large-scale unsupervised discovery of image patterns in YouTube videos[5]
- The creation of artificial agents capable of playing Atari video games and the Asian board game GO with human-like skill[6,7]
- State-of-the-art language translation via the BERT model developed by Google[8]

The models developed in these studies exploded in complexity along with the size of the datasets they were applied to (see *Table 2.2* to get a sense of the immense scale of some of these models). As industrial use cases required robust and scalable frameworks to develop and deploy new neural networks, several academic groups and large technology companies invested in the development of generic toolkits for the implementation of deep learning models. These software libraries codified common patterns into reusable abstractions, allowing even complex models to be often embodied in relatively simple experimental scripts.

Model Name	Year	# Parameters
AlexNet	2012	61M
YouTube CNN	2012	1B
Inception	2014	5M
VGG-16	2014	138M
BERT	2018	340M
GPT-3	2020	175B

Table 2.2: Number of parameters by model by year

Some of the early examples of these frameworks include Theano,[9] a Python package developed at the University of Montreal, and Torch,[10] a library written in the Lua language that was later ported to Python by researchers at Facebook, and TensorFlow, a C++ runtime with Python bindings developed by Google[11].

Setting Up a TensorFlow Lab

In this book, we will primarily use TensorFlow 2.0, due to its widespread adoption and its convenient high-level interface, **Keras**, which abstracts much of the repetitive plumbing of defining routine layers and model architectures.

TensorFlow is an open-source version of an internal tool developed at Google called **DistBelief**.[12] The DistBelief framework consisted of distributed workers (independent computational processes running on a cluster of machines) that would compute forward and backward gradient descent passes on a network (a common way to train neural networks we will discuss in *Chapter 3, Building Blocks of Deep Neural Networks*), and send the results to a **Parameter Server** that aggregated the updates. The neural networks in the DistBelief framework were represented as a **Directed Acyclic Graph (DAG)**, terminating in a loss function that yielded a scalar (numerical value) comparing the network predictions with the observed target (such as image class or the probability distribution over a vocabulary representing the most probable next word in a sentence in a translation model).

> A DAG is a software data structure consisting of nodes (**operations**) and data (**edges**) where information only flows in a single direction along the edges (thus `directed`) and where there are no loops (hence `acyclic`).

While DistBelief allowed Google to productionize several large models, it had limitations:

- First, the Python scripting interface was developed with a set of pre-defined layers corresponding to underlying implementations in C++; adding novel layer types required coding in C++, which represented a barrier to productivity.
- Secondly, while the system was well adapted for training feed-forward networks using basic **Stochastic Gradient Descent (SGD)** (an algorithm we will describe in more detail in *Chapter 3, Building Blocks of Deep Neural Networks*) on large-scale data, it lacked flexibility for accommodating recurrent, reinforcement learning, or adversarial learning paradigms – the latter of which is crucial to many of the algorithms we will implement in this book.
- Finally, this system was difficult to *scale down* – to run the same job, for example, on a desktop with GPUs as well as a distributed environment with multiple cores per machine, and deployment also required a different technical stack.

Jointly, these considerations prompted the development of TensorFlow as a generic deep learning computational framework: one that could allow scientists to flexibly experiment with new layer architectures or cutting-edge training paradigms, while also allowing this experimentation to be run with the same tools on both a laptop (for early-stage work) and a computing cluster (to scale up more mature models), while also easing the transition between research and development code by providing a common runtime for both.

Though both libraries share the concept of the computation graph (networks represented as a graph of operations (nodes) and data (edges)) and a dataflow programming model (where matrix operations pass through the directed edges of a graph and have operations applied to them), TensorFlow, unlike DistBelief, was designed with the edges of the graph being tensors (n-dimensional matrices) and nodes of the graph being atomic operations (addition, subtraction, nonlinear convolution, or queues and other advanced operations) rather than fixed layer operations – this allows for much greater flexibility in defining new computations and even allowing for mutation and stateful updates (these being simply additional nodes in the graph).

The dataflow graph in essence serves as a "placeholder" where data is slotted into defined variables and can be executed on single or multiple machines. TensorFlow optimizes the constructed dataflow graph in the C++ runtime upon execution, allowing optimization, for example, in issuing commands to the GPU. The different computations of the graph can also be executed across multiple machines and hardware, including CPUs, GPUs, and TPUs (custom tensor processing chips developed by Google and available in the Google Cloud computing environment)[11], as the same computations described at a high level in TensorFlow are implemented to execute on multiple backend systems.

Because the dataflow graph allows mutable state, in essence, there is also no longer a centralized parameter server as was the case for DistBelief (though TensorFlow can also be run in a distributed manner with a parameter server configuration), since different nodes that hold state can execute the same operations as any other worker nodes. Further, control flow operations such as loops allow for the training of variable-length inputs such as in recurrent networks (see *Chapter 3, Building Blocks of Deep Neural Networks*). In the context of training neural networks, the gradients of each layer are simply represented as additional operations in the graph, allowing optimizations such as velocity (as in the RMSProp or ADAM optimizers, described in *Chapter 3, Building Blocks of Deep Neural Networks*) to be included using the same framework rather than modifying the parameter server logic. In the context of distributed training, TensorFlow also has several checkpointing and redundancy mechanisms ("backup" workers in case of a single task failure) that make it suited to robust training in distributed environments.

TensorFlow 2.0

While representing operations in the dataflow graph as primitives allows flexibility in defining new layers within the Python client API, it also can result in a lot of "boilerplate" code and repetitive syntax. For this reason, the high-level API *Keras*[14] was developed to provide a high-level abstraction; layers are represented using Python classes, while a particular runtime environment (such as TensorFlow or Theano) is a "backend" that executes the layer, just as the atomic TensorFlow operators can have different underlying implementations on CPUs, GPUs, or TPUs. While developed as a framework-agnostic library, Keras has been included as part of TensorFlow's main release in version 2.0. For the purposes of readability, we will implement most of our models in this book in Keras, while reverting to the underlying TensorFlow 2.0 code where it is necessary to implement particular operations or highlight the underlying logic. Please see *Table 2.3* for a comparison between how various neural network algorithm concepts are implemented at a low (TensorFlow) or high (Keras) level in these libraries.

Object	TensorFlow implementation	Keras implementation
Neural network layer	Tensor computation	Python layer classes
Gradient calculation	Graph runtime operator	Python optimizer class
Loss function	Tensor computation	Python loss function
Neural network model	Graph runtime session	Python model class instance

Table 2.3: TensorFlow and Keras comparison

To show you the difference between the abstraction that Keras makes versus TensorFlow 1.0 in implementing basic neural network models, let's look at an example of writing a convolutional layer (see *Chapter 3, Building Blocks of Deep Neural Networks*) using both of these frameworks. In the first case, in TensorFlow 1.0, you can see that a lot of the code involves explicitly specifying variables, functions, and matrix operations, along with the gradient function and runtime session to compute the updates to the networks.

This is a multilayer perceptron in TensorFlow 1.0[15]:

```
X = tf.placeholder(dtype=tf.float64)
Y = tf.placeholder(dtype=tf.float64)
num_hidden=128

# Build a hidden layer
W_hidden = tf.Variable(np.random.randn(784, num_hidden))
b_hidden = tf.Variable(np.random.randn(num_hidden))
p_hidden = tf.nn.sigmoid( tf.add(tf.matmul(X, W_hidden), b_hidden) )
```

```python
# Build another hidden layer
W_hidden2 = tf.Variable(np.random.randn(num_hidden, num_hidden))
b_hidden2 = tf.Variable(np.random.randn(num_hidden))
p_hidden2 = tf.nn.sigmoid( tf.add(tf.matmul(p_hidden, W_hidden2), b_hidden2) )

# Build the output layer
W_output = tf.Variable(np.random.randn(num_hidden, 10))
b_output = tf.Variable(np.random.randn(10))
p_output = tf.nn.softmax( tf.add(tf.matmul(p_hidden2, W_output),
        b_output) )

loss = tf.reduce_mean(tf.losses.mean_squared_error(
        labels=Y,predictions=p_output))
accuracy=1-tf.sqrt(loss)
minimization_op = tf.train.AdamOptimizer(learning_rate=0.01).minimize(loss)

feed_dict = {
    X: x_train.reshape(-1,784),
    Y: pd.get_dummies(y_train)
}
with tf.Session() as session:
    session.run(tf.global_variables_initializer())

    for step in range(10000):
        J_value = session.run(loss, feed_dict)
        acc = session.run(accuracy, feed_dict)
        if step % 100 == 0:
            print("Step:", step, " Loss:", J_value," Accuracy:", acc)

        session.run(minimization_op, feed_dict)
    pred00 = session.run([p_output], feed_dict={X: x_test.reshape(-1,784)})
```

In contrast, the implementation of the same convolutional layer in Keras is vastly simplified through the use of abstract concepts embodied in Python classes, such as layers, models, and optimizers. Underlying details of the computation are encapsulated in these classes, making the logic of the code more readable.

Setting Up a TensorFlow Lab

Note also that in TensorFlow 2.0 the notion of running sessions (**lazy execution**, in which the network is only computed if explicitly compiled and called) has been dropped in favor of eager execution, in which the session and graph are called dynamically when network functions such as `call` and `compile` are executed, with the network behaving like any other Python class without explicitly creating a `session` scope. The notion of a global namespace in which variables are declared with `tf.Variable()` has also been replaced with a **default garbage collection mechanism**.

This is a multilayer perceptron layer in Keras[15]:

```python
import TensorFlow as tf
from TensorFlow.keras.layers import Input, Dense
from keras.models import Model

l = tf.keras.layers

model = tf.keras.Sequential([
    l.Flatten(input_shape=(784,)),
    l.Dense(128, activation='relu'),
    l.Dense(128, activation='relu'),
    l.Dense(10, activation='softmax')
])

model.compile(loss='categorical_crossentropy',
              optimizer='adam',
              metrics = ['accuracy'])

model.summary()

model.fit(x_train.reshape(-1,784),pd.get_dummies(y_train),nb_epoch=15,batch_size=128,verbose=1)
```

Now that we have covered some of the details of what the TensorFlow library is and why it is well-suited to the development of deep neural network models (including the generative models we will implement in this book), let's get started building up our research environment. While we could simply use a Python package manager such as pip to install TensorFlow on our laptop, we want to make sure our process is as robust and reproducible as possible – this will make it easier to package our code to run on different machines, or keep our computations consistent by specifying the exact versions of each Python library we use in an experiment. We will start by installing an **Integrated Development Environment** (IDE) that will make our research easier – VSCode.

VSCode

Visual Studio Code (**VSCode**) is an open-source code editor developed by Microsoft Corporation which can be used with many programming languages, including Python. It allows debugging and is integrated with version control tools such as Git; we can even run Jupyter notebooks (which we will describe later in this chapter) within VSCode. Instructions for installation vary by whether you are using a Linux, macOS, or Windows operating system: please see individual instructions at https://code.visualstudio.com for your system. Once installed, we need to clone a copy of the source code for the projects in this book using Git, with the command:

```
git clone git@github.com:PacktPublishing/Hands-On-Generative-AI-with-Python-and-TensorFlow-2.git
```

This command will copy the source code for the projects in this book to our laptop, allowing us to locally run and modify the code. Once you have the code copied, open the GitHub repository for this book using VSCode (*Figure 2.1*). We are now ready to start installing some of the tools we will need; open the file `install.sh`.

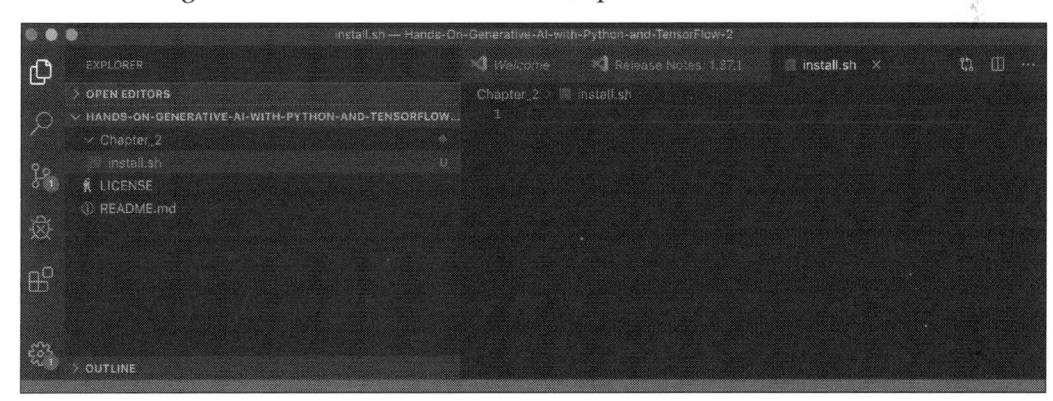

Figure 2.1: VSCode IDE

One feature that will be of particular use to us is the fact that VSCode has an integrated (*Figure 2.2*) terminal where we can run commands: you can access this by selecting **View**, then **Terminal** from the drop-down list, which will open a command-line prompt:

Figure 2.2: VSCode terminal

Select the **TERMINAL** tab, and **bash** for the interpreter; you should now be able to enter normal commands. Change the directory to Chapter_2, where we will run our installation script, which you can open in VSCode.

The installation script we will run will download and install the various components we will need in our end-to-end TensorFlow lab; the overarching framework we will use for these experiments will be the Kubeflow library, which handles the various data and training pipelines that we will utilize for our projects in the later chapters of this volume. In the rest of this chapter, we will describe how Kubeflow is built on Docker and Kubernetes, and how to set up Kubeflow on several popular cloud providers.

Kubernetes, the technology which Kubeflow is based on, is fundamentally a way to manage containerized applications created using **Docker**, which allows for reproducible, lightweight execution environments to be created and persisted for a variety of applications. While we will make use of Docker for creating reproducible experimental runtimes, to understand its place in the overall landscape of virtualization solutions (and why it has become so important to modern application development), let us take a detour to describe the background of Docker in more detail.

Docker: A lightweight virtualization solution

A consistent challenge in developing robust software applications is to make them run the same on a machine different than the one on which they are developed. These differences in environments could encompass a number of variables: operating systems, programming language library versions, and hardware such as CPU models.

Traditionally, one approach to dealing with this heterogeneity has been to use a **Virtual Machine** (**VM**). While VMs are useful to run applications on diverse hardware and operating systems, they are also limited by being **resource-intensive** (*Figure 2.3*): each VM running on a host requires the overhead resources to run a completely separate operating system, along with all the applications or dependencies within the guest system.

Chapter 2

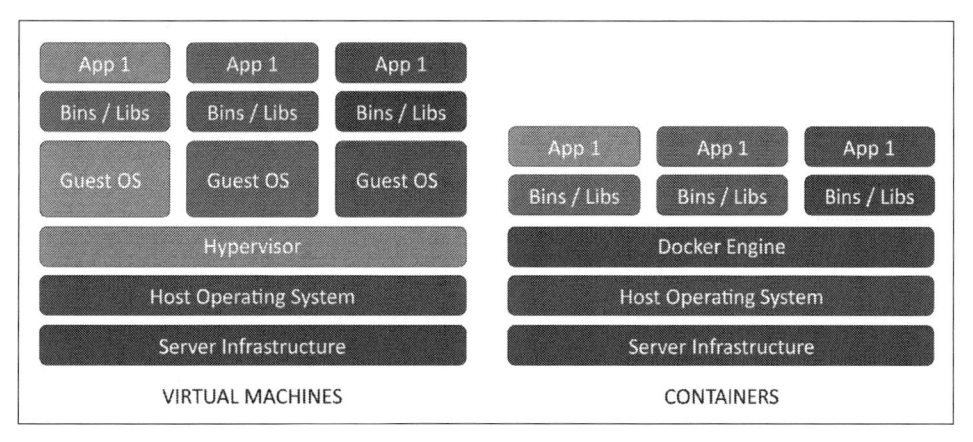

Figure 2.3: Virtual machines versus containers[16]

However, in some cases this is an unnecessary level of overhead; we do not necessarily need to run an entirely separate operating system, rather than just a consistent environment, including libraries and dependencies within a single operating system. This need for a **lightweight framework** to specify runtime environments prompted the creation of the **Docker project** for containerization in 2013. In essence, a container is an environment for running an application, including all dependencies and libraries, allowing reproducible deployment of web applications and other programs, such as a database or the computations in a machine learning pipeline. For our use case, we will use it to provide a reproducible Python execution environment (Python language version and libraries) to run the steps in our generative machine learning pipelines.

We will need to have Docker installed for many of the examples that will appear in the rest of this chapter and the projects in this book. For instructions on how to install Docker for your particular operating system, please refer to the directions at (https://docs.docker.com/install/). To verify that you have installed the application successfully, you should be able to run the following command on your terminal, which will print the available options:

```
docker run hello-world
```

Important Docker commands and syntax

To understand how Docker works, it is useful to walk through the template used for all Docker containers, a **Dockerfile**. As an example, we will use the TensorFlow container notebook example from the Kubeflow project (https://github.com/kubeflow/kubeflow/blob/master/components/example-notebook-servers/jupyter-tensorflow-full/cpu.Dockerfile).

This file is a set of instructions for how Docker should take a base operating environment, add dependencies, and execute a piece of software once it is packaged:

```
FROM public.ecr.aws/j1r0q0g6/notebooks/notebook-servers/jupyter-tensorflow:master-abf9ec48

# install - requirements.txt
COPY --chown=jovyan:users requirements.txt /tmp/requirements.txt
RUN python3 -m pip install -r /tmp/requirements.txt --quiet --no-cache-dir \
  && rm -f /tmp/requirements.txt
```

While the exact commands will differ between containers, this will give you a flavor for the way we can use containers to manage an application – in this case running a Jupyter notebook for interactive machine learning experimentation using a consistent set of libraries. Once we have installed the Docker runtime for our particular operating system, we would execute such a file by running:

```
Docker build -f <Dockerfilename> -t <image name:tag>
```

When we do this, a number of things happen. First, we retrieve the base filesystem, or image, from a remote repository, which is not unlike the way we collect JAR files from Artifactory when using Java build tools such as Gradle or Maven, or Python's pip installer. With this filesystem or image, we then set required variables for the Docker build command such as the username and TensorFlow version, and runtime environment variables for the container. We determine what shell program will be used to run the command, then we install dependencies we will need to run TensorFlow and the notebook application, and we specify the command that is run when the Docker container is started. Then we save this snapshot with an identifier composed of a base image name and one or more tags (such as version numbers, or, in many cases, simply a timestamp to uniquely identify this image). Finally, to actually start the notebook server running this container, we would issue the command:

```
Docker run <image name:tag>
```

By default, Docker will run the executable command in the Dockerfile file; in our present example, that is the command to start the notebook server. However, this does not have to be the case; we could have a Dockerfile that simply builds an execution environment for an application, and issue a command to run within that environment. In that case, the command would look like:

```
Docker run <image name:tag> <command>
```

The `Docker` run commands allow us to test that our application can successfully run within the environment specified by the `Dockerfile`; however, we usually want to run this application in the cloud where we can take advantage of distributed computing resources or the ability to host web applications exposed to the world at large, not locally. To do so, we need to move our image we have built to a remote repository, which may or may not be the same one we pulled the initial image from, using the push command:

```
Docker push <image name:tag>
```

Note that the image name can contain a reference to a particular registry, such as a local registry or one hosted on one of the major cloud providers such as **Elastic Container Service** (**ECS**) on AWS, **Azure Kubernetes Service** (**AKS**), or Google Container Registry. Publishing to a remote registry allows developers to share images, and us to make containers accessible to deploy in the cloud.

Connecting Docker containers with docker-compose

So far we have only discussed a few basic Docker commands, which would allow us to run a single service in a single container. However, you can probably appreciate that in the "real world" we usually need to have one or more applications running concurrently – for example, a website will have both a web application that fetches and processes data in response to activity from an end user and a database instance to log that information. In complex applications, the website might even be composed of multiple small web applications or **microservices** that are specialized to particular use cases such as the front end, user data, or an order management system. For these kinds of applications, we will need to have more than one container communicating with each other. The docker-compose tool (https://docs.docker.com/compose/) is written with such applications in mind: it allows us to specify several Docker containers in an application file using the YAML format. For example, a configuration for a website with an instance of the Redis database might look like:

```
version: '3'
services:
  web:
    build: .
    ports:
     - "5000:5000"
    volumes:
     - .:/code
     - logvolume01:/var/log
```

```
    links:
     - redis
   redis:
     image: redis
 volumes:
   logvolume01: {}
```

Code 2.1: A yaml input file for Docker Compose

The two application containers here are web and the redis database. The file also specified the volumes (disks) linked to these two applications. Using this configuration, we can run the command:

```
docker-compose up
```

This starts all the containers specified in the YAML file and allows them to communicate with each other. However, even though Docker containers and docker-compose allow us to construct complex applications using consistent execution environments, we may potentially run into issues with robustness when we deploy these services to the cloud. For example, in a web application, we cannot be assured that the virtual machines that the application is running on will persist over long periods of time, so we need processes to manage self-healing and redundancy. This is also relevant to distributed machine learning pipelines, in which we do not want to have to kill an entire job because one node in a cluster goes down, which requires us to have backup logic to restart a sub-segment of work. Also, while Docker has the docker-compose functionality to link together several containers in an application, it does not have robust rules for how communication should happen among those containers, or how to manage them as a unit. For these purposes, we turn to the Kubernetes library.

Kubernetes: Robust management of multi-container applications

The Kubernetes project – sometimes abbreviated as k8s – was born out of an internal container management project at Google known as **Borg**. Kubernetes comes from the Greek word for navigator, as denoted by the seven-spoke wheel of the project's logo.[18] Kubernetes is written in the Go programming language and provides a robust framework to deploy and manage Docker container applications on the underlying resources managed by cloud providers (such as **Amazon Web Services (AWS)**, Microsoft Azure, and **Google Cloud Platform (GCP)**).

Kubernetes is fundamentally a tool to control applications composed of one or more Docker containers deployed in the cloud; this collection of containers is known as a **pod**. Each pod can have one or more copies (to allow redundancy), which is known as a **replicaset**. The two main components of a Kubernetes deployment are a **control plane** and **nodes**. The control plane hosts the centralized logic for deploying and managing pods, and consists of (*Figure 2.4*):

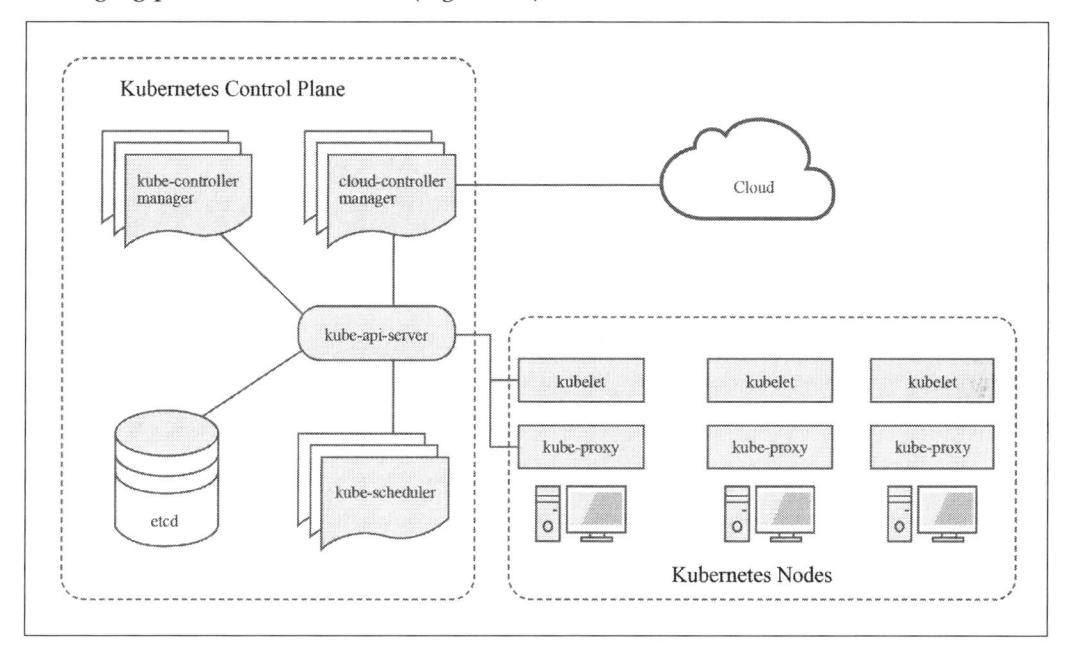

Figure 2.4: Kubernetes components[18]

- **Kube-api-server**: This is the main application that listens to commands from the user to deploy or update a pod, or manages external access to pods via `ingress`.
- **Kube-controller-manager**: An application to manage functions such as controlling the number of replicas per pod.
- **Cloud-controller-manager**: Manages functions particular to a cloud provider.
- **Etcd**: A key-value store that maintains the environment and state variables of different pods.
- **Kube-scheduler**: An application that is responsible for finding workers to run a pod.

While we could set up our own control plane, in practice we will usually have this function managed by our cloud provider, such as Google's **Google Kubernetes Engine (GKE)** or Amazon's **Elastic Kubernetes Services (EKS)**. The Kubernetes nodes – the individual machines in the cluster – each run an application known as a **kubelet**, which monitors the pod(s) running on that node.

Now that we have a high-level view of the Kubernetes system, let's look at the important commands you will need to interact with a Kubernetes cluster, update its components, and start and stop applications.

Important Kubernetes commands

In order to interact with a Kubernetes cluster running in the cloud, we typically utilize the **Kubernetes command-line tool** (**kubectl**). Instructions for installing kubectl for your operating system can be found at (https://kubernetes.io/docs/tasks/tools/install-kubectl/). To verify that you have successfully installed kubectl, you can again run the help command in the terminal:

```
kubectl --help
```

Like Docker, kubectl has many commands; the important one that we will use is the apply command, which, like docker-compose, takes in a YAML file as input and communicates with the Kubernetes control plane to start, update, or stop pods:

```
kubectl apply -f <file.yaml>
```

As an example of how the apply command works, let us look at a YAML file for deploying a web server (nginx) application:

```
apiVersion: v1
kind: Service
metadata:
  name: my-nginx-svc
  labels:
    app: nginx
spec:
  type: LoadBalancer
  ports:
  - port: 80
  selector:
    app: nginx
---
apiVersion: apps/v1
```

```
kind: Deployment
metadata:
  name: my-nginx
  labels:
    app: nginx
spec:
  replicas: 3
  selector:
    matchLabels:
      app: nginx
  template:
    metadata:
      labels:
        app: nginx
    spec:
      containers:
      - name: nginx
        image: nginx:1.7.9
        ports:
        - containerPort: 80
```

The resources specified in this file are created on the Kubernetes cluster nodes in the order in which they are listed in the file. First, we create the load balancer, which routes external traffic between copies of the `nginx` web server. The `metadata` is used to tag these applications for querying later using kubectl. Secondly, we create a set of 3 `replicas` of the `nginx` pod, using a consistent container (image `1.7.9`), which uses port `80` on their respective containers.

The same set of physical resources of a Kubernetes cluster can be shared among several **virtual** clusters using **namespaces** – this allows us to segregate resources among multiple users or groups. This can allow, for example, each team to run their own set of applications and logically behave as if they are the only users. Later, in our discussion of **Kubeflow**, we will see how this feature can be used to logically partition projects on the same Kubeflow instance.

Kustomize for configuration management

Like most code, we most likely want to ultimately store the YAML files we use to issue commands to Kubernetes in a version control system such as Git. This leads to some cases where this format might not be ideal: for example, in a machine learning pipeline, we might perform hyperparameter searches where the same application is being run with slightly different parameters, leading to a glut of duplicate command files.

Or, we might have arguments, such as AWS account keys, that for security reasons we do not want to store in a text file. We might also want to increase reuse by splitting our command into a base and additions; for example, in the YAML file shown in *Code 2.1*, if we wanted to run ngnix alongside different databases, or specify file storage in the different cloud object stores provided by Amazon, Google, and Microsoft Azure.

For these use cases, we will make use of the Kustomize tool (https://kustomize.io), which is also available through kubectl as:

```
kubectl apply -k <kustomization.yaml>
```

Alternatively, we could use the Kustomize command-line tool. A kustomization.yaml is a template for a Kubernetes application; for example, consider the following template for the training job in the Kubeflow example repository (https://github.com/kubeflow/pipelines/blob/master/manifests/kustomize/sample/kustomization.yaml):

```
apiVersion: kustomize.config.k8s.io/v1beta1
kind: Kustomization

bases:
  # Or
# github.com/kubeflow/pipelines/manifests/kustomize/env/gcp?ref=1.0.0
  - ../env/gcp
  # Kubeflow Pipelines servers are capable of
  # collecting Prometheus metrics.
  # If you want to monitor your Kubeflow Pipelines servers
  # with those metrics, you'll need a Prometheus server
  # in your Kubeflow Pipelines cluster.
  # If you don't already have a Prometheus server up, you
  # can uncomment the following configuration files for Prometheus.
  # If you have your own Prometheus server up already
  # or you don't want a Prometheus server for monitoring,
  # you can comment the following line out.
  # - ../third_party/prometheus
  # - ../third_party/grafana

# Identifier for application manager to apply ownerReference.
# The ownerReference ensures the resources get garbage collected
# when application is deleted.
commonLabels:
  application-crd-id: kubeflow-pipelines
```

```
# Used by Kustomize
configMapGenerator:
  - name: pipeline-install-config
    env: params.env
    behavior: merge

secretGenerator:
  - name: mysql-secret
    env: params-db-secret.env
    behavior: merge

# !!! If you want to customize the namespace,
# please also update
# sample/cluster-scoped-resources/kustomization.yaml's
# namespace field to the same value
namespace: kubeflow


#### Customization ###
# 1. Change values in params.env file
# 2. Change values in params-db-secret.env
# file for CloudSQL username and password
# 3. kubectl apply -k ./
####
```

We can see that this file refers to a base set of configurations in a separate kustomization.yaml file located at the relative path ../base. To edit variables in this file, for instance, to change the namespace for the application, we would run:

```
kustomize edit set namespace mykube
```

We could also add configuration maps to pass to the training job, using a key-value format, for example:

```
kustomize edit add configmap configMapGenerator --from-literal=myVar=myVal
```

Finally, when we are ready to execute these commands on Kubernetes, we can build the necessary kubectl command dynamically and apply it, assuming kustomization.yaml is in the current directory.

```
kustomize build . |kubectl apply -f -
```

Hopefully, these examples demonstrate how Kustomize provides a flexible way to generate the YAML we need for kubectl using a template; we will make use of it often in the process of parameterizing our workflows later in this book.

Now that we have covered how Kubernetes manages Docker applications in the cloud, and how Kustomize can allow us to flexibly reuse `kubectl yaml` commands, let's look at how these components are tied together in Kubeflow to run the kinds of experiments we will be undertaking later to create generative AI models in TensorFlow.

Kubeflow: an end-to-end machine learning lab

As was described at the beginning of this chapter, there are many components of an end-to-end `lab` for machine learning research and development (*Table 2.1*), such as:

- A way to manage and version library dependencies, such as TensorFlow, and package them for a reproducible computing environment
- Interactive research environments where we can visualize data and experiment with different settings
- A systematic way to specify the steps of a pipeline – data processing, model tuning, evaluation, and deployment
- Provisioning of resources to run the modeling process in a distributed manner
- Robust mechanisms for snapshotting historical versions of the research process

As we described earlier in this chapter, TensorFlow was designed to utilize distributed resources for training. To leverage this capability, we will use the Kubeflow projects. Built on top of Kubernetes, Kubeflow has several components that are useful in the end-to-end process of managing machine learning applications. To install Kubeflow, we need to have an existing Kubernetes control plane instance and use kubectl to launch Kubeflow's various components. The steps for setup differ slightly depending upon whether we are using a local instance or one of the major cloud providers.

Running Kubeflow locally with MiniKF

If we want to get started quickly or prototype our application locally, we can avoid setting up a cloud account and instead use virtual machines to simulate the kind of resources we would provision in the cloud. To set up Kubeflow locally, we first need to install VirtualBox (https://www.virtualbox.org/wiki/Downloads) to run virtual machines, and Vagrant to run configurations for setting up a Kubernetes control plane and Kubeflow on VirtualBox VMs (https://www.vagrantup.com/downloads.html).

Once you have these two dependencies installed, create a new directory, change into it, and run:

```
vagrant init arrikto/minikf
vagrant up
```

This initializes the VirtualBox configuration and brings up the application. You can now navigate to http://10.10.10.10/ and follow the instructions to launch Kubeflow and Rok (a storage volume for data used in experiments on Kubeflow created by Arrikto). Once these have been provisioned, you should see a screen like this (*Figure 2.5*):

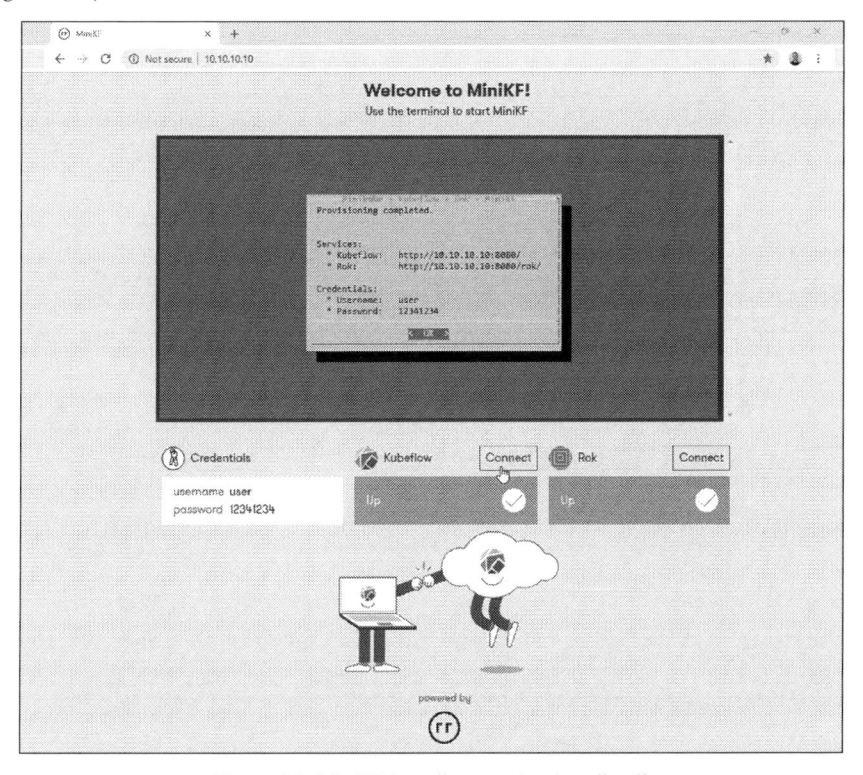

Figure 2.5: MiniKF install screen in virtualbox[19]

Setting Up a TensorFlow Lab

Log in to Kubeflow to see the dashboard with the various components (*Figure 2.6*):

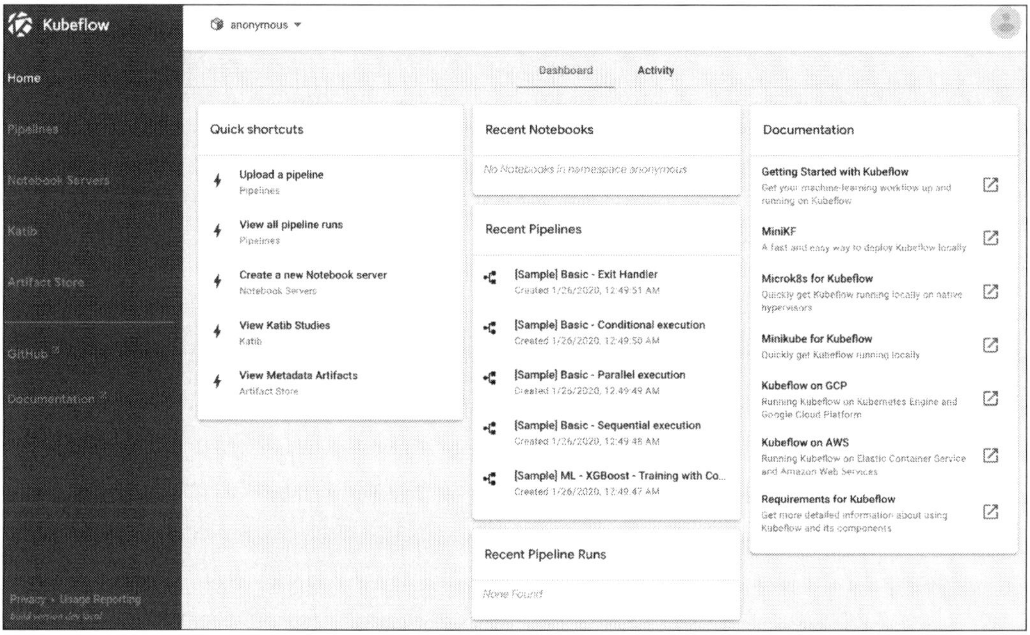

Figure 2.6: Kubeflow dashboard in MiniKF

We will return to these components later and go through the various functionalities available on Kubeflow, but first, let's walk through how to install Kubeflow in the cloud.

Installing Kubeflow in AWS

In order to run Kubeflow in AWS, we need a Kubernetes control plane available in the cloud. Fortunately, Amazon provides a managed service called EKS, which provides an easy way to provision a control plane to deploy Kubeflow. Follow the following steps to deploy Kubeflow on AWS:

1. **Register for an AWS account and install the AWS Command Line Interface**

    This is needed to interact with the various AWS services, following the instructions for your platform located at https://docs.aws.amazon.com/cli/latest/userguide/cli-chap-install.html. Once it is installed, enter:

    ```
    aws configure
    ```

    to set up your account and key information to provision resources.

[44]

2. **Install eksctl**

   This command-line utility allows us to provision a Kubernetes control plane in Amazon from the command line. Follow instructions at `https://docs.aws.amazon.com/cli/latest/userguide/cli-chap-install.html` to install.

3. **Install iam-authenticator**

   To allow kubectl to interact with EKS, we need to provide the correct permissions using the IAM authenticator to modify our kubeconfig. Please see the installation instructions at `https://docs.aws.amazon.com/eks/latest/userguide/install-aws-iam-authenticator.html`.

4. **Download the Kubeflow command-line tool**

   Links are located at the Kubeflow releases page (`https://github.com/kubeflow/kubeflow/releases/tag/v0.7.1`). Download one of these directories and unpack the tarball using:

   ```
   tar -xvf kfctl_v0.7.1_<platform>.tar.gz
   ```

5. **Build the configuration file**

   After entering environment variables for the Kubeflow application director (`${KF_DIR}`), the name of the deployment (`${KF_NAME}`), and the path to the base configuration file for the deployment (`${CONFIG_URI}`), which is located at `https://raw.githubusercontent.com/kubeflow/manifests/v0.7-branch/kfdef/kfctl_aws.0.7.1.yaml` for AWS deployments, run the following to generate the configuration file:

   ```
   mkdir -p ${KF_DIR}
   cd ${KF_DIR}
   kfctl build -V -f ${CONFIG_URI}
   ```

   This will generate a local configuration file locally named `kfctl_aws.0.7.1.yaml`. If this looks like Kustomize, that's because `kfctl` is using Kustomize under the hood to build the configuration. We also need to add an environment variable for the location of the local config file, `${CONFIG_FILE}`, which in this case is:

   ```
   export CONFIG_FILE=${KF_DIR}/kfctl_aws.0.7.1.yaml
   ```

6. **Launch Kubeflow on EKS**

   Use the following commands to launch Kubeflow:

   ```
   cd ${KF_DIR}
   rm -rf kustomize/
   kfctl apply -V -f ${CONFIG_FILE}
   ```

It will take a while for all the Kubeflow components to become available; you can check the progress by using the following command:

```
kubectl -n kubeflow get all
```

Once they are all available, we can get the URL address for the Kubeflow dashboard using:

```
kubectl get ingress -n istio-system
```

This will take us to the dashboard view shown in the MiniKF examples above. Note that in the default configuration, this address is open to the public; for secure applications, we need to add authentication using the instructions at https://www.kubeflow.org/docs/aws/authentication/.

Installing Kubeflow in GCP

Like AWS, **Google Cloud Platform** (GCP) provides a managed Kubernetes control plane, GKE. We can install Kubeflow in GCP using the following steps:

1. **Register for a GCP account and create a project on the console**

    This project will be where the various resources associated with Kubeflow will reside.

2. **Enable required services**

    The services required to run Kubeflow on GCP are:

    - Compute Engine API
    - Kubernetes Engine API
    - Identity and Access Management (IAM) API
    - Deployment Manager API
    - Cloud Resource Manager API
    - Cloud Filestore API
    - AI Platform Training & Prediction API

3. **Set up OAuth (optional)**

    If you wish to make a secure deployment, then, as with AWS, you must follow instructions to add authentication to your installation, located at (https://www.kubeflow.org/docs/gke/deploy/oauth-setup/). Alternatively, you can just use the name and password for your GCP account.

4. **Set up the GCloud CLI**

   This is parallel to the AWS CLI covered in the previous section. Installation instructions are available at https://cloud.google.com/sdk/. You can verify your installation by running:

   ```
   gcloud --help
   ```

5. **Download the kubeflow command-line tool**

   Links are located on the Kubeflow releases page (https://github.com/kubeflow/kubeflow/releases/tag/v0.7.1). Download one of these directories and unpack the tarball using:

   ```
   tar -xvf kfctl_v0.7.1_<platform>.tar.gz
   ```

6. **Log in to GCloud and create user credentials**

   We next need to create a login account and credential token we will use to interact with resources in our account.

   ```
   gcloud auth login
   gcloud auth application-default login
   ```

7. **Set up environment variable and deploy Kubeflow**

   As with AWS, we need to enter values for a few key environment variables: the application containing the Kubeflow configuration files (${KF_DIR}), the name of the Kubeflow deployment (${KF_NAME}), the path to the base configuration URI (${CONFIG_URI} – for GCP this is https://raw.githubusercontent.com/kubeflow/manifests/v0.7-branch/kfdef/kfctl_gcp_iap.0.7.1.yaml), the name of the Google project (${PROJECT}), and the zone it runs in (${ZONE}).

8. **Launch Kubeflow**

   The same as AWS, we use Kustomize to build the template file and launch Kubeflow:

   ```
   mkdir -p ${KF_DIR}
   cd ${KF_DIR}
   kfctl apply -V -f ${CONFIG_URI}
   ```

   Once Kubeflow is launched, you can get the URL to the dashboard using:

   ```
   kubectl -n istio-system get ingress
   ```

Installing Kubeflow on Azure

Azure is Microsoft Corporation's cloud offering, and like AWS and GCP, we can use it to install Kubeflow leveraging a Kubernetes control plane and computing resources residing in the Azure cloud.

1. **Register an account on Azure**

    Sign up at https://azure.microsoft.com – a free tier is available for experimentation.

2. **Install the Azure command-line utilities**

    See instructions for installation on your platform at https://docs.microsoft.com/en-us/cli/azure/install-azure-cli?view=azure-cli-latest. You can verify your installation by running the following on the command line on your machine:

    ```
    az
    ```

    This should print a list of commands that you can use on the console. To start, log in to your account with:

    ```
    az login
    ```

    And enter the account credentials you registered in *Step 1*. You will be redirected to a browser to verify your account, after which you should see a response like the following:

    ```
    "You have logged in. Now let us find all the subscriptions to
    which you have access": …
    [
    {
        "cloudName": …
        "id" ….
    …
        "user": {
    …
    }
    }
    ]
    ```

3. **Create the resource group for a new cluster**

   We first need to create the resource group where our new application will live, using the following command:

   ```
   az group create -n ${RESOURCE_GROUP_NAME} -l ${LOCATION}
   ```

4. **Create a Kubernetes resource on AKS**

   Now deploy the Kubernetes control plane on your resource group:

   ```
   az aks create -g ${RESOURCE_GROUP_NAME} -n ${NAME} -s ${AGENT_SIZE} -c ${AGENT_COUNT} -l ${LOCATION} --generate-ssh-keys
   ```

5. **Install Kubeflow**

   First, we need to obtain credentials to install Kubeflow on our AKS resource:

   ```
   az aks get-credentials -n ${NAME}  -g ${RESOURCE_GROUP_NAME}
   ```

6. **Install kfctl**

   Install and unpack the tarball directory:

   ```
   tar -xvf kfctl_v0.7.1_<platform>.tar.gz
   ```

7. **Set environment variables**

   As with AWS, we need to enter values for a few key environment variables: the application containing the Kubeflow configuration files (${KF_DIR}), the name of the Kubeflow deployment (${KF_NAME}), and the path to the base configuration URI (${CONFIG_URI} – for Azure, this is https://raw.githubusercontent.com/kubeflow/manifests/v0.7-branch/kfdef/kfctl_k8s_istio.0.7.1.yaml).

8. **Launch Kubeflow**

   The same as AWS, we use Kustomize to build the template file and launch Kubeflow:

   ```
   mkdir -p ${KF_DIR}
   cd ${KF_DIR}
   kfctl apply -V -f ${CONFIG_URI}
   ```

   Once Kubeflow is launched, you can use port forwarding to redirect traffic from local port 8080 to port 80 in the cluster to access the Kubeflow dashboard at localhost:8080 using the following command:

   ```
   kubectl port-forward svc/istio-ingressgateway -n istio-system 8080:80
   ```

Installing Kubeflow using Terraform

For each of these cloud providers, you'll probably notice that we have a common set of commands; creating a Kubernetes cluster, installing Kubeflow, and starting the application. While we can use scripts to automate this process, it would be desirable to, like our code, have a way to version control and persist different infrastructure configurations, allowing a reproducible recipe for creating the set of resources we need to run Kubeflow. It would also help us potentially move between cloud providers without completely rewriting our installation logic.

The template language **Terraform** (https://www.terraform.io/) was created by HashiCorp as a tool for **Infrastructure as a Service** (**IaaS**). In the same way that Kubernetes has an API to update resources on a cluster, **Terraform** allows us to abstract interactions with different underlying cloud providers using an API and a template language using a command-line utility and core components written in GoLang (*Figure 2.7*). Terraform can be extended using user-written plugins.

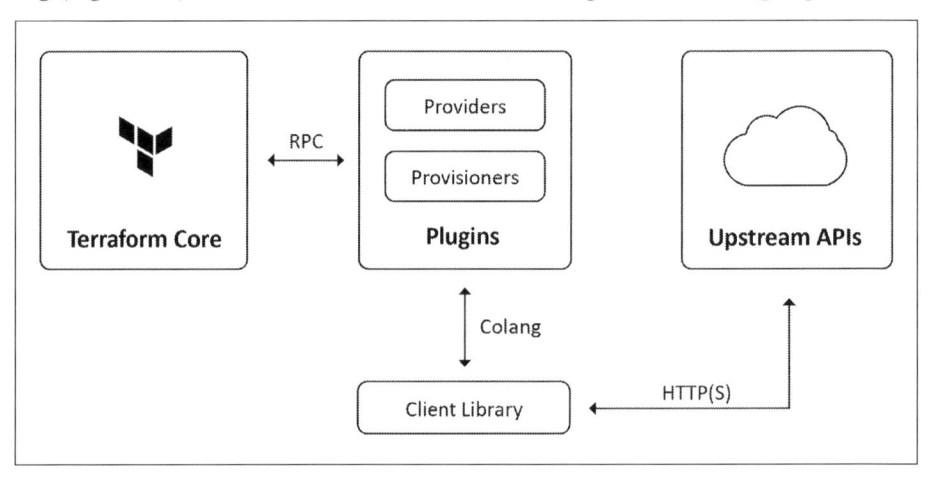

Figure 2.7: Terraform architecture[20]

Let's look at one example of installing Kubeflow using Terraform instructions on AWS, located at https://github.com/aws-samples/amazon-eks-machine-learning-with-terraform-and-kubeflow. Once you have established the required AWS resources and installed terraform on an EC2 container, the `aws-eks-cluster-and-nodegroup.tf` Terraform file is used to create the Kubeflow cluster using the command:

```
terraform apply
```

In this file are a few key components. One is variables that specify aspects of the deployment:

```
variable "efs_throughput_mode" {
   description = "EFS performance mode"
   default = "bursting"
   type = string
}
```

Another is a specification for which cloud provider we are using:

```
provider "aws" {
  region                 = var.region
  shared_credentials_file = var.credentials
resource "aws_eks_cluster" "eks_cluster" {
  name        = var.cluster_name
  role_arn    = aws_iam_role.cluster_role.arn
  version     = var.k8s_version

  vpc_config {
    security_group_ids = [aws_security_group.cluster_sg.id]
    subnet_ids         = flatten([aws_subnet.subnet.*.id])
  }

  depends_on = [
    aws_iam_role_policy_attachment.cluster_AmazonEKSClusterPolicy,
    aws_iam_role_policy_attachment.cluster_AmazonEKSServicePolicy,
  ]

  provisioner "local-exec" {
    command = "aws --region ${var.region} eks update-kubeconfig --name ${aws_eks_cluster.eks_cluster.name}"
  }

  provisioner "local-exec" {
    when    = destroy
    command = "kubectl config unset current-context"
  }

}
  profile    = var.profile
}
```

And another is resources such as the EKS cluster:

```
resource "aws_eks_cluster" "eks_cluster" {
  name     = var.cluster_name
  role_arn = aws_iam_role.cluster_role.arn
  version  = var.k8s_version

  vpc_config {
    security_group_ids = [aws_security_group.cluster_sg.id]
    subnet_ids         = flatten([aws_subnet.subnet.*.id])
  }

  depends_on = [
    aws_iam_role_policy_attachment.cluster_AmazonEKSClusterPolicy,
    aws_iam_role_policy_attachment.cluster_AmazonEKSServicePolicy,
  ]

  provisioner "local-exec" {
    command = "aws --region ${var.region} eks update-kubeconfig --name ${aws_eks_cluster.eks_cluster.name}"
  }

  provisioner "local-exec" {
    when    = destroy
    command = "kubectl config unset current-context"
  }

}
```

Every time we run the Terraform `apply` command, it walks through this file to determine what resources to create, which underlying AWS services to call to create them, and with which set of configuration they should be provisioned. This provides a clean way to orchestrate complex installations such as Kubeflow in a versioned, extensible template language.

Now that we have successfully installed Kubeflow either locally or on a managed Kubernetes control plane in the cloud, let us take a look at what tools are available on the platform.

Chapter 2

A brief tour of Kubeflow's components

Now that we have installed Kubeflow locally or in the cloud, let us take a look again at the Kubeflow dashboard (*Figure 2.8*):

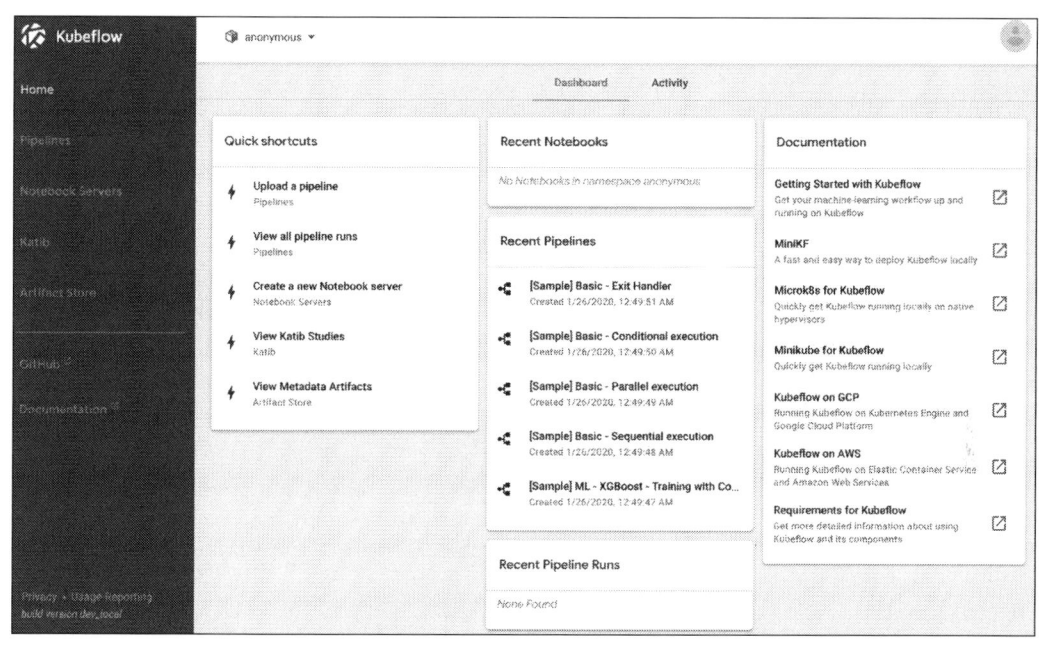

Figure 2.8: The Kubeflow dashboard

Let's walk through what is available in this toolkit. First, notice in the upper panel we have a dropdown with the name anonymous specified – this is the `namespace` for Kubernetes referred to earlier. While our default is anonymous, we could create several namespaces on our Kubeflow instance to accommodate different users or projects. This can be done at login, where we set up a profile (*Figure 2.9*):

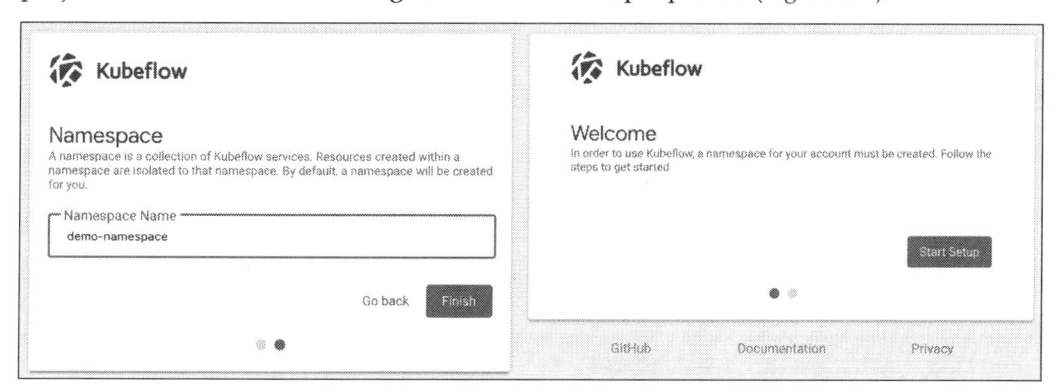

Figure 2.9: Kubeflow login page

[53]

Setting Up a TensorFlow Lab

Alternatively, as with other operations in Kubernetes, we can apply a namespace using a YAML file:

```
apiVersion: kubeflow.org/v1beta1
kind: Profile
metadata:
  name: profileName
spec:
  owner:
    kind: User
    name: userid@email.com
```

Using the `kubectl` command:

```
kubectl create -f profile.yaml
```

What can we do once we have a namespace? Let us look through the available tools.

Kubeflow notebook servers

We can use Kubeflow to start a Jupyter notebook server in a namespace, where we can run experimental code; we can start the notebook by clicking the **Notebook Servers** tab in the user interface and selecting **NEW SERVER** (*Figure 2.10*):

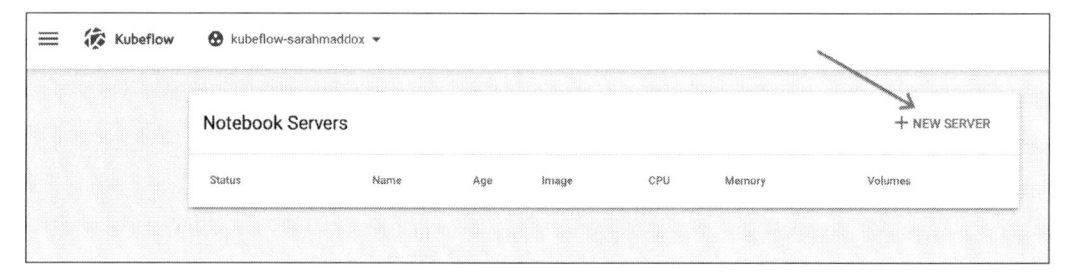

Figure 2.10: Kubeflow notebook creation

We can then specify parameters, such as which container to run (which could include the TensorFlow container we examined earlier in our discussion of Docker), and how many resources to allocate (*Figure 2.11*).

[54]

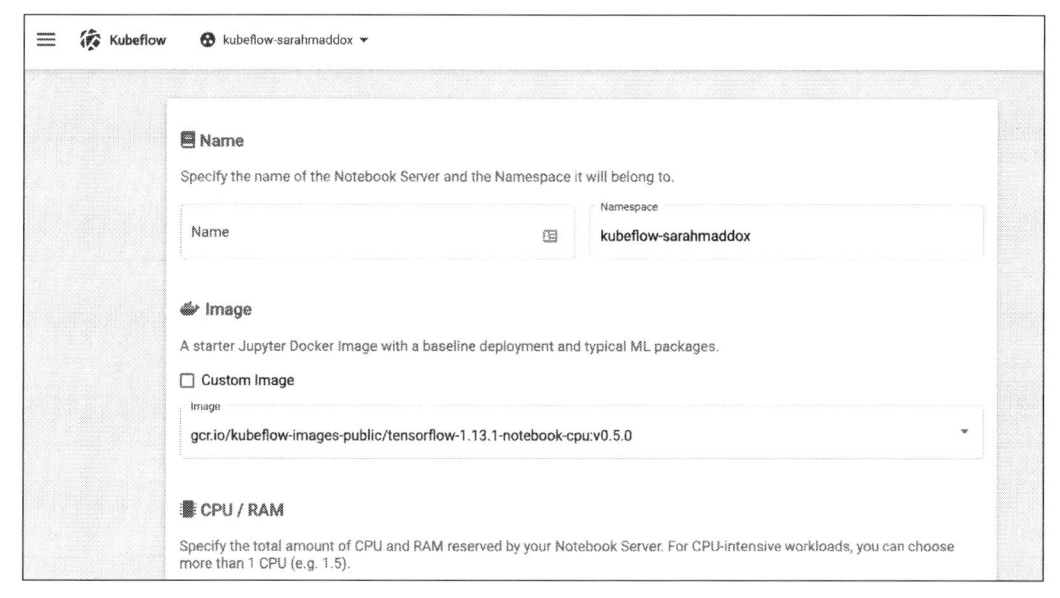

Figure 2.11: Kubeflow Docker resources panel

You can also specify a **Persistent Volume** (**PV**) to store data that remains even if the notebook server is turned off, and special resources such as GPUs.

Once started, if you have specified a container with TensorFlow resources, you can begin running models in the notebook server.

Kubeflow pipelines

For notebook servers, we gave an example of a single container (the notebook instance) application. Kubeflow also gives us the ability to run multi-container application workflows (such as input data, training, and deployment) using the **pipelines** functionality. Pipelines are Python functions that follow a **Domain Specific Language** (**DSL**) to specify components that will be compiled into containers.

Setting Up a TensorFlow Lab

If we click pipelines on the UI, we are brought to a dashboard (*Figure 2.12*):

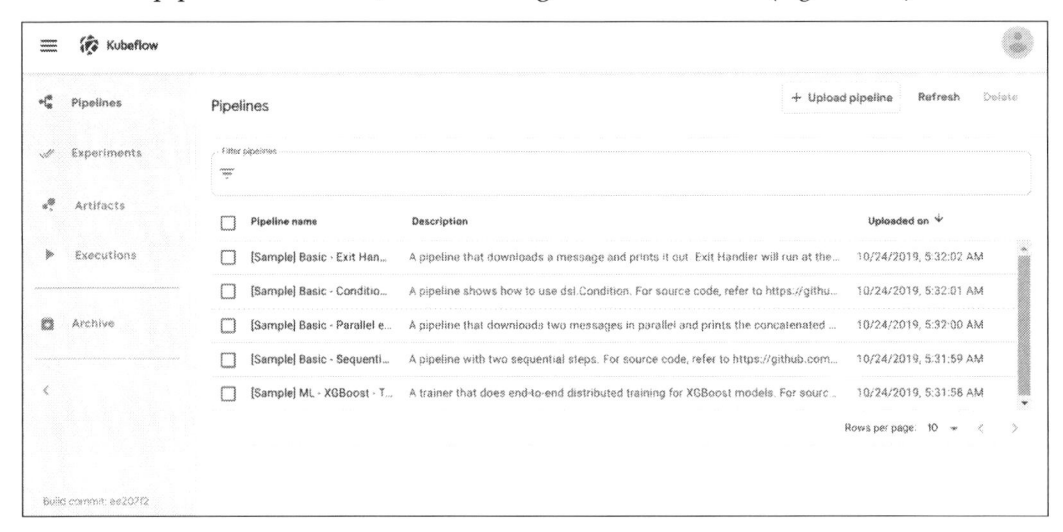

Figure 2.12: Kubeflow pipelines sashboard

Selecting one of these pipelines, we can see a visual overview of the component containers (*Figure 2.13*).

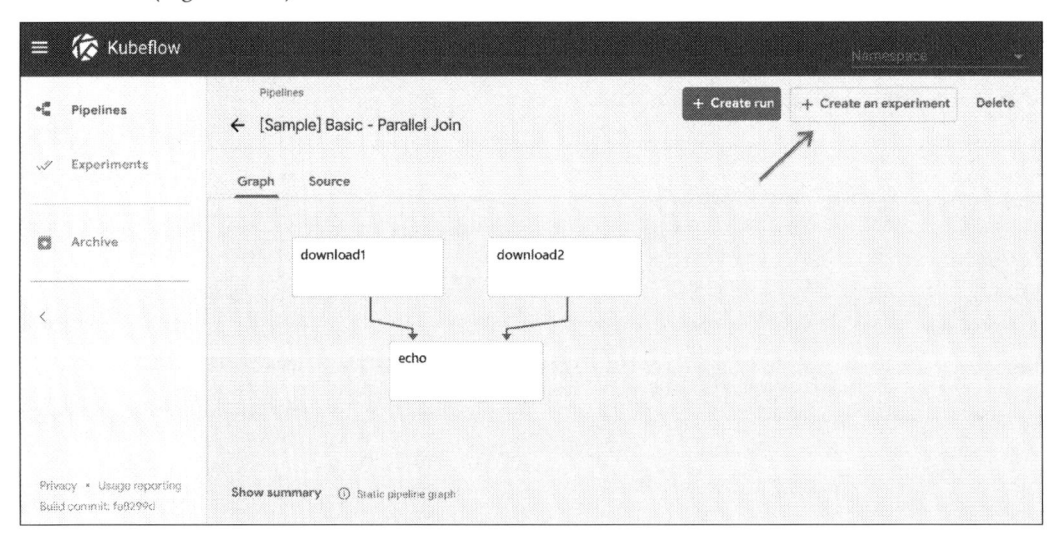

Figure 2.13: Kubeflow pipelines visualization

Chapter 2

After creating a new run, we can specify parameters for a particular instance of this pipeline (*Figure 2.14*).

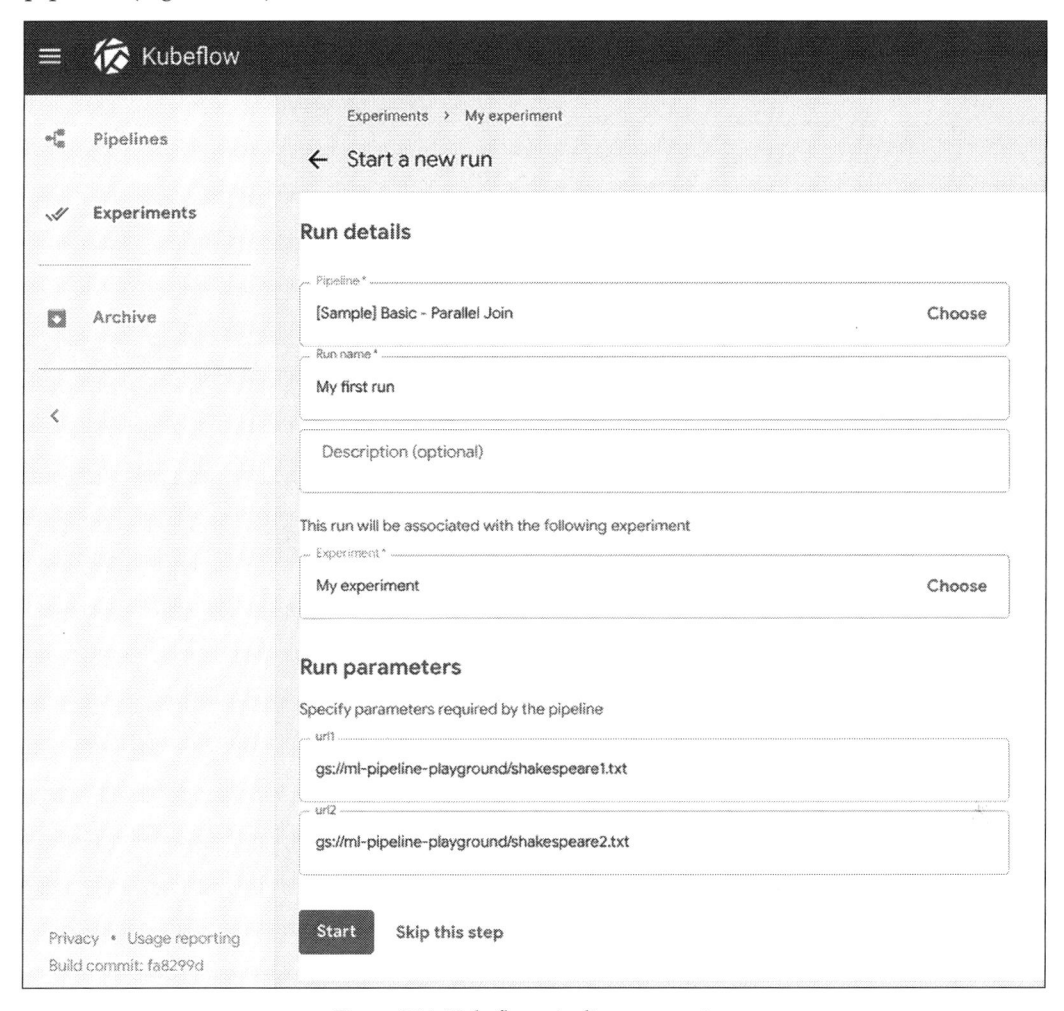

Figure 2.14: Kubeflow pipelines parameters

Setting Up a TensorFlow Lab

Once the pipeline is created, we can use the user interface to visualize the results (*Figure 2.15*):

Figure 2.15: Kubeflow pipeline results visualization

Under the hood, the Python code to generate this pipeline is compiled using the pipelines SDK. We could specify the components to come either from a container with Python code:

```
@kfp.dsl.component
def my_component(my_param):
  ...
  return kfp.dsl.ContainerOp(
    name='My component name',
    image='gcr.io/path/to/container/image'
```

or a function written in Python itself:
```
    )
or a function written in Python itself:
@kfp.dsl.python_component(
    name='My awesome component',
    description='Come and play',
)
def my_python_func(a: str, b: str) -> str:
```

For a pure Python function, we could turn this into an operation with the compiler:

```
my_op = compiler.build_python_component(
    component_func=my_python_func,
    staging_gcs_path=OUTPUT_DIR,
    target_image=TARGET_IMAGE)
```

We then use the `dsl.pipeline` decorator to add this operation to a pipeline:

```
@kfp.dsl.pipeline(
    name='My pipeline',
    description='My machine learning pipeline'
)
def my_pipeline(param_1: PipelineParam, param_2: PipelineParam):
    my_step = my_op(a='a', b='b')
```

We compile it using the following code:

```
kfp.compiler.Compiler().compile(my_pipeline, 'my-pipeline.zip')
```

and run it with this code:

```
client = kfp.Client()
my_experiment = client.create_experiment(name='demo')
my_run = client.run_pipeline(my_experiment.id, 'my-pipeline',
    'my-pipeline.zip')
```

We can also upload this ZIP file to the pipelines UI, where Kubeflow can use the generated YAML from compilation to instantiate the job.

Now that you have seen the process for generating results for a single pipeline, our next problem is how to generate the optimal parameters for such a pipeline. As you will see in *Chapter 3, Building Blocks of Deep Neural Networks*, neural network models typically have a number of configurations, known as **hyperparameters**, which govern their architecture (such as number of layers, layer size, and connectivity) and training paradigm (such as learning rate and optimizer algorithm). Kubeflow has a built-in utility for optimizing models for such parameter grids, called **Katib**.

Using Kubeflow Katib to optimize model hyperparameters

Katib is a framework for running multiple instances of the same job with differing inputs, such as in neural architecture search (for determining the right number and size of layers in a neural network) and hyperparameter search (finding the right learning rate, for example, for an algorithm). Like the other Kustomize templates we have seen, the TensorFlow job specifies a generic TensorFlow job, with placeholders for the parameters:

```
apiVersion: "kubeflow.org/v1alpha3"
kind: Experiment
metadata:
  namespace: kubeflow
  name: tfjob-example
spec:
  parallelTrialCount: 3
  maxTrialCount: 12
  maxFailedTrialCount: 3
  objective:
    type: maximize
    goal: 0.99
    objectiveMetricName: accuracy_1
  algorithm:
    algorithmName: random
  metricsCollectorSpec:
    source:
      fileSystemPath:
        path: /train
        kind: Directory
    collector:
      kind: TensorFlowEvent
  parameters:
    - name: --learning_rate
      parameterType: double
      feasibleSpace:
        min: "0.01"
        max: "0.05"
```

```
      - name: --batch_size
        parameterType: int
        feasibleSpace:
          min: "100"
          max: "200"
    trialTemplate:
      goTemplate:
        rawTemplate: |-
          apiVersion: "kubeflow.org/v1"
          kind: TFJob
          metadata:
            name: {{.Trial}}
            namespace: {{.NameSpace}}
          spec:
           tfReplicaSpecs:
            Worker:
              replicas: 1
              restartPolicy: OnFailure
              template:
                spec:
                  containers:
                    - name: tensorflow
                      image: gcr.io/kubeflow-ci/tf-mnist-with-
                              summaries:1.0
                      imagePullPolicy: Always
                      command:
                        - "python"
                        - "/var/tf_mnist/mnist_with_summaries.py"
                        - "--log_dir=/train/metrics"
                        {{- with .HyperParameters}}
                        {{- range .}}
                        - "{{.Name}}={{.Value}}"
                        {{- end}}
                        {{- end}}
```

which we can run using the familiar kubectl syntax:

```
kubectl apply -f https://raw.githubusercontent.com/kubeflow/katib/master/examples/v1alpha3/tfjob-example.yaml
```

or through the UI (*Figure 2.16*):

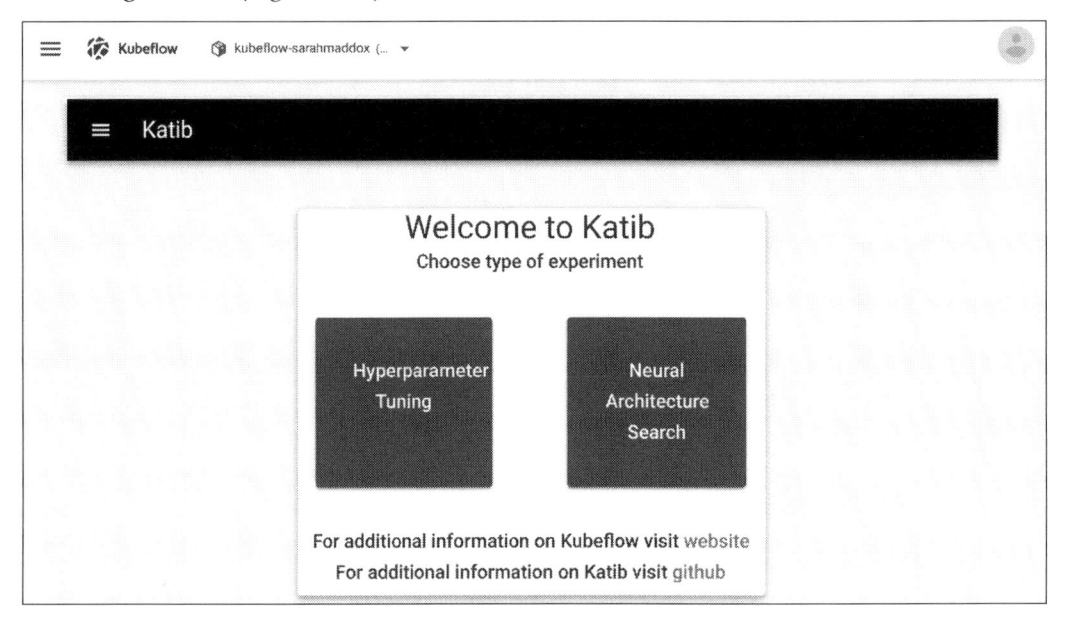

Figure 2.16: Katib UI on Kubeflow

where you can see a visual of the outcome of these multi-parameter experiments, or a table (*Figures 2.17* and *2.18*).

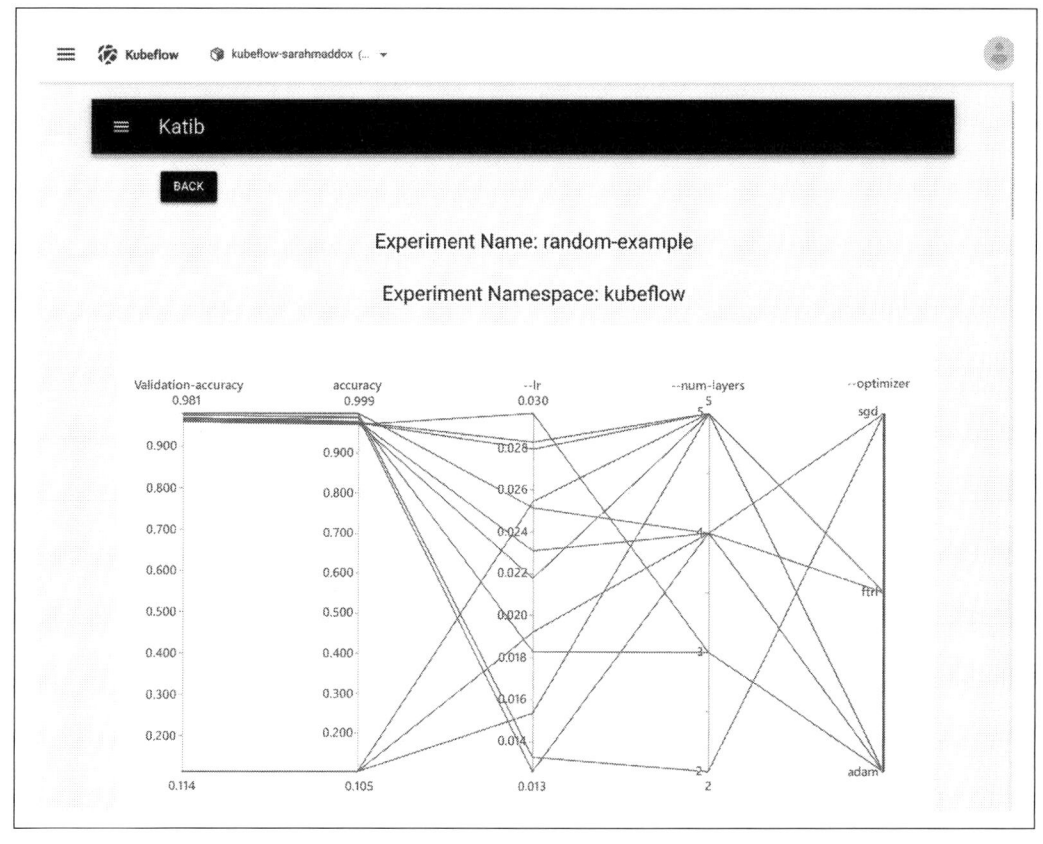

Figure 2.17: Kubeflow visualization for multi-dimensional parameter optimization

Setting Up a TensorFlow Lab

trialName	Validation-accuracy	accuracy	--lr	num-layers
random-example-4dj8tv57	0.976115	0.989531	0.0125707628996663537	4
random-example-556xhwh5	0.113854	0.105313	0.025437587023684788	5
random-example-bsb9lvbk	0.113854	0.105313	0.01921073871218211	4
random-example-ndjvxsb9	0.965864	0.986875	0.01828641157848641	3
random-example-psfgfdpc	0.966660	0.974531	0.02792704729276533	5

Figure 2.18: Kubeflow UI for multi-outcome experiments

Summary

In this chapter, we have covered an overview of what TensorFlow is and how it serves as an improvement over earlier frameworks for deep learning research. We also explored setting up an IDE, VSCode, and the foundation of reproducible applications, Docker containers. To orchestrate and deploy Docker containers, we discussed the Kubernetes framework, and how we can scale groups of containers using its API. Finally, I described Kubeflow, a machine learning framework built on Kubernetes which allows us to run end-to-end pipelines, distributed training, and parameter search, and serve trained models. We then set up a Kubeflow deployment using Terraform, an IaaS technology.

Before jumping into specific projects, we will next cover the basics of neural network theory and the TensorFlow and Keras commands that you will need to write basic training jobs on Kubeflow.

References

1. Abadi, Martín, et al. (2016) *TensorFlow: Large-Scale Machine Learning on Heterogeneous Distributed Systems*. arXiv:1603.04467. `https://arxiv.org/abs/1603.04467`.

2. Google. *TensorFlow*. Retrieved April 26, 2021, from `https://www.tensorflow.org/`

3. MATLAB, Natick, Massachusetts: The MathWorks Inc. `https://www.mathworks.com/products/matlab.html`

4. Krizhevsky A., Sutskever I., & Hinton G E. *ImageNet Classification with Deep Convolutional Neural Networks*. `https://papers.nips.cc/paper/4824-imagenet-classification-with-deepconvolutional-neural-networks.pdf`

5. Dean J., Ng A., (2012, Jun 26). *Using large-scale brain simulations for machine learning and A.I.*. Google | The Keyword. `https://blog.google/technology/ai/using-large-scale-brain-simulations-for/`

6. Mnih, V., Kavukcuoglu, K., Silver, D., Graves, A., Antonoglou, I., Wierstra, D., Riedmiller, M. (2013). *Playing Atari with Deep Reinforcement Learning*. arXiv:1312.5602. `https://arxiv.org/abs/1312.5602`

7. Silver D, Schrittwieser J, Simonyan K, Antonoglou I, Huang A, Guez A, Hubert T, Baker L, Lai M, Bolton A, Chen Y, Lillicrap T, Hui F, Sifre L, van den Driessche G, Graepel T, Hassabis D. (2017) *Mastering the game of Go without human knowledge*. Nature. 550(7676):354-359. `https://pubmed.ncbi.nlm.nih.gov/29052630/`

8. Devlin, J., Chang, M. W., Lee, K., & Toutanova, K. (2018). *Bert: Pre-training of deep bidirectional transformers for language understanding*. arXiv:1810.04805. `https://arxiv.org/abs/1810.04805`

9. Al-Rfou, R., et al. (2016). *Theano: A Python framework for fast computation of mathematical expressions*. arXiv. `https://arxiv.org/pdf/1605.02688.pdf`

10. Collobert R., Kavukcuoglu K., & Farabet C. (2011). *Torch7: A Matlab-like Environment for Machine Learning*. `http://ronan.collobert.com/pub/matos/2011_torch7_nipsw.pdf`

11. Abadi M., et al. (2015). *TensorFlow: Large-Scale Machine Learning on Heterogeneous Distributed Systems*. `download.tensorflow.org/paper/whitepaper2015.pdf`

12. Abadi, Martín, et al. (2016) *TensorFlow: Large-Scale Machine Learning on Heterogeneous Distributed Systems*. arXiv:1603.04467. `https://arxiv.org/abs/1603.04467`

13. Jouppi, N P, et al. (2017). *In-Datacenter Performance Analysis of a Tensor Processing Unit.* arXiv:1704.04760. https://arxiv.org/abs/1704.04760

14. van Merriënboer, B., Bahdanau, D., Dumoulin, V., Serdyuk, D., Warde-Farley, D., Chorowski, J., Bengio, Y. (2015). *Blocks and Fuel: Frameworks for deep learning.* arXiv:1506.00619. https://arxiv.org/pdf/1506.00619.pdf

15. https://stackoverflow.com/questions/57273888/keras-vs-TensorFlow-code-comparison-sources

16. Harris M. (2016). *Docker vs. Virtual Machine.* Nvidia developer blog. https://developer.nvidia.com/blog/nvidia-docker-gpu-server-application-deployment-made-easy/vm_vs_docker/

17. A visual play on words — the project's original code name was *Seven of Nine*, a Borg character from the series Star Trek: Voyager

18. Kubernetes Components. (2021, March 18) Kubernetes. https://kubernetes.io/docs/concepts/overview/components/

19. Pavlou C. (2019). *An end-to-end ML pipeline on-prem: Notebooks & Kubeflow Pipelines on the new MiniKF.* Medium | Kubeflow. https://medium.com/kubeflow/an-end-to-end-ml-pipeline-on-prem-notebooks-kubeflow-pipelines-on-the-new-minikf-33b7d8e9a836

20. Vargo S. (2017). *Managing Google Calendar with Terraform.* HashiCorp. https://www.hashicorp.com/blog/managing-google-calendar-with-terraform

3
Building Blocks of Deep Neural Networks

The wide range of generative AI models that we will implement in this book are all built on the foundation of advances over the last decade in *deep learning* and neural networks. While in practice we could implement these projects without reference to historical developments, it will give you a richer understanding of *how* and *why* these models work to retrace their underlying components. In this chapter, we will dive into this background, showing you how generative AI models are built from the ground up, how smaller units are assembled into complex architectures, how the loss functions in these models are optimized, and some current theories as to why these models are so effective. Armed with this background knowledge, you should be able to understand in greater depth the reasoning behind the more advanced models and topics that start in *Chapter 4, Teaching Networks to Generate Digits*, of this book. Generally speaking, we can group the building blocks of neural network models into a number of choices regarding how the model is constructed and trained, which we will cover in this chapter:

Which neural network architecture to use:

- Perceptron
- **Multilayer perceptron (MLP)**/feedforward
- **Convolutional Neural Networks (CNNs)**
- **Recurrent Neural Networks (RNNs)**
- **Long Short-Term Memory Networks (LSTMs)**
- **Gated Recurrent Units (GRUs)**

Which activation functions to use in the network:

- Linear
- Sigmoid
- Tanh
- ReLU
- PReLU

What optimization algorithm to use to tune the parameters of the network:

- **Stochastic Gradient Descent (SGD)**
- RMSProp
- AdaGrad
- ADAM
- AdaDelta
- Hessian-free optimization

How to initialize the parameters of the network:

- Random
- Xavier initialization
- He initialization

As you can appreciate, the products of these decisions can lead to a huge number of potential neural network variants, and one of the challenges of developing these models is determining the right search space within each of these choices. In the course of describing the history of neural networks we will discuss the implications of each of these model parameters in more detail. Our overview of this field begins with the origin of the discipline: the humble perceptron model.

Perceptrons – a brain in a function

The simplest neural network architecture – the perceptron – was inspired by biological research to understand the basis of mental processing in an attempt to represent the function of the brain with mathematical formulae. In this section we will cover some of this early research and how it inspired what is now the field of deep learning and generative AI.

From tissues to TLUs

The recent popularity of AI algorithms might give the false impression that this field is new. Many recent models are based on discoveries made decades ago that have been reinvigorated by the massive computational resources available in the cloud and customized hardware for parallel matrix computations such as **Graphical Processing Units (GPUs)**, **Tensor Processing Units (TPUs)**, and **Field Programmable Gate Array (FPGAs)**. If we consider research on neural networks to include their biological inspiration as well as computational theory, this field is over a hundred years old. Indeed, one of the first neural networks described appears in the detailed anatomical illustrations of 19th Century scientist Santiago Ramón y Cajal, whose illustrations based on experimental observations of layers of interconnected neuronal cells inspired the Neuron Doctrine – the idea that the brain is composed of individual, physically distinct and specialized cells, rather than a single continuous network.[1] The distinct layers of the retina observed by Cajal were also the inspiration for particular neural network architectures such as the CNN, which we will discuss later in this chapter.

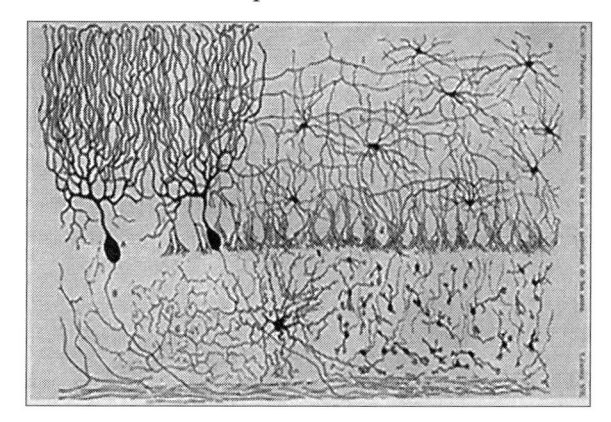

Figure 3.1: The networks of interconnected neurons illustrated by Santiago Ramón y Cajal[3]

This observation of simple neuronal cells interconnected in large networks led computational researchers to hypothesize how mental activity might be represented by simple, logical operations that, combined, yield complex mental phenomena. The original "automata theory" is usually traced to a 1943 article by Warren McCulloch and Walter Pitts of the Massachusetts Institute of Technology.[3] They described a simple model known as the **Threshold Logic Unit (TLU)**, in which binary inputs are translated into a binary output based on a threshold:

$$y = f(\sum_{i=1}^{N} W_i I_i)$$

where *I* is the input values, *W* is the weights with ranges from (0, 1) or (-1, 1), and f is a threshold function that converts these inputs into a binary output depending upon whether they exceed a threshold *T*:[4]

$$f(x) = 1 \; if \; x > T, else \; 0$$

Visually and conceptually, there is some similarity between McCulloch and Pitts' model and the biological neuron that inspired it (*Figure 3.2*). Their model integrates inputs into an output signal, just as the natural dendrites (short, input "arms" of the neuron that receive signals from other cells) of a neuron synthesize inputs into a single output via the axon (the long "tail" of the cell, which passes signals received from the dendrites along to other neurons). We might imagine that, just as neuronal cells are composed into networks to yield complex biological circuits, these simple units might be connected to simulate sophisticated decision processes.

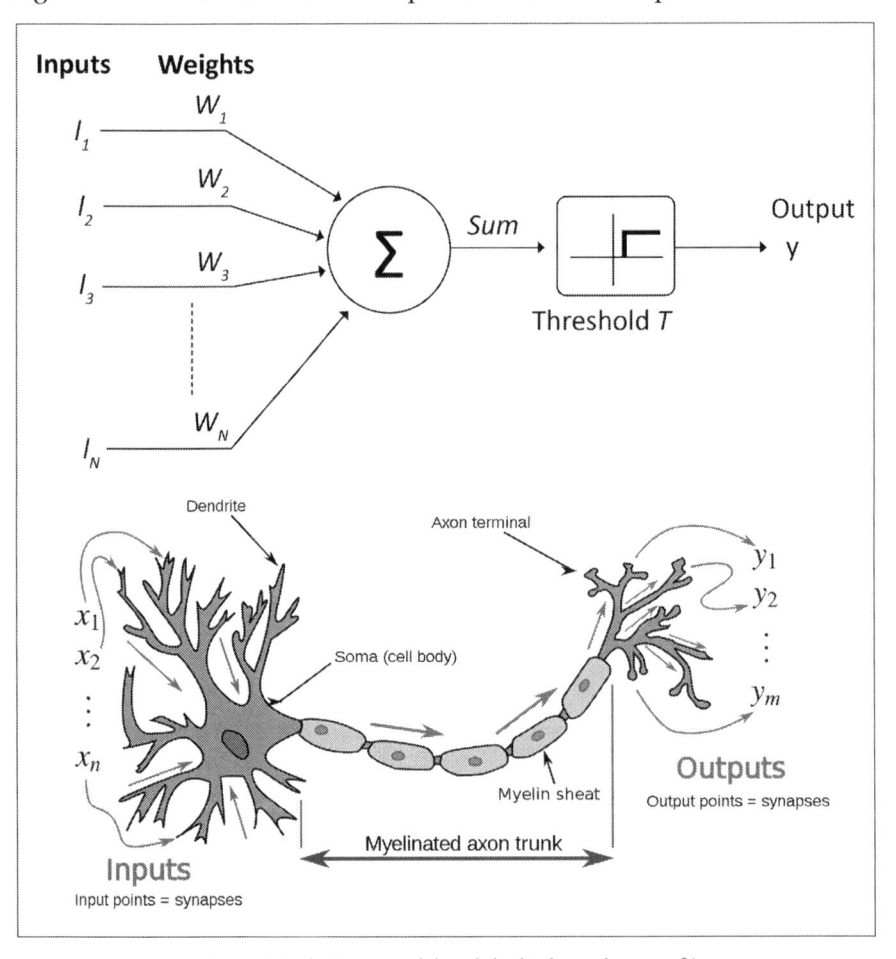

Figure 3.2: The TLU model and the biological neuron[5,6]

Indeed, using this simple model, we can already start to represent several logical operations. If we consider a simple case of a neuron with one input, we can see that a TLU can solve an identity or negation function (*Tables 3.1* and *3.2*).

For an identity operation that simply returns the input as output, the weight matrix would have 1s on the diagonal (or be simply the scalar 1, for a single numerical input, as illustrated in *Table 1*):

Identity	
Input	Output
1	1
0	0

Table 3.1: TLU logic for identity operations

Similarly, for a negation operation, the weight matrix could be a negative identity matrix, with a threshold at 0 flipping the sign of the output from the input:

Negation	
Input	Output
1	0
0	1

Table 3.2: TLU logic for negation operations

Given two inputs, a TLU could also represent operations such as AND and OR. Here, a threshold could be set such that combined input values either have to exceed 2 (to yield an output of 1) for an AND operation (*Table 3.3*) or 1 (to yield an output of 1 if either of the two inputs are 1) in an OR operation (*Table 3.4*).

AND		
Input 1	Input 2	Output
0	0	0
1	0	0
0	1	0
1	1	1

Table 3.3: TLU logic for AND operations

OR		
Input 1	Input 2	Output
0	0	0
1	0	1
0	1	1
1	1	1

Table 3.4: TLU logic for OR operations

However, a TLU cannot capture patterns such as Exclusive OR (XOR), which emits 1 if and *only if* the OR condition is true (*Table 3.5*).

XOR		
Input 1	Input 2	Output
0	0	0
1	0	1
0	1	1
1	1	0

Table 3.5: TLU logic for XOR operations

To see why this is true, consider a TLU with two inputs and positive weights of 1 for each unit. If the threshold value T is 1, then inputs of (0, 0), (1, 0), and (0, 1) will yield the correct value. What happens with (1, 1) though? Because the threshold function returns 1 for any inputs summing to greater than 1, it cannot represent XOR (*Table 3.5*), which would require a second threshold to compute a different output once a different, higher value is exceeded. Changing one or both of the weights to negative values won't help either; the problem is that the decision threshold operates only in one direction and can't be reversed for larger inputs.

Similarly, the TLU can't represent the negation of the Exclusive NOR, XNOR (*Table 3.6*):

XNOR		
Input 1	Input 2	Output
0	0	1
1	0	0
0	1	0
1	1	1

Table 3.6: TLU logic for XNOR operations

As with the XOR operation (Table 3.5), the impossibility of the XNOR operation (Table 3.6) being represented by a TLU function can be illustrated by considering a weight matrix of two 1s; for two inputs (1, 0) or (0, 1), we obtain the correct value if we set a threshold of 2 for outputting 1. As with the XOR operation, we run into a problem with an input of (0, 0), as we can't set a second threshold to output 1 at a sum of 0.

From TLUs to tuning perceptrons

Besides these limitations for representing the XOR and XNOR operations, there are additional simplifications that cap the representational power of the TLU model; the weights are fixed, and the output can only be binary (0 or 1). Clearly, for a system such as a neuron to "learn," it needs to respond to the environment and determine the relevance of different inputs based on feedback from prior experiences. This idea was captured in the 1949 book *Organization of Behavior* by Canadian Psychologist Donald Hebb, who proposed that the activity of nearby neuronal cells would tend to synchronize over time, sometimes paraphrased at Hebb's Law: *Neurons that fire together wire together*[7][8]. Building on Hebb's proposal that weights changed over time, researcher Frank Rosenblatt of the Cornell Aeronautical Laboratory proposed the perceptron model in the 1950s.[9] He replaced the fixed weights in the TLU model with adaptive weights and added a bias term, giving a new function:

$$y = f(\sum_{i=1}^{N} W_i X_i + b)$$

We note that the inputs *I* have been denoted *X* to underscore the fact that they could be any value, not just binary 0 or 1. Combining Hebb's observations with the TLU model, the weights of the perceptron would be updated according to a simple learning rule:

1. Start with a set of J samples *x(1) .... x(j)*. These samples all have a label y which is 0 or 1, giving labeled data *(y, x)(1) .... (y, x)(j)*. These samples could have either a single value, in which case the perceptron has a single input, or be a vector with length *N* and indices *i* for multi-value input.
2. Initialize all weights *w* to a small random value or 0.
3. Compute the estimated value, *yhat*, for all the examples *x* using the perceptron function.
4. Update the weights using a learning rate *r* to more closely match the input to the desired output for each step *t* in training:

$w_i(t+1) = w_i(t) + r(y_j - yhat_j)x_{j,i}$, for all J samples and N features. Conceptually, note that if y is 0 and the target is 1, we want to increase the value of the weight by some increment r; likewise, if the target is 0 and the estimate is 1, we want to decrease the weight so the inputs do not exceed the threshold.

5. Repeat *steps 3-4* until the difference between the predicted and actual outputs, y and $yhat$, falls below some desired threshold. In the case of a non-zero bias term, b, an update can be computed as well using a similar formula.

While simple, you can appreciate that many patterns could be learned from such a classifier, though still not the XOR function. However, by combining several perceptrons into multiple layers, these units could represent any simple Boolean function,[10] and indeed McCulloch and Pitts had previously speculated on combining such simple units into a universal computation engine, or Turing Machine, that could represent any operation in a standard programming language. However, the preceding learning algorithm operates on each unit independently, meaning it could be extended to networks composed of many layers of perceptrons (*Figure 3.3*).

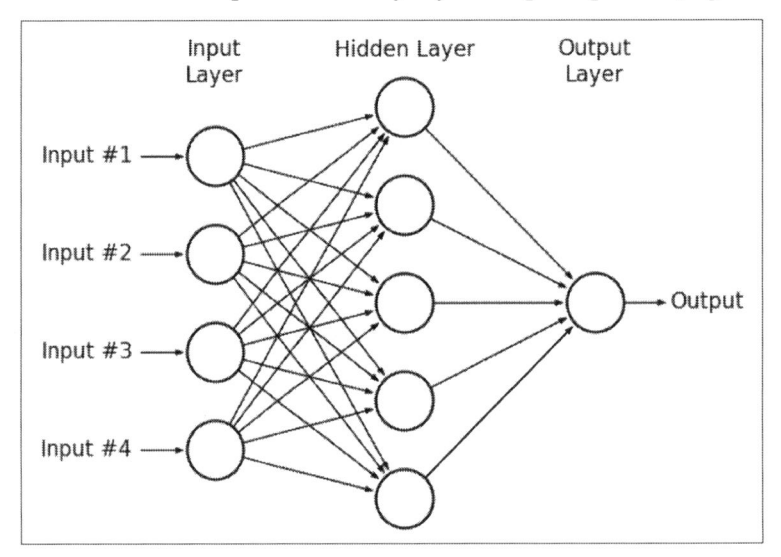

Figure 3.3: A multi-layer perceptron[11]

However, the 1969 book *Perceptrons*, by MIT computer scientists Marvin Minksy and Seymour Papert, demonstrated that a three-layer feed-forward network required complete (non-zero weight) connections between at least one of these units (in the first layer) and all inputs to compute all possible logical outputs[12]. This meant that instead of having a very sparse structure, like biological neurons, which are only connected to a few of their neighbors, these computational models required very dense connections.

While connective sparsity has been incorporated in later architectures, such as CNNs, such dense connections remain a feature of many modern models too, particularly in the *fully connected* layers that often form the second to last hidden layers in models. In addition to these models being computationally unwieldy on the hardware of the day, the observation that sparse models could not compute all logical operations was interpreted more broadly by the research community as *Perceptrons cannot compute XOR*. While erroneous,[13] this message led to a drought in funding for AI in subsequent years, a period sometimes referred to as the **AI Winter**[14].

The next revolution in neural network research would require a more efficient way to compute the required parameters updated in complex models, a technique that would become known as **backpropagation**.

Multi-layer perceptrons and backpropagation

While large research funding for neural networks declined until the 1980s after the publication of *Perceptrons*, researchers still recognized that these models had value, particularly when assembled into multi-layer networks, each composed of several perceptron units. Indeed, when the mathematical form of the output function (that is, the output of the model) was relaxed to take on many forms (such as a linear function or a sigmoid), these networks could solve both regression and classification problems, with theoretical results showing that 3-layer networks could effectively approximate any output.[15] However, none of this work addressed the practical limitations of computing the solutions to these models, with rules such as the perceptron learning algorithm described earlier proving a great limitation to the applied use of them.

Renewed interest in neural networks came with the popularization of the backpropagation algorithm, which, while discovered in the 1960s, was not widely applied to neural networks until the 1980s, following several studies highlighting its usefulness for learning the weights in these models.[16] As you saw with the perceptron model, a learning rule to update weights is relatively easy to derive as long as there are no "hidden" layers. The input is transformed once by the perceptron to compute an output value, meaning the weights can be directly tuned to yield the desired output. When there are hidden layers between the input and output, the problem becomes more complex: when do we change the internal weights to compute the activations that feed into the final output? How do we modify them in relation to the input weights?

Building Blocks of Deep Neural Networks

The insight of the backpropagation technique is that we can use the chain rule from calculus to efficiently compute the derivatives of each parameter of a network with respect to a loss function and, combined with a learning rule, this provides a scalable way to train multilayer networks.

Let's illustrate backpropagation with an example: consider a network like the one shown in *Figure 3.3*. Assume that the output in the final layer is computed using a sigmoidal function, which yields a value between 0 and 1:

$$\sigma(x) = \frac{1}{1 + e^{-x}}$$

Furthermore, the value y, the sum of the inputs to the final neuron, is a weighted sum of the sigmoidal inputs of the hidden units:

$$y = \sum_{i=1}^{N} \sigma(x_i) w_i$$

We also need a notion of when the network is performing well or badly at its task. A straightforward error function to use here is squared loss:

$$E = \frac{1}{2} \sum_{j=1}^{J} \sum_{k=1}^{K} (y_{j,k} - \widehat{y_{j,k}})^2$$

where *yhat* is the estimated value (from the output of the model) and *y* is the real value, summed over all the input examples *J* and the outputs of the network *K* (where *K=1*, since there is only a single output value). Backpropagation begins with a "forward pass" where we compute the values of all the outputs in the inner and outer layers, to obtain the estimated values of *yhat*. We then proceed with a backward step to compute gradients to update the weights.

Our overall objective is to compute partial derivatives for the weights w and bias terms b in each neuron: $\partial E/\partial w$ and $\partial E/\partial b$, which will allow us to compute the updates for b and w. Towards this goal, let's start by computing the update rule for the inputs in the final neuron; we want to date the partial derivative of the error E with respect to each of these inputs (in this example there are five, corresponding to the five hidden layer neurons), using the chain rule:

$$\frac{\partial E}{\partial x} = \frac{\partial E}{\partial y} \frac{\partial y}{\partial x}$$

We can get the value $\frac{\partial E}{\partial y}$ by differentiating the loss function:

$$\frac{\partial E}{\partial y} = 2 * \frac{1}{2} \sum_{j=1}^{J} \sum_{k=1}^{K} \left(y_{j,k} - \widehat{y_{J,k}} \right) = \sum_{j=1}^{J} \sum_{k=1}^{K} (y_{j,k} - \widehat{y_{J,k}})$$

which for an individual example is just the difference between the input and output value. For $\frac{\partial y}{\partial x}$, we need to take the partial derivative of the sigmoid function:

$$\frac{\partial y}{\partial x} = \frac{\partial}{\partial x} \left(\frac{1}{1+e^{-x}} \right) = \frac{(1+e^{-x})(0) - (1)(-e^{-x})}{(1+e^{-x})(1+e^{-x})} = \frac{e^{-x}}{(1+e^{-x})(1+e^{-x})}$$

$$= \left(\frac{1}{1+e^{-x}} \right) \left(\frac{e^{-x}}{1+e^{-x}} \right) = \left(\frac{1}{1+e^{-x}} \right) \left(\frac{1+e^{-x}}{1+e^{-x}} - \frac{1}{1+e^{-x}} \right)$$

$$= y(1-y)$$

Putting it all together, we have:

$$\frac{\partial E}{\partial x} = (y_{j,k} - \widehat{y_{J,k}}) \widehat{y_{J,k}} (1 - \widehat{y_{J,k}})$$

If we want to compute the gradient for a particular parameter of x, such as a weight w or bias term b, we need one more step:

$$\frac{\partial E}{\partial w} = \frac{\partial E}{\partial x} \frac{\partial x}{\partial w}$$

We already know the first term and x depends on w only through the inputs from the lower layers y since it is a linear function, so we obtain:

$$\frac{\partial E}{\partial w_{i,j}} = (y_{j,k} - \widehat{y_{J,k}}) \widehat{y_{J,k}} (1 - \widehat{y_{J,k}}) y_i$$

If we want to compute this derivative for one of the neurons in the hidden layer, we likewise take the partial derivative with respect to this input y_i, which is simply:

$$\frac{\partial E}{\partial y_i} = (y_{j,k} - \widehat{y_{J,k}}) \widehat{y_{J,k}} (1 - \widehat{y_{J,k}}) w_{i,j}$$

So, in total we can sum over all units that feed into this hidden layer:

$$\frac{\partial E}{\partial y_i} = \sum_{i,j} (y_{j,k} - \widehat{y_{J,k}}) \widehat{y_{J,k}} (1 - \widehat{y_{J,k}}) w_{i,j}$$

We can repeat this process recursively for any units in deeper layers to obtain the desired update rule, since we now know how to calculate the gradients for y or w at any layer. This makes the process of updating weights efficient since once we have computed the gradients through the backward pass we can combine consecutive gradients through the layers to get the required gradient at any depth of the network.

Now that we have the gradients for each w (or other parameter of the neuron we might want to calculate), how can we make a "learning rule" to update the weights? In their paper,[17] Hinton et al. noted that we could apply an update to the model parameters after computing gradients on each sample batch but suggested instead applying an update calculated after averaging over all samples. The gradient represents the direction in which the error function is changing with the greatest magnitude with respect to the parameters; thus, to update, we want to push the weight in the *opposite* direction, with $\Delta(w)$ the update, and e a small value (a step size):

$$\Delta w = -\epsilon \frac{\partial E}{\partial w}$$

Then at each time t during training we update the weight using this calculated gradient:

$$W(t+1) <- W(t) + \Delta W$$

Extending this approach, Hinton et al. proposed an exponentially weighted update of the current gradient plus prior updates:

$$\Delta w(t) = -\epsilon \frac{\partial E}{\partial w}(t) + \alpha \Delta w(t-1)$$

where alpha is a decay parameter to weight the contribution of prior updates ranging from 0 to 1. Following this procedure, we would initialize the weights in the network with some small random values, choose a step size e and iterate with forward and backward passes, along with updates to the parameters, until the loss function reaches some desired value.

Now that we have described the formal mathematics behind backpropagation, let us look at how it is implemented in practice in software packages such as TensorFlow 2.

Backpropagation in practice

While it is useful to go through this derivation in order to understand how the update rules for a deep neural network are derived, this would clearly quickly become unwieldy for large networks and complex architectures. It's fortunate, therefore, that TensorFlow 2 handles the computation of these gradients automatically. During the initialization of the model, each gradient is computed as an intermediate node between tensors and operations in the graph: as an example, see *Figure 3.4*:

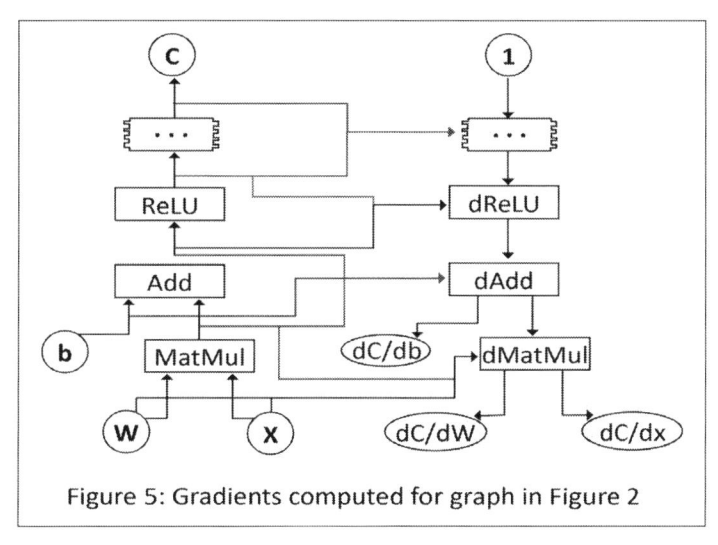

Figure 3.4: Inserting gradient operations into the TensorFlow graph[18]

The left side of the preceding figure shows a cost function C computed from the output of a **Rectified Linear Unit (ReLU)** – a type of neuron function we'll cover later in this chapter), which in turn is computed from multiplying a weight vector by an input x and adding a bias term b. On the right, you can see that this graph has been augmented by TensorFlow to compute all the intermediate gradients required for backpropagation as part of the overall control flow.

After storing these intermediate values, the task of combining them, as shown in the calculation in *Figure 3.4*, into a complete gradient through recursive operations falls to the GradientTape API. Under the hood, TensorFlow uses a method called **reverse-mode automatic differentiation** to compute gradients; it holds the dependent variable (the output y) fixed, and recursively computes backwards to the beginning of the network the required gradients.

For example, let's consider a neural network of the following form:

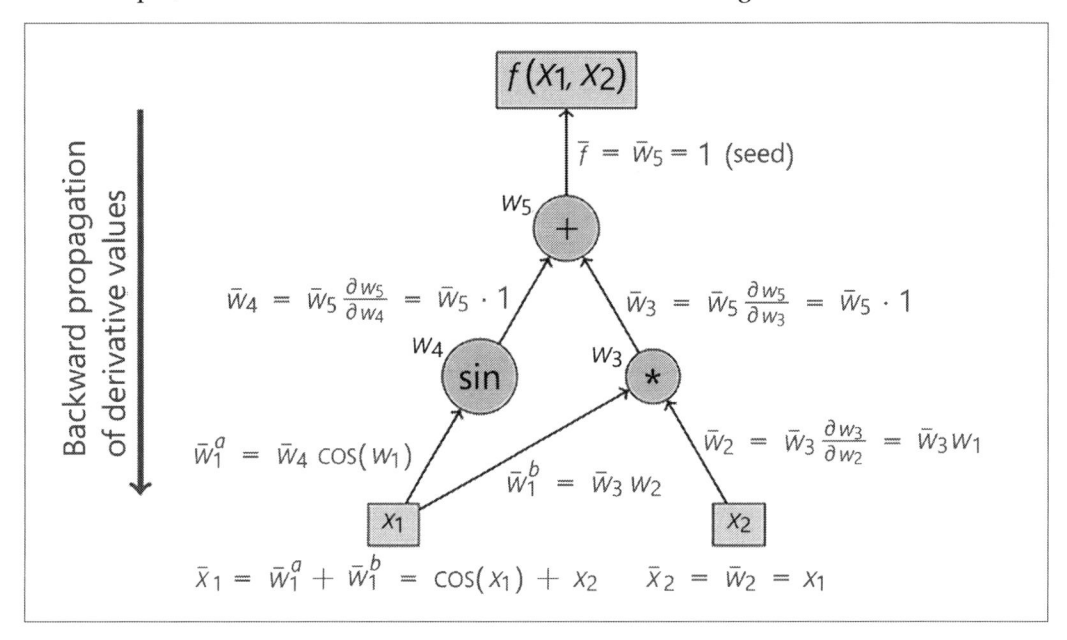

Figure 3.5: Reverse-mode automatic differentiation[19]

If we want to compute the derivative of the output y with respect to an input x we need to repeatedly substitute the outermost expression[20]:

$$\frac{\partial y}{\partial x} = \frac{\partial y}{\partial w_1}\frac{\partial w_1}{\partial x} = \left(\frac{\partial y}{\partial w_2}\frac{\partial w_2}{\partial w_1}\right)\frac{\partial w_1}{\partial x} = \left(\left(\frac{\partial y}{\partial w_3}\frac{\partial w_3}{\partial w_2}\right)\frac{\partial w_2}{\partial w_1}\right)\frac{\partial w_1}{\partial x} = \ldots$$

Thus, to compute the desired gradient we need to just traverse the graph from top to bottom, storing each intermediate gradient as we calculate it. These values are stored on a record, referred to as a tape in reference to early computers in which information was stored on a magnetic tape,[21] which is then used to replay the values for calculation. The alternative would be to use forward-mode automatic differentiation, computing from bottom to top. This requires two instead of one pass (for each branch feeding into the final value), but is conceptually simpler to implement and doesn't require the storage memory of reverse mode. More importantly, though, reverse-mode mimics the derivation of backpropagation that I described earlier.

The tape (also known as the **Wengert Tape**, after one of its developers) is actually a data structure that you can access in the TensorFlow Core API. As an example, import the core library:

```
from __future__ import absolute_import, division, print_function,
unicode_literals
import tensorflow as tf
```

The tape is then available using the tf.GradientTape() method, with which you can evaluate gradients with respect to intermediate values within the graph[22]:

```
x = tf.ones((2, 2))
with tf.GradientTape() as t:
  t.watch(x)
  y = tf.reduce_sum(x)
  z = tf.multiply(y, y)
# Use the tape to compute the derivative of z with respect to the
# intermediate value y.
dz_dy = t.gradient(z, y)
# note that the resulting derivative, 2*y, = sum(x)*2 = 8
assert dz_dy.numpy() == 8.0
```

By default, the memory resources used by GradientTape() are released once gradient() is called; however, you can also use the persistent argument to store these results[23]:

```
x = tf.constant(3.0)
with tf.GradientTape(persistent=True) as t:
  t.watch(x)
  y = x * x
  z = y * y
dz_dx = t.gradient(z, x)  # 108.0 (4*x^3 at x = 3)
dy_dx = t.gradient(y, x)  # 6.0
```

Now that you've seen how TensorFlow computes gradients in practice to evaluate backpropagation, let's return to the details of how the backpropagation technique evolved over time in response to challenges in practical implementation.

The shortfalls of backpropagation

While the backpropagation procedure provides a way to update interior weights within the network in a principled way, it has several shortcomings that made deep networks difficult to use in practice. One is the problem of **vanishing gradients**. In our derivation of the backpropagation formulas, you saw that gradients for weights deeper in the network are a product of successive partial derivatives from higher layers. In our example, we used the sigmoid function; if we plot out the value of the sigmoid and its first derivative, we can see a potential problem:

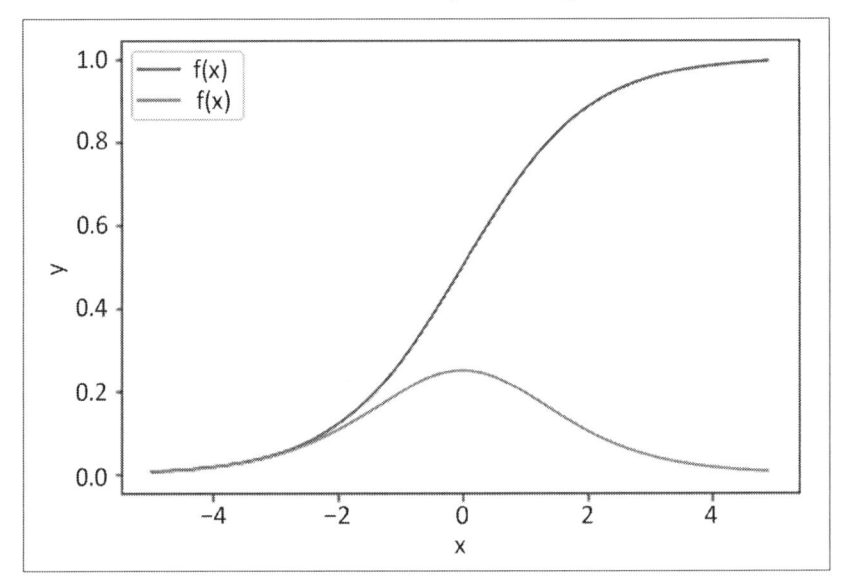

Figure 3.6: The sigmoid function and its gradient[24]

As the value of the sigmoid function increases or decreases towards the extremes (0 or 1, representing being either "off" or "on"), the values of the gradient vanish to near zero. This means that the updates to w and b, which are products of these gradients from hidden activation functions y, shrink towards zero, making the weights change little between iterations and making the parameters of the hidden layer neurons change very slowly during backpropagation. Clearly one problem here is that the sigmoid function saturates; thus, choosing another nonlinearity might circumvent this problem (this is indeed one of the solutions that was proposed as the ReLU, as we'll cover later).

Another problem is more subtle, and has to do with how the network utilizes its available free parameters. As you saw in *Chapter 1, An Introduction to Generative AI: "Drawing" Data from Models*, a posterior probability of a variable can be computed as a product of a likelihood and a prior distribution. We can see deep neural networks as a graphical representation of this kind of probability: the output of the neuron, depending upon its parameters, is a product of all the input values and the distributions on those inputs (the priors). A problem occurs when those values become tightly coupled. As an illustration, consider the competing hypotheses for a headache:

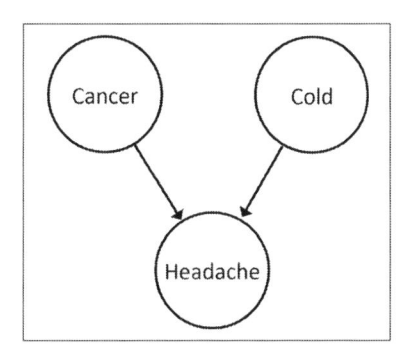

Figure 3.7: The explaining away effect

If a patient has cancer, the evidence is so overwhelming that whether they have a cold or not provides no additional value; in essence, the value of the two prior hypotheses becomes coupled because of the influence of one. This makes it intractable to compute the relative contribution of different parameters, particularly in a deep network; we will cover this problem in our discussion of Restricted Boltzmann Machine and Deep Belief Networks in *Chapter 4, Teaching Networks to Generate Digits*. As we will describe in more detail in that chapter, a 2006 study[25] showed how to counteract this effect, and was one of the first demonstrations of tractable inference in deep neural networks, a breakthrough that relied upon a generative model that produced images of hand-drawn digits.

Beyond these concerns, other challenges in the more widespread adoption of neural networks in the 1990s and early 2000s were the availability of methods such as Support Vector Machines[26], Gradient and Stochastic Gradient Boosting Models,[27] Random Forests,[28] and even penalized regression methods such as LASSO[29] and Elastic Net,[30] for classification and regression tasks.

While, in theory, deep neural networks had potentially greater representational power than these models since they built hierarchical representations of the input data through successive layers in contrast to the "shallow" representation given by a single transformation such as a regression weight or decision tree, in practice the challenges of training deep networks made these "shallow" methods more attractive for practical applications. This was coupled with the fact that larger networks required tuning thousands or even millions of parameters, requiring large-scale matrix calculations that were infeasible before the explosion of cheap compute resources – including GPUs and TPUs especially suited to rapid matrix calculations – available from cloud vendors made these experiments practical.

Now that we've covered the basics of training simple network architectures, let's turn to more complex models that will form the building blocks of many of the generative models in the rest of the book: CNNs and sequence models (RNNs, LSTMs, and others).

Varieties of networks: Convolution and recursive

Up until now we've primarily discussed the basics of neural networks by referencing feedforward networks, where every input is connected to every output in each layer. While these feedforward networks are useful for illustrating how deep networks are trained, they are only one class of a broader set of architectures used in modern applications, including generative models. Thus, before covering some of the techniques that make training large networks practical, let's review these alternative deep models.

Networks for seeing: Convolutional architectures

As noted at the beginning of this chapter, one of the inspirations for deep neural network models is the biological nervous system. As researchers attempted to design computer vision systems that would mimic the functioning of the visual system, they turned to the architecture of the retina, as revealed by physiological studies by neurobiologists David Huber and Torsten Weisel in the 1960s.[31] As previously described, the physiologist Santiago Ramon Y Cajal provided visual evidence that neural structures such as the retina are arranged in vertical networks:

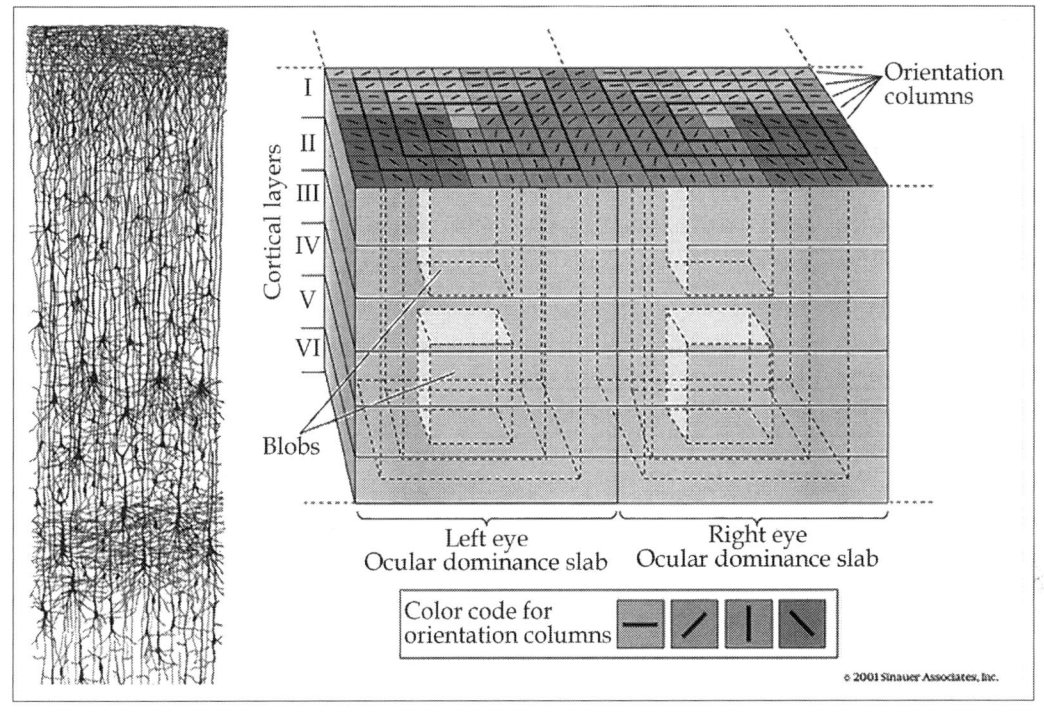

Figure 3.8: The "deep network" of the retina[32][33]

Huber and Weisel studied the retinal system in cats, showing how their perception of shapes is composed of the activity of individual cells arranged in a column. Each column of cells is designed to detect a specific orientation of an edge in an input image; images of complex shapes are stitched together from these simpler images.

Early CNNs

This idea of columns inspired early research into CNN architectures[34]. Instead of learning individual weights between units as in a feedforward network, this architecture (*Figure 3.9*) uses shared weights within a group of neurons specialized to detect a specific edge in an image. The initial layer of the network (denoted **H1**) consists of 12 groups of 64 neurons each. Each of these groups is derived by passing a 5 x 5 grid over the 16 x 16-pixel input image; each of the 64 5 x 5 grids in this group share the same weights, but are tied to different spatial regions of the input. You can see that there must be 64 neurons in each group to cover the input image if their receptive fields overlap by two pixels.

When combined, these 12 groups of neurons in layer **H1** form 12 8 x 8 grids representing the presence or absence of a particular edge within a part of the image – the 8 x 8 grid is effectively a down-sampled version of the image (*Figure 3.9*). This weight sharing makes intuitive sense in that the kernel represented by the weight is specified to detect a distinct color and/or shape, regardless of where it appears in the image. An effect of this down-sampling is a degree of positional invariance; we only know the edge occurred somewhere within a region of the image, but not the exact location due to the reduced resolution from downsampling. Because they are computed by multiplying a 5 x 5 matrix (kernel) with a part of the image, an operation used in image blurring and other transformations, these 5 x 5 input features are known as **convolutional kernels**, and give the network its name.

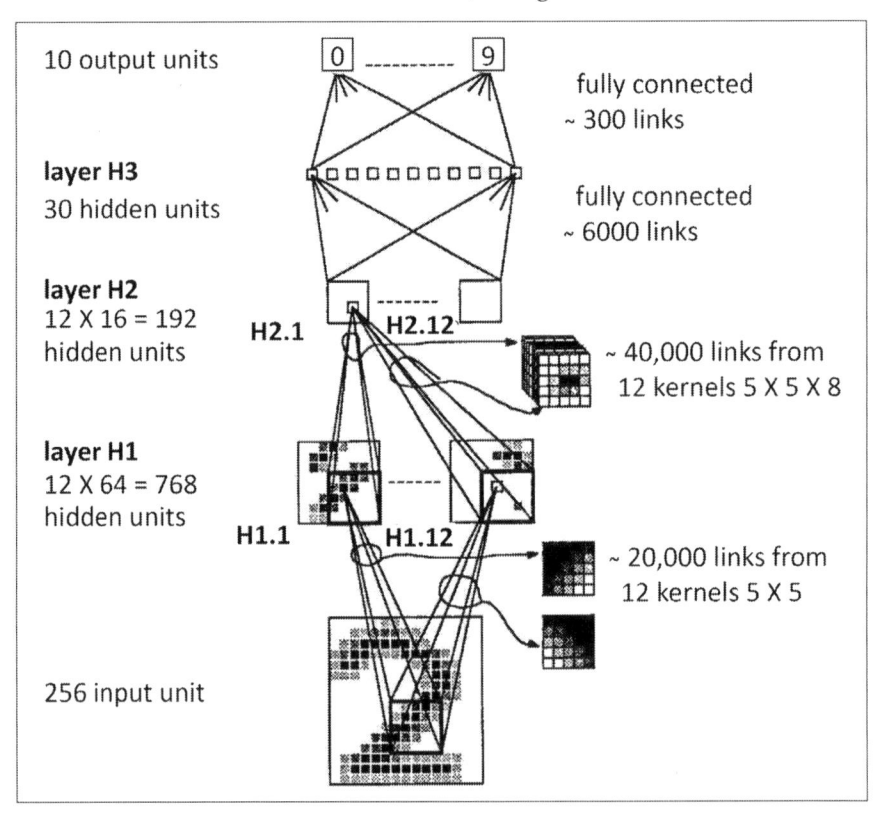

Figure 3.9: The CNN[35]

Once we have these 12 8 x 8 downsampled versions of the image, the next layer (**H2**) also has 12 groups of neurons; here, the kernels are 5 x 5 x 8 – they traverse the surface of an 8 x 8 map from **H1**, across 8 of the 12 groups. We need 16 neurons of these 5 x 5 x 8 groups since a 5 x 5 grid can be moved over four times up and down on an 8 x 8 grid to cover all the pixels in the 8 x 8 grid.

Just like deeper cells in the visual cortex, the deeper layers in the network integrate across multiple columns to combine information from different edge detectors together.

Finally, the third hidden layer of this network (**H3**) contains all-to-all connections between 30 hidden units and the 12 x 16 units in the **H2**, just as in a traditional feedforward network; a final output of 10 units classifies the input image as one of 10 hand-drawn digits.

Through weight sharing, the overall number of free parameters in this network is reduced, though it is still large in absolute terms. While backpropagation was used successfully for this task, it required a carefully designed network for a rather limited set of images with a restricted set of outcomes – for real-world applications, such as detecting objects from hundreds or thousands of possible categories, other approaches would be necessary.

AlexNet and other CNN innovations

A 2012 article that produced state-of-the-art results classifying the 1.3 million images in ImageNet into 1,000 classes using a model termed AlexNet demonstrates some of the later innovations that made training these kinds of models practical.[36] One, as I've alluded to before, is using ReLUs[37] in place of sigmoids or hyperbolic tangent functions. A ReLU is a function of the form:

$$y = max\,(0, x)$$

In contrast to the sigmoid function, or tanh, in which the derivative shrinks to 0 as the function is saturated, the ReLU function has a constant gradient and a discontinuity at 0 (*Figure 3.10*). This means that the gradient does not saturate and causes deeper layers of the network to train more slowly, leading to intractable optimization.

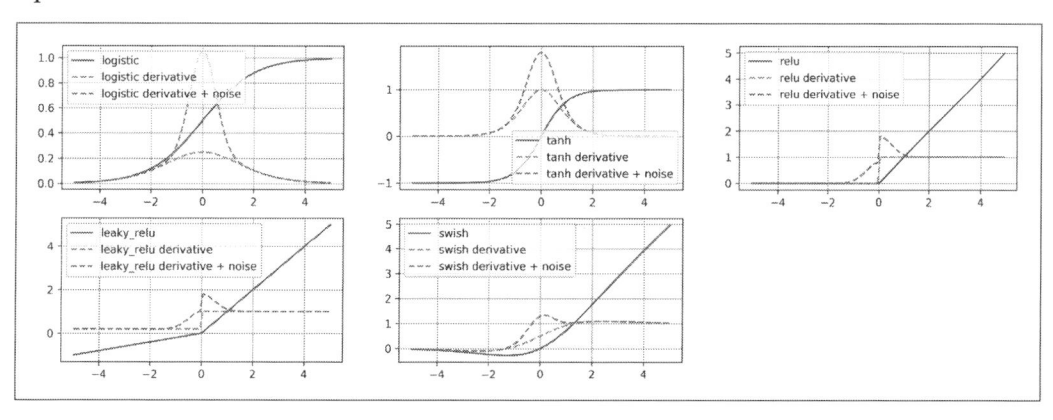

Figure 3.10: Gradients of alternative activation functions[38]

While advantageous due to non-vanishing gradients and their low computational requirements (as they are simply thresholded linear transforms), ReLU functions have the downside that they can "turn off" if the input falls below 0, leading again to a 0 gradient. This deficiency was resolved by later work in which a "leak" below 0 was introduced[39]:

$$y = x \text{ if } x > 0, else\ 0.01x$$

A further refinement is to make this threshold adaptive with a slope a, the **Parameterized Leak ReLU (PReLU)**[40]:

$$y = max(ax, x) \text{ if } a \leq 1$$

Another trick used by AlexNet is dropout.[41] The idea of dropout is inspired by ensemble methods in which we average the predictions of many models to obtain more robust results. Clearly for deep neural networks this is prohibitive; thus a compromise is to randomly set the values of a subset of neurons to 0 with a probability of 0.5. These values are reset with every forward pass of backpropagation, allowing the network to effectively sample different architectures since the "dropped out" neurons don't participate in the output in that pass.

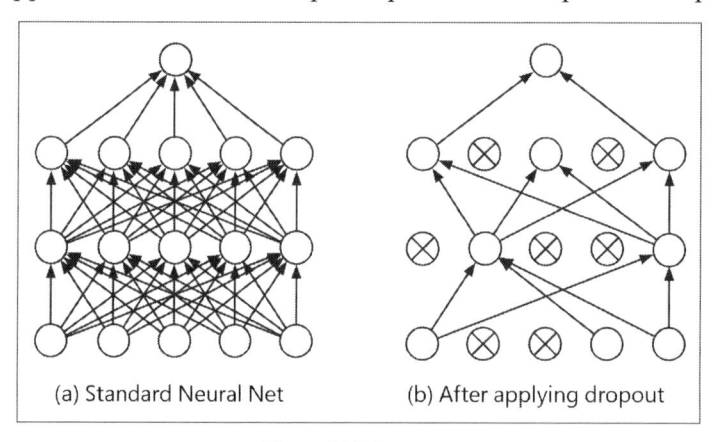

(a) Standard Neural Net   (b) After applying dropout

Figure 3.11: Dropout

Yet another enhancement used in AlexNet is local response normalization. Even though ReLUs don't saturate in the same manner as other units, the authors of the model still found value in constraining the range of output. For example, in an individual kernel, they normalized the input using values of adjacent kernels, meaning the overall response was rescaled[42]:

$$b_{x,y}^i = a_{x,y}^i / \left(k + \alpha \sum_{j=\max(0, i-n/2)}^{\min(N-1, i+n/2)} (a_{x,y}^j)^2 \right)^\beta$$

where *a* is the unnormalized output at a given *x*, *y* location on an image, the sum over *j* is over adjacent kernels, and *B*, *k*, and alpha are hyperparameters. This rescaling is reminiscent of a later innovation used widely in both convolutional and other neural network architectures, batch normalization[43]. Batch normalization also applies a transformation on "raw" activations within a network:

$$y(k) = \gamma_{(k)} X_{(k)} + \beta_{(k)}$$

where *x* is the unnormalized output, and *B* and *y* are scale and shift parameters. This transformation is widely applied in many neural network architectures to accelerate training, through the exact reason why it is effective remains a topic of debate.[44]

Now that you have an idea of some of the methodological advances that made training large CNNs possible, let's examine the structure of AlexNet to see some additional architectural components that we will use in the CNNs we implement in generative models in later chapters.

AlexNet architecture

While the architecture of AlexNet shown in *Figure 3.12* might look intimidating, it is not so difficult to understand once we break up this large model into individual processing steps. Let's start with the input images and trace how the output classification is computed for each image through a series of transformations performed by each subsequent layer of the neural network.

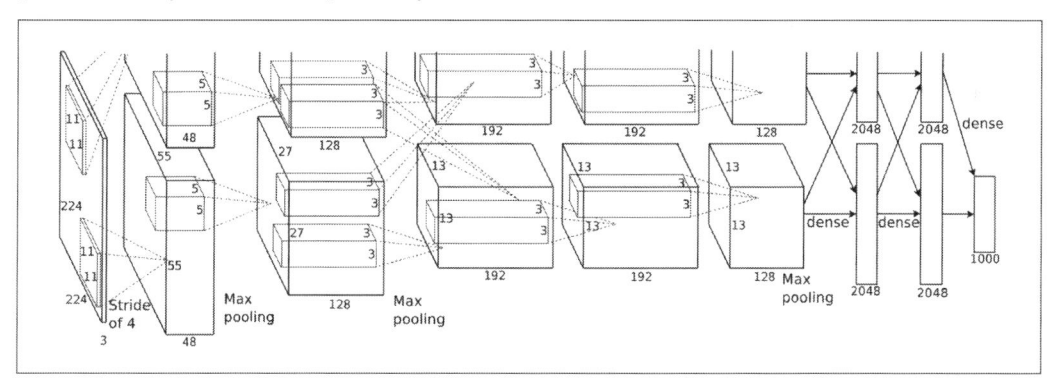

Figure 3.12: AlexNet

The input images to AlexNet are size 224 x 224 x 3 (for RGB channels). The first layer consists of groups of 96 units and 11 x 11 x 3 kernels; the output is response normalized (as described previously) and max pooled. Max pooling is an operation that takes the maximum value over an *n* x *n* grid to register whether a pattern appeared *anywhere* in the input; this is again a form of positional invariance.

Building Blocks of Deep Neural Networks

The second layer is also a set of kernels of size 5 x 5 x 8 in groups of 256. The third through to fifth hidden layers have additional convolutions, without normalization, followed by two fully connected layers and an output of size 1,000 representing the possible image classes in ImageNet. The authors of AlexNet used several GPUs to train the model, and this acceleration is important to the output.

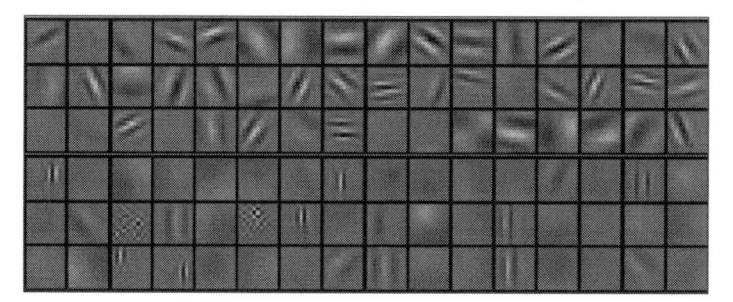

Figure 3.13: Image kernels from AlexNet

Looking at the features learned during training in the initial 11 x 11 x 3 convolutions (*Figure 3.13*), we can see recognizable edges and colors. While the authors of AlexNet don't show examples of neurons higher in the network that synthesize these basic features, an illustration is provided by another study in which researchers trained a large CNN to classify images in YouTube videos, yielding a neuron in the upper reaches of the network that appeared to be a cat detector (*Figure 3.14*).

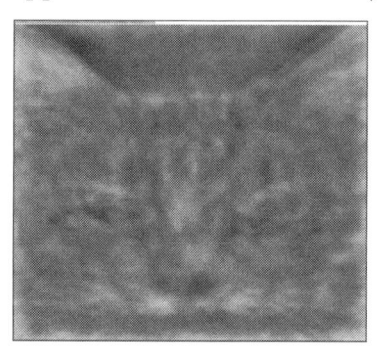

Figure 3.14: A cat detector learned from YouTube videos[45]

This overview should give you an idea of *why* CNN architectures look the way they do, and what developments have allowed them to become more tractable as the basis for image classifiers or image-based generative models over time. We will now turn to a second class of more specialized architectures – RNNs – that's used to develop time or sequence-based models.

Networks for sequence data

In addition to image data, natural language text has also been a frequent topic of interest in neural network research. However, unlike the datasets we've examined thus far, language has a distinct *order* that is important to its meaning. Thus, to accurately capture the patterns in language or time-dependent data, it is necessary to utilize networks designed for this purpose.

RNNs and LSTMs

Let's imagine we are trying to predict the next word in a sentence, given the words up until this point. A neural network that attempted to predict the next word would need to take into account not only the current word but a variable number of prior inputs. If we instead used only a simple feedforward MLP, the network would essentially process the entire sentence or each word as a vector. This introduces the problem of either having to pad variable-length inputs to a common length and not preserving any notion of correlation (that is, which words in the sentence are more relevant than others in generating the next prediction), or only using the last word at each step as the input, which removes the context of the rest of the sentence and all the information it can provide. This kind of problem inspired the "vanilla" RNN[46], which incorporates not only the current input but the prior step's hidden state in computing a neuron's output:

$$y = f(wx_t + uh_{t-1} + b)$$

One way to visualize this is to imagine each layer feeding recursively into the next timestep in a sequence. In effect, if we "unroll" each part of the sequence, we end up with a very deep neural network, where each layer shares the same weights.[47]

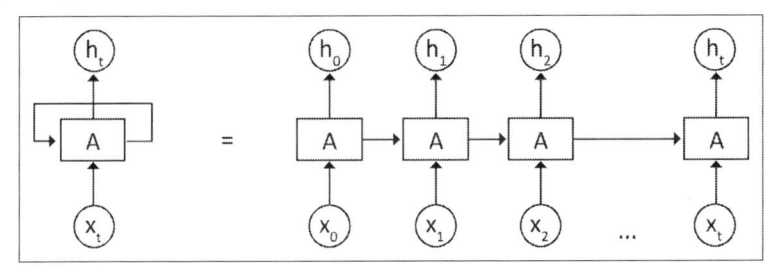

Figure 3.15: The unrolled RNN[48]

The same difficulties that characterize training deep feedforward networks also apply to RNNs; gradients tend to die out over long distances using traditional activation functions (or explode if the gradients become greater than 1).

Building Blocks of Deep Neural Networks

However, unlike feedforward networks, RNNs aren't trained with traditional backpropagation, but rather a variant known as **backpropagation through time** (**BPTT**): the network is unrolled, as before, and backpropagation is used, averaging over errors *at each time point* (since an "output," the hidden state, occurs at each step).[49] Also, in the case of RNNs, we run into the problem that the network has a very short memory; it only incorporates information from the most recent unit before the current one and has trouble maintaining long-range context. For applications such as translation, this is clearly a problem, as the interpretation of a word at the end of a sentence may depend on terms near the beginning, not just those directly preceding it.

The LSTM network was developed to allow RNNs to maintain a context or state over long sequences.[50]

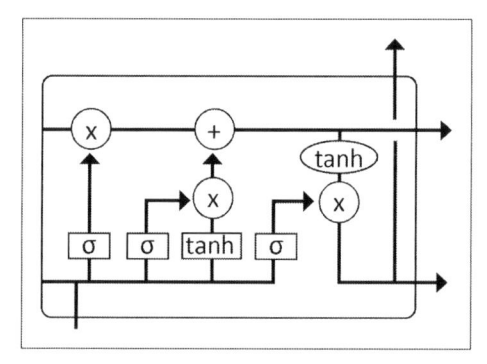

Figure 3.16: LSTM network

In a vanilla RNN, we only maintain a short-term memory h coming from the prior step's hidden unit activations. In addition to this short-term memory, the LSTM architecture introduces an additional layer c, the "long-term" memory, which can persist over many timesteps. The design is in some ways reminiscent of an electrical capacitor, which can use the c layer to store up or hold "charge," and discharge it once it has reached some threshold. To compute these updates, an LSTM unit consists of a number of related neurons, or gates, that act together to transform the input at each time step.

Given an input vector x, and the hidden state h, at the previous time t-1, at each time step an LSTM first computes a value from 0 to 1 for each element of c representing what fraction of information is "forgotten" of each element of the vector:

$$f = logistic(Wx_t + Uh_{t-1} + b)$$

We make a second, similar calculation to determine what from the input value to preserve:

$$i = logistic(Wx_t + Uh_{t-1} + b)$$

We now know which elements of c are updated; we can compute this update as follows:

$$c = f \circ c_{t-1} + i_t \circ tanh(Wx_t + Uh_{t-1} + b)$$

where ∘ is a Hadamard product (element-wise multiplication). In essence this equation tells us how to compute updates using the tanh transform, filter them using the input gate, and combine them with the prior time step's long-term memory using the forget gate to potentially filter out old values.

To compute the output at each time step, we compute another output gate:

$$o = logistic(Wx_t + Uh_{t-1} + b)$$

And to compute the final output at each step (the hidden layer fed as short-term memory to the next step) we have:

$$h = o_t \circ tanh(c_t)$$

Many variants of this basic design have been proposed; for example, the "peephole" LSTM substituted *h(t-1)* with *c(t-1)* (thus each operation gets to "peep" at the long-term memory cell),[51] while the GRU[52] simplifies the overall design by removing the output gate. What these designs all have in common is that they avoid the vanishing (or exploding) gradient difficulties seen during the training of RNNs, since the long-term memory acts as a buffer to maintain the gradient and propagate neuronal activations over many timesteps.

Building a better optimizer

In this chapter we have so far discussed several examples in which better neural network architectures allowed for breakthroughs; however, just as (and perhaps even more) important is the *optimization procedure* used to minimize the error function in these problems, which "learns" the parameters of the network by selecting those that yield the lowest error. Referring to our discussion of backpropagation, this problem has two components:

- **How to initialize the weights**: In many applications historically, we see that the authors used random weights within some range, and hoped that the use of backpropagation would result in at least a locally minimal loss function from this random starting point.

- **How to find the local minimum loss**: In basic backpropagation, we used gradient descent using a fixed learning rate and a first derivative update to traverse the potential solution space of weight matrices; however, there is good reason to believe there might be more efficient ways to find a local minimum.

In fact, both of these have turned out to be key considerations towards progress in deep learning research.

Gradient descent to ADAM

As we saw in our discussion of backpropagation, the original version proposed in 1986 for training neural networks averaged the loss over the *entire dataset* before taking the gradient and updating the weights. Obviously, this is quite slow and makes distributing the model difficult, as we can't split up the input data and model replicas; if we use them, each needs to have access to the whole dataset.

In contrast, SGD computes gradient updates after n samples, where n could a range from 1 to N, the size of the dataset. In practice, we usually perform *mini-batch* gradient descent, in which n is relatively small, and we randomize assignment of data to the n batches after each epoch (a single pass through the data).

However, SGD can be slow, leading researchers to propose alternatives that accelerate the search for a minimum. As seen in the original backpropagation algorithm, one idea is to use a form of exponentially weighted momentum that remembers prior steps and continues in promising directions. Variants have been proposed, such as *Nesterov Momentum*, which adds a term to increase this acceleration.[53]

$$v_{t+1} = \mu v_t - \varepsilon \nabla f(\theta_t + \mu v_t)$$

$$\theta_{t+1} = \theta_t + v_{t+1}$$

In comparison to the momentum term used in the original backpropagation algorithm, the addition of the current momentum term to the gradient helps keep the momentum component aligned with the gradient changes.

Another optimization, termed **Adaptive Gradient (Adagrad)**[54], scales the learning rate for each update by the running the sum of squares (G) of the gradient of that parameter; thus, elements that are frequently updated are downsampled, while those that are infrequently updated are pushed to update with greater magnitude:

$$\theta_{t+1,i} = \theta_{t,i} - \frac{\eta}{\sqrt{G_{t,ii} + \epsilon}} \cdot g_{t,i}$$

This approach has the downside that as we continue to train the neural network, the sum G will increase indefinitely, ultimately shrinking the learning rate to a very small value. To fix this shortcoming, two variant methods, RMSProp[55] (frequently applied to RNNs) and AdaDelta[56] impose fixed-width windows of n steps in the computation of G.

Adaptive Momentum Estimation (ADAM)[57] can be seen as an attempt to combine momentum and AdaDelta; the momentum calculation is used to preserve the history of past gradient updates, while the sum of decaying squared gradients within a fixed update window used in AdaDelta is applied to scale the resulting gradient.

The methods mentioned here all share the property of being *first order*: they involve only the first derivative of the loss with respect to the input. While simple to compute, this may introduce practical challenges with navigating the complex solution space of neural network parameters. As shown in *Figure 3.17*, if we visualize the landscape of weight parameters as a ravine, then first-order methods will either move too quickly in areas in which the curvature is changing quickly (the top image) overshooting the minima, or will change too slowly within the minima "ravine," where the curvature is low. An ideal algorithm would take into account not only the curvature but the *rate of change* of the curvature, allowing an optimizer order method to take larger step sizes when the curvature changes very slowly and vice versa (the bottom image).

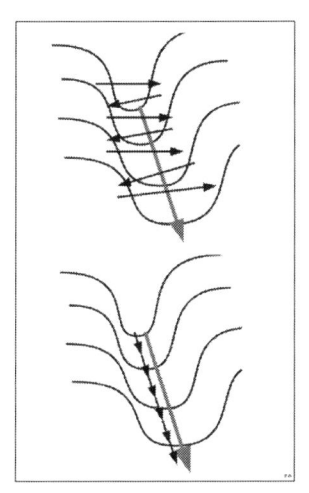

Figure 3.17: Complex landscapes and second-order methods[58]

Because they make use of the rate of change of the derivative (the **second derivative**), these methods are known as **second order**, and have demonstrated some success in optimizing neural network models.[59]

However, the computation required for each update is larger than for first-order methods, and because most second-order methods involve large matrix inversions (and thus memory utilization), approximations are required to make these methods scale. Ultimately, however, one of the breakthroughs in practically optimizing networks comes not just from the optimization algorithm, but how we initialize the weights in the model.

Xavier initialization

As noted previously, in earlier research it was common to initialize weights in a neural network with some range of random values. Breakthroughs in the training of Deep Belief Networks in 2006, as you will see in *Chapter 4, Teaching Networks to Generate Digits*, used pre-training (through a generative modeling approach) to initialize weights before performing standard backpropagation.

If you've ever used a layer in the TensorFlow Keras module, you will notice that the default initialization for layer weights draws from either a truncated normal or uniform distribution. Where does this choice come from? As I described previously, one of the challenges with deep networks using sigmoidal or hyperbolic activation functions is that they tend to become saturated, since the values for these functions are capped with very large or negative input. We might interpret the challenge of initializing networks then as keeping weights in such a range that they don't saturate the neuron's output. Another way to understand this is to assume that the input and output values of the neuron have similar variance; the signal is not massively amplifying or diminishing while passing through the neuron.

In practice, for a linear neuron, $y = wx + b$, we could compute the variance of the input and output as:

$$var(y) = var(wx + b)$$

The b is constant, so we are left with:

$$var(y) = var(w)var(x) + var(w)E(x)2 + var(x)E(w)2 = var(w)var(x)$$

Since there are N elements in the weight matrix, and we want $var(y)$ to equal $var(x)$, this gives:

$$1 = Nvar(x), var(w) = 1/N$$

Therefore, for a weight matrix w, we can use a truncated normal or uniform distribution with variance $1/N$ (the average number of input and output units, so the number of weights).[60] Variations have also been applied to ReLU units:[61] these methods are referred to by their original authors' names as Xavier or He initialization.

In summary, we've reviewed several common optimizers used under the hood in TensorFlow 2, and discussed how they improve upon the basic form of SGD. We've also discussed how clever weight initialization schemes work together with these optimizers to allow us to train ever more complex models.

Summary

In this chapter, we've covered the basic vocabulary of deep learning – how initial research into perceptrons and MLPs led to simple learning rules being abandoned for backpropagation. We also looked at specialized neural network architectures such as CNNs, based on the visual cortex, and recurrent networks, specialized for sequence modeling. Finally, we examined variants of the gradient descent algorithm proposed originally for backpropagation, which have advantages such as momentum, and described weight initialization schemes that place the parameters of the network in a range that is easier to navigate to a local minimum.

With this context in place, we are all set to dive into projects in generative modeling, beginning with the generation of MNIST digits using Deep Belief Networks in *Chapter 4, Teaching Networks to Generate Digits*.

References

1. López-Muñoz F., Boya J., Alamo C. (2006). *Neuron theory, the cornerstone of neuroscience, on the centenary of the Nobel Prize award to Santiago Ramón y Cajal.* Brain Research Bulletin. 70 (4–6): 391–405. https://pubmed.ncbi.nlm.nih.gov/17027775/
2. Ramón y Cajal, Santiago (1888). *Estructura de los centros nerviosos de las aves.*
3. McCulloch, W.S., Pitts, W. (1943). *A logical calculus of the ideas immanent in nervous activity.* Bulletin of Mathematical Biophysics 5, 115–133. https://doi.org/10.1007/BF02478259
4. Rashwan M., Ez R., reheem G. (2017). *Computational Intelligent Algorithms For Arabic Speech Recognition.* Journal of Al-Azhar University Engineering Sector. 12. 886-893. 10.21608/auej.2017.19198. http://wwwold.ece.utep.edu/research/webfuzzy/docs/kk-thesis/kk-thesis-html/node12.html
5. Rashwan M., Ez R., reheem G. (2017). *Computational Intelligent Algorithms For Arabic Speech Recognition.* Journal of Al-Azhar University Engineering Sector. 12. 886-893. 10.21608/auej.2017.19198. http://wwwold.ece.utep.edu/research/webfuzzy/docs/kk-thesis/kk-thesis-html/node12.html

6. *Artificial neuron*. Wikipedia. Retrieved April 26, 2021, from `https://en.wikipedia.org/wiki/Artificial_neuron`

7. Shackleton-Jones Nick. (2019, May 3). *How People Learn: Designing Education and Training that Works to Improve Performance*. Kogan Page. London, United Kingdom

8. Hebb, D. O. (1949). *The Organization of Behavior: A Neuropsychological Theory*. New York: Wiley and Sons

9. Rosenblatt, Frank (1957). *The Perceptron – a perceiving and recognizing automaton*. Report 85-460-1. Cornell Aeronautical Laboratory.

10. Marvin Minsky and Seymour Papert, 1972 (2nd edition with corrections, first edition 1969) *Perceptrons: An Introduction to Computational Geometry*, The MIT Press, Cambridge MA

11. Hassan, Hassan & Negm, Abdelazim & Zahran, Mohamed & Saavedra, Oliver. (2015). *Assessment of Artificial Neural Network for Bathymetry Estimation Using High Resolution Satellite Imagery in Shallow Lakes: Case Study El Burullus Lake*. International Water Technology Journal. 5.

12. Marvin Minsky and Seymour Papert, 1972 (2nd edition with corrections, first edition 1969) *Perceptrons: An Introduction to Computational Geometry*, The MIT Press, Cambridge MA

13. Pollack, J. B. (1989). "No Harm Intended: A Review of the Perceptrons expanded edition". *Journal of Mathematical Psychology*. 33 (3): 358–365.

14. Crevier, Daniel (1993), *AI: The Tumultuous Search for Artificial Intelligence*, New York, NY: BasicBooks.

15. Cybenko, G. *Approximation by superpositions of a sigmoidal function*. Math. Control Signal Systems 2, 303–314 (1989). `https://doi.org/10.1007/BF02551274`

16. Goodfellow, Ian; Bengio, Yoshua; Courville, Aaron (2016). *6.5 Back-Propagation and Other Differentiation Algorithms*. Deep Learning. MIT Press. pp. 200–220

17. Rumelhart, D., Hinton, G. & Williams, R. (1986) *Learning representations by back-propagating errors*. Nature 323, 533–536. `https://doi.org/10.1038/323533a0`

18. Guess A R., (2015, November 10). *Google Open-Sources Machine Learning Library, TensorFlow*. DATAVERSITY. `https://www.dataversity.net/google-open-sources-machine-learning-library-tensorflow/`

19. Berland (2007). *ReverseaccumulationAD.png*. Wikipedia. Available from: `https://commons.wikimedia.org/wiki/File:ReverseaccumulationAD.png`

20. *Automatic differentiation*. Wikipedia. https://en.wikipedia.org/wiki/Automatic_differentiation

21. R.E. Wengert (1964). *A simple automatic derivative evaluation program*. Comm. ACM. 7 (8): 463–464.;Bartholomew-Biggs, Michael; Brown, Steven; Christianson, Bruce; Dixon, Laurence (2000). *Automatic differentiation of algorithms*. Journal of Computational and Applied Mathematics. 124 (1–2): 171–190.

22. The TensorFlow Authors (2018). *automatic_differentiation.ipynb*. Available from: https://colab.research.google.com/github/tensorflow/tensorflow/blob/r1.9/tensorflow/contrib/eager/python/examples/notebooks/automatic_differentiation.ipynb#scrollTo=t09eeeR5prIJ

23. The TensorFlow Authors. *Introduction to gradients and automatic differentiation*. TensorFlow. Available from: https://www.tensorflow.org/guide/autodiff

24. Thomas (2018). *The vanishing gradient problem and ReLUs – a TensorFlow investigation*. Adventures in Machine Learning. Available from: https://adventuresinmachinelearning.com/vanishing-gradient-problem-tensorflow/

25. Hinton, Osindero, Yee-Whye (2005). *A Fast Learning Algorithm for Deep Belief Nets*. Univeristy of Toronto, Computer Science. Available from: http://www.cs.toronto.edu/~fritz/absps/ncfast.pdf

26. Cortes, C., Vapnik, V. *Support-vector networks*. Mach Learn 20, 273–297 (1995). https://doi.org/10.1007/BF00994018

27. Friedman, J. H. (February 1999). *Greedy Function Approximation: A Gradient Boosting Machine* (PDF)

28. Breiman, L. *Random Forests*. Machine Learning 45, 5–32 (2001). https://doi.org/10.1023/A:1010933404324

29. Tibshirani R. (1996). *Regression Shrinkage and Selection via the lasso*. Journal of the Royal Statistical Society. Series B (methodological). Wiley. 58 (1): 267–88.

30. Zou H., Hastie T. (2005). *Regularization and variable selection via the elastic net*. Journal of the Royal Statistical Society, Series B: 301–320

31. Hubel D. H., Wiesel T. N. (1962) *Receptive fields, binocular interaction and functional architecture in the cat's visual cortex*. J Physiol, 1962, 160: 106-154. https://doi.org/10.1113/jphysiol.1962.sp006837

32. http://charlesfrye.github.io/FoundationalNeuroscience/img/corticalLayers.gif

33. Wolfe, Kluender, Levy (2009). *Sensation and Perception*. Sunderland: Sinauer Associates Inc..

34. LeCun, Yann, et al. *Backpropagation applied to handwritten zip code recognition*. Neural computation 1.4 (1989): 541-551.

35. LeCun, Yann, et al. *Backpropagation applied to handwritten zip code recognition*. Neural computation 1.4 (1989): 541-551.

36. *ImageNet Classification with Deep Convolutional Neural Networks*: https://www.nvidia.cn/content/tesla/pdf/machine-learning/imagenet-classification-with-deep-convolutional-nn.pdf

37. Nair V., Hinton G E. (2010). *Rectified Linear Units Improve Restricted Boltzmann Machines*. Proceedings of the 27 th International Conference on Machine Learning, Haifa, Israel, 2010.

38. Agarap A F. (2019, September 5). *Avoiding the vanishing gradients problem using gradient noise addition*. Towards Data Science. https://towardsdatascience.com/avoiding-the-vanishing-gradients-problem-96183fd03343

39. Maas A L., Hannun A Y., Ng A Y. (2013). *Rectifer Nonlinearities Improve Neural Network Acoustic Models*. Proceedings of the 30 th International Conference on Machine Learning, Atlanta, Georgia, USA.

40. He, K., Zhang, X., Ren, S., Sun, J. (2015). *Delving Deep into Rectifiers: Surpassing Human-Level Performance on ImageNet Classification*. arXiv:1502.01852. https://arxiv.org/abs/1502.01852

41. Hinton, G E., Srivastava, N., Krizhevsky, A., Sutskever, I., Salakhutdinov, R R. (2012). *Improving neural networks by preventing co-adaptation of feature detectors*. arXiv:1207.0580. https://arxiv.org/abs/1207.0580

42. Krizhevsky A., Sutskever I., Hinton G E. (2012). *ImageNet Classification with Deep Convolutional Neural Networks*. Part of Advances in Neural Information Processing Systems 25 (NIPS 2012). https://papers.nips.cc/paper/2012/file/c399862d3b9d6b76c8436e924a68c45b-Paper.pdf

43. Ioffe, S., Szegedy, C. (2015). *Batch Normalization: Accelerating Deep Network Training by Reducing Internal Covariate Shift*. arXiv:1502.03167. https://arxiv.org/abs/1502.03167

44. Santurkar, S., Tsipras, D., Ilyas, A., Madry, A. (2019). *How Does Batch Normalization Help Optimization?*. arXiv:1805.11604. https://arxiv.org/abs/1805.11604

45. Dean J., Ng, A Y. (2012). *Using large-scale brain simulations for machine learning and A.I.*. The Keyword | Google. https://blog.google/technology/ai/using-large-scale-brain-simulations-for/

46. Rumelhart, D., Hinton, G. & Williams, R. (1986) *Learning representations by back-propagating errors*. Nature 323, 533–536. https://doi.org/10.1038/323533a0

47. LeCun, Y., Bengio, Y. & Hinton, (2015) G. *Deep learning*. Nature 521, 436–444. https://www.nature.com/articles/nature14539.epdf

48. Olah (2015). *Understanding LSTM Networks*. colah's blog. Available from: https://colah.github.io/posts/2015-08-Understanding-LSTMs/

49. Mozer, M. C. (1995). *A Focused Backpropagation Algorithm for Temporal Pattern Recognition*. In Chauvin, Y.; Rumelhart, D. (eds.). *Backpropagation: Theory, architectures, and applications*. ResearchGate. Hillsdale, NJ: Lawrence Erlbaum Associates. pp. 137–169

50. Greff K., Srivastava, R K., Koutník, J., Steunebrink, B R., Schmidhuber, J. (2017). *LSTM: A Search Space Odyssey*. arXiv:1503.04069v2. https://arxiv.org/abs/1503.04069v2

51. Gers FA, Schmidhuber E. *LSTM recurrent networks learn simple context-free and context-sensitive languages*. IEEE Trans Neural Netw. 2001;12(6):1333-40. doi: 10.1109/72.963769. PMID: 18249962.

52. Cho, K., van Merrienboer, B., Gulcehre, C., Bahdanau, D., Bougares, F., Schwenk, H., Bengio, Y. (2014). *Learning Phrase Representations using RNN Encoder-Decoder for Statistical Machine Translation*. arXiv:1406.1078. https://arxiv.org/abs/1406.1078

53. Sutskever, I., Martens, J., Dahl, G. & Hinton, G. (2013). *On the importance of initialization and momentum in deep learning*. Proceedings of the 30th International Conference on Machine Learning, in PMLR 28(3):1139-1147.

54. Duchi J., Hazan E., Singer Y. (2011). *Adaptive Subgradient Methods for Online Learning and Stochastic Optimization*. Journal of Machine Learning Research 12 (2011) 2121-2159.

55. Hinton, Srivastava, Swersky. *Neural Networks for Machine Learning*, Lecture 6a. Available from: http://www.cs.toronto.edu/~tijmen/csc321/slides/lecture_slides_lec6.pdf

56. Zeiler, M D. (2012). *ADADELTA: An Adaptive Learning Rate Method*. arXiv:1212.5701. https://arxiv.org/abs/1212.5701

57. Kingma, D P., Ba, J. (2017). *Adam: A Method for Stochastic Optimization*. arXiv:1412.6980. https://arxiv.org/abs/1412.6980

58. Martens J. (2010). *Deep Learning via Hessian-free Optimization*. ICML. Vol. 27. 2010.

59. Martens J. (2010). *Deep Learning via Hessian-free Optimization*. ICML. Vol. 27. 2010.
60. Glorot X., Bengio Y., (2010). *Understanding the difficulty of training deep feedforward neural networks*. Proceedings of the thirteenth international conference on artificial intelligence and statistics.
61. He, K., Zhang, X., Ren, S., Sun, J. (2015). *Delving Deep into Rectifiers: Surpassing Human-Level Performance on ImageNet Classification*. arXiv:1502.01852. https://arxiv.org/abs/1502.01852

4
Teaching Networks to Generate Digits

In the previous chapter, we covered the building blocks of neural network models. In this chapter, our first project will recreate one of the most groundbreaking models in the history of deep learning, **Deep Belief Network** (**DBN**). DBN was one of the first multi-layer networks for which a feasible learning algorithm was developed. Besides being of historical interest, this model is connected to the topic of this book because the learning algorithm makes use of a generative model in order to pre-train the neural network weights into a reasonable configuration prior to backpropagation.

In this chapter, we will cover:

- How to load the **Modified National Institute of Standards and Technology** (**MNIST**) dataset and transform it using TensorFlow 2's Dataset API.
- How a **Restricted Boltzmann Machine** (**RBM**) – a simple neural network – is trained by minimizing an "energy" equation that resembles formulas from physics to generate images.
- How to stack several RBMs to make a DBN and apply forward and backward passes to pre-train this network to generate image data.
- How to implement an end-to-end classifier by combining this pre-training with backpropagation "fine-tuning" using the TensorFlow 2 API.

Teaching Networks to Generate Digits

The MNIST database

In developing the DBN model, we will use a dataset that we have discussed before – the MNIST database, which contains digital images of hand-drawn digits from 0 to 9[1]. This database is a combination of two sets of earlier images from the **National Institute of Standards and Technology** (**NIST**): Special Database 1 (digits written by US high school students) and Special Database 3 (written by US Census Bureau employees),[2] the sum of which is split into 60,000 training images and 10,000 test images.

The original images in the dataset were all black and white, while the modified dataset normalized them to fit into a 20x20-pixel bounding box and removed jagged edges using anti-aliasing, leading to intermediary grayscale values in cleaned images; they are padded for a final resolution of 28x28 pixels.

In the original NIST dataset, all the training images came from Bureau employees, while the test dataset came from high school students, and the modified version mixes the two groups in the training and test sets to provide a less biased population for training machine learning algorithms.

Figure 4.1: Digits from the NIST dataset (left)[3] and MNIST (right)[4]

An early application of **Support Vector Machines** (**SMVs**) to this dataset yielded an error rate of 0.8%,[5] while the latest deep learning models have shown error rates as low as 0.23%.[6] You should note that these figures were obtained due to not only the discrimination algorithms used but also "data augmentation" tricks such as creating additional translated images where the digit has been shifted by several pixels, thus increasing the number of data examples for the algorithm to learn from. Because of its wide availability, this dataset has become a benchmark for many machine learning models, including Deep Neural Networks.

The dataset was also the benchmark for a breakthrough in training multi-layer neural networks in 2006, in which an error rate of 1.25% was achieved (without image translation, as in the preceding examples).[7] In this chapter, we will examine in detail how this breakthrough was achieved using a generative model, and explore how to build our own DBN that can generate MNIST digits.

Retrieving and loading the MNIST dataset in TensorFlow

The first step in training our own DBN is to construct our dataset. This section will show you how to transform the MNIST data into a convenient format that allows you to train a neural network, using some of TensorFlow 2's built-in functions for simplicity.

Let's start by loading the MNIST dataset in TensorFlow. As the MNIST data has been used for many deep learning benchmarks, TensorFlow 2 already has convenient utilities for loading and formatting this data. To do so, we need to first install the `tensorflow-datasets` library:

```
pip install tensorflow-datasets
```

After installing the package, we need to import it along with the required dependencies:

```
from __future__ import absolute_import
from __future__ import division
from __future__ import print_function
import matplotlib.pyplot as plt
import numpy as np
import tensorflow.compat.v2 as tf
import tensorflow_datasets as tfds
```

Now we can download the MNIST data locally from **Google Cloud Storage** (**GCS**) using the builder functionality:

```
mnist_builder = tfds.builder("mnist")
mnist_builder.download_and_prepare()
```

The dataset will now be available on disk on our machine. As noted earlier, this data is divided into a training and test dataset, which you can verify by taking a look at the `info` command:

```
info = mnist_builder.info
print(info)
```

This gives the following output:

```
tfds.core.DatasetInfo(
    name='mnist',
    version=3.0.1
    description='The MNIST database of handwritten digits.',
    homepage='http://yann.lecun.com/exdb/mnist/',
    features=FeaturesDict({
        'image': Image(shape=(28, 28, 1), dtype=tf.uint8),
        'label': ClassLabel(shape=(), dtype=tf.int64, num_classes=10),
    }),
    total_num_examples=70000,
    splits={
        'test': 10000,
        'train': 60000,
    },
    supervised_keys=('image', 'label'),
    citation="""@article{lecun2010mnist,
      title={MNIST handwritten digit database},
      author={LeCun, Yann and Cortes, Corinna and Burges, CJ},
      journal={ATT Labs [Online]. Available: http://yann. lecun. com/exdb/mnist},
      volume={2},
      year={2010}
    }""",
    redistribution_info=,
)
```

As you can see, the test dataset has 10,000 examples, the training dataset has 60,000 examples, and the images are 28x28 pixels with a label from one of 10 classes (0 to 9).

Let's start by taking a look at the training dataset:

```
mnist_train = mnist_builder.as_dataset(split="train")
```

We can visually plot some examples using the show_examples function:

```
fig = tfds.show_examples(info, mnist_train)
```

This gives the following figure:

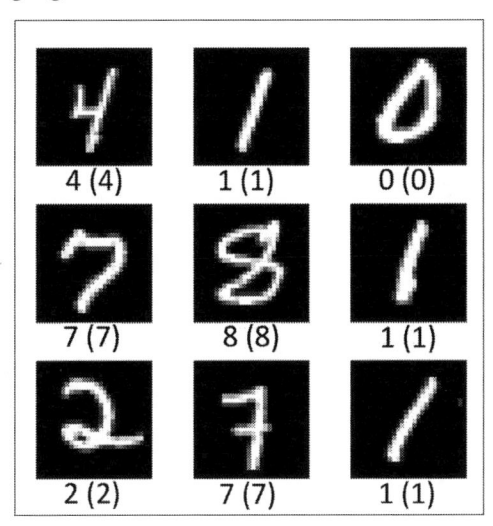

Figure 4.2: MNIST digit examples from the TensorFlow dataset

You can also see more clearly here the grayscale edges on the numbers where the anti-aliasing was applied to the original dataset to make the edges seem less jagged (the colors have also been flipped from the original example in *Figure 4.1*).

We can also plot an individual image by taking one element from the dataset, reshaping it to a 28x28 array, casting it as a 32-bit float, and plotting it in grayscale:

```
flatten_image = partial(flatten_image, label=True)

for image, label in mnist_train.map(flatten_image).take(1):
    plt.imshow(image.numpy().reshape(28,28).astype(np.float32),
               cmap=plt.get_cmap("gray"))
    print("Label: %d" % label.numpy())
```

This gives the following figure:

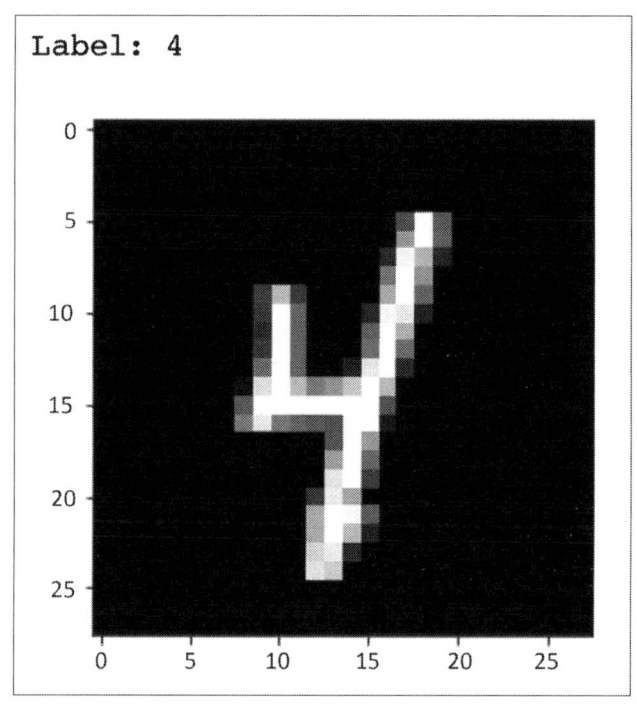

Figure 4.3: A MNIST digit in TensorFlow

This is nice for visual inspection, but for our experiments in this chapter, we will actually need to flatten these images into a vector. To do so, we can use the `map()` function, and verify that the dataset is now flattened; note that we also need to cast to a float for use in the RBM later. The RBM also assumes binary (0 or 1) inputs, so we need to rescale the pixels, which range from 0 to 256 to the range 0 to 1:

```
def flatten_image(x, label=True):
    if label:
        return (tf.divide(tf.dtypes.cast(tf.reshape(x["image"], 
(1,28*28)), tf.float32), 256.0) , x["label"])
    else:
        return (tf.divide(tf.dtypes.cast(tf.reshape(x["image"], 
(1,28*28)), tf.float32), 256.0))
for image, label in mnist_train.map(flatten_image).take(1):
    plt.imshow(image.numpy().astype(np.float32), cmap=plt.get_
cmap("gray"))
    print("Label: %d" % label.numpy())
```

This gives a 784x1 vector, which is the "flattened" version of the pixels of the digit "4":

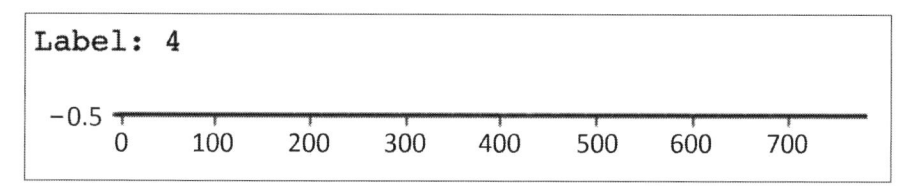

```
Label: 4
-0.5
     0    100   200   300   400   500   600   700
```

Figure 4.4: Flattening the MNIST digits in TensorFlow

Now that we have the MNIST data as a series of vectors, we are ready to start implementing an RBM to process this data and ultimately create a model capable of generating new images.

Restricted Boltzmann Machines: generating pixels with statistical mechanics

The neural network model that we will apply to the MNIST data has its origins in earlier research on how neurons in the mammalian brain might work together to transmit signals and encode patterns as memories. By using analogies to statistical mechanics in physics, this section will show you how simple networks can "learn" the distribution of image data and be used as building blocks for larger networks.

Hopfield networks and energy equations for neural networks

As we discussed in *Chapter 3, Building Blocks of Deep Neural Networks*, Hebbian Learning states, "Neurons that fire together, wire together",[8] and many models, including the multi-layer perceptron, made use of this idea in order to develop learning rules. One of these models was the **Hopfield network**, developed in the 1970-80s by several researchers[9][10]. In this network, each "neuron" is connected to every other by a symmetric weight, but no self-connections (there are only connections between neurons, no self-loops).

Unlike the multi-layer perceptrons and other architectures we studied in *Chapter 3, Building Blocks of Deep Neural Networks*, the Hopfield network is an undirected graph, since the edges go "both ways."

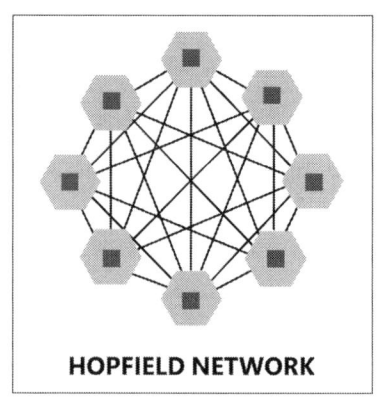

Figure 4.5: The Hopfield network

The neurons in the Hopfield network take on binary values, either (-1, 1) or (0, 1), as a thresholded version of the tanh or sigmoidal activation function:

$$s_i \leftarrow \begin{cases} +1 & \text{if } \Sigma_j w_{ij} s_j \geq \theta_i, \\ -1 & \text{otherwise.} \end{cases}$$

The threshold values (sigma) never change during training; to update the weights, a "Hebbian" approach is to use a set of n binary patterns (configurations of all the neurons) and update as:

$$w_{ij} = \frac{1}{n} \sum_{\mu=1}^{n} \epsilon_i^\mu \epsilon_j^\mu$$

where n is the number of patterns, and e is the binary activations of neurons i and j in a particular configuration. Looking at this equation, you can see that if the neurons share a configuration, the connection between them is strengthened, while if they are opposite signs (one neuron has a sign of +1, the other -1), it is weakened. Following this rule to iteratively strengthen or weaken a connection leads the network to converge to a stable configuration that resembles a "memory" for a particular activation of the network, given some input. This represents a model for associative memory in biological organisms – the kind of memory that links unrelated ideas, just as the neurons in the Hopfield network are linked together[11][12].

Besides representing biological memory, Hopfield networks also have an interesting parallel to electromagnetism. If we consider each neuron as a particle or "charge," we can describe the model in terms of a "free energy" equation that represents how the particles in this system mutually repulse/attract each other and where on the distribution of potential configurations the system lies relative to equilibrium:

$$E = -\frac{1}{2}\sum_{i,j} w_{ij} s_i s_j + \sum_i \theta_i s_i$$

where w is the weights between neurons i and j, s is the "states" of those neurons (either 1, "on," or -1, "off"), and sigma is the threshold of each neuron (for example, the value that its total inputs must exceed to set it to "on"). When the Hopfield network is in its final configuration, it also minimizes the value of the energy function computed for the network, which is lowered by units with an identical state(s) being connected strongly (w). The probability associated with a particular configuration is given by the **Gibbs measure**:

$$P(X = x) = \frac{1}{Z(\beta)} \exp(-\beta E(x))$$

Here, Z(B) is a normalizing constant that represents all possible configurations of the network, in the same respect as the normalizing constant in the Bayesian probability function you saw in *Chapter 1, An Introduction to Generative AI: "Drawing" Data from Models*.

Also notice in the energy function definition that the state of a neuron is only affected by local connections (rather than the state of every other neuron in the network, regardless of if it is connected); this is also known as the **Markov property**, since the state is "memoryless," depending only on its immediate "past" (neighbors). In fact, the *Hammersly-Clifford theorem* states that any distribution having this same memoryless property can be represented using the Gibbs measure.[13]

Modeling data with uncertainty with Restricted Boltzmann Machines

What other kinds of distributions might we be interested in? While useful from a theoretical perspective, one of the shortcomings of the Hopfield network is that it can't incorporate the kinds of uncertainty seen in actual physical or biological systems; rather than deterministically turning on or off, real-world problems often involve an element of chance – a magnet might flip polarity, or a neuron might fire at random.

This uncertainty, or *stochasticity*, is reflected in the *Boltzmann machine*,[14] a variant of the Hopfield network in which half the neurons (the "visible" units) receive information from the environment, while half (the "hidden" units) only receive information from the visible units.

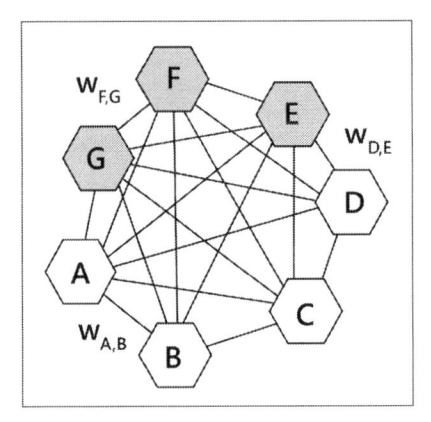

Figure 4.6: The Boltzmann machine

The Boltzmann machine randomly turns on (1) or off (0) each neuron by sampling, and over many iterations converges to a stable state represented by the minima of the energy function. This is shown schematically in *Figure 4.6*, in which the white nodes of the network are "off," and the blue ones are "on;" if we were to simulate the activations in the network, these values would fluctuate over time.

In theory, a model like this could be used, for example, to model the distribution of images, such as the MNIST data using the hidden nodes as a "barcode" that represents an underlying probability model for "activating" each pixel in the image. In practice, though, there are problems with this approach. Firstly, as the number of units in the Boltzmann network increases, the number of connections increases exponentially (for example, the number of potential configurations that has to be accounted for in the Gibbs measure's normalization constant explodes), as does the time needed to sample the network to an equilibrium state. Secondly, weights for units with intermediate activate probabilities (not strongly 0 or 1) will tend to fluctuate in a random walk pattern (for example, the probabilities will increase or decrease randomly but never stabilize to an equilibrium value) until the neurons converge, which also prolongs training.[15]

A practical modification is to remove some of the connections in the Boltzmann machine, namely those between visible units and between hidden units, leaving only connections between the two types of neurons. This modification is known as the RBM, shown in *Figure 4.7*[16]:

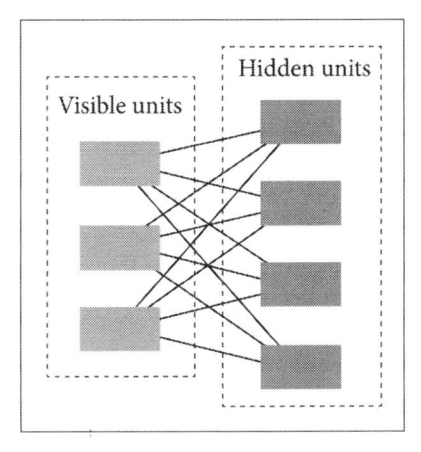

Figure 4.7: RBM

Imagine as described earlier that the visible units are input pixels from the MNIST dataset, and the hidden units are an encoded representation of that image. By sampling back and forth to convergence, we could create a generative model for images. We would just need a learning rule that would tell us how to update the weights to allow the energy function to converge to its minimum; this algorithm is **contrastive divergence** (CD). To understand why we need a special algorithm for RBMs, it helps to revisit the energy equation and how we might sample to get equilibrium for the network.

Contrastive divergence: Approximating a gradient

If we refer back to *Chapter 1, An Introduction to Generative AI: "Drawing" Data from Models*, creating a generative model of images using an RBM essentially involves finding the probability distribution of images, using the energy equation[17]:

$$p(x; \Theta) = \frac{1}{Z(\Theta)} f(x; \Theta)$$

where x is an image, theta is the parameters of the model (the weights and biases), and Z is the partition function:

$$Z(\Theta) = \int f(x; \Theta)\, dx$$

In order to find the parameters that optimize this distribution, we need to maximize the likelihood (product of each datapoint's probability under a density function) based on data:

$$p(\mathbf{X};\Theta) = \prod_{k=1}^{K} \frac{1}{Z(\Theta)} f(x_k;\Theta)$$

In practice, it's a bit easier to use the negative log likelihood, as this is represented by a sum:

$$E(\mathbf{X};\Theta) = \log Z(\Theta) - \frac{1}{K} \sum_{k=1}^{K} \log f(x_k;\Theta)$$

If the distribution f has a simple form, then we can just take the derivative of E with respect to parameters of f. For example, if f is a single normal distribution, then the values that maximize E with respect to mu (the mean) and sigma (the standard deviation) are, respectively, the sample mean and standard deviation; the partition function Z doesn't affect this calculation because the integral is 1, a constant, which becomes 0 once we take the logarithm.

If the distribution is instead a sum of N normal distributions, then the partial derivative of *mu(i)* (one of these distributions) with respect to f (the sum of all the N normal distributions) involves the mu and sigma of each other distribution as well. Because of this dependence, there is no closed-form solution (for example, a solution equation we can write out by rearranging terms or applying algebraic transformations) for the optimal value; instead, we need to use a gradient search method (such as the backpropagation algorithm we discussed in *Chapter 3, Building Blocks of Deep Neural Networks*) to iteratively find the optimal value of this function. Again, the integral of each of these N distributions is 1, meaning the partition function is the constant *log(N)*, making the derivative 0.

What happens if the distribution f is a product, instead of a sum, of normal distributions? The partition function Z is now no longer a constant in this equation with respect to theta, the parameters; the value will depend on how and where these functions overlap when computing the integral – they could cancel each other out by being mutually exclusive (0) or overlapping (yielding a value greater than 1). In order to evaluate gradient descent steps, we would need to be able to compute this partition function using numerical methods. In the RBM example, this partition function for the configuration of 28x28 MNIST digits would have 784 logistic units, and a massive number (2^{784}) of possible configurations, making it unwieldy to evaluate every time we want to take a gradient.

Is there any other way we could optimize the value of this energy equation without taking a full gradient? Returning to the energy equation, let's write out the gradient explicitly:

$$\frac{\partial E(\mathbf{X}; \Theta)}{\partial \Theta} = \frac{\partial \log Z(\Theta)}{\partial \Theta} - \frac{1}{K} \sum_{i=1}^{K} \frac{\partial \log f(x_i; \Theta)}{\partial \Theta}$$

$$= \frac{\partial \log Z(\Theta)}{\partial \Theta} - \langle \frac{\partial \log f(x; \Theta)}{\partial \Theta} \rangle_x$$

The partition function Z can be further written as a function of the integral involving X and the parameters of f:

$$\frac{\partial \log Z(\Theta)}{\partial \Theta} = \frac{1}{Z(\Theta)} \frac{\partial Z(\Theta)}{\partial \Theta}$$

$$= \frac{1}{Z(\Theta)} \frac{\partial}{\partial \Theta} \int f(x; \Theta) \, dx$$

$$= \frac{1}{Z(\Theta)} \int \frac{\partial f(x; \Theta)}{\partial \Theta} \, dx$$

$$= \frac{1}{Z(\Theta)} \int f(x; \Theta) \frac{\partial \log f(x; \Theta)}{\partial \Theta} \, dx$$

$$= \int p(x; \Theta) \frac{\partial \log f(x; \Theta)}{\partial \Theta} \, dx$$

$$= \langle \frac{\partial \log f(x; \Theta)}{\partial \Theta} \rangle_{p(x;\Theta)}$$

where < > represents an average over the observed data sampled from the distribution of x. In other words, we can approximate the integral by sampling from the data and computing the average, which allows us to avoid computing or approximating high-dimensional integrals.

While we can't directly sample from $p(x)$, we can use a technique known as **Markov Chain Monte Carlo (MCMC)** sampling to generate data from the target distribution $p(x')$. As was described in our discussion on Hopfield networks, the "Markov" property means that this sampling only uses the last sample as input in determining the probability of the next datapoint in the simulation – this forms a "chain" in which each successive sampled datapoint becomes input to the next.

The "Monte Carlo" in the name of this technique is a reference to a casino in the principality of Monaco, and denotes that, like the outcomes of gambling, these samples are generated through a random process. By generating these random samples, you can use N MCMC steps as an approximation of the average of a distribution that is otherwise difficult or impossible to integrate. When we put all of this together, we get the following gradient equation:

$$\frac{\partial E(\mathbf{X}; \Theta)}{\partial \Theta} = \langle \frac{\partial \log f(x; \Theta)}{\partial \Theta} \rangle_{\mathbf{X}^\infty} - \langle \frac{\partial \log f(x; \Theta)}{\partial \Theta} \rangle_{\mathbf{X}^0}$$

where X represents the data at each step in the MCMC chain, with X^0 being the input data. While in theory you might think it would take a large number of steps for the chain to converge, in practice it has been observed that even $N=1$ steps is enough to get a decent gradient approximation.[18]

Notice that the end result is a *contrast* between the input data and the sampled data; thus, the method is named **contrastive divergence** as it involves the difference between two distributions.

Applying this to our RBM example, we can follow this recipe to generate the required samples:

1. Take an input vector v
2. Compute a "hidden" activation h
3. Use the activation from (2) to generate a sampled visible state v'
4. Use (3) to generate a sampled hidden state h'
5. Compute the updates, which are simply the correlations of the visible and hidden units:

$$\Delta W = \epsilon(vh - v'h')$$

$$\Delta b = \epsilon(v - v')$$

$$\Delta c = \epsilon(h - h')$$

where b and c are the bias terms of visible and hidden units, respectively, and e is the learning rate.

This sampling is known as **Gibbs sampling**, a method in which we sample one unknown parameter of a distribution at a time while holding all others constant. Here we hold the visible or the hidden fixed and sample units in each step.

With CD, we now have a way to perform gradient descent to learn the parameters of our RBM model; as it turns out, we can potentially compute an even better model by stacking RBMs in what is called a DBN.

Stacking Restricted Boltzmann Machines to generate images: the Deep Belief Network

You have seen that an RBM with a single hidden layer can be used to learn a generative model of images; in fact, theoretical work has suggested that with a sufficiently large number of hidden units, an RBM can approximate *any* distribution with binary values.[19] However, in practice, for very large input data, it may be more efficient to add additional layers, instead of a single large layer, allowing a more "compact" representation of the data.

Researchers who developed DBNs also noted that adding additional layers can only lower the log likelihood of the lower bound of the approximation of the data reconstructed by the generative model.[20] In this case, the hidden layer output h of the first layer becomes the input to a second RBM; we can keep adding other layers to make a deeper network. Furthermore, if we wanted to make this network capable of learning not only the distribution of the image (x) but also the label – which digit it represents from 0 to 9 (y) – we could add yet another layer to a stack of connected RBMs that is a probability distribution (softmax) over the 10 possible digit classes.

A problem with training a very deep graphical model such as stacked RBMs is the "explaining-away effect" that we discussed in *Chapter 3, Building Blocks of Deep Neural Networks*. Recall that the dependency between variables can complicate inference of the state of hidden variables:

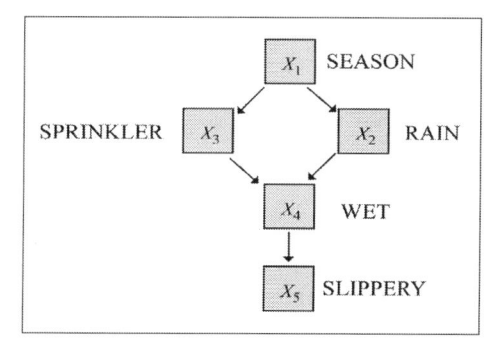

Figure 4.8: The explaining-away effect in a Bayesian network[21]

In *Figure 4.8*, the knowledge that the pavement is wet can be explained by a sprinkler being turned on, to the extent that the presence or absence of rain becomes irrelevant, meaning we can't meaningfully infer the probability that it is raining. This is equivalent to saying that the posterior distribution (*Chapter 1, An Introduction to Generative AI: "Drawing" Data from Models*) of the hidden units cannot be tractably computed, since they are correlated, which interferes with easily sampling the hidden states of the RBM.

One solution is to treat each of the units as independent in the likelihood function, which is known as *variational inference*; while this works in practice, it is not a satisfying solution given that we know that these units are in fact correlated.

But where does this correlation come from? If we sample the state of the visible units in a single-layer RBM, we set the states of each hidden unit randomly since they are independent; thus the *prior distribution* over the hidden units is independent. Why is the posterior then correlated? Just as the knowledge (data) that the pavement is wet causes a correlation between the probabilities of a sprinkler and rainy weather, the correlation between pixel values causes the posterior distribution of the hidden units to be non-independent. This is because the pixels in the images aren't set randomly; based on which digit the image represents, groups of pixels are more or less likely to be bright or dark. In the 2006 paper *A Fast Learning Algorithm for Deep Belief Nets*,[22] the authors hypothesized that this problem could be solved by computing a *complementary prior* that has exactly the opposite correlation to the likelihood, thus canceling out this dependence and making the posterior also independent.

To compute this *complementary prior*, we could use the posterior distribution over hidden units in a higher layer. The trick to generating such distributions is in a greedy, layer-wise procedure for "priming" the network of stacked RBMs in a multi-layer generative model, such that the weights can then be fine-tuned as a classification model. For example, let's consider a three-layer model for the MNIST data (*Figure 4.9*):

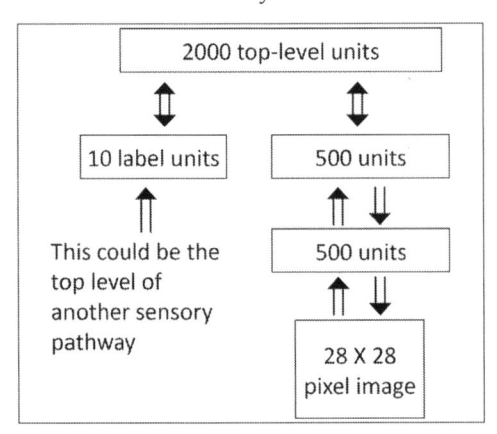

Figure 4.9: DBN architecture based on "A fast learning algorithm for deep belief nets" by Hinton et al.

The two 500-unit layers form representations of the MNIST digits, while the 2000- and 10-unit layers are "associative memory" that correlates labels with the digit representation. The two first layers have directed connections (different weights) for upsampling and downsampling, while the top layers have undirected weights (the same weight for forward and backward passes).

This model could be learned in stages. For the first 500-unit RBM, we would treat it as an undirected model by enforcing that the forward and backward weights are equal; we would then use CD to learn the parameters of this RBM. We would then fix these weights and learn a *second* (500-unit) RBM that uses the hidden units from the first layer as input "data," and repeat for the 2000-layer unit.

After we have "primed" the network, we no longer need to enforce that the weights in the bottom layers are tied, and can fine-tune the weights using an algorithm known as "wake-sleep."[23]

Firstly, we take input data (the digits) and compute the activations of the other layers all the way up until the connections between the 2000- and 10-unit layers. We compute updates to the "generative weights" (those that compute the activations that yield image data from the network) pointing downward using the previously given gradient equations. This is the "wake" phase because if we consider the network as resembling a biological sensory system, then it receives input from the environment through this forward pass.

For the 2000- and 10-unit layers, we use the sampling procedure for CD using the second 500-unit layer's output as "data" to update the undirected weights.

We then take the output of the 2000-layer unit and compute activations downward, updating the "recognition weights" (those that compute activations that lead to the classification of the image into one of the digit classes) pointing upward. This is called the "sleep" phase because it displays what is in the "memory" of the network, rather than taking data from outside.

We then repeat *these steps* until convergence.

Note that in practice, instead of using undirected weights in the top layers of the network, we could replace the last layer with directed connections and a softmax classifier. This network would then technically no longer be a DBN, but rather a regular Deep Neural Network that we could optimize with backpropagation. This is an approach we will take in our own code, as we can then leverage TensorFlow's built-in gradient calculations, and it fits into the paradigm of the Model API.

Now that we have covered the theoretical background to understand how a DBN is trained and how the pre-training approach resolves issues with the "explaining-away" effect, we will implement the whole model in code, showing how we can leverage TensorFlow 2's gradient tape functionality to implement CD as a custom learning algorithm.

Creating an RBM using the TensorFlow Keras layers API

Now that you have an appreciation of some of the theoretical underpinnings of the RBM, let's look at how we can implement it using the TensorFlow 2.0 library. For this purpose, we will represent the RBM as a custom layer type using the Keras layers API.

> Code in this chapter was adapted to TensorFlow 2 from the original Theano (another deep learning Python framework) code from deeplearning.net.

Firstly, we extend `tf.keras.layer`:

```
from tensorflow.keras import layers
import tensorflow_probability as tfp
class RBM(layers.Layer):
    def __init__(self, number_hidden_units=10, number_visible_units=None, learning_rate=0.1, cd_steps=1):
        super().__init__()
        self.number_hidden_units = number_hidden_units
        self.number_visible_units = number_visible_units
        self.learning_rate = learning_rate
        self.cd_steps = cd_steps
```

We input a number of hidden units, visible units, a learning rate for CD updates, and the number of steps to take with each CD pass. For the layers API, we are only required to implement two functions: `build()` and `call()`. `build()` is executed when we call `model.compile()`, and is used to initialize the weights of the network, including inferring the right size of the weights given the input dimensions:

```
def build(self, input_shape):
    if not self.number_visible_units:
        self.number_visible_units = input_shape[-1]
        self.w_rec = self.add_weight(shape=(self.number_visible_units,
self.number_hidden_units),
                            initializer='random_normal',
                            trainable=True)
        self.w_gen = self.add_weight(shape=(self.number_hidden_units,
self.number_visible_units),
                            initializer='random_normal',
                            trainable=True)
        self.hb = self.add_weight(shape=(self.number_hidden_units, ),
                            initializer='random_normal',
                            trainable=True)
        self.vb = self.add_weight(shape=(self.number_visible_units, ),
                            initializer='random_normal',
                            trainable=True)
```

We also need a way to perform both forward and reverse samples from the model. For the forward pass, we need to compute sigmoidal activations from the input, and then stochastically turn the hidden units on or off based on the activation probability between 1 and 0 given by that sigmoidal activation:

```
def forward(self, x):
    return tf.sigmoid(tf.add(tf.matmul(x, self.w), self.hb))

def sample_h(self, x):
    u_sample = tfp.distributions.Uniform().sample((x.shape[1],
                                            self.hb.shape[-1]))
    return tf.cast((x) > u_sample, tf.float32)
```

Likewise, we need a way to sample in reverse for the visible units:

```
def reverse(self, x):
    return tf.sigmoid(tf.add(tf.matmul(x, self.w_gen), self.vb))

def sample_v(self, x):
    u_sample = tfp.distributions.Uniform().sample((x.shape[1],
                                            self.vb.shape[-1]))
    return tf.cast(self.reverse(x) > u_sample, tf.float32)
```

We also implement `call()` in the RBM class, which provides the forward pass we would use if we were to use the `fit()` method of the Model API for backpropagation (which we can do for fine-tuning later in our deep belief model):

```
def call(self, inputs):
    return tf.sigmoid(tf.add(tf.matmul(inputs, self.w), self.hb))
```

To actually implement CD learning for each RBM, we need to create some additional functions. The first calculates the free energy, as you saw in the Gibbs measure earlier in this chapter:

```
def free_energy(self, x):
    return -tf.tensordot(x, self.vb, 1)\
    -tf.reduce_sum(tf.math.log(1+tf.math.exp(tf.add(tf.matmul(x, self.w), self.hb))), 1)
```

Note here that we could have used the Bernoulli distribution from `tensorflow_probability` in order to perform this sampling, using the sigmoidal activations as the probabilities; however, this is slow and would cause performance issues when we need to repetitively sample during CD learning. Instead, we use a speedup in which we sample an array of uniform random numbers the same size as the sigmoidal array and then set the hidden unit as 1 if it is greater than the random number. Thus, if a sigmoidal activation is 0.9, it has a 90% probability of being greater than a randomly sampled uniform number, and is set to "on." This has the same behavior as sampling a Bernoulli variable with a probability of 0.9, but is computationally much more efficient. The reverse and visible samples are computed similarly. Finally, putting these together allows us to perform both forward and reverse Gibbs samples:

```
def reverse_gibbs(self, x):
    return self.sample_h(self.sample_v(x))
```

To perform the CD updates, we make use of TensorFlow 2's eager execution and the `GradientTape` API you saw in *Chapter 3, Building Blocks of Deep Neural Networks*:

```
def cd_update(self, x):
    with tf.GradientTape(watch_accessed_variables=False) as g:
        h_sample = self.sample_h(x)
        for step in range(self.cd_steps):
            v_sample = tf.constant(self.sample_v(h_sample))
            h_sample = self.sample_h(v_sample)
        g.watch(self.w_rec)
        g.watch(self.hb)
        g.watch(self.vb)
```

```
        cost = tf.reduce_mean(self.free_energy(x)) - tf.reduce_
mean(self.free_energy(v_sample))
        w_grad, hb_grad, vb_grad = g.gradient(cost, [self.w_rec, self.
hb, self.vb])
        self.w_rec.assign_sub(self.learning_rate * w_grad)
        self.w_gen = tf.Variable(tf.transpose(self.w_rec)) # force
                                                           # tieing
        self.hb.assign_sub(self.learning_rate * hb_grad)
        self.vb.assign_sub(self.learning_rate * vb_grad)
        return self.reconstruction_cost(x).numpy()
```

We perform one or more sample steps, and compute the cost using the difference between the free energy of the data and the reconstructed data (which is cast as a constant using `tf.constant` so that we don't treat it as a variable during autogradient calculation). We then compute the gradients of the three weight matrices and update their values, before returning our reconstruction cost as a way to monitor progress. The reconstruction cost is simply the cross-entropy loss between the input and reconstructed data:

```
def reconstruction_cost(self, x):
    return tf.reduce_mean(
        tf.reduce_sum(tf.math.add(
            tf.math.multiply(x,tf.math.log(self.reverse(self.
forward(x)))),
tf.math.multiply(tf.math.subtract(1,x),tf.math.log(tf.math.
subtract(1,self.reverse(self.forward(x))))) 
        ), 1),)
```

which represents the formula:

$$-\frac{1}{N}\sum_{i=1}^{N}(y_n \log(\widehat{y_n}) + (1 - y_n)\log(\widehat{1 - y_n}))$$

where y is the target label, y-hat is the estimated label from the softmax function, and N is the number of elements in the dataset.

Note that we enforce the weights being equal by copying over the transposed value of the updated (recognition) weights into the generative weights. Keeping the two sets of weights separate will be useful later on when we perform updates only on the recognition (forward) or generative (backward) weights during the wake-sleep procedure.

Teaching Networks to Generate Digits

Putting it all together, we can initialize an RBM with 500 units like in Hinton's paper24, call build() with the shape of the flattened MNIST digits, and run successive epochs of training:

```
rbm = RBM(500)
rbm.build([784])
num_epochs=100

def train_rbm(rbm=None, data=mnist_train, map_fn=flatten_image,
              num_epochs=100, tolerance=1e-3, batch_size=32, shuffle_
buffer=1024):

    last_cost = None

    for epoch in range(num_epochs):
        cost = 0.0
        count = 0.0
        for datapoints in data.map(map_fn).shuffle(shuffle_buffer).batch(batch_size):
            cost += rbm.cd_update(datapoints)
            count += 1.0
        cost /= count
        print("epoch: {}, cost: {}".format(epoch, cost))
        if last_cost and abs(last_cost-cost) <= tolerance:
            break
        last_cost = cost

    return rbm

rbm = train_rbm(rbm, mnist_train, partial(flatten_image, label=False),
100, 0.5, 2000)
```

After ~25 steps, the model should converge, and we can inspect the results. One parameter of interest is the weight matrix w; the shape is 784 (28x28) by 500, so we could see each "column" as a 28x28 filter, similar to the kernels in the convolutional networks we studied in *Chapter 3, Building Blocks of Deep Neural Networks*. We can visualize a few of these to see what kinds of patterns they are recognizing in the images:

```
fig, axarr = plt.subplots(10,10)
plt.axis('off')

for i in range(10):
```

```
    for j in range(10):
        fig.axes[i*10+j].get_xaxis().set_visible(False)
        fig.axes[i*10+j].get_yaxis().set_visible(False)
        axarr[i,j].imshow(rbm.w_rec.numpy()[:,i*10+j].reshape(28,28),
cmap=plt.get_cmap("gray"))
```

This provides a set of filters:

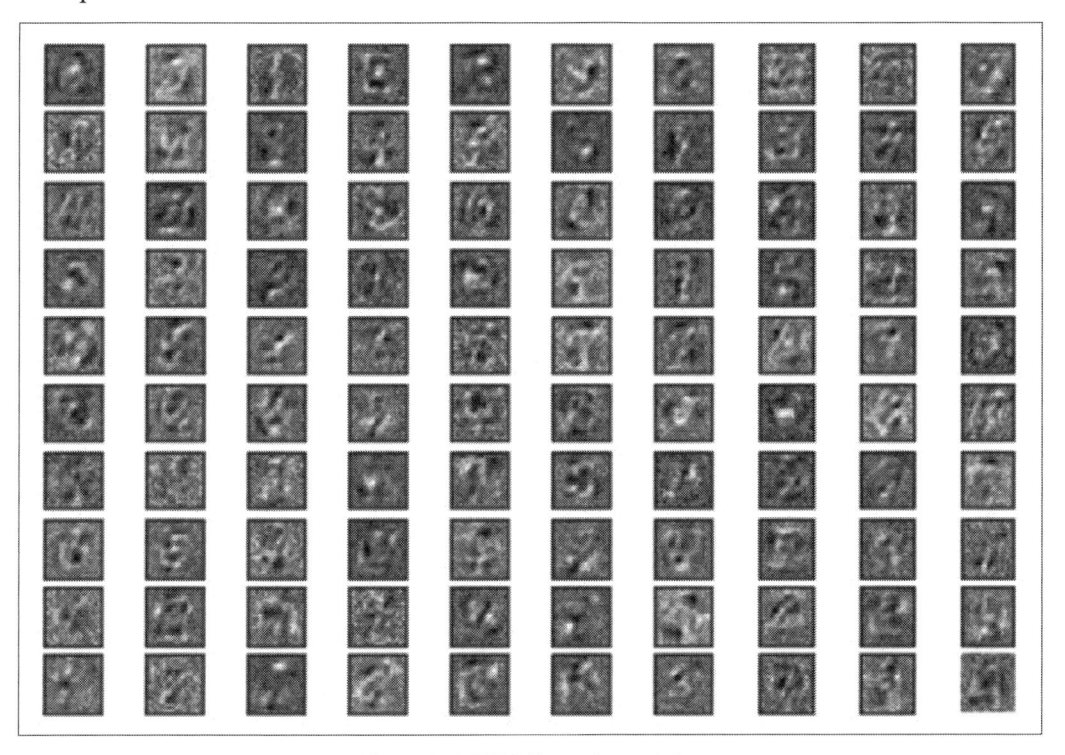

Figure 4.10: DBN filters after training

We can see that these filters appear to represent different shapes that we would find in a digit image, such as curves or lines. We can also observe the reconstruction of the images by sampling from our data:

```
i=0
for image, label in mnist_train.map(flatten_image).batch(1).take(10):
    plt.figure(i)
    plt.imshow(rbm.forward_gibbs(image).numpy().reshape(28,28).
astype(np.float32), cmap=plt.get_cmap("gray"))
    i+=1
    plt.figure(i)
```

Teaching Networks to Generate Digits

```
plt.imshow(image.numpy().reshape(28,28).astype(np.float32),
        cmap=plt.get_cmap("gray"))
i+=1
```

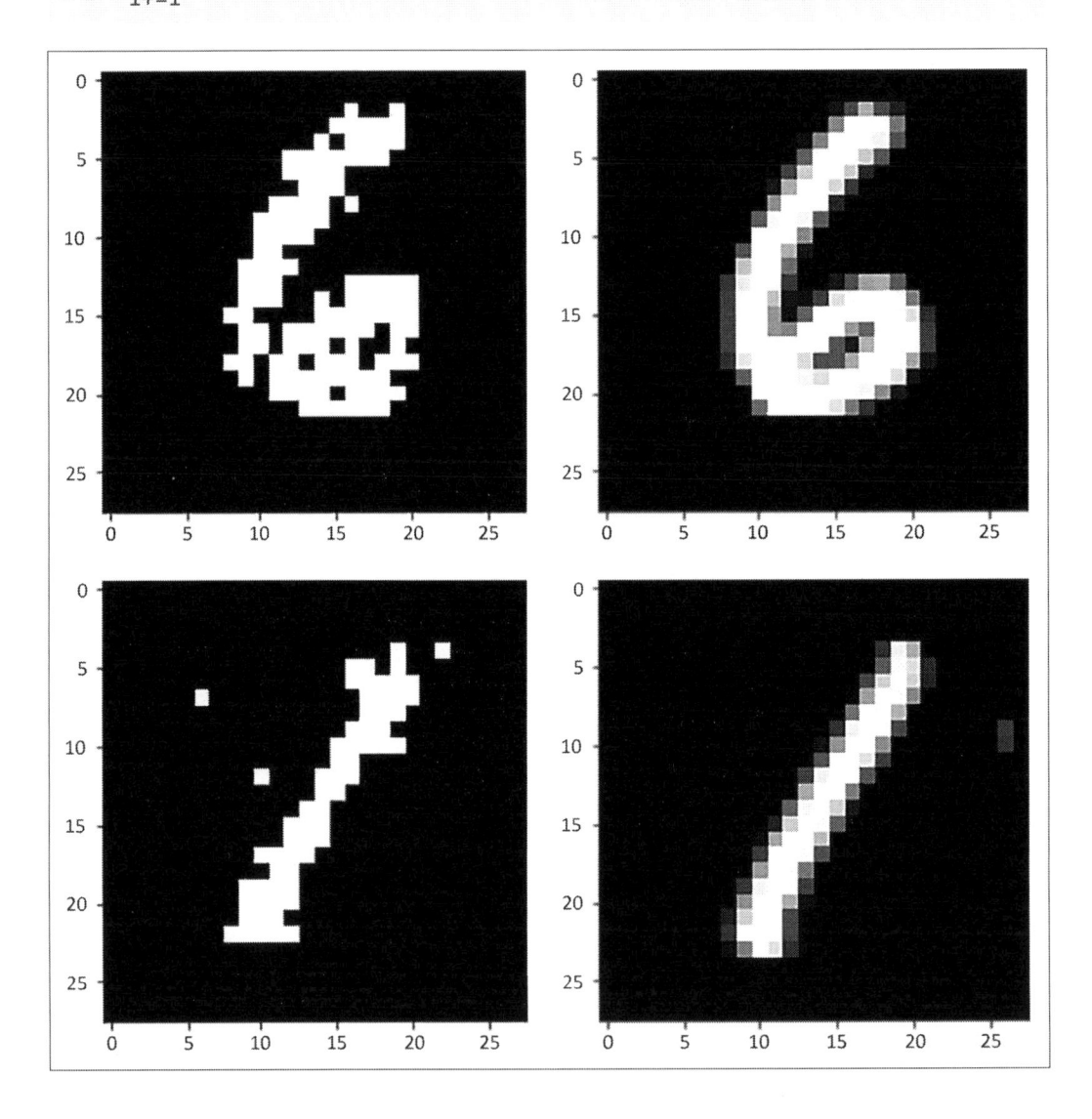

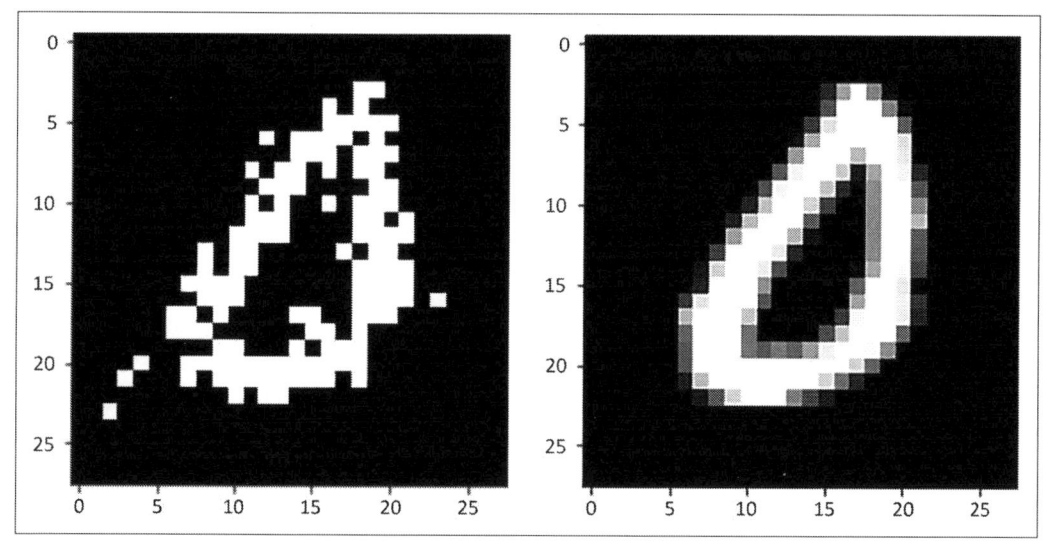

Figure 4.11: Original (right) and reconstructed (left) digits from DBN

We can see in *Figure 4.11* that the network has nicely captured the underlying data distribution, as our samples represent a recognizable binary form of the input images. Now that we have one layer working, let's continue by combining multiple RBMs in layers to create a more powerful model.

Creating a DBN with the Keras Model API

You have now seen how to create a single-layer RBM to generate images; this is the building block required to create a full-fledged DBN. Usually, for a model in TensorFlow 2, we only need to extend `tf.keras.Model` and define an initialization (where the layers are defined) and a `call` function (for the forward pass). For our DBN model, we also need a few more custom functions to define its behavior.

Teaching Networks to Generate Digits

First, in the initialization, we need to pass a list of dictionaries that contain the parameters for our RBM layers (`number_hidden_units, number_visible_units, learning_rate, cd_steps`):

```
class DBN(tf.keras.Model):
    def __init__(self, rbm_params=None, name='deep_belief_network',
                 num_epochs=100, tolerance=1e-3, batch_size=32,
shuffle_buffer=1024, **kwargs):
        super().__init__(name=name, **kwargs)
        self._rbm_params = rbm_params
        self._rbm_layers = list()
        self._dense_layers = list()
        for num, rbm_param in enumerate(rbm_params):
            self._rbm_layers.append(RBM(**rbm_param))
            self._rbm_layers[-1].build([rbm_param["number_visible_
units"]])
            if num < len(rbm_params)-1:
                self._dense_layers.append(
                    tf.keras.layers.Dense(rbm_param["number_hidden_
units"], activation=tf.nn.sigmoid))
            else:
                self._dense_layers.append(
                    tf.keras.layers.Dense(rbm_param["number_hidden_
units"], activation=tf.nn.softmax))
            self._dense_layers[-1].build([rbm_param["number_visible_
units"]])
        self._num_epochs = num_epochs
        self._tolerance = tolerance
        self._batch_size = batch_size
        self._shuffle_buffer = shuffle_buffer
```

Note at the same time that we also initialize a set of sigmoidal dense layers with a softmax at the end, which we can use for fine-tuning through backpropagation once we've trained the model using the generative procedures outlined earlier. To train the DBN, we begin a new code block to start the generative learning process for the stack of RBMs:

```
# pretraining:

        inputs_layers = []
        for num in range(len(self._rbm_layers)):

            if num == 0:
```

```
                inputs_layers.append(inputs)
                self._rbm_layers[num] = \
                    self.train_rbm(self._rbm_layers[num],
                                    inputs)
            else:   # pass all data through previous layer
                inputs_layers.append(inputs_layers[num-1].map(
                    self._rbm_layers[num-1].forward))
                self._rbm_layers[num] = \
                    self.train_rbm(self._rbm_layers[num],
                                    inputs_layers[num])
```

Notice that for computational efficiency, we generate the input for each layer past the first by passing every datapoint through the prior layer in a forward pass using the map() function for the Dataset API, instead of having to generate these forward samples repeatedly. While this takes more memory, it greatly reduces the computation required. Each layer in the pre-training loop calls back to the CD loop you saw before, which is now a member function of the DBN class:

```
def train_rbm(self, rbm, inputs,
            num_epochs, tolerance, batch_size, shuffle_buffer):
    last_cost = None
    for epoch in range(num_epochs):
        cost = 0.0
        count = 0.0
        for datapoints in inputs.shuffle(shuffle_buffer).batch(batch_size).take(1):
            cost += rbm.cd_update(datapoints)
            count += 1.0
        cost /= count
        print("epoch: {}, cost: {}".format(epoch, cost))
        if last_cost and abs(last_cost-cost) <= tolerance:
            break
        last_cost = cost
    return rbm
```

Once we have pre-trained in a greedy manner, we can proceed to the wake-sleep step. We start with the upward pass:

```
# wake-sleep:

    for epoch in range(self._num_epochs):
        # wake pass
        inputs_layers = []
        for num, rbm in enumerate(self._rbm_layers):
            if num == 0:
                inputs_layers.append(inputs)
            else:
                inputs_layers.append(inputs_layers[num-1].map(self._rbm_layers[num-1].forward))
        for num, rbm in enumerate(self._rbm_layers[:-1]):
            cost = 0.0
            count = 0.0
            for datapoints in inputs_layers[num].shuffle(
                self._shuffle_buffer).batch(self._batch_size):
                cost += self._rbm_layers[num].wake_update(datapoints)
                count += 1.0
            cost /= count
            print("epoch: {}, wake_cost: {}".format(epoch, cost))
```

Again, note that we gather a list of the transformed forward passes at each stage so that we have the necessary inputs for the update formula. We've now added a function, wake_update, to the RBM class, which will compute updates only for the generative (downward) weights, in every layer except the last (the associate, undirected connections):

```
def wake_update(self, x):
    with tf.GradientTape(watch_accessed_variables=False) as g:
        h_sample = self.sample_h(x)
        for step in range(self.cd_steps):
            v_sample = self.sample_v(h_sample)
            h_sample = self.sample_h(v_sample)
        g.watch(self.w_gen)
        g.watch(self.vb)
        cost = tf.reduce_mean(self.free_energy(x)) - tf.reduce_mean(self.free_energy_reverse(h_sample))
    w_grad, vb_grad = g.gradient(cost, [self.w_gen, self.vb])

    self.w_gen.assign_sub(self.learning_rate * w_grad)
```

```
        self.vb.assign_sub(self.learning_rate * vb_grad)
        return self.reconstruction_cost(x).numpy()
```

This is almost identical to the CD update, except that we are only updating the generative weights and the visible unit bias terms. Once we compute the forward pass, we then perform a contrastive update on the associate memory in the top layer:

```
# top-level associative:
        self._rbm_layers[-1] = self.train_rbm(self._rbm_layers[-1],
            inputs_layers[-2].map(self._rbm_layers[-2].forward),
            num_epochs=self._num_epochs,
            tolerance=self._tolerance, batch_size=self._batch_size,
            shuffle_buffer=self._shuffle_buffer)
```

We then need to compute the data for the reverse pass of the wake-sleep algorithm; we do this by again applying a mapping to the last layer input:

```
reverse_inputs = inputs_layers[-1].map(self._rbm_layers[-1].forward)
```

For the sleep pass, we need to traverse the RBM in reverse, updating only the non-associative (undirected) connections. We first need to map the required input for each layer in reverse:

```
reverse_inputs_layers = []
        for num, rbm in enumerate(self._rbm_layers[::-1]):
            if num == 0:
                reverse_inputs_layers.append(reverse_inputs)
            else:
                reverse_inputs_layers.append(
                    reverse_inputs_layers[num-1].map(
                    self._rbm_layers[len(self._rbm_layers)-num].
reverse))
```

Then we perform a backward traversal of the layers, only updating the non-associative connections:

```
for num, rbm in enumerate(self._rbm_layers[::-1]):
            if num > 0:
                cost = 0.0
                count = 0.0
                for datapoints in reverse_inputs_layers[num].shuffle(
                    self._shuffle_buffer).batch(self._batch_size):
                    cost += self._rbm_layers[len(self._rbm_layers)-1-
num].sleep_update(datapoints)
```

```
            count += 1.0
        cost /= count
        print("epoch: {}, sleep_cost: {}".format(epoch, cost))
```

Once we are satisfied with the training progress, we can tune the model further using normal backpropagation. The last step in the wake-sleep procedure is to set all the dense layers with the results of the trained weights from the RBM layers:

```
for dense_layer, rbm_layer in zip(dbn._dense_layers, dbn._rbm_layers):
    dense_layer.set_weights([rbm_layer.w_rec.numpy(), rbm_layer.hb.numpy()]
```

We have included a forward pass for a neural network in the DBN class using the call function():

```
def call(self, x, training):
    for dense_layer in self._dense_layers:
        x = dense_layer(x)
    return x
```

This can be used in the fit() call in the TensorFlow API:

```
dbn.compile(loss=tf.keras.losses.CategoricalCrossentropy())
dbn.fit(x=mnist_train.map(lambda x: flatten_image(x, label=True)).batch(32), )
```

This begins to train the now pre-trained weights using backpropagation, to fine-tune the discriminative power of the model. One way to conceptually understand this fine-tuning is that the pre-training procedure guides the weights to a reasonable configuration that captures the "shape" of the data, which backpropagation can then tune for a particular classification task. Otherwise, starting from a completely random weight configuration, the parameters are too far from capturing the variation in the data to be efficiently navigated to an optimal configuration through backpropagation alone.

You have seen how to combine multiple RBMs in layers to create a DBN, and how to run a generative learning process on the end-to-end model using the TensorFlow 2 API; in particular, we made use of the gradient tape to allow us to record and replay the gradients using a non-standard optimization algorithm (for example, not one of the default optimizers in the TensorFlow API), allowing us to plug a custom gradient update into the TensorFlow framework.

Summary

In this chapter, you learned about one of the most important models from the beginnings of the deep learning revolution, the DBN. You saw that DBNs are constructed by stacking together RBMs, and how these undirected models can be trained using CD.

The chapter then described a greedy, layer-wise procedure for priming a DBN by sequentially training each of a stack of RBMs, which can then be fine-tuned using the wake-sleep algorithm or backpropagation. We then explored practical examples of using the TensorFlow 2 API to create an RBM layer and a DBN model, illustrating the use of the `GradientTape` class to compute updates using CD.

You also learned how, following the wake-sleep algorithm, we can compile the DBN as a normal Deep Neural Network and perform backpropagation for supervised training. We applied these models to MNIST data and saw how an RBM can generate digits after training converges, and has features resembling the convolutional filters described in *Chapter 3, Building Blocks of Deep Neural Networks*.

While the examples in the chapter involved significantly extending the basic layer and model classes of the TensorFlow Keras API, they should give you an idea of how to implement your own low-level alternative training procedures. Going forward, we will mostly stick to using the standard `fit()` and `predict()` methods, starting with our next topic, Variational Autoencoders, a sophisticated and computationally efficient way to generate image data.

References

1. LeCun, Yann; Léon Bottou; Yoshua Bengio; Patrick Haffner (1998). *Gradient-Based Learning Applied to Document Recognition*. Proceedings of the IEEE. 86 (11): 2278–2324
2. LeCun, Yann; Corinna Cortes; Christopher J.C. Burges. *MNIST handwritten digit database, Yann LeCun, Corinna Cortes, and Chris Burges*
3. NIST's original datasets: https://www.nist.gov/system/files/documents/srd/nistsd19.pdf
4. https://upload.wikimedia.org/wikipedia/commons/thumb/2/27/MnistExamples.png/440px-MnistExamples.png
5. LeCun, Yann; Léon Bottou; Yoshua Bengio; Patrick Haffner (1998). *Gradient-Based Learning Applied to Document Recognition*. Proceedings of the IEEE. 86 (11): 2278–2324

6. D. Ciregan, U. Meier and J. Schmidhuber, (2012) *Multi-column deep neural networks for image classification*, 2012 IEEE Conference on Computer Vision and Pattern Recognition, pp. 3642-3649. https://ieeexplore.ieee.org/document/6248110

7. Hinton GE, Osindero S, Teh YW. (2006) *A fast learning algorithm for deep belief nets*. Neural Comput. 18(7):1527-54. https://www.cs.toronto.edu/~hinton/absps/fastnc.pdf

8. Hebb, D. O. (1949). *The Organization of Behavior: A Neuropsychological Theory*. New York: Wiley and Sons

9. Gurney, Kevin (2002). *An Introduction to Neural Networks*. Routledge

10. Sathasivam, Saratha (2008). *Logic Learning in Hopfield Networks*.

11. Hebb, D. O.. *The organization of behavior: A neuropsychological theory*. Lawrence Erlbaum, 2002.

12. Suzuki, Wendy A. (2005). *Associative Learning and the Hippocampus*. Psychological Science Agenda. American Psychological Association. https://www.apa.org/science/about/psa/2005/02/suzuki

13. Hammersley, J. M.; Clifford, P. (1971), Markov fields on finite graphs and lattices; Clifford, P. (1990), *Markov random fields in statistics*, in Grimmett, G. R.; Welsh, D. J. A. (eds.), *Disorder in Physical Systems: A Volume in Honour of John M. Hammersley*, Oxford University Press, pp. 19–32

14. Ackley, David H; Hinton, Geoffrey E; Sejnowski, Terrence J (1985), *A learning algorithm for Boltzmann machines* (PDF), Cognitive Science, 9 (1): 147–169

15. *Boltzmann machine*. Wikipedia. Retrieved April, 26, 2021 from https://en.wikipedia.org/wiki/Boltzmann_machine

16. Smolensky, Paul (1986). *Chapter 6: Information Processing in Dynamical Systems: Foundations of Harmony Theory* (PDF). In Rumelhart, David E.; McLelland, James L. (eds.). *Parallel Distributed Processing: Explorations in the Microstructure of Cognition*, Volume 1: Foundations. MIT Press. pp. 194–281

17. Woodford O. *Notes on Contrastive Divergence*. http://www.robots.ox.ac.uk/~ojw/files/NotesOnCD.pdf

18. Hinton, G E. (2000). *Training Products of Experts by Minimizing Contrastive Divergence*. http://www.cs.utoronto.ca/~hinton/absps/nccd.pdf

19. Roux, N L., Bengio, Y. (2008). *Representational Power of Restricted Boltzmann Machines and Deep Belief Networks*. in Neural Computation, vol. 20, no. 6, pp. 1631-1649. https://www.microsoft.com/en-us/research/wp-content/uploads/2016/02/representational_power.pdf

20. Hinton, G E. (2000). *Training Products of Experts by Minimizing Contrastive Divergence.* http://www.cs.utoronto.ca/~hinton/absps/nccd.pdf

21. Pearl J., Russell S. (2000). *BAYESIAN NETWORKS.* https://ftp.cs.ucla.edu/pub/stat_ser/r277.pdf

22. Hinton GE, Osindero S, Teh YW. (2006) *A fast learning algorithm for deep belief nets.* Neural Comput. 18(7):1527-54. https://www.cs.toronto.edu/~hinton/absps/fastnc.pdf

23. Hinton GE, Osindero S, Teh YW. (2006) *A fast learning algorithm for deep belief nets.* Neural Comput. 18(7):1527-54. https://www.cs.toronto.edu/~hinton/absps/fastnc.pdf

24. Hinton GE, Osindero S, Teh YW. (2006) *A fast learning algorithm for deep belief nets.* Neural Comput. 18(7):1527-54. https://www.cs.toronto.edu/~hinton/absps/fastnc.pdf

5
Painting Pictures with Neural Networks Using VAEs

As you saw in *Chapter 4*, *Teaching Networks to Generate Digits*, deep neural networks are a powerful tool for creating generative models for complex data such as images, allowing us to develop a network that can generate images from the MNIST hand-drawn digit database. In that example, the data is relatively simple; images can only come from a limited set of categories (the digits 0 through 9) and are low-resolution grayscale data.

What about more complex data, such as color images drawn from the real world? One example of such "real world" data is the Canadian Institute for Advanced Research 10 class dataset, denoted as CIFAR-10.[1] It is a subset of 60,000 examples from a larger set of 80 million images, divided into ten classes – airplanes, cars, birds, cats, deer, dogs, frogs, horses, ships, and trucks. While still an extremely limited set in terms of the diversity of images we would encounter in the real world, these classes have some characteristics that make them more complex than MNIST. For example, the MNIST digits can vary in width, curvature, and a few other properties; the CIFAR-10 classes have a much wider potential range of variation for animal or vehicle photos, meaning we may require more complex models in order to capture this variation.

In this chapter, we will discuss a class of generative models known as **Variational Autoencoders** (**VAEs**), which are designed to make the generation of these complex, real-world images more tractable and tunable. They do this by using a number of clever simplifications to make it possible to sample over the complex probability distribution represented by real-world images in a way that is scalable.

Painting Pictures with Neural Networks Using VAEs

We will explore the following topics to reveal how VAEs work:

- How neural networks create low-dimensional representations of data, and some desirable properties of those representations
- How variational methods allow us to sample from complex data using these representations
- How using the reparameterization trick allows us to stabilize the variance of a neural network based on variational sampling—a VAE
- How we can use **Inverse Autoregressive Flow (IAF)** to tune the output of a VAE
- How to implement VAE/IAF in TensorFlow

Creating separable encodings of images

In *Figure 5.1*, you can see an example of images from the CIFAR-10 dataset, along with an example of an early VAE algorithm that can generate fuzzy versions of these images based on a random number input:

Figure 5.1: CIFAR-10 sample (left), VAE (right)[2]

More recent work on VAE networks has allowed these models to generate much better images, as you will see later in this chapter. To start, let's revisit the problem of generating MNIST digits and how we can extend this approach to more complex data.

Recall from *Chapter 1, An Introduction to Generative AI: "Drawing" Data from Models* and *Chapter 4, Teaching Networks to Generate Digits* that the RBM (or DBN) model in essence involves learning the posterior probability distribution for images (x) given some latent "code" (z), represented by the hidden layer(s) of the network, the "marginal likelihood" of x:[3]

$$p(x) = \int p(z)p(x|z)dz$$

We can see z as being an "encoding" of the image x (for example, the activations of the binary hidden units in the RBM), which can be decoded (for example, run the RBM in reverse in order to sample an image) to get a reconstruction of x. If the encoding is "good," the reconstruction will be close to the original image. Because these networks encode and decode representations of their input data, they are also known as "autoencoders."

The ability of deep neural networks to capture the underlying structure of complex data is one of their most attractive features; as we saw with the DBN model in *Chapter 4, Teaching Networks to Generate Digits*, it allows us to improve the performance of a classifier by creating a better underlying model for the distribution of the data. It can also be used to simply create a better way to "compress" the complexity of data, in a similar way to **principal component analysis (PCA)** in classical statistics. In *Figure 5.2*, you can see how the stacked RBM model can be used as a way to encode the distribution of faces, for example.

Painting Pictures with Neural Networks Using VAEs

We start with a "pre-training" phase to create a 30-unit encoding vector, which we then calibrate by forcing it to reconstruct the input image, before fine-tuning with standard backpropagation:

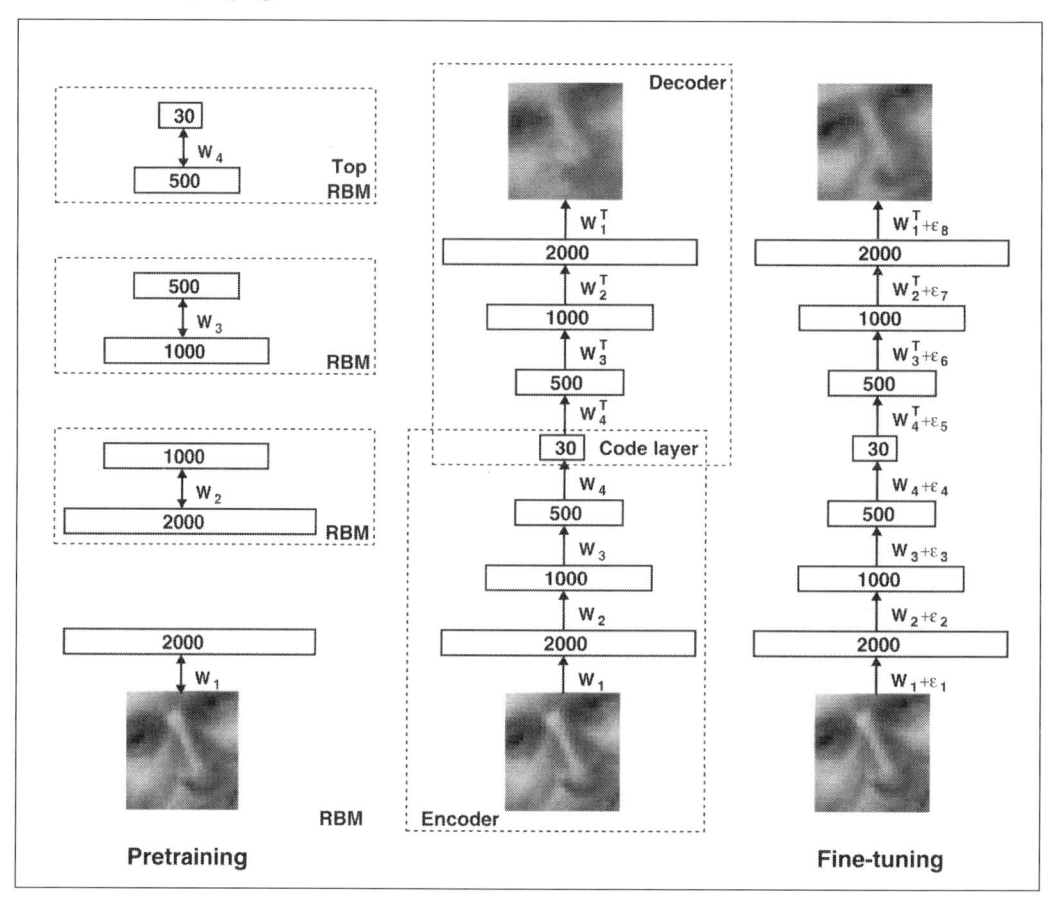

Figure 5.2: Using a DBN as an autoencoder[4]

As an example of how the stacked RBM model can more effectively represent the distribution of images, the authors of the paper *Reducing the Dimensionality of Data with Neural Networks*, from which *Figure 5.2* is derived, demonstrated using a two-unit code for the MNIST digits compared to PCA:

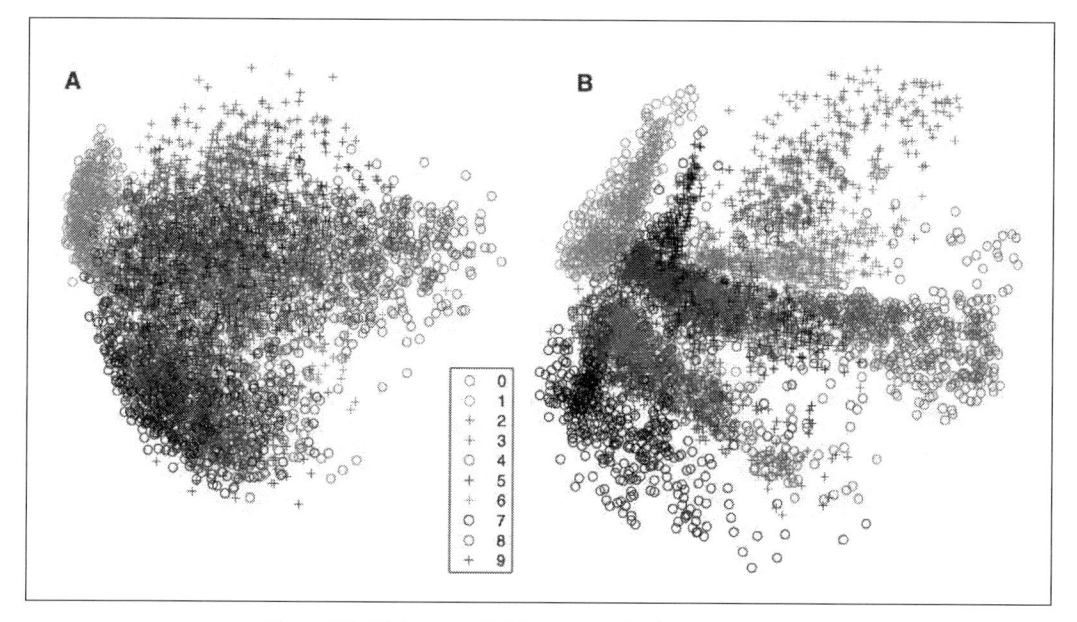

Figure 5.3: PCA versus RBM autoencoder for MNIST digits[5]

On the left, we see the digits 0-9 (represented by different shades and shapes) encoded using 2-dimensional PCA. Recall that PCA is generated using a low-dimensional factorization of the covariance matrix of the data:

$$Cov(X) = U \times V$$

Where $Cov(X)$ is the same height/width M as the data (for example, 28 by 28 pixels in MNIST) and U and V are both lower dimensional ($M \times k$ and $k \times M$), where k is much smaller than M. Because they have a smaller number of rows/columns k than the original data in one dimension, U and V are lower-dimensional representations of the data, and we can get an encoding of an individual image by projecting it onto these k vectors, giving a k unit encoding of the data. Since the decomposition (and projection) is a linear transformation (multiplying two matrices), the ability of the PCA components to distinguish data well depends on the data being linearly separable (we can draw a hyperplane through the space between groups—that space could be two-dimensional or N dimensional, like the 784 pixels in the MNIST images).

Painting Pictures with Neural Networks Using VAEs

As you can see in *Figure 5.3*, PCA yields overlapping codes for the images, showing that it is challenging to represent digits using a two-component linear decomposition, in which vectors representing the same digit are close together, while those representing different digits are clearly separated. Conceptually, the neural network is able to capture more of the variation between images representing different digits than PCA, as shown by its ability to separate the representations of these digits more clearly in a two-dimensional space.

As an analogy to understand this phenomenon, consider a very simple two-dimensional dataset consisting of parallel hyperbolas (2nd power polynomials) (*Figure 5.4*):

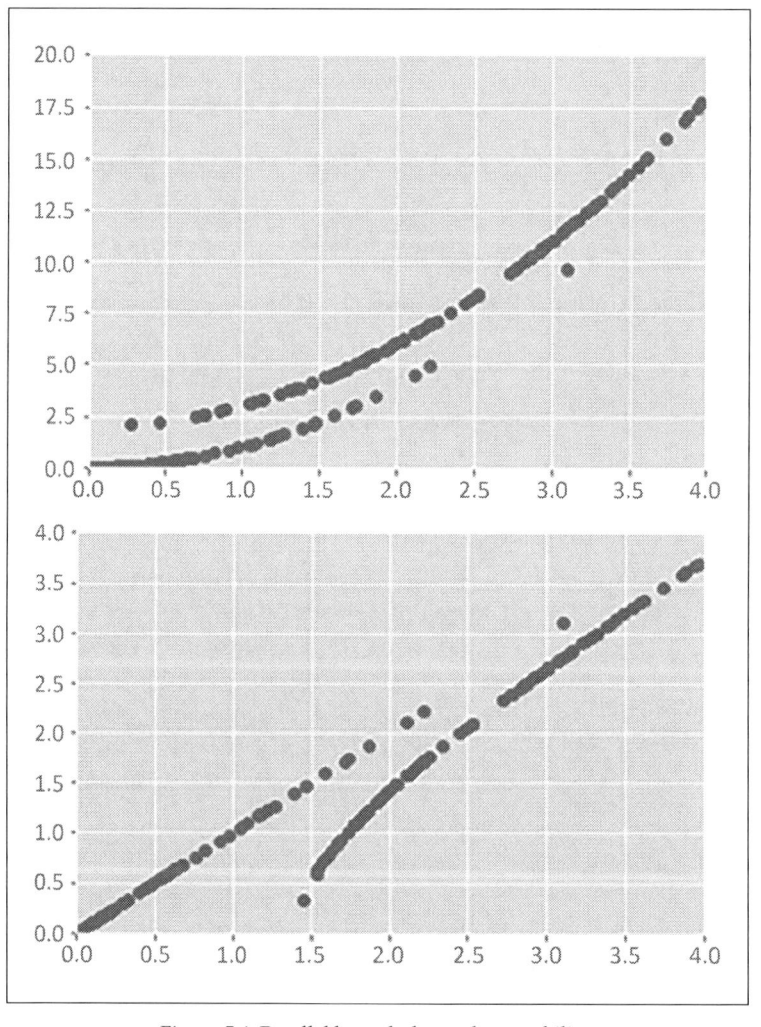

Figure 5.4: Parallel hyperbolas and separability

At the top, even though we have two distinct classes, we cannot draw a straight line through two-dimensional space to separate the two groups; in a neural network, the weight matrix in a single layer before the nonlinear transformation of a sigmoid or tanh is, in essence, a linear boundary of this kind. However, if we apply a nonlinear transformation to our 2D coordinates, such as taking the square root of the hyperbolas, we can create two separable planes (*Figure 5.4, bottom*).

A similar phenomenon is at play with our MNIST data: we need a neural network in order to place these 784-digit images into distinct, separable regions of space. This goal is achieved by performing a non-linear transformation on the original, overlapping data, with an objective function that rewards increasing the spatial separation among vectors encoding the images of different digits. A separable representation thus increases the ability of the neural network to differentiate image classes using these representations. Thus, in *Figure 5.3*, we can see on the right that applying the DBN model creates the required non-linear transformation to separate the different images.

Now that we've covered how neural networks can compress data into numerical vectors and what some desirable properties of those vector representations are, we'll examine how to optimally compress information in these vectors. To do so, each element of the vector should encode distinct information from the others, a property we can achieve using a variational objective. This variational objective is the building block for creating VAE networks.

The variational objective

We previously covered several examples of how images can be compressed into numerical vectors using neural networks. This section will introduce the elements that allow us to create effective encodings to sample new images from a space of random numerical vectors, which are principally efficient inference algorithms and appropriate objective functions. Let's start by quantifying more rigorously what makes such an encoding "good" and allows us to recreate images well. We will need to maximize the posterior:

$$p(z|x) = p(x|z)p(z)/p(x)$$

A problem occurs when the probability of x is extremely high dimensional, which, as you saw, can occur in even simple data such as binary MNIST digits, where we have 2^ (number of pixels) possible configurations that we would need to integrate over (in a mathematical sense of integrating over a probability distribution) to get a measure of the probability of an individual image; in other words, the density $p(x)$ is intractable, making the posterior $p(z|x)$, which depends on $p(x)$, likewise intractable.

In some cases, such as you saw in *Chapter 4, Teaching Networks to Generate Digits*, we can use simple cases such as binary units to compute an approximation such as contrastive divergence, which allows us to still compute a gradient even if we can't calculate a closed form. However, this might also be challenging for very large datasets, where we would need to make many passes over the data to compute an average gradient using **Contrastive Divergence (CD)**, as you saw previously in *Chapter 4, Teaching Networks to Generate Digits*.[6]

If we can't calculate the distribution of our encoder $p(z|x)$ directly, maybe we could optimize an approximation that is "close enough"—let's called this $q(z|x)$. Then, we could use a measure to determine if the distributions are close enough. One useful measure of closeness is whether the two distributions encode similar information; we can quantify information using the Shannon Information equation:

$$I(p(x)) = -\log(p(x))$$

Consider why this is a good measure: as $p(x)$ decreases, an event becomes rarer, and thus observation of the event communicates more information about the system or dataset, leading to a positive value of $-\log(p(x))$. Conversely, as the probability of an event nears 1, that event encodes less information about the dataset, and the value of $-\log(p(x))$ becomes 0 (*Figure 5.5*):

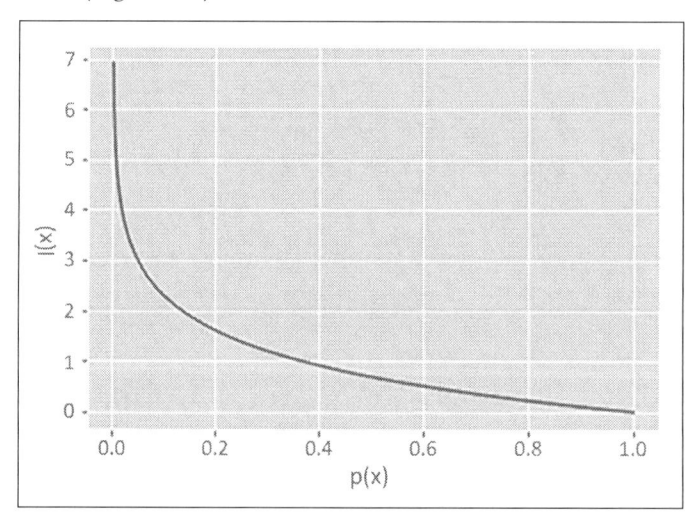

Figure 5.5: Shannon information

Thus, if we wanted to measure the difference between the information encoded in two distributions, p and q, we could use the difference in their information:

$$I(p(x)) - I(q(x)) = -\log(p(x)) + \log(q(x)) = \log(q(x)/p(x))$$

Finally, if we want to find the expected difference in information between the distributions for all elements of x, we can take the average over $p(x)$:

$$E\big((I(p(x)) - I(q(x)))\big) = \int p(x) log\left(\frac{q(x)}{p(x)}\right) dx$$

This quantity is known as the **Kullback Leibler (KL) Divergence**. It has a few interesting properties:

1. It is not symmetric: $KL(p(x), q(x))$ does not, in general, equal $KL(q(x), p(x))$, so the "closeness" is measured by mapping one distribution to another in a particular direction.
2. Whenever $q(x)$ and $p(x)$ match, the term is 0, meaning they are a minimum distance from one another. Likewise, $KL(p(x), q(x))$ is 0 only if p and q are identical.
3. If $q(x)$ is 0 or $p(x)$ is 0, then KL is undefined; by definition, it only computes relative information over the range of x where the two distributions match.
4. KL is always greater than 0.

If we were to use the KL divergence to compute how well an approximation $q(z,x)$ is of our intractable $p(z|x)$, we could write:

$$KL(q,p) = \int q(z|x) log\left(\frac{p(z|x)}{q(z|x)}\right) dx$$

and:

$$KL(q,p) = E_{q(z|x)}[log(q(z|x)) - log(p(z|x))]$$
$$= E_{q(z|x)}[log(q(z|x)) - log(p(x|z)p(z)/p(x))]$$

Now we can write an expression for our intractable $p(x)$ as well: since $log(p(x))$ does not depend on $q(z|x)$, the expectation with respect to $p(x)$ is simply $log(p(x))$. Thus, we can represent the objective of the VAE, learning the marginal distribution of $p(x)$, using the KL divergence:

$$log(p(x)) = KL(q,p) - E_{q(z|x)}[log(q(z|x)) - log(p(x|z)p(z))]$$

The second term is also known as the **Variational Lower Bound**, which is also referred to as the **Evidence Lower Bound (ELBO)**; since $KL(q,p)$ is strictly greater than 0, $log(p(x))$ is strictly greater than or (if $KL(q,p)$ is 0) equal to this value.

To explain what this objective is doing, notice that the expectation introduces a difference between $q(z|x)$ (*encoding x*) and $p(x|z)p(z)$ (the joint probability of the data and the encoding); thus we want to minimize a lower bound that is essentially the gap between the probability of the encoding and the joint probability of the encoding and data, with an error term given by $KL(q,p)$, the difference between a tractable approximation and intractable form of the encoder $p(z|x)$. We can imagine the functions $Q(z|x)$ and $P(x|z)$ being represented by two deep neural networks; one generates the latent code $z(Q)$, and the other reconstructs x from this code (P). We can imagine this as an autoencoder setup, as above with the stacked RBM models, with an encoder and decoder:

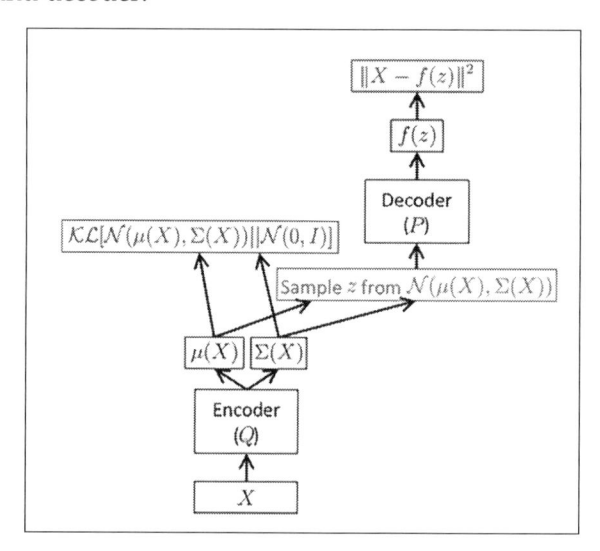

Figure 5.6: Autoencoder/Decoder of an un-reparameterized VAE[7]

We want to optimize the parameters of the encoder Q and the decoder P to minimize the reconstruction cost. One way to do this is to construct Monte Carlo samples to optimize the parameters ϕ of Q using gradient descent:

$$\nabla_\phi \mathbb{E}_{q_\phi(\mathbf{z})}[f(\mathbf{z})] = \mathbb{E}_{q_\phi(\mathbf{z})}[f(\mathbf{z})\nabla_{q_\phi(\mathbf{z})}\log q_\phi(\mathbf{z})] \simeq \frac{1}{L}\sum_{l=1}^{\mathcal{L}} f(\mathbf{z})\left[\nabla_{q_\phi(\mathbf{z}^{(l)})}\log q_\phi(\mathbf{z}^{(l)})\right]$$

Where we sample z:

$$\mathbf{z}^{(l)} \sim q_\phi(\mathbf{z}|\mathbf{x}^{(i)})$$

However, it has been found in practice that a large number of samples may be required in order for the variance of these gradient updates to stabilize.[8]

We also have a practical problem here: even if we could choose enough samples to get a good approximation of the gradients for the encoder, our network contains a stochastic, non-differentiable step (sampling z) that we can't backpropagate through, in a similar way we couldn't backpropagate through the stochastic units in the RBM in *Chapter 4, Teaching Networks to Generate Digits*. Thus, our reconstruction error depends on samples from z, but we can't backpropagate through the step that generates these samples to tune the network end to end. Is there a way we can create a differentiable decoder/encoder architecture while also reducing the variance of sample estimates? One of the main insights of the VAE is to enable this through the "reparameterization trick."

The reparameterization trick

In order to allow us to backpropagate through our autoencoder, we need to transform the stochastic samples of z into a deterministic, differentiable transformation. We can do this by reparameterizing z as a function of a noise variable ε:

$$\tilde{z} = g_\phi(\epsilon, x) \text{ with } \epsilon \sim p(\epsilon)$$

Once we have sampled from ε, the randomness in z no longer depends on the parameters of the variational distribution Q (the encoder), and we can backpropagate end to end. Our network now looks like *Figure 5.7*, and we can optimize our objective using random samples of ε (for example, a standard normal distribution). This reparameterization moves the "random" node out of the encoder/decoder framework so we can backpropagate through the whole system, but it also has a subtler advantage; it reduces the variance of these gradients. Note that in the un-reparameterized network, the distribution of z depends on the parameters of the encoder distribution Q; thus, as we are changing the parameters of Q, we are also changing the distribution of z, and we would need to potentially use a large number of samples to get a decent estimate.

By reparameterizing, z now depends only on our simpler function, g, with randomness introduced through sampling ε from a standard normal (that doesn't depend on Q); hence, we've removed a somewhat circular dependency, and made the gradients we are estimating more stable:

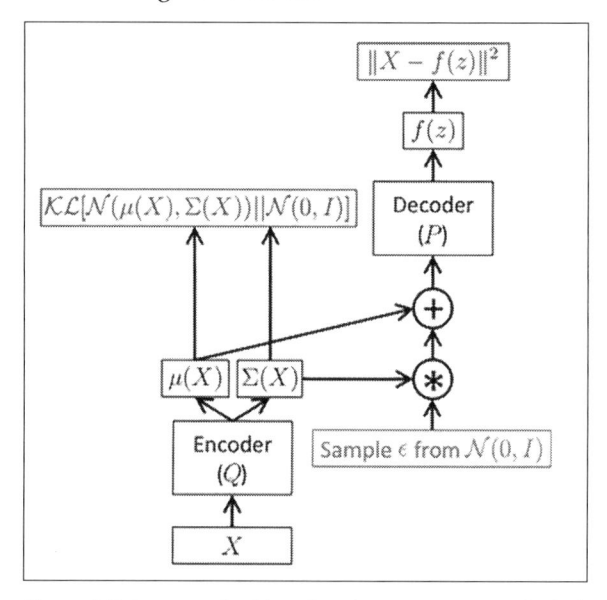

Figure 5.7: Autoencoder/decoder of a reparameterized VAE[9]

Now that you have seen how the VAE network is constructed, let's discuss a further refinement of this algorithm that allows VAEs to sample from complex distributions: **Inverse Autoregressive Flow (IAF)**.

Inverse Autoregressive Flow

In our discussion earlier, it was noted that we want to use $q(z|x)$ as a way to approximate the "true" $p(z|x)$ that would allow us to generate an ideal encoding of the data, and thus sample from it to generate new images. So far, we've assumed that $q(z|x)$ has a relatively simple distribution, such as a vector of Gaussian distribution random variables that are independent (a diagonal covariance matrix with 0s on the non-diagonal elements). This sort of distribution has many benefits; because it is simple, we have an easy way to generate new samples by drawing from random normal distributions, and because it is independent, we can separately tune each element of the latent vector z to influence parts of the output image.

However, such a simple distribution may not fit the desired output distribution of data well, increasing the KL divergence between $p(z|x)$ and $q(z|x)$. Is there a way we can keep the desirable properties of $q(z|x)$ but "transform" z so that it captures more of the complexities needed to represent x?

One approach is to apply a series of autoregressive transformations to z to turn it from a simple to a complex distribution; by "autoregressive," we mean that each transformation utilizes both data from the previous transformation and the current data to compute an updated version of z. In contrast, the basic form of VAE that we introduced above has only a single "transformation:" from z to the output (though z might pass through multiple layers, there is no recursive network link to further refine that output). We've seen such transformations before, such as the LSTM networks in *Chapter 3, Building Blocks of Deep Neural Networks*, where the output of the network is a combination of the current input and a weighted version of prior time steps.

An attractive property of the independent $q(z|x)$ distributions we discussed earlier, such as independent normals, is that they have a very tractable expression for the log likelihood. This property is important for the VAE model because its objective function depends on integrating over the whole likelihood function, which would be cumbersome for more complex log likelihood functions. However, by constraining a transformed z to computation through a series of autoregressive transformations, we have the nice property that the log-likelihood of step t only depends on $t-1$, thus the Jacobian (gradient matrix of the partial derivative between t and $t-1$) is lower triangular and can be computed as a sum:

$$\log q(\mathbf{z}_T|\mathbf{x}) = \log q(\mathbf{z}_0|\mathbf{x}) - \sum_{t=1}^{T} \log \det \left| \frac{d\mathbf{z}_t}{d\mathbf{z}_{t-1}} \right|$$

What kinds of transformations f could be used? Recall that after the parameterization trick, z is a function of a noise element e and the mean and standard deviation output by the encoder Q:

$$\mathbf{z}_0 = \boldsymbol{\mu}_0 + \boldsymbol{\sigma}_0 \odot \boldsymbol{\epsilon}$$

If we apply successive layers of transformation, step t becomes the sum of μ and the element-wise product of the prior layer z and the sigmoidal output σ:

$$\mathbf{z}_t = \boldsymbol{\mu}_t + \boldsymbol{\sigma}_t \odot \mathbf{z}_{t-1}$$

In practice, we use a neural network transformation to stabilize the estimate of the mean at each step:

$$[m_t, s_t] \leftarrow \text{AutoregressiveNN}[t](\mathbf{Z}_t, \mathbf{h}; \theta)$$

$$\sigma_t = \text{sigmoid}(s_t)$$

$$\mathbf{z}_t = \sigma_t \odot \mathbf{z}_{t-1} + (1 - \sigma_t) \odot m_t$$

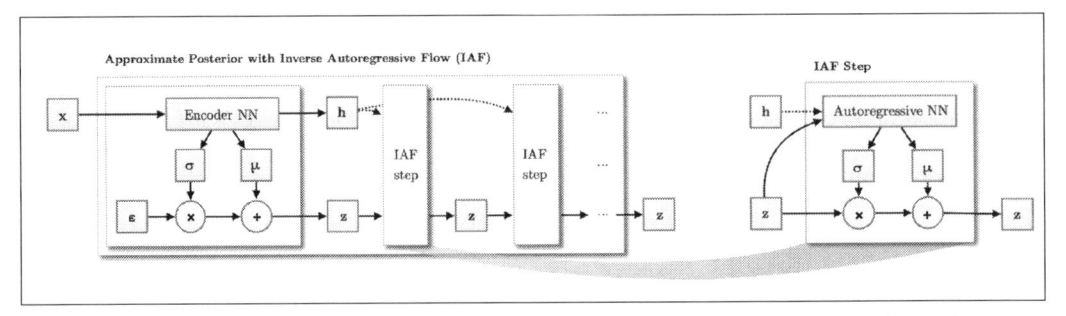

Figure 5.8: IAF networks[6]

Again, note the similarity of this transformation to the LSTM networks discussed in *Chapter 3, Building Blocks of Deep Neural Networks*. In *Figure 5.8*, there is another output (*h*) from the encoder *Q* in addition to the mean and standard deviation in order to sample *z*. H is, in essence, "accessory data" that is passed into each successive transformation and, along with the weighted sum that is being calculated at each step, represents the "persistent memory" of the network in a way reminiscent of the LSTM.

Importing CIFAR

Now that we've discussed the underlying theory of VAE algorithms, let's start building a practical example using a real-world dataset. As we discussed in the introduction, for the experiments in this chapter, we'll be working with the Canadian Institute for Advanced Research (CIFAR) 10 dataset.[10] The images in this dataset are part of a larger 80 million "small image" dataset[11], most of which do not have class labels like CIFAR-10. For CIFAR-10, the labels were initially created by student volunteers[12], and the larger tiny images dataset allows researchers to submit labels for parts of the data.

Like the MNIST dataset, CIFAR-10 can be downloaded using the TensorFlow dataset's API:

```
import tensorflow.compat.v2 as tf
import tensorflow_datasets as tfds
cifar10_builder = tfds.builder("cifar10")
cifar10_builder.download_and_prepare()
```

This will download the dataset to disk and make it available for our experiments. To split it into training and test sets, we can use the following commands:

```
cifar10_train = cifar10_builder.as_dataset(split="train")
cifar10_test = cifar10_builder.as_dataset(split="test")
```

Let's inspect one of the images to see what format it is in:

```
cifar10_train.take(1)
```

The output tells us that each image in the dataset is of format `<DatasetV1Adapter shapes: {image: (32, 32, 3), label: ()}, types: {image: tf.uint8, label: tf.int64}>`: Unlike the MNIST dataset we used in *Chapter 4, Teaching Networks to Generate Digits*, the CIFAR images have three color channels, each with 32 x 32 pixels, while the label is an integer from 0 to 9 (representing one of the 10 classes). We can also plot the images to inspect them visually:

```
from PIL import Image
import numpy as np
import matplotlib.pyplot as plt
for sample in cifar10_train.map(lambda x: flatten_image(x, label=True)).take(1):
    plt.imshow(sample[0].numpy().reshape(32,32,3).astype(np.float32),
               cmap=plt.get_cmap("gray")
               )
    print("Label: %d" % sample[1].numpy())
```

This gives the following output:

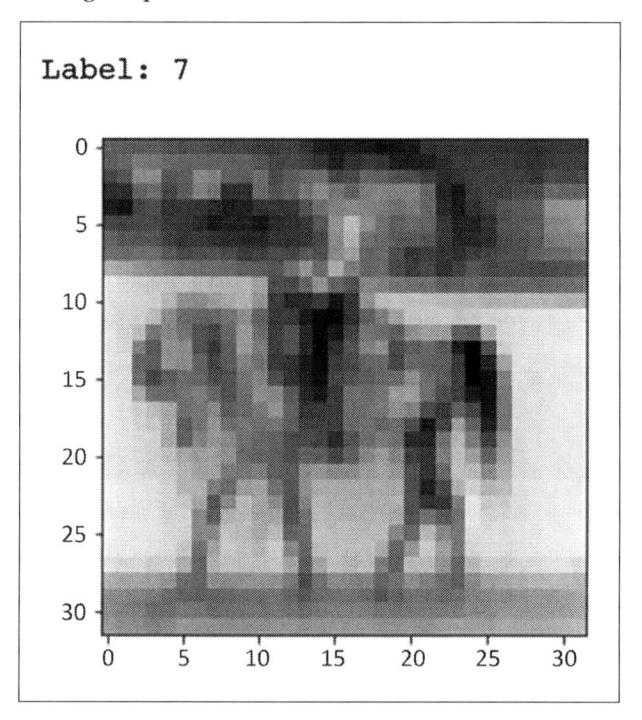

Figure 5.9: The output

Like the RBM model, the VAE model we'll build in this example has an output scaled between 1 and 0 and accepts flattened versions of the images, so we'll need to turn each image into a vector and scale it to a maximum of 1:

```
def flatten_image(x, label=False):
    if label:
        return (tf.divide(
            tf.dtypes.cast(
                tf.reshape(x["image"], (1, 32*32*3)), tf.float32),
                256.0),
            x["label"])
    else:
        return (
            tf.divide(tf.dtypes.cast(
                tf.reshape(x["image"], (1, 32*32*3)), tf.float32),
                256.0))
```

This results in each image being a vector of length 3072 (32*32*3), which we can reshape once we've run the model to examine the generated images.

Creating the network from TensorFlow 2

Now that we've downloaded the CIFAR-10 dataset, split it into test and training data, and reshaped and rescaled it, we are ready to start building our VAE model. We'll use the same Model API from the Keras module in TensorFlow 2. The TensorFlow documentation contains an example of how to implement a VAE using convolutional networks (https://www.tensorflow.org/tutorials/generative/cvae), and we'll build on this code example; however, for our purposes, we will implement simpler VAE networks using MLP layers based on the original VAE paper, *Auto-Encoding Variational Bayes*[13], and show how we adapt the TensorFlow example to also allow for IAF modules in decoding.

In the original article, the authors propose two kinds of models for use in the VAE, both MLP feedforward networks: Gaussian and Bernoulli, with these names reflecting the probability distribution functions used in the MLP network outputs in their finals layers The Bernoulli MLP can be used as the decoder of the network, generating the simulated image x from the latent vector z. The formula for the Bernoulli MLP is:

$$\log p(\mathbf{x}|\mathbf{z}) = \sum_{i=1}^{D} x_i \log y_i + (1 - x_i) \cdot \log(1 - y_i)$$

$$\text{where } y = f_\sigma(\mathbf{W}_1 \tanh(\mathbf{W}_1 \mathbf{z} + \mathbf{b}_1) + \mathbf{b}_2)$$

Where the first line is the cross-entropy function we use to determine if the network generates an approximation of the original image in reconstruction, while y is a feedforward network with two layers: a tanh transformation followed by a sigmoidal function to scale the output between 0 and 1. Recall that this scaling is why we had to normalize the CIFAR-10 pixels from their original values.

We can easily create this Bernoulli MLP network using the Keras API:

```
class BernoulliMLP(tf.keras.Model):
    def __init__(self, input_shape, name='BernoulliMLP', hidden_dim=10, latent_dim=10, **kwargs):
        super().__init__(name=name, **kwargs)
        self._h = tf.keras.layers.Dense(hidden_dim,
                                        activation='tanh')
        self._y = tf.keras.layers.Dense(latent_dim,
```

```
                            activation='sigmoid')
    def call(self, x):
        return self._y(self._h(x)), None, None
```

We just need to specify the dimensions of the single hidden layer and the latent output (z). We then specify the forward pass as a composition of these two layers. Note that in the output, we've returned three values, with the second two set as None. This is because in our end model, we could use either the BernoulliMLP or GaussianMLP as the decoder. If we used the GaussianMLP, we return three values, as we will see below; the example in this chapter utilizes a binary output and cross-entropy loss so we can use just the single output, but we want the return signatures for the two decoders to match.

The second network type proposed by the authors in the original VAE paper was a Gaussian MLP, whose formulas are:

$$\log p(\mathbf{x}|\mathbf{z}) = \log \mathcal{N}(x; \boldsymbol{\mu}, \sigma^2 \mathbf{I})$$

$$\text{where } \boldsymbol{\mu} = \mathbf{W}_4 \mathbf{h} + \mathbf{b}_4$$

$$\log \sigma^2 = \mathbf{W}_5 \mathbf{h} + \mathbf{b}_5$$

$$\mathbf{h} = \tanh(\mathbf{W}_3 \mathbf{z} + \mathbf{b}_3)$$

This network can be used as either the encoder (generating the latent vector z) or the decoder (generating the simulated image x) in the network. The equations above assume that it is used as the decoder, and for the encoder we just switch the x and z variables. As you can see, this network has two types of layers, a hidden layer given by a tanh transformation of the input, and two output layers, each given by linear transformations of the hidden layer, which are used as the inputs of a lognormal likelihood function. Like the Bernoulli MLP, we can easily implement this simple network using the TensorFlow Keras API:

```
class GaussianMLP(tf.keras.Model):
    def __init__(self, input_shape, name='GaussianMLP', hidden_dim=10,
latent_dim=10, iaf=False, **kwargs):
        super().__init__(name=name, **kwargs)
        self._h = tf.keras.layers.Dense(hidden_dim,
                                        activation='tanh')
        self._mean = tf.keras.layers.Dense(latent_dim)
        self._logvar = tf.keras.layers.Dense(latent_dim)
        self._iaf_output = None
        if iaf:
            self._iaf_output = tf.keras.layers.Dense(latent_dim)
```

```
    def call(self, x):
        if self._iaf_output:
            return self._mean(self._h(x)), self._logvar(self._h(x)),
                self._iaf_output(self._h(x))
        else:
            return self._mean(self._h(x)), self._logvar(self._h(x)),
                None
```

As you can see, to implement the call function, we must return the two outputs of the model (the mean and log variance of the normal distribution we'll use to compute the likelihood of z or x). However, recall that for the IAE model, the encoder has to have an additional output h, which is fed into each step of the normalizing flow:

$$[\mu, \sigma, h] \leftarrow \text{EncoderNN}(\mathbf{x}; \theta)$$

To allow for this additional output, we include a third variable in the output, which gets set to a linear transformation of the input if we set the IAF options to True, and is none if False, so we can use the GaussianMLP as an encoder in networks both with and without IAF.

Now that we have both of our subnetworks defined, let's see how we can use them to construct a complete VAE network. Like the sub-networks, we can define the VAE using the Keras API:

```
class VAE(tf.keras.Model):
    def __init__(self, input_shape, name='variational_autoencoder',
                latent_dim=10, hidden_dim=10, encoder='GaussianMLP',
                decoder='BernoulliMLP', iaf_model=None,
                number_iaf_networks=0,
                iaf_params={},
                num_samples=100, **kwargs):
        super().__init__(name=name, **kwargs)
        self._latent_dim = latent_dim
        self._num_samples = num_samples
        self._iaf = []
        if encoder == 'GaussianMLP':
            self._encoder = GaussianMLP(input_shape=input_shape,
                                        latent_dim=latent_dim,
                                        iaf=(iaf_model is not None),
                                        hidden_dim=hidden_dim)
        else:
            raise ValueError("Unknown encoder type: {}".format(encoder))
        if decoder == 'BernoulliMLP':
```

```
                self._decoder = BernoulliMLP(input_shape=(1,latent_dim),
                                            latent_dim=input_shape[1],
                                            hidden_dim=hidden_dim)
            elif decoder == 'GaussianMLP':
                self._encoder = GaussianMLP(input_shape=(1,latent_dim),
                                            latent_dim=input_shape[1],
                                            iaf=(iaf_model is not None),
                                            hidden_dim=hidden_dim)
            else:
                raise ValueError("Unknown decoder type: {}".
    format(decoder))
            if iaf_model:
                self._iaf = []
                for t in range(number_iaf_networks):
                    self._iaf.append(
                        iaf_model(input_shape==(1,latent_dim*2),
                                  **iaf_params))
```

As you can see, this model is defined to contain both an encoder and decoder network. Additionally, we allow the user to specify whether we are implementing IAF as part of the model, in which case we need a stack of autoregressive transforms specified by the iaf_params variable. Because this IAF network needs to take both z and h as inputs, the input shape is twice the size of the latent_dim (z). We allow the decoder to be either the GaussianMLP or BernoulliMLP network, while the encoder is the GaussianMLP.

There are a few other functions of this model class that we need to cover; the first are simply the encoding and decoding functions of the VAE model class:

```
def encode(self, x):
        return self._encoder.call(x)
    def decode(self, z, apply_sigmoid=False):
        logits, _, _ = self._decoder.call(z)
        if apply_sigmoid:
            probs = tf.sigmoid(logits)
            return probs
        return logits
```

For the encoder, we simply call (run the forward pass for) the encoder network. To decode, you will notice that we specify three outputs. The article that introduced VAE models, *Autoencoding Variational Bayes*, provided examples of a decoder specified as either a **Gaussian Multilayer Perceptron (MLP)** or Benoulli output. If we used a Gaussian MLP, the decoder would yield the value, mean, and standard deviation vectors for the output, and we need to transform that output to a probability (0 to 1) using the sigmoidal transform. In the Bernoulli case, the output is already in the range 0 to 1, and we don't need this transformation (`apply_sigmoid=False`).

Once we've trained the VAE network, we'll want to use sampling in order to generate random latent vectors (z) and run the decoder to generate new images. While we could just run this as a normal function of the class in the Python runtime, we'll decorate this function with the `@tf.function` annotation, which will allow it to be executed in the TensorFlow graph runtime (just like any of the `tf` functions, such as `reduce_sum` and `multiply`), making using of GPU and TPU devices if they are available. We sample a value from a random normal distribution, for a specified number of samples, and then apply the decoder to generate new images:

```
@tf.function
    def sample(self, eps=None):
        if eps is None:
            eps = tf.random.normal(shape=(self._num_samples,
                                          self.latent_dim))
        return self._decoder.call(eps, apply_sigmoid=False)
```

Finally, recall that the "reparameterization trick" is used to allow us to backpropagate through the value of z and reduce the variance of the likelihood of z. We need to implement this transformation, which is given by:

```
def reparameterize(self, mean, logvar):
        eps = tf.random.normal(shape=mean.shape)
        return eps * tf.exp(logvar * .5) + mean
```

In the original paper, *Autoencoding Variational Bayes*, this is given by:

$$z^{(i,l)} = \mu^{(i)} + \sigma^{(i)} \odot \epsilon^{(l)} \text{ and } \epsilon^{(l)} \sim \mathcal{N}(0, \mathbf{I})$$

where i is a data point in x and l is a sample from the random distribution, here, a normal. In our code, we multiply by 0.5 because we are computing the **log variance** (or standard deviation squared), and $log(s\wedge 2) = log(s)2$, so the 0.5 cancels the 2, leaving us with $exp(log(s)) = s$, just as we require in the formula.

Painting Pictures with Neural Networks Using VAEs

We'll also include a class property (with the @property decorator) so we can access the array of normalizing transforms if we implement IAF:

```
@property
    def iaf(self):
        return self._iaf
```

Now, we'll need a few additional functions to actually run our VAE algorithm. The first computes the log normal **probability density function (pdf)**, used in the computation of the variational lower bound, or ELBO:

```
def log_normal_pdf(sample, mean, logvar, raxis=1):
    log2pi = tf.math.log(2. * np.pi)
    return tf.reduce_sum(
        -.5 * ((sample - mean) ** 2. * tf.exp(-logvar) + \
        logvar + log2pi), axis=raxis)
```

We now need to utilize this function as part of computing the loss with each minibatch gradient descent pass in the process of training the VAE. As with the sample method, we'll decorate this function with the @tf.function annotation so it will be executed on the graph runtime:

```
@tf.function
def compute_loss(model, x):
    mean, logvar, h = model.encode(x)
    z = model.reparameterize(mean, logvar)
    logqz_x = log_normal_pdf(z, mean, logvar)
    for iaf_model in model.iaf:
        mean, logvar, _ = iaf_model.call(tf.concat([z, h], 2))
        s = tf.sigmoid(logvar)
        z = tf.add(tf.math.multiply(z,s), tf.math.multiply(mean,(1-s)))
        logqz_x -= tf.reduce_sum(tf.math.log(s))

    x_logit = model.decode(z)
    cross_ent = tf.nn.sigmoid_cross_entropy_with_logits(logits=x_logit, labels=x)
    logpx_z = -tf.reduce_sum(cross_ent, axis=[2])
    logpz = log_normal_pdf(z, 0., 0.)
    return -tf.reduce_mean(logpx_z + logpz - logqz_x)
```

Let's unpack a bit of what is going on here. First, we can see that we call the encoder network on the input (a minibatch of flattened images, in our case) to generate the needed mean, logvariance, and, if we are using IAF in our network, the accessory input h that we'll pass along with each step of the normalizing flow transform.

We apply the "reparameterization trick" on the inputs in order to generate the latent vector z, and apply a lognormal pdf to get the $logq(z|x)$.

If we are using IAF, we need to iteratively transform z using each network, and pass in the h (accessory input) from the decoder at each step. Then we apply the loss from this transform to the initial loss we computed, as per the algorithm given in the IAF paper:[14]

$$\begin{aligned}
&\textbf{for } t \leftarrow 1 \textbf{ to } T \textbf{ do} \\
&\quad [\mathbf{m}, \mathbf{s}] \leftarrow \text{AutoregressiveNN}[t](\mathbf{z}, \mathbf{h}; \boldsymbol{\theta}) \\
&\quad \boldsymbol{\sigma} \leftarrow \text{sigmoid}(\mathbf{s}) \\
&\quad \mathbf{z} \leftarrow \boldsymbol{\sigma} \odot \mathbf{z} + (1 - \boldsymbol{\sigma}) \odot \mathbf{m} \\
&\quad l \leftarrow l - \text{sum}(\log \boldsymbol{\sigma}) \\
&\textbf{end}
\end{aligned}$$

Once we have the transformed or untransformed z, we decode it using the decoder network to get the reconstructed data, x, from which we calculate a cross-entropy loss. We sum these over the minibatch and take the lognormal pdf of z evaluated at a standard normal distribution (the prior), before computing the expected lower bound.

Recall that the expression for the variational lower bound, or ELBO, is:

$$-E_{q(z|x)}[log(q(z|x)) - log(p(x|z)p(z))]$$

So, our minibatch estimator is a sample of this value:

Now that we have these ingredients, we can run the stochastic gradient descent using the GradientTape API, just as we did for the DBN in *Chapter 4, Teaching Networks to Generate Digits* passing in an optimizer, model, and minibatch of data (x):

```
@tf.function
def compute_apply_gradients(model, x, optimizer):
    with tf.GradientTape() as tape:
        loss = compute_loss(model, x)
    gradients = tape.gradient(loss, model.trainable_variables)
    optimizer.apply_gradients(zip(gradients, model.trainable_variables))
```

To run the training, first we need to specify a model using the class we've built. If we don't want to use IAF, we could do this as follows:

```
model = VAE(input_shape=(1,3072), hidden_dim=500, latent_dim=500)
```

If we want to use IAF transformations, we need to include some additional arguments:

```
model = VAE(input_shape=(1,3072), hidden_dim=500, latent_dim=500,
    iaf_model=GaussianMLP, number_iaf_networks=3,
    iaf_params={'latent_dim': 500, 'hidden_dim': 500, 'iaf': False})
```

With the model created, we need to specify a number of epochs, an optimizer (in this instance, Adam, as we described in *Chapter 3, Building Blocks of Deep Neural Networks*). We split our data into minibatches of 32 elements, and apply gradient updates after each minibatch for the number of epochs we've specified. At regular intervals, we output the estimate of the ELBO to verify that our model is getting better:

```
import time as time
epochs = 100
optimizer = tf.keras.optimizers.Adam(1e-4)
for epoch in range(1, epochs + 1):
    start_time = time.time()
    for train_x in cifar10_train.map(
            lambda x: flatten_image(x, label=False)).batch(32):
        compute_apply_gradients(model, train_x, optimizer)
    end_time = time.time()
    if epoch % 1 == 0:
        loss = tf.keras.metrics.Mean()
        for test_x in cifar10_test.map(
            lambda x: flatten_image(x, label=False)).batch(32):
            loss(compute_loss(model, test_x))
    elbo = -loss.result()
    print('Epoch: {}, Test set ELBO: {}, '
        'time elapse for current epoch {}'.format(epoch,
                                    elbo,
                                    end_time - start_time))
```

We can verify that the model is improving by looking at updates, which should show an increasing ELBO:

```
Epoch: 1, Test set ELBO: -2151.757080078125, time elapse for current epoch 61.974515199661255
Epoch: 2, Test set ELBO: -2061.24560546875, time elapse for current epoch 58.04972314834595
Epoch: 3, Test set ELBO: -2038.94970703125, time elapse for current epoch 60.04802680015564
Epoch: 4, Test set ELBO: -2026.10546875, time elapse for current epoch 60.26771402359009
Epoch: 5, Test set ELBO: -2018.3909912109375, time elapse for current epoch 58.40106797218323
Epoch: 6, Test set ELBO: -2013.5391845703125, time elapse for current epoch 58.88316321372986
Epoch: 7, Test set ELBO: -2009.5238037109375, time elapse for current epoch 58.35735893249512
Epoch: 8, Test set ELBO: -2005.8297119140625, time elapse for current epoch 60.940675020217896
Epoch: 9, Test set ELBO: -2003.8834228515625, time elapse for current epoch 59.65025997161865
Epoch: 10, Test set ELBO: -2002.408203125, time elapse for current epoch 61.06896686553955
Epoch: 11, Test set ELBO: -2001.0401611328125, time elapse for current epoch 58.0478720664978
Epoch: 12, Test set ELBO: -2000.0992431640625, time elapse for current epoch 58.393925189971924
Epoch: 13, Test set ELBO: -1998.7967529296875, time elapse for current epoch 58.945866107940674
Epoch: 14, Test set ELBO: -1997.6968994140625, time elapse for current epoch 58.28441119194031
Epoch: 15, Test set ELBO: -1996.740966796875, time elapse for current epoch 58.37646412849426
Epoch: 16, Test set ELBO: -1995.9884033203125, time elapse for current epoch 60.18032097816467
Epoch: 17, Test set ELBO: -1995.2236328125, time elapse for current epoch 59.59520673751831
Epoch: 18, Test set ELBO: -1994.47021484375, time elapse for current epoch 59.842689037323
Epoch: 19, Test set ELBO: -1993.89697265625, time elapse for current epoch 60.1396849155426
Epoch: 20, Test set ELBO: -1993.309326171875, time elapse for current epoch 59.13459086418152
```

To examine the output of the model, we can first look at the reconstruction error; does the encoding of the input image by the network approximately capture the dominant patterns in the input image, allowing it to be reconstructed from its vector z? We can compare the raw image to its reconstruction formed by passing the image through the encoder, applying IAF, and then decoding it:

```
for sample in cifar10_train.map(lambda x: flatten_image(x,
label=False)).batch(1).take(10):
    mean, logvar, h = model.encode(sample)
    z = model.reparameterize(mean, logvar)
    for iaf_model in model.iaf:
        mean, logvar, _ = iaf_model.call(tf.concat([z, h], 2))
        s = tf.sigmoid(logvar)
        z = tf.add(tf.math.multiply(z,s), tf.math.multiply(mean,(1-s)))

    plt.figure(0)
    plt.imshow((sample.numpy().reshape(32,32,3)).astype(np.float32),
            cmap=plt.get_cmap("gray"))
    plt.figure(1)
    plt.imshow((model.decode(z).numpy().reshape(32,32,3)).astype(np.
float32), cmap=plt.get_cmap("gray"))
```

Painting Pictures with Neural Networks Using VAEs

For the first few CIFAR-10 images, we get the following output, showing that we have captured the overall pattern of the image (although it is fuzzy, a general downside to VAEs that we'll address in our discussion of **Generative Adversarial Networks (GANs)** in future chapters):

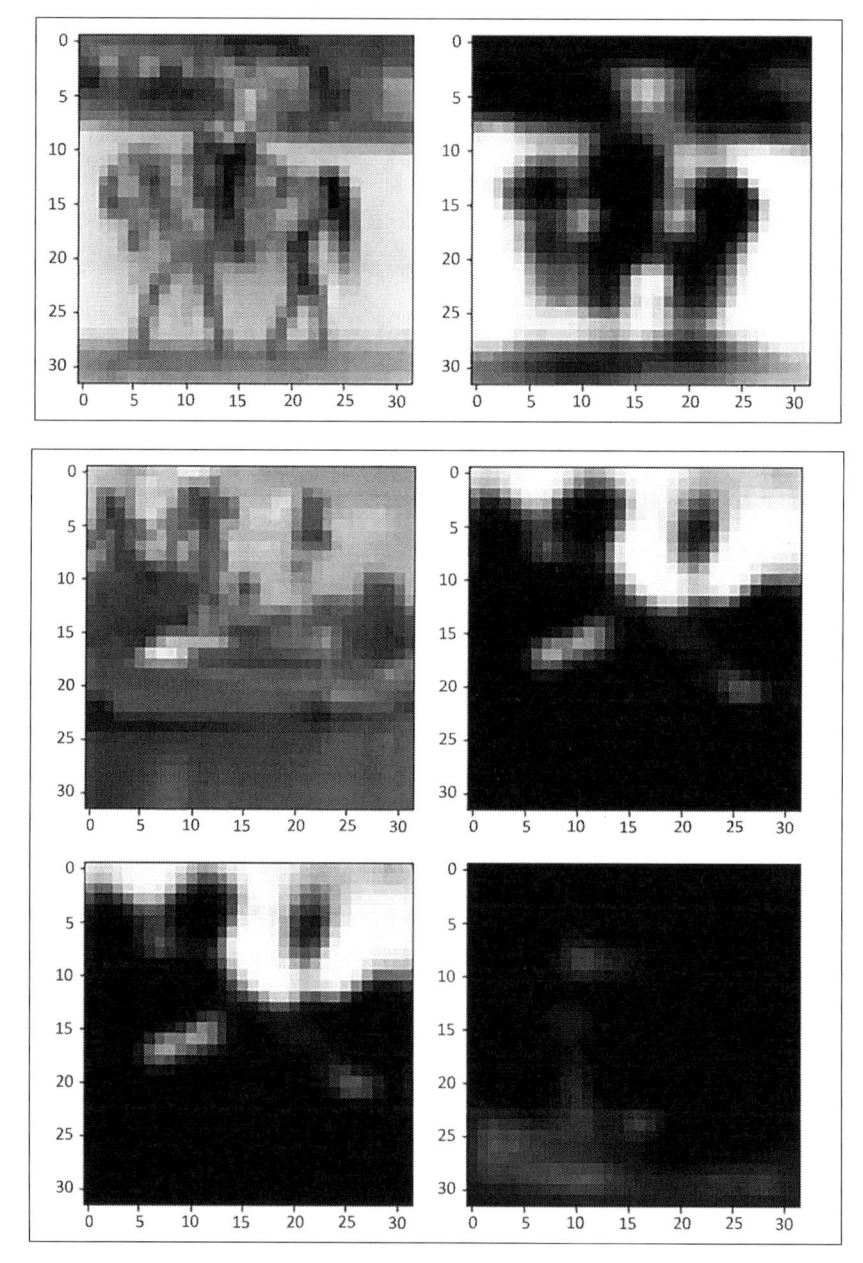

Figure 5.10: The output for the CIFAR-10 images

What if we wanted to create entirely new images? Here we can use the "sample" function we defined previously in *Creating the network from TensorFlow 2* to create batches of new images from randomly generated *z* vectors, rather than the encoded product of CIFAR images:

```
plt.imshow((model.sample(10)).numpy().reshape(32,32,3)).astype(np.
float32), cmap=plt.get_cmap("gray"))
```

This code will produce output like the following, which shows a set of images generated from vectors of random numbers:

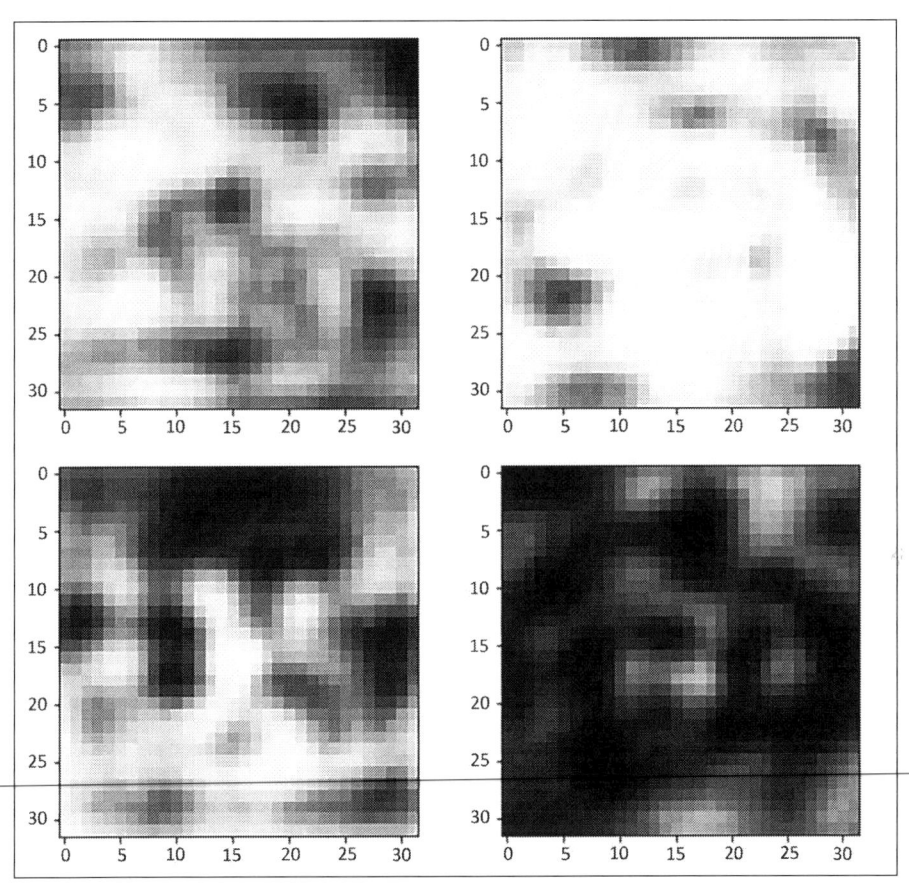

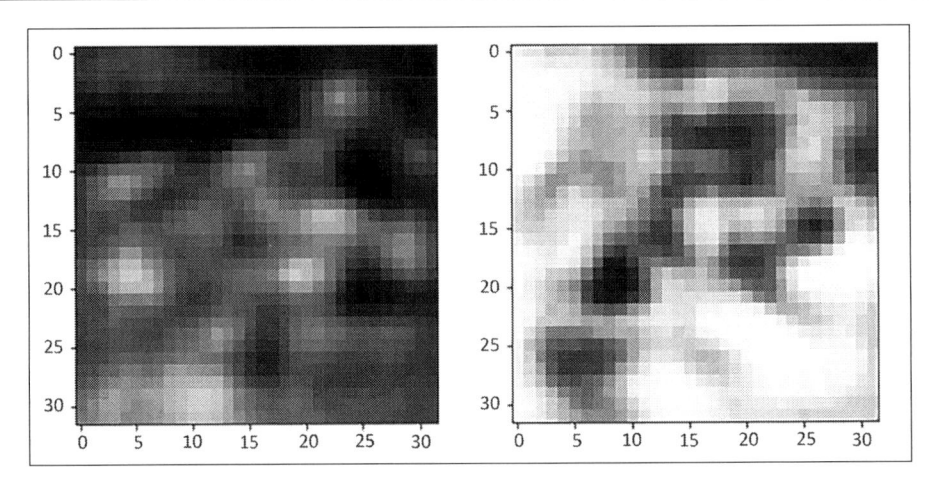

Figure 5.11: Images generated from vectors of random numbers

These are, admittedly, a bit blurry, but you can appreciate that they show structure and look comparable to some of the "reconstructed" CIFAR-10 images you saw previously. Part of the challenge here, as we'll discuss more in subsequent chapters, is the loss function itself: the cross-entropy function, in essence, penalizes each pixel for how much it resembles the input pixel. While this might be mathematically correct, it doesn't capture what we might think of as conceptual "similarity" between an input and reconstructed image. For example, an input image could have a single pixel set to infinity, which would create a large difference between it and a reconstruction that set that pixel to 0; however, a human, looking at the image, would perceive both as being identical. The objective functions used for GANs, described in *Chapter 6, Image Generation with GANs*, capture this nuance more accurately.

Summary

In this chapter, you saw how deep neural networks can be used to create representations of complex data such as images that capture more of their variance than traditional dimension reduction techniques, such as PCA. This is demonstrated using the MNIST digits, where a neural network can spatially separate the different digits in a two-dimensional grid more cleanly than the principal components of those images. The chapter showed how deep neural networks can be used to approximate complex posterior distributions, such as images, using variational methods to sample from an approximation of an intractable distribution, leading to a VAE algorithm based on minimizing the variational lower bound between the true and approximate posterior.

You also learned how the latent vector from this algorithm can be reparameterized to have lower variance, leading to better convergence in stochastic minibatch gradient descent. You saw how the latent vectors generated by encoders in these models, which are usually independent, can be transformed into more realistic correlated distributions using IAF. Finally, we implemented these models on the CIFAR-10 dataset and showed how they can be used to reconstruct the images and generate new images from random vectors.

The next chapter will introduce GANs and show how we can use them to add stylistic filters to input images, using the StyleGAN model.

References

1. Eckersley P., Nasser Y. *Measuring the Progress of AI Research*. EFF. Retrieved April 26, 2021, https://www.eff.org/ai/metrics#Measuring-the-Progress-of-AI-Research and CIFAR-10 datasets, https://www.cs.toronto.edu/~kriz/

2. Malhotra P. (2018). Autoencoder-Implementations. GitHub repository. https://www.piyushmalhotra.in/Autoencoder-Implementations/VAE/

3. Kingma, D P., Welling, M. (2014). *Auto-Encoding Variational Bayes*. arXiv:1312.6114. https://arxiv.org/pdf/1312.6114.pdf

4. Hinton G. E., Salakhutdinov R. R. (2006). *Reducing the Dimensionality of Data with Neural Networks*. ScienceMag. https://www.cs.toronto.edu/~hinton/science.pdf

5. Hinton G. E., Salakhutdinov R. R. (2006). *Reducing the Dimensionality of Data with Neural Networks*. ScienceMag. https://www.cs.toronto.edu/~hinton/science.pdf

6. Kingma, D P., Welling, M. (2014). *Auto-Encoding Variational Bayes*. arXiv:1312.6114. https://arxiv.org/pdf/1312.6114.pdf

7. Doersch, C. (2016). *Tutorial on Variational Autoencoders*. arXiv:1606.05908. https://arxiv.org/pdf/1606.05908.pdf

8. Paisley, J., Blei, D., Jordan, M. (2012). *Variational Bayesian Inference with Stochastic Search*. https://icml.cc/2012/papers/687.pdf

9. Doersch, C. (2016). *Tutorial on Variational Autoencoders*. arXiv:1606.05908. https://arxiv.org/pdf/1606.05908.pdf

10. Angelov, Plamen; Gegov, Alexander; Jayne, Chrisina; Shen, Qiang (2016-09-06). *Advances in Computational Intelligence Systems: Contributions Presented at the 16th UK Workshop on Computational Intelligence*, September 7–9, 2016, Lancaster, UK. Springer International Publishing. pp. 441–. ISBN 9783319465623. Retrieved January 22, 2018.

11. TinyImages: http://groups.csail.mit.edu/vision/TinyImages/

12. Krizhevsky A. (2009). *Learning Multiple Layers of Features from Tiny Images.* http://citeseerx.ist.psu.edu/viewdoc/download?doi=10.1.1.222.9220&rep=rep1&type=pdf

13. Kingma, D P., Welling, M. (2014). *Auto-Encoding Variational Bayes.* arXiv:1312.6114. https://arxiv.org/pdf/1312.6114.pdf

14. Kingma, D P., Salimans, T., Jozefowicz, R., Chen, X., Sutskever, I., Welling, M. (2016). *Improving Variational Inference with Inverse Autoregressive Flow.* arXiv:1606.04934. https://arxiv.org/pdf/1606.04934.pdf

6
Image Generation with GANs

Generative modeling is a powerful concept that provides us with immense potential to approximate or model underlying processes that generate data. In the previous chapters, we covered concepts associated with deep learning in general and more specifically related to **restricted Boltzmann machines** (**RBMs**) and **variational autoencoders** (**VAEs**). This chapter will introduce another family of generative models called **Generative Adversarial Networks** (**GANs**).

Heavily inspired by the concepts of game theory and picking up some of the best components from previously discussed techniques, GANs provide a powerful framework for working in the generative modeling space. Since their invention in 2014 by Goodfellow et al., GANs have benefitted from tremendous research and are now being used to explore creative domains such as art, fashion, and photography.

The following are two amazing high-quality samples from a variant of GANs called StyleGAN (*Figure 6.1*). The photograph of the kid is actually a fictional person who does not exist. The art sample is also generated by a similar network. StyleGANs are able to generate high-quality sharp images by using the concept of progressive growth (we will cover this in detail in later sections). These outputs were generated using the StyleGAN2 model trained on datasets such as the **Flickr-Faces-HQ** or **FFHQ** dataset.

Image Generation with GANs

Figure 6.1: Imagined by a GAN (StyleGAN2) (Dec 2019) - Karras et al. and Nvidia[2]

This chapter will cover:

- The taxonomy of generative models
- A number of improved GANs, such as DCGAN, Conditional-GAN, and so on
- The progressive GAN setup and its various components
- Some of the challenges associated with GANs
- Hands-on examples

The taxonomy of generative models

Generative models are a class of models in the unsupervised machine learning space. They help us to model the underlying distributions responsible for generating the dataset under consideration. There are different methods/frameworks to work with generative models. The first set of methods correspond to models that represent data with an explicit density function. Here we define a probability density function, $p\theta$, explicitly and develop a model that increases the maximum likelihood of sampling from this distribution.

There are two further types within explicit density methods, *tractable* and *approximate* density methods. PixelRNNs are an active area of research for tractable density methods. When we try to model complex real-world data distributions, for example, natural images or speech signals, defining a parametric function becomes challenging. To overcome this, you learned about RBMs and VAEs in *Chapter 4, Teaching Networks to Generate Digits*, and *Chapter 5, Painting Pictures with Neural Networks Using VAEs*, respectively. These techniques work by approximating the underlying probability density functions explicitly. VAEs work towards maximizing the likelihood estimates of the lower bound, while RBMs use Markov chains to make an estimate of the distribution. The overall landscape of generative models can be described using *Figure 6.2*:

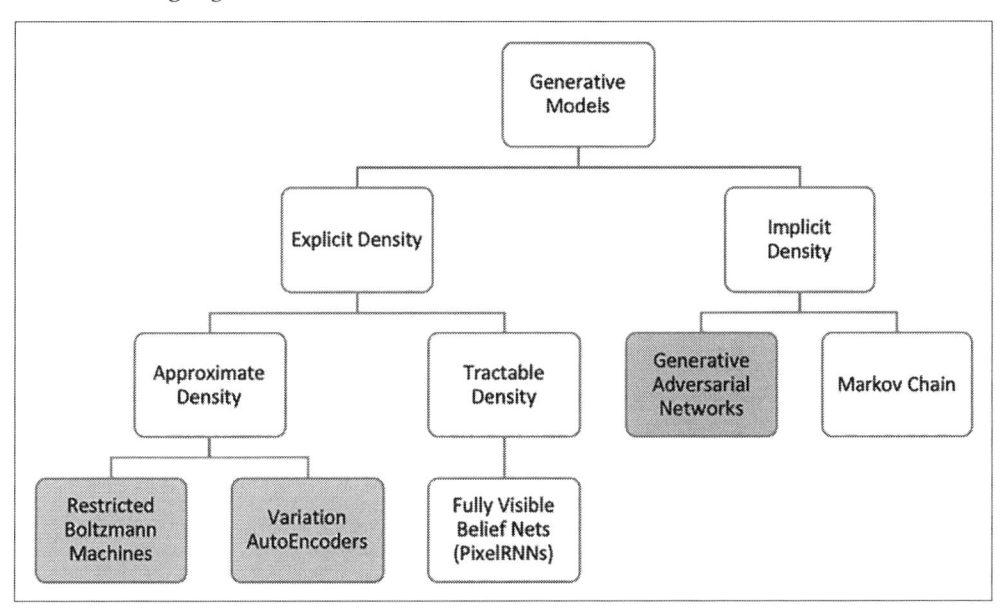

Figure 6.2: The taxonomy of generative models[3]

GANs fall under implicit density modeling methods. The implicit density functions give up the property of explicitly defining the underlying distribution but work by defining methods to draw samples from such distributions. The GAN framework is a class of methods that can sample directly from the underlying distributions. This alleviates some of the complexities associated with the methods we have covered so far, such as defining underlying probability distribution functions and the quality of outputs. Now that you have a high-level understanding of generative models, let's dive deeper into the details of GANs.

Generative adversarial networks

GANs have a pretty interesting origin story. It all began as a discussion/argument in a bar with Ian Goodfellow and friends discussing work related to generating data using neural networks. The argument ended with everyone downplaying each other's methods. Goodfellow went back home and coded the first version of what we now call a GAN. To his amazement, the code worked on the first try. A more verbose description of the chain of events was shared by Goodfellow himself in an interview with *Wired* magazine.

As mentioned, GANs are implicit density functions that sample directly from the underlying distribution. They do this by defining a two-player game of adversaries. The adversaries compete against each other under well-defined reward functions and each player tries to maximize its rewards. Without going into the details of game theory, the framework can be explained as follows.

The discriminator model

This model represents a differentiable function that tries to maximize a probability of 1 for samples drawn from the training distribution. This can be any classification model, but we usually prefer a deep neural network for this. This is the throw-away model (similar to the decoder part of autoencoders).

The discriminator is also used to classify whether the output from the generator is real or fake. The main utility of this model is to help develop a robust generator. We denote the discriminator model as D and its output as $D(x)$. When it is used to classify output from the generator model, the discriminator model is denoted as $D(G(z))$, where $G(z)$ is the output from the generator model.

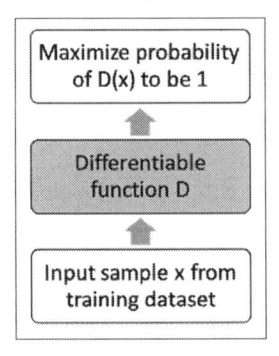

Figure 6.3: The discriminator model

The generator model

This is the primary model of interest in the whole game. This model generates samples that are intended to resemble the samples from our training set. The model takes random unstructured noise as input (typically denoted as z) and tries to create a varied set of outputs. The generator model is usually a differentiable function; it is often represented by a deep neural network but is not restricted to that.

We denote the generator as G and its output as $G(z)$. We typically use a lower-dimensional z as compared to the dimension of the original data, x, that is, $z_{dim} \leq x_{dim}$. This is done as a way of compressing or encoding real-world information into lower-dimensional space.

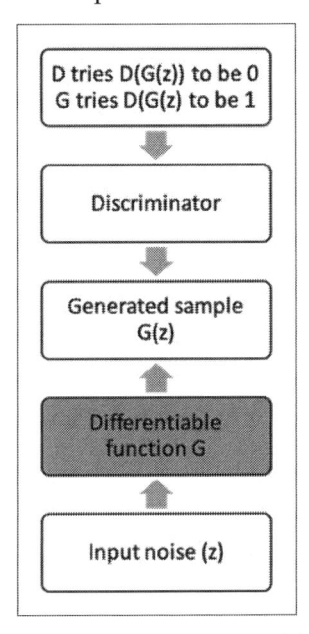

Figure 6.4: The generator model

In simple words, the generator trains to generate samples good enough to fool the discriminator, while the discriminator trains to properly classify real (training samples) versus fake (output from the generator). Thus, this game of adversaries uses a generator model, G, which tries to make $D(G(z))$ as close to 1 as possible. The discriminator is incentivized to make $D(G(z))$ close to 0, where 1 denotes real and 0 denotes fake samples. The GAN model achieves equilibrium when the generator starts to easily fool the discriminator, that is, the discriminator reaches its saddle point. While, in theory, GANs have several advantages over other methods in the family tree described previously, they pose their own set of problems. We will discuss some of them in the upcoming sections.

Training GANs

Training a GAN is like playing this game of two adversaries. The generator is learning to generate good enough fake samples, while the discriminator is working hard to discriminate between real and fake. More formally, this is termed as the minimax game, where the value function $V(G, D)$ is described as follows:

$$min_G max_D V(G,D) = E_{x \sim p_{data}} \log \log D(x) + E_{z \sim p_z} \log \log (1 - D(G(z)))$$

This is also called the zero-sum game, which has an equilibrium that is the same as the Nash equilibrium. We can better understand the value function $V(G, D)$ by separating out the objective function for each of the players. The following equations describe individual objective functions:

$$J^D = -\frac{1}{2} \{ E_{x \sim p_{data}} \log \log D(x) + E_z \log \log (1 - D(G(z))) \}$$

$$J^G = -J^D$$

where J^D is the discriminator objective function in the classical sense, J^G is the generator objective equal to the negative of the discriminator, and p_{data} is the distribution of the training data. The rest of the terms have their usual meaning. This is one of the simplest ways of defining the game or corresponding objective functions. Over the years, different ways have been studied, some of which we will cover in this chapter.

The objective functions help us to understand the aim of each of the players. If we assume both probability densities are non-zero everywhere, we can get the optimal value of $D(x)$ as:

$$D(x) = \frac{p_{data}}{p_{data}(x) + p_z(x)}$$

We will revisit this equation in the latter part of the chapter. For now, the next step is to present a training algorithm wherein the discriminator and generator models train towards their respective objectives. The simplest yet widely used way of training a GAN (and by far the most successful one) is as follows.

Repeat the following steps N times. N is the number of total iterations:

1. Repeat steps k times:
    - Sample a minibatch of size m from the generator: $\{z_1, z_2, \ldots z_m\} = p_{model}(z)$

- Sample a minibatch of size m from the actual data: $\{x_1, x_2, \ldots x_m\} = p_{data}(x)$
   - Update the discriminator loss, J^D

2. Set the discriminator as non-trainable
3. Sample a minibatch of size m from the generator: $\{z_1, z_2, \ldots z_m\} = p_{model}(z)$
4. Update the generator loss, J^G

In their original paper, Goodfellow et al. used $k=1$, that is, they trained discriminator and generator models alternately. There are some variants and hacks where it is observed that training the discriminator more often than the generator helps with better convergence.

The following figure (*Figure 6.5*) showcases the training phases of the generator and discriminator models. The smaller dotted line is the discriminator model, the solid line is the generator model, and the larger dotted line is the actual training data. The vertical lines at the bottom demonstrate the sampling of data points from the distribution of z, that is, $x = p_{model}(z)$. The lines point to the fact that the generator contracts in the regions of high density and expands in the regions of low density. Part **(a)** shows the initial stages of the training phase where the discriminator (*D*) is a partially correct classifier. Parts **(b)** and **(c)** show how improvements in D guide changes in the generator, G. Finally, in part **(d)** you can see where $p_{model} = p_{data}$ and the discriminator is no longer able to differentiate between fake and real samples, that is, $D(x) = \dfrac{1}{2}$:

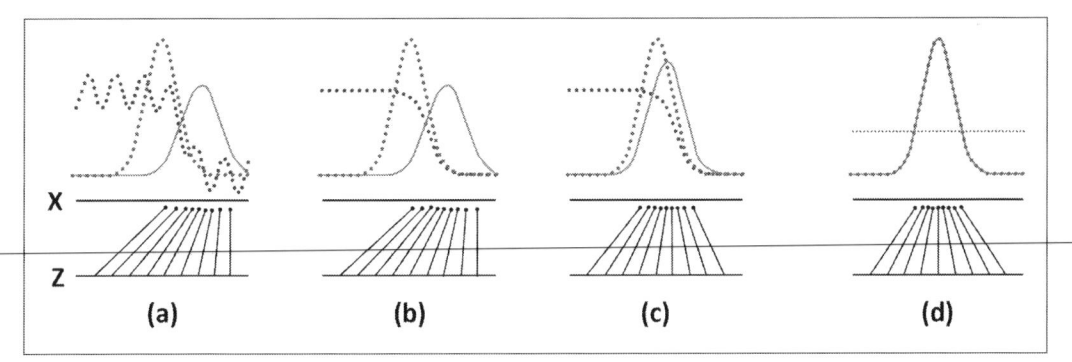

Figure 6.5: The training process for GAN[4]

Non-saturating generator cost

In practice, we do not train the generator to minimize $log(1 - D(G(z)))$ as this function does not provide sufficient gradients for learning. During the initial learning phases, where G is poor, the discriminator is able to classify the fake from the real with high confidence. This leads to the saturation of $log(1 - D(G(z)))$, which hinders improvements in the generator model. We thus tweak the generator to maximize $log(D(G(z)))$ instead:

$$J^G = E_{z \sim p_z} log(D(G(z)))$$

This provides stronger gradients for the generator to learn. This is shown in *Figure 6.6*. The x-axis denotes $D(G(z))$. The top line shows the objective, which is minimizing the likelihood of the discriminator being correct. The bottom line (updated objective) works by maximizing the likelihood of the discriminator being wrong.

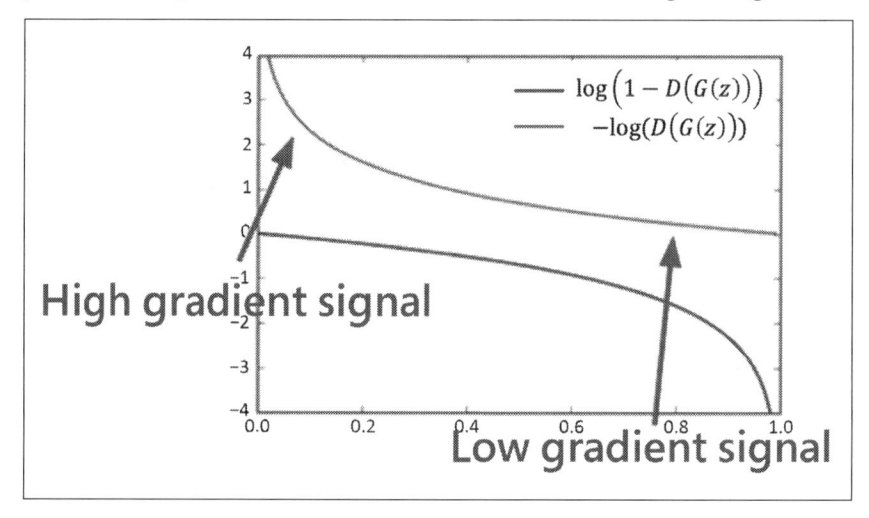

Figure 6.6: Generator objective functions[5]

Figure 6.6 illustrates how a slight change helps achieve better gradients during the initial phases of training.

Maximum likelihood game

The minimax game can be transformed into a maximum likelihood game where the aim is to maximize the likelihood of the generator probability density. This is done to ensure that the generator probability density is similar to the real/training data probability density. In other words, the game can be transformed into minimizing the divergence between p_z and p_{data}. To do so, we make use of **Kullback-Leibler divergence (KL divergence)** to calculate the similarity between two distributions of interest. The overall value function can be denoted as:

$$\theta = arg_{min} D_{KL}(p_{data}(x) \| p_g(z))$$

The cost function for the generator transforms to:

$$J^G = -\frac{1}{2} E_z exp\left(\sigma^{-1}(D(G(z)))\right)$$

One important point to note is that KL divergence is not a symmetric measure, that is, $KL(p_{data} \| p_g) \neq KL(p_g \| p_{data})$. The model typically uses $KL(p_g \| p_{data})$ to achieve better results.

The three different cost functions discussed so far have slightly different trajectories and thus lead to different properties at different stages of training. These three functions can be visualized as shown in *Figure 6.7*:

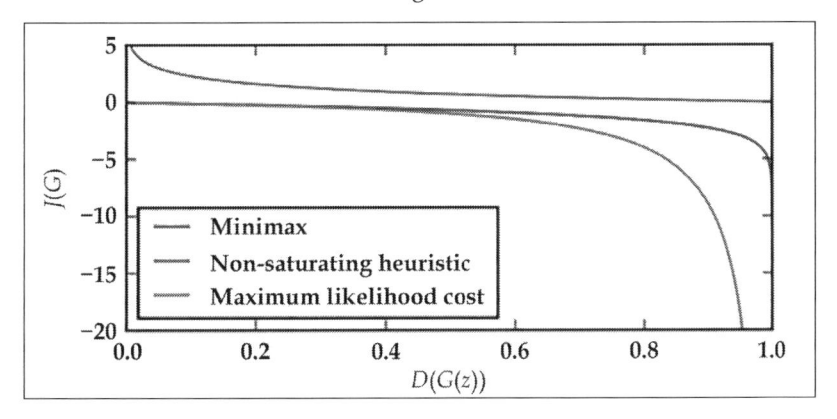

Figure 6.7: Generator cost functions[6]

Vanilla GAN

We have covered quite a bit of ground in understanding the basics of GANs. In this section, we will apply that understanding and build a GAN from scratch. This generative model will consist of a repeating block architecture, similar to the one presented in the original paper. We will try to replicate the task of generating MNIST digits using our network.

The overall GAN setup can be seen in *Figure 6.8*. The figure outlines a generator model with noise vector z as input and repeating blocks that transform and scale up the vector to the required dimensions. Each block consists of a dense layer followed by Leaky ReLU activation and a batch-normalization layer. We simply reshape the output from the final block to transform it into the required output image size.

Image Generation with GANs

The discriminator, on the other hand, is a simple feedforward network. This model takes an image as input (a real image or the fake output from the generator) and classifies it as real or fake. This simple setup of two competing models helps us to train the overall GAN.

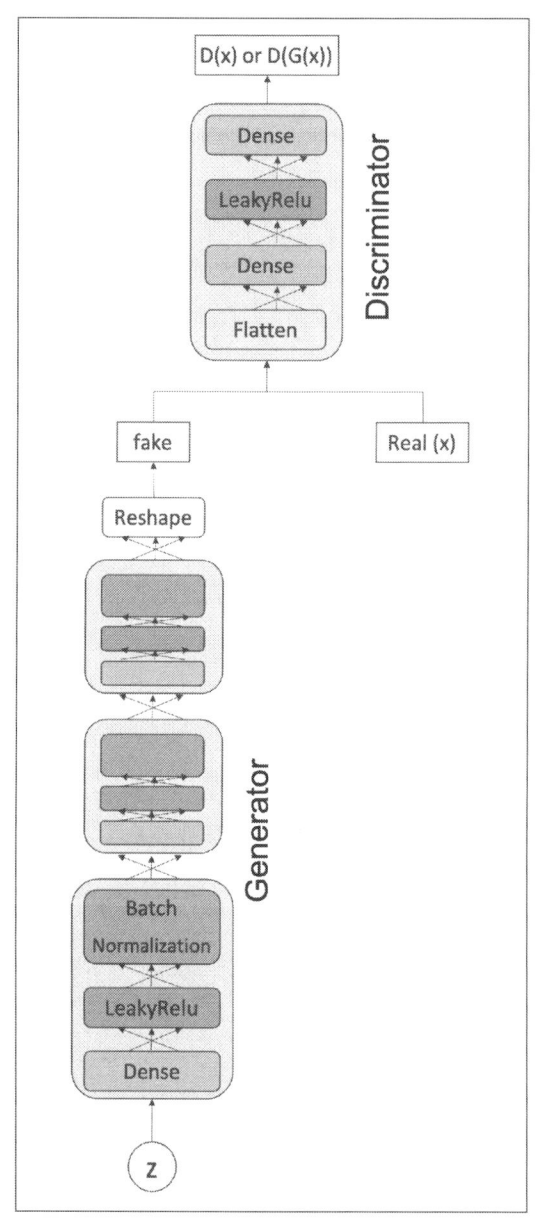

Figure 6.8: Vanilla GAN architecture

We will be relying on TensorFlow 2 and using the high-level Keras API wherever possible. The first step is to define the discriminator model. In this implementation, we will use a very basic **multi-layer perceptron (MLP)** as the discriminator model:

```
def build_discriminator(input_shape=(28, 28,), verbose=True):
    """
    Utility method to build a MLP discriminator
    Parameters:
        input_shape:
            type:tuple. Shape of input image for classification.
                        Default shape is (28,28)->MNIST
        verbose:
            type:boolean. Print model summary if set to true.
                        Default is True
    Returns:
        tensorflow.keras.model object
    """
    model = Sequential()
    model.add(Input(shape=input_shape))
    model.add(Flatten())
    model.add(Dense(512))
    model.add(LeakyReLU(alpha=0.2))
    model.add(Dense(256))
    model.add(LeakyReLU(alpha=0.2))
    model.add(Dense(1, activation='sigmoid'))

    if verbose:
        model.summary()

    return model
```

We will use the sequential API to prepare this simple model, with just four layers and the final output layer with sigmoid activation. Since we have a binary classification task, we have only one unit in the final layer. We will use binary cross-entropy loss to train the discriminator model.

The generator model is also a multi-layer perceptron with multiple layers scaling up the noise vector z to the desired size. Since our task is to generate MNIST-like output samples, the final reshape layer will convert the flat vector into a 28x28 output shape. Note that we will make use of batch normalization to stabilize model training. The following snippet shows a utility method for building the generator model:

```
def build_generator(z_dim=100, output_shape=(28, 28), verbose=True):
    """
```

Image Generation with GANs

```
        Utility method to build a MLP generator
        Parameters:
            z_dim:
                type:int(positive). Size of input noise vector to be
                            used as model input.
                            Default value is 100
            output_shape:   type:tuple. Shape of output image .
                            Default shape is (28,28)->MNIST
            verbose:
                type:boolean. Print model summary if set to true.
                            Default is True
        Returns:
            tensorflow.keras.model object
    """
    model = Sequential()
    model.add(Input(shape=(z_dim,)))
    model.add(Dense(256, input_dim=z_dim))
    model.add(LeakyReLU(alpha=0.2))
    model.add(BatchNormalization(momentum=0.8))
    model.add(Dense(512))
    model.add(LeakyReLU(alpha=0.2))
    model.add(BatchNormalization(momentum=0.8))
    model.add(Dense(1024))
    model.add(LeakyReLU(alpha=0.2))
    model.add(BatchNormalization(momentum=0.8))
    model.add(Dense(np.prod(output_shape), activation='tanh'))
    model.add(Reshape(output_shape))

    if verbose:
        model.summary()
    return model
```

We simply use these utility methods to create generator and discriminator model objects. The following snippet uses these two model objects to create the GAN object as well:

```
discriminator = build_discriminator()
discriminator.compile(loss='binary_crossentropy',
                      optimizer=Adam(0.0002, 0.5),
                      metrics=['accuracy'])

generator=build_generator()
z_dim = 100 #noise
```

```
z = Input(shape=(z_dim,))
img = generator(z)

# For the combined model we will only train the generator
discriminator.trainable = False

# The discriminator takes generated images as input
# and determines validity
validity = discriminator(img)

# The combined model  (stacked generator and discriminator)
# Trains the generator to fool the discriminator
gan_model = Model(z, validity)
gan_model.compile(loss='binary_crossentropy', optimizer=Adam(0.0002, 0.5))
```

The final piece of the puzzle is defining the training loop. As described in the previous section, we will train both (discriminator and generator) models alternatingly. Doing so is straightforward with high-level Keras APIs. The following code snippet first loads the MNIST dataset and scales the pixel values between -1 and +1:

```
# Load MNIST train samples
(X_train, _), (_, _) = datasets.mnist.load_data()

# Rescale to [-1, 1]
  X_train = X_train / 127.5 - 1
```

For each training iteration, we first sample real images from the MNIST dataset equal to our defined batch size. The next step involves sampling the same number of z vectors. We use these sampled z vectors to generate output from our generator model. Finally, we calculate the discriminator loss on both real and generated samples. These steps are explained in the following snippet:

```
idx = np.random.randint(0, X_train.shape[0], batch_size)
real_imgs = X_train[idx]

# pick random noise samples (z) from a normal distribution
noise = np.random.normal(0, 1, (batch_size, z_dim))

# use generator model to generate output samples
fake_imgs = generator.predict(noise)

# calculate discriminator loss on real samples
disc_loss_real = discriminator.train_on_batch(real_imgs, real_y)
```

Image Generation with GANs

```
# calculate discriminator loss on fake samples
disc_loss_fake = discriminator.train_on_batch(fake_imgs, fake_y)

# overall discriminator loss
discriminator_loss = 0.5 * np.add(disc_loss_real, disc_loss_fake)
```

Training the generator is straightforward. We prepare a stacked model object that resembles the GAN architecture we discussed previously. Simply using the `train_on_batch` helps us to calculate the generator loss and improve it, as shown in the following snippet:

```
# train generator
# pick random noise samples (z) from a normal distribution
noise = np.random.normal(0, 1, (batch_size, z_dim))

# use trained discriminator to improve generator
gen_loss = gan_model.train_on_batch(noise, real_y)
```

We train our vanilla GAN for about 30,000 iterations. The following (*Figure 6.9*) are model outputs at different stages of the training. You can clearly see how the sample quality improves as we move from one stage to another.

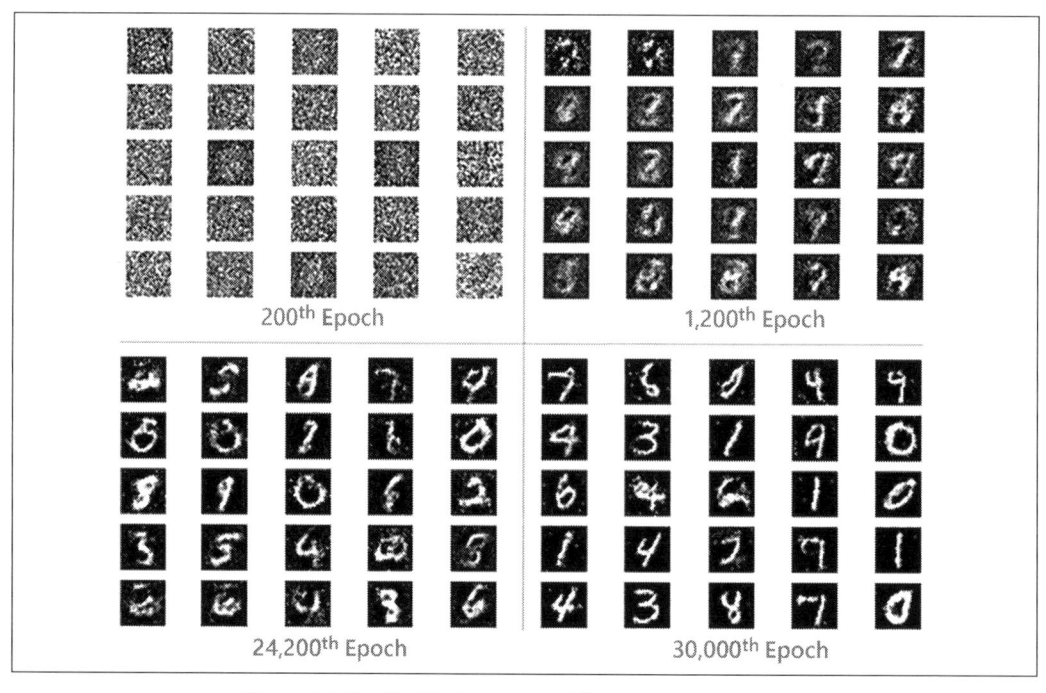

Figure 6.9: Vanilla GAN output at different stages of training

[180]

The results from vanilla GAN are encouraging yet leave space for further improvements. In the next section, we will explore some improved architectures to enhance the generative capabilities of GANs.

Improved GANs

Vanilla GAN proved the potential of adversarial networks. The ease of setting up the models and the quality of the output sparked much interest in this field. This led to a lot of research in improving the GAN paradigm. In this section, we will cover a few of the major improvements in developing GANs.

Deep Convolutional GAN

Published in 2016, this work by Radford et al. introduced several key contributions to improve GAN outputs apart from focusing on convolutional layers, which are discussed in the original GAN paper. The 2016 paper emphasized using deeper architectures instead. *Figure 6.10* shows the generator architecture for a **Deep Convolutional GAN (DCGAN)** (as proposed by the authors). The generator takes the noise vector as input and then passes it through a repeating setup of up-sampling layers, convolutional layers, and batch normalization layers to stabilize the training.

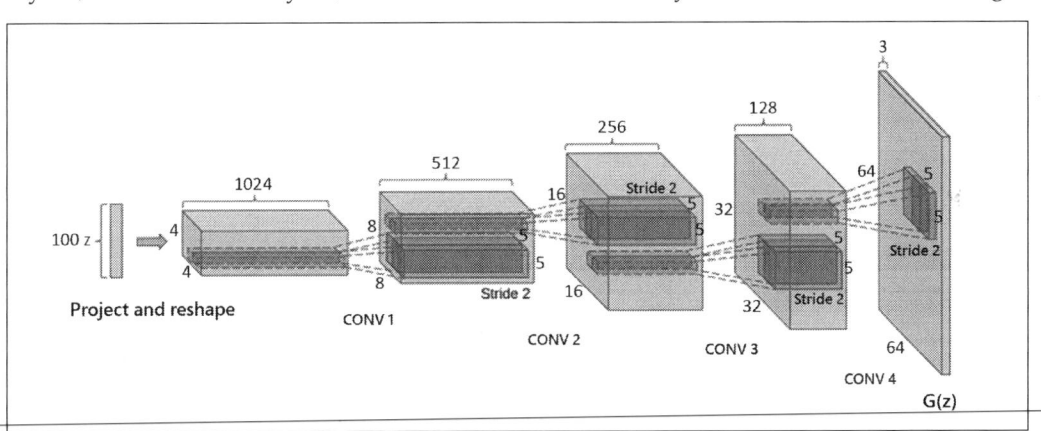

Figure 6.10: DCGAN generator architecture[7]

Until the introduction of DCGANs, the output image resolution was quite limited. A Laplacian pyramid or LAPGAN was proposed to generate high-quality images, but it also suffered from certain fuzziness in the output. The DCGAN paper also made use of another important invention, the batch normalization layer. Batch normalization was presented after the original GAN paper and proved useful in stabilizing the overall training by normalizing the input for each unit to have zero mean and unit variance. To get higher-resolution images, it made use of strides greater than 1 while moving the convolutional filters.

Image Generation with GANs

Let's start by preparing the discriminator model. CNN-based binary classifiers are simple models. One modification we make here is to use strides longer than 1 to down-sample the input between layers instead of using pooling layers. This helps in providing better stability for the training of the generator model. We also rely on batch normalization and Leaky ReLU for the same purposes (although these were not used in the original GAN paper). Another important aspect of this discriminator (as compared to the vanilla GAN discriminator) is the absence of fully connected layers.

The generator model is quite different to what you saw for vanilla GAN. Here we only need the input vector's dimension to start with. We make use of reshaping and up-sampling layers to modify the vector into a two-dimensional image and increase its resolution, respectively. Similar to DCGAN's discriminator, we do not have any fully connected layers apart from the input layer, which is reshaped into an image. The following code snippet shows how to build a generator model for DCGAN:

```python
def build_dc_generator(z_dim=100, verbose=True):
    model = Sequential()
    model.add(Input(shape=(z_dim,)))
    model.add(Dense(128 * 7 * 7, activation="relu", input_dim=z_dim))
    model.add(Reshape((7, 7, 128)))
    model.add(UpSampling2D())
    model.add(Conv2D(128, kernel_size=3, padding="same"))
    model.add(BatchNormalization(momentum=0.8))
    model.add(Activation("relu"))
    model.add(UpSampling2D())
    model.add(Conv2D(64, kernel_size=3, padding="same"))
    model.add(BatchNormalization(momentum=0.8))
    model.add(Activation("relu"))
    model.add(Conv2D(1, kernel_size=3, padding="same"))
    model.add(Activation("tanh"))

    if verbose:
        model.summary()

    return model
```

Chapter 6

The training loop is exactly the same as vanilla GAN. For brevity, we'll skip the snippet for the training loop. It is available in the GitHub repository. The following are output samples from DCGAN at different intervals (*Figure 6.11*).

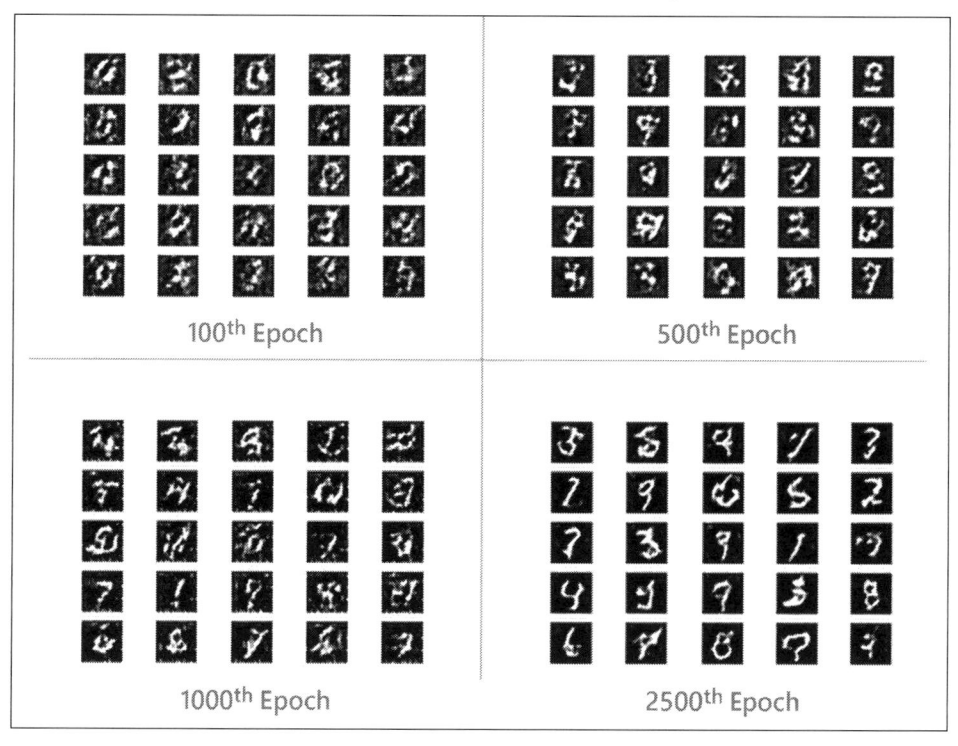

Figure 6.11: DCGAN output at different stages of training

The results show how DCGAN is able to generate the required set of outputs in fewer training cycles. While it is difficult to make much out of the quality of generated images (given the nature of the MNIST dataset), in principle, DCGAN should be able to generate better quality output than vanilla GAN.

Image Generation with GANs

Vector arithmetic

The ability to manipulate the latent vectors by addition, subtraction, and so on to generate meaningful output transformations is a powerful tool. The authors of the DCGAN paper showed that indeed the z representative space of the generator obeys such a rich linear structure. Similar to vector arithmetic in the NLP domain, where word2vec generates a vector similar to "Queen" upon performing the manipulation "King" - "Man" + "Woman," DCGAN allows the same in the visual domain. The following is an example from the DCGAN paper (*Figure 6.12*):

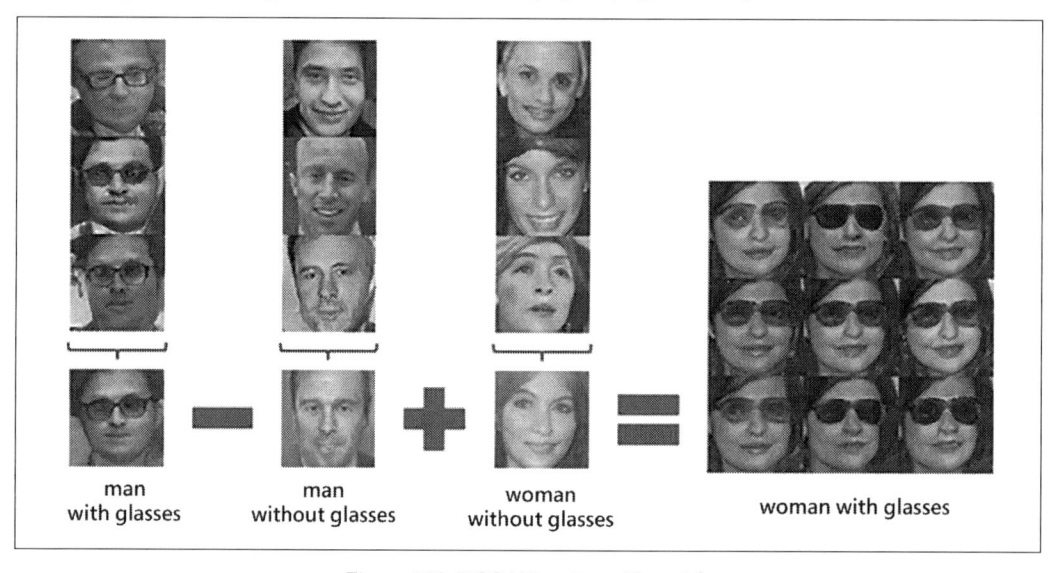

Figure 6.12: DCGAN vector arithmetic[8]

The example shows that we can generate examples of "woman with glasses" by performing the simple manipulation of "man with glasses" - "man without glasses" + "woman without glasses." This opens up the possibility of generating complex samples without the need for huge amounts of training data. Though unlike word2vec, where a single vector is sufficient, in this case, we average at least three samples to achieve stable outputs.

Conditional GAN

GANs are powerful systems that can generate realistic samples from the domain of training. In the previous sections, you saw vanilla GAN and DCGAN generate realistic samples from the MNIST dataset. These architectures have also been used to generate samples that resemble human faces and even real-world items (from training on CIFAR10 and so on). However, they miss out on the ability to control the samples we would like to generate.

In simple words, we can use a trained generator to generate any number of samples required, yet we cannot control it to generate a specific type of example. **Conditional GANs (CGANs)** are the class of GANs that provide us with precisely the control needed to generate a specific class of examples. Developed by Mirza et al. in 2014[9], they are some of the earliest enhancements to the original GAN architecture from Goodfellow et al.

CGANs work by training the generator model to generate fake samples conditioned on specific characteristics of the output required. The discriminator, on the other hand, needs to do some extra work. It needs to learn not only to differentiate between fake and real but also to mark out samples as fake if the generated sample and its conditioning characteristics do not match.

In their work *Conditional Adversarial Networks*, Mirza et al. pointed towards using class labels as additional conditioning input to both generator and discriminator models. We denote the conditioning input as y and transform the value function for the GAN minimax game as follows:

$$min_G max_D V(G,D) = E_{x \sim p_{data}} \log \log D(x|y) + E_{z \sim p_z} \log \log (1 - D(G(z|y)))$$

where $\log \log D(x|y)$ is the discriminator output for a real sample, x, conditioned on y and similarly $\log \log (1 - D(G(z|y)))$ is the discriminator output for a fake sample, $G(z)$, conditioned on y. Note that the value function is only slightly changed from the original minimax equation for vanilla GAN. Thus, we can leverage the improved cost functions for the generator as well as the other enhancements we discussed in the previous sections. The conditioning information, y (the class label, for example), is provided as an additional input to both the models and the rest is taken care of by the GAN setup itself. *Figure 6.13* shows the architectural setup for a Conditional GAN.

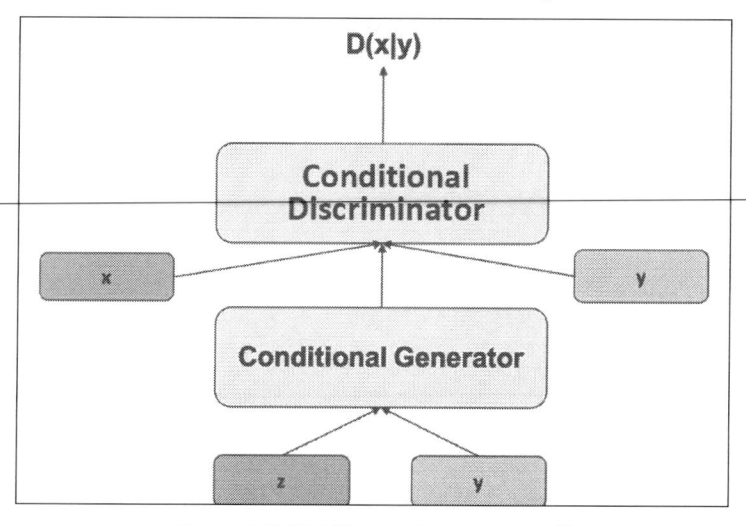

Figure: 6.13 CGAN generator architecture[10]

Image Generation with GANs

Keeping the implementation as close to the original implementation of CGAN as possible, we will now develop conditioned generator and discriminator models as MLPs. You are encouraged to experiment with DCGAN-like architectures conditioned on class labels. Since we would have multiple inputs to each of the constituent models, we will make use of the Keras functional API to define our models. We will be developing CGAN to generate MNIST digits.

The following snippet shows a multi-input MLP generator network. The network uses an embedding layer to transform the class labels as conditioned input for the generator. We perform an element-wise multiplication of the two inputs, the noise vector *z* and the class label *y*'s embedding output, using the **multiply** layer. Please note that this is different from the original implementation, which concatenates vectors *z* and *y*. Changes as compared to vanilla GAN's generator have been highlighted for ease of understanding:

```
def build_conditional_generator(z_dim=100, output_shape=(28, 28),
                                num_classes=10, verbose=True):
    """
    Utility method to build a MLP generator
    Parameters:
        z_dim:
            type:int(positive). Size of input noise vector to be
                                used as model input.
                                Default value is 100
        output_shape:   type:tuple. Shape of output image .
                        Default shape is (28,28)->MNIST
        num_classes:    type:int. Number of unique class labels.
                        Default is 10->MNIST digits
        verbose:
            type:boolean. Print model summary if set to true.
                        Default is True
    Returns:
        tensorflow.keras.model object
    """
    noise = Input(shape=(z_dim,))
    label = Input(shape=(1,), dtype='int32')
    label_embedding = Flatten()(Embedding(num_classes, z_dim)(label))
    model_input = multiply([noise, label_embedding])

    mlp = Dense(256, input_dim=z_dim)(model_input)
    mlp = LeakyReLU(alpha=0.2)(mlp)
    mlp = BatchNormalization(momentum=0.8)(mlp)
    mlp = Dense(512)(mlp)
```

```
    mlp = LeakyReLU(alpha=0.2)(mlp)
    mlp = Dense(1024)(mlp)
    mlp = LeakyReLU(alpha=0.2)(mlp)
    mlp = BatchNormalization(momentum=0.8)(mlp)
    mlp = Dense(np.prod(output_shape), activation='tanh')(mlp)
    mlp = Reshape(output_shape)(mlp)

    model = Model([noise, label], mlp)

    if verbose:
        model.summary()
    return model
```

Similar to the generator, we develop a multi-input discriminator network and combine the real input image along with the embedded class label vector using element-wise multiplication. The following snippet shows the discriminator network. Changes as compared to vanilla GAN's discriminator have been highlighted:

```
def build_conditional_discriminator(input_shape=(28, 28,),
                                    num_classes=10, verbose=True):
    """
    Utility method to build a conditional MLP discriminator
    Parameters:
        input_shape:
            type:tuple. Shape of input image for classification.
                        Default shape is (28,28)->MNIST
        num_classes:   type:int. Number of unique class labels.
                        Default is 10->MNIST digits
        verbose:
            type:boolean. Print model summary if set to true.
                        Default is True
    Returns:
        tensorflow.keras.model object
    """

    img = Input(shape=input_shape)
    flat_img = Flatten()(img)

    label = Input(shape=(1,), dtype='int32')
    label_embedding = Flatten()(Embedding(num_classes,
                                np.prod(input_shape))(label))
```

```
model_input = multiply([flat_img, label_embedding])

mlp = Dense(512, input_dim=np.prod(input_shape))(model_input)
mlp = LeakyReLU(alpha=0.2)(mlp)
mlp = Dense(512)(mlp)
mlp = LeakyReLU(alpha=0.2)(mlp)
mlp = Dropout(0.4)(mlp)
mlp = Dense(512)(mlp)
mlp = LeakyReLU(alpha=0.2)(mlp)
mlp = Dropout(0.4)(mlp)
mlp = Dense(1, activation='sigmoid')(mlp)

model = Model([img, label], mlp)

if verbose:
    model.summary()

return model
```

The training loop for CGAN is very similar to the ones we have seen so far, with a couple of minor changes. We need to provide additional conditioning inputs to both models (class labels in this case). The following snippet shows updated segments from the original training loop:

```
def train(generator=None,discriminator=None,gan_model=None,
          epochs=1000, batch_size=128, sample_interval=50,
          z_dim=100):
    # Load MNIST train samples
    (X_train, y_train), (_, _) = datasets.mnist.load_data()

    # Rescale -1 to 1
    X_train = X_train / 127.5 - 1
    X_train = np.expand_dims(X_train, axis=3)
    y_train = y_train.reshape(-1, 1)

    # Prepare GAN output labels
    real_y = np.ones((batch_size, 1))
    fake_y = np.zeros((batch_size, 1))

    for epoch in range(epochs):
        # train disriminator
```

```python
        # pick random real samples from X_train
        idx = np.random.randint(0, X_train.shape[0], batch_size)
        real_imgs, labels = X_train[idx], y_train[idx]

        # pick random noise samples (z) from a normal distribution
        noise = np.random.normal(0, 1, (batch_size, z_dim))
        # use generator model to generate output samples
        fake_imgs = generator.predict([noise, labels])

        # calculate discriminator loss on real samples
        disc_loss_real = discriminator.train_on_batch([real_imgs, labels], real_y)

        # calculate discriminator loss on fake samples
        disc_loss_fake = discriminator.train_on_batch([fake_imgs, labels], fake_y)

        # overall discriminator loss
        discriminator_loss = 0.5 * np.add(disc_loss_real, disc_loss_fake)

        # train generator
        # pick random noise samples (z) from a normal distribution
        noise = np.random.normal(0, 1, (batch_size, z_dim))

        # pick random labels for conditioning
        sampled_labels = np.random.randint(0, 10, batch_size).reshape(-1, 1)

        # use trained discriminator to improve generator
        gen_loss = gan_model.train_on_batch([noise, sampled_labels], real_y)

        # training updates
        print ("%d [Discriminator loss: %f, acc.: %.2f%%] [Generator loss: %f]" % (epoch, discriminator_loss[0],
            100*discriminator_loss[1], gen_loss))

        # If at save interval => save generated image samples
        if epoch % sample_interval == 0:
            sample_images(epoch,generator)
```

Image Generation with GANs

Once trained, CGAN can be asked to generate examples of a specific class. *Figure 6.14* shows the output for different class labels across the training epochs.

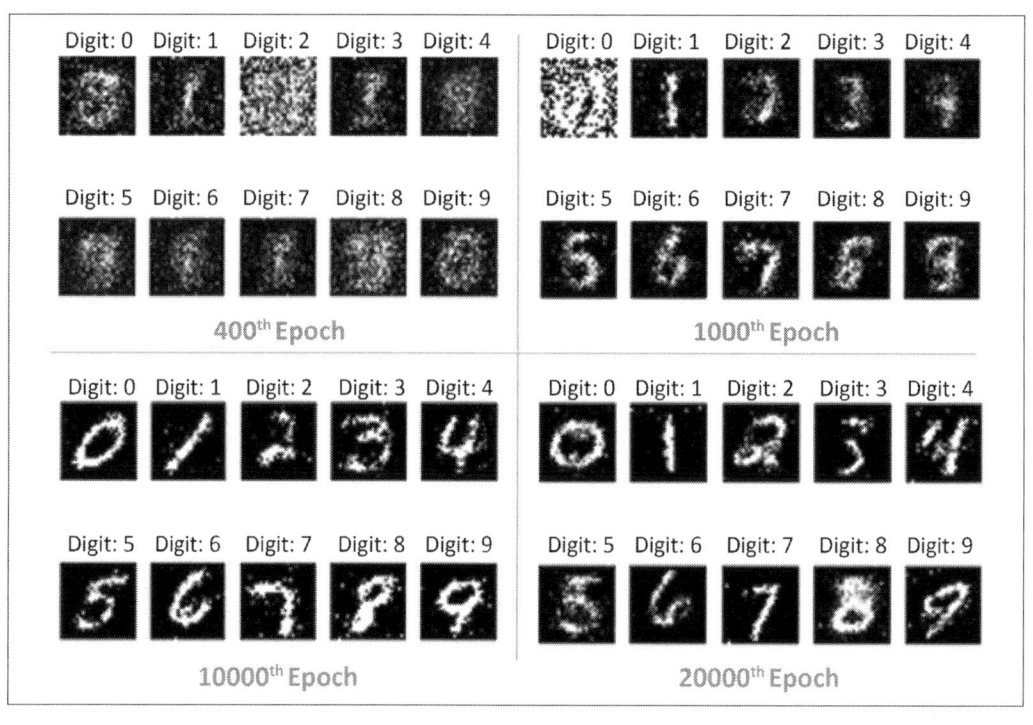

Figure 6.14: CGAN output at different stages of training

One major advantage apparent from *Figure 6.14* is the additional control that CGANs provide us with. As discussed, using additional inputs, we are able to easily control the generator to generate specific digits. This opens up a long list of use cases, some of which we will cover in later chapters of the book.

Wasserstein GAN

The improved GANs we have covered so far were mostly focused upon architectural enhancements to improve results. Two major issues with the GAN setup are the stability of the minimax game and the unintuitiveness of the generator loss. These issues arise due to the fact that we train the discriminator and generator networks alternatingly and at any given moment, the generator loss is indicative of the discriminator's performance so far.

Wasserstein GAN (or W-GAN) was an attempt by Arjovsky et al. to overcome some of the issues with the GAN setup. This is one of a few deep learning papers that are deeply rooted in theoretical foundations to explain the impact of their work (apart from empirical results). The main difference between typical GANs and W-GANs is the fact that W-GANs treat the discriminator as a critic (deriving from reinforcement learning; see *Chapter 11, Composing Music with Generative Models*). Hence, instead of simply classifying input images as real or fake, the W-GAN discriminator (or critic) generates a score to inform the generator about the realness or fakeness of the input image.

The maximum likelihood game we discussed in the initial sections of the chapter explained the task as one where we try to minimize the divergence between p_z and p_{data} using KL divergence, that is, $\theta = arg_{min} D_{KL}(p_{data}(x) \parallel p_g(z))$. Apart from being asymmetric, KL divergence also has issues when the distributions are too far off or completely disjointed. To overcome these issues, W-GANs make use of **Earth Mover's (EM)** distance or Wasserstein distance. Simply put, EM distance is the minimum cost to move or transport mass from distribution p to q. For the GAN setup, we can imagine this as the minimum cost of moving from the generator distribution (p_z) to the real distribution (p_{data}). Mathematically, this can be stated as the infimum (or greatest lower bound, denoted as *inf*) for any transport plan (denoted as W(*source, destination*), that is:

$$W(p_{data}, p_z) = inf_{\gamma \in \Pi(p_{data}, p_z)} E_{(x,y) \sim \gamma}[\|x - y\|]$$

Since this is intractable, the authors used Kantorovich-Rubinstein duality to simplify the calculations. The simplified form is denoted as:

$$W(p_{data}, p_z) = sup_{\|f\|_{L \leq 1}} E_{x \sim p_{data}}[f(x)] - E_{x \sim p_z}[f(x)]$$

where *sup* is the supremum or least upper bound and *f* is a 1-Lipschitz function that imposes certain constraints. A great many details are required to fully understand the details and impact of using Wasserstein distance. You are encouraged to go through the paper for an in-depth understanding of the associated concepts or refer to `https://vincentherrmann.github.io/blog/wasserstein/`.

Image Generation with GANs

For brevity, we will focus on implementation-level changes that help in achieving a stable trainable architecture. A comparison of gradient updates of a GAN and W-GAN is shown in *Figure 6.15*:

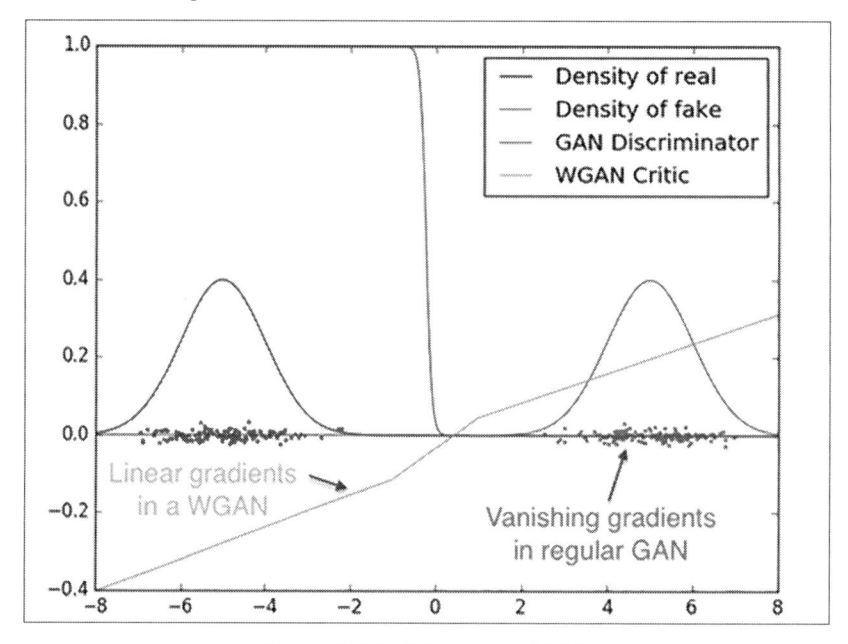

Figure 6.15: W-GAN versus GAN[11]

The figure explains the vanishing gradients in the case of the GAN discriminator when the input is bimodal Gaussian, while the W-GAN critic has a smooth gradient throughout.

To transform this understanding into implementation-level details, the following are the key changes in W-GAN:

- The discriminator is termed as the critic, which generates and outputs a score of realness or fakeness.
- The final layer in the critic/discriminator is a linear layer (instead of sigmoid).
- -1 denotes real labels, while 1 denotes fake labels. These are expressed as positive and negative critics in the literature. We otherwise use 1 and 0 for real and fake labels, respectively.

- We replace classification loss (binary cross-entropy) with Wasserstein loss.
- The critic model is allowed to train for a greater number of cycles compared to the generator model. This is done because in the case of W-GANs, a stable critic better guides the generator; the gradients are much smoother. The authors trained the critic model five times per generator cycle.
- The weights of the critic layers are clipped within a range. This is required in order to maintain the 1-Lipschitz constraint. The authors used the range of -0.01 to 0.01.
- RMSProp is the recommended optimizer to allow stable training. This is in contrast to the usage of Adam as an optimizer for the typical case.

With these changes, the authors noted a significant improvement in training stability and better feedback for the generator. *Figure 6.16* (from the paper) shows how the generator takes cues from a stable critic to train better. The results improve as the training epochs increase. The authors experimented with both MLP-based generators as well as convolutional generators and found similar results.

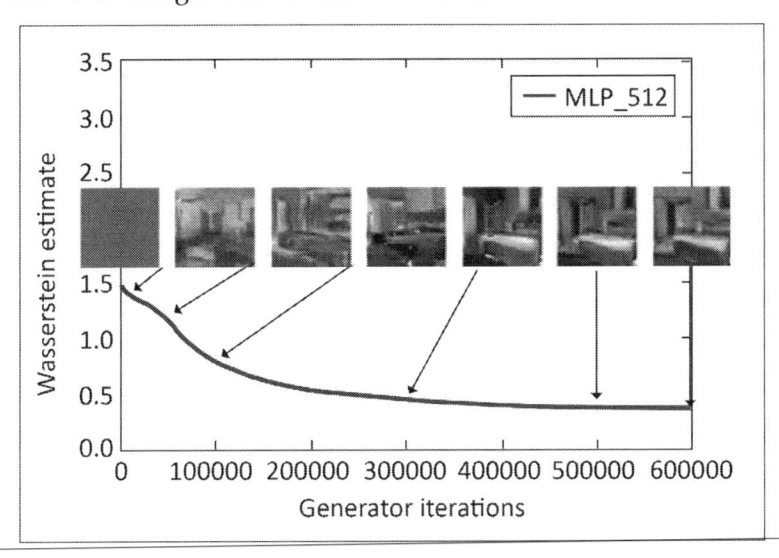

Figure 6.16: W-GAN generator loss and output quality[12]

Since we can use any generator and discriminator with minor modifications, let's get to some of the implementation details. First and foremost is the Wasserstein loss. We calculate it by taking a mean of the critic score and the ground truth labels. This is shown in the following snippet:

```
def wasserstein_loss(y_true, y_pred):
    """
    Custom loss function for W-GAN
    Parameters:
        y_true: type:np.array. Ground truth
        y_pred: type:np.array. Predicted score
    """
    return K.mean(y_true * y_pred)
```

The major change for the discriminator is its final layer and its weight clipping. While the change of activation function for the last layer is straightforward, the weight clipping can be a bit challenging to implement at first. With the Keras API, this can be done in two ways: by sub-classing the Constraint class and using it as an additional argument for all layers or by iterating through the layers during the training loop. While the first approach is much cleaner, we'll use the second approach as it is easier to understand.

```
# Clip critic weights
for l in discriminator.layers:
    weights = l.get_weights()
    weights = [np.clip(w, -clip_value, clip_value) for w in weights]
    l.set_weights(weights)
```

With these changes, we train our W-GAN to generate MNIST digits. The following (*Figure 6.17*) are the output samples during different stages of training:

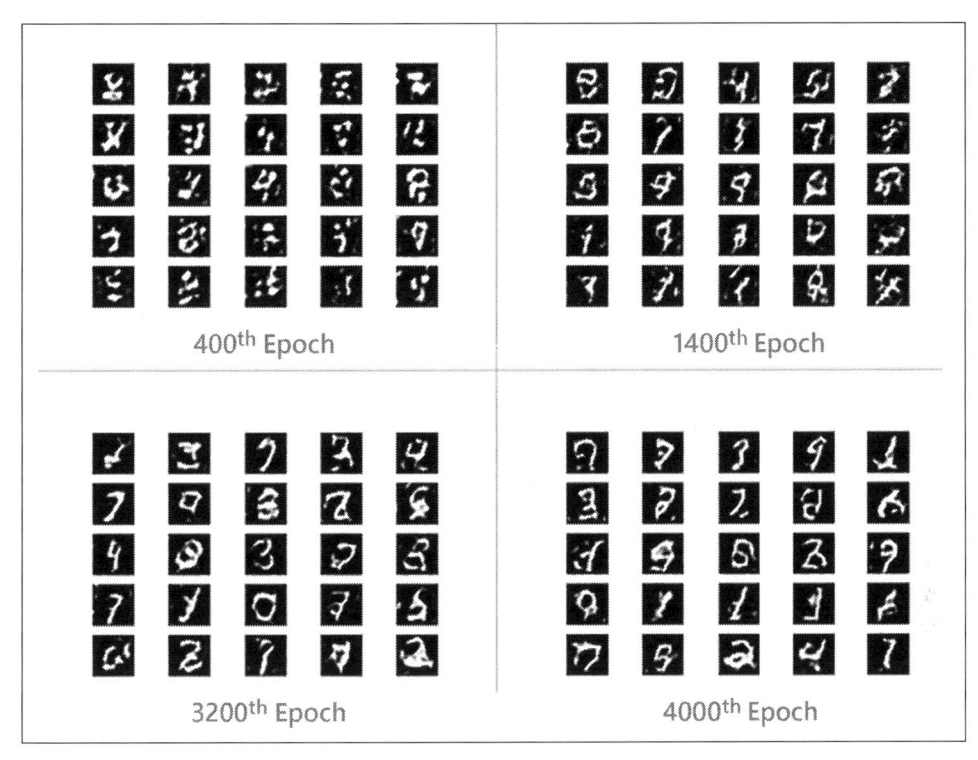

Figure 6.17: W-GAN output at different stages of training

The promised stable training backed up by theoretical proofs is not free from its own set of issues. Mostly, the issues are due to the constraints of keeping the calculations tractable. Some of these concerns were addressed in a recent work titled *Improved Training of Wasserstein GAN*[13] by Gulrajani et al. in 2017. This work presented a few tricks, with the most important one being gradient penalty (or, as the authors refer to it, W-GAN-GP). You are encouraged to go through this interesting work as well to better understand the contributions.

Now that we have covered quite a few improvements, let's move towards a slightly more complex setup called Progressive GAN. In the next section, we will go through the details of this highly effective architecture to generate high-quality outputs.

Progressive GAN

GANs are powerful systems to generate high-quality samples, examples of which we have seen in the previous sections. Different works have utilized this adversarial setup to generate samples from different distributions like CIFAR10, celeb_a, LSUN-bedrooms, and so on (we covered examples using MNIST for explanation purposes). There have been some works that focused on generating higher-resolution output samples, like Lap-GANs, but they lacked perceived output quality and presented a larger set of challenges for training. Progressive GANs or Pro-GANs or PG-GANs were presented by Karras et al. in their work titled *GANs for Improved Quality, Stability, and Variation*[14] at ICLR-2018, as a highly effective method for generating high-quality samples.

The method presented in this work not only mitigated many of the challenges present in earlier works but also brought about a very simple solution to crack this problem of generating high-quality output samples. The paper also presented a number of very impactful contributions, some of which we will cover in detail in the following subsections.

The overall method

The software engineering way of solving tough technical problems is often to break them down into simpler granular tasks. Pro-GANs also target the complex problem of generating high-resolution samples by breaking down the task into smaller and simpler problems to solve. The major issue with high-resolution images is the huge number of modes or details such images have. It makes it very easy to differentiate between generated samples and the real data (perceived quality issues). This inherently makes the task of building a generator, with enough capacity to train well on such datasets along with memory requirements, a very tough one.

To tackle these issues, Karras et al. presented a method to grow both generator and discriminator models as the training progresses from lower to higher resolutions gradually. This is shown in *Figure 6.18*. They noted that this progressive growth of models has various advantages, such as the ability to generate high-quality samples, faster training, and lesser memory requirements (compared to directly training a GAN to generate high-resolution output).

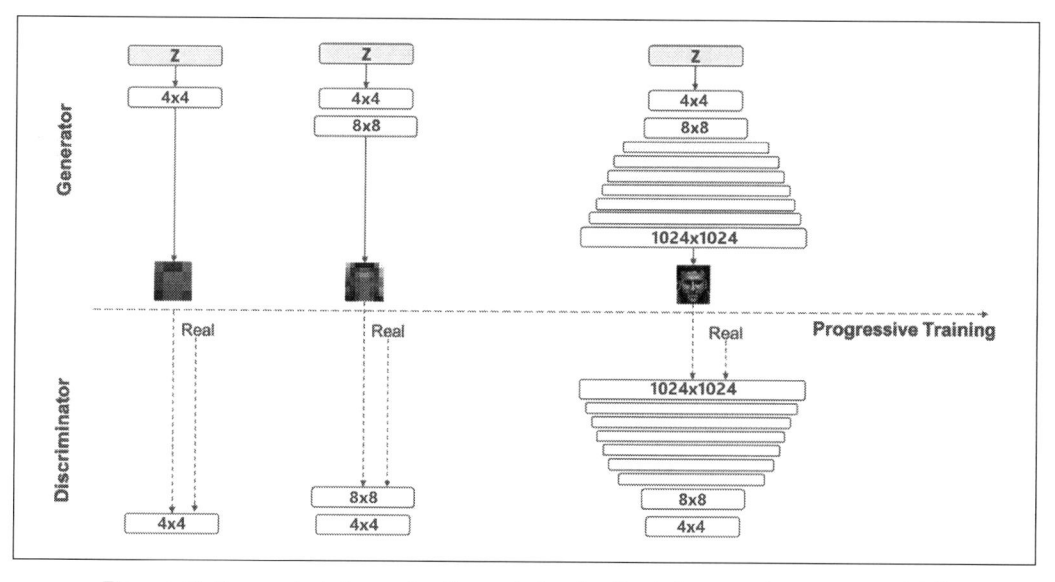

Figure 6.18: Progressively increasing the resolution for discriminator and generator models[15]

> Generating higher-resolution images step by step was not an entirely new idea. A lot of prior works used similar techniques, yet the authors pointed out that their work was most similar to the layer-wise training of autoencoders[16].

The system learns by starting with lower-resolution samples and a generator-discriminator set up as mirror images of each other (architecture-wise). At a lower resolution (say 4x4), the training is much simpler and stable as there are fewer modes to learn. We then increase the resolution step by step by introducing additional layers for both models. This step-by-step increase in resolution limits the complexity of the task at hand rather than forcing the generator to learn all modes at once. This finally enables Pro-GANs to generate megapixel-size outputs, which all start from a very low-resolution initial point.

In the following subsections, we will cover the important contributions and implementation-level details. Note that the training time and compute requirements, despite improvements, for Pro-GANs are huge. The authors mentioned a training time of up to a week on multiple GPUs to generate said megapixel outputs. Keeping the requirements in check, we will cover component-level details but use TensorFlow Hub to present the trained model (instead of training one from scratch). This will enable us to focus on the important details and leverage pre-built blocks as required.

Progressive growth-smooth fade-in

Pro-GANs were introduced as networks that increase the resolution step by step by adding additional layers to generator and discriminator models. But how does that actually work? The following is a step-by-step explanation:

- The generator and discriminator models start with a resolution of 4x4 each. Both networks perform their designated tasks of generating and discriminating the pre-scaled samples.
- We train these models for a number of epochs until the performance saturates. At this point, additional layers are added to both networks.
- The generator gets an additional upscaling layer to generate 8x8 samples while the discriminator gets an additional downscaling layer.
- The move from one step to the next (that is, from 4x4 to 8x8) is done gradually using an overlay factor, α. *Figure 6.19* shows the transition pictorially.

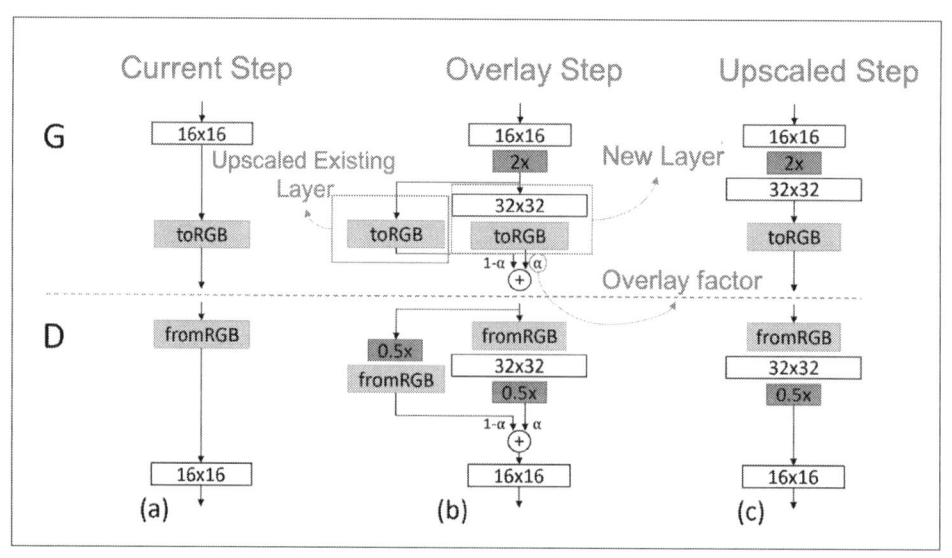

Figure 6.19: Smooth fade-in[17]

- The existing layers are upscaled and transitioned with a factor of 1-α, while the newly added layer is multiplied with a factor of α. The value of α ranges between 0 and 1, which is gradually increased from 0 towards 1 to increase the contribution from the newly added layers.
- The same process is followed for the discriminator, where the transition moves it gradually from the existing setup to newly added layers.
- It is important to note that all layers are trained (existing upscaled and newly added ones) throughout the training process.

The authors started from a 4x4 resolution and, step by step, increased it to finally take it to megapixel levels.

Minibatch standard deviation

Existing approaches rely on normalization techniques such as batch normalization, virtual normalization, and so on. These techniques use trainable parameters to compute minibatch-level statistics in order to maintain similarity across samples. Apart from adding additional parameters and compute load, these normalization methods do not completely alleviate issues.

The authors of Pro-GAN introduced a simplified solution that does not require any trainable parameters. The proposed minibatch standard deviation method was introduced to improve the diversity of minibatches. From the last layer of the discriminator, the method computes the standard deviation of each spatial location (pixel location x, y). For a given batch of size B with images shaped H x W x C (height, width, and channels), a total of $B * H * W * C$ standard deviations are calculated. The next step involves averaging these standard deviations and concatenating them to the layer's output. This is designed to be the same for each example in the minibatch.

Equalized learning rate

The authors of Pro-GAN briefly mentioned that they focused on simpler weight initialization methods compared to the current trend of identifying custom initialization methods. They used an $N(0,1)$ standard normal distribution for the initialization of weights and then explicitly scaled at runtime. The scaling was performed as $\hat{w}_i = \frac{w_i}{c}$, where c is the per-layer normalization constant from the *He's* initializer. They also pointed out issues with momentum-based optimizers such as Adam and RMSProp that get mitigated with this equalized learning rate method.

Pixelwise normalization

The enhancements mentioned so far either focus on the discriminator or the overall GAN training. This normalization technique is applied to the generator model. The authors pointed out that this method helps to prevent instability in the training process along with mode-collapse issues. As the name suggests, they proposed the application of the normalization per spatial location (or per pixel, denoted as (x, y)). The normalization equation is given as:

$$b_{x,y} = \frac{a_{x,y}}{\sqrt{\frac{1}{N}\sum_{j=0}^{N-1}(a_{x,y}^{j})^2 + \epsilon}}$$

where $\epsilon = 10^{-8}$, N is the number of feature maps, and a and b are the original and normalized feature vectors, respectively. This strange-looking normalization equation helps in preventing huge random changes in magnitude effectively.

TensorFlow Hub implementation

As mentioned earlier, despite the long list of effective contributions, Pro-GANs require huge amounts of compute to generate quality results. The official implementation on GitHub[18] mentions a training time of two weeks on a single GPU for the CelebA-HQ dataset. This is beyond the time and effort available for most people. The following (*Figure 6.20*) is a snapshot of the generator and discriminator model architectures; each of them has about 23 million parameters!

Generator	Act.	Output shape	Params
Latent vector	–	512 × 1 × 1	–
Conv 4 × 4	LReLU	512 × 4 × 4	4.2M
Conv 3 × 3	LReLU	512 × 4 × 4	2.4M
Upsample	–	512 × 8 × 8	–
Conv 3 × 3	LReLU	512 × 8 × 8	2.4M
Conv 3 × 3	LReLU	512 × 8 × 8	2.4M
Upsample	–	512 × 16 × 16	–
Conv 3 × 3	LReLU	512 × 16 × 16	2.4M
Conv 3 × 3	LReLU	512 × 16 × 16	2.4M
Upsample	–	512 × 32 × 32	–
Conv 3 × 3	LReLU	512 × 32 × 32	2.4M
Conv 3 × 3	LReLU	512 × 32 × 32	2.4M
Upsample	–	512 × 64 × 64	–
Conv 3 × 3	LReLU	256 × 64 × 64	1.2M
Conv 3 × 3	LReLU	256 × 64 × 64	590k
Upsample	–	256 × 128 × 128	–
Conv 3 × 3	LReLU	128 × 128 × 128	295k
Conv 3 × 3	LReLU	128 × 128 × 128	148k
Upsample	–	128 × 256 × 256	–
Conv 3 × 3	LReLU	64 × 256 × 256	74k
Conv 3 × 3	LReLU	64 × 256 × 256	37k
Upsample	–	64 × 512 × 512	–
Conv 3 × 3	LReLU	32 × 512 × 512	18k
Conv 3 × 3	LReLU	32 × 512 × 512	9.2k
Upsample	–	32 × 1024 × 1024	–
Conv 3 × 3	LReLU	16 × 1024 × 1024	4.6k
Conv 3 × 3	LReLU	16 × 1024 × 1024	2.3k
Conv 1 × 1	linear	3 × 1024 × 1024	51
Total trainable parameters			23.1M

Discriminator	Act.	Output shape	Params
Input image	–	3 × 1024 × 1024	–
Conv 1 × 1	LReLU	16 × 1024 × 1024	64
Conv 3 × 3	LReLU	16 × 1024 × 1024	2.3k
Conv 3 × 3	LReLU	32 × 1024 × 1024	4.6k
Downsample	–	32 × 512 × 512	–
Conv 3 × 3	LReLU	32 × 512 × 512	9.2k
Conv 3 × 3	LReLU	64 × 512 × 512	18k
Downsample	–	64 × 256 × 256	–
Conv 3 × 3	LReLU	64 × 256 × 256	37k
Conv 3 × 3	LReLU	128 × 256 × 256	74k
Downsample	–	128 × 128 × 128	–
Conv 3 × 3	LReLU	128 × 128 × 128	148k
Conv 3 × 3	LReLU	256 × 128 × 128	295k
Downsample	–	256 × 64 × 64	–
Conv 3 × 3	LReLU	256 × 64 × 64	590k
Conv 3 × 3	LReLU	512 × 64 × 64	1.2M
Downsample	–	512 × 32 × 32	–
Conv 3 × 3	LReLU	512 × 32 × 32	2.4M
Conv 3 × 3	LReLU	512 × 32 × 32	2.4M
Downsample	–	512 × 16 × 16	–
Conv 3 × 3	LReLU	512 × 16 × 16	2.4M
Conv 3 × 3	LReLU	512 × 16 × 16	2.4M
Downsample	–	512 × 8 × 8	–
Conv 3 × 3	LReLU	512 × 8 × 8	2.4M
Conv 3 × 3	LReLU	512 × 8 × 8	2.4M
Downsample	–	512 × 4 × 4	–
Minibatch stddev	–	513 × 4 × 4	–
Conv 3 × 3	LReLU	512 × 4 × 4	2.4M
Conv 4 × 4	LReLU	512 × 1 × 1	4.2M
Fully-connected	linear	1 × 1 × 1	513
Total trainable parameters			23.1M

Figure 6.20: Generator and discriminator model summary[19]

Hence, we will focus on the pretrained Pro-GAN model available through TensorFlow Hub. TensorFlow Hub is a repository of a large number of deep learning models that can be easily downloaded and used for various downstream tasks using the TensorFlow ecosystem. The following is a miniature example to showcase how we can use the Pro-GAN model.

The first step is to load the required libraries. With TensorFlow Hub, the only additional `import` required is:

```
import tensorflow_hub as hub
```

Image Generation with GANs

We used TensorFlow Hub version 0.12.0 with TensorFlow version 2.4.1. Make sure your versions are in sync otherwise there might be slight changes with respect to syntax. The next step is to load the model. We set a seed for our TensorFlow session to ensure the reproducibility of results:

```
tf.random.set_seed(12)
pro_gan = hub.load("https://tfhub.dev/google/progan-128/1").signatures['default']
```

Loading a pretrained model using TensorFlow Hub is as simple as the preceding code. The next step is about randomly sampling a latent vector (*z*) from a normal distribution. The model requires the latent vector to be of size 512. Once we have the latent vector, we pass it to our generator to get the output:

```
vector = tf.random.normal([1, 512])
sample_image = pro_gan(vector)['default'][0]
np_img = sample_image.numpy()
plt.figure(figsize=(6,6))
plt.imshow(np_img)
```

The following is a sample face generated from the pretrained Pro-GAN model (*Figure 6.21*):

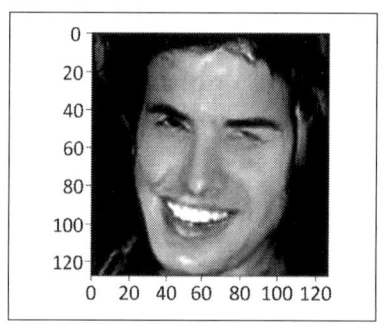

Figure 6.21: Sample face using pretrained Pro-GAN from TF Hub

We wrote a simple sampling function, similar to one we have been using throughout the chapter to generate a few additional faces. This additional experiment helps us to understand the diversity of human faces this model has been able to capture and, of course, its triumph over issues such as mode collapse (more on this in the next section). The following image (*Figure 6.22*) is a sample of 25 such faces:

Figure 6.22: 25 faces generated using Pro-GAN

If you are curious, TensorFlow Hub provides a training mechanism to train such models from scratch. Also, the Pro-GAN authors have open-sourced their implementation. You are encouraged to go through it.

We have covered a lot of ground to understand different architectures and their ability to generate images. In the next section, we will cover some of the challenges associated with GANs.

Challenges

GANs provide an alternative method of developing generative models. Their design inherently helps in mitigating the issues we discussed with some of the other techniques. However, GANs are not free from their own set of issues. The choice to develop models using concepts of game theory is fascinating yet difficult to control. We have two agents/models trying to optimize opposing objectives, which can lead to all sorts of issues. Some of the most common challenges associated with GANs are as follows.

Training instability

GANs play a minimax game with opposing objectives. No wonder this leads to oscillating losses for generator and discriminator models across batches. A GAN setup that is training well will typically have a higher variation in losses initially but, eventually, it will stabilize and so will the loss of the two competing models. Yet it is very common for GANs (especially vanilla GANs) to spiral out of control. It is difficult to determine when to stop the training or to estimate an equilibrium state.

Mode collapse

Mode collapse refers to a failure state where the generator finds one or only a small number of samples that are enough to fool the discriminator. To understand this better, let's take the example of a hypothetical dataset of temperatures from two cities, city **A** and city **B**. Let's also assume city **A** is at a higher altitude and remains cold mostly while city **B** is near the equator and has high temperatures. Such a dataset might have a temperature distribution as shown in *Figure 6.23*. The distribution is bimodal, that is, it has two peaks: one for city **A** and one for city **B** (due to their different weather conditions).

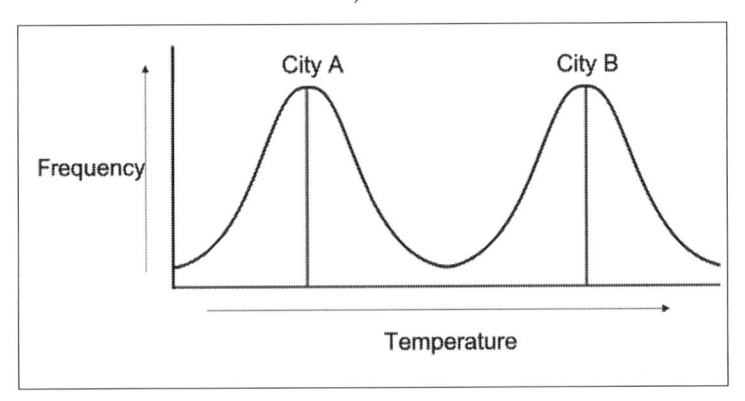

Figure 6.23: Bimodal distribution of the temperatures of two cities

Now that we have our dataset, assume we are tasked with training a GAN that can mimic this distribution. In the perfect scenario, we will have the GAN generate samples of temperatures from city **A** and city **B** with roughly equal probability. However, a commonly occurring issue is that of mode collapse: the generator ends up generating samples only from a single mode (say, only city **B**). This happens when:

- The generator learns to fool the discriminator by generating realistic-looking samples from city **B** only
- The discriminator tries to counter this by learning that all outputs for city **A** are real and tries to classify samples from city **B** as real or fake
- The generator then flips to city **A**, abandoning the mode for city **B**
- The discriminator now assumes all samples for city **B** are real and tries to classify samples for city **A** instead
- This cycle keeps on repeating

This cycle repeats as the generator is never incentivized enough to cover both modes. This limits the usefulness of the generator as it exhibits poor diversity of output samples. In a real-world setting, mode collapse varies from complete collapse (that is, all generated samples are identical) to partial collapse (that is, a few modes are captured).

We have trained different GAN architectures in the chapter so far. The MNIST dataset is also multimodal in nature. A complete collapse for such a dataset would result in the GAN generating only a single digit as output, while a partial collapse would mean only a few digits were generated (out of 10). *Figure 6.24* shows the two scenarios for vanilla GAN:

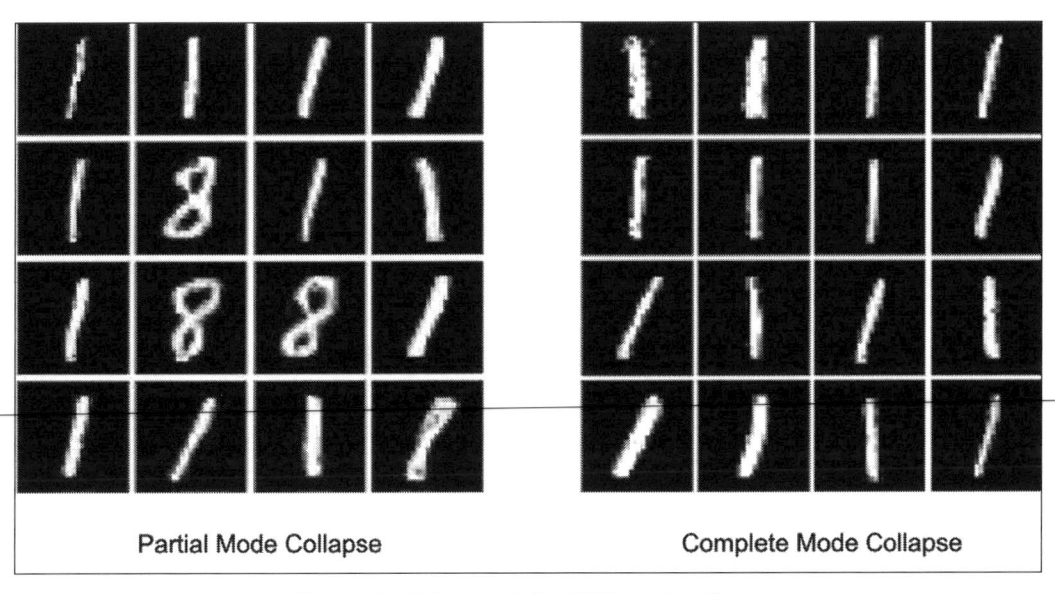

Figure 6.24: Failure mode for GAN - mode collapse

Figure 6.24 shows how mode collapse can lead to limited diversity in the samples that a GAN can generate.

Uninformative loss and evaluation metrics

Neural networks train using gradient descent and improve upon the loss values. Yet in the case of GANs (except W-GAN and related architectures), the loss values are mostly uninformative. We would assume that as training progresses, the generator loss would keep on decreasing while the discriminator would hit a saddle point, but this is not the case. The main reason is the alternate training cycles for generator and discriminator models. The generator loss at any given point is compared against the discriminator trained so far, thus making it difficult to compare the generator's performance across training epochs. You should note that in the case of W-GAN, critic loss in particular is the guiding signal for improving the generator model.

Apart from these issues, GANs also need a strict evaluation metric to understand the output quality of the samples. Inception score is one such way of calculating the output quality, yet there is scope for identifying better evaluation metrics in this space.

Summary

In this chapter, you were introduced to a new class of generative models called Generative Adversarial Networks. Inspired by concepts of game theory, GANs present an implicit method of modeling the data generation probability density. We started the chapter by first placing GANs in the overall taxonomy of generative models and comparing how these are different from some of the other methods we have covered in earlier chapters. Then we moved onto understanding the finer details of how GANs actually work by covering the value function for the minimax game, as well as a few variants like the non-saturating generator loss and the maximum likelihood game. We developed a multi-layer-perceptron-based vanilla GAN to generate MNIST digits using TensorFlow Keras APIs.

In the next section, we touched upon a few improved GANs in the form of Deep Convolutional GANs, Conditional GANs, and finally, Wasserstein GANs. We not only explored major contributions and enhancements, but also built some code bases to train these improved versions. The next section involved an advanced variant called Progressive GANs. We went through the nitty-gritty details of this advanced setup and used a pretrained model to generate fake faces. In the final section, we discussed a few common challenges associated with GANs.

This chapter was the foundation required before we jump into some even more advanced architectures in the upcoming chapters. We will cover additional topics in the computer vision space such as style transfer methods, face-swap/deep-fakes, and so on. We will also cover topics in domains such as text and audio. Stay tuned!

References

1. Goodfellow, I J., Pouget-Abadie, J., Mirza, M., Xu, B., Warde-Farley, D., Ozair, S., Courville, A., Bengio, Y. (2014). *Generative Adversarial Networks*. arXiv:1406.2661. https://arxiv.org/abs/1406.2661

2. Samples: https://thispersondoesnotexist.com/ (left) and https://thisartworkdoesnotexist.com/ (right)

3. Adapted from *Ian Goodfellow, Tutorial on Generative Adversarial Networks, 2017*

4. Goodfellow, I J., Pouget-Abadie, J., Mirza, M., Xu, B., Warde-Farley, D., Ozair, S., Courville, A., Bengio, Y. (2014). *Generative Adversarial Networks*. arXiv:1406.2661. https://arxiv.org/abs/1406.2661

5. Adapted from lecture 13 CS231: http://cs231n.stanford.edu/slides/2017/cs231n_2017_lecture13.pdf

6. Goodfellow, I J., Pouget-Abadie, J., Mirza, M., Xu, B., Warde-Farley, D., Ozair, S., Courville, A., Bengio, Y. (2014). *Generative Adversarial Networks*. arXiv:1406.2661. https://arxiv.org/abs/1406.2661

7. Radford, A., Metz, L., Chintala, S. (2015). *Unsupervised Representation Learning with Deep Convolutional Generative Adversarial Networks*. arXiv:1511.06434. https://arxiv.org/abs/1511.06434

8. Radford, A., Metz, L., Chintala, S. (2015). *Unsupervised Representation Learning with Deep Convolutional Generative Adversarial Networks*. arXiv:1511.06434. https://arxiv.org/abs/1511.06434

9. Mirza, M., Osindero, S. (2014). *Conditional Generative Adversarial Nets*. arXiv:1411.1784. https://arxiv.org/abs/1411.1784

10. Mirza, M., Osindero, S. (2014). *Conditional Generative Adversarial Nets*. arXiv:1411.1784. https://arxiv.org/abs/1411.1784

11. Arjovsky, M., Chintala, S., Bottou, L. (2017). *Wasserstein GAN*. arXiv:1701.07875. https://arxiv.org/abs/1701.07875

12. Arjovsky, M., Chintala, S., Bottou, L. (2017). *Wasserstein GAN*. arXiv:1701.07875. https://arxiv.org/abs/1701.07875

13. Gulrajani, I., Ahmed, F., Arjovsky, M., Courville, A. (2017). *Improved Training of Wasserstein GANs*. arXiv:1704.00028. https://arxiv.org/abs/1704.00028

14. Karras, T., Aila, T., Laine, S., Lehtinen, J. (2017). "*Progressive Growing of GANs for Improved Quality, Stability, and Variation*". arXiv:1710.10196. https://arxiv.org/abs/1710.10196

15. Karras, T., Aila, T., Laine, S., Lehtinen, J. (2017). *Progressive Growing of GANs for Improved Quality, Stability, and Variation*. arXiv:1710.10196. https://arxiv.org/abs/1710.10196

16. Bengio Y., Lamblin P., Popovici D., Larochelle H. (2006). *Greedy Layer-Wise Training of Deep Networks*. In Proceedings of the 19th International Conference on Neural Information Processing Systems (NIPS'06). MIT Press, Cambridge, MA, USA, 153–160. https://dl.acm.org/doi/10.5555/2976456.2976476

17. Karras, T., Aila, T., Laine, S., Lehtinen, J. (2017). *Progressive Growing of GANs for Improved Quality, Stability, and Variation*. arXiv:1710.10196. https://arxiv.org/abs/1710.10196

18. Progressive GAN official implementation: https://github.com/tkarras/progressive_growing_of_gans

19. Karras, T., Aila, T., Laine, S., Lehtinen, J. (2017). *Progressive Growing of GANs for Improved Quality, Stability, and Variation*. arXiv:1710.10196. https://arxiv.org/abs/1710.10196

7
Style Transfer with GANs

Neural networks are improving in a number of tasks involving analytical and linguistic skills. Creativity is one sphere where humans have had an upper hand. Not only is art subjective and has no defined boundaries, it is also difficult to quantify. Yet this has not stopped researchers from exploring the creative capabilities of algorithms. There have been several successful attempts at creating, understanding, and even copying art or artistic styles over the years, a few examples being *Deep Dream*[1] and *Neural Style Transfer.*[2]

Generative models are well suited to tasks associated with imagining and creating. **Generative Adversarial Networks (GANs)** in particular have been studied and explored in detail for the task of style transfer over the years. One such example is presented in *Figure 7.1*, where the CycleGAN architecture has been used to successfully transform photographs into paintings using the styles of famous artists such as Monet and Van Gogh.

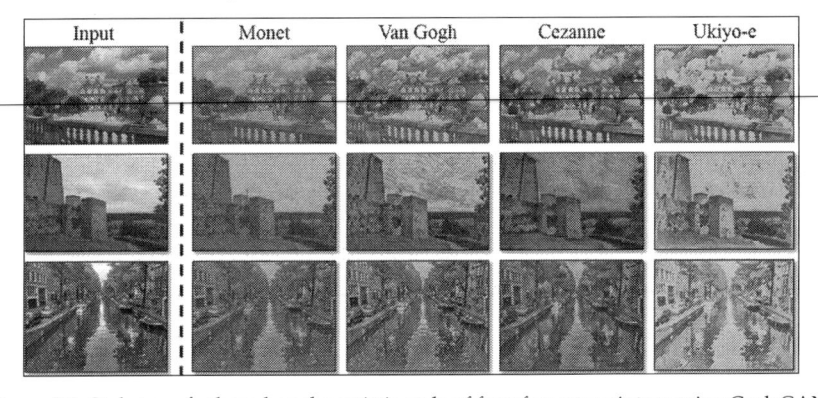

Figure 7.1: Style transfer based on the artistic style of four famous painters using CycleGAN[3]

Figure 7.1 gives us a visual sense of how style transfer works. The samples show that the CycleGAN model is able to preserve the details and structures of the input image, yet transforms it in a way that mimics famous painters' works. In other words, style transfer is a technique that transforms an input image such that it adopts the visual style of another/reference image.

In this chapter, we will cover style transfer methods using different GAN architectures. We will focus on the following aspects:

- Image-to-image paired style transfer techniques
- Image-to-image unpaired style transfer techniques
- Related works

We will cover the internal workings of different GAN architectures and key contributions that have enabled the style transfer setup. We will also build and train these architectures from scratch to get a better understanding of how they work.

> All code snippets presented in this chapter can be run directly in Google Colab. For reasons of space, import statements for dependencies have not been included, but readers can refer to the GitHub repository for the full code: https://github.com/PacktPublishing/Hands-On-Generative-AI-with-Python-and-TensorFlow-2

Let's get started by looking at paired style transfer.

Paired style transfer using pix2pix GAN

In *Chapter 6, Image Generation with GANs*, we discussed a number of innovations related to GAN architectures that led to improved results and better control of the output class. One of those innovations was conditional GANs. This simple yet powerful addition to the GAN setup enabled us to navigate the latent vector space and control the generator to generate specific outputs. We experimented with a simple MNIST conditional GAN where we were able to generate the output of our choice.

In this section, we will cover a variant of conditional GANs in the context of style transfer. We will go through details of the pix2pix architecture, discuss the important components and also train a paired style transfer network of our own. We will close this section with some amazing and innovative use cases of such a capability.

Style transfer is an intriguing research area, pushing the boundaries of creativity and deep learning together. In their work titled *Image-to-Image Translation with Conditional Adversarial Networks*,[4] Isola and Zhu et al. present a conditional GAN network that is able to learn task-specific loss functions and thus work across datasets. As the name suggests, this GAN architecture takes a specific type of image as input and transforms it into a different domain. It is called pair-wise style transfer as the training set needs to have matching samples from both source and target domains. This generic approach is shown to effectively synthesize high-quality images from label maps and edge maps, and even colorize images. The authors highlight the importance of developing an architecture capable of understanding the dataset at hand and learning mapping functions without the need for hand-engineering (which has been the case typically).

This work presents a number of contributions on top of the conditional GAN architecture. Some of these contributions have been used in other works as well, with the authors citing the required references in their work. We encourage readers to go through these for an in-depth understanding. We will now cover each component of the pix2pix GAN setup in detail.

The U-Net generator

Deep convolutional generators were explored as part of the DC-GAN setup in *Chapter 6, Image Generation with GANs*. Since CNNs are optimized for computer vision tasks, using them for generator as well as discriminator architectures has a number of advantages. This work focuses on two related architectures for the generator setup. The two choices are the vanilla encoder-decoder architecture and the encoder-decoder architecture with skip connections. The architecture with skip connections has more in common with the U-Net model[5] than the encoder-decoder setup. Hence, the generator in the pix2pix GAN is termed a U-Net generator. See *Figure 7.2* for reference:

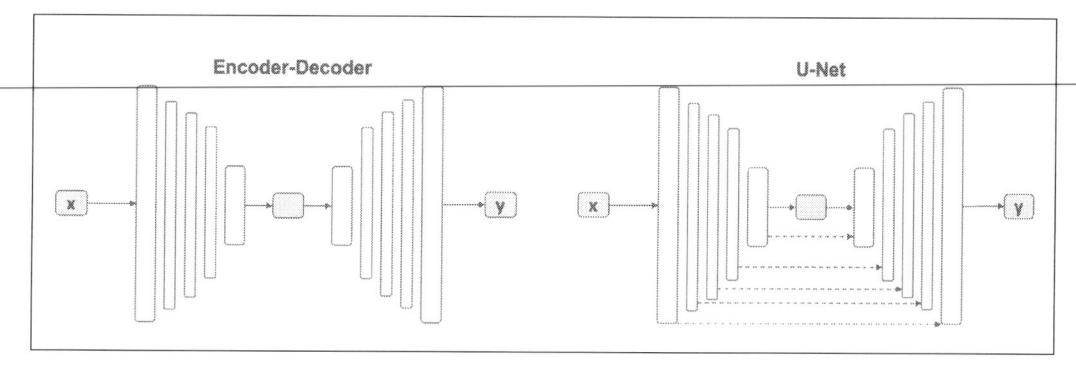

Figure 7.2: (left) Encoder-decoder generator. (right) Encoder-decoder with skip connections, or a U-Net generator

A typical encoder (in the encoder-decoder setup) takes an input and passes it through a series of downsampling layers to generate a condensed vector form. This condensed vector is termed the bottleneck features. The decoder part then upsamples the bottleneck features to generate the final output. This setup is extremely useful in a number of scenarios, such as language translation and image reconstruction. The bottleneck features condense the overall input into a lower-dimensional space.

Theoretically, the bottleneck features capture all the required information, but practically this becomes difficult when the input space is large enough.

Additionally, for our task of image-to-image translation, there are a number of important features that need to be consistent between the input and output images. For example, if we are training our GAN to generate aerial photos out of outline maps, the information associated with roads, water bodies, and other low-level information needs to be preserved between inputs and outputs, as shown in *Figure 7.3*:

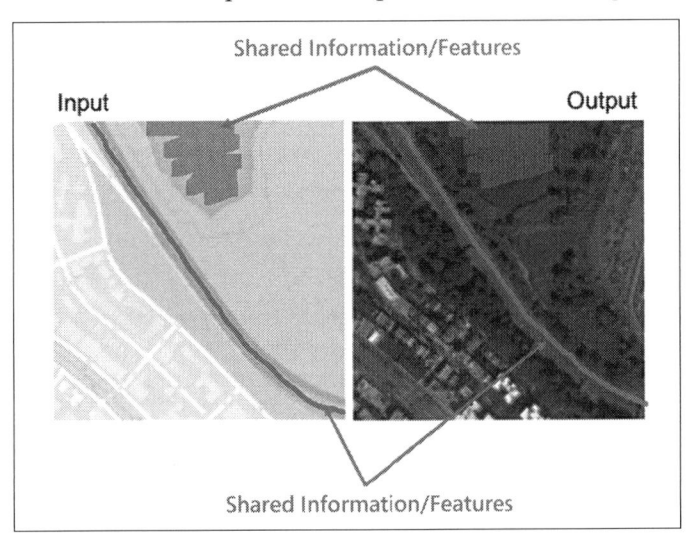

Figure 7.3: The U-Net architecture enables the generator to ensure features are consistent between the input and the generated output

The U-Net architecture uses skip connections to shuttle important features between the input and output (see *Figures 7.2* and *7.3*). In the case of the pix2pix GAN, skip connections are added between every i^{th} down-sampling layer and $(n - i)^{th}$ over-sampling layer, where n is the total number of layers in the generator. The skip connection leads to the concatenation of all channels from the ith to $(n - i)^{th}$ layers, with the ith layers being appended to the $(n - i)^{th}$ layers:

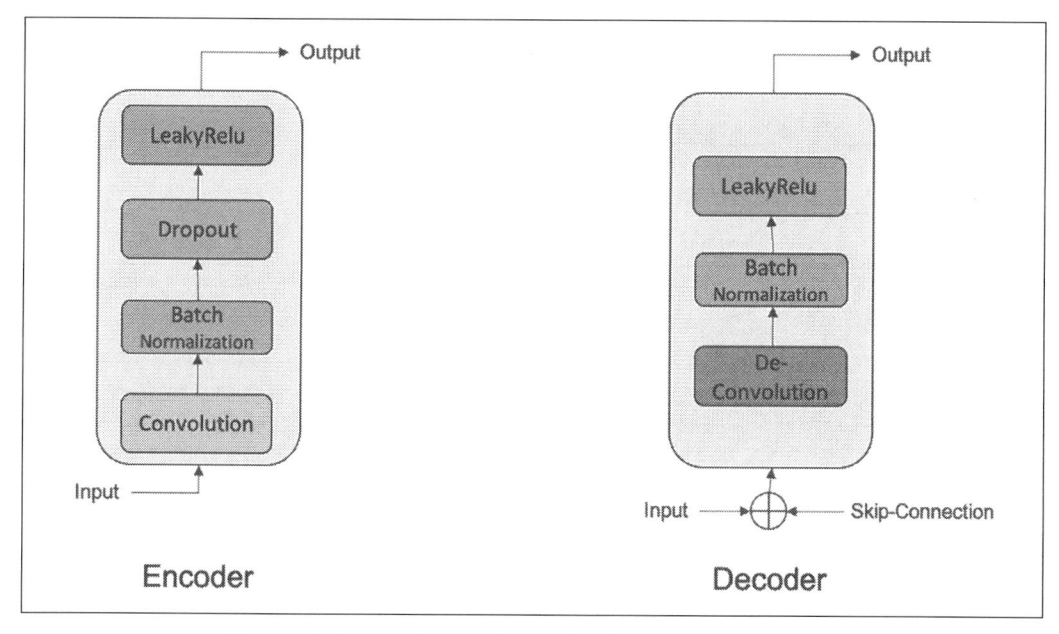

Figure 7.4: The encoder and decoder blocks of the U-Net generator

The generator presented in the paper follows a repeating block structure for both encoder and decoder parts. Each encoder block consists of a convolutional layer followed by a batch normalization layer, dropout layer, and leaky ReLU activation. Every such block downsamples by a factor of 2, using a stride of 2.

The decoder blocks use a transposed-convolution layer followed by batch normalization and leaky ReLU activation. Each block upsamples by a factor of 2. A simplified setup of encoder and decoder blocks is shown in *Figure 7.4*. As mentioned earlier, each of these blocks is connected using a skip connection as well. Equipped with this knowledge about the generator, let's get onto implementation details.

Firstly, let us prepare utility methods for downsampling and upsampling blocks of the U-Net generator. The downsampling block uses a stack comprised of convolutional layers, followed by leaky ReLU activation, and finally an optional batch normalization layer.

The `downsample_block` helper function below takes input parameters for the number of filters required, kernel size, and whether we need batch normalization or not:

```
def downsample_block(incoming_layer,
                    num_filters,
                    kernel_size=4,
                    batch_normalization=True):

    downsample_layer = Conv2D(num_filters,
                        kernel_size=kernel_size,
                        strides=2, padding='same')(incoming_layer)
    downsample_layer = LeakyReLU(alpha=0.2)(downsample_layer)
    if batch_normalization:
        downsample_layer = BatchNormalization(momentum=0.8)(downsample_layer)
    return downsample_layer
```

The next helper function is the upsampling block. Each upsampling block is a stack comprised of an upsampling layer followed by a convolutional 2D layer, an optional dropout layer, and finally the batch normalization layer.

As mentioned earlier, the decoder part of the network also makes use of skip connections from the encoder layers. Apart from the input parameters for the number of filters, kernel size, and so on, we also provide an additional parameter for the skip connection. The following snippet implements this `upsample_block` function:

```
def upsample_block(incoming_layer,
                  skip_input_layer,
                  num_filters,
                  kernel_size=4,
                  dropout_rate=0):
    upsample_layer = UpSampling2D(size=2)(incoming_layer)
    upsample_layer = Conv2D(num_filters,
                        kernel_size=kernel_size,
                        strides=1,
                        padding='same',
                        activation='relu')(upsample_layer)
    if dropout_rate:
        upsample_layer = Dropout(dropout_rate)(upsample_layer)
    upsample_layer = BatchNormalization(momentum=0.8)(upsample_layer)
    upsample_layer = Concatenate()([upsample_layer, skip_input_layer])
    return upsample_layer
```

In the next snippet, we leverage these methods to prepare our generator model. We start by defining the input layer with a specific input shape. The next step is to prepare the encoder. For this, we will use the helper function `downsample_block()`. We stack seven such blocks with an increasing number of filters.

The final piece of the puzzle is to prepare the decoder. For this, we stack seven decoder blocks using the `upsample_block()` function, with skip connections from the encoder layers. The following snippet implements this:

```
def build_generator(img_shape,channels=3,num_filters=64):
    # Image input
    input_layer = Input(shape=img_shape)

    # Downsampling
    down_sample_1 = downsample_block(input_layer,
                                    num_filters,
                                    batch_normalization=False)
    # rest of the downsampling blocks have batch_normalization=true
    down_sample_2 = downsample_block(down_sample_1, num_filters*2)
    down_sample_3 = downsample_block(down_sample_2, num_filters*4)
    down_sample_4 = downsample_block(down_sample_3, num_filters*8)
    down_sample_5 = downsample_block(down_sample_4, num_filters*8)
    down_sample_6 = downsample_block(down_sample_5, num_filters*8)
    down_sample_7 = downsample_block(down_sample_6, num_filters*8)

    # Upsampling blocks with skip connections
    upsample_1 = upsample_block(down_sample_7, down_sample_6,
                                num_filters*8)
    upsample_2 = upsample_block(upsample_1, down_sample_5,
                                num_filters*8)
    upsample_3 = upsample_block(upsample_2, down_sample_4,
                                num_filters*8)
    upsample_4 = upsample_block(upsample_3, down_sample_3,
                                num_filters*8)
    upsample_5 = upsample_block(upsample_4, down_sample_2,
                                num_filters*2)
    upsample_6 = upsample_block(upsample_5, down_sample_1, num_filters)

    upsample_7 = UpSampling2D(size=2)(upsample_6)
    output_img = Conv2D(channels,
                        kernel_size=4,
                        strides=1,
                        padding='same',
                        activation='tanh')(upsample_7)

    return Model(input_layer, output_img)
```

This shows the ease with which we can leverage building blocks to form complex architectures such as the U-Net generator. Let us now understand the details associated with the discriminator for pix2pix.

The Patch-GAN discriminator

A typical discriminator works by taking an input image and classifies it as fake or real, that is, generates a single output scalar. In the case of a conditional discriminator, there are two inputs, the first being the conditional input and the second the generated sample (from the generator) for classification. For our image-to-image transfer use case, the discriminator is provided with a source image (conditional input) as well as the generated sample, and its aim is to predict whether the generated sample is a plausible transformation of the source or not.

The authors of pix2pix propose a Patch-GAN setup for the discriminator, which takes the two required inputs and generates an output of size N x N. *Figure 7.5* illustrates the concept of Patch-GAN in a simplified manner.

A typical discriminator simply classifies the complete input as either fake or real (as shown on the left in *Figure 7.5*). In the case of Patch-GAN, the discriminator divides the whole input into a number of smaller patches. These patches are then individually classified as fake or real (as shown on the right in *Figure 7.5*). Each x_{ij} element of the N x N output signifies whether the corresponding patch *ij* in the generated image is real or fake. Each output patch can be traced back to its initial input patch based on the effective receptive field for each of the layers. We will code a short snippet to calculate the receptive field for a given N x N input:

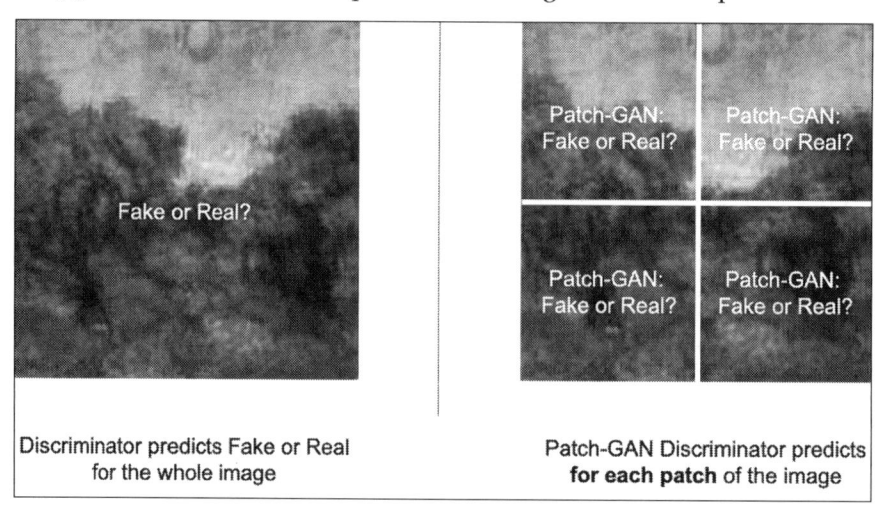

Figure 7.5: Simplified illustration to understand the workings of a Patch-GAN discriminator

The configuration presented in the paper uses three Patch-GAN layers using a kernel size of 4 x 4 and a stride of 2. The final two layers use a kernel size of 4 x 4 with a stride of 1. This leads to a 70 x 70 Patch-GAN setup, that is, each output pixel/cell/element in the $N \times N$ output matrix corresponds to a 70 x 70 patch of the input image. Each such 70 x 70 patch has high overlaps as the input image has a size of 256 x 256. To understand this better, let's work through the calculation of effective receptive fields using the following snippet:

```python
def get_receptive_field(output_size, ksize, stride):
    return (output_size - 1) * stride + ksize

last_layer = get_receptive_field(output_size=1, ksize=4, stride=1)
# Receptive field: 4

fourth_layer = get_receptive_field(output_size=last_layer, ksize=4,
stride=1)
# Receptive field: 7

third_layer = get_receptive_field(output_size=fourth_layer, ksize=4,
stride=2)
# Receptive field: 16

second_layer = get_receptive_field(output_size=third_layer, ksize=4,
stride=2)
# Receptive field: 34

first_layer = get_receptive_field(output_size=second_layer, ksize=4,
stride=2)
# Receptive field: 70

print(first_layer)
```

The snippet shows the calculation for understanding how each output pixel corresponds to a patch of size 70 x 70 in the initial input image.

The intuitive way of understanding this is to assume that the model prepares multiple overlapping patches of the input image and tries to classify each patch as fake or real, then averages them to prepare the overall result. This is shown to improve the overall output quality of the generated images.

The authors experiment with different patch sizes ranging from 1 x 1 (Pixel-GAN) to 256 x 256 (Image-GAN), but they report best results with the 70 x 70 configuration (Patch-GAN) and little to no improvements beyond it.

Intuitively, we can perhaps reason why: in style transfer, the goal is to copy local characteristics from the source image onto the target image, so the patch size needs to best serve this goal; a pixel-level patch size is too narrow and loses sight of larger characteristics, while an image-level patch size is insensitive to local variation within the image.

Let's now prepare our Patch-GAN discriminator using TensorFlow 2. The first step is to prepare a utility for defining a discriminator block consisting of a convolutional layer, leaky ReLU, and an optional batch normalization layer:

```
def discriminator_block(incoming_layer,
                        num_filters,
                        kernel_size = 4,
                        batch_normalization=True):

    disc_layer = Conv2D(num_filters,
                        kernel_size = kernel_size,
                        strides=2,
                        padding='same')(incoming_layer)
    disc_layer = LeakyReLU(alpha = 0.2)(disc_layer)
    if batch_normalization:
        disc_layer = BatchNormalization(momentum = 0.8)(disc_layer)
    return disc_layer
```

We will use these blocks to prepare the Patch-GAN discriminator as follows. The snippet below prepares a discriminator model that takes in two inputs (the generator's output and the conditioning image) followed by four discriminator blocks with an increasing number of filters:

```
def build_discriminator(img_shape,num_filters=64):
    input_img = Input(shape=img_shape)
    cond_img = Input(shape=img_shape)

    # Concatenate input and conditioning image by channels
    # as input for discriminator
    combined_input = Concatenate(axis=-1)([input_img, cond_img])

    # First discriminator block does not use batch_normalization
    disc_block_1 = discriminator_block(combined_input,
                                       num_filters,
                                       batch_normalization=False)
    disc_block_2 = discriminator_block(disc_block_1, num_filters*2)
    disc_block_3 = discriminator_block(disc_block_2, num_filters*4)
```

```
    disc_block_4 = discriminator_block(disc_block_3, num_filters*8)

    output = Conv2D(1, kernel_size=4, strides=1, padding='same')(disc_
block_4)

    return Model([input_img, cond_img], output)
```

Similar to the generator, we now have a function to build the required Patch-GAN discriminator. The next step is to understand the objective functions used to train the overall setup.

Loss

We discussed conditional GANs in detail in *Chapter 6, Image Generation with GANs*, where we introduced the overall conditional GAN objective function. Here it is again:

$$\mathcal{L}_{CGAN}(G,D) = min_G max_D V(G,D) = E_{x \sim p_{data}} log\, D(x|y) + E_{z \sim p_z} log(1 - D(G(z|y)))$$

The authors observe that the typical way of utilizing L1 and L2 regularization methods to improve output quality works by capturing low frequencies only, that is, local structures that contribute to the overall crispness of the generated image. L1 regularization helps prevent blurring compared to L2 regularization. Therefore, we can formulate L1 regularization as:

$$\mathcal{L}_{L1}(G) = E_{x,y,z} \|x - G(z|y)\|_1$$

where x is the source image, y is the conditioned input, and z is the noise vector. Coupling the U-Net setup with L1 regularization leads to the generation of sharp output images, where the GAN handles high frequencies while the L1 assists with low frequencies. The updated objective function can be stated as:

$$\mathcal{L}_{CGAN}^* = min_G max_D \mathcal{L}_{CGAN}(G,D) + \lambda \mathcal{L}_{L1}(G)$$

Similar to improvements suggested in the original GAN paper, pix2pix also maximizes $log(D(G(z|y)))$ instead of minimizing $log(1 - D(G(z|y)))$. This results in better feedback from gradient curves (refer to the section *Training GANs* in *Chapter 6, Image Generation with GANs*).

Training pix2pix

We now have all the required components ready. The final piece of the puzzle is to combine the generator and discriminator into a training loop for preparing the pix2pix GAN network.

We attach relevant loss functions to each of the component networks as well:

```
def train(generator,
          discriminator,
          gan,
          patch_gan_shape,
          epochs,
          path='/content/maps',
          batch_size = 1,
          sample_interval = 50):

    # Ground truth shape/Patch-GAN outputs
    real_y = np.ones((batch_size,) + patch_gan_shape)
    fake_y = np.zeros((batch_size,) + patch_gan_shape)

    for epoch in range(epochs):
      print("Epoch={}".format(epoch))
      for idx, (imgs_source, imgs_cond) in enumerate(batch_
generator(path=path, batch_size=batch_size,
                  img_res=[IMG_HEIGHT, IMG_WIDTH])):
          # train discriminator
          # generator generates outputs based on
          # conditioned input images
          fake_imgs = generator.predict([imgs_cond])

          # calculate discriminator loss on real samples
          disc_loss_real = discriminator.train_on_batch([imgs_source,
                                                         imgs_cond],
                                                        real_y)

          # calculate discriminator loss on fake samples
          disc_loss_fake = discriminator.train_on_batch([fake_imgs,
                                                         imgs_cond],
                                                        fake_y)

          # overall discriminator loss
          discriminator_loss = 0.5 * np.add(disc_loss_real,
                                            disc_loss_fake)

          # train generator
          gen_loss = gan.train_on_batch([imgs_source, imgs_cond],
                                        [real_y, imgs_source])

          # training updates every 50 iterations
```

```
            if idx % 50 == 0:
                print ("[Epoch {}/{}] [Discriminator loss: {}, accuracy:
 {}] [Generator loss: {}]".format(epoch, epochs,
                                               discriminator_loss[0],
                                               100*discriminator_loss[1],
                                               gen_loss[0]))


            # Plot and Save progress every few iterations
            if idx % sample_interval == 0:
                plot_sample_images(generator=generator,
                                   path=path,
                                   epoch=epoch,
                                   batch_num=idx,
                                   output_dir='images')
```

The above function takes the generator, discriminator, and the combined pix2pix GAN model object as inputs. Based on the size of the Patch-GAN discriminator, we define NumPy arrays for holding fake and real output predictions.

Similar to the way we trained GANs in the previous chapter, we loop through multiple iterations by first using the generator to generate a fake sample and then using this to get discriminator output. Finally, these outputs are used to calculate the loss and update the corresponding model weights.

Now that we have the training loop, the following snippet prepares the discriminator and GAN networks:

```
IMG_WIDTH = 256
IMG_HEIGHT = 256

# build discriminator
discriminator = build_discriminator(img_shape=(IMG_HEIGHT,IMG_WIDTH,3),
                                    num_filters=64)
discriminator.compile(loss='mse',
                      optimizer=Adam(0.0002, 0.5),
                      metrics=['accuracy'])

# build generator and GAN objects
generator = build_generator(img_shape=(IMG_HEIGHT,IMG_WIDTH,3),
                            channels=3,
                            num_filters=64)

source_img = Input(shape=(IMG_HEIGHT,IMG_WIDTH,3))
cond_img = Input(shape=(IMG_HEIGHT,IMG_WIDTH,3))
```

```
fake_img = generator(cond_img)

discriminator.trainable = False
output = discriminator([fake_img, cond_img])

gan = Model(inputs=[source_img, cond_img], outputs=[output, fake_img])
gan.compile(loss=['mse', 'mae'],
            loss_weights=[1, 100],
            optimizer=Adam(0.0002, 0.5))
```

The training loop is simple and similar to what we used in the previous chapter: for every epoch, we alternate between training the discriminator and the generator. The hyperparameters used are as stated in the pix2pix paper. The outputs from the model at different stages of training are showcased in *Figure 7.6*:

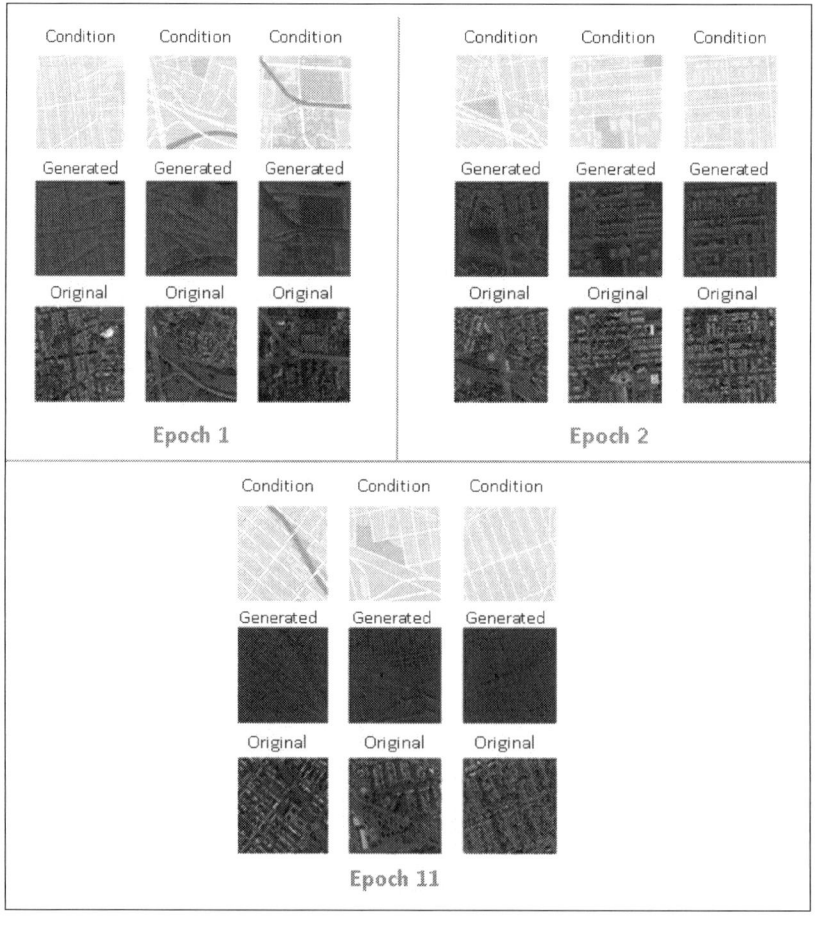

Figure 7.6: Pix2pix-generated outputs at different stages of training

Unlike the simpler architectures we trained in *Chapter 6, Image Generation with GANs*, despite being far more complex, the pix2pix GAN trains faster and stabilizes to far better results in fewer iterations. The outputs showcased in *Figure 7.6* show the model's ability to learn the mapping and generate high-quality outputs right from the first epoch. This can all be attributed to some of the innovations discussed in the previous sections.

Now that we've seen how to set up and train a pix2pix GAN for paired style transfer, let's look at some of the things it can be used for.

Use cases

The image-to-image translation setup opens up a lot of use cases and applications in the real world. The pix2pix setup provides a generic framework that can be applied to a number of image-to-image translation use cases without specifically engineering the architectures or loss functions. In their work, Isola and Zhu et al. present a number of interesting studies to showcase these capabilities.

This conditional GAN setup of the pix2pix GAN is capable of performing tasks such as:

- Building façade generation from label inputs
- Colorization of black and white images
- Transforming satellite/aerial map input images to Google Maps-like outputs
- Semantic segmentation tasks such as street view to segment labels
- Sketch to image tasks such as sketch to photo, sketch to portrait, sketch to cat, sketch to colored Pokémon, and even outline to fashion objects such as shoes, bags, and so on
- Background removal
- In-painting or image completion
- Thermal to RGB image translation
- Day to night scene and summer to winter scene conversion

Style Transfer with GANs

Some of the types of translations performed in the paper are shown in *Figure 7.7* for reference:

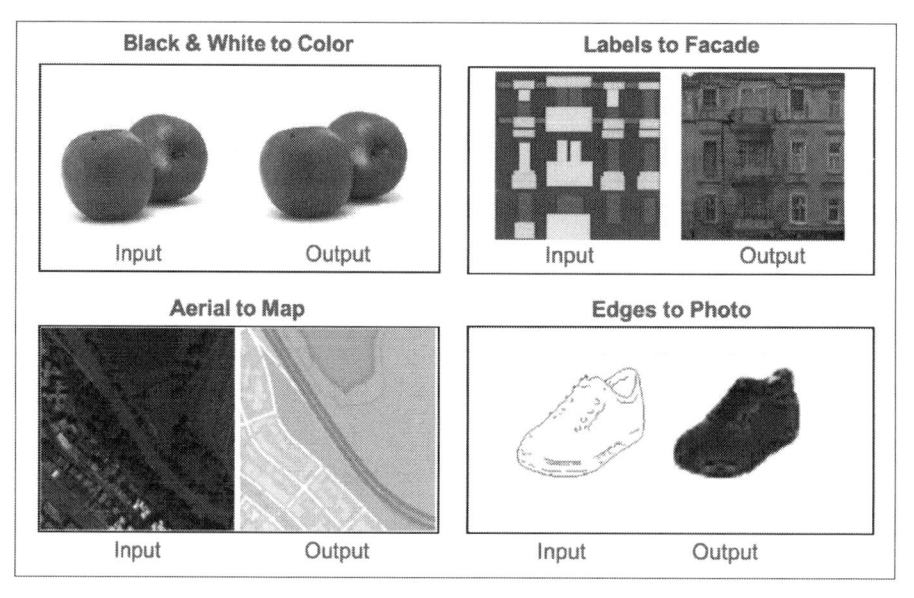

Figure 7.7: A few examples of different image-to-image translation tasks using pix2pix

As mentioned earlier, the pix2pix architecture is highly optimized and trains even on very small datasets. This enables many more creative use cases experimented with by the community and other researchers; the authors have developed a website for the paper where they showcase such use cases. We encourage readers to visit the website for more details: https://phillipi.github.io/pix2pix/.

Having discussed paired style transfer, next we're going to look at unpaired style transfer.

Unpaired style transfer using CycleGAN

Paired style transfer is a powerful setup with a number of use cases, some of which we discussed in the previous section. It provides the ability to perform cross-domain transfer given a pair of source and target domain datasets. The pix2pix setup also showcased the power of GANs to understand and learn the required loss functions without the need for manually specifying them.

While being a huge improvement over hand-crafted loss functions and previous works, paired style transfer is limited by the availability of paired datasets. Paired style transfer requires the input and output images to be structurally the same even though the domains are different (aerial to map, labels to scene, and so on). In this section, we will focus on an improved style transfer architecture called CycleGAN.

CycleGAN improves upon paired style transfer architecture by relaxing the constraints on input and output images. CycleGAN explores the unpaired style transfer paradigm where the model actually tries to learn the stylistic differences between source and target domains without explicit pairing between input and output images.

Zhu and Park et al. describe this unpaired style transfer as similar to our ability to imagine how Van Gogh or Monet would have painted a particular scene, without having actually seen a side-by-side example. Quoting from the paper[3]:

> *Instead, we have knowledge of the set of Monet paintings and of the set of landscape photographs. We can reason about the stylistic differences between these two sets, and thereby imagine what a scene might look like if we were to translate it from one set into the other.*

This provides a nice advantage as well as opening up additional use cases where an exact pairing of source and target domains is either not available or we do not have enough training examples.

Overall setup for CycleGAN

In the case of paired style transfer, the training dataset consists of paired samples, denoted as $\{x_i, y_i\}$, where x_i and y_i have correspondence between them. This is shown in *Figure 7.8 (a)* for reference:

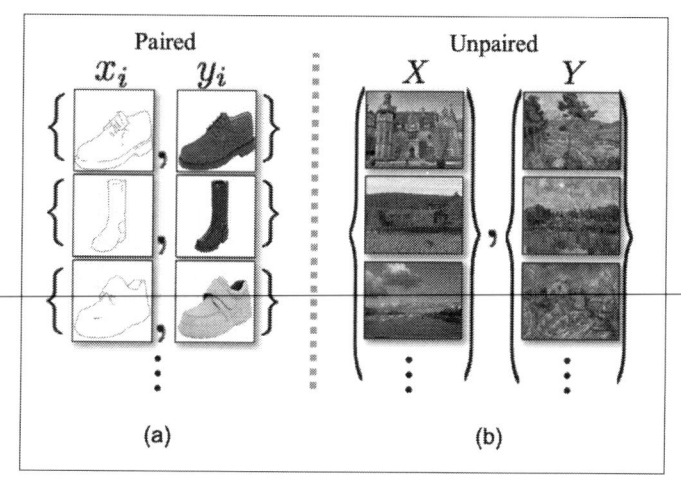

Figure 7.8: (a) Paired training examples. (b) Unpaired training examples. (Source: Zhu and Park et al. Unpaired Image-to-Image Translation using Cycle-Consistent Adversarial Networks, Figure 2)

Style Transfer with GANs

For CycleGAN, the training dataset consists of unpaired samples from the source set, denoted as $\{x_i\}_{i=1}^{N}$, and target set $\{y_j\}_{j=1}^{M}$, with no specific information regarding which x_i matches which y_j. See *Figure 7.8 (b)* for reference.

In the previous chapter, we discussed how GANs learn a mapping $G: X \to Y$ such that the output $\hat{y} = G(x)$ is indistinguishable from $y \in Y$. While this works well for other scenarios, it is not so good for unpaired image-to-image translation tasks. Due to the lack of paired samples, we cannot use the L1 loss as before to learn a G, so we need to formulate a different loss for unpaired style transfer. In general, when we learn the function $G(x)$, it is one of the numerous possibilities for learning Y. In other words, for a given X and Y, there are infinitely many Gs that will have the same distribution over $\hat{y}$.

In order to reduce the search space and add more constraints in our search for the best possible generator G, the authors introduced a property called **cycle consistency**. Mathematically, assume we have two generators, G and F, such that $G: X \to Y$ and $F: Y \to X$. In the best possible setting, G and F would be inverses of each other and should be bijections, that is, one-to-one. For CycleGAN, the authors train both generators, G and F, simultaneously for adversarial loss along with cycle consistency constraints to encourage $F(G(x)) \approx x$ and $G(F(y)) \approx y$. This results in the successful training of the unpaired style transfer GAN setup.

Please note that similar to the generators, we have two sets of discriminators as well in this setup, D_Y for G and D_X for F. The intuition behind this setup of having a pair of generators/discriminators is that we can learn the best possible translation from the source domain to target only if we are able to do the same in reverse order as well. *Figure 7.9* demonstrates the concept of cycle consistency pictorially:

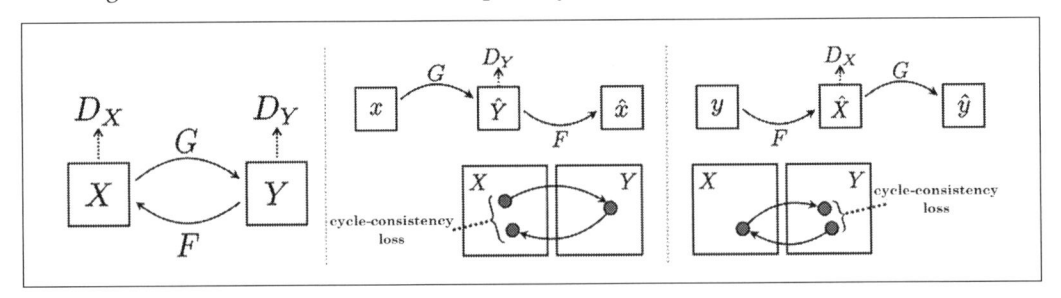

Figure 7.9: High-level schematic for CycleGAN[3]

The first section (left-most) of *Figure 7.9* depicts the CycleGAN setup. The setup shows two pairs of generators and discriminators, G & D_Y and F & D_X.

The middle section of *Figure 7.9* shows CycleGAN's forward cycle training. Input x is transformed to $\hat{Y}$ using G, and then F tries to regenerate the original input as $\hat{x}$. This pass updates G and D_Y. The cycle consistency loss helps to reduce the distance between x and its regenerated form $\hat{x}$.

Similarly, the third section (right-most) of *Figure 7.9* showcases the backward pass where y is transformed to X and then G tries to regenerate the original input as $\hat{y}$.

To better understand how the unpaired training setup works, let's walk through a generic example. Assume the task is to translate from English to French. A setup where the model has learned the best possible mapping of English to French would be the one which when reversed (that is, French to English) results in the original sentence.

Let's now look under the hood and understand each component in detail in the coming subsections.

Adversarial loss

A typical GAN uses adversarial loss to train a generator that is smart enough to fool a discriminator. In the case of CycleGAN, as we have two sets of generators and discriminators, we need some tweaking of the adversarial loss. Let us take it step by step.

For the first generator-discriminator set in our CycleGAN, that is, $G: X \rightarrow Y$, the adversarial loss can be defined as:

$$\mathcal{L}_{GAN}(G, D_Y, X, Y) = min_G max_{D_Y} V(G, D_Y, X, Y)$$

$$\Rightarrow \mathcal{L}_{GAN} = E_{y \sim p_{data}} \log D_Y(y) + E_{x \sim p_{data}} \log(1 - D_Y(G(x)))$$

Similarly, the second-generator-discriminator $F: Y \rightarrow X$ set is given as:

$$\mathcal{L}_{GAN}(F, D_X, Y, X) = min_G max_{D_X} V(F, D_X, Y, X)$$

Together, these two objectives form the first two terms of the overall objective for CycleGAN. One additional change to both sets of generator-discriminators is the minimization part. Instead of using the standard negative log likelihood, the choice is made in favor of least squares loss. It is denoted as:

$$\mathcal{L}_{GAN}(G, D, X, Y) = E_{y \sim p_{data}} \left[(D(G(y)) - 1)^2\right] + E_{x \sim p_{data}} \left[(D(G(x)))^2\right]$$

The least squares loss is observed to be more stable and leads to better quality output samples.

Cycle loss

We introduced the concept of cycle consistency earlier; now we'll see how to implement it explicitly. In their paper for CycleGAN, authors Zhu and Park et al. highlight that adversarial loss is not enough for the task of unpaired image-to-image translation. Not only is the search space too wide, but with enough capacity, the generator can fall into mode-collapse without learning about the actual characteristics of the source and target domains.

To reduce the search space and ensure the learned mappings are good enough, the CycleGAN setup should be able to generate the original input x after being processed through both G and F, that is, $x \to G(x) \to F(G(x)) \approx x$ as well as the reverse path of $y \to F(y) \to G(F(y)) \approx y$. These are termed as forward and backward cycle consistencies respectively. The overall cycle consistency loss is an L1 loss defined as:

$$\mathcal{L}_{cyc}(G,F) = E_{x \sim p_{data}} \|F(G(x)) - x\|_1 + E_{y \sim p_{data}} \|G(F(y)) - y\|_1$$

This loss ensures that the reconstruction of the original input from the generated output is as close as possible.

Identity loss

The authors for CycleGAN also observed a specific issue with the overall setup with respect to colored objects. Without any constraints specifically for colors, the G and F generators were found to be introducing different tints while going through the forward and backward cycles when none was necessary. To reduce this unwanted behavior, a regularization term called **identity loss** was introduced. See *Figure 7.10* showcasing this particular effect in action:

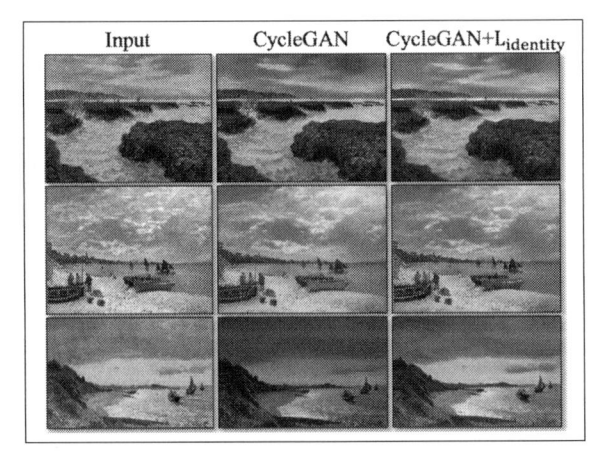

Figure 7.10 Impact of identity loss on CycleGAN performance. The outputs correspond to those of the generator G(x). (Source: Zhu and Park et al. Unpaired Image-to-Image Translation using Cycle-Consistent Adversarial Networks, Figure 9)

As is evident from the middle column in *Figure 7.10*, without the additional constraint of the identity loss, CycleGAN introduces unnecessary tints in its outputs. Thus, the identity loss, defined as $\mathcal{L}_{Identity}$, can be stated as:

$$\mathcal{L}_{Identity}(G, F) = E_{x \sim p_{data}} \|F(x) - x\|_1 + E_{y \sim p_{data}} \|G(y) - y\|_1$$

In simple words, this loss regularizes the generators to be near an identity mapping when real samples from the target domain are used as inputs for generation.

Overall loss

The overall objective of CycleGAN is simply a weighted sum of the different losses we discussed in the previous subsections, namely, the adversarial loss, the cycle consistency loss, and the identity loss. The overall objective is defined as:

$$\mathcal{L}_{cycleGAN}(G, F, D_X, D_Y) = \mathcal{L}_{GAN}(G, D_Y, X, Y) + \mathcal{L}_{GAN}(F, D_X, Y, X) + \lambda \mathcal{L}_{cyc}(G, F) + \eta \mathcal{L}_{Identity}(G, F)$$

The paper highlights different values for λ and η for different experiments. We will explicitly mention the value used for these regularization terms when we prepare our model from scratch.

Hands-on: Unpaired style transfer with CycleGAN

We discussed the overall setup for CycleGAN and its key innovations in the form of cycle consistency loss and identity loss, which enable unpaired style transfer. In this section, we will implement it, part by part, and train a couple of CycleGANs to convert apples to oranges and photos to Van Gogh paintings.

Generator setup

Let us begin with the generator. Similar to the pix2pix GAN, CycleGAN also makes use of U-Net generators (pay attention, there are two of them in this setup).

The first step is to prepare utility methods for upsampling and downsampling blocks. One important difference here is the use of **instance normalization** in place of the batch normalization layer. Instance normalization works by normalizing each channel in each training sample. This is in contrast to batch normalization, where normalization is done across the whole mini-batch and across all input features. See *Chapter 6, Image Generation with GANs*, for more details on instance normalization.

The following snippet prepares utilities for the two types of blocks. The function `downsample_block()` prepares a stack composed of a convolutional layer followed by leaky ReLU activation and an instance normalization layer. The function takes the number of filters and kernel size as inputs:

```
def downsample_block(incoming_layer,
                     num_filters,
                     kernel_size=4):
    downsample_layer = Conv2D(num_filters,
                        kernel_size=kernel_size,
                        strides=2, padding='same')(incoming_
layer)
    downsample_layer = LeakyReLU(alpha=0.2)(downsample_layer)
    downsample_layer = InstanceNormalization()(downsample_layer)
    return downsample_layer
```

Similarly, the following snippet shows the `upsample_block()` function. This function prepares a stack consisting of an upsampling layer followed by a convolutional layer, optional dropout, and instance normalization layer. Each upsampling block takes input from the previous layer as well as a skip connection as input:

```
def upsample_block(incoming_layer,
                   skip_input_layer,
                   num_filters,
                   kernel_size=4,
                   dropout_rate=0):

    upsample_layer = UpSampling2D(size=2)(incoming_layer)
    upsample_layer = Conv2D(num_filters,
                        kernel_size=kernel_size,
                        strides=1,
                        padding='same',
                        activation='relu')(upsample_layer)
    if dropout_rate:
        upsample_layer = Dropout(dropout_rate)(upsample_layer)
    upsample_layer = InstanceNormalization()(upsample_layer)
    upsample_layer = Concatenate()([upsample_layer, skip_input_layer])
    return upsample_layer
```

The U-Net generators used here are shallower compared to the pix2pix setup, yet perform equally well (see the section on *Cycle loss*). The following snippet demonstrates the method to build the generator:

```python
def build_generator(img_shape, channels=3, num_filters=32):
    # Image input
    input_layer = Input(shape=img_shape)
    
    # Downsampling
    down_sample_1 = downsample_block(input_layer, num_filters)
    down_sample_2 = downsample_block(down_sample_1, num_filters*2)
    down_sample_3 = downsample_block(down_sample_2,num_filters*4)
    down_sample_4 = downsample_block(down_sample_3,num_filters*8)
    
    # Upsampling
    upsample_1 = upsample_block(down_sample_4, down_sample_3,
                                                num_filters*4)
    upsample_2 = upsample_block(upsample_1, down_sample_2,
                                                num_filters*2)
    upsample_3 = upsample_block(upsample_2, down_sample_1, num_filters)
    
    upsample_4 = UpSampling2D(size=2)(upsample_3)
    output_img = Conv2D(channels,
                        kernel_size=4,
                        strides=1,
                        padding='same',
                        activation='tanh')(upsample_4)
    
    return Model(input_layer, output_img)
```

As we can see, the generator consists of four downsampling and four upsampling blocks, followed by a Conv2D layer that outputs the target image. Now let's build the discriminator.

Discriminator setup

Just like the generators, the discriminators used in CycleGAN make use of contributions from the pix2pix paper. The discriminators are Patch-GANs and the following code listing demonstrates a method for constructing a discriminator block as well as a method for building the discriminators:

```python
def discriminator_block(incoming_layer,
                        num_filters,
                        kernel_size=4,
                        instance_normalization=True):
```

```
    disc_layer = Conv2D(num_filters,
                        kernel_size=kernel_size,
                        strides=2,
                        padding='same')(incoming_layer)
    disc_layer = LeakyReLU(alpha=0.2)(disc_layer)
    if instance_normalization:
        disc_layer = InstanceNormalization()(disc_layer)
    return disc_layer


def build_discriminator(img_shape,num_filters=64):
    input_layer = Input(shape=img_shape)
    
    disc_block_1 = discriminator_block(input_layer,
                                        num_filters,
                                        instance_normalization=False)
    disc_block_2 = discriminator_block(disc_block_1, num_filters*2)
    disc_block_3 = discriminator_block(disc_block_2, num_filters*4)
    disc_block_4 = discriminator_block(disc_block_3, num_filters*8)
    
    output = Conv2D(1, kernel_size=4, strides=1, padding='same')(disc_block_4)
    
    return Model(input_layer, output)
```

We now have the building blocks ready. Let's use them to build the overall CycleGAN architecture.

GAN setup

We use these methods to prepare two sets of generators and discriminators required for mapping from domain A to B and then back from B to A. The following snippet does exactly this:

```
generator_filters = 32
discriminator_filters = 64

# input shape
channels = 3
input_shape = (IMG_HEIGHT, IMG_WIDTH, channels)

# Loss weights
lambda_cycle = 10.0
```

```python
lambda_identity = 0.1 * lambda_cycle

optimizer = Adam(0.0002, 0.5)

patch = int(IMG_HEIGHT / 2**4)
patch_gan_shape = (patch, patch, 1)

# Discriminators
disc_A = build_discriminator(input_shape,discriminator_filters)
disc_A.compile(loss='mse',
    optimizer=optimizer,
    metrics=['accuracy'])

disc_B = build_discriminator(input_shape,discriminator_filters)
disc_B.compile(loss='mse',
    optimizer=optimizer,
    metrics=['accuracy'])


# Generators
gen_AB = build_generator(input_shape,channels, generator_filters)
gen_BA = build_generator(input_shape, channels, generator_filters)

# CycleGAN
img_A = Input(shape=input_shape)
img_B = Input(shape=input_shape)

# generate fake samples from both generators
fake_B = gen_AB(img_A)
fake_A = gen_BA(img_B)

# reconstruct original samples from both generators
reconstruct_A = gen_BA(fake_B)
reconstruct_B = gen_AB(fake_A)

# generate identity samples
identity_A = gen_BA(img_A)
identity_B = gen_AB(img_B)

# disable discriminator training
disc_A.trainable = False
disc_B.trainable = False
```

```
# use discriminator to classify real vs fake
output_A = disc_A(fake_A)
output_B = disc_B(fake_B)

# Combined model trains generators to fool discriminators
gan = Model(inputs=[img_A, img_B],
            outputs=[output_A, output_B,
                    reconstruct_A, reconstruct_B,
                    identity_A, identity_B ])
gan.compile(loss=['mse', 'mse','mae', 'mae','mae', 'mae'],
            loss_weights=[1, 1,
                          lambda_cycle, lambda_cycle,
                          lambda_identity, lambda_identity ],
            optimizer=optimizer)
```

We just created objects for both pairs of generators and discriminators. We combine them in the gan object by defining the required inputs and outputs. Let's implement the training loop next.

The training loop

The final piece of the puzzle is to write a custom training loop. This loop first uses both generators to generate fake samples, which are then used to update the discriminators in both directions (that is, A to B and B to A). We finally use the updated discriminators to train the overall CycleGAN. The following snippet shows the training loop:

```
def train(gen_AB,
          gen_BA,
          disc_A,
          disc_B,
          gan,
          patch_gan_shape,
          epochs,
          path='/content/{}'.format(dataset_name),
          batch_size=1,
          sample_interval=50):

    # Adversarial loss ground truths
    real_y = np.ones((batch_size,) + patch_gan_shape)
    fake_y = np.zeros((batch_size,) + patch_gan_shape)

    for epoch in range(epochs):
```

```python
        print("Epoch={}".format(epoch))
        for idx, (imgs_A, imgs_B) in enumerate(batch_generator(path,
                                                    batch_size,
                                    image_res=[IMG_HEIGHT, IMG_WIDTH])):

            # train discriminators

            # generate fake samples from both generators
            fake_B = gen_AB.predict(imgs_A)
            fake_A = gen_BA.predict(imgs_B)

            # Train the discriminators
            # (original images = real / translated = Fake)
            disc_A_loss_real = disc_A.train_on_batch(imgs_A, real_y)
            disc_A_loss_fake = disc_A.train_on_batch(fake_A, fake_y)
            disc_A_loss = 0.5 * np.add(disc_A_loss_real,
                                    disc_A_loss_fake)

            disc_B_loss_real = disc_B.train_on_batch(imgs_B, real_y)
            disc_B_loss_fake = disc_B.train_on_batch(fake_B, fake_y)
            disc_B_loss = 0.5 * np.add(disc_B_loss_real,
                                    disc_B_loss_fake)

            # Total disciminator loss
            discriminator_loss = 0.5 * np.add(disc_A_loss, disc_B_loss)

            # train generator
            gen_loss = gan.train_on_batch([imgs_A, imgs_B],
                                        [
                                        real_y, real_y,
                                        imgs_A, imgs_B,
                                        imgs_A, imgs_B
                                        ]
                                    )

            # training updates every 50 iterations
            if idx % 50 == 0:
                print ("[Epoch {}/{}] [Discriminator loss: {}, accuracy: {}][Generator loss: {}, Adversarial Loss: {}, Reconstruction Loss: {}, Identity Loss: {}]".format(idx,
                            epoch,
                            discriminator_loss[0],
                            100*discriminator_loss[1],
```

```
                    gen_loss[0],
                    np.mean(gen_loss[1:3]),
                    np.mean(gen_loss[3:5]),
                    np.mean(gen_loss[5:6])))

    # Plot and Save progress every few iterations
    if idx % sample_interval == 0:
      plot_sample_images(gen_AB,
                         gen_BA,
                         path=path,
                         epoch=epoch,
                         batch_num=idx,
                         output_dir='images')
```

The training loop for CycleGAN is mostly similar to that of pix2pix with a few additions. As we have two pairs of generators and discriminators, the function takes all four models as input along with a combined gan object. The training loop starts with the generation of fake samples from both generators and then uses them to update weights for their corresponding discriminators. These are then combined to train the overall GAN model as well.

Using the components described in this section, we experimented with two sets of style transfer datasets, turning apples into oranges and turning photographs into Van Gogh paintings. *Figure 7.11* shows the output of the apples to oranges experiment through different stages of training:

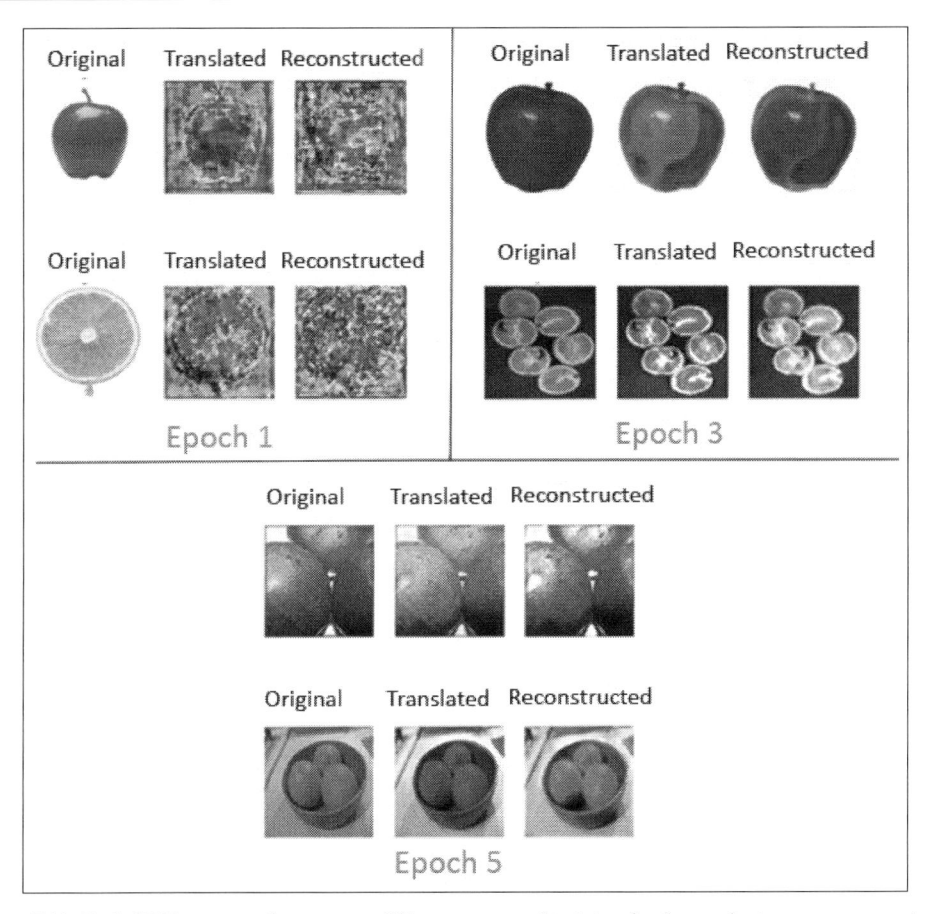

Figure 7.11: CycleGAN generated outputs at different stages of training for the apples to oranges experiment

Similarly, *Figure 7.12* shows how CycleGAN learns to transform photographs into Van Gogh style artwork:

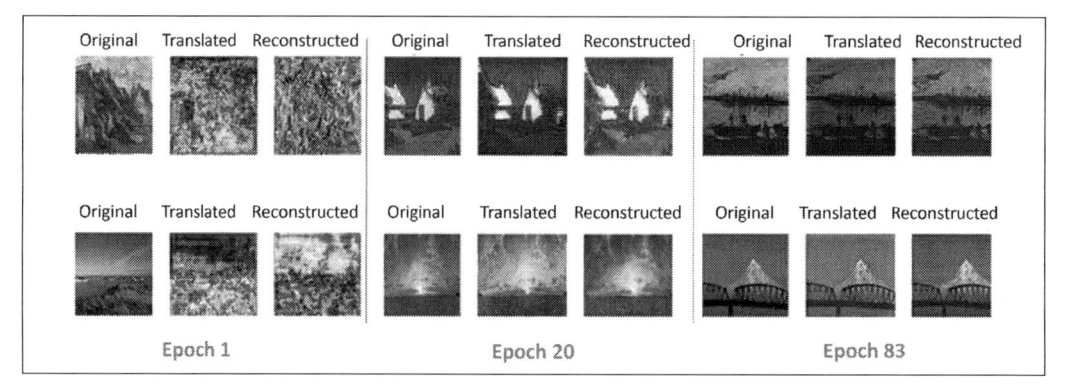

Figure 7.12: CycleGAN generated outputs at different stages of training for the photographs to Van Gogh style paintings experiment

As is evident from the samples above (*Figures 7.11* and *7.12*), CycleGAN seems to have picked up the nuances from both domains without having paired training samples. This is a good leap forward in cases where paired samples are hard to get.

Another important observation from the two experiments is the amount of training required. While both experiments used exactly the same setup and hyperparameters, the apples to oranges experiment trained much faster compared to the photograph to Van Gogh style painting setup. This could be attributed to the large number of modes in the case of the second experiment, along with diversity in the training samples.

This ends our section on unpaired style transfer. Now we're going to explore some work relating to and branching off from both paired and unpaired style transfer.

Related works

Style transfer is an amusing field and a lot of parallel research is going on across different research groups to improve the state of the art. The two most influential works in the paired and unpaired style transfer space have been discussed in this chapter so far. There have been a few more related works in this space that are worth discussing.

In this section, we will briefly discuss two more works in the unpaired image-to-image translation space that have similar ideas to CycleGAN. Specifically, we will touch upon the DiscoGAN and DualGAN setups, as they present similar ideas with minor changes.

Chapter 7

It is important to note that there are a number of other works in the same space. We limit our discussion to only a few of them for the sake of completeness and consistency. Readers are encouraged to explore other interesting architectures as well.

DiscoGAN

Kim and Cha et al. presented a model that discovers cross-domain relations with GANs called DiscoGAN.[6] The task of transforming black and white images to colored images, satellite images to map-like images, and so on can also termed *cross-domain transfer*, as well as style transfer.

As we've seen already, cross-domain transfer has a number of applications in the real world. Domains such as autonomous driving and healthcare have started to leverage deep learning techniques, yet many use cases fall short because of the unavailability of larger datasets. Unpaired cross-domain transfer works such as DiscoGAN (and CycleGAN) can be of great help in such domains.

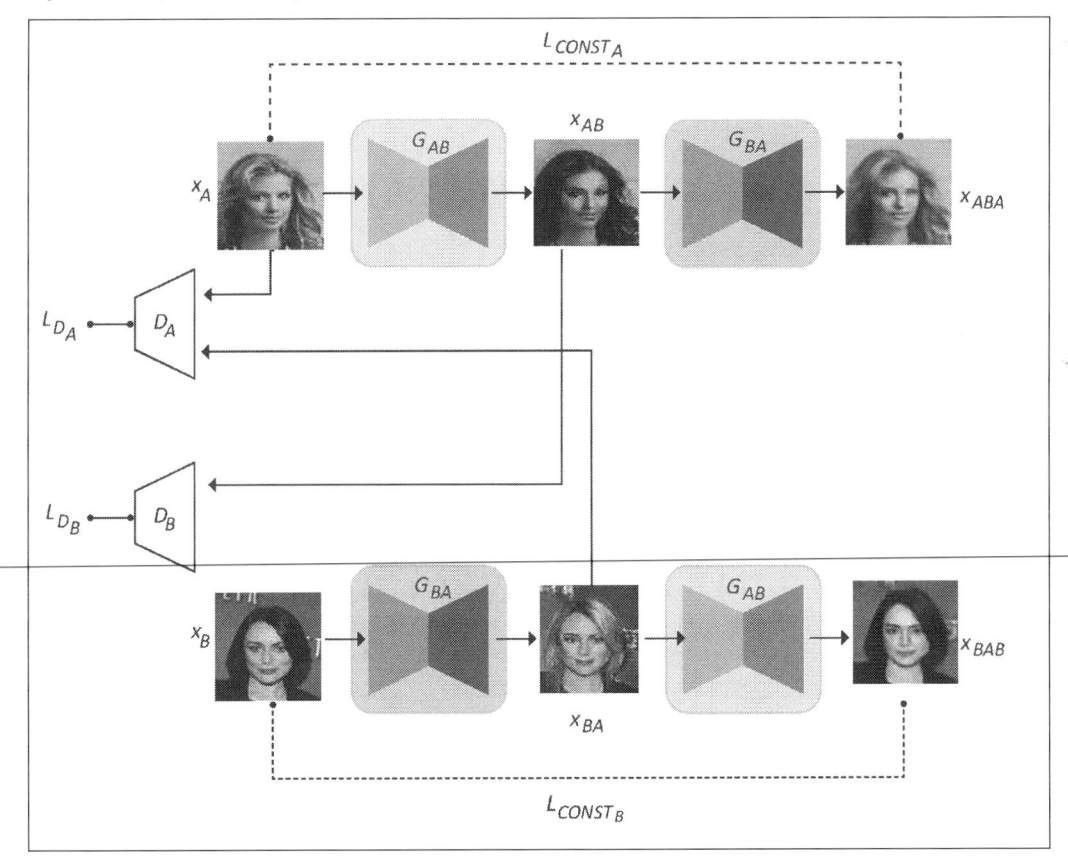

Figure 7.13: DiscoGAN setup[6]

[239]

Published about the same time as CycleGAN, DiscoGAN has a number of similarities and a few slight differences in performing unpaired style transfer. Like CycleGAN, DiscoGAN achieves cross-domain transfer with the help of two pairs of generators and discriminators. The generator in the first pair transforms images from domain A to B (denoted as G_{AB}) and the discriminator (denoted as D_B) classifies whether the generated output (denoted as x_{AB}) is real or fake.

The second generator-discriminator pair is the crux of the paper. By enforcing that the system regenerates the original input image from the generated output (x_{AB}), DiscoGAN is able to learn the required cross-domain representations without the need for explicit pairs. This reconstruction of original samples is achieved using the second generator (denoted as G_{BA}) and its corresponding discriminator (D_A). The overall setup is represented in *Figure 7.13* for reference.

As shown in *Figure 7.13*, to learn cross-domain representations, DiscoGAN not only transforms images from domain A to x_{AB} and then reconstructs them back, but also does the same for images in domain B as well (that is, B to x_{BA} and reconstruct back). This two-way mapping, also called a bijection, along with the reconstruction loss and adversarial loss, helps achieve state-of-the-art results. The authors note that setups that only rely on reconstruction loss without the additional pipeline (B to x_{BA} and reconstruction) still lead to failure modes such as mode collapse.

Unlike CycleGAN, where we noted that the reconstruction loss is an L1 loss and a weighted sum of forward and backward reconstruction, DiscoGAN explores and uses the reconstruction loss slightly differently. The DiscoGAN paper mentions that the reconstruction loss could be any of the distance measures, such as mean squared error, cosine distance, or hinge loss. As shown in the following equations, the generators then use the reconstruction loss in their training separately:

$$L_{G_{AB}} = L_{GAN_B} + L_{CONST_A}$$

$$L_{G_{BA}} = L_{GAN_A} + L_{CONST_B}$$

where L_{GAN_i} represents the original adversarial loss and L_{CONST_i} is the reconstruction loss for each of the GAN pairs.

The generators make use of an encoder-decoder setup with convolutional and deconvolutional layers (or transposed convolutions) to downsample and upsample intermediate representations/feature maps. The decoder, on the other hand, is similar to the encoder part of the generator, consisting of convolutional layers with the final layer being a sigmoid for classification.

The authors of DiscoGAN present a number of well-documented experiments to understand how their proposed architecture handles mode-collapse. One such experiment is the car-to-car mapping experiment. In this setup, the authors explore how three architectures, that is, the original GAN, the GAN with reconstruction loss, and DiscoGAN, handle various modes. The mapping experiment transforms the input image of a car with specific rotation (azimuth) to a different rotation angle.

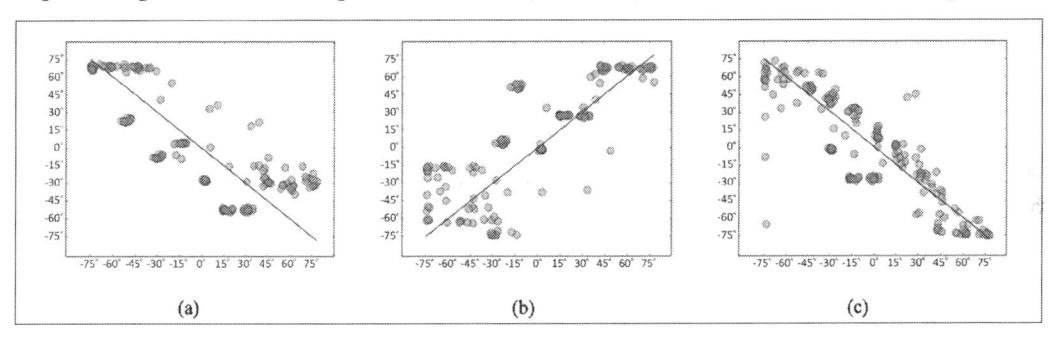

Figure 7.14: Car-to-car mapping experiment to understand mode collapse under different settings. (a) Original GAN, (b) GAN with reconstruction loss, (c) DiscoGAN setup.

As noted in *Figure 7.14 (a)* and *(b)*, both the GAN and GAN with reconstruction loss suffer from mode collapse; the clustered dots in both cases represent the fact that these architectures have been able to learn only a few modes, or car orientations (the line being the ground truth). Conversely, *Figure 7.14 (c)* shows that DiscoGAN learns a better representation of various modes, with the dots spread across the line.

Style Transfer with GANs

Setting up DiscoGAN is fairly straightforward. Using the utilities described in the chapter so far, we trained a DiscoGAN setup to learn an edges-to-shoes mapping.

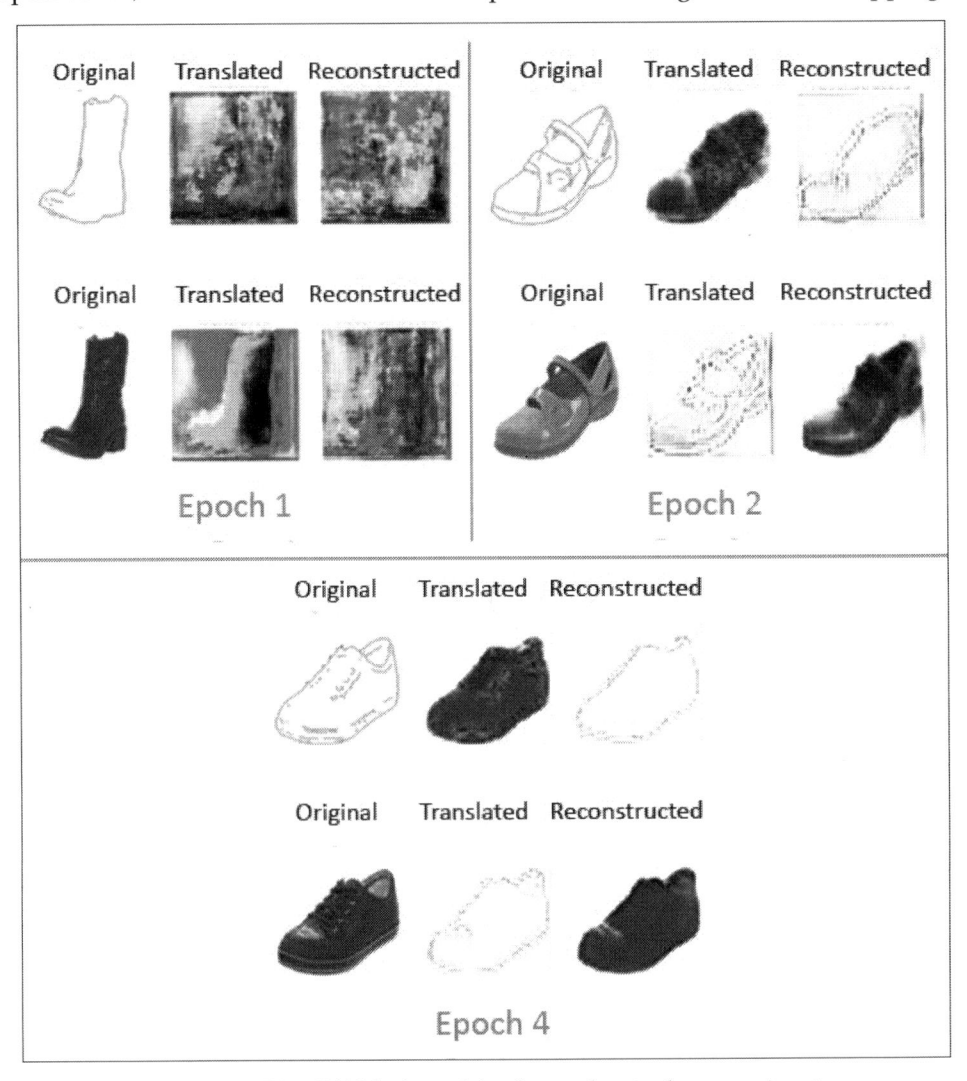

Figure 7.15: DiscoGAN during training for an edges-to-shoes experiment

Figure 7.15 shows the training progress of our model. It starts with a random mapping to understand boundary shapes and a few colors. Training for longer periods achieves even better results, as shown by the authors in their paper.

DualGAN

DualGAN is the latest in the family of unpaired image-to-image translation architectures. It approaches this task of unpaired image-to-image translation from a slightly different perspective compared to DiscoGAN and CycleGAN. Authors Yi and Zhang et al. present their work titled *DualGAN: Unsupervised Dual Learning for Image-to-Image Translation*[7] inspired by a seminal paper on *Dual Learning for Machine Translation*.[8] Quoting from the paper, the idea behind looking at image-to-image translation as a dual learning task goes as follows:

> *Our approach is inspired by dual learning from natural language processing. Dual learning trains two "opposite" language translators (e.g., English-to-French and French-to-English) simultaneously by minimizing the re-construction loss resulting from a nested application of the two translators. The two translators represent a primal-dual pair and the nested application forms a closed loop, allowing the application of reinforcement learning. Specifically, the reconstruction loss measured over monolingual data (either English or French) would generate informative feedback to train a bilingual translation model.*

Though not explicitly cited in the CycleGAN paper, the ideas seem to have quite a bit of overlap. The setup for DualGAN, as expected, also uses two pairs of generator-discriminator. The pairs are termed as primal-GAN and dual-GAN. *Figure 7.16* presents the overall setup for DualGAN:

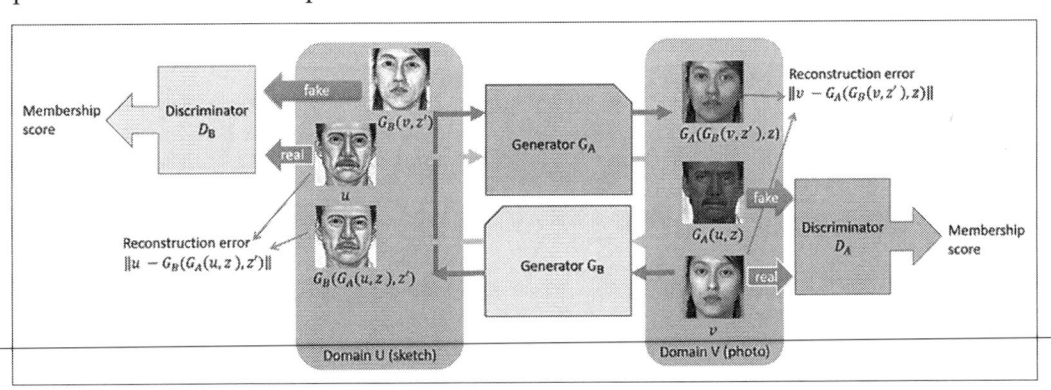

Figure 7.16: DualGAN setup[7]

The primal GAN (denoted as G_A) takes input u from domain U and learns to transform this into v from domain V, and the dual GAN does the reverse of this. The two feedback signals from this setup are termed the reconstruction error and the membership score. The membership score is similar to the adversarial loss in CycleGAN, where the aim of G_A is to generate outputs $G_A(u, z)$ that are good enough to fool D_A.

Style Transfer with GANs

The reconstruction loss represents the learned ability of G_B to reconstruct the original input u from the generated output $G_A(u, z)$. The reconstruction loss is similar to the cycle consistency loss for CycleGAN, apart from differences in problem formulation compared to CycleGAN, and a slight difference in training setup as well. The DualGAN setup makes use of Wasserstein loss to train. They report that using Wasserstein loss helps achieve stable models easily. *Figure 7.17* shows a few experiments from the DualGAN paper:

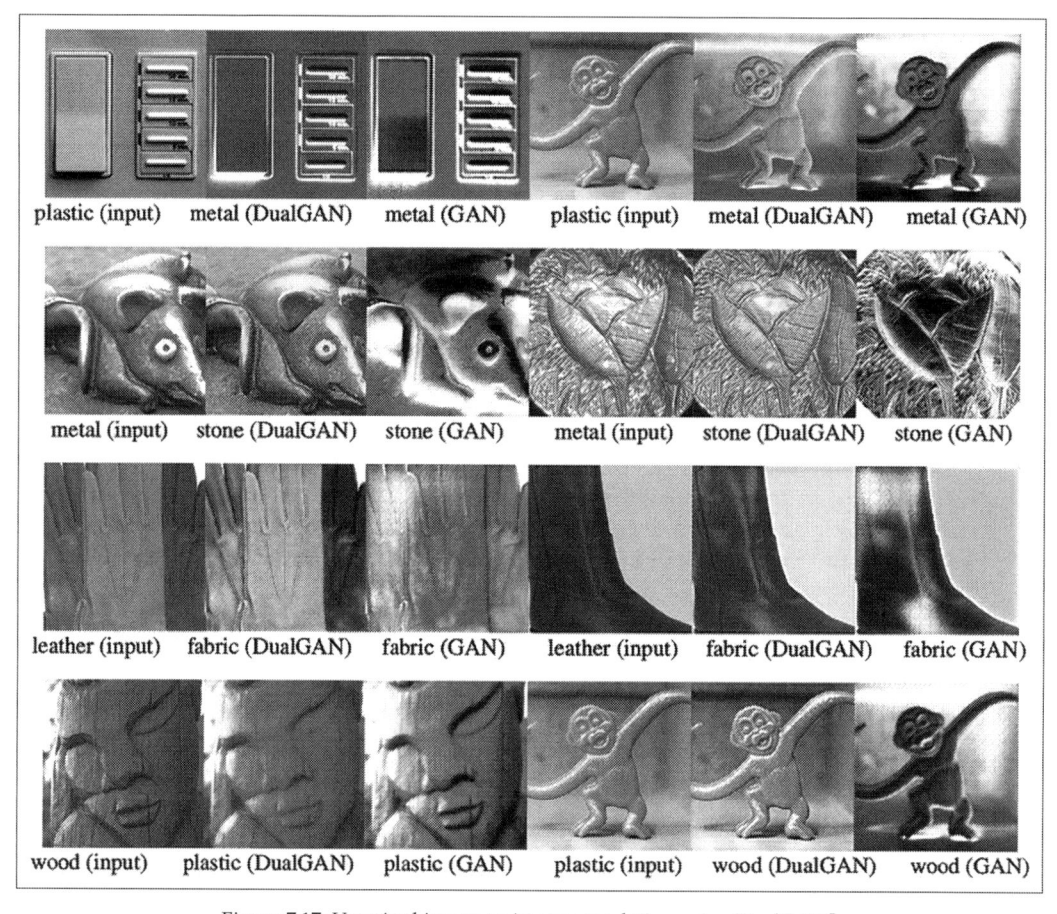

Figure 7.17: Unpaired image-to-image translation using DualGAN[7]

The DualGAN setup also makes use of U-Net style generators and Patch-GAN style discriminators, and the impact of these tricks is seen in the quality of the output.

Summary

In this chapter, we explored the creative side of GAN research through the lenses of image-to-image translation tasks. While the creative implications are obvious, such techniques also open up avenues to improve the research and development of computer vision models for domains where datasets are hard to get.

We started off the chapter by understanding the paired image-to-image translation task. This task provides training data where the source and destination domains have paired training samples. We explored this task using the pix2pix GAN architecture. Through this architecture, we explored how the encoder-decoder architecture is useful for developing generators that can produce high-fidelity outputs. The pix2pix paper took the encoder-decoder architecture one step further by making use of skip-connections or a U-Net style generator.

This setup also presented another powerful concept, called the Patch-GAN discriminator, which works elegantly to assist the overall GAN with better feedback signal for different style transfer use cases. We used these concepts to build and train our own pix2pix GAN from scratch to transfigure satellite images to Google Maps-like outputs. Our training results were good-quality outputs using very few training samples and training iterations. This faster and stable training was observed to be a direct implication of different innovations contributed by the authors of this work. We also explored various other use cases that can be enabled using pix2pix style architectures.

In the second part of the chapter, we extended the task of image-to-image translation to work in the unpaired setting. The unpaired training setup is no doubt a more complex problem to solve, yet it opens up a lot more avenues. The paired setup is good for cases where we have explicit pairs of samples in both source and target domains, but most real-life scenarios do not have such datasets.

We explored the unpaired image-to-image translation setup through CycleGAN architecture. The authors of CycleGAN presented a number of intuitive yet powerful contributions that enable the unpaired setup to work. We discussed the concepts of cycle-consistency loss and identity loss as regularization terms for the overall adversarial loss. We specifically discussed how identity loss helps improve the overall reconstruction of samples and thus the overall quality of output. Using these concepts, we built the CycleGAN setup from scratch using TensorFlow-Keras APIs. We experimented with two datasets, apples to oranges and photographs to Van Gogh style paintings. The results were exceptionally good in both cases with unpaired samples.

We discussed a couple of related works in the final section of the chapter, the DiscoGAN and DualGAN architectures. Along with CycleGAN, these two architectures form the overall family of unpaired image-to-image translation GANs. We discussed how these architectures present similar ideas from slightly different perspectives. We also discussed how slight differences in their problem formulation and overall architectures impact the final results.

In this chapter, we built upon the concepts related to GANs and particularly conditional GANs that we discussed in *Chapter 6, Image Generation with GANs*. We discussed a number of innovations and contributions that make use of simple building blocks to enable some amazing use cases. The next set of chapters will push the boundaries of generative models even further into domains such as text and audio. Fasten your seat belts!

References

1. Mordvintsev, A., McDonald, K., Rudolph, L., Kim, J-S., Li, J., & daviga404. (2015). deepdream. GitHub repository. https://github.com/google/deepdream

2. Gatys, L.A., Ecker, A.S., & Bethge, M. (2015). *A Neural Algorithm of Artistic Style*. arXiv. https://arxiv.org/abs/1508.06576

3. Zhu, J-Y., Park, T., Isola, P., & Efros, A.A. (2017). *Unpaired Image-to-Image Translation using Cycle-Consistent Adversarial Networks*. arXiv. https://arxiv.org/abs/1703.10593

4. Isola, P., Zhu, J-Y., Zhou, T., & Efros, A.A. (2017). *Image-to-Image Translation with Conditional Adversarial Networks*. 2017 IEEE Conference on Computer Vision and Pattern Recognition (CVPR), 2017, pp. 5967-5976. https://ieeexplore.ieee.org/document/8100115

5. Ronneberger, O., Fisher, P., & Brox, T. (2015). *U-net: Convolutional Networks for Biomedical Image Segmentation*. MICCAI, 2015. https://arxiv.org/abs/1505.04597

6. Kim, T., Cha, M., Kim, H., Lee, J.K., & Kim, J. (2017). *Learning to Discover Cross-Domain Relations with Generative Adversarial Networks*. International Conference on Machine Learning (ICML) 2017. https://arxiv.org/abs/1703.05192

7. Yi, Z., Zhang, H., Tan, P., & Gong, M. (2017). *DualGAN: Unsupervised Dual Learning for Image-to-Image Translation*. ICCV 2017. https://arxiv.org/abs/1704.02510v4

8. Xia, Y., He, D., Qin, T., Wang, L., Yu, N., Liu, T-Y., & Ma, W-Y. (2016). *Dual Learning for Machine Translation*. NIPS 2016. https://arxiv.org/abs/1611.00179

8
Deepfakes with GANs

Manipulating videos and photographs to edit artifacts has been in practice for quite a long time. If you have seen movies like *Forrest Gump* or *Fast and Furious 7*, chances are you did not even notice that the scenes with John F. Kennedy or Paul Walker in their respective movies were fake and edited into the movies as required.

You may recall one particular scene from the movie *Forrest Gump*, where Gump meets John F. Kennedy. The scene was created using complex visual effects and archival footage to ensure high-quality results. Hollywood studios, spy agencies from across the world, and media outlets have been making use of editing tools such as Photoshop, After Effects, and complex custom visual effects/CGI (computer generated imagery) pipelines to come up with such compelling results. While the results have been more or less believable in most instances, it takes a huge amount of manual effort and time to edit each and every detail, such as scene lighting, face, eyes, and lip movements, as well as shadows, for every frame of the scene.

Along the same lines, there is a high chance you might have come across a Buzzfeed video[1] where former US president Barack Obama says "Killmonger was right" (Killmonger is one of Marvel Cinematic Universe's villains). While obviously fake, the video does seem real in terms of its visual and audio aspects. There are a number of other examples where prominent personalities can be seen making comments they would usually not.

Keeping ethics aside, there is one major difference between Gump meeting John F. Kennedy and Barack Obama talking about Killmonger. As mentioned earlier, the former is the result of painstaking manual work done using complex visual effects/CGI. The latter, on the other hand, is the result of a technology called **deepfakes**. A portmanteau of the words *deep learning* and *fake*, *deepfake* is a broad term used to describe AI-enabled technology that is used to generate the examples we discussed.

In this chapter, we will cover different concepts, architectures, and components associated with deepfakes. We will focus on the following topics:

- Overview of the deepfakes technological landscape
- The different forms of deepfaking: replacement, re-enactment, and editing
- Key features leveraged by different architectures
- A high-level deepfakes workflow
- Swapping faces using autoencoders
- Re-enacting Obama's face movements using pix2pix
- Challenges and ethical issues
- A brief discussion of off-the-shelf implementations

We will cover the internal workings of different GAN architectures and key contributions that have enabled deepfakes. We will also build and train these architectures from scratch to get a better understanding of them. Deepfakes are not limited to videos or photographs, but are also used to generate fake text (news articles, books) and even audio (voice clips, phone calls). In this chapter, we will focus on videos/images only and the term *deepfakes* refers to related use cases, unless stated otherwise.

> All code snippets presented in this chapter can be run directly in Google Colab. For reasons of space, import statements for dependencies have not been included, but readers can refer to the GitHub repository for the full code: `https://github.com/PacktPublishing/Hands-On-Generative-AI-with-Python-and-TensorFlow-2`.

Let's begin with an overview of deepfakes.

Deepfakes overview

Deepfakes is an all-encompassing term representing content generated using artificial intelligence (in particular, deep learning) that seems realistic and authentic to a human being. The generation of fake content or manipulation of existing content to suit the needs and agenda of the entities involved is not new. In the introduction, we discussed a few movies where CGI and painstaking manual effort helped in generating realistic results. With advancements in deep learning and, more specifically, generative models, it is becoming increasingly difficult to differentiate between what is real and what is fake.

Generative Adversarial Networks (**GANs**) have played a very important role in this space by enabling the generation of sharp, high-quality images and videos. Works such as https://thispersondoesnotexist.com, based on StyleGAN, have really pushed the boundaries in terms of the generation of high-quality realistic content. A number of other key architectures (some of which we discussed in *Chapter 6, Image Generation with GANs*, and *Chapter 7, Style Transfer with GANs*) have become key building blocks for different deepfake setups.

Deepfakes have a number of applications, which can be categorized into creative, productive, and unethical or malicious use cases. The following are a few examples that highlight the different use cases of deepfakes.

Creative and productive use cases:

- **Recreating history and famous personalities**: There are a number of historical figures we would love to interact with and learn from. With the ability to manipulate and generate realistic content, deepfakes are just the right technology for such use cases. A large-scale experiment of this type was developed to bring famous surrealist painter Salvador Dali back to life. The Dali Museum, in collaboration with the ad agency GS&P, developed an exhibition entitled Dali Lives.[2] The exhibition used archival footage and interviews to train a deepfake setup on thousands of hours of videos. The final outcome was a re-enactment of Dali's voice and facial expressions. Visitors to the museum were greeted by Dali, who then shared his life's stories with them. Toward the end, Dali even proposed a selfie with the visitors, and the output photographs were realistic selfies indeed.

- **Movie translation**: With the likes of Netflix becoming the norm these days, viewers are watching far more cross-lingual content than ever before. While subtitles and manual dubbing are viable options, they leave a lot to be desired. With deepfakes, using AI to autogenerate dubbed translations of any video is easier than ever. The social initiative known as *Malaria Must Die* created a powerful campaign leveraging a similar technique to help David Beckham, a famous footballer, speak in nine different languages to help spread awareness.[3] Similarly, deepfakes have been used by a political party in India, where a candidate is seen speaking in different languages as part of his election campaign.[4]

- **Fashion**: Making use of GANs and other generative models to create new styles and fashion content is not new. With deepfakes, researchers, bloggers, and fashion houses are taking the fashion industry to new levels. We now have AI-generated digital models that are adorning new fashion line-ups and help in reducing costs. This technology is even being used to create renderings of models personalized to mimic a buyer's body type, to improve the chances of a purchase.[5]

- **Video game characters**: Video games have improved a lot over the years, with many modern games presenting cinema class graphics. Traditionally, human actors have been leveraged to create characters within such games. However, there is now a growing trend of using deepfakes and related technologies to develop characters and storylines. The developers of the game *Call of Duty* released a trailer showing former US president Ronald Reagan playing one of the characters in the game.[6]

- **Stock images**: Marketing flyers, advertisements, and official documents sometimes require certain individuals to be placed alongside the rest of the content. Traditionally, actual actors and models have been used. There are also stock image services that license such content for commercial use. With works such as https://thispersondoesnotexist.com, it is now very easy to generate a new face or personality as per our requirements, without any actual actors or models.

Malicious use cases:

- **Pornography**: The ability to generate fake content as per our requirements has grave consequences. Indeed, deepfakes came into the public eye when, in 2017, a notorious fake pornographic video was posted by a Reddit user with a celebrity's face swapped on.[7] After this, there have been whole communities working toward generating such fake videos, which can be very damaging to the public image of the people they depict.
- **Impersonation**: We've already discussed a fake video of former US president Barack Obama talking about a number of topics and things he would usually avoid. Creating such videos to impersonate public figures, politicians, and so on can have huge consequences.

Deepfakes entail realistic looking content that can be categorized into a number of subcategories. In the next section, we will present a discussion on the different categories to better understand the overall landscape.

Modes of operation

Generating believable fake content requires taking care of multiple aspects to ensure that the results are as authentic as possible. A typical deepfake setup requires a **source**, **a target**, and **the generated content**.

- The source, denoted with subscript s, is the driver identity that controls the required output
- The target, denoted with subscript t, is the identity being faked
- The generated content, denoted with subscript g, is the result following the transformation of the source to the target.

Now that we have some basic terminology in place, let's dive deeper and understand different ways of generating fake content.

Replacement

This is the most widely used form of generating fake content. The aim is to replace specific content of the target (x_t) with that from the source (x_s). Face replacement has been an active area of research for quite some time now. *Figure 8.1* shows Donald Trump's face being replaced with Nicolas Cage's. The figure displays both source (x_s) and target (x_t) identities, while the generated content (x_g) is shown in the last column:

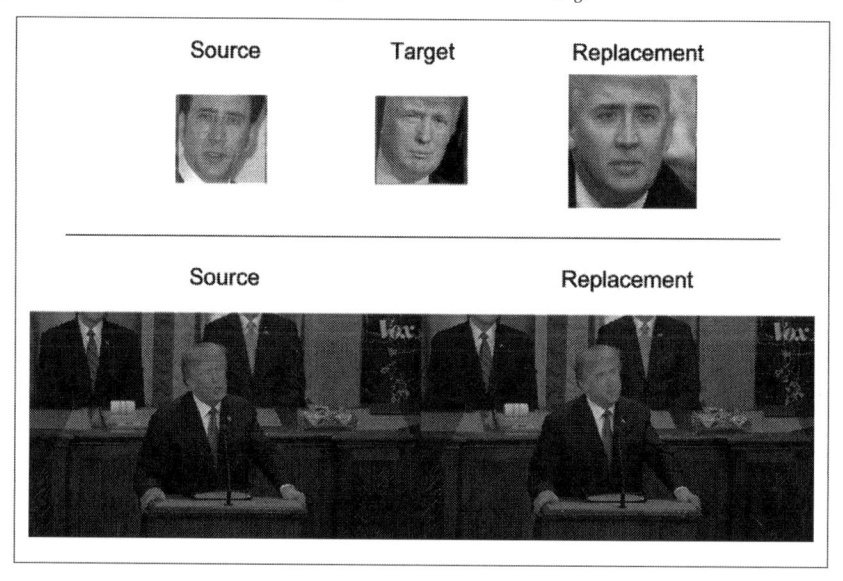

Figure 8.1: Face replacement[8]

Replacement techniques can be broadly categorized into:

- **Transfer**: This is a basic form of replacement where the content of x_s (for example, the face in the case of face replacement) is transferred to x_t. The transfer method is mostly leveraged in a coarse context, in other words, the replacement is not as clean or smooth as one would expect. For example, for clothes shopping, users might be interested in visualizing themselves in different outfits. Such applications can afford to leave out very detailed information yet still give users the required experience.
- **Swap**: This is a slightly more sophisticated type of replacement where the transfer to x_t is guided by certain characteristics of x_t itself. For instance, in *Figure 8.1*, the bottom row shows Nicolas Cage's face getting swapped onto Donald Trump's face. The replacement image maintains the characteristics of Trump's (the target image's) hair, pose, and so on.

The replacement mode, despite sounding trivial, is not so simple, since any models need to focus on a number of factors relating to image lighting, skin colors, occlusions, and shadows. The handling of some of these aspects will be discussed in later sections of this chapter.

Re-enactment

Replacement methods yield impressive results, but the generated content leaves scope for improvement. Re-enactment methods are utilized to capture characteristics such as the pose, expression, and gaze of the target to improve upon the believability of the generated content. Re-enactment techniques focus on the following aspects to improve the quality of the fake content:

- **Gaze**: The aim is to focus on the eyes and the position of the eyelids. Techniques in this area try to re-enact the generated output's gaze based on the source's eye movements/gaze. This is useful in improving photographs or maintaining eye contact in videos.
- **Mouth**: Re-enacting lips and the mouth region of a face improves the believability of the generated content. In this case, the mouth movements of x_t are conditioned on the mouth movements of x_s. In certain cases, the source input x_s could be speech or other audio. Mouth re-enactment methods are also called BoI methods.
- **Expression**: This is a more generic form of re-enactment that often includes other re-enactment aspects such as the eyes, mouth, and pose. These are used to drive the expression of x_t on the basis of x_s.
- **Pose**: Pose re-enactments, for both the head and the body, are all-encompassing methods that consider the positioning of the head and the whole body. In this case as well, the source drives the target and yields more believable results.

These re-enactments are better depicted in *Figure 8.2*, where we have the source (x_s) and target (x_t) shown on the left of the figure. The right side of the figure shows how different aspects of the source impact the generated content. Please note that *Figure 8.2* is for illustrative purposes only and the results are not mere copy and paste editing of the target content. We will see more evolved examples as we progress through the chapter.

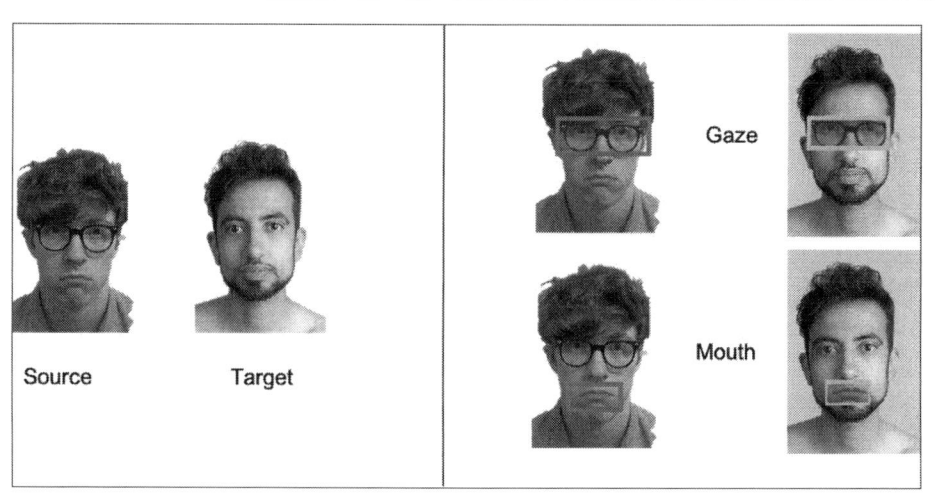

Figure 8.2: Re-enactment methods. Impacted regions are highlighted for each re-enactment

Specific regions that are the focus of different types of re-enactments have been highlighted specifically in *Figure 8.2*. As mentioned earlier, it is quite apparent that expression re-enactments encompass the eye and mouth regions as well.

Editing

Deepfakes do not necessarily concern replacement or re-enactment. Another application of deepfakes is to add, remove, or alter certain aspects of the target entity to serve specific objectives. Editing could involve manipulation of clothing, age, ethnicity, gender, hair, and so on. A few possible edits are depicted in the following figure:

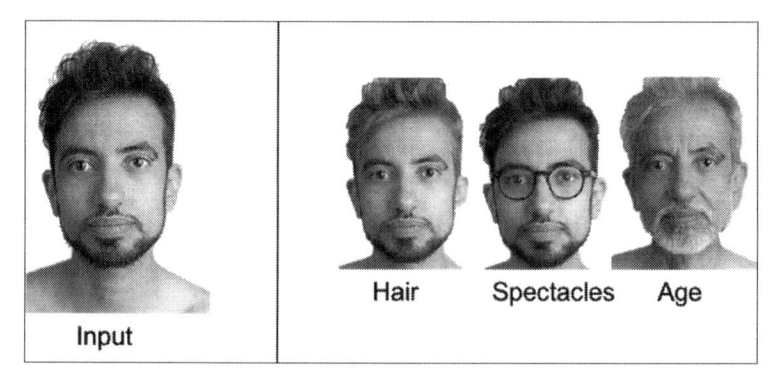

Figure 8.3: Deepfakes in Edit mode. The left image is the base input for transformation. The right image depicts three different edits: hair, spectacles, and age.

The edits on the right-hand side of *Figure 8.3* showcase how certain attributes of the input image can be transformed to generate fake content. There are a number of benign use cases that are either for fun (apps such as **FaceApp** and **REFACE**) or have commercial value (eyewear and cosmetics brands). Yet there are a number of malicious applications (pornography, fake identities, and so on) that undermine and raise questions about the use of such tools.

We have covered the basics of the different modes of generating fake content and discussed the major areas of focus for each of the modes. In the next section, we will discuss what features play a role in training such models and how we leverage them.

Key feature set

The human face and body are key entities in this task of fake content generation. While deep learning architectures usually do not require hand-crafted features, a little nudge goes a long way when complex entities are involved. Particularly when dealing with the human face, apart from detecting the overall face in a given image or video, a deepfake solution also needs to focus on the eyes, mouth, and other features. We discussed different modes of operation in the previous section, where we highlighted the importance of different sections of a face and their impact on improving the believability of the fake content generated.

In this section, we will briefly cover a few important features leveraged by different deepfake solutions. These are:

- Facial Action Coding System (FACS)
- 3D Morphable Model (3DMM)
- Facial landmarks

We will also undertake a couple of hands-on exercises to better understand these feature sets.

Facial Action Coding System (FACS)

Developed by Carl-Herman Hjortsjö in 1969, and later adopted and refined by Ekamn et al. in 1978, Facial Action Coding System, or FACS, is an anatomy-based system for understanding facial movements. It is one of the most extensive and accurate coding systems for analyzing facial muscles to understand expressions and emotions.

Figure 8.4 depicts a few specific muscle actions and their associated meanings.

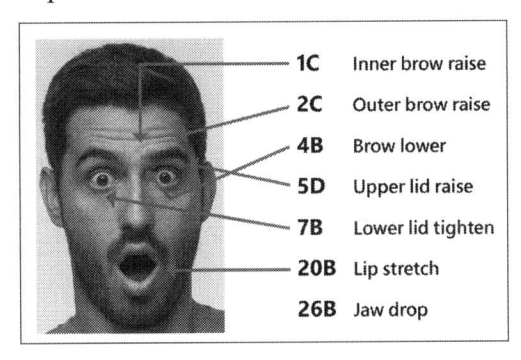

Figure 8.4: A sample set of action marking using FACS

FACS consists of a detailed manual that is used by human coders to manually code each facial expression. The muscular activities are grouped into what are called Action Units, or AUs. These AUs represent muscular activities corresponding to facial expressions. A few sample AUs are described in *Figure 8.4*, pointing to the movement of eyebrows, lips, and other parts of the face.

Although the original FACS system required human coders, there are automated systems now available to computationally determine the correct AUs. Works such as the following leverage automated AUs to generate realistic results:

- *GANimation: Anatomically-aware Facial Animation from a Single Image*[9]
- *High-Resolution Face Swapping for Visual Effects*[10]
- *3D Guided Fine-Grained Face Manipulation*[11]

Even though FACS provides a fine-grained understanding of a given face's expressions, the complexity of the overall system limits its usage outside of professional animation/CGI/VFX studios.

3D Morphable Model

3D Morphable Model, or 3DMM for short, is a method of inferring a complete 3D facial surface from a 2D image. Originally proposed by Blanz, Vetter, et al. in their work entitled *A Morphable Model for the Synthesis of 3D Faces*,[12] this is a powerful statistical method that can model human face shape and texture along with pose and illumination.

The technique works by transforming the input image into a face mesh. The face mesh consists of vertices and edges that determine the shape and texture of each section of the face. The mesh helps in parameterizing the pose and expressions with a set of vectors and matrices. These vectors, or the 3D reconstruction itself, can then be used as input features for our fake content generation models.

Facial landmarks

FACS and 3DMM-based features are highly accurate and expressive in terms of defining the characteristics of a human face (and body in general). Yet these methods are computationally expensive and sometimes even require human intervention (for example, FACS coding) for proper results. Facial landmarks are another feature set which are simple yet powerful, and are being used by a number of recent works to achieve state-of-the-art results.

Facial landmarks are a list of important facial features, such as the nose, eyebrows, mouth, and the corners of the eyes. The goal is the detection of these key features using some form of a regression model. The most common method is to leverage a predefined set of positions on the face or body that can be efficiently tracked using trained models.

A facial landmark detection task can be broken down into the following two-step approach:

- The first step involves localization of a face (or faces) in a given image
- The second step goes granular to identify key facial structures of the identified face(s)

These two steps can be thought of as special cases of shape prediction. There are a couple of different methods we can use to detect facial landmarks as features for the task of fake content generation. In the following subsections, we will cover three of the most widely used methods: OpenCV, dlib, and MTCNN.

Facial landmark detection using OpenCV

OpenCV is a computer vision library aimed at handling real-time tasks. It is one of the most popular and widely used libraries, with wrappers available in a number of languages, Python included. It consists of a number of extensions and contrib-packages, such as the ones for face detection, text manipulation, and image processing. These packages enhance its overall capabilities.

Facial landmark detection can be performed using OpenCV in a few different ways. One of the ways is to leverage Haar Cascade filters, which make use of histograms followed by an SVM for object detection. OpenCV also supports a DNN-based method of performing the same task.

Facial landmark detection using dlib

Dlib is another cross-platform library which provides more or less similar functionality to OpenCV. The major advantage dlib offers over OpenCV is a list of pretrained detectors for faces as well as landmarks. Before we get onto the implementation details, let's learn a bit more about the landmark features.

Facial landmarks are granular details on a given face. Even though each face is unique, there are certain attributes that help us to identify a given shape as a face. This precise list of common traits is codified into what is called the **68-coordinate** or **68-point system**. This point system was devised for annotating the iBUG-300W dataset. This dataset forms the basis of a number of landmark detectors available through dlib. Each feature is given a specific index (out of 68) and has its own (x, y) coordinates. The 68 indices are indicated in *Figure 8.5*.

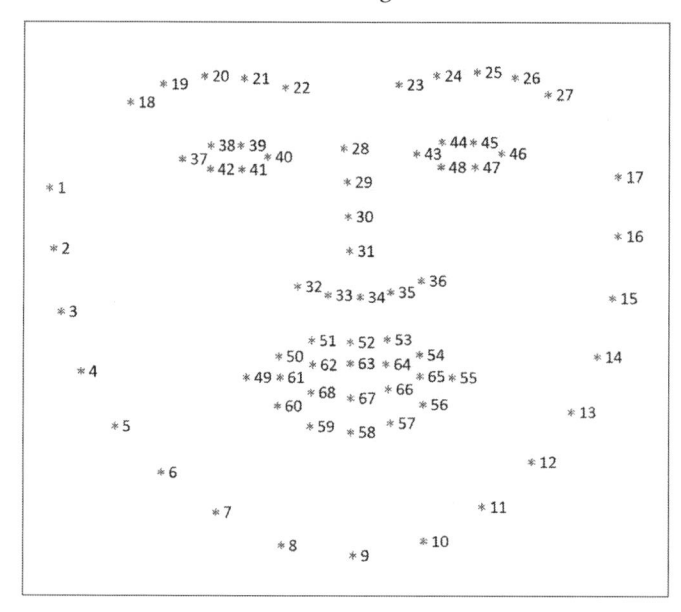

Figure 8.5: The 68-point annotations from the iBUG-300W dataset

Chapter 8

As depicted in the figure, each index corresponds to a specific coordinate and a set of indices mark a facial landmark. For instance, indices 28-31 correspond to the nose bridge and the detectors try to detect and predict the corresponding coordinates for those indices.

> Setting up dlib is a bit of an involved process, especially if you are on a Windows machine. Refer to setup guides such as:
>
> - https://www.pyimagesearch.com/2017/03/27/how-to-install-dlib/
> - https://medium.com/analytics-vidhya/how-to-install-dlib-library-for-python-in-windows-10-57348ba1117f

Let's now leverage this 68-coordinate system of facial landmarks to develop a short demo application for detecting facial features. We will make use of pretrained detectors from dlib and OpenCV to build this demo. The following snippet shows how a few lines of code can help us identify different facial landmarks easily:

```
detector = dlib.get_frontal_face_detector()
predictor = dlib.shape_predictor("shape_predictor_68_face_landmarks.dat")

image = cv2.imread('nicolas_ref.png')

# convert to grayscale
gray = cv2.cvtColor(image, cv2.COLOR_BGR2GRAY)
faces = detector(gray)

# identify and mark features
for face in faces:
    x1 = face.left()
    y1 = face.top()
    x2 = face.right()
    y2 = face.bottom()
    landmarks = predictor(gray, face)
    for n in range(0, 68):
        x = landmarks.part(n).x
        y = landmarks.part(n).y
        cv2.circle(image, (x, y), 2, (255, 0, 0), -1)
```

The preceding code takes in an image of a face as input, converts it to grayscale, and marks the aforementioned 68 points onto the face using a dlib detector and predictor. Once we have these functions ready, we can execute the overall script. The script pops open a video capture window. The video output is overlaid with facial landmarks, as shown in *Figure 8.6*:

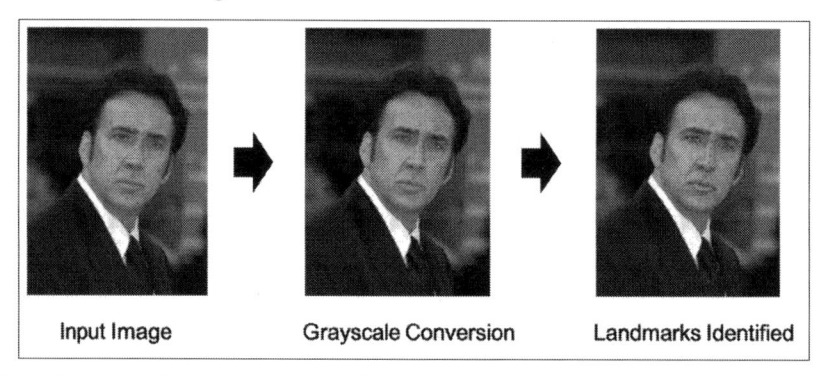

Figure 8.6: A sample video capture with facial landmark detection using pretrained detectors

As you can see, the pretrained facial landmark detector seems to be doing a great job. With a few lines of code, we were able to get specific facial features. In the later sections of the chapter, we will leverage these features for training our own deepfake architectures.

Facial landmark detection using MTCNN

There are a number of alternatives to OpenCV and dlib for face and facial landmark detection tasks. One of the most prominent and well performing ones is called **MTCNN**, short for **Multi-Task Cascaded Convolutional Networks**. Developed by Zhang, Zhang et al.,[13] MTCNN is a complex deep learning architecture consisting of three cascaded networks. Together, these three networks help with the tasks of face and landmark identification. A discussion of the details of MTCNN are beyond the scope of this book, but we will briefly talk about its salient aspects and build a quick demo. Interested readers are requested to go through the original cited work for details.

The MTCNN setup, as mentioned earlier, makes use of three cascaded networks called P-Net, R-Net, and O-Net. Without going into much detail, the setup first builds a pyramid of the input image, i.e. the input image is scaled to different resolutions. The Proposal-Net, or P-Net, then takes these as input and outputs a number of potential bounding boxes that might contain a face. With some pre-processing steps in between, the Refine-Net, or R-Net, then refines the results by narrowing them down to the most probable bounding boxes.

The final output is generated by Output-Net, or O-Net. O-Net outputs the final bounding boxes containing faces, along with landmark coordinates for the eyes, nose, and mouth.

Let's now try out this state-of-the-art architecture to identify faces and corresponding landmarks. Luckily for us, MTCNN is available as a pip package, which is straightforward to use. In the following code listing, we will build a utility function to leverage MTCNN for our required tasks:

```python
def detect_faces(image, face_list):
    plt.imshow(cv2.cvtColor(image, cv2.COLOR_BGR2RGB))
    ax = plt.gca()
    for face in face_list:
        # mark faces
        x, y, width, height = face['box']
        rect = Rectangle((x, y), width, height, fill=False,
                                                color='orange')
        ax.add_patch(rect)
        # mark Landmark features
        for key, value in face['keypoints'].items():
            dot = Circle(value, radius=12, color='red')
            ax.add_patch(dot)
    plt.show()

# instantiate the detector
detector = MTCNN()

# load sample image
image = cv2.imread('trump_ref.png')

# detect face and facial Landmarks
faces = detector.detect_faces(image)

# visualize results
detect_faces(image, faces)
```

As showcased in the code listing, the predictions from the MTCNN detector outputs two items for each detected face – the bounding box for the face and five coordinates for each facial landmark. Using these outputs, we can leverage OpenCV to add markers on the input image to visualize the predictions.

Figure 8.7 depicts the sample output from this exercise.

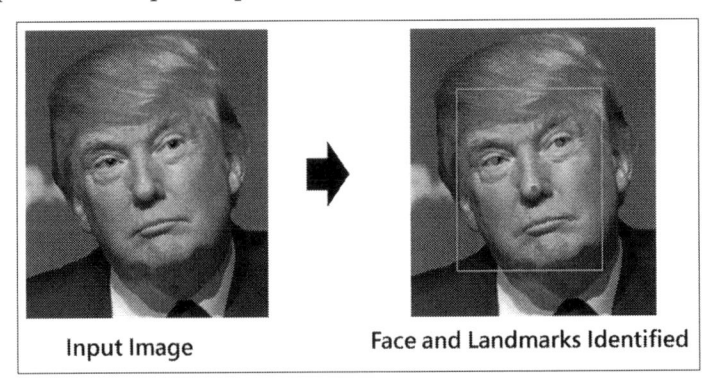

Figure 8.7: MTCNN-based face and facial landmark detection

As shown in the figure, MTCNN seems to have detected all the faces in the image along with the facial landmarks properly. With a few lines of code, we were able to use a state-of-the-art complex deep learning network to quickly generate the required outputs. Similar to the dlib/OpenCV exercise in the previous section, we can leverage MTCNN to identify key features which can be used as inputs for our fake content generation models.

Another easy-to-use deep learning-based library for face detection and recognition is called `face_recognition`. This is a pip-installable package that provides straightforward APIs for both the tasks. For the task of face recognition (where the primary aim is to identify a person apart from just detecting a face), it makes use of VGGFace. VGGFace is a deep learning architecture developed by the Visual Geometry Group at Oxford University. It makes use of a VGG-style backbone to extract facial features. These features can then be leveraged for similarity matching. We will make use of this package in later sections of the chapter.

Now that we have developed an understanding of different modes, along with different ways of identifying and extracting relevant features, let's get started with building a few such architectures of our own from scratch. In the coming sections, we will discuss a high-level flow for building a deepfake model and common architectures employed for this purpose, followed by hands-on training of a couple of these from scratch.

High-level workflow

Fake content generation is a complex task consisting of a number of components and steps that help in generating believable content. While this space is seeing quite a lot of research and hacks that improve the overall results, the setup can largely be explained using a few common building blocks. In this section, we will discuss a common high-level flow that describes how a deepfake setup uses data to train and generate fake content. We will also touch upon a few common architectures used in a number of works as basic building blocks.

As discussed earlier, a deepfake setup requires a source identity (x_s) which drives the target identity (x_t) to generate fake content (x_g). To understand the high-level flow, we will continue with this notation, along with the concepts related to the key feature set discussed in the previous section. The steps are as follows:

- **Input processing**
  - The input image (x_s or x_t) is processed using a face detector that identifies and crops the face
  - The cropped face is then used to extract intermediate representations or features

- **Generation**
  - The intermediate representation along with a driving signal (x_s or another face) is used to generate a new face

- **Blending**
  - A blending function then merges the generated face into the target as cleanly as possible

Respective works employ additional interim or post-processing steps to improve the overall results. *Figure 8.8* depicts the main steps in detail:

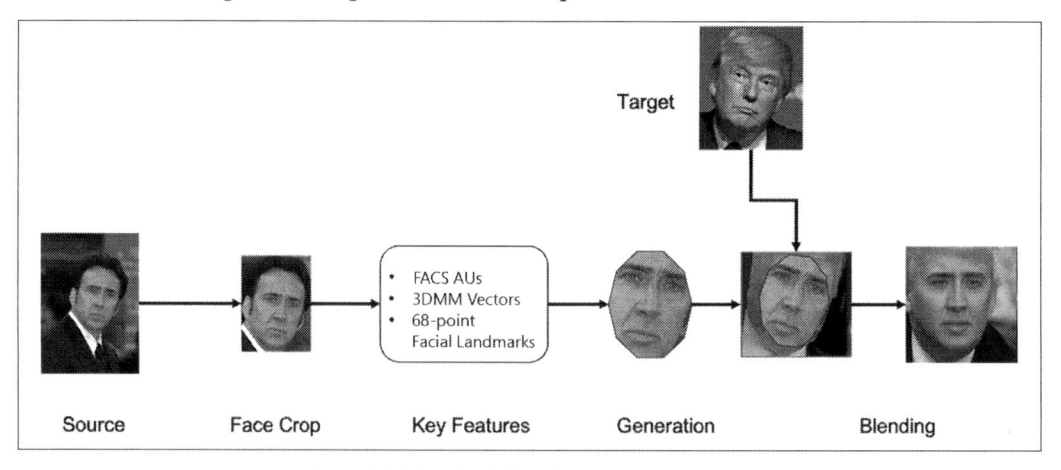

Figure 8.8: High-level flow for creating deepfakes

As shown in the figure, we use a photograph of Nicolas Cage as input and transform him into a fake photograph resembling Donald Trump. The key components used for each of these steps could be any of the various components presented so far in the chapter. For instance, the face crop step could leverage either dlib or MTCNN, and similarly, the key features used for the generation process could be either FACS AUs, facial landmarks, or the 3DMM vectors.

So far, we have covered aspects related to face cropping and key features which can be used in this fake content generation process. The next step in this process of deepfakes is the final output image, or video generation. Generative modeling is something we have covered in quite some depth in previous chapters, from variational autoencoders to different types of GANs. For the task of fake content generation, we will build upon these architectures. Readers should note that the deepfakes task is a special case, or rather a restricted use case, of different models we have covered in these previous chapters.

Let's now have a look at some of the most common architectures that are leveraged by different deepfake works.

Common architectures

Most deepfake setups leverage known architectures with certain tweaks as building blocks for generating fake content. We have discussed most of these architectures in detail in *Chapters 4, 5, 6,* and *7*. The following is a brief reiteration of the most commonly leveraged architectures for generating images or videos.

Encoder-Decoder (ED)

An encoder-decoder architecture consists of two components, an encoder and a decoder. The encoder component consists of a sequence of layers that start from the actual higher dimensional input, such as an image. The encoder then narrows the input down to a lower dimensional space or a vector representation, rightly termed **bottleneck features**. The decoder component takes the bottleneck features and decodes or transforms them to a different or the same vector space as the input. A typical ED architecture is depicted here:

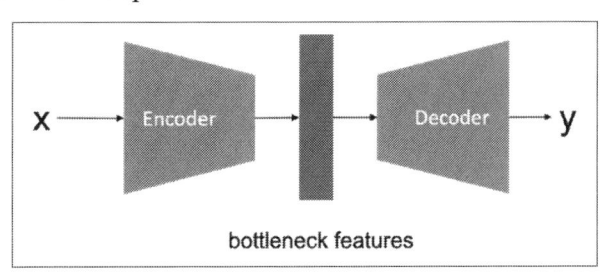

Figure 8.9: A typical encoder-decoder architecture

A special case of ED architecture is called an **autoencoder**. An autoencoder takes the input, transforms it into bottleneck features, and then reconstructs the original input as the output. Such networks are useful in learning feature representation on inputs. Another variant of ED architecture is called the **variational autoencoder**, or VAE. A VAE learns the posterior distribution of the decoder given the input space. We have seen in *Chapter 5, Painting Pictures with Neural Networks using VAEs*, how VAEs are better at learning and untangling representations, and better at generating content overall (as compared to autoencoders).

Generative Adversarial Networks (GANs)

GANs are implicit density modeling networks which have been used to generate very high-quality outputs in recent works. Without going into much detail, a GAN setup consists of two competing models, a generator and a discriminator. The generator is tasked with generating real-looking content based on a driving signal (noise vector, conditional inputs, and so on). The discriminator, on the other hand, is tasked with distinguishing fake from real. The two networks play a minimax game until we achieve an equilibrium state, with the generator being able to generate good enough samples to fool the discriminator.

A typical GAN is depicted in *Figure 8.10*:

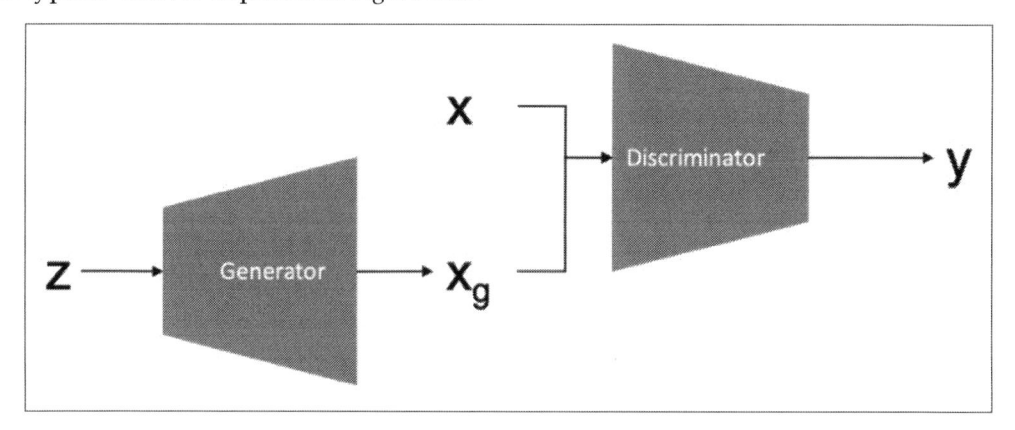

Figure 8.10: A typical GAN architecture

GANs are effective at generating high-quality outputs, and they have been the subject of significant research over the years. Improvements have led to some really powerful variants that have pushed the boundaries even further. Two of the most widely used variants in the context of deepfakes are **CycleGAN** and **pix2pix**. Both architectures were designed for image-to-image translation tasks. Pix2pix is a paired translation network, while CycleGAN does not require any pairing of the training samples. The effectiveness and simplicity of both these architectures make them perfect candidates for the task of deepfakes. We discussed both these architectures in detail in *Chapter 7, Style Transfer with GANs*; we encourage you to take a quick look at the previous chapter for a better understanding of the remaining sections in this chapter.

We have covered all the required building blocks in fair detail so far. Let's now leverage this understanding to implement a couple of deepfake setups from scratch.

Replacement using autoencoders

Deepfakes are an interesting and powerful use of technology that is both useful and dangerous. In previous sections, we discussed different modes of operations and key features that can be leveraged, as well as common architectures. We also briefly touched upon the high-level flow of different tasks required to achieve the end results. In this section, we will focus on developing a face swapping setup using an autoencoder as our backbone architecture. Let's get started.

Task definition

The aim of this exercise is to develop a face swapping setup. As discussed earlier, face swapping is a type of replacement mode operation in the context of deepfake terminology. In this setup, we will focus on transforming Nicolas Cage (a Hollywood actor) into Donald J. Trump (former US president). In the upcoming sections, we will present each sub-task necessary for the preparation of data, training our models, and finally, the generation of swapped fake output images.

Dataset preparation

The first and foremost task is data preparation. Since the aim is to develop a face swapper for Nicolas Cage and Donald Trump, we need datasets containing images of each of them. This task of data collection itself can be time-consuming and challenging for a number of reasons. Firstly, photographs could be restricted by licensing and privacy issues. Secondly, it is challenging to find good quality datasets that are publicly available. Finally, there is the challenge associated with identifying specific faces in photographs, as there could be multiple faces in a given photograph belonging to different people.

For copyright reasons, we cannot publish the training datasets that have been used to obtain the exact output in this chapter, as they have been scraped from a variety of online sources. However, websites that might prove useful for obtaining similar datasets are:

- https://github.com/deepfakes/faceswap/
- http://cs.binghamton.edu/~ncilsal2/DeepFakesDataset/
- https://www.kaggle.com/c/deepfake-detection-challenge/overview

Assuming we already have the raw datasets collected, we can proceed to the next set of tasks: face detection and identification.

The first task is to define an entity class to hold face-related objects. We need such a class as we will need to pass images, extracted faces, and face landmarks, as well as transformations, through the pipeline. We define a class, `DetectedFace`, as shown in the following code snippet:

```
# Entity class
class DetectedFace(object):
    def __init__(self, image, x, w, y, h, landmarks):
        self.image = image
        self.x = x
        self.w = w
```

```
        self.y = y
        self.h = h
        self.landmarks = landmarks

    def landmarksAsXY(self):
        return [(p.x, p.y) for p in self.landmarks.parts()]
```

Abstracting these frequently used properties into an object (class) enables us to reduce the number of individual parameters needed to pass between different utilities. We discussed the face_recognition library in the *Key feature set* section. We will leverage the pose prediction model from this library to predict face locations using dlib's shape_predictor. The following snippet instantiates the predictor objects:

```
predictor_68_point_model = face_recognition_models.pose_predictor_
model_location()
pose_predictor = dlib.shape_predictor(predictor_68_point_model)
```

We use these objects to identify faces using the 68-point landmark detector from dlib. The following snippet shows the detect_faces utility method:

```
def detect_faces(frame):
    face_locations = face_recognition.face_locations(frame)
    landmarks = _raw_face_landmarks(frame, face_locations)

    for ((y, right, bottom, x), landmarks) in zip(face_locations,
landmarks):
        yield DetectedFace(frame[y: bottom, x: right],
                           x, right - x, y, bottom - y, landmarks)
```

This method takes an image as input and generates DetectedFace objects as outputs. Readers should note that we are yielding objects of type DetectedFace. The yield keyword ensures lazy execution, meaning objects are created when required. This ensures smaller memory requirements. The DetectedFace object, on the other hand, abstracts the extracted face and corresponding landmarks.

Chapter 8

Let's now use these utilities to see how we can identify faces in a given image. The following snippet loads a sample image and then makes use of the detect_faces function to extract all the faces in the input image:

```
# Load Sample Image
image = cv2.imread('sample_image.jpg')
plt.imshow(cv2.cvtColor(image , cv2.COLOR_BGR2RGB))
plt.axis('off');

# Detect faces and visualize them all
detected_faces = [face for face in detect_faces(image)]
```

We iterate the generator object returned by the detect_faces method to visualize all the identified faces. In the following snippet, we perform this visualization:

```
for face in detected_faces:
    plt.imshow(cv2.cvtColor(face.image , cv2.COLOR_BGR2RGB))
    plt.axis('off');
    plt.show()
```

The sample image used for face identification and extraction is showcased in the following figure:

Figure 8.11: Sample image for face identification and extraction

[269]

Deepfakes with GANs

As visible in *Figure 8.11*, there are two faces corresponding to Donald Trump and Narendra Modi. The extracted faces using the `detect_faces` utility method are shown in *Figure 8.12*:

Figure 8.12: Extracted faces from sample image

Now that we have identified the faces (face detection), the next task is to perform face recognition (recognise a specific person's face). Since we are aiming to develop a face swapping architecture involving Donald Trump and Nicolas Cage, it is imperative that we should have the ability to extract only relevant faces from the input images. To do so, we will make use of VGGFace-based face recognition. The following snippet shows a helper class, `FaceFilter`, which helps us to do so:

```python
class FaceFilter():
    def __init__(self, reference_file_path, threshold=0.65):
        """
        Works only for single face images
        """
        image = face_recognition.load_image_file(reference_file_path)
        self.encoding = face_recognition.face_encodings(image)[0]
        self.threshold = threshold

    def check(self, detected_face):
        encodings = face_recognition.face_encodings(detected_face.image)
        if len(encodings) > 0:
            encodings = encodings[0]
            score = face_recognition.face_distance([self.encoding],
                                                    encodings)
        else:
            print("No faces found in the image!")
            score = 0.8
        return score <= self.threshold
```

In the preceding code, the `FaceFilter` class requires a reference image as an input. This is intuitive; this reference serves as a ground truth to compare against in order to confirm whether or not we've found the right face. As mentioned earlier, the `face_recognition` package makes use of VGGFace to generate encoding for any image. We do this for the reference image and extract a vector representation for it. The check function in the `FaceFilter` class is then used to perform a similarity check (using metrics such as Euclidean distance or cosine similarity) between any new image and the reference image. If the similarity is below a certain threshold, it returns `False`.

The following snippet creates an object of type `FaceFilter` using a reference image. We then iterate through the list of `detected_faces` to see which faces actually belong to Donald Trump:

```
face_filter = FaceFilter('trump_ref.png')

for face in detected_faces:
  if face_filter.check(face):
    plt.title("Matching Face")
    plt.imshow(cv2.cvtColor(face.image , cv2.COLOR_BGR2RGB))
    plt.axis('off');
    plt.show()
```

The sample image, reference image, and recognized face are shown in *Figure 8.13*:

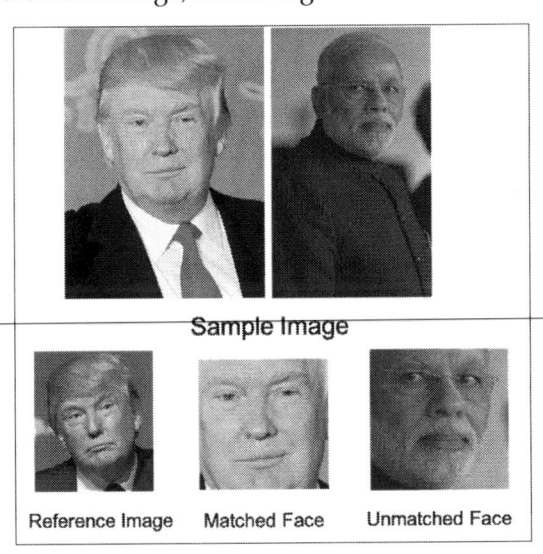

Figure 8.13: Sample image, reference image, matched face, and unmatched face

Deepfakes with GANs

As shown in the figure, our `FaceFilter` class was able to identify which face belongs to Donald Trump and which doesn't. This is extremely useful for creating our datasets.

It is often observed that the alignment and crop of a face has a direct impact on the quality of the trained model. For this reason, we make use of a helper class to align the extracted faces. The following snippet shows the `Extract` class, which takes in the extracted face as input and generates an aligned output; in other words, we align the orientation of the cropped/extracted face with that of the reference image:

```python
class Extract(object):
    def extract(self, image, face, size):
        if face.landmarks is None:
            print("Warning! landmarks not found. Switching to crop!")
            return cv2.resize(face.image, (size, size))

        alignment = get_align_mat(face)
        return self.transform(image, alignment, size, padding=48)

    def transform(self, image, mat, size, padding=0):
        mat = mat * (size - 2 * padding)
        mat[:, 2] += padding
        return cv2.warpAffine(image, mat, (size, size))
```

The extract method in the `Extract` class takes in the whole image, along with the `DetectFace` object, as input. It also takes in a size parameter to resize the images to the required dimensions. We make use of cv2's `warpAffine` and skimage's `transform` methods to perform the alignment. Interested readers are requested to check out the official documentation of these libraries for more details. For now, we can consider these as helper functions that allow us to extract and align the detected faces. *Figure 8.14* shows the output after alignment:

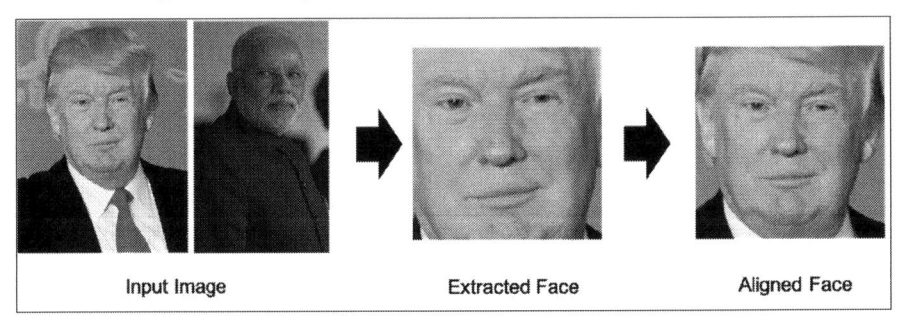

Figure 8.14: Transformation from the input image to the extracted face and finally, the aligned face

The transformation depicted in the figure highlights subtle differences between the raw extracted face and the aligned face. This transformation works for any face pose and helps align faces for better results.

Now that we understand the step-by-step tasks, let's put everything in order to generate the required datasets. The following snippet combines all these steps into a single method for ease of use:

```python
def get_faces(reference_image,image,extractor,debug=False):
    faces_count = 0
    facefilter = FaceFilter(reference_image)
    for face in detect_faces(image):
        if not facefilter.check(face):
            print('Skipping not recognized face!')
            continue
        resized_image = extractor.extract(image, face, 256)
        if debug:
            imgplot = plt.imshow(cv2.cvtColor(resized_image,
                                              cv2.COLOR_BGR2RGB))
            plt.show()

        yield faces_count, face
        faces_count +=1
```

We next use the get_faces method to write a high-level function which takes the raw images as input, along with other required objects, to extract and dump the relevant faces into an output directory. This is shown in the following snippet:

```python
def create_face_dataset(reference_face_filepath,
                        input_dir,
                        output_dir,
                        extractor,
                        included_extensions=included_extensions):
    image_list = [fn for fn in glob.glob(input_dir+"/*.*") \
                  if any(fn.endswith(ext) for ext in included_extensions)]
    print("Total Images to Scan={}".format(len(image_list)))
    positive_ctr = 0
    try:
        for filename in image_list:
            image = cv2.imread(filename)
            for idx, face in get_faces(reference_face_
 filepath,image,extractor):
                resized_image = extractor.extract(image, face, 256)
```

```
                    output_file = output_dir+"/"+str(filename).split("/")[-1]
                    cv2.imwrite(output_file, resized_image)
                    positive_ctr += 1
        except Exception as e:
            print('Failed to extract from image: {}. Reason: {}'.
    format(filename, e))
        print("Images with reference face={}".format(positive_ctr))
```

We use `create_face_dataset` to scan through raw images of Donald Trump and Nicolas Cage to create the required datasets for us.

Autoencoder architecture

We prepared our datasets for both Donald Trump and Nicolas Cage using the tools presented in the previous section. Let's now work toward a model architecture that learns the task of face swapping.

We presented a few common architectures in earlier sections of the book. The encoder-decoder setup is one such setup widely used for deepfake tasks. For our current task of face swapping, we will develop an autoencoder setup to learn and swap faces. As has been the norm, we will make use of TensorFlow and Keras to prepare the required models.

Before we get onto actual architecture code, let's briefly recap how this setup works. A typical autoencoder has two components, an encoder and a decoder. The encoder takes an image as input and compresses it down to a lower dimensional space. This compressed representation is called an embedding, or bottleneck features. The decoder works in the reverse manner. It takes the embedding vector as input and tries to reconstruct the image as output. In short, an autoencoder can be described as:

$$f(x) = decoder(encoder(x)) \approx x'$$

The autoencoder takes x as input and tries to generate a reconstruction x' such that $x \approx x'$.

With this brief overview of the autoencoder architecture, let's get started with developing the required functions for both encoders and decoders. The following snippet shows a function that creates downsampling blocks for the encoder part:

```
def conv(x, filters):
    x = Conv2D(filters, kernel_size=5, strides=2, padding='same')(x)
    x = LeakyReLU(0.1)(x)
    return x
```

The downsampling block makes use of a two-dimensional convolutional layer followed by leaky ReLU activation. The encoder will make use of multiple such repeating blocks followed by fully connected and reshaping layers. We finally make use of an upsampling block to transform the output into an 8x8 image with 512 channels. The following snippet shows the upsampling block:

```python
def upscale(x, filters):
    x = Conv2D(filters * 4, kernel_size=3, padding='same')(x)
    x = LeakyReLU(0.1)(x)
    x = UpSampling2D()(x)
    return x
```

The upsampling block is composed of a two-dimensional convolution, LeakyReLU, and finally an UpSampling2D layer. We use both the downsampling and upsampling blocks to create the encoder architecture, which is presented in the following snippet:

```python
def Encoder(input_shape, encoder_dim):
    input_ = Input(shape=input_shape)
    x = input_
    x = conv(x, 128)
    x = conv(x, 256)
    x = conv(x, 512)
    x = conv(x, 1024)
    x = Dense(encoder_dim)(Flatten()(x))
    x = Dense(4 * 4 * 1024)(x)
    # Passed flattened X input into 2 dense layers, 1024 and 1024*4*4
    x = Reshape((4, 4, 1024))(x)
    # Reshapes X into 4,4,1024
    x = upscale(x, 128)
    return Model(input_, x)
```

The decoder, on the other hand, has a simpler setup. We make use of a few upsampling blocks followed by a convolutional layer to reconstruct the input image as its output. The following snippet shows the function for the decoder:

```python
def Decoder(input_shape=(8, 8, 512)):
    input_ = Input(shape=input_shape)
    x = input_
    x = upscale(x, 256)
    x = upscale(x, 128)
    x = upscale(x, 64)
    x = Conv2D(3, kernel_size=5, padding='same', activation='sigmoid')(x)
    return Model(input_, x)
```

Deepfakes with GANs

For our task of face swapping, we develop two autoencoders, one for each identity, in other words, one for Donald Trump and one for Nicolas Cage. The only trick is that both autoencoders share the same encoder. Yes, this architectural setup requires us to develop two autoencoders with specific decoders but a common encoder.

This trick works for a few simple reasons. Let's discuss this a bit more. Let's assume we have two autoencoders, Autoencoder-A and Autoencoder-B, composed of a common encoder but the respective decoders of Decoder-A and Decoder-B. This setup is depicted in the following figure:

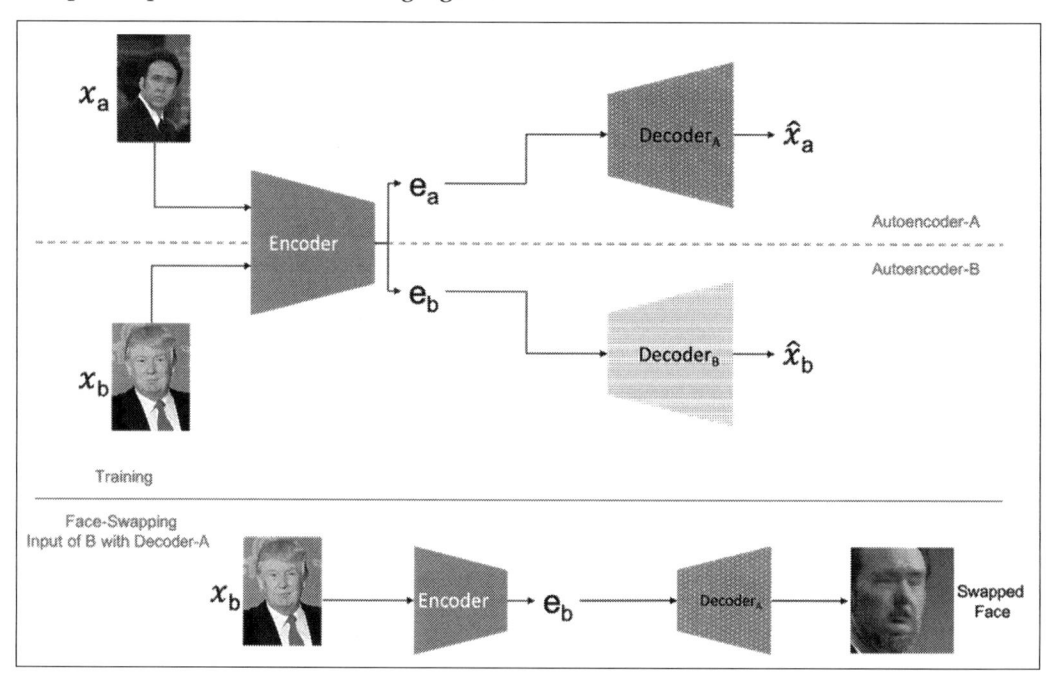

Figure 8.15: Replacement using autoencoders

The details regarding how this setup works are as follows:

- Both autoencoders learn to reconstruct their respective inputs as they train using backpropagation.
- Each autoencoder tries to minimize the reconstruction error. In our case, we will make use of **mean absolute error** (**MAE**) as our metric.
- Since both autoencoders have the same encoder, the encoder learns to understand both kinds of faces and transforms them into the embedding space.

Chapter 8

- Transforming the input images by aligning and warping the faces ensures that the encoder is able to learn representations of both kinds of faces.
- The respective decoders, on the other hand, are trained to make use of the embeddings to reconstruct the images.

Once both the encoders are trained to our satisfaction, we proceed to face swapping. Let's consider the scenario where we're swapping the face of person B onto the face of person A:

- We start with an image of person B. The input is encoded into a lower dimensional space by the encoder. Now, in place of using the decoder for B, we swap it with the decoder of A itself, i.e. Decoder-A. This is essentially Autoencoder-A with input from the dataset of person B.
- Face swapping using B as input for Autoencoder-A works because Autoencoder-A treats the face of B as if it were a warped version of face A itself (due to the common encoder in place).
- Thus, Decoder-A of Autoencoder-A generates an output image which seems like a look-alike of A with the characteristics of B.

Let's leverage this understanding to create the required autoencoders. The following snippet presents autoencoders for both types of faces:

```
ENCODER_DIM = 1024
IMAGE_SHAPE = (64, 64, 3)

encoder = Encoder(IMAGE_SHAPE,ENCODER_DIM)
decoder_A = Decoder()
decoder_B = Decoder()

optimizer = Adam(lr=5e-5, beta_1=0.5, beta_2=0.999) #orig adam 5e-5
x = Input(shape=IMAGE_SHAPE)

autoencoder_A = Model(x, decoder_A(encoder(x)))
autoencoder_B = Model(x, decoder_B(encoder(x)))

autoencoder_A.compile(optimizer=optimizer, loss='mean_absolute_error')
autoencoder_B.compile(optimizer=optimizer, loss='mean_absolute_error')
```

We have two autoencoders that take 3 channel input images, each 64x64 in size. The encoder transforms these images into embeddings of size 8x8x512, while the decoder uses these embeddings to reconstruct output images of shape 64x64x3. In the next section, we'll train these autoencoders.

Training our own face swapper

Now that we have both the autoencoders in place, we need to prepare a custom training loop to train both networks together. However, before we get to the training loop, there are a few other utilities we need to define.

The input datasets we have created for both personalities contain their faces under different lighting conditions, face positions, and other settings. Yet these cannot be exhaustive in nature. To ensure that we capture a larger variation of each type of face, we'll make use of a few augmentation methods. The following snippet presents a function that applies random transformations to an input image:

```python
def random_transform(image,
                     rotation_range,
                     zoom_range,
                     shift_range,
                     random_flip):
    h, w = image.shape[0:2]
    rotation = np.random.uniform(-rotation_range, rotation_range)
    scale = np.random.uniform(1 - zoom_range, 1 + zoom_range)
    tx = np.random.uniform(-shift_range, shift_range) * w
    ty = np.random.uniform(-shift_range, shift_range) * h
    mat = cv2.getRotationMatrix2D((w // 2, h // 2), rotation, scale)
    mat[:, 2] += (tx, ty)
    result = cv2.warpAffine(image, mat, (w, h),
                            borderMode=cv2.BORDER_REPLICATE)
    if np.random.random() < random_flip:
        result = result[:, ::-1]
    return result
```

The `random_transform` function helps us to generate different warps of the same input face. This method ensures that we have enough variation for training our networks.

The next function required is a batch generator. Since we are dealing with images and large networks, it is imperative that we keep in mind the resource requirements. We make use of lazy execution utilities such as `yield` to keep memory/GPU requirements as low as possible. The following snippet shows our batch generator for the training process:

```python
def minibatch(image_list, batchsize):
    length = len(image_list)
    epoch = i = 0
    shuffle(image_list)
```

```
    while True:
        size = batchsize
        if i + size > length:
            shuffle(image_list)
            i = 0
            epoch += 1
        images = np.float32([read_image(image_list[j])
                             for j in range(i, i + size)])
        warped_img, target_img = images[:, 0, :, :, :],
                                 images[:, 1, :, :, :]
        i += size
        yield epoch, warped_img, target_img


def minibatchAB(image_list, batchsize):
    batch = minibatch(image_list, batchsize)
    for ep1, warped_img, target_img in batch:
        yield ep1, warped_img, target_img
```

Now that we have the batch generator along with the augmentation functions, let's prepare a training loop. This is shown in the following snippet:

```
def train_one_step(iter,batch_genA,batch_genB,autoencoder_A,autoencoder_B):
    epoch, warped_A, target_A = next(batch_genA)
    epoch, warped_B, target_B = next(batch_genB)
    loss_A = autoencoder_A.train_on_batch(warped_A, target_A)
    loss_B = autoencoder_B.train_on_batch(warped_B, target_B)

    print("[#{0:5d}] loss_A: {1:.5f}, loss_B: {2:.5f}".format(iter,
loss_A, loss_B))
```

```
ctr = 10000
batchsize = 64
save_interval = 100
model_dir = "models"

fn_imgA = get_image_paths('nicolas_face')
fn_imgB = get_image_paths('trump_face')

batch_genA = minibatchAB(fn_imgA, batchsize)
batch_genB = minibatchAB(fn_imgB, batchsize)
for epoch in range(0, ctr):
```

```
        save_iteration = epoch % save_interval == 0

        train_one_step(epoch,batch_genA,batch_genB,autoencoder_A,autoencode
r_B)

        if save_iteration:
            print("{}/{}".format(epoch,ctr))
            save_weights('models',encoder,decoder_A,decoder_B)
```

We train both the autoencoders for about 10,000 steps, or until the loss stabilizes. We utilize a batch size of 64 and save checkpoint weights every 100 epochs. Readers are free to play around with these parameters depending on their infrastructure setup.

Results and limitations

We have now trained the respective autoencoders for Nicolas Cage (Autoencoder-A) and Donald Trump (Autoencoder-B). The final step is to transform Nicolas Cage into Donald Trump. We described the steps earlier; we will use the autoencoder for Donald Trump with the input as Nicolas Cage, thereby generating an output that seems like a Nicolas Cage version of Donald Trump.

But before we get to the task of output generation, we require a few additional utilities. We discussed an additional step called **blending**. This step is performed post-output generation to ensure that the generated replacement and the original face seamlessly combine into a single image. Refer back to *Figure 8.8* for a visual reminder of the concept of blending. For our task, we prepare a blending class called Convert. The class is presented in the following snippet:

```
class Convert():
    def __init__(self, encoder,
                 blur_size=2,
                 seamless_clone=False,
                 mask_type="facehullandrect",
                 erosion_kernel_size=None,
                 **kwargs):
        self.encoder = encoder

        self.erosion_kernel = None
        if erosion_kernel_size is not None:
            self.erosion_kernel = cv2.getStructuringElement(
                cv2.MORPH_ELLIPSE, (erosion_kernel_size, erosion_
kernel_size))
```

```
        self.blur_size = blur_size
        self.seamless_clone = seamless_clone
        self.mask_type = mask_type.lower()

    def patch_image(self, image, face_detected):

        size = 64
        image_size = image.shape[1], image.shape[0]

        # get face alignment matrix
        mat = np.array(get_align_mat(face_detected)).reshape(2, 3) * size

        # perform affine transformation to
        # transform face as per alignment matrix
        new_face = self.get_new_face(image, mat, size)

        # get face mask matrix
        image_mask = self.get_image_mask(image, new_face,
                                        face_detected, mat,
                                        image_size)

        return self.apply_new_face(image,
                                   new_face,
                                   image_mask,
                                   mat,
                                   image_size,
                                   size)
```

The patch_image method relies on a few utility functions also defined in the class, get_new_face, apply_new_face and get_image_mask:

```
    def apply_new_face(self,
                       image,
                       new_face,
                       image_mask,
                       mat,
                       image_size,
                       size):
        base_image = np.copy(image)
        new_image = np.copy(image)
        # perform affine transformation for better match
        cv2.warpAffine(new_face, mat, image_size, new_image,
```

Deepfakes with GANs

```
                            cv2.WARP_INVERSE_MAP, cv2.BORDER_TRANSPARENT)

        outimage = None
        if self.seamless_clone:
            masky, maskx = cv2.transform(np.array([size / 2, size /
2]).reshape(1, 1, 2), cv2.invertAffineTransform(mat)).reshape(2).
astype(int)
            outimage = cv2.seamlessClone(new_image.astype(np.uint8),
base_image.astype(np.uint8), (image_mask * 255).astype(np.uint8),
(masky, maskx), cv2.NORMAL_CLONE)
        else:
            # apply source face on the target image's mask
            foreground = cv2.multiply(image_mask,
                                      new_image.astype(float))

            # keep background same
            background = cv2.multiply(1.0 - image_mask,
                                      base_image.astype(float))

            # merge foreground and background components
            outimage = cv2.add(foreground, background)

        return outimage

    def get_new_face(self, image, mat, size):
        # function to align input image based on
        # base image face matrix
        face = cv2.warpAffine(image, mat, (size, size))
        face = np.expand_dims(face, 0)
        new_face = self.encoder(face / 255.0)[0]

        return np.clip(new_face * 255, 0, 255).astype(image.dtype)

    def get_image_mask(self, image, new_face, face_detected, mat,
image_size):
        # function to get mask/portion of image covered by face
        face_mask = np.zeros(image.shape, dtype=float)
        if 'rect' in self.mask_type:
            face_src = np.ones(new_face.shape, dtype=float)
            cv2.warpAffine(face_src, mat, image_size, face_mask,
                           cv2.WARP_INVERSE_MAP, cv2.BORDER_TRANSPARENT)
```

```python
        hull_mask = np.zeros(image.shape, dtype=float)
        if 'hull' in self.mask_type:
            hull = cv2.convexHull(np.array(face_detected.
landmarksAsXY()).reshape(
                (-1, 2)).astype(int)).flatten().reshape((-1, 2))
            cv2.fillConvexPoly(hull_mask, hull, (1, 1, 1))

        if self.mask_type == 'rect':
            image_mask = face_mask
        elif self.mask_type == 'faceHull':
            image_mask = hull_mask
        else:
            image_mask = ((face_mask * hull_mask))

        # erode masked image to improve blending
        if self.erosion_kernel is not None:
            image_mask = cv2.erode(image_mask, self.erosion_kernel,
                                   iterations=1)

        # blur masked image to improve blending
        if self.blur_size != 0:
            image_mask = cv2.blur(image_mask, (self.blur_size,
                                               self.blur_size))

        return image_mask
```

This class takes in multiple parameters to improve the blending results. The parameters control aspects such as the size of the blurring kernel, the type of patch (such as rectangular or polygon), and the erosion kernel size. The class also takes the encoder as input. The class method `patch_image` does its magic with the help of transformation functions from the cv2 library and the parameters we set during instantiation. We use the following `convert` function to process each input face of type A and transform it into type B:

```python
def convert(converter, item,output_dir):
    try:
        (filename, image, faces) = item
        image1 = None
        for idx, face in faces:
            image1 = converter.patch_image(image, face)
        if np.any(image1):
          output_file = output_dir+"/"+str(filename).split("/")[-1]
```

```
            cv2.imwrite(str(output_file), image1)
    except Exception as e:
        print('Failed to convert image: {}. Reason: {}'.
format(filename, e))
```

We use these methods to loop through the dataset of Nicolas Cage's faces to generate blended outputs. The following snippet shows the objects of the `Convert` class and an inference loop to generate output:

```
conv_name = "Masked"
swap_model = False
blur_size = 2
seamless_clone = False
mask_type = "facehullandrect"
erosion_kernel_size = None
smooth_mask = True
avg_color_adjust = True

faceswap_converter = Convert(model_swapper(False,autoencoder_A,autoencoder_B),
    blur_size = blur_size,
    seamless_clone = seamless_clone,
    mask_type = mask_type,
    erosion_kernel_size = erosion_kernel_size,
    smooth_mask = smooth_mask,
    avg_color_adjust = avg_color_adjust
)

list_faces=get_list_images_faces('nicolas_face',
                                 'nicolas_ref.png',extractor)

for item in list_faces:
    #print(item)
    convert(faceswap_converter, item,'face_swaps_trump')
```

The generated outputs are depicted in the following figure:

Figure 8.16: Nicolas Cage transformed as Donald Trump

The swapped output faces are encouraging, but not as seamless as we would have expected. Still, we can see that the model has learned to identify and swap the right portions of the face. The blending step has also tried to match the skin tone, face pose, and other aspects to make the results as realistic as possible.

This seems like a good start, but leaves a lot for improvement. Here are a few limitations of our setup:

- The quality of the swapped output is directly related to the capabilities of the trained autoencoders. Since there is no component to track how realistic the reconstructed outputs are, it is difficult to nudge the autoencoders in the right direction. Using a GAN would be a possible enhancement to provide a positive feedback to the overall training process.
- The outputs are a bit blurry. This is due to the difference in the actual input resolution and the generated output (64x64). Another reason for the blurry output is the use of MAE as a simple loss function. Research has shown that composite and complex losses help improve final output quality.
- The limited dataset is another reason for restricted output quality. We leveraged augmentation techniques to work around the limitation, but it is not a substitute for larger datasets.

In this section, we developed a face swapping deepfake architecture from scratch. We went through a step-by-step approach to understand every component and step in the overall pipeline that swaps Nicolas Cage with Donald Trump. In the next section, we will use a more complex setup to try our hand at a different mode of operation.

The code presented in this section is based on the original deepfake work as well as a simplified implementation of Olivier Valery's code, which is available on GitHub at the following link: https://github.com/OValery16/swap-face.

Now that we have trained our own face swapper, illustrating the replacement mode of operation, we can move onto the re-enactment mode.

Re-enactment using pix2pix

Re-enactment is another mode of operation for the deepfakes setup. It is supposedly better at generating believable fake content compared to the replacement mode. In earlier sections, we discussed different techniques used to perform re-enactment, i.e. by focusing on gaze, expressions, the mouth, and so on.

We also discussed image-to-image translation architectures in *Chapter 7, Style Transfer with GANs*. Particularly, we discussed in detail how the pix2pix GAN is a powerful architecture which enables paired translation tasks. In this section, we will leverage the pix2pix GAN to develop a face re-enactment setup from scratch. We will work toward building a network where we can use our own face, mouth, and expressions to control Barack Obama's (former US president) face. We will go through each and every step, starting right from preparing the dataset, to defining the pix2pix architecture, to finally generating the output re-enactment. Let's get started.

Dataset preparation

We will be using the pix2pix GAN as the backbone network for our current task of re-enactment. While pix2pix is a powerful network that trains with very few training samples, there is a restriction that requires the training samples to be paired. In this section, we will use this restriction to our advantage.

Since the aim is to analyze a target face and control it using a source face, we can leverage what is common between faces to develop a dataset for our use case. The common characteristics between different faces are the presence of facial landmarks and their positioning. In the *Key feature set* section, we discussed how simple and easy it is to build a facial landmark detection module using libraries such as dlib, cv2, and MTCNN.

For our current use case, we will prepare paired training samples consisting of pairs of landmarks and their corresponding images/photographs. For generating re-enacted content, we can then simply extract facial landmarks of the source face/controlling entity and use pix2pix to generate high quality actual output based on the target person.

In our case, the source/controlling personality could be you or any other person, while the target personality is Barack Obama.

To prepare our dataset, we will extract frames and corresponding landmarks of each frame from a video. Since we want to train our network to be able to generate high-quality coloured output images based on landmark inputs, we need a video of Barack Obama. You could download this from various different sources on the internet. Please note that this exercise is again for academic and educational purposes only. Kindly use any videos carefully and with caution.

Generating a paired dataset of landmark and video frames is a straightforward application of the code snippets given in the *Facial landmarks* section. To avoid repetition, we leave this as an exercise for the reader. Please note that complete code is available in the code repository for this book. We generated close to 400 paired samples from one of the speeches of Barack Obama. *Figure 8.17* presents a few of these samples:

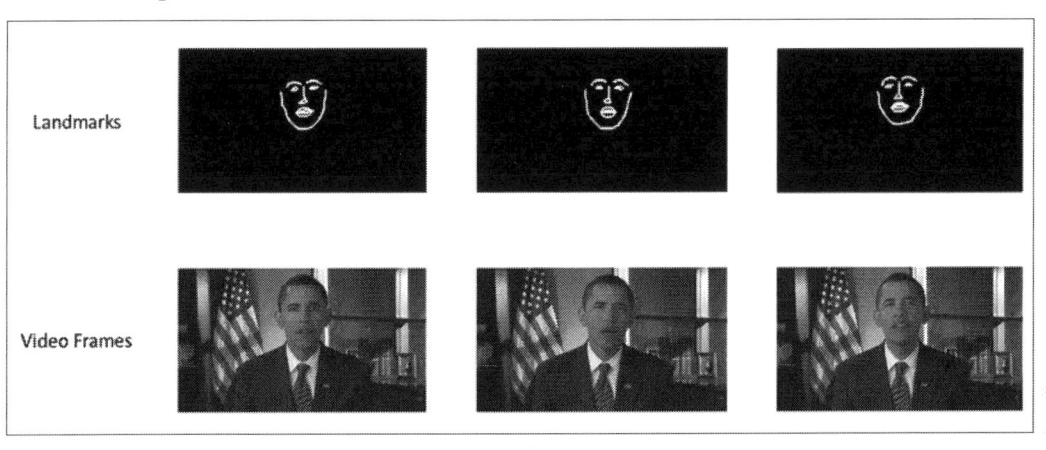

Figure 8.17: Paired training samples consisting of facial landmarks and corresponding video frames

We can see how the landmarks capture the position of the head along with the movement of the lips, eyes, and other facial landmarks. We are thus able to generate a paired training dataset in almost no time. Let's now move on to network setup and training.

Pix2pix GAN setup and training

We discussed the pix2pix architecture along with its sub-components and objective functions in detail in *Chapter 7, Style Transfer with GANs*. In this section, we will briefly touch upon them for the sake of completeness.

Similar to a typical GAN, pix2pix also consists of generator and discriminator networks. Both networks are trained alternatively until we achieve a stable performance from the generator. In the case of the pix2pix GAN, we have a U-Net style generator. In other words, the generator consists of a number of skip connections between its downsampling and upsampling layers. This ensures that important features and local characteristics are carried along to the output layers. The following snippet shows a function, build_generator, that prepares the generator network:

```
def build_generator(img_shape,channels=3,num_filters=64):
    # Image input
    input_layer = Input(shape=img_shape)

    # Downsampling
    down_sample_1 = downsample_block(input_layer,
                                    num_filters,
                                    batch_normalization=False)
    # rest of the downsampling blocks have batch_normalization=true
    down_sample_2 = downsample_block(down_sample_1, num_filters*2)
    down_sample_3 = downsample_block(down_sample_2, num_filters*4)
    down_sample_4 = downsample_block(down_sample_3, num_filters*8)
    down_sample_5 = downsample_block(down_sample_4, num_filters*8)
    down_sample_6 = downsample_block(down_sample_5, num_filters*8)
    down_sample_7 = downsample_block(down_sample_6, num_filters*8)

    # Upsampling blocks with skip connections
    upsample_1 = upsample_block(down_sample_7, down_sample_6,
                                num_filters*8)
    upsample_2 = upsample_block(upsample_1, down_sample_5,
                                num_filters*8)
    upsample_3 = upsample_block(upsample_2, down_sample_4,
                                num_filters*8)
    upsample_4 = upsample_block(upsample_3, down_sample_3,
                                num_filters*8)
    upsample_5 = upsample_block(upsample_4, down_sample_2,
                                num_filters*2)
    upsample_6 = upsample_block(upsample_5, down_sample_1, num_filters)

    upsample_7 = UpSampling2D(size=2)(upsample_6)
    output_img = Conv2D(channels,
                        kernel_size=4,
                        strides=1,
```

```
                    padding='same',
                    activation='tanh')(upsample_7)

    return Model(input_layer, output_img)
```

Please note that we are reusing the utility functions prepared as part of *Chapter 7, Style Transfer with GANs*. Unlike the generator, which has a specific setup, the discriminator network for pix2pix is a fairly straightforward implementation. We present the discriminator network in the following snippet:

```
def build_discriminator(img_shape,num_filters=64):
    input_img = Input(shape=img_shape)
    cond_img = Input(shape=img_shape)

    # Concatenate input and conditioning image by channels
    # as input for discriminator
    combined_input = Concatenate(axis=-1)([input_img, cond_img])

    # First discriminator block does not use batch_normalization
    disc_block_1 = discriminator_block(combined_input,
                                       num_filters,
                                       batch_normalization=False)
    disc_block_2 = discriminator_block(disc_block_1, num_filters*2)
    disc_block_3 = discriminator_block(disc_block_2, num_filters*4)
    disc_block_4 = discriminator_block(disc_block_3, num_filters*8)

    output = Conv2D(1, kernel_size=4, strides=1, padding='same')(disc_block_4)

    return Model([input_img, cond_img], output)
```

As shown in the snippet, the discriminator network uses repeating blocks consisting of convolutional, LeakyReLU, and batch normalization layers. The output is a *patch-GAN* kind of setup that divides the whole output into several overlapping patches to calculate fake versus real. The patch-GAN ensures high-quality outputs that feel more realistic.

We use these two functions to prepare our generator, discriminator, and GAN network objects. The objects are created as shown in the following snippet:

```
IMG_WIDTH = 256
IMG_HEIGHT = 256

discriminator = build_discriminator(img_shape=(IMG_HEIGHT,IMG_WIDTH,3),
```

Deepfakes with GANs

```
                              num_filters=64)
discriminator.compile(loss='mse',
                      optimizer=Adam(0.0002, 0.5),
                      metrics=['accuracy'])

generator = build_generator(img_shape=(IMG_HEIGHT,IMG_WIDTH,3),
                            channels=3,
                            num_filters=64)

source_img = Input(shape=(IMG_HEIGHT,IMG_WIDTH,3))
cond_img = Input(shape=(IMG_HEIGHT,IMG_WIDTH,3))
fake_img = generator(cond_img)

discriminator.trainable = False
output = discriminator([fake_img, cond_img])

gan = Model(inputs=[source_img, cond_img], outputs=[output, fake_img])
gan.compile(loss=['mse', 'mae'],
            loss_weights=[1, 100],
            optimizer=Adam(0.0002, 0.5))
```

The training loop is straightforward; we make use of the three network objects (discriminator, generator, and the overall GAN model) and alternately train the generator and discriminator. Note that the facial landmarks dataset is used as input, while the video frames are output for this training process. The training loop is presented in the following snippet:

```
def train(generator,
          discriminator,
          gan,
          patch_gan_shape,
          epochs,
          path='/content/data',
          batch_size=1,
          sample_interval=50):

    # Ground truth shape/Patch-GAN outputs
    real_y = np.ones((batch_size,) + patch_gan_shape)
    fake_y = np.zeros((batch_size,) + patch_gan_shape)

    for epoch in range(epochs):
      print("Epoch={}".format(epoch))
      for idx, (imgs_source, imgs_cond) in enumerate(batch_
```

```python
           generator(path=path,
                     batch_size=batch_size,
                     img_res=[IMG_HEIGHT, IMG_WIDTH])):
            # train discriminator
            # generator generates outputs based on
            # conditioned input images
            fake_imgs = generator.predict([imgs_cond])

            # calculate discriminator loss on real samples
            disc_loss_real = discriminator.train_on_batch([imgs_source,
                                                           imgs_cond],
                                                          real_y)
            # calculate discriminator loss on fake samples
            disc_loss_fake = discriminator.train_on_batch([fake_imgs,
                                                           imgs_cond],
                                                          fake_y)
            # overall discriminator loss
            discriminator_loss = 0.5 * np.add(disc_loss_real, disc_loss_fake)

            # train generator
            gen_loss = gan.train_on_batch([imgs_source, imgs_cond], [real_y, imgs_source])

            # training updates every 50 iterations
            if idx % 50 == 0:
                print ("[Epoch {}/{}] [Discriminator loss: {}, accuracy: {}] [Generator loss: {}]".format(epoch, epochs,
                                                      discriminator_loss[0],
                                                      100*discriminator_loss[1],
                                                      gen_loss[0]))

            # Plot and Save progress every few iterations
            if idx % sample_interval == 0:
                plot_sample_images(generator=generator,
                                   path=path,
                                   epoch=epoch,
                                   batch_num=idx,
                                   output_dir='images')
```

In the preceding snippet, we train the discriminator and generator models of this pix2pix setup with paired training examples. Pix2pix is a highly optimized GAN which requires very few resources overall. With only 400 samples and 200 epochs, we trained our landmarks-to-video frame GAN.

Figures 8.18 and *8.19* showcase the training progress of this setup:

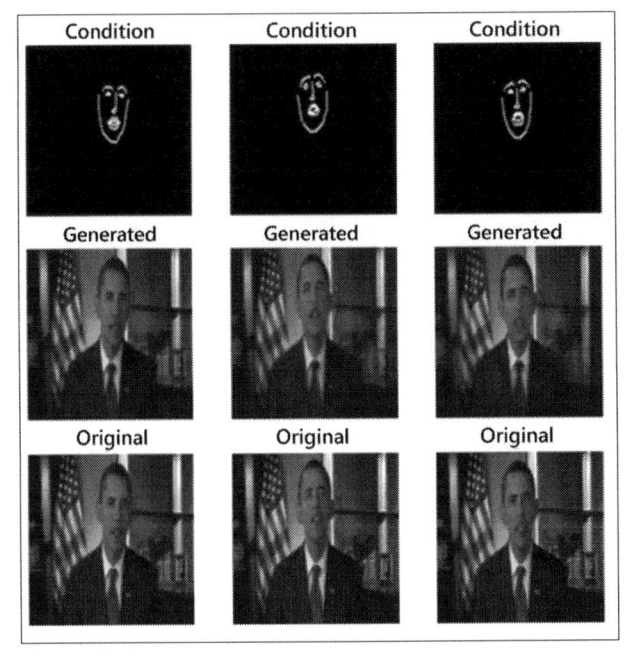

Figure 8.18: Training progress for pix2pix GAN for face re-enactment (epoch 1)

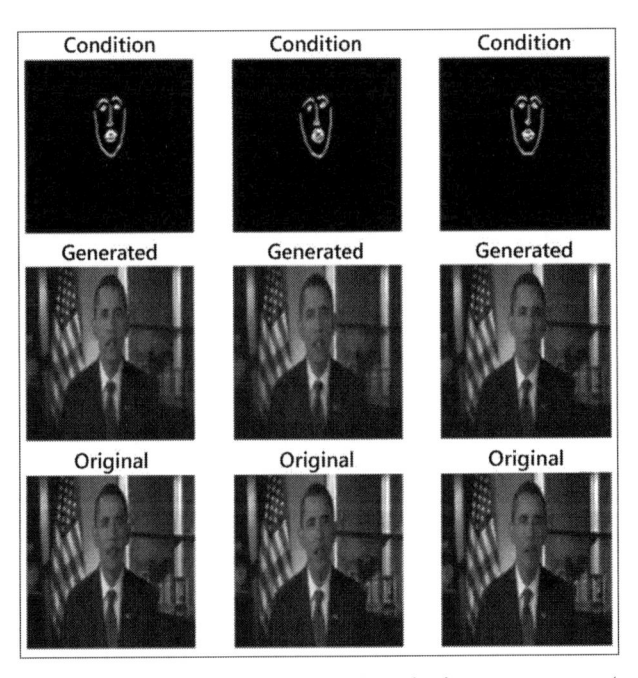

Figure 8.19: Training progress for the pix2pix GAN for face re-enactment (epoch 40)

Chapter 8

As we can see in the preceding figures, the model is able to capture key facial features and their positioning, along with the background details. In the initial iterations (*Figure 8.18*), the model seems to be having difficulty in generating the mouth region, but as the training progresses, it learns to fill it with the right set of details (*Figure 8.19*).

Now that we have our GAN trained for the required task, let's perform some re-enactments in the next section.

Results and limitations

In the chapter so far, we have dealt mostly with images or photographs as input. Since the pix2pix GAN is a very efficient implementation, it can be leveraged to generate outputs in near-real time. This capability therefore implies that we can use such a trained model to perform re-enactments using a live video feed. In other words, we can use a live video feed of ourselves to re-enact Barack Obama's face movements and expressions.

To perform live video re-enactment, we will make use of OpenCV. OpenCV has video capture APIs that make it very easy to capture individual video frames and manipulate them as required. We also make use of the 68-point facial landmark detection from dlib, as we have been doing in the chapter so far. The following snippet presents the get_landmarks and get_obama functions:

```
CROP_SIZE = 256
DOWNSAMPLE_RATIO = 4

def get_landmarks(black_image,gray,faces):
    for face in faces:
        detected_landmarks = predictor(gray, face).parts()
        landmarks = [[p.x * DOWNSAMPLE_RATIO, p.y * DOWNSAMPLE_RATIO]
for p in detected_landmarks]

        jaw = reshape_for_polyline(landmarks[0:17])
        left_eyebrow = reshape_for_polyline(landmarks[22:27])
        right_eyebrow = reshape_for_polyline(landmarks[17:22])
        nose_bridge = reshape_for_polyline(landmarks[27:31])
        lower_nose = reshape_for_polyline(landmarks[30:35])
        left_eye = reshape_for_polyline(landmarks[42:48])
        right_eye = reshape_for_polyline(landmarks[36:42])
        outer_lip = reshape_for_polyline(landmarks[48:60])
        inner_lip = reshape_for_polyline(landmarks[60:68])
```

```
        color = (255, 255, 255)
        thickness = 3

        cv2.polylines(black_image, [jaw], False, color, thickness)
        cv2.polylines(black_image, [left_eyebrow], False, color,
                    thickness)
        cv2.polylines(black_image, [right_eyebrow], False, color,
                    thickness)
        cv2.polylines(black_image, [nose_bridge], False, color,
                    thickness)
        cv2.polylines(black_image, [lower_nose], True, color,
                    thickness)
        cv2.polylines(black_image, [left_eye], True, color, thickness)
        cv2.polylines(black_image, [right_eye], True, color, thickness)
        cv2.polylines(black_image, [outer_lip], True, color, thickness)
        cv2.polylines(black_image, [inner_lip], True, color, thickness)
    return black_image

def get_obama(landmarks):
    landmarks = (landmarks/127.5)-1
    landmarks = tf.image.resize(landmarks, [256,256]).numpy()
    fake_imgs = generator.predict(np.expand_dims(landmarks,axis=0))
    return fake_imgs
```

These functions help extract and draw facial landmarks from a given frame, and use those landmarks to generate output of colored frames using the pix2pix GAN.

The next step is to use these functions to process the live video feed and generate re-enacted output samples. This manipulation is fast enough to enhance the believability of the fake content. The following snippet presents the manipulation loop:

```
cap = cv2.VideoCapture(0)
fps = video.FPS().start()
k = 0
display_plots = True
display_cv2 = True
while True:
    k += 1
    ret, frame = cap.read(0)
    if np.all(np.array(frame.shape)):
        frame_resize = cv2.resize(frame, None, fx=1 / DOWNSAMPLE_RATIO,
fy=1 / DOWNSAMPLE_RATIO)
```

```python
            gray = cv2.cvtColor(frame_resize, cv2.COLOR_BGR2GRAY)
            faces = detector(gray, 1)
            black_image = np.zeros(frame.shape, np.uint8)
            landmarks = get_landmarks(black_image.copy(),gray,faces)
            img_tgt = (landmarks/127.5)-1
            img_tgt = tf.image.resize(img_tgt, [256,256]).numpy()
            obama = generator.predict(np.expand_dims(img_tgt,axis=0))[0]
            try:
                obama = 0.5 * obama + 0.5
                gen_imgs = np.concatenate([np.expand_dims(cv2.
cvtColor(rescale_frame(frame_resize), cv2.COLOR_RGB2BGR),axis=0),
                        np.expand_dims(rescale_frame(obama),axis=0),
                        np.expand_dims(rescale_frame(landmarks),axis=0)])
                if display_plots:
                    titles = ['Live', 'Generated', 'Landmarks']
                    rows, cols = 1, 3
                    fig, axs = plt.subplots(rows, cols)
                    for j in range(cols):
                        if j!=1:
                            axs[j].imshow(gen_imgs[j].astype(int))
                        else:
                            axs[j].imshow(gen_imgs[j])
                        axs[j].set_title(titles[j])
                        axs[j].axis('off')
                    plt.show()
                if display_cv2:
                    cv2.imshow('synthetic obama', cv2.cvtColor(gen_imgs[1],
cv2.COLOR_BGR2RGB))
                    #cv2.imshow('Landmark', rescale_frame(landmarks))
            except Exception as ex:
                print(ex)
            fps.update()
            if cv2.waitKey(1) & 0xFF == ord('q'):
                break

fps.stop()
print('[INFO] elapsed time (total): {:..2f}'.format(fps.elapsed()))
print('[INFO] approx. FPS: {:..2f}'.format(fps.fps()))

cap.release()
cv2.destroyAllWindows()
```

The preceding snippet brings all the pieces into place for video capture and manipulation using the pix2pix GAN. Upon executing the video capture and manipulation loop, we are able to generate some promising results. Some of the re-enactments are depicted in the following figure:

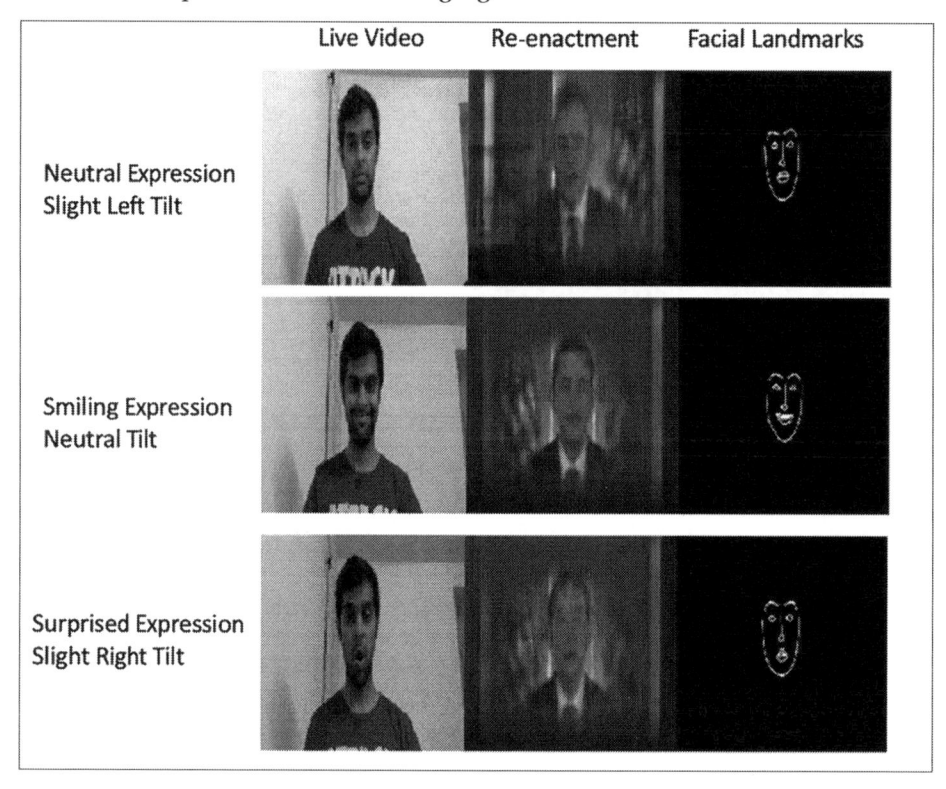

Figure 8.20: Re-enactment using live video as the source and Obama as the target using the pix2pix GAN

Figure 8.20 presents how seamlessly the overall setup works. We are able to capture a live video, convert it into facial landmarks, and then generate re-enactments using the pix2pix GAN. It is apparent how, in the live video, there are no objects in the background, but our network is able to generate the American flag correctly. The samples also showcase how the model is able to capture expressions and head tilt nicely.

Though the results are encouraging, they are far from being perceived as real or believable. The following are a few limitations associated with the approach we discussed in this section:

- The outputs in *Figure 8.20* are a bit fuzzy. They turn completely blank or incomprehensible if the head is tilted quite a lot or if the person in the live video feed is too close or too far from the camera. This issue is mostly because the pix2pix GAN has learned the relative size and position of facial landmarks with respect to the training dataset. This can be improved by performing face alignment and using tighter crops for both the input and inference stages.
- The model's generated content is highly dependent upon the training data. Since our training dataset is derived from a speech, there is limited head movement and very limited facial expression. Thus, if you try to move the head a bit too much or present an expression that isn't in the training dataset, the model makes a very poor guess. A larger dataset with more variability can help fix this issue.

We have seen how a powerful image-to-image translation GAN architecture can be reused for the task of re-enactment.

In the last two sections, we covered a number of interesting hands-on exercises to develop replacement and re-enactment architectures from scratch. We discussed some of the issues with our setup and how we could improve upon them. In the following section, we will discuss some of the challenges associated with deepfake systems.

Challenges

In this section, we will discuss some of the common challenges associated with deepfake architectures, beginning with a brief discussion on the ethical issues associated with this technology.

Ethical issues

Even though generating fake content is not a new concept, the word "deepfake" came into the limelight in 2017 when a Reddit user by the name u/deepfakes posted fake pornographic videos with celebrity faces superimposed on them using deep learning. The quality of the content and the ease with which the user was able to generate them created huge uproar on news channels across the globe. Soon, u/deepfakes released an easy-to-setup application called **FakeApp** that enabled users to generate such content with very little knowledge of how deep learning works. This led to a number of fake videos and objectionable content. This, in turn, helped people gain traction on issues associated with identity theft, impersonation, fake news, and so on.

Soon, interest picked up within the academic community, which not only helped to improve the technology but also insisted on its ethical use. While there are malicious and objectionable content creators making use of these techniques, a number of industry and research projects are underway to detect such fake content, such as Microsoft's deepfake detection tool and Deepware.[14][15]

Technical challenges

Ethical issues aside, let's also discuss a few challenges that are quite apparent for a typical deepfake setup: generalization, occlusions, and temporal issues.

Generalization

Deepfake architectures are generative models at their core, which are highly dependent on the training dataset used. These architectures typically also require huge amounts of training samples, which could be hard to get, especially for the target (or victim in the case of malicious use). Another issue is the paired training setup. Typically, a model trained for one source and target pair is not so easy to use for another pair of source and target personalities.

Work on efficient architectures that can train with smaller amounts of training data is an active area of research. The development of CycleGAN and other unpaired translation architectures is also helping in overcoming the paired training bottleneck.

Occlusions

The source or target inputs might have artifacts around them that obstruct certain features. This could be due to hand movements, hair, eyewear, or other objects. Another type of occlusion occurs due to dynamic changes in the mouth and eye region. This can lead to inconsistent facial features or weird cropped imagery. Certain works are focusing on avoiding such issues by making use of segmentation, in-painting, and other related techniques. One example of such a work is *First Order Motion Model for Image Generation* by Siarohin et al.[16]

Temporal issues

Deepfake architectures work on a frame-by-frame basis (when it comes to video inputs). This results in jitter, flickering, or complete incoherence between subsequent frames. We saw an example of this with the re-enactment exercise using the pix2pix GAN in the previous section. The model is unable to generate coherent output for unseen scenarios. To improve upon this, some researchers are trying to use RNNs (recurrent neural networks) with GANs to generate coherent outputs. Examples of this include:

- *MoCoGAN: Decomposing Motion and Content for Video Generation*[17]
- *Video-to-Video Synthesis*[18]

Off-the-shelf implementations

In this chapter, we covered a step-by-step approach to developing two different deepfake architectures for replacement and re-enactment. Although the implementations are easy to understand and execute, they require quite a bit of understanding and resources to generate high-quality results.

Since the release of u/deepfakes' content in 2017, a number of open source implementations have come out to simplify the use of this technology. While dangerous, most of these projects highlight the ethical implications and caution developers and users in general against the malicious adoption of such projects. While it is beyond the scope of this chapter, we list a few well-designed and popular implementations in this section. Readers are encouraged to go through specific projects for more details.

- **FaceSwap**[19]
  The developers of this project claim this implementation is close to the original implementation by u/deepfakes, with enhancements over the years to improve output content quality. This project provides a detailed documentation and step-by-step guide for preparing the training dataset and generating the fake content. They also share pretrained networks for speeding up the training process. This project has a graphical interface for completely novice users.

- **DeepFaceLab**[20]
  This is one of the most extensive, detailed, and popular deepfakes projects available on the internet. This project is based on the recent paper with the same name presented in May 2020. The project consists of a detailed user guide, video tutorials, a very mature GUI, pretrained models, Colab notebooks, datasets, and even Docker images for quick deployment.
- **FaceSwap-GAN**[21]
  A simple, yet effective, implementation using an ED+GAN setup. This project provides utilities and ready-to-use notebooks for quickly training your own models. The project also provides pretrained models for direct use or transfer learning.

There are a number of Android and iOS apps that work along the same lines and lower the entry barrier to a bare minimum. Today, anybody with a smartphone or a little understanding of technical concepts can use or train such setups with ease.

Summary

Deepfakes are a complicated subject both ethically and technically. In this chapter, we discussed the deepfake technology in general to start with. We presented an overview of what deepfakes are all about and briefly touched upon a number of productive as well as malicious use cases. We presented a detailed discussion on different modes of operation of different deepfake setups and how each of these impacts the overall believability of generated content. While deepfakes is an all-encompassing term associated with videos, images, audio, text, and so on, we focused on visual use cases only in this chapter.

Given our scope, we discussed various feature sets leveraged by different works in this space. In particular, we discussed the Facial Action Coding System (FACS), 3D Morphable Models (3DMM), and facial landmarks. We also discussed how we can perform facial landmark detection using libraries such as dlib and MTCNN. We then presented a high-level flow of tasks to be performed for a deepfakes pipeline. In conjunction with this, we discussed a few common architectures that are widely used to develop such systems.

The second part of the chapter leveraged this understanding to present two hands-on exercises to develop deepfake pipelines from scratch. We first worked toward developing an autoencoder-based face swapping architecture. Through this exercise, we worked through a step by step approach for preparing the dataset, training the networks, and finally generating the swapped outputs. The second exercise involved using the pix2pix GAN to perform re-enactment using live video as the source and Barack Obama as the target. We discussed issues and ways of overcoming the issues we faced with each of these implementations.

In the final section, we presented a discussion about the ethical issues and challenges associated with deepfake architectures. We also touched on a few popular off-the-shelf projects that allow anyone and everyone with a computer or a smartphone to generate fake content.

We covered a lot of ground in this chapter and worked on some very exciting use cases. It is important that we reiterate how vital it is to be careful when we are using technology as powerful as this. The implications and consequences could be very dangerous for the entities involved, so we should be mindful of how this knowledge is used.

While this chapter focused on visual aspects, we will shift gears and move on to text in the next two chapters. The Natural Language Processing space is brimming with some exciting research and use cases. We will focus on some of the path-breaking textual generative works next. Stay tuned.

References

1. BuzzFeedVideo. (2018, April 17). *You Won't Believe What Obama Says In This Video! ;)* [Video]. YouTube. https://www.youtube.com/watch?v=cQ54GDm1eL0&ab_channel=BuzzFeedVideo

2. Lee, D. (2019, May 10). *Deepfake Salvador Dalí takes selfies with museum visitors.* The Verge. https://www.theverge.com/2019/5/10/18540953/salvador-dali-lives-deepfake-museum

3. Malaria Must Die. (2020). *A World Without Malaria.* Malaria Must Die. https://malariamustdie.com/

4. Lyons, K. (2020, February 18). *An Indian politician used AI to translate his speech into other languages to reach more voters.* The Verge. https://www.theverge.com/2020/2/18/21142782/india-politician-deepfakes-ai-elections

5. Dietmar, J. (2019, May 21). *GANs And Deepfakes Could Revolutionize The Fashion Industry.* Forbes. https://www.forbes.com/sites/forbestechcouncil/2019/05/21/gans-and-deepfakes-could-revolutionize-the-fashion-industry/?sh=2502d4163d17

6. Statt, N. (2020, August 27). *Ronald Reagan sends you to do war crimes in the latest Call of Duty: Black Ops Cold War trailer.* The Verge. https://www.theverge.com/2020/8/27/21403879/call-of-duty-black-ops-cold-war-gamescom-2020-trailer-ronald-reagan

7. Cole, S. (2017, December 11). *AI-Assisted Fake Porn Is Here and We're All Fucked.* Vice. https://www.vice.com/en/article/gydydm/gal-gadot-fake-ai-porn

8. dfaker & czfhhh. (2020). *df.* GitHub repository. https://github.com/dfaker/df

9. Pumarola, A., Agudo, A., Martinez, A.M., Sanfeliu, A., & Moreno-Noguer, F. (2018). *GANimation: Anatomically-aware Facial Animation from a Single Image.* ECCV 2018. https://arxiv.org/abs/1807.09251

10. Naruniec, J., Helminger, L., Schroers, C., & Weber, R.M. (2020). *High-Resolution Neural Face Swapping for Visual Effects.* Eurographics Symposium on Rendering 2020. https://s3.amazonaws.com/disney-research-data/wp-content/uploads/2020/06/18013325/High-Resolution-Neural-Face-Swapping-for-Visual-Effects.pdf

11. Geng, Z., Cao, C., & Tulyakov, S. (2019). *3D Guided Fine-Grained Face Manipulation.* arXiv. https://arxiv.org/abs/1902.08900

12. Blanz, V., & Vetter, T. (1999). *A morphable model for the synthesis of 3D faces.* SIGGRAPH '99: Proceedings of the 26th annual conference on Computer graphics and interactive techniques. 187-194. https://cseweb.ucsd.edu/~ravir/6998/papers/p187-blanz.pdf

13. Kaipeng, Z., Zhang, Z., Li, Z., & Qiao, Y. (2016). *Joint Face Detection and Alignment using Multi-task Cascaded Convolutional Networks.* IEEE Signal Processing Letters (SPL), vol. 23, no. 10, pp. 1499-1503, 2016. https://kpzhang93.github.io/MTCNN_face_detection_alignment/

14. Burt, T., & Horvitz, E. (2020, September 1). *New Steps to Combat Disinformation.* Microsoft blog. https://blogs.microsoft.com/on-the-issues/2020/09/01/disinformation-deepfakes-newsguard-video-authenticator/

15. Deepware. (2021). *Deepware - Scan & Detect Deepfake Videos With a Simple tool.* https://deepware.ai/

16. Siarohin, A., Lathuiliere, S., Tulyakov, S., Ricci, E., & Sebe, N. (2019). *First Order Motion Model for Image Animation.* NeurIPS 2019. https://aliaksandrsiarohin.github.io/first-order-model-website/

17. Tulyakov, S., Liu, M-Y., Yang, X., & Kautz, J. (2017). *MoCoGAN: Decomposing Motion and Content for Video Generation.* arXiv. https://arxiv.org/abs/1707.04993

18. Wang, T-C., Liu, M-Y., Zhu, J-Y., Liu, G., Tao, A., Kautz, J., Catanzaro, B. (2018). *Video-to-Video Synthesis.* NeurIPS, 2018. https://arxiv.org/abs/1808.06601

19. torzdf & 77 other contributors. (2021). faceswap. GitHub repository. `https://github.com/Deepfakes/faceswap`

20. iperov & 18 other contributors. (2021). DeepFaceLab. GitHub repository. `https://github.com/iperov/DeepFaceLab`

20. shaoanlu, silky, clarle, & Ja1r0. (2019). faceswap-GAN. GitHub repository. `https://github.com/shaoanlu/faceswap-GAN`

9
The Rise of Methods for Text Generation

In the preceding chapters, we discussed different methods and techniques to develop and train generative models. Particularly, in *Chapter 6, Image Generation with GANs*, we discussed the taxonomy of generative models and introduced explicit and implicit classes. Throughout this book, our focus has been on developing generative models in the vision space, utilizing image and video datasets. The advancements in the field of deep learning for computer vision and ease of understanding were the major reasons behind such a focused introduction.

In the past couple of years though, **Natural Language Processing** (**NLP**) or processing of textual data has seen great interest and research. Text is not just another unstructured type of data; there's a lot more to it than what meets the eye. Textual data is a representation of our thoughts, ideas, knowledge, and communication.

In this chapter and the next, we will focus on understanding concepts related to NLP and generative models for textual data. We will cover different concepts, architectures, and components associated with generative models for textual data, with a focus on the following topics in this chapter:

- A brief overview of traditional ways of representing textual data
- Distributed representation methods
- RNN-based text generation
- LSTM variants and convolutions for text

We will cover the internal workings of different architectures and key contributions that have enabled text generation use cases. We will also build and train these architectures to get a better understanding of them. Readers should also note that while we will go deep into key contributions and related details across *Chapter 9, The Rise of Methods for Text Generation*, and *Chapter 10, NLP 2.0: Using Transformers to Generate Text*, some of these models are extremely large to train on commodity hardware. We will make use of certain high-level Python packages wherever necessary to avoid complexity.

> All code snippets presented in this chapter can be run directly in Google Colab. For reasons of space, import statements for dependencies have not been included, but readers can refer to the GitHub repository for the full code: https://github.com/PacktPublishing/Hands-On-Generative-AI-with-Python-and-TensorFlow-2.

Before we get into the modeling aspects, let's get started by understanding how to represent textual data.

Representing text

Language is one of the most complex aspects of our existence. We use language to communicate our thoughts and choices. Every language is defined with a list of characters called the alphabet, a vocabulary, and a set of rules called grammar. Yet it is not a trivial task to understand and learn a language. Languages are complex and have fuzzy grammatical rules and structures.

Text is a representation of language that helps us communicate and share. This makes it a perfect area of research to expand the horizons of what artificial intelligence can achieve. Text is a type of unstructured data that cannot directly be used by any of the known algorithms. Machine learning and deep learning algorithms in general work with numbers, matrices, vectors, and so on. This, in turn, raises the question: how can we represent text for different language-related tasks?

Bag of Words

As we mentioned earlier, every language consists of a defined list of characters (alphabet), which are combined to form words (vocabulary). Traditionally, **Bag of Words** (**BoW**) has been one of the most popular methods for representing textual information.

BoW is a simple and flexible approach to transforming text into vector form. This transformation helps not only in extracting features from raw text, but also in making it fit for consumption by different algorithms and architectures. As the name suggests, the BoW model of representation utilizes each word as a basic unit of measurement. A BoW model describes the occurrence of words within a given corpus of text. To build a BoW model for representation, we require two major things:

- **A vocabulary**: A collection of known words from the corpus of text to be analyzed.
- **A measure of occurrence**: Something that we choose based upon the application/task at hand. For instance, counting the occurrence of each word, known as term frequency, is one such measure.

A detailed discussion related to the BoW model is beyond the scope of this chapter. We are presenting a high-level overview as a primer before more complex topics are introduced later in this chapter.

The BoW model is called a "bag" to highlight the simplicity and the fact that we overlook any ordering of the occurrences. In other words, the BoW model discards any order or structure-related information of the words in a given text. This might sound like a big issue but until recently, the BoW model remained quite a popular and effective choice for representing textual data. Let's have a quick look at a few examples to understand how this simple method works.

"Some say the world will end in fire,
Some say in ice.
From what I have tasted of desire
I hold with those who favour fire."

The preceding snippet is a short excerpt from the poem *Fire and Ice* by Robert Frost. We'll use these few lines of text to understand how the BoW model works. The following is a step-by-step approach:

1. **Define a vocabulary**:

    The first and foremost step is to define a list of known words from our corpus. For ease of understanding and practical reasons, we can ignore the case and punctuation marks for now. The vocabulary, or unique words, thus are {some, say, the, world, will, end, in, fire, ice, from, what, i, have, tasted, of, desire, hold, with, those, who, favour}.

    This vocabulary is a set of 21 unique words in a corpus of 26 words.

2. **Define a metric of occurrence**:

   Once we have the vocabulary set, we need to define how we will measure the occurrence of each word from the vocabulary. As we mentioned earlier, there are a number of ways to do so. One such metric is simply checking if a specific word is present or absent. We use a 0 if the word is absent or a 1 if it is present. The sentence "some say ice" can thus be scored as:

   - some: 1
   - say: 1
   - the: 0
   - world: 0
   - will: 0
   - end: 0
   - in: 0
   - fire: 0
   - ice: 1

   Hence, the overall vector will look like [1, 1, 0, 0, 0, 0, 0, 0, 1].

   There are a few other metrics that have been developed over the years. The most widely used metrics are:

   - Term frequency
   - TF-IDF, as seen in *Chapter 7, Style Transfer with GANs*
   - Hashing

These steps provide a high-level glimpse into how the BoW model helps us represent textual data as numbers or vectors. The overall vector representation of our excerpt from the poem is depicted in the following table:

	some	from	have	say	will	----	fire	ice	tasted	favour	hold
some say the world will end in fire	1	0	0	1	1		1	0	0	0	0
some say in ice	1	0	0	1	0		0	1	0	0	0
from what i have tasted of desire	0	1	1	0	0		0	0	1	0	0
i hold with those who favour fire	0	0	0	0	0		1	0	0	1	1

Figure 9.1: BoW representation

Each row in the matrix corresponds to one line from the poem, while the unique words from the vocabulary form the columns. Each row thus is simply the vector representation of the text under consideration.

There are a few additional steps involved in improving the outcome of this method. The refinements are related to vocabulary and scoring aspects. Managing the vocabulary is very important; often, a corpus of text can increase in size quite rapidly. A few common methods of handling vocabularies are:

- Ignoring punctuation marks
- Ignoring case
- Removing frequently occurring words (or stopwords) like *a*, *an*, *the*, *this*, and so on
- Methods to use the root form of words, such as *stop* in place of *stopping*. Stemming and lemmatization are two such methods
- Handling spelling mistakes

We already discussed different scoring methods and how they help in capturing certain important features. BoW is simple, yet is an effective tool that serves as a good starting point for most NLP tasks. Yet there are a few issues which can be summarized as follows:

- **Missing context**:

    As we mentioned earlier, the BoW model does not consider the ordering or structure of the text. By simply discarding information related to ordering, the vectors lose out on capturing the context in which the underlying text was used. For instance, the sentences "I am sure about it" and "Am I sure about it?" would have identical vector representations, yet they express different thoughts. Expanding BoW models to include n-grams (contiguous terms) instead of singular terms does help in capturing some context, but in a very limited way.

- **Vocabulary and sparse vectors**:

    As the corpus size increases, so does the vocabulary. The steps required to manage vocabulary size require a lot of oversight and manual effort. Due to the way this model works, a large vocabulary leads to very sparse vectors. Sparse vectors pose issues with modeling and computation requirements (space and time). Aggressive pruning and vocabulary management steps do help to a certain extent but can lead to the loss of important features as well.

Here, we discussed how the BoW model helps in transforming text into vector form, along with a few issues with this setup. In the next section, we will move on to a few more involved representation methods that alleviate some of these issues.

Distributed representation

The Bag of Words model is an easy-to-understand way of transforming words into vector form. This process is generally termed *vectorization*. While it is a useful method, the BoW model has its limitations when it comes to capturing context, along with sparsity-related issues. Since deep learning architectures are becoming de facto state-of-the-art systems in most spaces, it is obvious that we should be leveraging them for NLP tasks as well. Apart from the issues mentioned earlier, the sparse and large (wide) vectors from the BoW model are another aspect which can be tackled using neural networks.

A simple alternative that handles the sparsity issue can be implemented by encoding each word as a unique number. Continuing with the example from the previous section, "some say ice", we could assign 1 to "some", 2 to "say", 3 to "ice", and so on. This would result in a dense vector, [1, 2, 3]. This is an efficient utilization of space and we end up with vectors where all the elements are full. However, the limitation of missing context still remains. Since the numbers are arbitrary, they hardly capture any context on their own. On the contrary, arbitrarily mapping numbers to words is not very interpretable.

> **Interpretability** is an important requirement when it comes to NLP tasks. For computer vision use cases, visual cues are good enough indicators for understanding how a model is perceiving or generating outputs (though quantification is also a problem there, but we can skip it for now). For NLP tasks, since the textual data is first required to be transformed into a vector, it is important to understand what those vectors capture and how they are used by the models.

In the coming sections, we will cover some of the popular vectorization techniques that try to capture context while limiting the sparsity of the vectors as well. Please note that there are a number of other methods (such as SVD-based methods and co-occurrence matrices) as well that help in vectorizing textual data. In this section, we will be covering only those which are helpful in understanding later sections of this chapter.

Word2vec

The English Oxford dictionary has about 600k unique words and is growing year on year. Yet those words are not independent terms; they have some relationship to each other. The premise of the word2vec model is to learn high-quality vector representations that capture context. This is better summarized by the famous quote by J.R. Firth *"you shall know a word by the company it keeps"*.

In their work titled *Efficient Estimation of Word Representations in Vector Space*, Mikolov et al.[1] present two different models that learn vector representations of words from a large corpus. Word2Vec is a software implementation of these models which is classified as an iterative approach to learning such embeddings. Instead of taking the whole corpus into account in one go, this approach tries to iteratively learn to encode each word's representation, along with its context. This idea of learning word representations as dense context vectors is not a new one. It was first proposed by Rumelhart et al. in 1990[2]. They presented how a neural network is able to learn representations, with similar words ending up in the same clusters. The ability to have vector forms of words that capture some notion of similarity is quite a powerful one. Let's see in detail how the word2vec models achieve this.

Continuous Bag of Words (CBOW) Model

The Continuous Bag of Words model is an extension of the Bag of Words model we discussed in the previous section. The key aspect of this model is the context window. A context window is defined as a sliding window of a fixed size moving along a sentence. The word in the middle is termed the *target*, and the terms to its left and right within the window are the *context terms*. The CBOW model works by predicting the target term, given its context terms.

For instance, let's consider a reference sentence, "some say the *world* will end in fire". If we have a window size of 4 and a target term of *world*, the context terms would be {say, the} and {will, end}. The model inputs are tuples of the form (context terms, target term), which are then passed through a neural network to learn the embeddings.

This process is depicted in the following diagram:

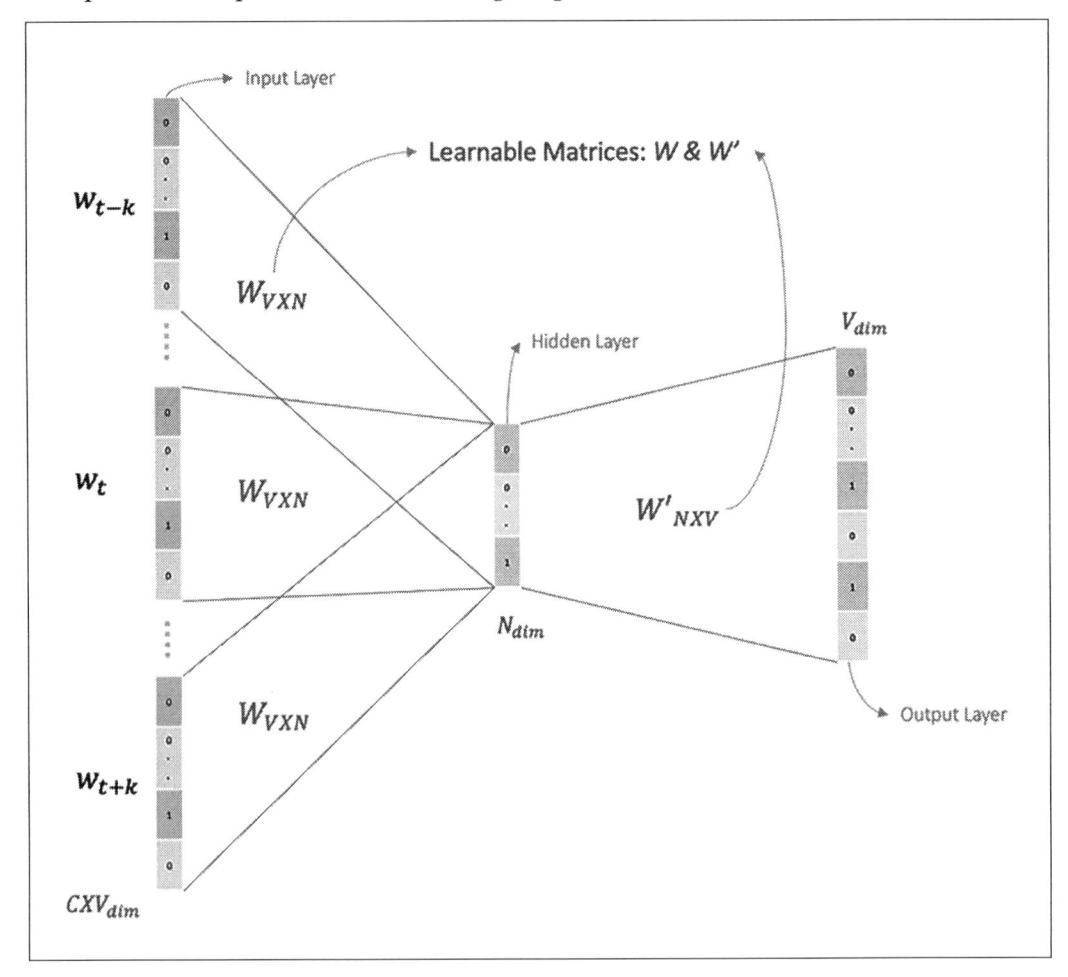

Figure 9.2: Continuous Bag of Words model setup

As shown in the preceding diagram, the context terms, denoted as $w_{t\pm i}$, are passed as input to the model to predict the target term, denoted as w_t. The overall working of the CBOW model can be explained as follows:

1. For a vocabulary of size V, a context window of size C is defined. C could be 4, 6, or any other size. We also define two matrices W and W' to generate input and output vectors, respectively. The matrix W is VxN, while W' is NxV in dimensions. N is the size of the embedding vector.
2. The context terms ($w_{t\pm i}$) and the target term (y) are transformed into one-hot encodings (or label-encodings) and training data is prepared in the form of tuples: ($w_{t\pm i}, y$).
3. We average the context vectors to get $v' = \frac{\sum w_{t\pm k}}{2C}$.
4. The final output scoring vector z is calculated as a dot product between the average vector v' and the output matrix W'.
5. The output scoring vector is transformed into a probability using a softmax function; that is, $y' = softmax(z)$, where y' should correspond to one of the terms in the vocabulary.
6. The final aim would be to train the neural network such that y' and the actual target y become as close as possible.

The authors proposed using a cost function such as cross-entropy to train the network and learn such embeddings.

Skip-gram model

The skip-gram model is the second variant presented in the paper for learning word embeddings. In essence, this model works in exactly the opposite way to the CBOW model. In other words, in the case of skip-gram, we input a word (center/target word) and predict the context terms as the model output. Let's use the same example as before, "some say the *world* will end in fire". Here, we will start with *world* as our input term and train a model to predict {say, the, will, end} as context terms with high probability.

The Rise of Methods for Text Generation

The following diagram depicts the skip-gram model; as expected, this is a mirror image of the CBOW setup we discussed in *Figure 9.2*:

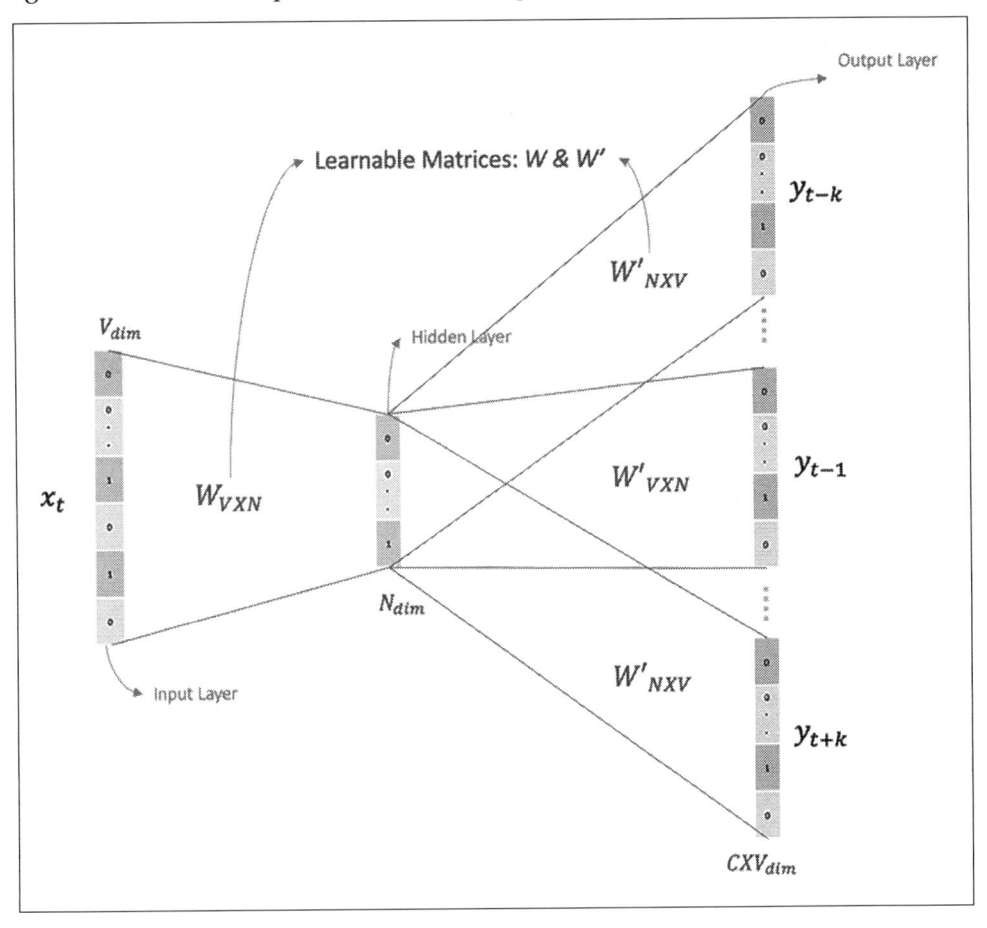

Figure 9.3: Skip-gram model setup

The step by step working skip-gram model can be explained as follows:

1. For a vocabulary of size V, a context window of size C is defined. C could be 4, 6, or any other size. We also define two matrices W and W' to generate input and output vectors, respectively. The matrix W is VxN, while W' is NxV in dimensions. N is the size of the embedding vector.
2. Generate the one-hot encoded representation of the center word x.
3. We get the word embedding representation of x by taking a dot product of x and W. The embedded representation is given as $v = W.x$.

4. We generate the output score vector z by taking a dot product of W' and v; that is, $z = W'.v$.
5. The scoring vector is transformed into output probabilities using a softmax layer to generate y'.
6. The final aim would be to train the neural network such that y' and the actual context y become as close as possible.

In the case of skip-gram, we have multiple input-output training pairs for any given center word. This model treats all context terms equally, irrespective of their distance from the center word in the context window. This allows us to use cross-entropy as the cost function with a strong conditional independence assumption.

In order to improve the outcomes and speed up the training process, the authors introduced some simple yet effective tricks. Concepts such as *negative sampling*, *noise contrastive estimation* and *hierarchical softmax* are a few such techniques which have been leveraged. For a detailed understanding of CBOW and skip-gram, readers are requested to go through the cited paper by Mikolov et al.,[1] where the authors have given detailed explanations of each of the steps.

For ease of understanding, let's make use of a well-known Python library called gensim to prepare our own word vectors. The first step is to prepare a dataset. For our exercise, we'll make use of the **20newsgroup** dataset, available as part of the sklearn library. This dataset contains news articles on different topics. The following snippet uses nltk to clean up this dataset and prepare it for the next steps. The text cleanup process is limited to lowercasing, removing special characters, and stop word removal only:

```
# import statements and code for the function normalize_corpus
# have been skipped for brevity. See corresponding
# notebook for details.

cats = ['alt.atheism', 'sci.space']
newsgroups_train = fetch_20newsgroups(subset='train',
                                      categories=cats,
                                      remove=('headers', 'footers',
                                              'quotes'))

norm_corpus = normalize_corpus(newsgroups_train.data)
```

The next step is to tokenize each news article into words. We split sentences into words using spaces. The following snippet first tokenizes text and then uses `gensim` to train a skip-gram word2vec model:

```
# tokenize corpus
tokenized_corpus = [nltk.word_tokenize(doc) for doc in norm_corpus]

# Set values for various parameters
embedding_size = 32    # Word vector dimensionality
context_window = 20    # Context window size
min_word_count = 1     # Minimum word count
sample = 1e-3          # Downsample setting for frequent words
sg = 1                 # skip-gram model

w2v_model = word2vec.Word2Vec(tokenized_corpus, size=embedding_size,
                              window=context_window,
                              min_count =min_word_count,
                              sg=sg, sample=sample, iter=200)
```

Just a few lines of code and we have our word2vec representations of our vocabulary ready. Upon checking, we find that there are 19,000 unique words in our vocabulary, and that we have a vector representation for each. The following snippet shows how we can get the vector representation of any word. We will also demonstrate how to get words that are most similar to a given word:

```
# get word vector
w2v_model.wv['sun']
```

```
array([ 0.607681, 0.2790227, 0.48256198, 0.41311446, 0.9275479,
       -1.1269532, 0.8191313, 0.03389674, -0.23167856, 0.3170586,
        0.0094937, 0.1252524, -0.5247988, -0.2794391, -0.62564677,
       -0.28145587, -0.70590997, -0.636148, -0.6147065, -0.34033248,
        0.11295943, 0.44503215, -0.37155458, -0.04982868, 0.34405553,
        0.49197063, 0.25858226, 0.354654, 0.00691116, 0.1671375,
        0.51912665, 1.0082873 ], dtype=float32)
```

```
# get similar words
w2v_model.wv.most_similar(positive=['god'])
```

```
[('believe', 0.8401427268981934),
 ('existence', 0.8364629149436951),
 ('exists', 0.8211747407913208),
 ('selfcontradictory', 0.8076522946357727),
 ('gods', 0.7966105937957764),
 ('weak', 0.7965559959411621),
 ('belief', 0.7767481803894043),
 ('disbelieving', 0.7757835388183594),
 ('exist', 0.77425217628479),
 ('interestingly', 0.7742466926574707)]
```

The preceding outputs show a 32-dimensional vector for the word *sun*. We also display words that are most similar to the word *god*. We can clearly see that words such as believe, existence, and so on seem to be the most similar, which makes sense given the dataset we used. For interested readers, we have a 3-dimensional vector space representation using TensorBoard showcased in the corresponding notebook. The TensorBoard representation helps us visually understand the embedding space and see how these vectors interact.

GloVe

The word2vec models helped in improving performance for various NLP tasks. Continuing with the same momentum, another important implementation called GloVe came into the picture. GloVe or *Global Vectors for Word Representation* was published by Pennington et al. in 2014 to improve upon the known word representation techniques.[3]

As we've seen, word2vec models work by considering the local context (a defined window) of the words in the vocabulary. Even though this works remarkably well, it is a bit rough around the edges. The fact that words may mean different things in different contexts requires us to understand not just the local but the global context as well. GloVe tries to work upon the global context while learning the word vectors.

There are classical techniques for this, such as **Latent Semantic Analysis (LSA)**, which are based on matrix factorization and do a good job at capturing global context, but are not so good at things such as vector math.

GloVe is a method which tries to get the best of both worlds in order to learn better word representations. The GloVe algorithm consists of the following steps:

1. Prepare a word co-occurrence matrix X, such that each element, x_{ij}, represents how often the word j appears in the context of the word i. GloVe makes use of two fixed size windows that help in capturing context before the word and context after the word.

2. The co-occurrence matrix X is updated with a decay factor to penalize terms that are farther apart in the context. The decay factor is defined as $\alpha = \frac{1}{offset}$, where offset is the distance from the word under consideration.

3. Then, we prepare the GloVe equation as the following soft constraint:

$$w_i^T w_j + b_i + b_j = \log(X_{ij})$$

Here, w_i is the vector for the main word, w_j is the vector for the context word, and b_i, b_j are the corresponding bias terms.

4. The final step is to use the preceding constraint to define the cost function, which is given as:

$$J = \sum_{i=1}^{V} \sum_{j=1}^{V} f(X_{ij})(w_i^T w_j + b_i + b_j - \log(X_{ij}))^2$$

Here, f is a weighting function, defined as:

$$f = \begin{cases} \left(\frac{X_{ij}}{X_{max}}\right)^Y & \text{if } X_{ij} < X_{max} \\ 1 & \text{otherwise} \end{cases}$$

The authors of the paper achieved the best results with $Y = \frac{3}{4}$.

Similar to word2vec models, GloVe embeddings also achieve good results and the authors present results where they show GloVe outperforming word2vec. They attribute this to better problem formulation and the global context being captured.

In practice, both models perform more or less similarly. As larger vocabularies are required to get better embeddings (for both word2vec and GloVe), for most practical use cases, pretrained embeddings are available and used.

Pretrained GloVe vectors are available through a number of packages, such as spacy. Interested readers may wish to explore the spacy package for more details.

FastText

Word2Vec and GloVe are powerful methods which have nice properties when it comes to encoding words in the vector space. Both techniques work nicely when it comes to getting vector representation of words that are in the vocabulary, but they do not have clear answers for terms that are outside of the vocabulary.

The word is the fundamental unit in the case of the word2vec and GloVe methods. This assumption is challenged and improved upon in the FastText implementation. The word representation aspect of FastText is based on the paper, *Enriching Word Vectors with Subword Information* by Bojanowski et al. in 2017.[4] This work decomposes each word into a set of n-grams. This helps in capturing and learning vector representations of different combinations of characters, as opposed to the whole word in earlier techniques.

For instance, if we consider the word "India" and *n=3* for the n-gram setup, it will decompose the word into {<india>, <in, ind, ndi, dia, ia>}. The symbols "<" and ">" are special characters to denote the start and end of the original word. This helps in differentiating between <in>, which represents the whole word, and <in, which is an n-gram. This approach helps FastText generate embeddings for *out of vocabulary* terms as well. This can be done by adding and averaging the vector representation of required n-grams.

FastText is shown to drastically improve performance when it comes to use cases where there is a high chance of new/out of vocabulary terms. FastText was developed by researchers at **Facebook AI Research** (**FAIR**), which shouldn't come as a surprise as the kind of content generated on social media platforms such as Facebook is huge and ever-changing.

With its added improvements come a few disadvantages as well. Since the basic unit in this case is an n-gram, the amount of time required to train/learn such representations is higher than previous techniques. The n-gram approach also increases the amount of memory required to train such a model. However, the authors of the paper point out that a hashing trick helps in controlling the memory requirements to a certain extent.

For ease of understanding, let's again make use of our well-known Python library, gensim. We will extend upon the same dataset and pre-processing steps that we performed for the word2vec model exercise in the previous section. The following snippet prepares the FastText model object:

```
# Set values for various parameters
embedding_size = 32    # Word vector dimensionality
context_window = 20    # Context window size
```

```
min_word_count = 1    # Minimum word count
sample = 1e-3         # Downsample setting for frequent words
sg = 1                # skip-gram model

ft_model = FastText(tokenized_corpus, size=embedding_size,
                    window=context_window, min_count = min_word_count,
sg=sg, sample=sample, iter=100)
```

The word2vec model fails to return a vector representation of the word "sunny" as it is not in the trained vocabulary. The following snippet shows how FastText is still able to generate a vector representation:

```
# out of vocabulary
ft_model.wv['sunny']
```

```
array([-0.16000476,  0.3925578, -0.6220364, -0.14427347, -1.308504,
        0.611941,   1.2834805,  0.5174112, -1.7918613, -0.8964722,
       -0.23748468, -0.81343293, 1.2371198,  1.0380564, -0.44239333,
        0.20864521, -0.9888209,  0.89212966, -1.1963437,  0.738966,
       -0.60981965, -1.1683533, -0.7930039,  1.0648874,  0.5561004,
       -0.28057176, -0.37946936, 0.02066167,  1.3181996,  0.8494686,
       -0.5021836,  -1.0629338], dtype=float32)
```

This showcases how FastText improves upon word2vec- and GloVe-based representation techniques. We can easily handle out of vocabulary terms, all the while ensuring context-based dense representations.

Let's now use this understanding to develop a text generation model.

Text generation and the magic of LSTMs

In the previous sections, we discussed different ways of representing textual data in order to make it fit for consumption by different NLP algorithms. In this section, we will leverage this understanding of text representation to work our way toward building text generation models.

So far, we have built models using feedforward networks consisting of different kinds and combinations of layers. These networks work with one training example at a time, which is independent of other training samples. We say that the samples are **independent and identically distributed**, or **IID**. Language, or text, is a bit different.

As we discussed in the previous sections, words change their meaning based on the context they are being used in. In other words, if we were to develop and train a language generation model, we would have to ensure the model understands the context of its input.

Recurrent Neural Networks (RNNs) are a class of neural networks that allow previous outputs to be used as inputs, along with memory or hidden units. This awareness of previous inputs helps in capturing context, and provides us with the ability to handle variable-length input sequences (sentences are hardly ever of the same length). A typical RNN is depicted in the following diagram, in both actual and unrolled form:

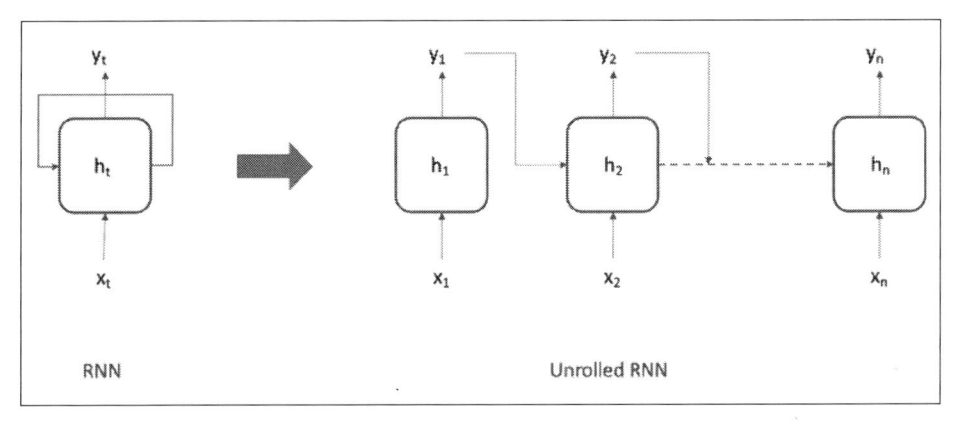

Figure 9.4: A typical RNN

As shown in *Figure 9.4*, at time t_1, input x_1 generates output y_1. At time t_2, x_2 along with y_1 (the previous output) generate output y_2, and so on. Unlike typical feedforward networks where every input is independent of the others, RNN introduces the notion of previous outputs impacting the current and upcoming ones.

> RNNs have a few different variants to them, namely, **Gated Recurrent Units** (**GRUs**) and **Long Short-Term Memory** (**LSTMs**). The vanilla RNN described previously works in auto-regressive settings well. Yet it has issues with longer context windows (vanishing gradients). GRUs and LSTMs try to overcome such issues by using different gates and memory units. Introduced by Hochreiter and Schmidhuber in 1997, LSTMs can remember information from really long sequence-based data. LSTMs consist of three gates called input, output, and forget gates. This is depicted in the following diagram.
>
> Figure 9.5: Different gates of an LSTM cell
>
> For a detailed understanding of LSTMs, you may refer to `http://colah.github.io/posts/2015-08-Understanding-LSTMs/`.

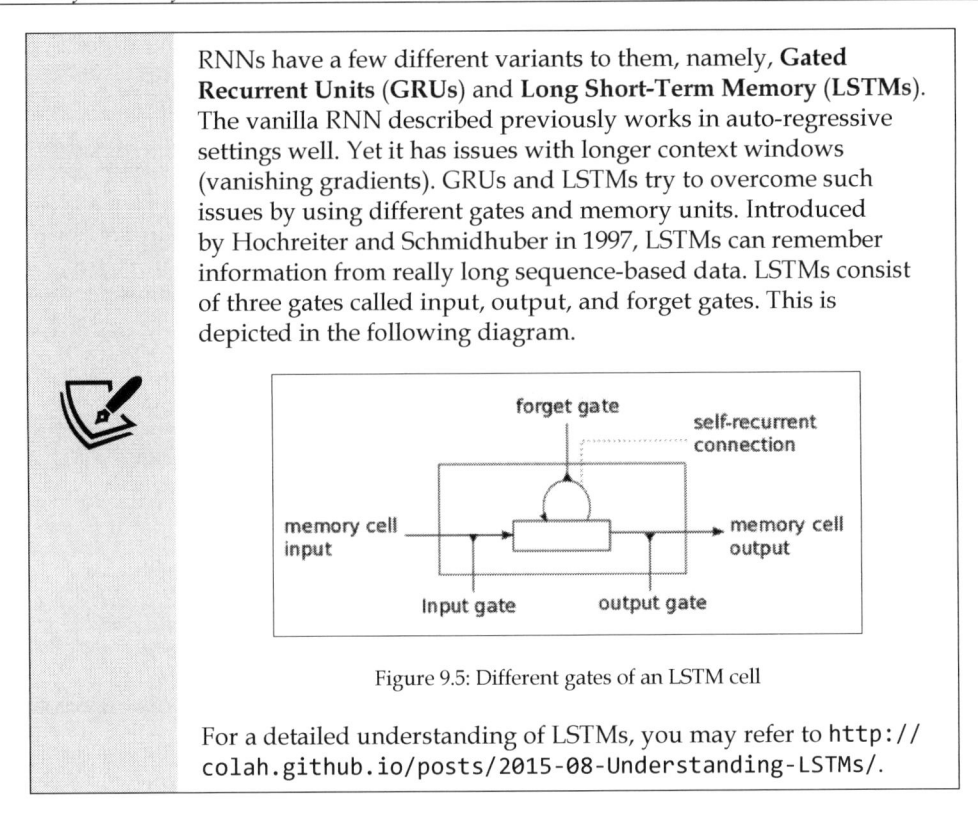

We will now focus on defining the task of text generation more formally.

Language modeling

NLP-based solutions are quite effective and can be seen all around us. The most prominent example is the autocomplete feature on most smartphone keyboards, search engines (Google, Bing, and so on), and even word processors (like MS Word).

Autocomplete is a common name for a formal concept called *language modeling*. In simple words, a language model takes certain text as the input context to generate the next set of words as the output. This is interesting because a language model tries to understand the input context, the language structure, and rules to predict the next word(s). We use it in the form of text completion utilities on search engines, chat platforms, emails, and more all the time. Language models are a perfect real-life application of NLP and showcase the power of RNNs. In this section, we will work toward building an understanding, as well as training an RNN-based language model for text generation.

Let's get started by understanding the process of generating a training dataset. We can do this with the help of the following image. This image depicts a word-level language model; that is, a model for which a word is the basic unit. Along the same lines, we can develop character-level, phrase-level, or even document-level models:

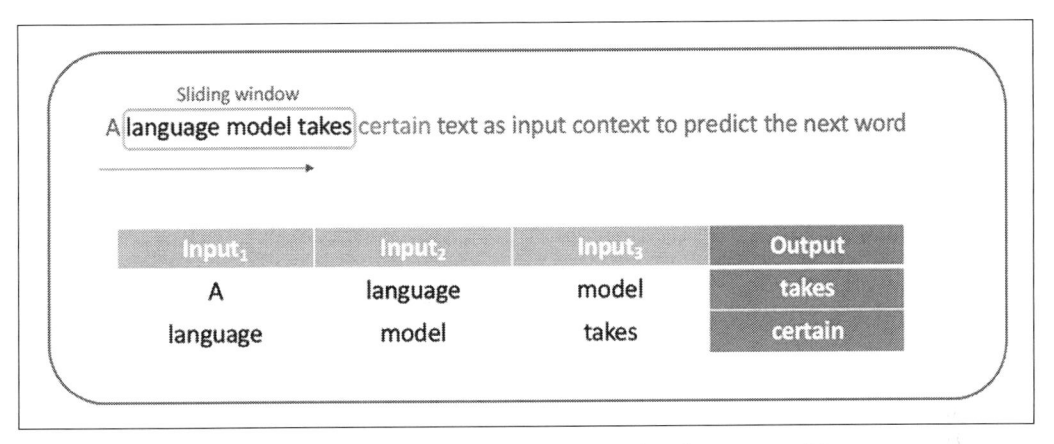

Figure 9.6: Training data generation process for a language model

As we mentioned earlier, a language model looks at the context to generate the next set of words. This context is also called a sliding window, which moves across the input sentence from left to right (right to left for languages that are written from right to left). The sliding window depicted in *Figure 9.6* spans three words, which act as input. The corresponding output for each training data point is the immediate next word after the window (or a set of words if the aim is to predict the next phrase). We thus prepare our training dataset, which consists of tuples of the form ({context terms}, next_word). The sliding window helps us to generate a good number of training samples from every sentence in the training dataset without explicit labeling.

This training dataset is then used to train an RNN-based language model. In practice, we typically use LSTMs or GRU units in place of vanilla RNN units. We discussed earlier that RNNs have the ability to auto-regress on previous timestep values. In the context of language models, we auto-regress on the context terms and the model generates the corresponding next word. We then make use of **backpropagation through time** (**BPTT**) to update model weights through gradient descent until the required performance is achieved. We discussed BPTT in detail in *Chapter 3, Building Blocks of Deep Neural Networks*.

We now have a fair understanding of what a language model is and what steps are involved in preparing the training dataset, along with the model setup. Let's now implement some of these concepts using TensorFlow and Keras.

Hands-on: Character-level language model

We discussed the basics of language modeling in the previous section. In this section, we will build and train our own language model, but with a twist. In contrast to the discussion in the previous section, here, we will work at the character level, not at the word level. In simple words, we will work toward building a model that takes a few characters as input (context) to generate the next set of characters. This choice of a more granular language model is for the ease of training such a model. A character-level language model needs to worry about a much smaller vocabulary, or number of unique characters, compared to a word-level language model.

To build our language model, the first step is to get a dataset to use as a training source. Project Gutenberg is a volunteer effort to digitize historical works and make them available as free downloads. Since we need lots of data to train a language model, we will pick one of the biggest available books, *War and Peace* by Leo Tolstoy. This book is available for download at the following URL:

https://www.gutenberg.org/ebooks/2600

The following snippet loads the book's content for use as our source dataset:

```
datafile_path = r'warpeace_2600-0.txt'
# Load the text file
text = open(datafile_path, 'rb').read().decode(encoding='utf-8')
print ('Book contains a total of {} characters'.format(len(text)))
```

```
Book contains a total of 3293673 characters
```

```
vocab = sorted(set(text))
print ('{} unique characters'.format(len(vocab)))
```

```
108 unique characters
```

The next step is to prepare our dataset for the model. As we discussed in the *Representing text* section, textual data is transformed into vectors using word representation models. One way to do so is to first transform them into one-hot encoded vectors, which are then transformed into dense representations using models such as word2vec. The other way is to transform them into an arbitrary numerical representation first and then train an embedding layer along with the rest of the RNN-based language model. In this case, we are using the latter approach of training an embedding layer alongside the rest of the model.

The following snippet prepares a mapping of individual characters to their integer mapping:

```
char2idx = {u:i for i, u in enumerate(vocab)}
idx2char = np.array(vocab)

text_as_int = np.array([char2idx[c] for c in text])

print('{')
for char,_ in zip(char2idx, range(20)):
    print('  {:4s}: {:3d},'.format(repr(char), char2idx[char]))
print('   ...\n}')
```

```
{
  '\n':   0,
  '\r':   1,
  ' ' :   2,
  '!' :   3,
  ...
```

As you can see, each unique character is mapped to an integer; for instance, \n is mapped to 0, ! is mapped to 3, and so on.

For optimal memory utilization, we can make use of the tf.data API to slice our data into manageable slices. We restrict our input sequences to 100 characters long, and this API helps us create contiguous slices of this dataset. This is showcased in the following code snippet:

```
seq_length = 100
examples_per_epoch = len(text)//(seq_length+1)

# Create training examples / targets
char_dataset = tf.data.Dataset.from_tensor_slices(text_as_int)

for i in char_dataset.take(10):
    print(idx2char[i.numpy()])
```

```
B
O
O
K
```

The Rise of Methods for Text Generation

```
O
N
E
...
```

The char_dataset object helps us generate sample batches as needed during training time. Earlier in this section, we introduced how a language model generates the next word or character based on the context window. Keeping this concept in mind, in the following snippet, we write a utility function split_input_target to prepare the target output as a one-position-shifted transformation of the input itself. In this way, we will be able to generate consecutive (input, output) training pairs using just a single shift in position:

```python
def split_input_target(chunk):
    """
    Utility which takes a chunk of input text and target
    as one position shifted form of input chunk.
    Parameters:
        chunk: input list of words
    Returns:
        Tuple-> input_text(i.e. chunk minus
        last word),target_text(input chunk minus the first word)
    """
    input_text = chunk[:-1]
    target_text = chunk[1:]
    return input_text, target_text

dataset = sequences.map(split_input_target)

for input_example, target_example in  dataset.take(1):
    print ('Input data: ', repr(''.join(idx2char[input_example.
numpy()])))
    print ('Target data:', repr(''.join(idx2char[target_example.
numpy()])))
```

```
Input data:   '\r\nBOOK ONE: 1805\r\n\r\n\r\n\r\n\r\n\r\nCHAPTER I\r\n\
r\n"Well, Prince, so Genoa and Lucca are now just family estat'
Target data:  '\nBOOK ONE: 1805\r\n\r\n\r\n\r\n\r\n\r\nCHAPTER I\r\n\r\
n"Well, Prince, so Genoa and Lucca are now just family estate'
```

[326]

The sample output showcases the one-shift difference between the input and target sequences. Next, we make use of a utility function to define our language model itself. The following snippet defines a function `build_model` that prepares a single layer LSTM-based language model:

```
def build_model(vocab_size, embedding_dim, rnn_units, batch_size):
    """
    Utility to create a model object.
    Parameters:
        vocab_size: number of unique characters
        embedding_dim: size of embedding vector.
        This typically in powers of 2, i.e. 64, 128, 256 and so on
        rnn_units: number of GRU units to be used
        batch_size: batch size for training the model
    Returns:
        tf.keras model object
    """
    model = tf.keras.Sequential([
    tf.keras.layers.Embedding(vocab_size, embedding_dim,
                        batch_input_shape=[batch_size, None]),
    tf.keras.layers.LSTM(rnn_units,
                    return_sequences=True,
                    stateful=True,
                    recurrent_initializer='glorot_uniform'),
    tf.keras.layers.Dense(vocab_size)
  ])
    return model

# Length of the vocabulary in chars
vocab_size = len(vocab)

# The embedding dimension
embedding_dim = 256

# Number of RNN units
rnn_units = 1024

model = build_model(
  vocab_size = len(vocab),
  embedding_dim=embedding_dim,
  rnn_units=rnn_units,
  batch_size=BATCH_SIZE)
```

We have created the model object. As is apparent from the snippet, the model is a stack of embedding, LSTM, and dense layers. The embedding layer helps transform raw text into vector form, and is followed by the LSTM and dense layers, which learn context and language semantics.

The next set of steps involve defining a loss function and compiling the model. We will be using sparse categorical cross-entropy as our loss function. The following snippet defines the loss function and compiles the model; we are using the Adam optimizer for minimization:

```
def loss(labels, logits):
    return tf.keras.losses.sparse_categorical_crossentropy(labels, logits, from_logits=True)

model.compile(optimizer='adam', loss=loss)
```

Since we are using TensorFlow with the high-level Keras API, training the model is as simple as calling the `fit` function. We train the model for just 10 epochs, using the `ModelCheckpoint` callback to save the model's weights every epoch, as shown in the following snippet:

```
# Directory where the checkpoints will be saved
checkpoint_dir = r'data/training_checkpoints'
# Name of the checkpoint files
checkpoint_prefix = os.path.join(checkpoint_dir, "ckpt_{epoch}")

checkpoint_callback=tf.keras.callbacks.ModelCheckpoint(
    filepath=checkpoint_prefix,
    save_weights_only=True)


EPOCHS = 10
history = model.fit(dataset, epochs=EPOCHS, callbacks=[checkpoint_callback])
```

```
Epoch 1/10
254/254 [==============================] - 38s 149ms/step - loss: 2.4388
```

```
Epoch 2/10
254/254 [==============================] - 36s 142ms/step - loss:
1.7407
 .
 .
 .
Epoch 10/10
254/254 [==============================] - 37s 145ms/step - loss:
1.1530
```

Congratulations, you've trained your very first language model. Now, we'll use it to generate some fake text. Before we do that, though, we need to understand how we can decode the output generated by our model.

Decoding strategies

Earlier on, we transformed all the textual data into suitable vector forms for training and inference purposes. Now that we have a trained model, the next step is to input some context words and generate the next word as output. This output generation step is formally known as the **decoding step**. It is termed "decoding" because the model outputs a vector which has to be processed to get the actual word as output. There are a few different decoding techniques; let's briefly discuss the popular ones: greedy decoding, beam search, and sampling.

Greedy decoding

This is the simplest and fastest decoding strategy. As the name suggests, greedy decoding is a method which picks up the highest probability term at every prediction step.

While this is fast and efficient, being greedy does create a few issues while generating text. By focusing on only the highest probability outputs, the model may generate inconsistent or incoherent outputs. In the case of character-language models, this may even result in outputs that are non-dictionary words. Greedy decoding also limits the variance of outputs, which may result in repetitive content as well.

Beam search

Beam search is a widely used alternative to greedy decoding. This decoding strategy, instead of picking the highest probability term, keeps track of *n* possible outputs at every timestep. The following diagram illustrates the beam search decoding strategy. It shows multiple beams forming from step 0, creating a tree-like structure:

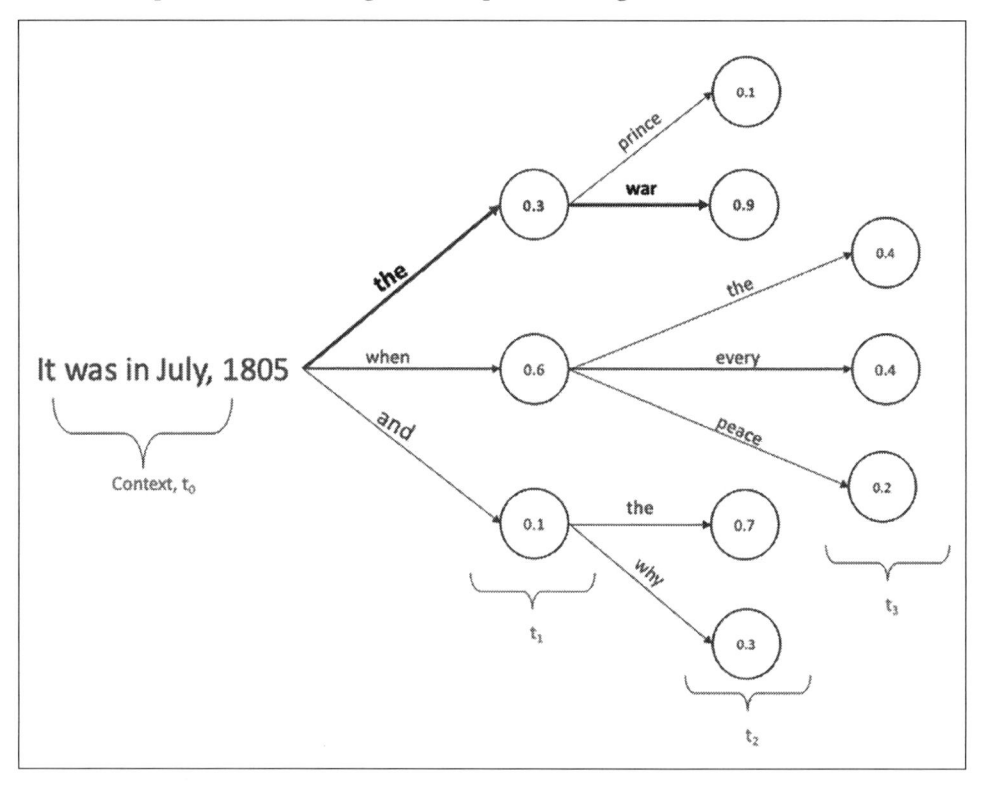

Figure 9.7: Beam search-based decoding strategy

As shown in *Figure 9.7*, the beam search strategy works by keeping track of *n* predictions at every timestep and finally selects the path with the **overall** highest probability, highlighted with bold lines in the figure. Let's analyze the beam search decoding example used in the preceding diagram step by step, assuming a beam size of 2.

At time step t_0:

1. The model predicts the following three words (with probabilities) as (**the**, 0.3), (**when**, 0.6), and (**and**, 0.1).
2. In the case of greedy decoding, we would have selected "when" as it has the highest probability.
3. In this case, we will keep track of the top two outputs as our beam size is 2.

At time step t_2:

1. We repeat the same steps; that is, we keep track of the top two outputs from each of the two beams.
2. The beam-wise scores are calculated by multiplying the probabilities along the branches, like so:
   - *(when, 0.6) –> (the, 0.4) = 0.6*0.4 = 0.24*
   - *(the, 0.3) –> (war, 0.9) = 0.3*0.9 = 0.27*

Based on the above discussion, the final output generated is "It was July, 1805 *the war*". This output had a final probability of 0.27 in comparison to an output like "It was July, 1805 *when the*", which had a score of 0.24, and is what greedy decoding would have given us.

This decoding strategy drastically improves upon the naïve greedy decoding strategy we discussed in the previous section. This, in a way, provides the language model with additional capabilities to pick the best possible outcome.

Sampling

Sampling is a process wherein a predefined a number of observations are selected from a larger population. As an improvement over greedy decoding, a random sampling decoding method can be employed to address the variation/repetition issue. In general, a sampling-based decoding strategy helps in selecting the next word conditioned on the context so far, that is:

$$w_t \sim P(w_t|w_{1:t-1})$$

Here, w_t is the output at time step t that's been conditioned on words that are generated until time step $t-1$. Continuing with the example from our previous decoding strategies, the following image highlights how a sampling-based decoding strategy would select the next word:

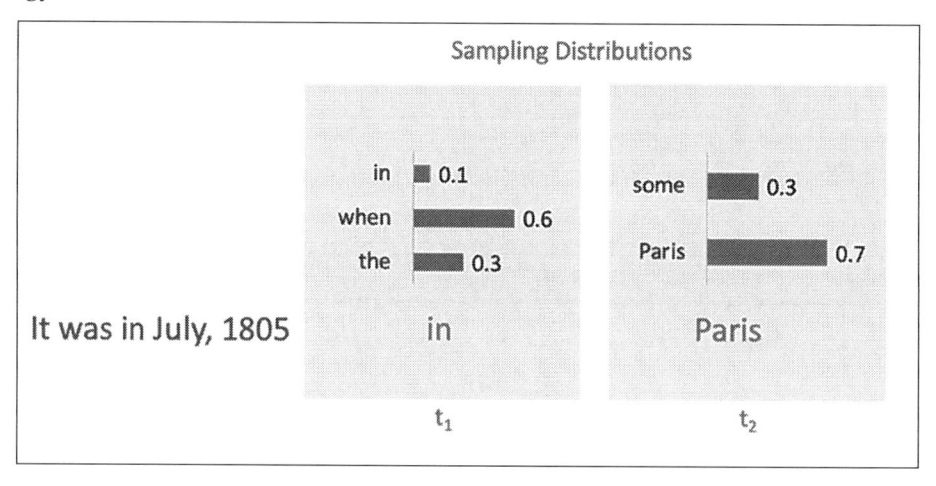

Figure 9.8: Sampling-based decoding strategy

As shown in *Figure 9.8*, this method picks a random word at every timestep from the given conditional probability. In the case of our example, the model ended by randomly selecting **in** and then **Paris** as subsequent outputs. If you notice carefully, at timestep t_1, the model ends up selecting the word with the least probability. This brings in a much-required randomness associated with the way humans use language. Holtzman et al. in their work titled *The Curious Case of Neural Text Degeneration*[5] present this exact argument by stating that humans do not always simply use the words with the highest probability. They present different scenarios and examples to highlight how language is a random choice of words and not a typical high probability curve formed by beam search or greedy decoding.

This brings us to an important parameter called *temperature*.

Temperature

As we discussed earlier, a sampling-based decoding strategy helps with improving the randomness of the output. However, too much randomness is also not ideal, as it can lead to gibberish and incoherent results. To control this amount of randomness, we can introduce a tunable parameter called temperature. This parameter helps to increase the likelihood of high probability terms while reducing the likelihood of low probability ones, which leads to sharper distributions. High temperature leads to more randomness, while lower temperature brings in predictability. An important point to note is that this can be applied to any decoding strategy.

Top-k sampling

Beam search and sampling-based decoding strategies both have their own set of advantages and disadvantages. Top-*k* sampling is a hybrid strategy which takes the best of both worlds to provide an even more sophisticated decoding method. In simple terms, at every timestep, instead of selecting a random word, we keep track of the *top k terms* (similar to beam search) and redistribute the probabilities among them. This gives the model an additional chance of generating coherent samples.

Hands-on: Decoding strategies

Now that we have a decent enough understanding of some of the most widely used decoding strategies, it's time to see them in action.

The first step is to prepare a utility function generate_text to generate the next word based on a given decoding strategy, as shown in the following code snippet:

```
def generate_text(model, mode='greedy', context_string='Hello',
    num_generate=1000,
                  temperature=1.0):
    """
    Utility to generate text given a trained model and context
    Parameters:
        model: tf.keras object trained on a sufficiently sized corpus
        mode: decoding mode. Default is greedy. Other mode is
            sampling (set temperature)
        context_string: input string which acts as context for the
                        model
        num_generate: number of characters to be generated
        temperature: parameter to control randomness of outputs
    Returns:
        string : context_string+text_generated
    """

    # vectorizing: convert context string into string indices
    input_eval = [char2idx[s] for s in context_string]
    input_eval = tf.expand_dims(input_eval, 0)

    # String for generated characters
    text_generated = []
    model.reset_states()
    # Loop till required number of characters are generated
    for i in range(num_generate):
```

```
        predictions = model(input_eval)
        predictions = tf.squeeze(predictions, 0)
        if mode == 'greedy':
          predicted_id = np.argmax(predictions[0])

        elif mode == 'sampling':
          # temperature helps control the character
          # returned by the model.
          predictions = predictions / temperature
          # Sampling over a categorical distribution
          predicted_id = tf.random.categorical(predictions,
                                        num_samples=1)[-1,0].numpy()

        # predicted character acts as input for next step
        input_eval = tf.expand_dims([predicted_id], 0)
        text_generated.append(idx2char[predicted_id])
    return (context_string + ''.join(text_generated))
```

The code first transforms raw input text into integer indices. We then use the model to make predictions which are manipulated based on the mode selected, greedy or sampling. We already have a character-language model trained from the previous exercise, along with a utility to help us generate the next word based on a decoding strategy of choice. We use both of these in the following snippet to understand the different outputs that are generated using different strategies:

```
# greedy decoding
print(generate_text(model, context_string=u"It was in July, 1805
",num_generate=50,mode="greedy"))

# sampled decoding with different temperature settings
print(generate_text(model, context_string=u"It was in July, 1805
",num_generate=50, mode="sampling", temperature=0.3))

print(generate_text(model, context_string=u"It was in July, 1805
",num_generate=50, mode="sampling",temperature=0.9))
```

The results of using the same seed with different decoding strategies are showcased in the following screenshot:

Greedy Decoding	**It was in July, 1805-** CHAPTER XII The former conditions of
Sampled @ 0.3	**It was in July, 1805,** "Yes, I say, sir, and so it is the same thing!" said the countess, with a smile of the same time
Sampled @ 0.9	**It was in July, 1805,** I spoke to them, and Bonaparte was foreshed the effect one another; intelligent, or by asking to

Figure 9.9: Text generation based on different decoding strategies. The text in bold is the seed text, followed by the output text generated by the model.

This output highlights some of the issues as well as the salient features of all the decoding strategies we've discussed so far. We can see how the increase in temperature makes the model more expressive. We can also observe that the model has learned to pair up quotation marks and even use punctuation. The model also seems to have learned how to use capitalization. The added expressiveness of the temperature parameter comes at the cost of the stability of the model. Thus, there is usually a trade-off between expressiveness and stability.

This concludes our first method for generating text; we leveraged RNNs (LSTMs in particular) to generate text using different decoding strategies. Next, we will look at some variations of the LSTM model, as well as convolutions.

LSTM variants and convolutions for text

RNNs are extremely useful when it comes to handling sequential datasets. We saw in the previous section how a simple model effectively learned to generate text based on what it learned from the training dataset.

Over the years, there have been a number of enhancements in the way we model and use RNNs. In this section, we will discuss two widely used variants of the single-layer LSTM network we discussed in the previous section: stacked and bidirectional LSTMs.

Stacked LSTMs

We are well aware of how the depth of a neural network helps it learn complex and abstract concepts when it comes to computer vision tasks. Along the same lines, a stacked LSTM architecture, which has multiple layers of LSTMs stacked one after the other, has been shown to give considerable improvements. Stacked LSTMs were first presented by Graves et al. in their work *Speech Recognition with Deep Recurrent Neural Networks*.[6] They highlight the fact that depth – multiple layers of RNNs – has a greater impact on performance compared to the number of units per layer.

Though there isn't any theoretical proof to explain this performance gain, empirical results help us understand the impact. These enhancements can be attributed to the model's capacity to learn complex features and even abstract representations of inputs. Since there is a time component associated with LSTMs and RNNs in general, deeper networks learn the ability to operate at different time scales as well.[7]

As we are making use of the high-level Keras API, we can easily extend the architecture we used in the previous section to add additional LSTM layers. The following snippet modifies the `build_model` function to do just that:

```
def build_model(vocab_size, embedding_dim, rnn_units, batch_size,is_
bidirectional=False):
    """
    Utility to create a model object.
    Parameters:
        vocab_size: number of unique characters
        embedding_dim: size of embedding vector. This typically in
                        powers of 2, i.e. 64, 128, 256 and so on
        rnn_units: number of LSTM units to be used
        batch_size: batch size for training the model
    Returns:
        tf.keras model object
    """
    model = tf.keras.Sequential()
    model.add(tf.keras.layers.Embedding(vocab_size, embedding_dim,
                        batch_input_shape=[batch_size, None]))
    if is_bidirectional:
       model.add(tf.keras.layers.Bidirectional(tf.keras.layers.LSTM(rnn_
units,
```

```
                         return_sequences=True,
                         stateful=True,
                         recurrent_initializer='glorot_uniform')))
    else:
        model.add(tf.keras.layers.LSTM(rnn_units,
                         return_sequences=True,
                         stateful=True,
                         recurrent_initializer='glorot_uniform'))
        model.add(tf.keras.layers.LSTM(rnn_units,
                         return_sequences=True,
                         stateful=True,
                         recurrent_initializer='glorot_uniform'))
    model.add(tf.keras.layers.Dense(vocab_size))
    return model
```

The dataset, training loop, and even the inference utilities remain as-is. For brevity, we have skipped presenting those code snippets again. We will discuss the bidirectional argument that we introduce here shortly.

Now, let's see how the results look for this deeper LSTM-based language model. The following screenshot demonstrates the results from this model:

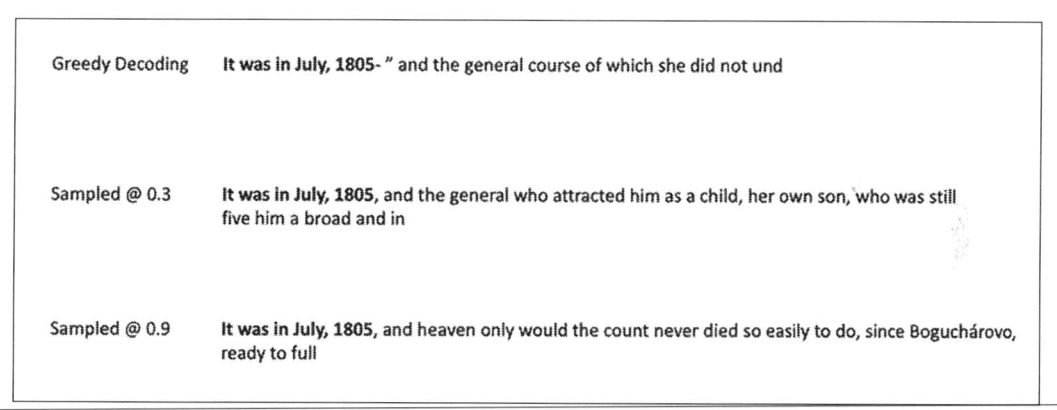

Greedy Decoding	It was in July, 1805-" and the general course of which she did not und
Sampled @ 0.3	It was in July, 1805, and the general who attracted him as a child, her own son, who was still five him a broad and in
Sampled @ 0.9	It was in July, 1805, and heaven only would the count never died so easily to do, since Bogucharóvo, ready to full

Figure 9.10: Text generation based on different decoding strategies for the stacked-LSTM based language model

We can clearly see how the generated text is picking up the writing style of the book, capitalization, punctuation, and other aspects better than the outputs shown in *Figure 9.9*. This highlights some of the advantages we discussed regarding deeper RNN architectures.

Bidirectional LSTMs

The second variant that's very widely used nowadays is the bidirectional LSTM. We have already discussed how LSTMs, and RNNs in general, condition their outputs by making use of previous timesteps. When it comes to text or any sequence data, this means that the LSTM is able to make use of past context to predict future timesteps. While this is a very useful property, this is not the best we can achieve. Let's illustrate why this is a limitation through an example:

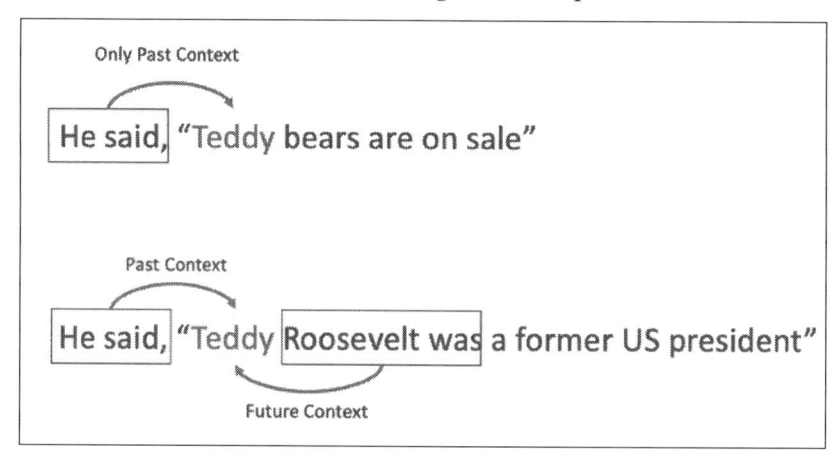

Figure 9.11: Looking at both past and future context windows for a given word

As is evident from this example, without looking at what is to the right of the target word "Teddy", the model would not pick up the context properly. To handle such scenarios, bidirectional LSTMs were introduced. The idea behind them is pretty simple and straightforward. A bidirectional LSTM (or biLSTM) is a combination of two LSTM layers that work simultaneously. The first is the usual forward LSTM, which takes the input sequence in its original order. The second one is called the backward LSTM, which takes **a reversed copy** of the sequence as input. The following diagram showcases a typical biLSTM setup:

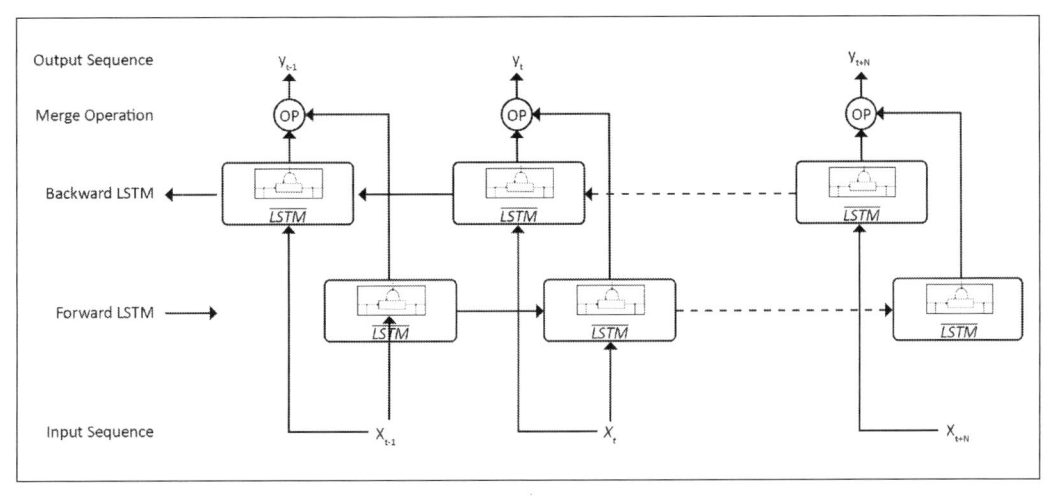

Figure 9.12: Bidirectional LSTM setup

As depicted in *Figure 9.12*, the forward and backward LSTMs work in tandem to process the original and reversed copy of the input sequences. Since we have two LSTM cells working on different contexts at any given time step, we need a way of defining the output that will be used by the downstream layers in the network. The outputs can be combined via summation, multiplication, concatenation, or even averaging of hidden states. Different deep learning frameworks might set different defaults, but the most widely used method is concatenation of the biLSTM outputs. Please note that, similar to biLSTM, we can make use of bi-RNNs or even bi-GRUs (**Gated Recurrent Units**).

The biLSTM setup has advantages compared to a normal LSTM, as the former can look at the future context as well. This advantage also becomes a limitation when it is not possible to peek into the future. For the current use case of text generation, biLSTMs are leveraged in an encoder-decoder type of architecture. We make use of biLSTMs to learn better embeddings of the inputs, but the decoding stage (where we use these embeddings to guess the next word) only uses the normal LSTMs. Similar to earlier hands-on exercises, we can train this network using the same set of utilities. We leave this as an exercise for you; for now, we will move on to convolutions.

Convolutions and text

RNNs are extremely powerful and expressive when it comes to *sequence-to-sequence* tasks such as text generation. Yet they meet a few challenges:

1. RNNs suffer from vanishing gradients when the context window is very wide. Though LSTMs and GRUs overcome that to a certain extent, the context windows are still fairly small compared to the typical non-local interaction of words we see in normal usage.
2. The recurrence aspect of RNNs makes them sequential and eventually slow for training as well as inference.
3. The architecture we covered in the previous section tries to encode the whole input context (or seed text) into a single vector, which is then used by the decoder to generate the next set of words. This creates limitations when the seed/context is pretty long, as does the fact that the RNN pays a lot more attention to the last set of inputs in the context.
4. RNNs have a larger memory footprint compared to other types of neural network architectures; that is, they require more parameters and hence more memory during their implementation.

On the other hand, we have convolutional networks, which are battle-tested in the field of computer vision. State-of-the-art architectures make use of CNNs to extract features and perform well on different vision tasks. The success of CNNs led researchers to explore their application to NLP tasks as well.

The main idea behind using CNNs for text is to first try to create vector representations of **a set of words** rather than individual words. More formally, the idea is to generate a vector representation of every sub-sequence of words in a given sentence.

Let's consider a sample sentence, "Flu outbreak forces schools to close". The aim would be to first break down this sentence into all possible sub-sequences, such as "Flu outbreak forces", "outbreak forces schools",..., "schools to close", and then generate a vector representation of each of these sub-sequences. Though such sub-sequences may or may not carry much meaning, they provide us with a way to understand words in different contexts, as well as their usage. Since we already understand how to prepare dense vector representation of words (see the *Distributed representation* section), let's build on top of that to understand how CNNs can be leveraged.

Continuing with the preceding example, *Figure 9.13 (A)* depicts each of the words in their vector form. The vectors are only 4-dimensional for ease of understanding:

	word vectors (1x4)			
flu	-0.4	-0.4	0.2	0.3
outbreak	0.1	0.2	-0.1	-0.1
forces	0.5	0.2	-0.3	-0.1
schools	0.2	-0.3	0.4	0.1
to	0.3	-0.3	0.1	0.1
close	-0.1	-0.3	-0.2	-0.4

(A)

Kernel Movement

Kernel-1 size 3:
3	1	2	-3
1	1	-1	1
-1	2	1	-3

Kernel-2 size 3:
1	0	0	1
1	0	-1	-1
0	1	0	1

(B)

	Kernel-1	Kernel-2
flu outbreak forces	-1.9	0.3
outbreak forces schools	0.8	0.7
forces schools to	-0.2	0.1
schools to close	1.3	-0.3

(C)

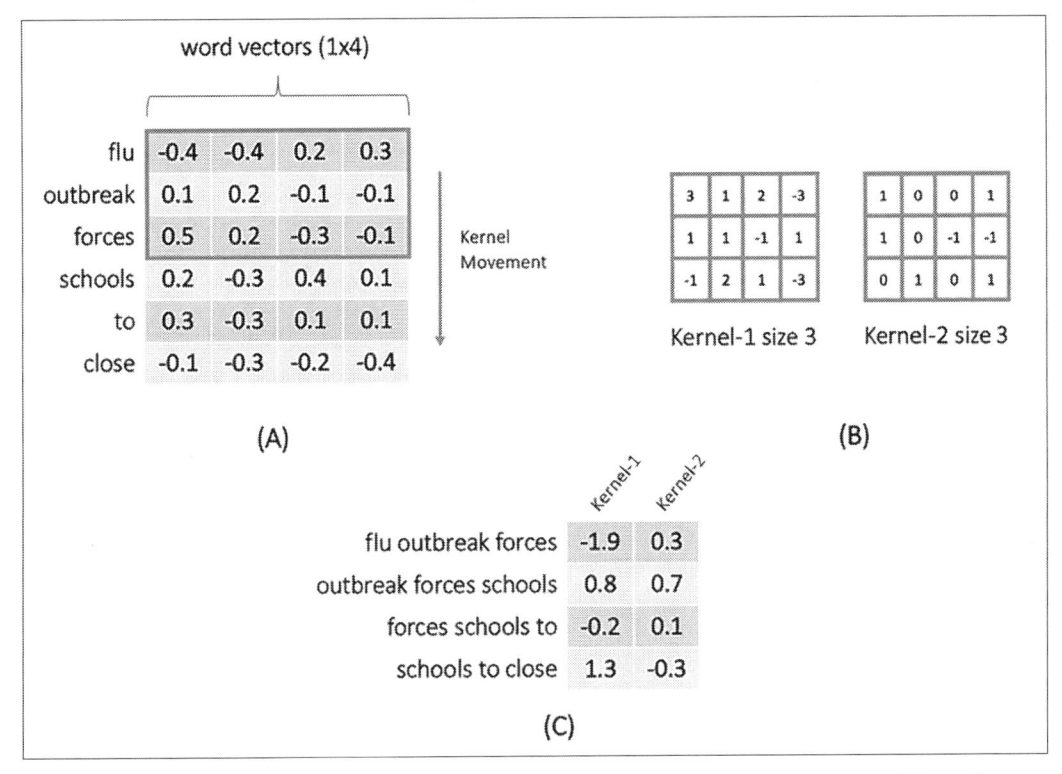

Figure 9.13: (A) Vector representation (1x4) of each word in sample sentence. (B) Two kernels/filters of size 3 each. (C) Phrase vectors of dimension 1x2 each after taking the Hadamard product, followed by the sum for each kernel with stride 1.

The two kernels, each of size 3, are depicted in *Figure 9.13 (B)*. The kernels in the case of text/NLP use cases are chosen to be as wide as the word vector dimension. The size of 3 signifies the context window each kernel is focusing on. Since the kernel width is the same as the word-vector width, we move the kernel along the words in the sentence. This constraint on size and movement in one direction only is the reason these convolutional filters are termed 1-D convolutions. The output phrase vectors are depicted in *Figure 9.13 (C)*.

Similar to deep convolutional neural networks for computer vision use cases, the above setup enables us to stack 1-D convolutional layers for NLP use cases as well. The greater depth allows the models to capture not just more complex representations but also a wider context window (this is analogous to an increase in the receptive field for a vision model with depth).

Using CNNs for NLP use cases also improves computation speed, as well as reducing the memory and time requirements to train such networks. In fact, these are some of the advantages that are explored by the following works for NLP tasks using 1-D CNNs:

- *Natural Language Processing (almost) from Scratch*, Collobert et al.[8]
- *Character-level Convolutional Networks for Text Classification*, Zhang et al.[9]
- *Convolutional Neural Networks for Sentence Classification*, Kim[10]
- *Recurrent Convolutional Neural Networks for Text Classification*, Lai and Xu et al.[11]

So far, we've discussed how CNNs can be used to extract features and capture a larger context for NLP use cases. Language-related tasks, especially text generation, have a certain temporal aspect associated with them. Hence, the next obvious question is, can we leverage CNNs for understanding temporal features, just like RNNs do?

Researchers have been exploring the use of CNNs for temporal or sequential processing for quite some time. While we discussed how CNNs are a good choice for capturing the context of a given word, this presents a problem for certain use cases. For instance, tasks such as language modeling/text generation require models to understand context, but only from one side. In simple words, a language model works by looking at words that have already been processed (past context) to generate future words. But a CNN can span to future timesteps as well.

Digressing a bit from the NLP domain, the works by Van den Oord et al. on PixelCNNs[12] and WaveNets[13] are particularly important to understand the use of CNNs in a temporal setting. They present the concept of **causal convolutions** to ensure CNNs only utilize past and not future context. This concept is highlighted in the following diagram:

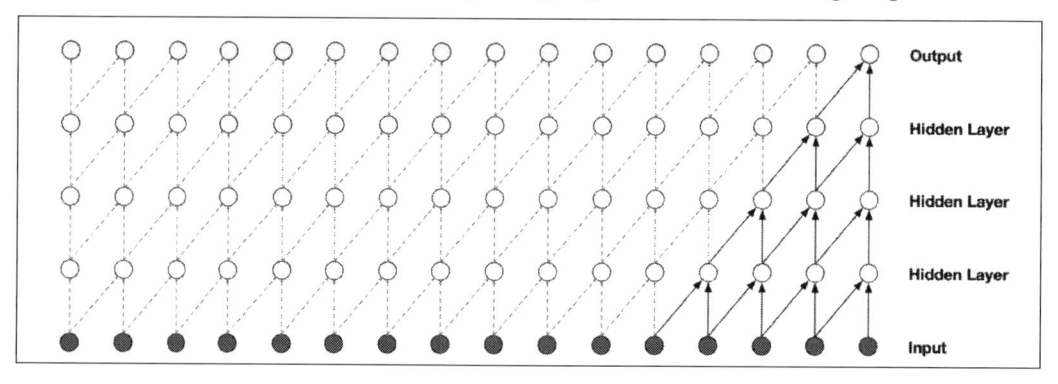

Figure 9.14: Causal padding for CNNs
Based on Van den Oord et al.[13] Figure 2

Causal convolutions ensure that the model, at any given time step t, makes predictions of the type $p(x_{t+1} \mid x_{1:t})$ and doesn't depend on future timesteps x_{t+1}, $x_{t+2} \ldots x_{t+T}$, as depicted in *Figure 9.14*. During training, conditional predictions for all timesteps can be made in parallel; the generation/inference step is sequential though; the output at every timestep is fed back into the model for the next timestep's prediction.

Since this setup does not have any recurrent connections, the model trains faster, even for longer sequences. The setup for causal convolutions originated for image and audio generation use cases but has been extended to NLP use cases as well. The authors of the WaveNet paper additionally made use of a concept called *dilated convolutions* to give the model larger receptive fields without requiring very deep architectures.

This idea of using CNNs to capture and use temporal components has opened up doors for further exploration.

Before we move on to the more involved concepts of attention and transformer architectures in the next chapter, it is important to highlight some important works which preceded them:

- *Neural Machine Translation in Time* by Kalchbrenner et al.[14] presents the ByteNet neural translation model based on encoder-decoder architecture. The overall setup makes use of 1-D causal convolutions, along with dilated kernels, to provide state-of-the-art performance on English to German translation tasks.
- Dauphin et al. presented a language model based on Gated Convolutions in their work titled *Language Modeling with Gated Convolutional Networks*.[15] They observed that their Gated Convolutions provide remarkable training speedup and lower memory footprint.
- Works by Gehring et al.[16] and Lea et al.[17] explored these ideas further and provided even better results.
- Interested readers may also explore the paper titled *An Empirical Evaluation of Generic Convolutional and Recurrent Networks for Sequence Modeling* by Bai et al.[18] This paper provides a nice overview of RNN- and CNN-based architectures for sequence modeling tasks.

This concludes our discussion of the building blocks of older architectures for language modeling.

Summary

Congratulations on completing a complex chapter involving a large number of concepts. In this chapter, we covered various concepts associated with handling textual data for the task of text generation. We started off by developing an understanding of different text representation models. We covered most of the widely used representation models, from Bag of Words to word2vec and even FastText.

The next section of the chapter focused on developing an understanding of RNN-based text generation models. We briefly discussed what comprises a language model and how we can prepare a dataset for such a task. We then trained a character-based language model to generate synthetic text samples. We touched upon different decoding strategies and used them to understand different outputs from our RNN based-language model. We also delved into a few variants, such as stacked LSTMs and bidirectional LSTM-based language models. Finally, we discussed the usage of convolutional networks in the NLP space.

In the next chapter, we will focus on the building blocks of some of the most recent and powerful architectures in the NLP domain, including attention and transformers

References

1. Mikolov, T., Chen, K., Corrado, G., & Dean, J. (2013). *Efficient Estimation of Word Representations in Vector Space*. arXiv. https://arxiv.org/abs/1301.3781

2. Rumelhart, D.E., & McClelland, J.L. (1987). *Distributed Representations*, in Parallel Distributed Processing: Explorations in the Microstructure of Cognition: Foundations, pp.77-109. MIT Press. https://web.stanford.edu/~jlmcc/papers/PDP/Chapter3.pdf

3. Pennington, J., Socher, R., & Manning, C.D. (2014). *GloVe: Global Vectors for Word Representation*. Proceedings of the 2014 Conference on Empirical Methods in Natural Language Processing (EMNLP). https://nlp.stanford.edu/pubs/glove.pdf

4. Bojanowski, P., Grave, E., Joulin, A., & Mikolov, T. (2017). *Enriching Word Vectors with Subword Information*. arXiv. https://arxiv.org/abs/1607.04606

5. Holtzman, A., Buys, J., Du, L., Forbes, M., & Choi, Y. (2019). *The Curious Case of Neural Text Degeneration*. arXiv. https://arxiv.org/abs/1904.09751

6. Graves, A., Mohamed, A., & Hinton, G. (2013). *Speech Recognition with Deep Recurrent Neural Networks*. arXiv. https://arxiv.org/abs/1303.5778

7. Pascanu, R., Gulcehre, C., Cho, K., & Bengio, Y. (2013). *How to Construct Deep Recurrent Neural Networks*. arXiv. https://arxiv.org/abs/1312.6026

8. Collobert, R., Weston, J., Karlen, M., Kavukcuoglu, K., & Kuksa, P. (2011). *Natural Language Processing (almost) from Scratch*. arXiv. https://arxiv.org/abs/1103.0398

9. Zhang, X., Zhao, J., & LeCun, Y. (2015). *Character-level Convolutional Networks for Text Classification*. arXiv. https://arxiv.org/abs/1509.01626

10. Kim, Y. (2014). *Convolutional Neural Networks for Sentence Classification*. arXiv. https://arxiv.org/abs/1408.5882

11. Lai, S., Xu, L., Liu, K., & Zhao, J. (2015). *Recurrent Convolutional Neural Networks for Text Classification*. Proceedings of the Twenty-Ninth AAAI Conference on Artifical Intelligence. http://zhengyima.com/my/pdfs/Textrcnn.pdf

12. van den Oord, A., Kalchbrenner, N., Vinyals, O., Espeholt, L., Graves, A., & Kavukcuoglu, K. (2016). *Conditional Image Generation with PixelCNN Decoders*. arXiv. https://arxiv.org/abs/1606.05328

13. van den Oord, A., Dieleman, S., Simonyan, K., Vinyals, O., Graves, A., Kalchbrenner, N., Senior, A., Kavukcuoglu, K. (2016). *WaveNet: A Generative Model for Raw Audio*. https://arxiv.org/abs/1609.03499

14. Kalchbrenner, N., Espeholt, L., Simonyan, K., van den Oord, A., Graves, A., & Kavukcuoglu, K. (2016). *Neural Machine Translation in Linear Time*. arXiv. https://arxiv.org/abs/1609.03499

15. Dauphin, Y.N., Fan, A., Auli, M., & Grangier, D. (2016). *Language Modeling with Gated Convolutional Networks*. arXiv. https://arxiv.org/abs/1612.08083

16. Gehring, J., Auli, M., Grangier, D., Yarats, D., & Dauphin, Y.N. (2017). *Convolutional Sequence to Sequence Learning*. arXiv. https://arxiv.org/abs/1705.03122

17. Lea, C., Flynn, M.D., Vidal, R., Reiter, A., & Hager, G.D. (2016). *Temporal Convolutional Networks for Action Segmentation and Detection*. arXiv. https://arxiv.org/abs/1611.05267

18. Bai, S., Kolter, J.Z., & Koltun, V. (2018). *An Empirical Evaluation of Generic Convolutional and Recurrent Networks for Sequence Modeling*. arXiv. https://arxiv.org/abs/1803.01271

10
NLP 2.0: Using Transformers to Generate Text

As we saw in the previous chapter, the NLP domain has seen some remarkable leaps in the way we understand, represent, and process textual data. From handling long-range dependencies/sequences using LSTMs and GRUs to building dense vector representations using word2vec and friends, the field in general has seen drastic improvements. With word embeddings becoming almost the de facto representation method and LSTMs as the workhorse for NLP tasks, we were hitting some roadblocks in terms of further enhancement. This setup of using embeddings with LSTM made the best use of encoder-decoder (and related architectures) style models.

We saw briefly in the previous chapter how certain improvements were achieved due to the research and application of CNN-based architectures for NLP use cases. In this chapter, we will touch upon the next set of enhancements that led to the development of current state-of-the-art transformer architectures. We will focus on:

- An overview of attention and how transformers changed the NLP landscape
- The GPT series of models, with a step-by-step guide to preparing a text-generation pipeline based on GPT-2

We will be covering topics such as attention, self-attention, contextual embeddings, and finally transformer architectures.

> All code snippets presented in this chapter can be run directly in Google Colab. For reasons of space, import statements for dependencies have not been included, but readers can refer to the GitHub repository for the full code: https://github.com/PacktPublishing/Hands-On-Generative-AI-with-Python-and-TensorFlow-2.

Let's first turn our attention to attention.

Attention

The LSTM-based architecture we used to prepare our first language model for text generation had one major limitation. The RNN layer (generally speaking, it could be LSTM, or GRU, etc.) takes in a context window of a defined size as input and encodes all of it into a single vector. This bottleneck vector needs to capture a lot of information in itself before the decoding stage can use it to start generating the next token.

Attention is one of the most powerful concepts in the deep learning space that really changed the game. The core idea behind the attention mechanism is to make use of all interim hidden states of the RNN to decide which one to focus upon before it is used by the decoding stage. A more formal way of presenting attention is:

> *Given a vector of values (all the hidden states of the RNN) and a query vector (this could be the decoder state), attention is a technique to compute a weighted sum of the values, dependent on the query.*

The weighted sum acts as a selective summary of the information contained in the hidden states (value vectors) and the query decides which values to focus on. The roots of the attention mechanism can be found in the research associated with **Neural Machine Translation** (**NMT**) architectures. NMT models particularly struggled with alignment issues and this is where attention greatly helped. For instance, translation of a sentence from English to French may not match words one-to-one. Attention is not limited to NMT use cases only and is widely used across other NLP tasks, such as text generation and classification.

The idea is pretty straightforward, but how do we implement and use it? *Figure 10.1* depicts a sample scenario of how an attention mechanism works. The figure demonstrates an unrolled RNN at time step *t*.

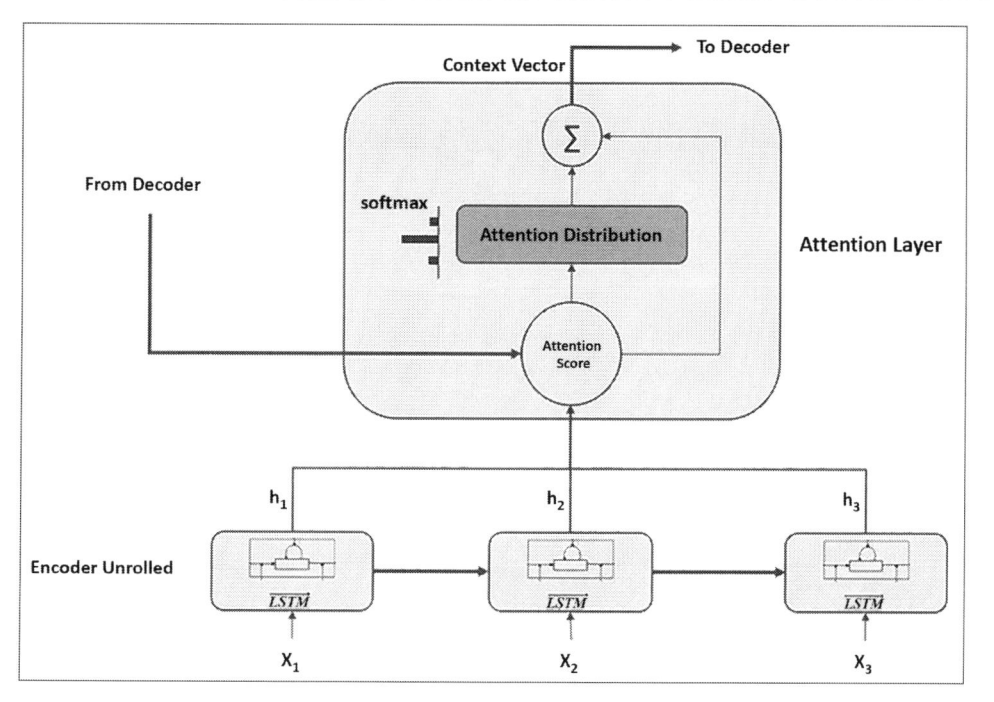

![Figure 10.1]

Figure 10.1: A simple RNN with an attention mechanism

Referring to the figure, let us understand step-by-step how attention is calculated:

1. Let the RNN encoder hidden states be denoted as $h_1, h_2 \ldots, h_N$ and the current output vector as s_t.

2. We first calculate the *attention score* e^t for time step t as:

$$e^t = [s_t^T h_1, s_t^T h_2, \ldots, s_t^T h_N]$$

This step is also called the alignment step.

3. We then transform this score into the *attention distribution*: $\alpha^t = softmax(e^t)$.

4. Using the softmax function helps us to transform the score into a probability distribution that sums to 1.

5. The final step is to calculate the attention vector, denoted as a_t, also called a context vector, by taking a weighted sum of encoder hidden states with α^t:

$$a_t = \sum_{i=1}^{N} \alpha_i^t h_i$$

Once we have the attention vector, we can then simply concatenate it with the decoder state vector from the previous time step and continue to decode the vector as previously.

Different variants of the attention mechanism have been explored by various researchers so far. A couple of important points to note are:

- The aforementioned steps for the attention calculation are the same across all variants.
- However, the difference lies in the way the attention score (denoted as e^t) is calculated.

Widely used attention scoring functions are content-based attention, additive attention, dot-product, and scaled dot-product. Readers are encouraged to explore these further for better understanding.

Contextual embeddings

The big leap from BoW-based text representation models to unsupervised dense representation techniques such as word2vec, GloVe, fastText, and so on was the secret sauce to improve deep learning model performance on NLP tasks. Yet these representations had a few limitations, which we'll remind ourselves of:

- Words can have different meanings depending on the context in which they are used. These techniques result in the same vector representation regardless of the context. This can be rectified a bit by using very strong word-sense disambiguation methods (such as the usage of supervised learning algorithms to disambiguate words), but inherently, this isn't captured by any of the known techniques.
- Words can have different uses, semantics, and syntactic behaviors, yet the word representation remains the same.

If we think about this carefully, the architecture that we prepared in the previous chapter using LSTMs was trying to solve these issues internally. To elaborate further, let us do a quick recap of the architecture we built:

- We started off with our input text being transformed into character or word embeddings.
- These embeddings were then passed through an LSTM layer (or a stack of LSTM layers or even bi-LSTM layers) and the final hidden state was transformed and decoded to generate the next token.

While the starting point leverages pre-trained embeddings, which have the same representation of any given word in every context, the LSTM layers bring in the context. The set of LSTM layers analyzes the sequence of tokens and each layer tries to learn concepts related to *language syntax*, *semantics*, and so on. This provides the much-required context to each token's (word or character) representation.

The **TagLM** architecture by Peters et al. in 2017[1] was one of the first works that provided an insight into how we could combine pre-trained word embeddings with a pre-trained neural language model to generate context-aware embeddings for downstream NLP tasks.

The big breakthrough that changed the NLP landscape came in the form of **ELMo**, or **Embeddings from Language Models**. The ELMo architecture was presented by Peters et al. in their work titled *Deep Contextualized Word Representations* in 2018.[2] Without going into too much detail, the main highlights of the ELMo architecture were:

- The model used a bi-LSTM-based language model.
- Character CNNs were used to generate embeddings, in place of pre-trained word vectors, which made use of huge 4096 LSTM units but transformed into smaller 512-sized vectors using feedforward layers.
- The model made use of residual layers to help carry the gradient between deep layers of the architecture. This helped prevent issues like vanishing gradients.
- The main innovation was to make use of all the hidden bi-LSTM layers for generating input representation. Unlike previous works, where only the final LSTM layer was used to fetch the representation of the input, this work took a weighted average of all the hidden layers' hidden states. This helped the model learn contextual word embeddings where each layer contributed to things like syntax and semantics.

The main reason ELMo got so much attention was not the fact that it helped improve the performance by a certain factor. The contextual embeddings learned by ELMo helped it improve state-of-the-art performance using previous architectures on not just a couple of NLP tasks, but *almost all of them* (see paper for details).

The **ULMFiT** model by Howard and Ruder in 2018 was based on similar concepts and helped introduce, or rather push, widespread application of *transfer learning* in the NLP domain.[3]

Self-attention

We've already briefly discussed the attention mechanism and its impact on improving NLP models in general. In this section, we will talk about a successive improvement upon the attention mechanism called self-attention.

Self-attention was proposed by Cheng et al. in their paper titled *Long Short-Term Memory Networks for Machine Reading* in 2016.[4] The concept of self-attention builds upon the general idea of attention. Self-attention enables a model to learn the correlation between the current token (character or word or sentence, etc.) and its context window. In other words, it is an attention mechanism that relates different positions of a given sequence so as to generate a representation of the same sequence. Imagine this as a way of transforming word embeddings in the context of the given sentence/sequence. The concept of self-attention as presented in the original paper itself is depicted in *Figure 10.2*.

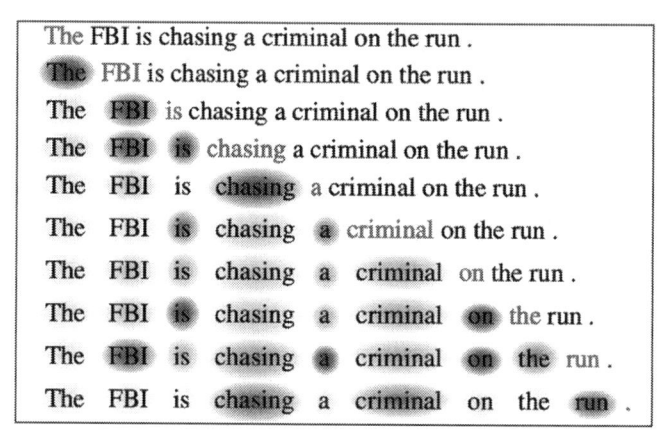

```
The FBI is chasing a criminal on the run .
The FBI is chasing a criminal on the run .
The FBI is chasing a criminal on the run .
The FBI is chasing a criminal on the run .
The FBI is chasing a criminal on the run .
The FBI is chasing a criminal on the run .
The FBI is chasing a criminal on the run .
The FBI is chasing a criminal on the run .
The FBI is chasing a criminal on the run .
The FBI is chasing a criminal on the run .
```

Figure 10.2: Self-attention[4]

Let us try and understand the self-attention output presented in this figure. Each row/sentence represents the state of the model at every time step, with the current word highlighted in red. Blue represents the attention of the model, with the intensity of focus depicted by the shade of blue. Thus, each word in the context of the current word gets to contribute to the embeddings of the current word to a certain extent.

> Interested readers may explore a notebook by the Google Brain team that showcases a framework called Tensor2Tensor (now deprecated in favor of JAX). This notebook presents an interactive visualization to help understand the concept of self-attention: https://colab.research.google.com/github/tensorflow/tensor2tensor/blob/master/tensor2tensor/notebooks/hello_t2t.ipynb.

This concept forms one of the core building blocks of the transformer architecture we are about to discuss next.

Transformers

The culmination of concepts such as attention, contextual embeddings, and recurrence-free architectures led to what we now call **transformer architectures**. The transformer architecture was presented in the seminal paper *Attention is All You Need* by Vaswani et al. back in 2017.[5] This work represented a complete paradigm shift in the NLP space; it presented not just a powerful architecture but also a smart use of some of the recently developed concepts that helped it beat state-of-the-art models by a margin across different benchmarks.

> We will cover the internals of the transformer architecture briefly. For a step-by-step explanation, readers may refer to *Illustrated Transformer* by Jay Alammar: https://jalammar.github.io/illustrated-transformer/.

At the core, a transformer is a recurrence- and convolution-free attention-based encoder-decoder architecture. It *solely depends upon the attention mechanism* to learn local and global dependencies and thus enables massive parallelization. Let us now have a look at the main contributions of this work.

Overall architecture

As mentioned earlier, a transformer is an encoder-decoder architecture at its core. Yet unlike known encoder-decoder architectures in the NLP domain, this work presented a stacked encoder-decoder setup.

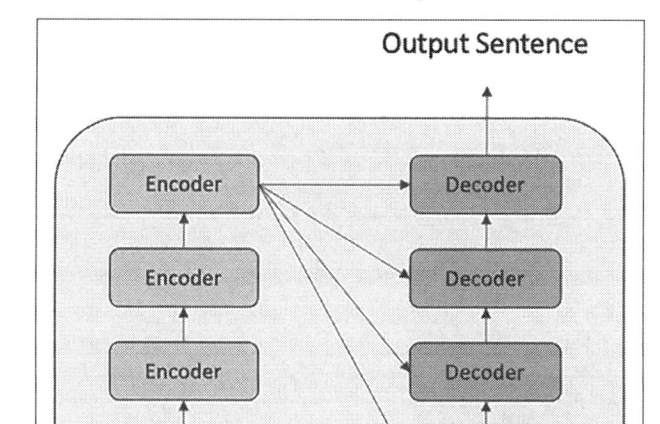

Figure 10.3 shows the high-level transformer setup.

Figure 10.3: A high-level schematic of the transformer architecture

As shown in the figure, the architecture makes use of multiple encoder blocks stacked on top of each other. The decoder itself consists of stacked decoding blocks, and the final encoder block feeds into each of the decoder blocks. The important thing to note here is that neither the encoder nor the decoder blocks are comprised of recurrent or convolutional layers. *Figure 10.4 (A)* outlines the encoder block and *Figure 10.4 (B)* the decoder block. Dotted lines denote residual connections between different sets of layers. The original paper presented the transformer architecture with 6 identical encoder blocks and decoder blocks each.

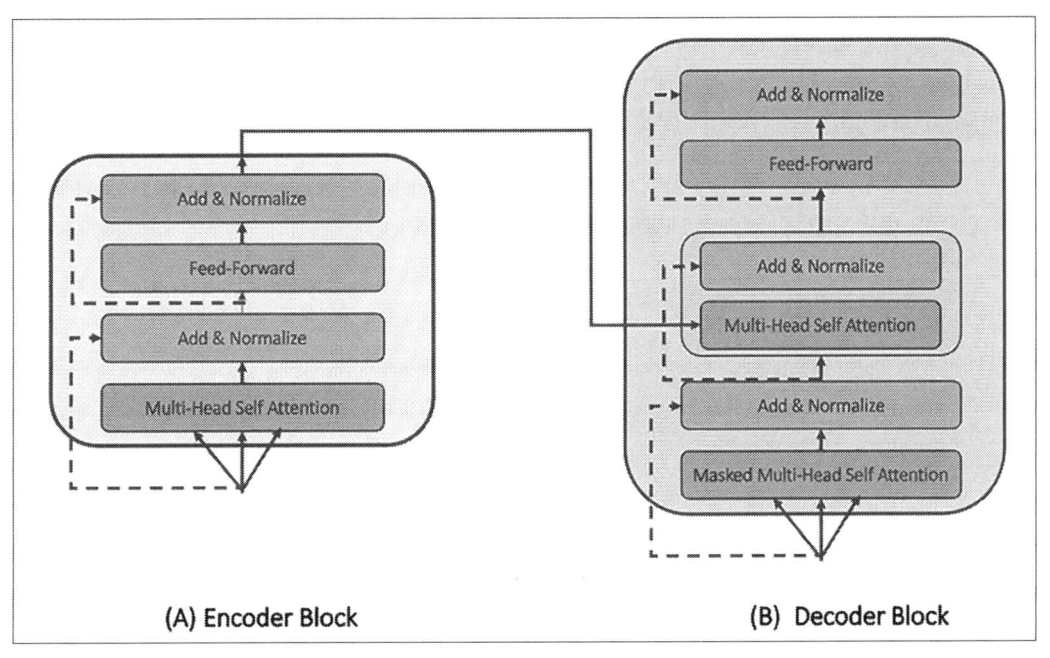

Figure 10.4: A) Encoder block, B) Decoder block used in the transformer architecture

The encoder block, as shown in *Figure 10.4 (A)*, consists of a layer for calculating self-attention followed by normalization and feed-forward layers. There are skip connections between these layers. The decoder block is almost the same as the encoder block, with one additional sub-block consisting of self-attention and normalization layers. This additional sub-block takes input from the last encoder block to ensure that the encoder's attention is propagated to the decoding blocks.

The first layer in the decoder block carries a slight modification. This multi-head self-attention layer is masked for future timesteps/contexts. This ensures the model does not attend to future positions of the target while decoding the current token. Let's spend a bit more time trying to understand the multi-head self-attention component.

Multi-head self-attention

We discussed the concept of self-attention in the previous section. In this section, we will discuss how the transformer architecture implements self-attention and its related parameters. While presenting the concept of attention, we discussed it in terms of the query vector (decoder state, denoted as q) and the value vectors (the encoder's hidden state, denoted as v).

In the case of transformers, this is modified a bit. We make use of encoder states or input tokens as both query and value vectors (self-attention) along with an additional vector called the *key* vector (denoted as k). The key, value, and query vectors are of the same dimension in this case.

The transformer architecture makes use of the *scaled dot-product* as its attention mechanism. This scoring function is defined as:

$$Attention(Q, K, V) = softmax\left(\frac{QK^T}{\sqrt{n}}\right)V$$

where the attention output is calculated first as the dot product QK^T between the query and key vectors Q and K (these are actually matrices, but we will explain that in a bit). The dot product tries to capture the similarity of the query with encoder states, which is then scaled by the square root of the dimension n of the input vector. This scaling factor is introduced to ensure the gradients are propagated properly, since vanishing gradients are observed for large embedding vectors. The softmax operation transforms the score into a probability distribution summing to 1. The final step is to calculate the product of the weighted sum of the encoder states (the value vector V this time) with the output of the softmax. This overall operation is depicted in *Figure 10.5*:

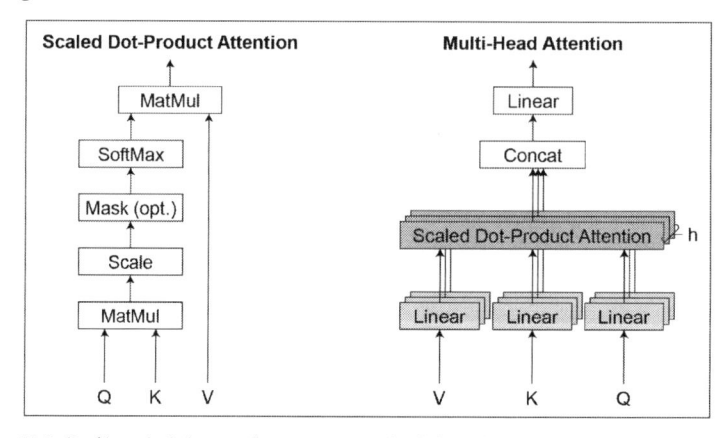

Figure 10.5: (Left) scaled dot product attention, (right) multi-head self-attention combining several self-attention layers in parallel.

In place of using a single attention head per encoder block, the model makes use of multiple attention heads in parallel (as depicted in *Figure 10.5 (right)*). The authors mention in the paper that "multi-head attention allows the model to jointly attend to information from different representation subspaces at different positions. With a single attention head, averaging inhibits this." In other words, multi-head attention allows the model to learn different aspects of every word in the input, that is, one attention head could be capturing the impact of the relationships with prepositions, the other one could be focusing on its interactions with verbs, and so on. As each attention head would have its own set of *Q*, *K*, and *V* vectors, in practice these are implemented as matrices with each row corresponding to a specific head.

> A highly intuitive visual explanation of multi-head self-attention is presented here for reference: https://www.youtube.com/watch?v=-9vVhYEXeyQ&ab_channel=Peltarion.

One may think that due to the multi-head setup, the number of parameters would suddenly blow out of proportion and slow down the training process. To counteract this, the authors made use of smaller-dimensional vectors (size 64) by first projecting the larger input embeddings into a smaller dimension. They then made use of 8 heads in the original implementation. This resulted in a final concatenated vector (from all attention heads) of the same dimension as it would be with a single attention head with a larger input embedding vector. This neat trick helps the model capture a lot more semantics in the same space without any impact on the overall training speed. The overall transformer architecture uses multiple such encoder blocks with each of them containing multi-head attention layers.

Positional encodings

The transformer model is devoid of any recurrence or convolutional layers, so in order to ensure that the model understands the importance of the sequence of the inputs, the concept of *positional embeddings* was used. The authors chose to use the following method to generate positional encodings:

$$PE(pos, 2i) = \sin\left(pos / 10000^{\frac{2i}{d_{model}}}\right)$$

$$PE(pos, 2i+1) = \cos\left(pos / 10000^{\frac{2i}{d_{model}}}\right)$$

where *pos* is the position of the input token, *i* is the dimension, and d_{model} is the length of the input embedding vector. The authors use sine for even positions and cosine for odd ones. The positional encoding vector dimension is kept the same as the input vector and both vectors are summed up before they are fed into the encoder or decoder blocks.

The combination of multi-head self-attention along with positional encodings helps the transformer network build highly contextual representations of input sequences. This, along with the completely attention-based architecture, enables the transformer to not only beat the state-of-the-art models on a number of benchmarks, but also form the basis of a whole family of transformer-based models. In the next section, we will briefly touch upon this family of transformers.

BERT-ology

The transformer architecture ushered in completely unheard-of performance benchmarks in the NLP domain. This recurrence-free setup led to research into and the development of a whole family of transformer-based architectures. One of the initial and most successful ones is the BERT model. **BERT**, or **Bi-Directional Encoder Representations from Transformers**, was presented by Devlin et al., a team at Google AI in 2018.[6]

The model drastically improved upon the benchmarks set by the transformer model. BERT also helped push the transfer-learning envelope in the NLP domain by showcasing how a pre-trained model can be fine-tuned for various tasks to provide state-of-the-art performance. In computer vision use cases, we can use a large pre-trained network such as VGG or ResNet as a feature extractor with a classification layer, or we can fine-tune the whole network for the given task. We can do the same thing using BERT as well.

The BERT model makes use of a transformer-style encoder with a different number of encoder blocks depending on the model size. The authors presented two models, BERT-base with 12 blocks and BERT-large with 24 blocks. Both of these models have larger feedforward networks (768 and 1024 respectively) and a greater number of attention heads (12 and 16 respectively) compared to the original transformer setup.

Another major change from the original transformer implementation is the bi-directional masked language model objective. A typical language model ensures causality, that is, the decoding process only looks at the past context and not future time steps. The authors of BERT tweaked this objective to build context from both directions, i.e. the objective of *predicting masked words* along with *next sentence prediction*. This is depicted in *Figure 10.6*:

Chapter 10

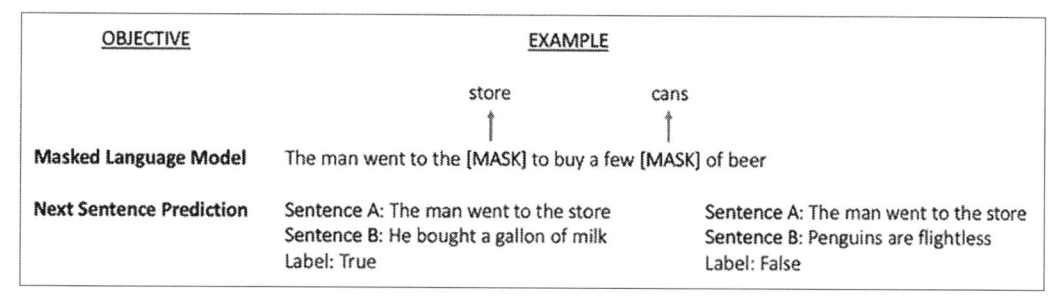

OBJECTIVE	EXAMPLE	
Masked Language Model	store ↑ cans ↑ The man went to the [MASK] to buy a few [MASK] of beer	
Next Sentence Prediction	Sentence A: The man went to the store Sentence B: He bought a gallon of milk Label: True	Sentence A: The man went to the store Sentence B: Penguins are flightless Label: False

Figure 10.6: BERT training objectives of a masked language model and next sentence prediction

As shown in the figure, the *masked language model* randomly masks out 15% of tokens for the training process. They train the model on a huge corpus and then fine-tune it for different tasks on GLUE (https://gluebenchmark.com/) and other related benchmarks. As reported in the paper, the model outperforms all previous architectures by a good margin.

The success of BERT led to a series of improved models that tweaked certain aspects with respect to embeddings, encoder layers, and so on to provide incremental performance improvements. Models such as RoBERTa[7], ALBERT[8], DistilBERT[9], XLNet[10], and so on share the core idea and build upon it to provide improvements.

As BERT does not conform to causality, it cannot be used for typical language modeling tasks such as text generation. In the next section, we will discuss a parallel architectural family of transformers from OpenAI.

GPT 1, 2, 3…

OpenAI is an AI research group that has been in the spotlight for quite some time because of their newsworthy works such as GPT, GPT-2, and the recently released GPT-3. In this section, we will walk through a brief discussion related to these architectures and their novel contributions. Toward the end, we will use a pre-trained version of GPT-2 for our task of text generation.

Generative pre-training: GPT

The first model in this series is called **GPT**, or **Generative Pre-Training**. It was released in 2018, about the same time as the BERT model. The paper[11] presents a task-agnostic architecture based on the ideas of transformers and unsupervised learning. The GPT model was shown to beat several benchmarks such as GLUE and SST-2, though the performance was overtaken by BERT, which was released shortly after this.

GPT is essentially a language model based on the *transformer-decoder* we presented in the previous chapter (see the section on *Transformers*). Since a language model can be trained in an unsupervised fashion, the authors of this model made use of this unsupervised approach to train on a very large corpus and then fine-tuned it for specific tasks. The authors used the **BookCorpus** dataset,[12] which contains over 7,000 unique, unpublished books across different genres. This dataset, the authors claim, allows the model to learn long-range information due to the presence of long stretches of contiguous text. This is seen to be better than the 1B Word Benchmark dataset used by earlier works, which misses out on long-range information due to shuffled sentences. The overall GPT setup is depicted in the following figure:

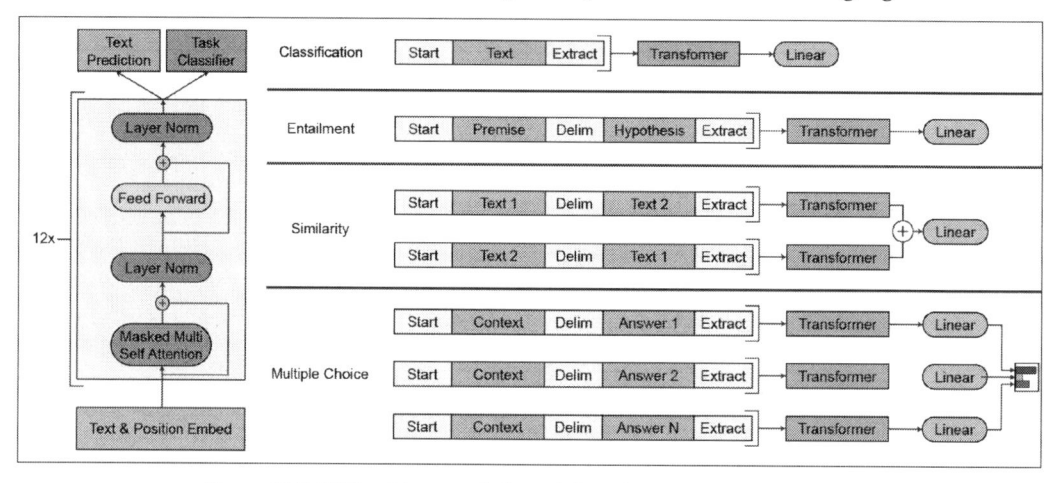

Figure 10.7: GPT architecture (left), task-based setup using GPT (right)

As shown in *Figure 10.7 (left)*, the GPT model is similar to the original transformer-decoder. The authors make use of 12 decoder blocks (as opposed to 6 in the original transformer) with 768-dimensional states and 12 self-attention heads each. Since the model uses masked self-attention, it maintains the causal nature of the language model and hence can be used for text generation as well. For the rest of the tasks showcased in *Figure 10.7 (right)*, essentially the same pre-trained language model is used with minimal task-specific preprocessing of inputs and final task-specific layers/objectives.

GPT-2

GPT was superseded by an even more powerful model called GPT-2. Radford et al. presented the GPT-2 model as part of their work titled *Language Models are Unsupervised Multi-task Learners* in 2019.[13] The largest GPT-2 variant is a huge 1.5 billion parameter transformer-based model which was able to perform remarkably well on various NLP tasks.

The most striking aspect of this work is that the authors showcase how a model trained in an unsupervised fashion (language modeling) achieves state-of-the-art performance in a *few-shot* setting. This is particularly important because, in comparison to GPT and even BERT, GPT-2 does not require any fine-tuning on specific tasks.

Similar to GPT, the secret sauce for GPT-2 is its dataset. The authors prepared a massive 40 GB dataset by crawling 45 million outbound links from a social networking site called Reddit. They performed some heuristic-based cleaning, de-duplication, and removal of Wikipedia articles (of course, why not?) to end up with roughly 8 million documents. This dataset is called the **WebText** dataset.

The overall architecture of GPT-2 remains the same as GPT, with minor changes such as the placement of layer normalization at the start of each sub-block and an additional layer normalization after the final self-attention block. The four variants of the model leveraged 12, 24, 36, and 48 layers respectively. The vocabulary was also expanded to cover 50,000 words and the context window was expanded to 1,024 tokens (as compared to 512 for GPT).

GPT-2 was so performant as a language model that the authors initially decided against releasing the pre-trained model for the general good.[14] They eventually did release it, citing the fact that no ill-intentioned use had been found so far. It is important to note that it isn't just an ethical issue. The sheer size of the data and the model make it nearly impossible for most people to even think about training such a model. *Figure 10.8* depicts the size of some recent NLP models and the amount of compute required to train them:

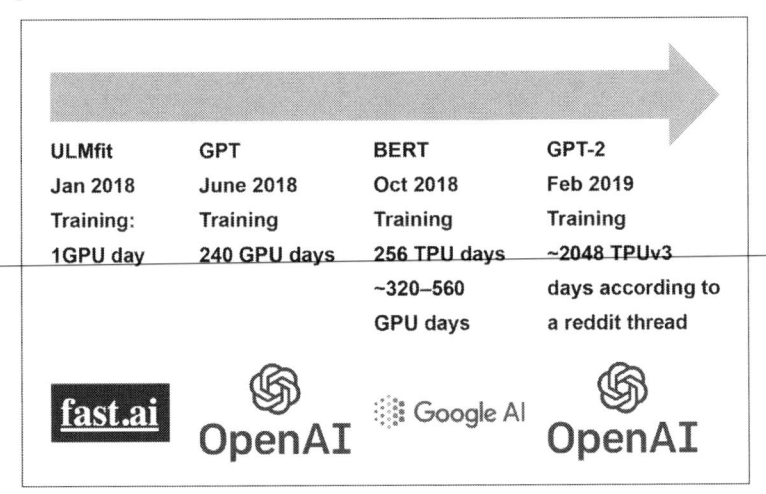

Figure 10.8: Scale of NLP models[15]

TPUs are multiple times faster than typical GPUs and, as shown in the figure, GPT-2 requires 2048 TPU days to train on the reported dataset. Compare this against 256 TPU days for the large BERT model.

> Interested readers may explore the official implementation of GPT-2 here: https://github.com/openai/gpt-2.
>
> While the official implementation was made for TensorFlow 1.14, an unofficial implementation using TensorFlow 2.x is available at this link:
>
> https://akanyaani.github.io/gpt-2-tensorflow2.0/

Thankfully, as the pre-trained model was released, researchers at Hugging Face decided to work toward democratizing the transformer architectures. The `transformer` package from Hugging Face is a high-level wrapper that enables us to use these massive NLP models with a few lines of code. The library also provides a web app for exploring different transformer-based models. *Figure 10.9* is a snapshot of the paragraph generated by this web app when provided with a "GPT is" seed:

> GPT2 is a large-scale language model with a vocabulary of 8,000,000 sentences in length (Mikolov et al., 2007). We are currently working on a model that allows to train both parallel and hybrid WGPT models, and we plan to make it available for both languages in the future. This would be a major breakthrough in the area of automated language generation, as it will significantly speed up the training process. The training process involves two components : parallel and hybrid . While using parallel, users will run W GPT with up to four instances on parallel.
>
> **Written by Transformer** · transformer.huggingface.co

Figure 10.9: A sample output using GPT-2 based on the Hugging Face transformer package[16]

The generated text in the figure shows how impressively GPT-2 works. In the first sentence, the model does a remarkable job and even follows a proper convention for citing a previous work (although the citation itself isn't correct). The content does not make much sense, but syntactically it is on the mark and quite coherent with respect to the minimal seed text we provided as input.

We will now leverage the `transformers` package to build a text generation pipeline of our own based on GPT-2, and see how well our model can do.

Hands-on with GPT-2

Keeping with the theme of some of the previous chapters where we were generating fake content using various complex architectures, let's generate some fake headlines using GPT-2. The million-headlines dataset contains over a million headlines from ABC News Australia, collected over a period of 17 years. The dataset is available at the following links:

`https://dataverse.harvard.edu/dataset.xhtml?persistentId=doi:10.7910/DVN/SYBGZL`

`https://www.kaggle.com/therohk/million-headlines`

We will be using the `transformers` library from Hugging Face to fine-tune GPT-2 on this dataset. At a high level, this task of fake headline generation is the same as the language modeling task we worked on in the initial sections of *Chapter 9*, *The Rise of Methods for Text Generation*. Since we are using the `transformers` package, the steps relating to training dataset creation, tokenization, and finally training the model are abstracted with high-level APIs.

> The `transformers` library works with both TensorFlow and PyTorch backends. For this particular case, we are using the default retraining setup based on PyTorch. The library is constantly improving and at the time of writing, the stable version 3.3.1 has issues with fine-tuning GPT-2 using TensorFlow. Since `transformers` is a high-level library, readers will not notice much difference in the following code snippets.

The first step, as always, is to read the dataset at hand and transform it into the required format. We need not prepare the word-to-integer and reverse mappings on our own. The `Tokenizer` class from the `transformers` library handles that for us. The following snippet prepares the dataset and required objects:

```
import pandas as pd
from sklearn.model_selection import train_test_split
from transformers import AutoTokenizer
from transformers import TextDataset,DataCollatorForLanguageModeling

# Get dataset
news = pd.read_csv('abcnews-date-text.csv')
X_train, X_test= train_test_split(news.headline_text.tolist(),test_size=0.33, random_state=42)

# Write the headlines from training dataset
```

```
with open('train_dataset.txt','w') as f:
    for line in X_train:
        f.write(line)
        f.write("\n")

# Write the headlines from testing dataset
with open('test_dataset.txt','w') as f:
    for line in X_test:
        f.write(line)
        f.write("\n")

# Prepare tokenizer object
tokenizer = AutoTokenizer.from_pretrained("gpt2",pad_token='<pad>')

train_path = 'train_dataset.txt'
test_path = 'test_dataset.txt'

# Utility method to prepare DataSet objects
def load_dataset(train_path,test_path,tokenizer):
    train_dataset = TextDataset(
          tokenizer=tokenizer,
          file_path=train_path,
          block_size=4)

    test_dataset = TextDataset(
          tokenizer=tokenizer,
          file_path=test_path,
          block_size=4)

    data_collator = DataCollatorForLanguageModeling(
        tokenizer=tokenizer, mlm=False,
    )
    return train_dataset,test_dataset,data_collator

train_dataset,test_dataset,data_collator = load_dataset(train_path,
test_path, tokenizer)
```

In the above snippet, we use `sklearn` to split our dataset into training and test segments, which are then transformed into usable form using the `TextDataset` class. The `train_dataset` and `test_dataset` objects are simple generator objects that will be used by the `Trainer` class to fine-tune our model. The following snippet prepares the setup for training the model:

```
from transformers import Trainer,TrainingArguments,AutoModelWithLMHead

model = AutoModelWithLMHead.from_pretrained("gpt2")

training_args = TrainingArguments(
    output_dir="./headliner",   # The output directory
    overwrite_output_dir=True,  # overwrite the content of
                                # the output directory
    num_train_epochs=1,         # number of training epochs
    per_device_train_batch_size=4, # batch size for training
    per_device_eval_batch_size=2,  # batch size for evaluation
    eval_steps = 400, # Number of update steps
                      # between two evaluations.
    save_steps=800,   # after # steps model is saved
    warmup_steps=500, # number of warmup steps for
                      # learning rate scheduler
)

trainer = Trainer(
    model=model,
    args=training_args,
    data_collator=data_collator,
    train_dataset=train_dataset,
    eval_dataset=test_dataset,
    prediction_loss_only=True,
)
```

We make use of the class `AutoModelWithLMHead` as a high-level wrapper for GPT-2 with a language model objective. The `Trainer` class simply iterates through training steps based on the parameters set using the `TrainingArguments` class.

The next step is to simply call the `train` function and let the fine-tuning begin. The following snippet shows training steps for GPT-2:

```
trainer.train()
{'loss': 6.99887060546875, 'learning_rate': 5e-05, 'epoch': 0.0010584004182798454, 'total_flos': 5973110784000, 'step': 500}
{'loss': 6.54750146484375, 'learning_rate': 4.994702390916932e-05, 'epoch': 0.0021168008365596907, 'total_flos': 11946221568000, 'step': 1000}
{'loss': 6.5059072265625, 'learning_rate': 4.989404781833863e-05, 'epoch': 0.003175201254839536, 'total_flos': 17919332352000, 'step': 1500}
```

```
{'loss': 6.46778125, 'learning_rate': 4.9841071727507945e-05, 'epoch':
0.0042336016731193814, 'total_flos': 23892443136000, 'step': 2000}
{'loss': 6.339587890625, 'learning_rate': 4.978809563667726e-05,
'epoch': 0.005292002091399226, 'total_flos': 29865553920000, 'step':
2500}
{'loss': 6.3247421875, 'learning_rate': 4.973511954584657e-05, 'epoch':
0.006350402509679072, 'total_flos': 35838664704000, 'step': 3000}
```

As GPT-2 is a huge model, fine-tuning it for a few epochs could take hours on very fast GPUs. For the purpose of this exercise, we let it train for a few hours, all the while saving interim checkpoints. The following snippet shows the `pipeline` object along with the utility function `get_headline`, which we need to generate headlines using this fine-tuned model:

```
from transformers import pipeline

headliner = pipeline('text-generation',
          model='./headliner',
          tokenizer='gpt2',
          config={'max_length':8})

# Utility method
def get_headline(headliner_pipeline, seed_text="News"):
  return headliner_pipeline(seed_text)[0]['generated_text'].split('\n')
[0]
```

Let us now generate some fake headlines to see how good or bad our GPT-2 model is. *Figure 10.10* showcases a few fake headlines generated using our model:

> **AG Calls for** public to vote on kangaroo tax avoidance
>
> **China decides** to help indigenous population in the process of drought
>
> **Wildfire** warnings warn farmers in champs in Melbourne
>
> **City Council** prepares against development crisis

Figure 10.10: Fake headlines using fine-tuned GPT-2. Text in bold is the seed text.

The generated output showcases the potential of GPT-2 and transformer-based architectures in general. Readers should compare this against the LSTM-based variants we trained in the initial sections of *Chapter 9, The Rise of Methods for Text Generation*. The model shown here is able to pick up a few nuances associated with news headlines. For instance, it is generating short and crisp sentences, picking up words such as *kangaroo*, *indigenous*, and even *Melbourne*, which are all relevant in an Australian context, the domain of our training dataset. All of this was captured by the model with only a few epochs of training. The possibilities are endless.

Mammoth GPT-3

The OpenAI group did not just stop after the massive success of GPT-2. Rather, GPT-2 demonstrated how model capacity (parameter size) and larger datasets can lead to impressive results. The recently published paper titled *Language Models are Few Shot Learners* by Brown et al. was released in May 2020.[17] This paper introduces the mammoth 175 billion-parameter GPT-3 model.

GPT-3 is orders of magnitude larger (10x) than any previous language model and explores the transformer architecture to its limits. In this work, the authors present 8 different variants of the model, starting from a 125 million-parameter, 12-layer "GPT-3 small" to a 175 billion-parameter, 96-layer GPT-3 model.

The model architecture is the same as GPT-2, but with one major change (aside from the increase in embedding size, attention heads, and layers). This major change is the use of alternating dense and locally banded sparse attention patterns in transformer blocks. This sparse attention technique is similar to the one presented for sparse transformers (see *Generating Long Sequences with Sparse Transformers*, Child et al.[18]).

Similar to earlier GPT models, the authors had to prepare an even larger dataset for this third iteration. They prepared a 300 billion-token dataset based on existing datasets like Common Crawl (filtered for better content), WebText2 (a larger version of WebText used for GPT-2), Books1 and Books2, and the Wikipedia dataset. They sampled each dataset in proportion to the dataset's quality.

The authors compare the overall learning paradigm of NLP models, and machine learning in general, with the way humans learn. Despite the improved performance and capacity of language models over the years, the state-of-the-art models still require task-specific fine-tuning. To showcase the capabilities of GPT-3, they evaluate the model in *few-shot*, *one-shot*, and *zero-shot modes*. The fine-tuning mode is left as a future exercise for the time being.

The three evaluation modes can be summarised as follows:

- **Zero-shot**: Given only a natural language description of the task, i.e. without being shown any examples of correct output, the model predicts the answer.
- **One-shot**: As well as a description of the task, the model is shown one example of the task.
- **Few-shot**: As well as a description of the task, the model is shown a few examples of the task.

In each case, no gradient updates are performed (as we are only evaluating, not training, the model in any of these modes). *Figure 10.11* shows sample settings for each of the evaluation modes with the task being translation of text from English to Spanish.

```
Zero-shot
            Task Description: Translate English to Spanish
                      Prompt: water =>


One-shot
            Task Description: Translate English to Spanish
                     Example: with milk => con leche
                      Prompt: water =>


Few-shot
            Task Description: Translate English to Spanish
                     Example: with milk => con leche
                     Example: cat and dog => gato y perro
                     Example: I speak English => Yo hablo inglés
                      Prompt: water =>
```

Figure 10.11: Evaluation modes for GPT-3

As shown in the figure, in zero-shot mode, the model is presented with the task description and a prompt for translation. Similarly, for one-shot and few-shot modes the model is presented with one and a few examples respectively before presenting a prompt for actual translation. The authors observe that GPT-3 achieves promising results in zero-shot and one-shot settings. In a few-shot setting, the model is mostly competitive and for certain tasks even surpasses the current state-of-the-art.

Aside from the usual NLP tasks, GPT-3 seems to showcase some extraordinary capabilities on tasks which otherwise require rapid adaptation or on-the-fly reasoning. The authors observe that GPT-3 is able to perform reasonably well on tasks such as unscrambling words, performing three-digit arithmetic, and even using novel words in a sentence after seeing them defined just once. The authors also observe that the news articles generated by GPT-3 in the few-shot setting are good enough to cause difficulties for human evaluators when distinguishing them from human-generated articles. It would be interesting to test out GPT-3 against the fine-tuned GPT-2 we prepared in the previous section.

The model is huge enough to require a dedicated high-performance cluster to train it as described in the paper. The authors present a discussion on the amount of compute and energy required to train this huge model. In its current state, the model remains out of bounds for most of us. OpenAI plans to expose the model in the form of an API, but details are sketchy at the time of writing this chapter.

Summary

In this chapter, we introduced some of the core ideas that have dominated recent models for NLP, like the *attention* mechanism, *contextual embeddings*, and *self-attention*. We then used this foundation to learn about the *transformer* architecture and its internal components. We briefly discussed BERT and its family of architectures.

In the next section of the chapter, we presented a discussion on the transformer-based language models from OpenAI. We discussed the architectural and dataset-related choices for GPT and GPT-2. We also used the `transformer` package from Hugging Face to develop our own GPT-2-based text generation pipeline. We finally closed the chapter with a brief discussion on the latest and greatest language model, GPT-3. We discussed various motivations behind developing such a huge model and its long list of capabilities, which go beyond the list of traditionally tested benchmarks.

This chapter, along with *Chapter 9, The Rise of Methods for Text Generation*, showcased how NLP is a field of study of its own. Yet, concepts from computer vision and deep learning/machine learning in general cross-pollinate to push the boundaries.

In the next chapter, we will shift our focus to understanding the audio landscape and how generative models work in the audio domain.

References

1. Peters, M.E., Ammar, W., Bhagavatula, C., & Power, R. (2017). *Semi-supervised sequence tagging with bidirectional language models.* arXiv. https://arxiv.org/abs/1705.00108

2. Peters, M.E., Neumann, M., Iyyer, M., Gardner, M., Clark, C., Lee, K., & Zettlemoyer, L. (2018). *Deep contexualized word representations.* arXiv. https://arxiv.org/abs/1802.05365

3. Howard, J., & Ruder, S. (2018). *Universal Language Model Fine-tuning for Text Classification.* arXiv. https://arxiv.org/abs/1801.06146

4. Cheng, J., Dong, L., & Lapata, M. (2016). *Long Short-Term Memory-Networks for Machine Reading.* arXiv. https://arxiv.org/abs/1601.06733

5. Vaswani, A., Shazeer, N., Parmar, N., Uszkoreit, J., Jones, L., Gomez, A.N., Kaiser, L., & Polosukhin, I. (2017). *Attention Is All You Need.* arXiv. https://arxiv.org/abs/1706.03762

6. Devlin, J., Chang, M-W., Lee, K., & Toutanova, K. (2018). *BERT: Pre-training of Deep Bidirectional Transformers for Language Understanding.* arXiv. https://arxiv.org/abs/1810.04805

7. Liu, Y., Ott, M., Goyal, N., Du, J., Joshi, M., Chen, D., Levy, O., Lewis, M., Zettlemoyer, L., & Stoyanov, V. (2019). *RoBERTa: A Robustly Optimized BERT Pretaining Approach.* arXiv. https://arxiv.org/abs/1907.11692

8. Lan, Z., Chen, M., Goodman, S., Gimpel, K., Sharma, P., & Soricut, R. (2019). *ALBERT: A Lite BERT for Self-supervised Learning of Language Representations.* arXiv. https://arxiv.org/abs/1909.11942

9. Sanh, V., Debut, L., Chaumond, J., & Wolf, T. (2019) *DistilBERT, a distilled version of BERT: smaller, faster, cheaper and lighter.* arXiv. https://arxiv.org/abs/1910.01108

10. Yang, Z., Dai, Z., Yang, Y., Carbonell, J., Salakhutdinov, R., & Le, Q.V. (2019). *XLNet: Generalized Autoregressive Pretraining for Language Understanding.* arXiv. https://arxiv.org/abs/1906.08237

11. Radford, A. (2018, June 11). *Improving Language Understanding with Unsupervised Learning.* OpenAI. https://openai.com/blog/language-unsupervised/

12. Zhu, Y., Kiros, R., Zemel, R., Salakhutdinov, R., Urtasun, R., Torralba, A., & Fidler, S. (2015). *Aligning Books and Movies: Towards Story-like Visual Explanations by Watching Movies and Reading Books.* arXiv. https://arxiv.org/abs/1506.06724

13. Radford, A., Wu, J., Child, R., Luan, D., Amodei, D., & Sutskever, I. (2019). *Language Models are Unsupervised Multitask Learners*. OpenAI. https://cdn.openai.com/better-language-models/language_models_are_unsupervised_multitask_learners.pdf

14. Radford, A., Wu, J., Amodei, D., Amodei, D., Clark, J., Brundage, M., & Sutskever, I. (2019, February 14). *Better Language Models and Their Implications*. OpenAI. https://openai.com/blog/better-language-models/

15. stanfordonline. (2019, March 21). *Stanford CS224N: NLP with Deep Learning | Winter 2019 | Lecture 13 – Contextual Word Embeddings* [Video]. YouTube. https://www.youtube.com/watch?v=S-CspeZ8FHc&ab_channel=stanfordonline

16. Hugging Face. (n.d.). *gpt2 abstract*. Retrieved April 22, 2021, from https://transformer.huggingface.co/doc/arxiv-nlp/ByLHXHhnBJtBLOpRENZmulqc/edit

17. Brown, T.B., Mann, B., Ryder, N., Subbiah, M., Kaplan, J., Dhariwal, P., Neelakantan, A., Shyam, P., Sastry, G., Askell, A., Agarwal, S., Herbert-Voss, A., Krueger, G., Henighan, T., Child, R., Ramesh, A., Ziegler, D., Wu, J., Winter, C., Hesse, C., Chen, M., Sigler, E., Litwin, M., Gray, S., Chess, B., Clark, J., Berner, C., McCandlish, S., Radford, A., Sutskever, I., & Amodei, D. (2020). "*Language Models are Few-Shot Learners*". arXiv. https://arxiv.org/abs/2005.14165

18. Child, R., Gray, S., Radford, A., & Sutskever, I. (2019). *Generating Long Sequences with Sparse Transformers*. arXiv. https://arxiv.org/abs/1904.10509

11
Composing Music with Generative Models

In the preceding chapters, we discussed a number of generative models focused on tasks such as image, text, and video generation. In the contexts of very basic MNIST digit generation to more involved tasks like mimicking Barack Obama, we explored a number of complex works along with their novel contributions, and spent time understanding the nuances of the tasks and datasets involved.

We saw, in the previous chapters on text generation, how improvements in the field of computer vision helped usher in drastic improvements in the NLP domain as well. Similarly, audio is another domain where the cross-pollination of ideas from computer vision and NLP domains has broadened the perspective. Audio generation is not a new field, but thanks to research in the deep learning space, this domain has seen some tremendous improvements in recent years as well.

Audio generation has a number of applications. The most prominent and popular ones nowadays are a series of smart assistants (Google Assistant, Apple Siri, Amazon Alexa, and so on). These virtual assistants not only try to understand natural language queries but also respond in a very human-like voice. Audio generation also finds applications in the field of assistive technologies, where text-to-speech engines are used for reading content onscreen for people with reading disabilities.

Leveraging such technologies in the field of music generation is increasingly being explored as well. The acquisition of AI-based royalty-free music generation service Jukedeck by ByteDance (the parent company of social network TikTok) speaks volumes for this field's potential value and impact.[1]

In fact, AI-based music generation is a growing trend with a number of competing solutions and research work. Commercial offerings for computer-aided music generation, such as Apple's GarageBand,[2] provide a number of easy-to-use interfaces for novices to compose high-quality music tracks with just a few clicks. Researchers on Google's project Magenta[3] are pushing the boundaries of music generation to new limits by experimenting with different technologies, tools, and research projects to enable people with little to no knowledge of such complex topics to generate impressive pieces of music on their own.

In this chapter, we will cover different concepts, architectures, and components associated with generative models for audio data. In particular, we will limit our focus to music generation tasks only. We will concentrate on the following topics:

- A brief overview of music representations
- RNN-based music generation
- A simple setup to understand how GANs can be leveraged for music generation
- Polyphonic music generation based on MuseGAN

> All code snippets presented in this chapter can be run directly in Google Colab. For reasons of space, import statements for dependencies have not been included, but readers can refer to the GitHub repository for the full code: https://github.com/PacktPublishing/Hands-On-Generative-AI-with-Python-and-TensorFlow-2.

We will begin with an introduction to the task of music generation.

Getting started with music generation

Music generation is an inherently complex and difficult task. Doing so with the help of algorithms (machine learning or otherwise) is even more challenging. Nevertheless, music generation is an interesting area of research with a number of open problems and fascinating works.

In this section, we will build a high-level understanding of this domain and understand a few important and foundational concepts.

Computer-assisted music generation or, more specifically, deep music generation (due to the use of deep learning architectures) is a multi-level learning task composed of score generation and performance generation as its two major components. Let's briefly discuss each of these components:

- **Score generation**: A score is a symbolic representation of music that can be used/read by humans or systems to produce music. To draw an analogy, we can safely consider the relationship between scores and music to be similar to that between text and speech. Music scores consist of discrete symbols which can effectively convey music. Some works use the term *AI Composer* to denote models associated with the task of score generation.
- **Performance generation**: Continuing with the text-speech analogy, performance generation (analogous to speech) is where performers use scores to generate music using their own characteristics of tempo, rhythm, and so on. Models associated with the task of performance generation are sometimes termed *AI Performers* as well.

We can realize different use cases or tasks based on which component is being targeted. *Figure 11.1* highlights a few such tasks that are being researched in the context of music generation:

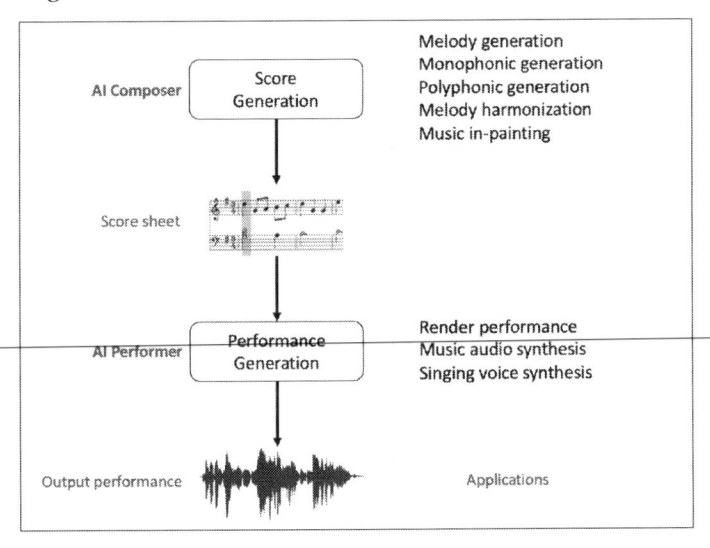

Figure 11.1: Different components of music generation and associated list of tasks

As shown in the figure, by focusing on score generation alone, we can work toward tasks such as melody generation and melody harmonization, as well as music in-painting (associated with filling in missing or lost information in a piece of music). Apart from the composer and the performer, there is also research being done toward building AI DJs. Similar to human disc jockeys (DJs), AI DJs make use of pre-existing music components to create medleys, mashups, remixes, and even highly personalized playlists.

In the coming sections, we will work mainly toward building our own score generation models or AI Composers. Now that we have a high-level understanding of the overall music generation landscape, let's focus on understanding how music is represented.

Representing music

Music is a work of art that represents mood, rhythm, emotions, and so on. Similar to text, which is a collection of alphabets and grammatical rules, music scores have their own notation and set of rules. In the previous chapters, we discussed how textual data is first transformed into usable vector form before it can be leveraged for any NLP task. We would need to do something similar in the case of music as well.

Music representation can be categorized into two main classes: continuous and discrete. The continuous representation is also called the **audio domain representation**. It handles music data as waveforms. An example of this is presented in *Figure 11.2 (a)*. Audio domain representation captures rich acoustic details such as timbre and articulation.

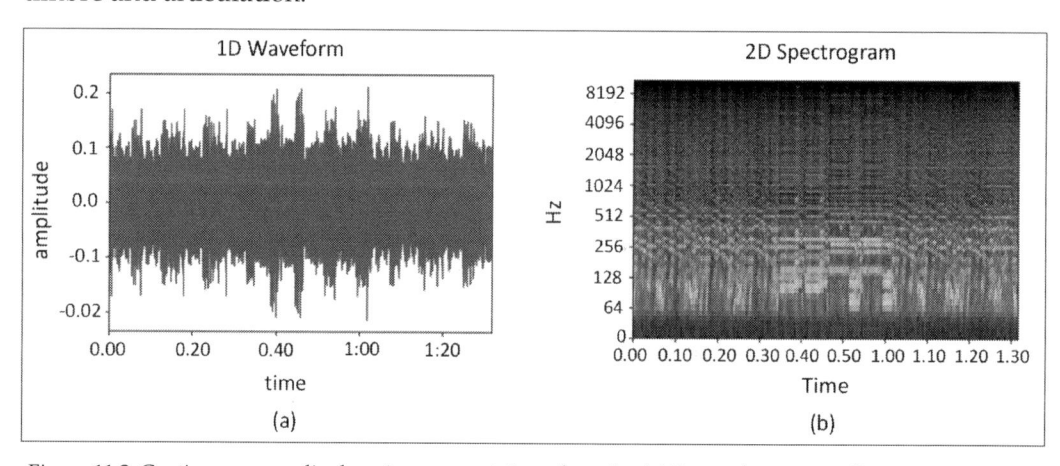

Figure 11.2: Continuous or audio domain representation of music. a) 1D waveforms are a direct representation of audio signals. b) 2D representations of audio data can be in the form of spectrograms with one axis as time and second axis as frequency

As shown in the figure, audio domain representations can be directly as 1D waveforms or 2D spectrograms:

- The 1D waveform is a direct representation of the audio signal, with the *x*-axis as time and the *y*-axis as changes to the signal
- The 2D spectrogram introduces time as the *x*-axis and frequency as the *y*-axis

We typically use **Short-Time Fourier Transformation** (**STFT**) to convert from 1D waveform to 2D spectrogram. Based on how we achieve the final spectrogram, there are different varieties such as Mel-spectrograms or magnitude spectrograms.

On the other hand, discrete or **symbolic representation** makes use of discrete symbols to capture information related to pitch, duration, chords, and so on. Even though less expressive than audio-domain representation, symbolic representation is widely used across different music generation works. This popularity is primarily due to the ease of understanding and handling such a representation. *Figure 11.3* showcases a sample symbolic representation of a music score:

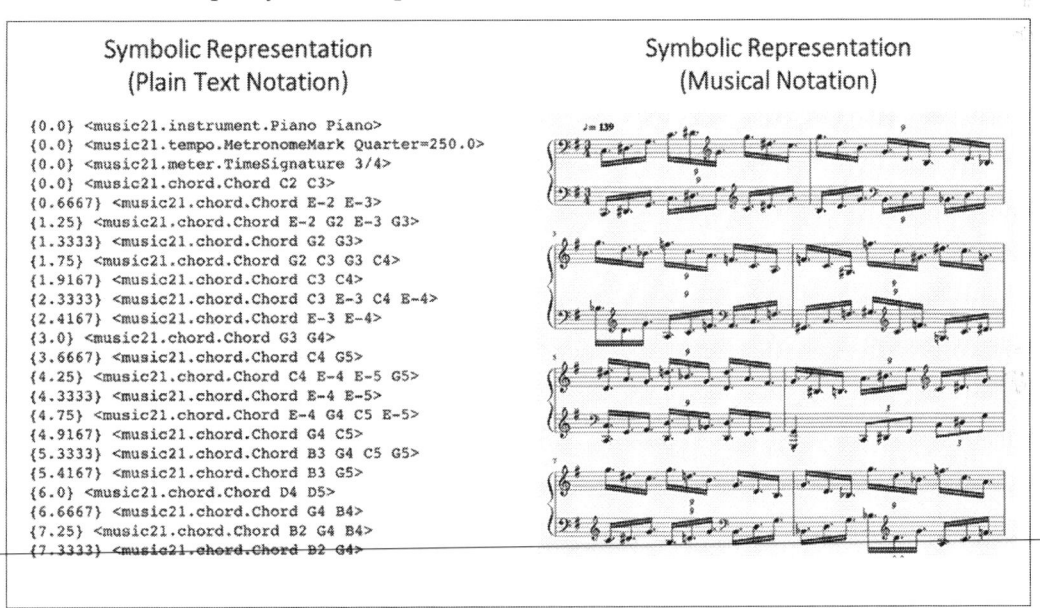

```
Symbolic Representation
(Plain Text Notation)

{0.0}    <music21.instrument.Piano Piano>
{0.0}    <music21.tempo.MetronomeMark Quarter=250.0>
{0.0}    <music21.meter.TimeSignature 3/4>
{0.0}    <music21.chord.Chord C2 C3>
{0.6667} <music21.chord.Chord E-2 E-3>
{1.25}   <music21.chord.Chord E-2 G2 E-3 G3>
{1.3333} <music21.chord.Chord G2 G3>
{1.75}   <music21.chord.Chord G2 C3 G3 C4>
{1.9167} <music21.chord.Chord C3 C4>
{2.3333} <music21.chord.Chord C3 E-3 C4 E-4>
{2.4167} <music21.chord.Chord E-3 E-4>
{3.0}    <music21.chord.Chord G3 G4>
{3.6667} <music21.chord.Chord C4 G5>
{4.25}   <music21.chord.Chord C4 E-4 E-5 G5>
{4.3333} <music21.chord.Chord E-4 E-5>
{4.75}   <music21.chord.Chord E-4 G4 C5 E-5>
{4.9167} <music21.chord.Chord G4 C5>
{5.3333} <music21.chord.Chord B3 G4 C5 G5>
{5.4167} <music21.chord.Chord B3 G5>
{6.0}    <music21.chord.Chord D4 D5>
{6.6667} <music21.chord.Chord G4 B4>
{7.25}   <music21.chord.Chord B2 G4 B4>
{7.3333} <music21.chord.Chord B2 G4>
```

Figure 11.3: Discrete or symbolic representation of music

As shown in the figure, a symbolic representation captures information using various symbols/positions. **MIDI**, or **Musical Instrument Digital Interface**, is an interoperable format used by musicians to create, compose, perform, and share music. It is a common format used by various electronic musical instruments, computers, smartphones, and even software to read and play music files.

The symbolic representation can be designed to capture a whole lot of events such as *note-on, note-off, time shift, bar, track*, and so on. To understand the upcoming sections and the scope of this chapter, we will only focus on two main events, note-on and note-off. The MIDI format captures 16 channels (numbered 0 to 15), 128 notes, and 128 loudness settings (also called velocity). There are a number of other formats as well, but for the purposes of this chapter, we will leverage MIDI-based music files only as these are widely used, expressive, interoperable, and easy to understand.

To interact with, manipulate, and finally generate music, we require an interface for MIDI files. We'll make use of `music21` as our library of choice for loading and processing MIDI files in Python. In the following code snippet, we load a sample MIDI file using `music21`. We then use its utility function to visualize the information in the file:

```
from music21 import converter
midi_filepath = 'Piano Sonata No.27.mid'

midi_score = converter.parse(midi_filepath).chordify()

# text-form
print(midi_score.show('text'))

# piano-roll form
print(midi_score.show())
```

We have covered quite some ground so far in terms of understanding the overall music generation landscape and a few important representation techniques. Next, we will get started with music generation itself.

Music generation using LSTMs

As we saw in the previous section, music is a continuous signal, which is a combination of sounds from various instruments and voices. Another characteristic is the presence of structural recurrent patterns which we pay attention to while listening. In other words, each musical piece has its own characteristic coherence, rhythm, and flow.

Such a setup is similar to the case of text generation we saw in *Chapter 9, The Rise of Methods for Text Generation*. In the case of text generation, we saw the power and effectiveness of LSTM-based networks. In this section, we will extend a stacked LSTM network for the task of music generation.

Chapter 11

To keep things simple and easy to implement, we will focus on a single instrument/monophonic music generation task. Let's first look at the dataset and think about how we would prepare it for our task of music generation.

Dataset preparation

MIDI is an easy-to-use format which helps us extract a symbolic representation of music contained in the files. For the hands-on exercises in this chapter, we will make use of a subset of the massive public MIDI dataset collected and shared by reddit user *u/midi_man*, which is available at this link:

https://www.reddit.com/r/WeAreTheMusicMakers/comments/3ajwe4/the_largest_midi_collection_on_the_internet/

The subset is based on classical piano pieces by great musicians such as Beethoven, Bach, Bartok, and the like. The subset can be found in a zipped folder, `midi_dataset.zip`, along with the code in this book's GitHub repository.

As mentioned previously, we will make use of `music21` to process the subset of this dataset and prepare our data for training the model. As music is a collection of sounds from various instruments and voices/singers, for the purpose of this exercise we will first use the `chordify()` function to extract chords from the songs. The following snippet helps us to get a list of MIDI scores in the required format:

```
from music21 import converter

data_dir = 'midi_dataset'

# list of files
midi_list = os.listdir(data_dir)

# Load and make list of stream objects
original_scores = []
for midi in tqdm(midi_list):
    score = converter.parse(os.path.join(data_dir,midi))
    original_scores.append(score)

# Merge notes into chords
original_scores = [midi.chordify() for midi in tqdm(original_scores)]
```

Once we have the list of scores, the next step is to extract notes and their corresponding timing information. For extracting these details, `music21` has simple-to-use interfaces such as `element.pitch` and `element.duration`.

The following snippet helps us extract such information from MIDI files and prepare two parallel lists:

```
# Define empty lists of lists
original_chords = [[] for _ in original_scores]
original_durations = [[] for _ in original_scores]
original_keys = []

# Extract notes, chords, durations, and keys
for i, midi in tqdm(enumerate(original_scores)):
    original_keys.append(str(midi.analyze('key')))
    for element in midi:
        if isinstance(element, note.Note):
            original_chords[i].append(element.pitch)
            original_durations[i].append(element.duration.quarterLength)
        elif isinstance(element, chord.Chord):
            original_chords[i].append('.'.join(str(n) for n in element.pitches))
            original_durations[i].append(element.duration.quarterLength)
```

We take one additional step to reduce the dimensionality. While this is an optional step, we recommend this in order to keep the task tractable as well as to keep the model training requirements within limits. The following snippet reduces the list of notes/chords and duration to only songs in the *C major key*:

```
# Create list of chords and durations from songs in C major
major_chords = [c for (c, k) in tqdm(zip(original_chords, original_keys)) if (k == 'C major')]
major_durations = [c for (c, k) in tqdm(zip(original_durations, original_keys)) if (k == 'C major')]
```

Now we have pre-processed our dataset, the next step is to transform the notes/chords and duration-related information into consumable form. As we did in the case of text generation, one simple method is to create a mapping of symbols to integers. Once transformed into integers, we can use them as inputs to an embedding layer of the model, which gets fine-tuned during the training process itself. The following snippet prepares the mapping and presents a sample output as well:

```
def get_distinct(elements):
    # Get all pitch names
    element_names = sorted(set(elements))
    n_elements = len(element_names)
    return (element_names, n_elements)
```

```
def create_lookups(element_names):
    # create dictionary to map notes and durations to integers
    element_to_int = dict((element, number) for number, element in enumerate(element_names))
    int_to_element = dict((number, element) for number, element in enumerate(element_names))

    return (element_to_int, int_to_element)

# get the distinct sets of notes and durations
note_names, n_notes = get_distinct([n for chord in major_chords for n in chord])
duration_names, n_durations = get_distinct([d for dur in major_durations for d in dur])
distincts = [note_names, n_notes, duration_names, n_durations]

with open(os.path.join(store_folder, 'distincts'), 'wb') as f:
    pickle.dump(distincts, f)

# make the lookup dictionaries for notes and durations and save
note_to_int, int_to_note = create_lookups(note_names)
duration_to_int, int_to_duration = create_lookups(duration_names)
lookups = [note_to_int, int_to_note, duration_to_int, int_to_duration]

with open(os.path.join(store_folder, 'lookups'), 'wb') as f:
    pickle.dump(lookups, f)

print("Unique Notes={} and Duration values={}".format(n_notes,n_durations))
```

```
Unique Notes=2963 and Duration values=18
```

We now have the mapping ready. In the following snippet, we prepare the training dataset as sequences of length 32 with their corresponding target as the very next token in the sequence:

```
# Set sequence length
sequence_length = 32

# Define empty array for training data
train_chords = []
train_durations = []
target_chords = []
```

```
target_durations = []

# Construct train and target sequences for chords and durations
# hint: refer back to Chapter 9 where we prepared similar
# training data
# sequences for an LSTM-based text generation network
for s in range(len(major_chords)):
    chord_list = [note_to_int[c] for c in major_chords[s]]
    duration_list = [duration_to_int[d] for d in major_durations[s]]
    for i in range(len(chord_list) - sequence_length):
        train_chords.append(chord_list[i:i+sequence_length])
        train_durations.append(duration_list[i:i+sequence_length])
        target_chords.append(chord_list[i+1])
        target_durations.append(duration_list[i+1])
```

As we've seen, the dataset preparation stage was mostly straightforward apart from a few nuances associated with the handling of MIDI files. The generated sequences and their corresponding targets are shown in the following output snippet for reference:

```
print(train_chords[0])
```

```
array([ 935, 1773, 2070, 2788,  244,  594, 2882, 1126,  152, 2071,
       2862, 2343, 2342,  220,  221, 2124, 2123, 2832, 2584,  939,
       1818, 2608, 2462,  702,  935, 1773, 2070, 2788,  244,  594,
       2882, 1126])
```

```
print(target_chords[0])
```

```
1773
```

```
print(train_durations[0])
```

```
array([ 9, 9, 9, 12, 5, 8, 2, 9, 9, 9, 9, 5, 5, 8, 2,
       5, 5, 9, 9, 7, 3, 2, 4, 3, 9, 9, 9, 12, 5, 8,
       2, 9])
```

```
print(target_durations[0])
```

```
9
```

The transformed dataset is now a sequence of numbers, just like in the text generation case. The next item on the list is the model itself.

LSTM model for music generation

As mentioned earlier, our first music generation model will be an extended version of the LSTM-based text generation model from *Chapter 9*, *The Rise of Methods for Text Generation*. Yet there are a few caveats that we need to handle and necessary changes that need to be made before we can use the model for this task.

Unlike text generation (using Char-RNN) where we had only a handful of input symbols (lower- and upper-case alphabets, numbers), the number of symbols in the case of music generation is pretty large (~500). Add to this list of symbols a few additional ones required for time/duration related information as well. With this larger input symbol list, the model requires more training data and capacity to learn (capacity in terms of the number of LSTM units, embedding size, and so on).

The next obvious change we need to take care of is the model's capability to take two inputs for every timestep. In other words, the model should be able to take the notes as well as duration information as input at every timestep and generate an output note with its corresponding duration. To do so, we leverage the functional tensorflow.keras API to prepare a multi-input multi-output architecture in place.

As discussed in detail in *Chapter 9*, *The Rise of Methods for Text Generation*, stacked LSTMs have a definite advantage in terms of being able to learn more sophisticated features over networks with a single LSTM layer. In addition to that, we also discussed **attention mechanisms** and how they help in alleviating issues inherent to RNNs, such as difficulties in handling long-range dependencies. Since music is composed of local as well as global structures which are perceivable in the form of rhythm and coherence, attention mechanisms can certainly make an impact. The following code snippet prepares a multi-input stacked LSTM network in the manner discussed:

```
def create_network(n_notes, n_durations, embed_size = 100,
                                        rnn_units = 256):
    """ create the structure of the neural network """

    notes_in = Input(shape = (None,))
    durations_in = Input(shape = (None,))

    x1 = Embedding(n_notes, embed_size)(notes_in)
    x2 = Embedding(n_durations, embed_size)(durations_in)

    x = Concatenate()([x1,x2])

    x = LSTM(rnn_units, return_sequences=True)(x)
```

```
        x = LSTM(rnn_units, return_sequences=True)(x)

        # attention
        e = Dense(1, activation='tanh')(x)
        e = Reshape([-1])(e)
        alpha = Activation('softmax')(e)

        alpha_repeated = Permute([2, 1])(RepeatVector(rnn_units)(alpha))

        c = Multiply()([x, alpha_repeated])
        c = Lambda(lambda xin: K.sum(xin, axis=1), output_shape=(rnn_
units,))(c)


        notes_out = Dense(n_notes, activation = 'softmax', name = 'pitch')
(c)
        durations_out = Dense(n_durations, activation = 'softmax', name =
'duration')(c)

        model = Model([notes_in, durations_in], [notes_out, durations_out])
        model.compile(loss=['sparse_categorical_crossentropy',
                            'sparse_categorical_crossentropy'],
optimizer=RMSprop(lr = 0.001))

        return model
```

The model prepared using the preceding snippet is a multi-input network (one input each for notes and durations respectively). Each of the inputs is transformed into vectors using respective embedding layers. We then concatenate both inputs and pass them through a couple of LSTM layers followed by a simple attention mechanism. After this point, the model again diverges into two outputs (one for the next note and the other for the duration of that note). Readers are encouraged to use keras utilities to visualize the network on their own.

Training this model is as simple as calling the fit() function on the keras model object. We train the model for about 100 epochs. *Figure 11.4* depicts the learning progress of the model across different epochs:

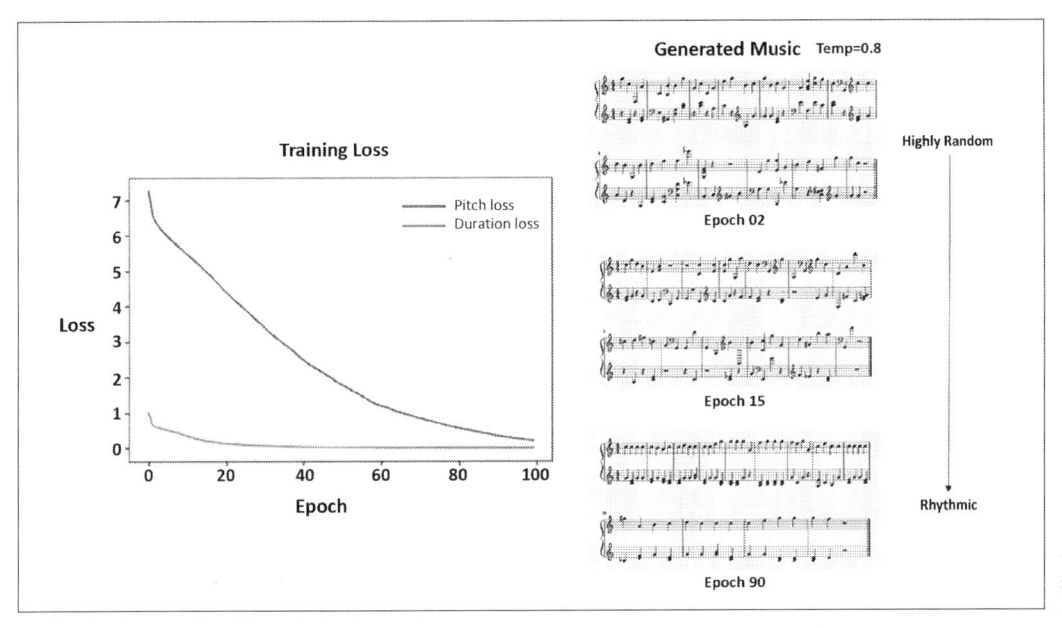

Figure 11.4: Model output as the training progresses across epochs

As shown in the figure, the model is able to learn a few repeating patterns and generate music. Here, we made use of temperature-based sampling as our decoding strategy. As discussed in *Chapter 9, The Rise of Methods for Text Generation*, readers can experiment with techniques such as greedy decoding, pure sampling-based decoding, and other such strategies to see how the output music quality changes.

This was a very simple implementation of music generation using deep learning models. We drew analogies with concepts learned in the previous two chapters on text generation. Next, let's do some music generation using adversarial networks.

Music generation using GANs

In the previous section, we tried our hand at music generation using a very simple LSTM-based model. Now, let's raise the bar a bit and try to see how we can generate music using a GAN. In this section, we will leverage the concepts related to GANs that we have learned in the previous chapters and apply them to generating music.

We've already seen that music is continuous and sequential in nature. LSTMs or RNNs in general are quite adept at handling such datasets. We have also seen that, over the years, various types of GANs have been proposed to train deep generative networks efficiently.

Combining the power of LSTMs and GAN-based generative networks, Mogren et al. presented *Continuous Recurrent Neural Networks with Adversarial Training: C-RNN-GAN*[4] in 2016 as a method for music generation. This is a straightforward yet effective implementation for music generation. As in the previous section, we will keep things simple and focus only on monophonic music generation, even though the original paper mentions using features such as tone length, frequency, intensity, and time apart from music notes. The paper also mentions a technique called *feature mapping* to generate polyphonic music (using the C-RNN-GAN-3 variant). We will only focus on understanding the basic architecture and pre-processing steps and not try to implement the paper as-is. Let's begin with defining each of the components of our music-generating GAN.

Generator network

The generator network in this setup is a simple stack of multiple dense, leaky ReLU, and batch normalization layers. We start off with a random vector z of a given dimension and pass it through different non-linearities to achieve a final output of desired shape. This stack is shown in the following snippet, where we use `tensorflow.keras` to prepare our generator model:

```python
def build_generator(latent_dim,seq_shape):

    model = Sequential()
    model.add(Dense(256, input_dim=latent_dim))
    model.add(LeakyReLU(alpha=0.2))
    model.add(BatchNormalization(momentum=0.8))
    model.add(Dense(512))
    model.add(LeakyReLU(alpha=0.2))
    model.add(BatchNormalization(momentum=0.8))
    model.add(Dense(1024))
    model.add(LeakyReLU(alpha=0.2))
    model.add(BatchNormalization(momentum=0.8))
    model.add(Dense(np.prod(seq_shape), activation='tanh'))
    model.add(Reshape(seq_shape))
    model.summary()

    noise = Input(shape=(latent_dim,))
    seq = model(noise)

    return Model(noise, seq)
```

The generator model is a fairly straightforward implementation which highlights the effectiveness of a GAN-based generative model. Next, let us prepare the discriminator model.

Discriminator network

In a GAN setup, the discriminator's job is to differentiate between real and generated (or fake) samples. In this case, since the sample to be checked is a musical piece, the model needs to have the ability to handle sequential input.

In order to handle sequential input samples, we use a simple stacked RNN network. The first recurrent layer is an LSTM layer with 512 units, followed by a bi-directional LSTM layer. The bi-directionality of the second layer helps the discriminator learn about the context better by viewing what came before and after a particular chord or note. The recurrent layers are followed by a stack of dense layers and a final sigmoid layer for the binary classification task. The discriminator network is presented in the following code snippet:

```
def build_discriminator(seq_shape):

    model = Sequential()
    model.add(LSTM(512, input_shape=seq_shape, return_sequences=True))
    model.add(Bidirectional(LSTM(512)))
    model.add(Dense(512))
    model.add(LeakyReLU(alpha=0.2))
    model.add(Dense(256))
    model.add(LeakyReLU(alpha=0.2))
    model.add(Dense(1, activation='sigmoid'))
    model.summary()

    seq = Input(shape=seq_shape)
    validity = model(seq)

    return Model(seq, validity)
```

As shown in the snippet, the discriminator is also a very simple model consisting of a few recurrent and dense layers. Next, let us combine all these components and train the overall GAN.

Training and results

The first step is to instantiate the generator and discriminator models using the utilities we presented in the previous sections. Once we have these objects, we combine the generator and discriminator into a stack to form the overall GAN. The following snippet presents the instantiation of the three networks:

```
rows = 100
seq_length = rows
seq_shape = (seq_length, 1)
latent_dim = 1000

optimizer = Adam(0.0002, 0.5)

# Build and compile the discriminator
discriminator = build_discriminator(seq_shape)
discriminator.compile(loss='binary_crossentropy', optimizer=optimizer,
metrics=['accuracy'])

# Build the generator
generator = build_generator(latent_dim,seq_shape)

# The generator takes noise as input and generates note sequences
z = Input(shape=(latent_dim,))
generated_seq = generator(z)

# For the combined model we will only train the generator
discriminator.trainable = False

# The discriminator takes generated images as input and determines
validity
validity = discriminator(generated_seq)

# The combined model  (stacked generator and discriminator)
# Trains the generator to fool the discriminator
gan = Model(z, validity)
gan.compile(loss='binary_crossentropy', optimizer=optimizer)
```

As we have done in the previous chapters, the discriminator training is first set to `false` before it is stacked into the GAN model object. This ensures that only the generator weights are updated during the generation cycle and not the discriminator weights. We prepare a custom training loop just as we have presented a number of times in previous chapters.

For the sake of completeness, we present it again here for reference:

```python
def train(latent_dim,
          notes,
          generator,
          discriminator,
          gan,
          epochs,
          batch_size=128,
          sample_interval=50):

    disc_loss =[]
    gen_loss = []

    n_vocab = len(set(notes))
    X_train, y_train = prepare_sequences(notes, n_vocab)

    # ground truths
    real = np.ones((batch_size, 1))
    fake = np.zeros((batch_size, 1))

    for epoch in range(epochs):

        idx = np.random.randint(0, X_train.shape[0], batch_size)
        real_seqs = X_train[idx]

        noise = np.random.normal(0, 1, (batch_size, latent_dim))

        # generate a batch of new note sequences
        gen_seqs = generator.predict(noise)

        # train the discriminator
        d_loss_real = discriminator.train_on_batch(real_seqs, real)
        d_loss_fake = discriminator.train_on_batch(gen_seqs, fake)
        d_loss = 0.5 * np.add(d_loss_real, d_loss_fake)

        #  train the Generator
        noise = np.random.normal(0, 1, (batch_size, latent_dim))
        g_loss = gan.train_on_batch(noise, real)

        # visualize progress
        if epoch % sample_interval == 0:
           print ("%d [D loss: %f, acc.: %.2f%%] [G loss: %f]" % (epoch, d_loss[0],100*d_loss[1],g_loss))
           disc_loss.append(d_loss[0])
```

Composing Music with Generative Models

```
        gen_loss.append(g_loss)

    generate(latent_dim, generator, notes)
    plot_loss(disc_loss,gen_loss)
```

We have used the same training dataset as in the previous section. We train our setup for about 200 epochs with a batch size of 64. *Figure 11.5* is a depiction of discriminator and generator losses over training cycles, along with a few outputs at different intervals:

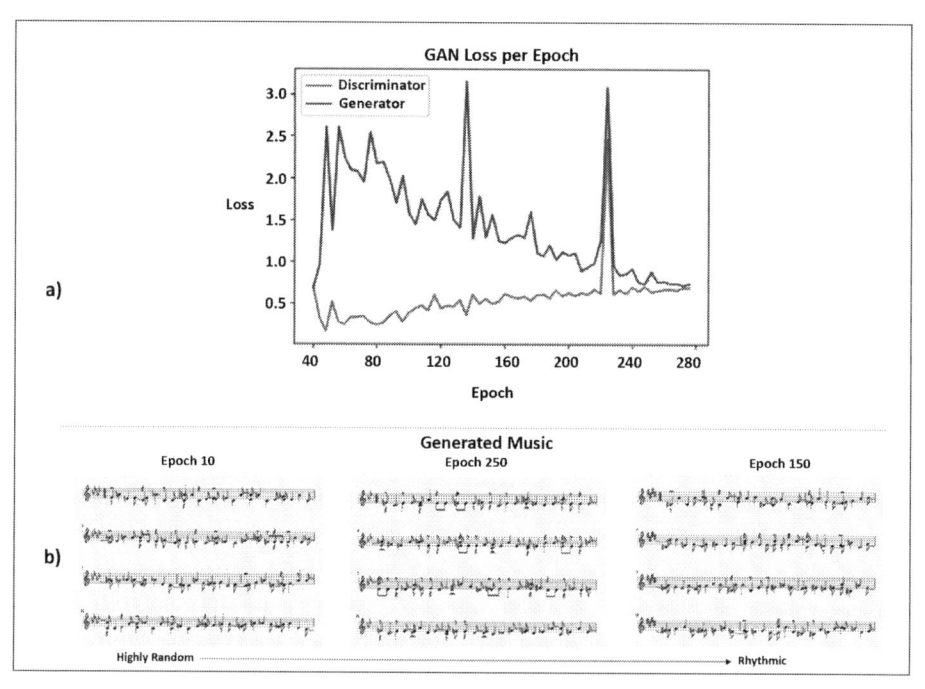

Figure 11.5: a) Discriminator and generator losses as the training progresses over time. b) The output from the generator model at different training intervals

The outputs shown in the figure highlight the potential of a GAN-based music generation setup. Readers may choose to experiment with different datasets or even the details mentioned in the C-RNN-GAN paper by Mogren et al. The generated MIDI files can be played using the MuseScore app.

The output from this GAN-based model as compared to the LSTM-based model from the previous section might feel a bit more refined (though this is purely subjective given our small datasets). This could be attributed to GANs' inherent ability to better model the generation process compared to an LSTM-based model. Please refer to *Chapter 6, Image Generation with GANs*, for more details on the topology of generative models and their respective strengths.

Now that we have seen two variations of monophonic music generation, let us graduate toward polyphonic music generation using MuseGAN.

MuseGAN – polyphonic music generation

The two models we have trained so far have been simplified versions of how music is actually perceived. While limited, both the attention-based LSTM model and the C-RNN-GAN based model helped us to understand the music generation process very well. In this section, we will build on what we've learned so far and make a move toward preparing a setup which is as close to the actual task of music generation as possible.

In 2017, Dong et al. presented a GAN-type framework for multi-track music generation in their work titled *MuseGAN: Multi-track Sequential Generative Adversarial Networks for Symbolic Music Generation and Accompaniment*.[5] The paper is a detailed explanation of various music-related concepts and how Dong and team tackled them. To keep things within the scope of this chapter and without losing details, we will touch upon the important contributions of the work and then proceed toward the implementation. Before we get onto the "how" part, let's understand the three main properties related to music that the MuseGAN work tries to take into account:

- **Multi-track interdependency**: As we know, most songs that we listen to are usually composed of multiple instruments such as drums, guitars, bass, vocals, and so on. There is a high level of interdependency in how these components play out for the end-user/listener to perceive coherence and rhythm.

- **Musical texture**: Musical notes are often grouped into chords and melodies. These groupings are characterized by a high degree of overlap and not necessarily chronological ordering (this simplification of chronological ordering is usually applied in most known works associated with music generation). The chronological ordering comes not only as part of the need for simplification but also as a generalization from the NLP domain, language generation in particular.

- **Temporal structure**: Music has a hierarchical structure where a song can be seen as being composed of paragraphs (at the highest level). A paragraph is composed of various phrases, which are in turn composed of multiple bars, and so on. *Figure 11.6* depicts this hierarchy pictorially:

Composing Music with Generative Models

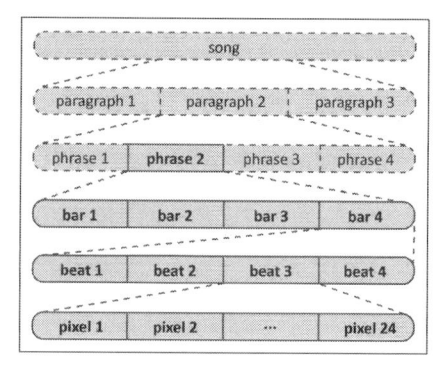

Figure 11.6: Temporal structure of a song

- As shown in the figure, a bar is further composed of beats and at the lowest level, we have pixels. The authors of MuseGAN mention a bar as the compositional unit, as opposed to notes, which we have been considering the basic unit so far. This is done in order to account for grouping of notes from the multi-track setup.

MuseGAN works toward solving these three major challenges through a unique framework based on three music generation approaches. These three basic approaches make use of jamming, hybrid, and composer models. We will briefly explain these now.

Jamming model

If we were to extrapolate the simplified-monophonic GAN setup from the previous section to a polyphonic setup, the simplest method would be to make use of multiple generator-discriminator combinations, one for each instrument. The jamming model is precisely this setup, where M multiple independent generators prepare music from their respective random vectors. Each generator has its own critic/discriminator, which helps in training the overall GAN. This setup is depicted in *Figure 11.7*:

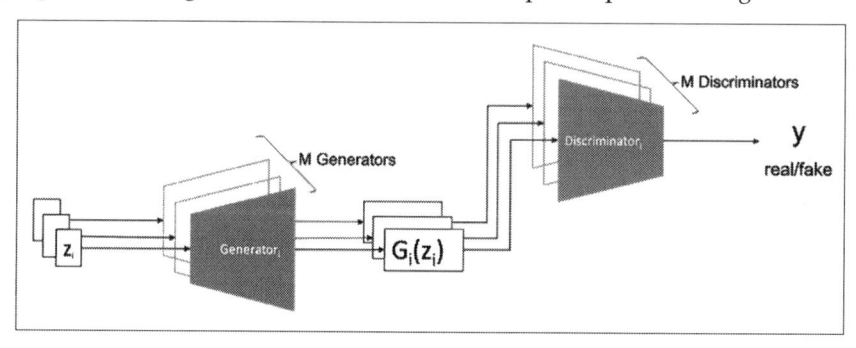

Figure 11.7: Jamming model composed of M generator and discriminator pairs for generating multi-track outputs

As shown in the preceding figure, the jamming setup imitates a grouping of musicians who create music by improvising independently and without any predefined arrangement.

Composer model

As the name suggests, this setup assumes that the generator is a typical human composer capable of creating multi-track piano rolls, as shown in *Figure 11.8*:

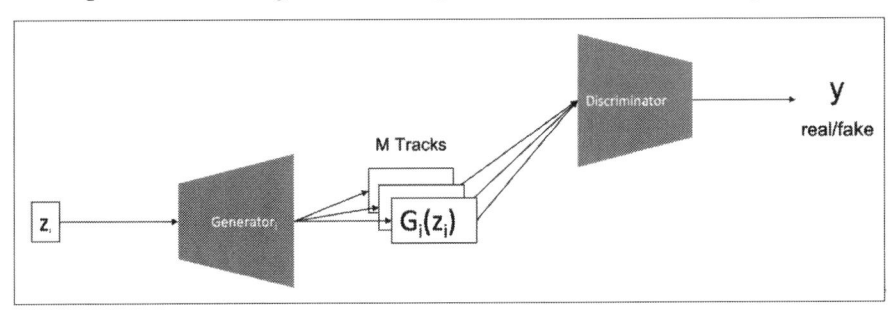

Figure 11.8: Composer model composed of a single generator capable of generating M tracks and a single discriminator for detecting fake versus real samples

As shown in the figure, the setup only has a single discriminator to detect real or fake (generated) samples. This model requires only one common random vector z as opposed to M random vectors in the previous jamming model setup.

Hybrid model

This is an interesting take that arises by combining the jamming and composer models. The hybrid model has M independent generators that make use of their respective random vectors, which are also called *intra-track random vectors*. Each generator also takes an additional random vector called the *inter-track random vector*. This additional vector is supposed to imitate the composer and help in the coordination of the independent generators. *Figure 11.9* depicts the hybrid model, with M generators each taking intra-track and inter-track random vectors as input:

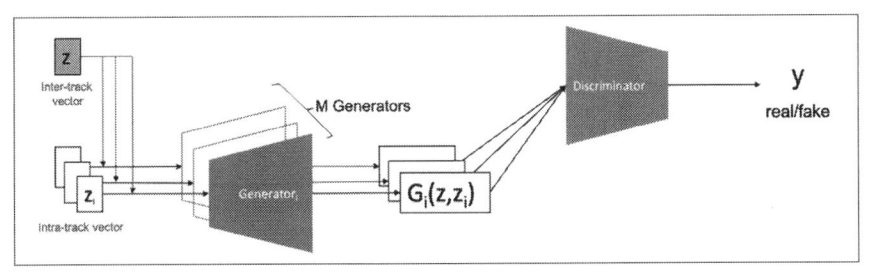

Figure 11.9: Hybrid model composed of M generators and a single discriminator. Each generator takes two inputs in the form of inter-track and intra-track random vectors

As shown in the figure, the hybrid model with its M generators works with only a single discriminator to predict whether a sample is real or fake. The advantage of combining both jamming and composer models is in terms of flexibility and control at the generator end. Since we have M different generators, the setup allows for flexibility to choose different architectures (different input sizes, filters, layers, and so on) for different tracks, as well as additional control via the inter-track random vector to manage coordination amongst them.

Apart from these three variants, the authors of MuseGAN also present a temporal model, which we discuss next.

Temporal model

The temporal structure of music was one of the three aspects we discussed as top priorities for the MuseGAN setup. The three variants explained in the previous sections, jamming, composer, and hybrid models, all work at the bar level. In other words, each of these models generates multi-track music bar by bar, but possibly with no coherence or continuity between two successive bars. This is different from the hierarchical structure where a group of bars makes up a phrase, and so on.

To maintain coherence and the temporal structure of the song being generated, the authors of MuseGAN present a temporal model. While generating from scratch (as one of the modes), this additional model helps in generating fixed-length phrases by taking bar-progression as an additional dimension. This model consists of two sub-components, the temporal structure generator G_{temp} and the bar generator G_{bar}. This setup is presented in *Figure 11.10*:

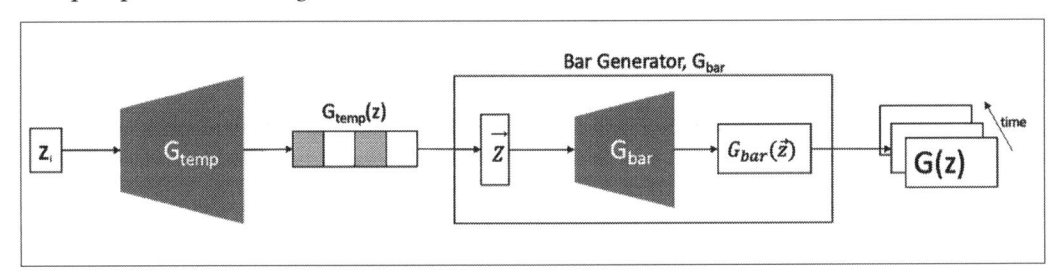

Figure 11.10: Temporal model with its two sub-components, temporal structure generator G_{temp} and bar generator G_{bar}

The temporal structure generator maps a noise vector z to a sequence of latent vectors $\vec{z} = \{\vec{z^t}\}_{t=1}^{T}$. This latent vector $\vec{z}$ carries temporal information and is then used by G_{bar} to generate music bar by bar. The overall setup for the temporal model is formulated as follows:

$$G(z) = \{G_{bar}(G_{temp}(z)^t)\}_{t=1}^{T}$$

The authors note that this setup is similar to some of the works on video generation, and cite references for further details. The authors also mention another setting where a conditional setup is presented for the generation of temporal structure by learning from a human-generated track sequence.

We have covered details on the specific building blocks for the MuseGAN setup. Let's now dive into how these components make up the overall system.

MuseGAN

The overall MuseGAN setup is a complex architecture composed of a number of moving parts. To bring things into perspective, the paper presents experiments with jamming, composer, and hybrid generation approaches at a very high level. To ensure temporal structure, the setup makes use of the two-step temporal model approach we discussed in the previous section. A simplified version of the MuseGAN architecture is presented in *Figure 11.11*:

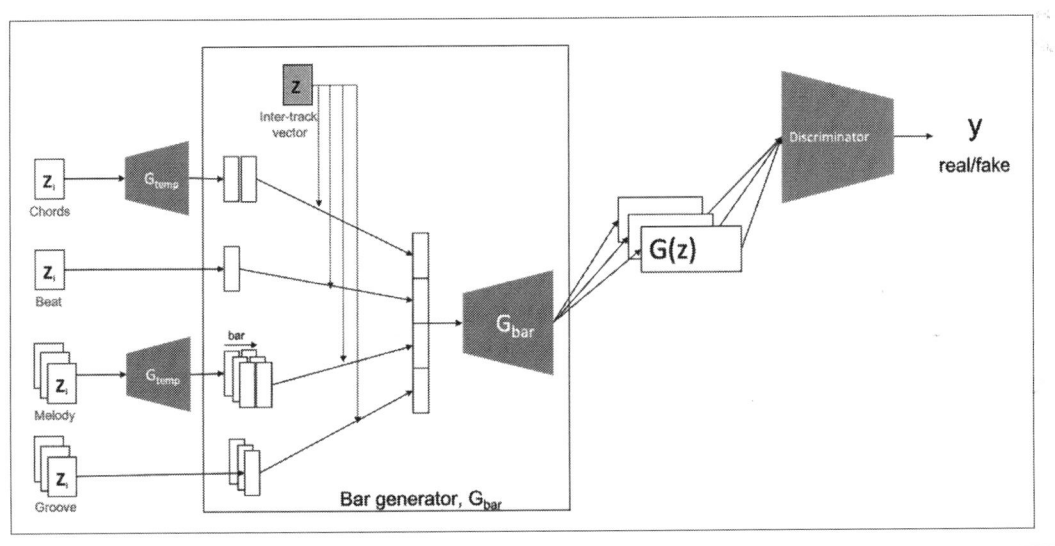

Figure 11.11: Simplified MuseGAN architecture consisting of a hybrid model with M generators and a single discriminator, along with a two-stage temporal model for generating phrase coherent output

As shown in the figure, the setup makes use of a temporal model for certain tracks and direct random vectors for others. The outputs from temporal models, as well as direct inputs, are then concatenated (or summed) before they are passed to the bar generator model.

The bar generator then creates music bar by bar and is evaluated using a critic or discriminator model. In the coming section, we will briefly touch upon implementation details for both the generator and critic models.

> Please note that the implementation presented in this section is close to the original work but not an exact replication. We have taken certain shortcuts in order to simplify and ease the understanding of the overall architecture. Interested readers may refer to official implementation details and the code repository mentioned in the cited work.

Generators

As mentioned in the previous section, the generator setup depends on whether we are using the jamming, composer, or hybrid approach. For simplicity, we will focus only on the hybrid setup where we have multiple generators, one for each track.

One set of generators focuses on tracks which require temporal coherence; for instance, components such as melody are long sequences (more than one bar long) and coherence between them is an important factor. For such tracks, we use a temporal architecture as shown in the following snippet:

```python
def build_temporal_network(z_dim, n_bars, weight_init):

    input_layer = Input(shape=(z_dim,), name='temporal_input')
    x = Reshape([1, 1, z_dim])(input_layer)

    x = Conv2DTranspose(
        filters=512,
        kernel_size=(2, 1),
        padding='valid',
        strides=(1, 1),
        kernel_initializer=weight_init
    )(x)
    x = BatchNormalization(momentum=0.9)(x)
    x = Activation('relu')(x)

    x = Conv2DTranspose(
        filters=z_dim,
        kernel_size=(n_bars - 1, 1),
        padding='valid',
        strides=(1, 1),
        kernel_initializer=weight_init
    )(x)
    x = BatchNormalization(momentum=0.9)(x)
    x = Activation('relu')(x)
```

```
        output_layer = Reshape([n_bars, z_dim])(x)

        return Model(input_layer, output_layer)
```

As shown, the temporal model firstly reshapes the random vector to desired dimensions, then passes it through transposed convolutional layers to expand the output vector so that it spans the length of specified bars.

For the tracks where we do not require inter-bar coherence, we directly use the random vector *z* as-is. Groove or beat-related information covers such tracks in practice.

The outputs from the temporal generator and the direct random vectors are first concatenated to prepare a larger coordinated vector. This vector then acts as an input to the bar generator G_{bar} shown in the following snippet:

```
def build_bar_generator(z_dim, n_steps_per_bar, n_pitches, weight_
init):

    input_layer = Input(shape=(z_dim * 4,), name='bar_generator_input')

    x = Dense(1024)(input_layer)
    x = BatchNormalization(momentum=0.9)(x)
    x = Activation('relu')(x)

    x = Reshape([2, 1, 512])(x)

    x = Conv2DTranspose(
        filters=512,
        kernel_size=(2, 1),
        padding='same',
        strides=(2, 1),
        kernel_initializer=weight_init
    )(x)
    x = BatchNormalization(momentum=0.9)(x)
    x = Activation('relu')(x)

    x = Conv2DTranspose(
        filters=256,
        kernel_size=(2, 1),
        padding='same',
        strides=(2, 1),
```

```
            kernel_initializer=weight_init
    )(x)
    x = BatchNormalization(momentum=0.9)(x)
    x = Activation('relu')(x)

    x = Conv2DTranspose(
            filters=256,
            kernel_size=(2, 1),
            padding='same',
            strides=(2, 1),
            kernel_initializer=weight_init
    )(x)
    x = BatchNormalization(momentum=0.9)(x)
    x = Activation('relu')(x)

    x = Conv2DTranspose(
            filters=256,
            kernel_size=(1, 7),
            padding='same',
            strides=(1, 7),
            kernel_initializer=weight_init
    )(x)
    x = BatchNormalization(momentum=0.9)(x)
    x = Activation('relu')(x)

    x = Conv2DTranspose(
            filters=1,
            kernel_size=(1, 12),
            padding='same',
            strides=(1, 12),
            kernel_initializer=weight_init
    )(x)
    x = Activation('tanh')(x)

    output_layer = Reshape([1, n_steps_per_bar, n_pitches, 1])(x)

    return Model(input_layer, output_layer)
```

The snippet shows that the bar generator consists of a dense layer followed by batch-normalization, before a stack of transposed convolutional layers, which help to expand the vector along time and pitch dimensions.

Critic

The critic model is simpler compared to the generator we built in the previous section. The critic is basically a convolutional WGAN-GP model (similar to WGAN, covered in *Chapter 6, Image Generation with GANs*), which takes the output from the bar generator, as well as real samples, to detect whether the generator output is fake or real. The following snippet presents the critic model:

```
def build_critic(input_dim, weight_init, n_bars):

    critic_input = Input(shape=input_dim, name='critic_input')

    x = critic_input

    x = conv_3d(x,
                num_filters=128,
                kernel_size=(2, 1, 1),
                stride=(1, 1, 1),
                padding='valid',
                weight_init=weight_init)

    x = conv_3d(x,
                num_filters=64,
                kernel_size=(n_bars - 1, 1, 1),
                stride=(1, 1, 1),
                padding='valid',
                weight_init=weight_init)

    x = conv_3d(x,
                num_filters=64,
                kernel_size=(1, 1, 12),
                stride=(1, 1, 12),
                padding='same',
                weight_init=weight_init)

    x = conv_3d(x,
                num_filters=64,
                kernel_size=(1, 1, 7),
                stride=(1, 1, 7),
                padding='same',
                weight_init=weight_init)

    x = conv_3d(x,
```

```python
            num_filters=64,
            kernel_size=(1, 2, 1),
            stride=(1, 2, 1),
            padding='same',
            weight_init=weight_init)

x = conv_3d(x,
            num_filters=64,
            kernel_size=(1, 2, 1),
            stride=(1, 2, 1),
            padding='same',
            weight_init=weight_init)

x = conv_3d(x,
            num_filters=128,
            kernel_size=(1, 4, 1),
            stride=(1, 2, 1),
            padding='same',
            weight_init=weight_init)

x = conv_3d(x,
            num_filters=256,
            kernel_size=(1, 3, 1),
            stride=(1, 2, 1),
            padding='same',
            weight_init=weight_init)

x = Flatten()(x)

x = Dense(512, kernel_initializer=weight_init)(x)
x = LeakyReLU()(x)

critic_output = Dense(1,
                      activation=None,
                      kernel_initializer=weight_init)(x)

critic = Model(critic_input, critic_output)
return critic
```

One major point to note here is the use of 3D convolutional layers. We typically make use of 2D convolutions for a majority of tasks. In this case, since we have 4-dimensional inputs, a 3D convolutional layer is required for handling the data correctly.

We use these utilities to prepare 4 different generators, one for each track, into a common generator model object. In the next step, we prepare the training setup and generate some sample music.

Training and results

We have all the components ready. The final step is to combine them and train in the manner a typical WGAN-GP is trained. The authors of the paper mention that the model achieves stable performance if they update the generators once for every 5 updates of the discriminator. We follow a similar setup to achieve the results shown in *Figure 11.12*:

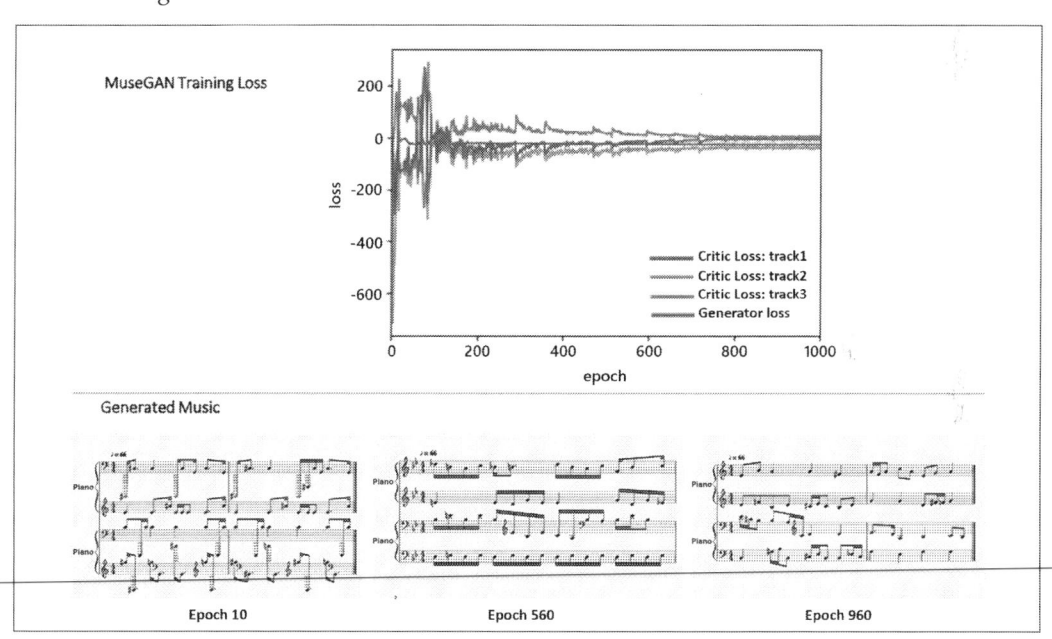

Figure 11.12: Results from MuseGAN setup showcase multi-track output, which seems to be coherent across bars and has a consistent rhythm to it

As shown in the figure, the multi-track polyphonic output from MuseGAN indeed seems quite impressive. We urge readers to use a MIDI player (or even MuseScore itself) to play the generated music samples in order to understand the complexity of the output, along with the improvement over the simpler models prepared in the earlier sections of the chapter.

Summary

Congratulations on completing yet another complex chapter. In this chapter, we covered quite a bit of ground in terms of building an understanding of music as a source of data, and then various methods of generating music using generative models.

In the first section of this chapter, we briefly discussed the two components of music generation, namely *score* and *performance generation*. We also touched upon different use cases associated with music generation. The next section focused on different methods for music representation. At a high level, we discussed continuous and discrete representation techniques. We primarily focused on *1D waveforms* and *2D spectrograms* as main representations in the audio or continuous domain. For symbolic or discrete representation, we discussed *notes/chords*-based sheet music. We also performed a quick hands-on exercise using the `music21` library to transform a given MIDI file into readable sheet music.

Once we had some basic understanding of how music can be represented, we turned toward building music generation models. The first and the simplest method we worked upon was based on a stacked LSTM architecture. The model made use of an attention mechanism and symbolic representation to generate the next set of notes. This LSTM-based model helped us to get a peek into the music generation process.

The next section focused on using a GAN setup to generate music. We designed our GAN similar to *C-RNN-GAN* presented by Mogren et al. The results were very encouraging and gave us a good insight into how an adversarial network can be used for the task of music generation.

During the first two hands-on exercises, we limited our music generation process to only monophonic music to keep things simple. In the final section of this chapter, our aim was to understand the complexities and techniques required to generate polyphonic/multi-track music. We discussed in detail *MuseGAN*, a polyphonic/multi-track GAN-based music generation architecture presented by Dong et al. in 2017. Dong and team discussed *multi-track interdependency*, *musical texture*, and *temporal structure* as three main aspects that should be handled by any multi-track music generation model. They presented three variants for music generation in the form of *jamming*, *composer*, and *hybrid models*. They also presented a discussion on *temporal* and *bar* generation models to bring things into perspective. The MuseGAN paper presents MuseGAN as a complex combination of these smaller components/models to handle multi-track/polyphonic music generation. We leveraged this understanding to build a simplified version of this work and generate polyphonic music of our own.

This chapter provided us with a look into yet another domain which can be handled using generative models. In the next chapter, we will level things up and focus on the exciting field of reinforcement learning. Using RL, we will build some cool applications as well. Stay tuned.

References

1. Butcher, M. (2019, July 23). *It looks like TikTok has acquired Jukedeck, a pioneering music AI UK startup*. TechCrunch. https://techcrunch.com/2019/07/23/it-looks-like-titok-has-acquired-jukedeck-a-pioneering-music-ai-uk-startup/

2. Apple. (2021). *GarageBand for Mac - Apple*. https://www.apple.com/mac/garageband/

3. Magenta. (n.d.) *Make Music and Art Using Machine Learning*. https://magenta.tensorflow.org/

4. Mogren, O. (2016). *C-RNN-GAN: Continuous recurrent neural networks with adversarial training*. Constructive Machine Learning Workshop (CML) at NIPS 2016 in Barcelona, Spain, December 10. https://arxiv.org/abs/1611.09904

5. Dong, H-W., Hsiao, W-Y., Yang, L-C., & Yang, Y-H. (2017). *MuseGAN: Multi-Track Sequential Generative Adversarial Networks for Symbolic Music Generation and Accompaniment*. The Thirty-Second AAAI Conference on Artificial Intelligence (AAAI-18). https://salu133445.github.io/musegan/pdf/musegan-aaai2018-paper.pdf

12
Play Video Games with Generative AI: GAIL

In the preceding chapters, we have seen how we can use generative AI to produce both simple (restricted Boltzmann machines) and sophisticated (variational autoencoders, generative adversarial models) images, musical notes (MuseGAN), and novel text (BERT, GPT-3).

In all these prior examples, we have focused on generating complex data using deep neural networks. However, neural networks can also be used to learn *rules* for how an entity (such as a video game character or a vehicle) should respond to an environment to optimize a reward; as we will describe in this chapter, this field is known as **reinforcement learning** (**RL**). While RL is not intrinsically tied to either deep learning or generative AI, the union of these fields has created a powerful set of techniques for optimizing complex behavioral functions.

In this chapter, we will show you how to apply GANs to learn optimal policies for different figures to navigate within the OpenAI simulation environment. To understand the powerful combination of these methods with traditional approaches in RL, we will first review the more general problem that RL is trying to solve: how to determine the right *action* for an entity given a *state*, yielding a new *state* and a *reward*. The rules that optimize such rewards are known as a *policy*. We will discuss the following topics:

- How deep neural networks were used to learn complex policies for high dimensional data such as the raw pixels from Atari video games.

- The problem of **inverse reinforcement learning** (IRL) – how to learn the reward function from observing examples of the policy as given by an "expert" agent that makes optimal decisions – this kind of algorithm, as we will describe in more detail, is therefore also known as *imitation learning*.
- How we can use the GAN training function to distinguish between expert and non-expert behavior (just as we distinguished between simulated and natural data in prior examples) to optimize a reward function.

Reinforcement learning: Actions, agents, spaces, policies, and rewards

Recall from *Chapter 1, An Introduction to Generative AI: "Drawing" Data from Models*, that most *discriminative AI* examples involve applying a continuous or discrete label to a piece of data. In the image examples we have discussed in this book, this could be applying a deep neural network to determine the digit represented by one of the MNIST images, or whether a CIFAR-10 image contains a horse. In these cases, the model produces a single output, a prediction with minimal error. In reinforcement learning, we also want to make such point predictions, but over many steps, and to optimize the total error over repeated uses.

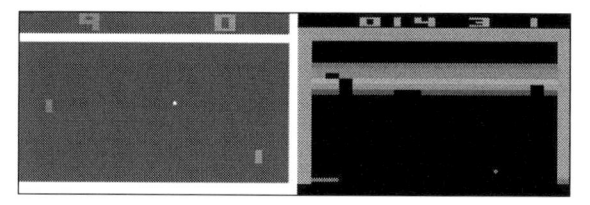

Figure 12.1: Atari video game examples[1]

As a concrete example, consider a video game with a player controlling a spaceship to shoot down alien vessels. The spaceship navigated by the player in this example is the *agent*; the set of pixels on the screen at any point in the game is the *state*. Based on this environment, the player needs to take the right *action* (for example, moving right, pressing fire) which will maximize the *reward* – here quite literally the score for the game. It is not just the next immediate action which we need to consider though, but all actions until the end of the game, since we can accumulate additional points as long as we do not run out of lives. Expert video game players learn how to react in different situations, a *policy* to follow when confronted with diverse scenarios during gameplay. The problem of RL is to determine a machine learning algorithm that can replicate the behavior of such a human expert, by taking a set of inputs (the current state of the game) and outputting the optimal action to increase the probability of winning.

Chapter 12

To formalize this description with some mathematical notation, we can denote the *environment*, such as the video game, in which an agent acts as ε, which outputs a set of data (pixels) at each point in time as the *state*, x_t. For each point of time in the game, the player (algorithm) selects an *action*, a_t, from a set of n actions $A = \{1, 2, \ldots N\}$; this is also known as the "action set" or "action space." While for clarity we limit our discussion in the chapter to discrete action spaces, there is theoretically no such restriction, and the theory works just as well for continuous actions (though the resulting RL problem is consequently more complex with an infinite space of possibilities). For each of these actions, the agent receives a reward, r_t, that can change the game score.

If we were to only consider the current screen, x_t, as the "state" of the system, then our decision relies only on the present, and the RL problem becomes a **Markov Decision Process (MDP)**, as the choice for the next action depends only on immediately available data and not on history (*Figure 12.2*). However, for the video game example given above, the current screen only is probably not enough information to determine the optimal action, because it is only *partially observable* – we don't know cases where an enemy starcraft may have moved off the screen (and thus where it might re-emerge). We also don't know what direction our ship is moving without comparing to prior examples, which might affect whether we need to change direction or not. If the current state of the environment contained all the information we need to know about the game – such as a game of cards in which all players show their hands – then we say that the environment is *fully observable*.[2]

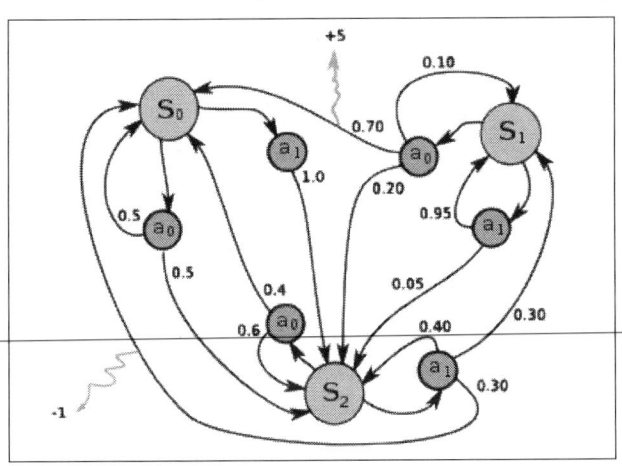

Figure 12.2: A Markov Decision Process (MDP)[3]. The transition (black arrows) between states (green circles) via actions with certain probabilities (orange circles) yields rewards (orange arrows).

Indeed, a human video game player does not rely only on the immediate state of the game to determine what to do next; they also rely on cues from prior points in the game, such as the point at which enemies went offscreen to anticipate them re-emerging.

Similarly, our algorithm will benefit from using a *sequence* of states and actions leading to the current state, $s = \{x_1..., x_t; a_1...a_{t-1}\}$, from the game as input to the current decision. In other words, the "state" becomes this sequence of prior states and actions, and we can still use the methods developed for MDPs to solve this RL problem.[1]

At each point in time, based on this state (history), we want to make the decision that will maximize *future reward*, R, at the end of the game. Intuitively, we are usually better at estimating the outcome of our immediate actions versus their effect far in the future, so we apply a discount to estimating the impact of actions taken near-term versus long-term using a *discount* term, γ, between 0 and 1 in our computation of expected reward:

$$R_t = \sum_{t'=t}^{T} \gamma^{t'-t} r'_t$$

Where t' is a timepoint between the current timepoint, t, and the end of the game, T. We can see that there are three potential interpretations of this future rewards function based on the value of γ:

- $\gamma = 0$. Future rewards have no impact on our decision, and we care only about the current rewards.
- $0 < \gamma < 1$. As we increase the distance between t' and t, the exponent of this multiplicative factor becomes greater and the discount term smaller, shrinking the future reward to 0 at infinity. In this case, we weight nearer-term goals more highly than longer-term goals.
- $\gamma = 1$. In this case, our environment could be deterministic, such that we don't need to discount future reward because there is no uncertainty about outcomes, but even in stochastic environments the use of $\gamma < 1$ or $\gamma = 1$ can be seen as a choice between regularizing the reward calculation (or not). When the discount factor is < 1, the algorithm is less affected by (potentially sparse) data over a longer horizon, so can be helpful in cases where the action space is very large and training on many future steps without this discounting could lead to overfitting on individual paths in that space.[4]

The goal of the RL problem we have described here is then to learn a *value function*, Q, which maximizes reward given a sequence and a *policy*, **π**, that associates sequences to actions – the convention of writing this as the "Q" function comes from the fact that the function evaluates the "quality" of decisions made by the RL algorithm[5]:

$$Q(s, a) = max_\pi E[R_t | s = s_t, a = a_t, \pi]$$

In other words, given a state (or, as in our case, a sequence of states) and a proposed action, the Q-function scores the proposed action based on the maximum total future reward R. This Q-function is generally not known, and we need to solve for it – however, the optimal Q-function obeys an important rule based on *dynamic programming* called the *principle of optimality*:

> "An optimal policy has the property that whatever the initial state and initial decision are, the remaining decisions must constitute an optimal policy with regard to the state resulting from the first decision."[6]

In others words, regardless of the starting state, once we transition to a new state as a result of the first action, all subsequent actions must be optimal under an optimal policy. If we write out this principle in mathematical form, it splits the value function into two parts in a recursive expression known as the *Bellman equation*:

$$Q^*(s,a) = E_{s' \sim \xi}[r + \gamma \max_{a'} Q^*(s',a')|s,a]$$

Where Q^* is the "optimal" Q-function, E is the expected value, and ξ is an environment from which future states s' are sampled. This expression says that the optimal Q-function should give the expected value for the current sequence and proposed action as the expectation of the sum of current reward r and the discounted future value of the next sequence of actions, $Q^*(s', a')$. This expression is also known as a functional expression because the solution is the function Q^*, and thus this general class of problems is known as "Q-learning."[7] One approach to solving for Q^* in Q-learning is through *value iteration*:

$$Q_{i+1}(s,a) = Q_i(s,a) + \alpha(r + \gamma \max_{a'} Q_i(s',a') - Q_i(s,a))$$

Where α is a *learning rate* that determines how quickly to modify the function with new information. If we run this update for a sufficiently large number of i and s, we could converge to the optimal value for Q, Q^*.[8,9] For simpler problems where we have only a small number of actions and states, we could create a table that gives the value of Q for any potential action. The entries in this table are randomly initialized for every $Q(s, a)$ and updated using the value iteration formula:

State/Action	A1	A2	A3	A4
S1	Q(S1, A1)			
S2				
S3				

Table 12.1: A lookup table for Q-learning. Each cell contains a Q value for a particular state (S) and action (A) pair. Values are randomly initialized and updated using value iteration.

However, as pointed out by prior authors,[1] for problems such as the video game scenario we have described, it is almost impossible to enumerate all potential sequences and actions. Also, because the likelihood of any particular sequence-action pair is very low, we would need to sample a huge number of examples to be able to accurately estimate the Q value using value iteration.

To make this problem more computationally feasible, we need to turn Q from a lookup table to a function that can *generalize* to estimate the value of state-action pairs that it hasn't seen based on similar examples to which it has been exposed. To do this, Q can be represented by a parameterized function with some parameters θ: the function can be linear, a tree model, or in modern applications even the deep neural networks that we have been studying in other parts of this book. In this case, our objective resembles more a classical learning algorithm, where we try to minimize:

$$L_i(\theta_i) = E_{s,a \sim p}[(y_i - Q(s, a, \theta_i))^2]$$

$$\text{With } y_i = E_{s' \sim \xi}[r + \gamma \max_{a'} Q^*(s', a', \theta_{i-1}) | s, a]$$

and p is a distribution of actions and sequences from a potentially very large space performed by an agent in an environment ξ. Since L is differentiable, we can optimize it using stochastic gradient descent, just like the deep learning algorithms we discussed in *Chapter 3, Building Blocks of Deep Neural Networks*:

$$\nabla_{\theta_i} L_i(\theta_i) = E_{s,a \sim p(.); s' \sim \xi}\left[\left(r + \gamma \max_{a'} Q(s', a'; \theta_{i-1}) - Q(s, a; \theta_i)\right) \nabla_{\theta_i} Q(s, a; \theta_i)\right]$$

By holding the parameters fixed and optimizing L, followed by constructing new samples from p and s, we have an algorithm that resembles the iterative updates for the value iteration Q-learning as given above.[10]

Where does this approach fit among the hierarchy of RL methods? Generally, RL methods are classified according to:

- Whether they use a static (offline) dataset or are trained on new data continuously delivered to the system (online).[11]
- Whether the policy function is updated with Q (on-policy) or independently (off-policy).[12]
- Whether the transition equations are explicitly modeled (model-based) or not (model-free).[12]

Among these possible RL algorithm variants, the version of Q-learning described above is classified as *off-policy, online, and model-free*. While we could use the values of Q as a policy for selecting the next action, our samples from $p(.)$ do not need to hold to this policy.

In practice, an epsilon greedy distribution is used for problems where we want to introduce some randomness into the algorithm to prevent it from getting stuck in local minima, such as deep Q-learning (introduced in a short while), which selects the "greedy" (maximizing Q) action with probability e, and a random action with probability $1-e$. Thus the policy we are learning (Q) is not strictly used to select actions (a) given this randomness. This approach is model-free because the neural network approximates the transition model, and is online because it is learned on a dynamically generated dataset, though could be trained using a static offline history of video game sessions as well.

In contrast, in *on-policy* Q-learning algorithms, such as **State-Action-Reward-State-Action (SARSA)** [13], we use direct updates for the Q-function as given for the value iteration steps described above. Unlike the off-policy example, we are not calculating the optimal Q based on a sample or exploratory selection of actions generated from the distribution p (sometimes known as the *behavioral policy*); instead, we are selecting actions based on a policy and potentially updating that policy as we learn Q.

Deep Q-learning

While the field of deep learning is independent of reinforcement learning methods such as the Q-learning algorithm, a powerful combination of these two approaches was applied in training algorithms to play arcade games at near-human level.[1] A major insight in this research was to apply a deep neural network to generate vector representations from the raw pixels of the video game, rather than trying to explicitly represent some features of the "state of the game"; this neural network is the Q-function for this RL algorithm.

Another key development was a technique called *experience replay*, wherein the history of states (here, pixels from video frames in a game), actions, and rewards is stored in a fixed-length list and re-sampled at random repeatedly, with some stochastic possibility to choose a non-optimal outcome using the epsilon-greedy approach described above. The result is that the value function updates are averaged over many samples of the same data, and correlations between consecutive samples (which could make the algorithm explore only a limited set of the solution space) are broken. Further, this "deep" Q-learning algorithm is implemented *off-policy* to avoid the potential circular feedback of generating optimal samples with a jointly optimized policy function.

Deep Q-learning is also *model-free*, in the sense we have no representation or model (such as a generative model that can simulate new frames of the game) of the environment E. In fact, as with the video game example, it could just be samples of historical data that represent the "internal state" of a game that is observed by a player.

Putting these pieces together, the deep Q-learning algorithm uses the following steps to learn to play Atari games[14]:

1. Create a list to store samples of (current state, action, reward, next state) as a "replay memory."
2. Randomly initialize the weights in the neural network representing the Q-function.
3. For a certain number of gameplay sequences, initialize a starting game screen (pixels) and a transformation of this input (such as the last four screens). This "window" of fixed-length history is important because otherwise the Q-network would need to accommodate arbitrarily sized input (very long or very short sequences of game screens), and this restriction makes it easier to apply a convolutional neural network to the problem.
4. For a certain number of steps (screens) in the game, use epsilon greedy sampling to choose the next action given the current screen and reward function computed through Q.
5. After updating the state, save this transition of (current state, action, reward, action, next state) into the replay memory.
6. Choose random sets of (current state, action, reward, next state) transitions from the replay memory, and compute their reward using the Q-function. Use stochastic gradient descent to update Q based on these transitions.
7. Continue *steps 3-6* for many games and gameplay steps until the weights in the Q-network converge.

While other applications of Q-learning have nuances tied to their specific domain, the general approach of using a deep neural network to approximate the Q-function on a large space of possible outcomes (rather than a small set of states and actions that can be represented in a table) has proved effective in many cases. Other examples in which deep Q-learning has been applied include:

- Processing the positions on a Go (an East Asian game resembling chess) gameboard using a CNN and applying Q-learning to determine the next best move in the game based on historical examples from human players; a model named "AlphaGo" was published in 2015.[15]
- An innovation on the AlphaGo release in 2017, named "AlphaGo Zero," where the program learns entirely from synthetic games (two RL agents playing each other) rather than historical examples from human players.[16]
- A more general form of AlphaGo Zero, "AlphaZero," which also mastered the games of Chess and Shogi using self-play.[17]

- AlphaStar, an RL algorithm that can beat human masters in the multi-player real-time strategy game StarCraft.[18]
- A model called "AlphaFold," which can predict the 3D structure of proteins from their 2D sequence – we will describe AlphaFold in more detail in *Chapter 13, Emerging Applications of Generative AI*.

We've thus far described Q-learning and its variants, and how deep learning augments Q-learning through deep Q-learning for complex environments and datasets. However, the problems we've described all share the common feature that we are able to express the reward function in defined mathematical terms (such as the score in a game). In many real-world scenarios – such as training an RL agent to drive a car – this reward function is not so easy to define. In these cases, rather than writing down a reward function, we might instead use examples of human drivers as an implicit representation of the reward – this is an approach known as inverse reinforcement learning, which we describe in more detail below.

Inverse reinforcement learning: Learning from experts

The example of deep Q-learning above relies upon an explicit reward function – the score in the game. We don't always have access to an explicit reward function though, including in important real-world scenarios such as self-driving cars. What "reward" value would we assign to a driver choosing to navigate one way or the other given the surrounding environment on the road? While we have an intuitive sense of what the "right" decision is, quantifying exhaustive rules for how we should score such a reward function would be challenging.

Instead of trying to determine the reward function, we could instead observe an expert driver perform complex maneuvers such as merging in multi-lane traffic and optimize an agent whose behavior mimics that of the expert. This is a more general problem known as *imitation learning*. One form of imitation learning is *behavioral cloning*,[19] which follows the following algorithm:

1. Collect a set of state, action pairs (s, a) from expert behavior.
2. Learn a policy function $a = \pi(s, a)$, where π is a supervised classification algorithm.

While this approach is straightforward, it requires a large amount of data in order to create a classifier that generalizes to unseen environments, particularly when the number of potential environments (as is the case for self-driving cars) is very large.[20]

In particular, the success of behavioral cloning depends on the future distribution of the environment being similar to the training data, which is particularly difficult when the results of the model can influence the distribution of later observations. For example, the choices made by a self-driving car on the road become further data for re-training the model, leading to a feedback loop of potentially compounding errors and data drift.[21]

An alternative is to learn an agent that tries to match the outcomes of an expert's *entire trajectory* rather than individual actions, as in behavioral cloning. The output of this algorithm is then a function that scores "expert behavior" on a trajectory higher than novice behavior. This approach is known as **inverse reinforcement learning** (IRL) since it reverses the common pattern (*Figure 12.3*) – on the left we see a typical feedback loop for an RL like we've described for the Atari-playing deep Q-network, where an agent (blue) observes a state (s) and using a reward function (R) chooses an action (a) that yields a transition (T) to a new state and a reward (r). In contrast, on the right, the rewards resulting from these states, actions, and transitions are represented implicitly by examples from an expert (E), and the agent (blue) instead learns to replicate this sequence through a learned reward function (R_E) rather than being explicitly "in the loop" of the algorithm. In other words, instead of learning policy from an explicit reward function, we observe an expert's behavior and infer a reward function that would lead to their observed actions.

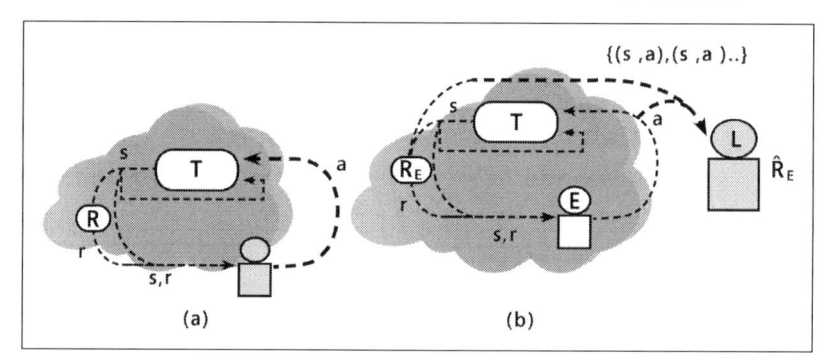

Figure 12.3: Reinforcement learning (a) and inverse reinforcement learning (b)[22]

How could we quantify the behavior of an "expert" through learning a reward function from scratch? If we re-examine our prior example of video game playing, we could examine sequences of pixel screens x and actions a ($x_1, a_1, x_2, a_2...$) from expert human play that form a complete session, and try to find a function f that would give us the total reward for a given game:

$$R = \sum_i f(s_i, a_i)$$

Chapter 12

We could then ask whether the given function f tends to replicate the behavior of an expert player versus other alternatives. However, there are inherent problems – multiple f's might give the same reward result, making it unclear which (of many possible solutions) would generalize best to new data.[23]

Alternatively, we could instead try to optimize an agent which will result in observed trajectories with the same probability as an expert; in other words, we would see the same distribution of sequences from following this agent as from drawing randomly from expert behavior, and the optimization algorithm is based on minimizing the difference between the proposed and the observed empirical distribution of sequences from the expert.[24] This expected distribution (either observed or generated by the agent) can be represented by:

$$\sum_{Path \zeta_i} P(\zeta_i) f_{\zeta_i} = \tilde{f}$$

Where P is the probability of trajectory (ζ), and f are the features of a state, such as the observed pixels in the video game example. We've removed the problem of solving for an ambiguous reward function, but we still are faced with the possibility that many agents could lead to the same behavior. We might even need a mixture of different policy or reward functions in order to mimic a given expert behavior, and it is unclear how to select these.

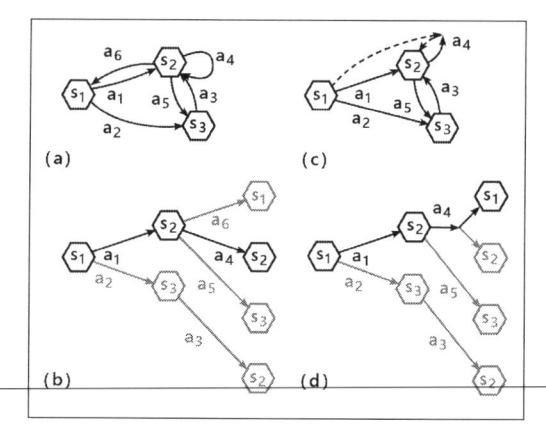

Figure 12.4: Path trajectories from a (non) deterministic MDP. (b) is a particular path (trajectory) from the deterministic MDP (a), while (d) is a sample path from a non-deterministic MDP (c), where there is ambiguity as to which state action a_4 might lead to.[23]

We can appeal to the partition function and Boltzmann distribution that we saw in *Chapter 4, Teaching Networks to Generate Digits*, when studying restricted Boltzmann machines. If we take the MDP represented by an RL agent and "unroll" the trajectories from following a particular set of actions in response to a set of states, we get a set of variable length paths in a tree diagram as depicted in *Figure 12.4*.

Many different distributions over the occurrence of these paths could be obtained by following different policies, and even with the same distribution of pixel features some of these policies might prefer one path over another based on a particular reward function. To resolve this ambiguity, we could optimize a reward function with parameters θ such that paths with the same reward function value based on these features receive the same preference, but we exponentially prefer a higher reward:

$$P(\zeta_i|\theta) = \frac{1}{Z(\theta)} e^{\theta^T f_{\zeta_i}} = \frac{1}{Z(\theta)} e^{\Sigma_{s_j \epsilon \zeta_i} \theta^T f_{s_j}}$$

This approach is known as *maximum entropy*; recall from *Chapter 4, Teaching Networks to Generate Digits*, that the Z is the partition function, which normalizes P to be a probability density over average trajectories f composed of steps s_j evaluated using a (here, linear) reward function θ^T.[25] Even in the case of non-deterministic outcomes (*Figure 12.4*, (b) and (d)), which could be the case, for example, in a video game where some of the behavior of enemy spacecraft is randomly generated by the computer, we could parameterize this equation in terms of the transition distribution T:[23]

$$P(\zeta|\theta, T) = \sum_{o \in T} P_T(o) \frac{e^{\theta^T f_\zeta}}{Z(\theta, o)} I_{\zeta \epsilon o} \approx \frac{e^{\theta^T f_\zeta}}{Z(\theta, T)} \prod_{s_{t+1}, a_t, s_t \epsilon \zeta} P_T(s_{t+1}|a_t, s_t)$$

Here, the distribution is similar to before, but we've added the probability P_T of observing outcome o based on actions a and states s using the transition model T. $I_{\zeta \epsilon o}$ denotes the indicator function, which evaluates to 1 when $\zeta \epsilon o$ and 0 otherwise. We could then optimize this equation to find the parameters of the reward function that maximize the likelihood of this function:

$$\theta^* = argmax_\theta L(\theta) = argmax_\theta \sum_{examples} \log P(\bar{\zeta}|\theta, T)$$

The gradients of this likelihood are just the difference between the expected feature counts (for example, distribution of pixels) from expert play and those obtained by following the proposed agent, based on the frequency of visiting a given state D:

$$\nabla L(\theta) = \bar{f} - \sum_\zeta P(\zeta|\theta, T) f_\zeta = \bar{f} - \sum_{s_i} D_{s_i} f_{s_i}$$

This gives us an objective to optimize, but there are options for what kind of P we would like to use. The one that we will study is the *maximal causal entropy*, where the probability of a given action (and thus, state and path distribution) is conditioned on the prior set of states and actions, just as in our prior video game example [26][27]:

$$E[-logP(A_{0:t_1}|S_{0:t_1})]$$

$$P(a_{0:t_1}|s_{0:t_1}) = \prod_{t=0}^{t_i} P(a_t|s_{0:t}, a_{0:t-1})$$

Because this entropy value could potentially be infinite if the path never terminates, we could apply a discount factor to make it finite[26]:

$$H^B(A_{0:\infty}||S_{0:\infty}) \triangleq E_{P_0,P,\pi}\left[\sum_{t=0}^{\infty} -B^t log\pi_t(A_i|S_{0:t}, A_{0:t-1})\right]$$

Where the discount factor B is applied to each time step t, with expectation over the distribution of initial states P_0 and subsequent states P subject to a policy π; $H(A \parallel S)$ denotes the causal entropy $H(A \parallel S) = E[-logP(A||S)]$; and $P(A \parallel S)$ is the causally conditioned probability $= \prod_{t=0}^{T} P(A_t|S_{0:t}, A_{0:t-1})$ (the probability conditioned on the prior actions in the sequence).

So at this point, we have an objective to optimize (discounted causal entropy), and the notion of computing a reward function for a particular agent that would make its behavior similar to an expert. What is the connection between this objective and generative AI? The answer is in how we can draw parallels between *discriminating* between an expert and learner, and generating samples from the learner – not unlike the GANs we studied in *Chapters 6, 7*, and *8*!

Adversarial learning and imitation

Given a set of expert observations (of a driver, or a champion video game player), we would like to find a reward function that assigns high reward to an agent that matches expert behavior, and low reward to agents that do not. At the same time, we want to choose such an agent's policy, π, under this reward function such that it is as informative as possible by maximizing entropy and preferring expert over non-expert choices. We'll show how both are achieved through an algorithm known as **Generative Adversarial Imitation Learning (GAIL)** published in 2016.[20]

In the following, instead of a "reward" function, we use a "cost" function to match the conventions used in the referenced literature on this topic, but it is just the negative of the reward function.

Putting these constraints together, we get[20]:

$$maximize_{c \in C} \left(\min_{\pi \in \Pi} -H(\pi) + E_\pi[c(s,a)] \right) - E_{\pi_E}[c(s,a)]$$

In the inner term, we are trying to find a policy that maximizes the discounted entropy:

$$H(\pi) \triangleq E_\pi[-log\pi(a|s)]$$

Thus leading to a large negative value, and minimizing the cost term. We want to maximize this whole expression over different potential cost functions by selecting one that not only satisfies the inner constraint but gives low cost expert-like behavior, thus maximizing the overall expression. Note that this inner term is also equivalent to an RL problem that seeks an agent whose behavior optimizes the objective:

$$RL(c) = argmin_{\pi \in \Pi} - H(\pi) + E_\pi[c(s,a)]$$

over the space of possible policies π, denoted Π. However, in order to limit the space of possible choices of c, we apply a regularization function $\Psi(c)$, which seeks a low-complexity c among many possible choices, and adds this constraint into the overall objective:

$$IRL_\psi(\pi_E) = argmax_{c \in R^{SxA}} - \psi(c) + (\min_{\pi \in \Pi} -H(\pi) + E_\pi[c(s,a)]) - E_{\pi_E}[c(s,a)]$$

We can see that we could alternate between optimizing c under a given policy (IRL) and optimizing a policy under that c (RL) – and that is exactly the approach we will follow. We can express the optimal policy, using the approach described before, as a measure of **occupancy** (ρ) of different states under that policy:

$$\rho_\pi(s,a) = \pi(a|s) \sum_{t=0}^{\infty} \gamma^t P(s_t = s|\pi)$$

Then the optimal point for the RL and IRL problem is equivalent to minimizing the difference between the learned and expert occupancy:

$$RL \circ IRL_\psi(\pi_E) = argmin_{\pi \in \Pi} \; -H(\pi) + \psi^*(\rho_\pi - \rho_{\pi_E})$$

where $\circ$ denotes a functional composition, $f \circ g(x) = f(g(x))$, here representing that the RL agent uses the IRL output as one of its arguments. However, the examples of the expert behavior that we receive are often limited, so we don't want to exactly mimic their distribution since that may cause the agent to overfit. Instead, we want to use a distance measure, such as the KL divergence or JS divergence we saw in Chapter 6, Image Generation with GANs, to quantify differences between the observed distribution of expert behavior and the distribution of actions taken by the IRL agent which tries to approximate that behavior:

$$\text{minimize}_\pi d_\psi(\rho_\pi, \rho_E) - H(\pi)$$

What regularizer function, $\Psi(c)$, should be used in this algorithm? The authors of the GAIL algorithm present a function that assigns low penalty if the cost is low, and high penalty otherwise. A regularizer function with this property, for which the full derivation is presented in the paper "Generative Adversarial Imitation Learning," is:

$$\psi_{GA}(c) \triangleq \begin{cases} E_{\pi_E}[g(c(s,a))] & \text{if } c < 0 \\ +\infty & \text{otherwise} \end{cases} \text{ where } g(x) = \begin{cases} -x - \log(1 - e^x) & \text{if } x < 0 \\ +\infty & \text{otherwise} \end{cases}$$

The intuition for this function is that it minimizes the difference between the causal entropy of the policy H with a penalty λ (for example, the likelihood of the learned policy) and the difference between the expert and learned policy state occupancies $D_{JS}(\rho_\pi, \rho_{\pi_E})$:

$$\text{minimize}_\pi \psi^*_{GA}(\rho_\pi - \rho_{\pi_E}) - \lambda H(\pi) = D_{JS}(\rho_\pi, \rho_{\pi_E}) - \lambda H(\pi)$$

This $D_{JS}(\rho_\pi, \rho_{\pi_E})$ or $\psi^*_{GA}(\rho_\pi - \rho_{\pi_E})$ can be written as the negative log loss of a binary classifier that distinguishes between expert (0) and learned (1) action-states pairs:

$$\max_{D \in (0,1)^{S \times A}} E_\pi[\log(D(s,a))] + E_{\pi_E}[\log(1 - D(s,a))]$$

The expression probably looks quite familiar from *Chapter 6, Image Generation with GANs*, as it resembles the objective function of a GAN as well for discriminating between generated and real data! Putting these terms together (the regularizer and the causal entropy), we see that the complete objective function is:

$$E_\pi[\log(D(s,a))] + E_{\pi_E}[\log(1 - D(s,a))] - \lambda H(\pi)$$

To optimize this objective function, the GAIL algorithm utilizes the following steps:

1. Prepare a set of expert trajectories and randomly initialize the discriminator and policy parameters.
2. Generate a set of trajectories for the RL agent under the current policy.
3. Update the discriminator parameters with a stochastic gradient descent step.
4. Update the policy parameters with gradient-based updates using an algorithm called **Trust Region Policy Optimization (TRPO)** published in 2015 – please consult the original article "Trust Region Policy Optimization" for more details on the form of this gradient update.[28]
5. Repeat *steps 2-4* of the algorithm until the values of the parameters of the policy and the discriminator converge.

Now that we've explained the intuition behind using generative AI in reinforcement learning, let's dive into a practical example of training a walking humanoid in a virtual environment.

Running GAIL on PyBullet Gym

For our code example in this chapter, we will train a virtual agent to navigate a simulated environment – in many RL papers, this environment is simulated using the Mujoco framework (http://www.mujoco.org/). **Mujoco** stands for **Multi joint dynamics with contacts** – it is a physics "engine" that allows you to create an artificial agent (such as a pendulum or bipedal humanoid), where a "reward" might be an ability to move through the simulated environment.

While it is a popular framework used for developing reinforcement learning benchmarks, such as by the research group OpenAI (see https://github.com/openai/baselines for some of these implementations), it is also closed source and requires a license for use. For our experiments, we will use PyBullet Gymperium (https://github.com/benelot/pybullet-gym), a drop-in replacement for Mujoco that allows us to run a physics simulator and import agents trained in Mujoco environments.

Figure 12.5: Examples from the Mujoco simulated environments (http://www.mujoco.org/)

To install Pybullet-Gym, you need to first install OpenAI Gym, using the following commands:

```
git clone https://github.com/openai/gym.git
cd gym
pip install -e .
```

Then install Pybullet:

```
git clone https://github.com/benelot/pybullet-gym.git
cd pybullet-gym
pip install -e .
```

To show how this simulated environment works, let's create a "hopper," one of the many virtual agents you can instantiate with the library:

```
import gym
import pybulletgym

env = gym.make('HopperMuJoCoEnv-v0')
env.render("human")
env.reset()
```

If the commands execute correctly, we will see the following output, an array giving the current observation (11-dimensional vector) vector of the walker.

```
    WalkerBase::__init__
    array([ 0.05650253, -0.00185301, -0.04258511,  0.03430916,  0.0476181 ,
            0.        ,  0.        ,  0.        ,  0.        ,  0.        ,
            0.        ], dtype=float32)
```

Figure 12.6: Observation vector of the walker

The call to render("human") will create a window showing the "hopper," a simple single-footed figure which moves in a simulated 3D environment (*Figure 12.7*):

Figure 12.7: PyGym hopper

We can run a few iterations of the hopper in its raw, "untrained" form, to get a sense of how it looks. In this simulation, we take up to 1,000 steps and visualize it using a pop-up window:

```
env.reset()

for t in range(1000):
    action = env.action_space.sample()
    _, _, done, _ = env.step(action)
    env.render("human")
    if done:
        break
```

We first clear the environment with reset(). Then, for up to 1,000 timesteps, we sample the action space (for example, the x, y, and z coordinates representing movements of the walking figure within the virtual environment). Then, we use that action to get an updated reward and observation, and render the result, until the movement completes.

This demonstration comes from a completely untrained hopper. For our GAIL implementation, we will need a hopper that has been successfully trained to walk as a sample of "expert" trajectories for the algorithm. For this purpose, we'll download a set of hopper data from the OpenAI site, at:

https://drive.google.com/drive/folders/1h3H4AY_ZBx08hz-Ct0Nxxus-V1melu1U

These contain a set of NumPy files, such as deterministic.trpo.Hopper.0.00.npz, that contain samples of data from reinforcement learning agents trained using the Trust Region Policy Optimization algorithm used in *Step 4* of the GAIL algorithm we discussed earlier.[28]

If we load this data, we can also visualize it using the Pybullet simulator, but this time we will see steps from the expert, rather than the random baseline agent:

```
import numpy as np
mujoco_hopper_np = np.load('deterministic.trpo.Hopper.0.00.npz')

for i_episode in range(20):
    observation = env.reset()
    episode = np.random.choice(mujoco_hopper_np['acs'].shape[0])
    for t in range(1000):
        env.render("human")
        action = mujoco_hopper_np = \
        np.load('deterministic.trpo.Hopper.0.00.npz')['acs'][episode]
```

```
            [t]
                observation, reward, done, info = env.step(action)
                if done:
                    print("Episode finished after {} timesteps".format(t+1))
                    break
        env.close()
```

This code loads the pre-trained hopper, initializes the virtual environment, and takes a maximum of 1,000 steps in which an action (the next move of the hopper) is determined using the hopper's trained policy function, and the environment state (position of the hopper) is updated based on that action. Note that here the policy function is deterministic, leading to the same outcome for any given action at time t. You can see the hopper now taking many steps:

Figure 12.8: The hopper moving with expert policy trained by TRPO

Let's take a closer look at what kinds of data are in this NumPy object we've loaded. You'll notice that the format, .npz, is a gzipped archive of compressed files. We can see the names of these archives by using the files parameter of the object mujoco_hopper_np:

```
print(mujoco_hopper_np.files)
```

which gives:

```
['ep_rets', 'obs', 'rews', 'acs']
```

The observations are 11-dimensional objects, which you can verify by looking at the dimension of obs:

```
print(mujoco_hopper_np['obs'].shape)
```

This array has 1,500 examples, each of 1,000 timesteps, which each have 11 dimensions representing different physical quantities (position of hinges, torque, and so on). The objective of the hopper task is to move the hopper forward as fast as possible, so the reward function is higher when the agent learns to move forward. If we examine the `acs` data, we see that it has three dimensions, corresponding to points in 3D space. This is a continuous action space, unlike the discrete examples we have discussed previously.

```
print(mujoco_hopper_np ['acs'].shape)
```

The `ep_rets` corresponds to the predicted reward in the future for an action at time t, and the rewards `rews` are the output of the reward function.

The agent: Actor-Critic network

To create our GAIL implementation, we'll first need to specify an agent.[29] This is an Actor-Critic architecture, consisting of two networks: one which learns the "value" of an observation (Critic), and another (Actor) which samples actions based on observations. These networks could be independent or share parameters; for our experiment, we'll have them share hidden and input layers but have separate output layers (*Figure 12.9*).

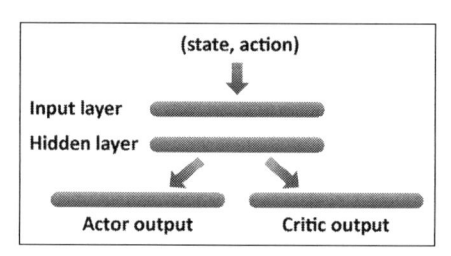

Figure 12.9: Actor-Critic architecture

Note the code for the GAIL implementation in this chapter is based on https://github.com/fangihsiao/GAIL-Tensorflow/blob/master/tf_gail.ipynb.

Below we define the `ActorCritic` class:

```
import tensorflow_probability as tfp
import tensorflow as tf
tfd = tfp.distributions

class ActorCritic(tf.keras.Model):
    def __init__(self, name='actor_critic', dim_actions=3, num_
layers=2, input_shape=(11), num_units=100, **kwargs):
        super().__init__(name=name, **kwargs)
```

```python
        self._num_layers = num_layers
        self._num_units = num_units
        self._dim_actions = dim_actions
        self._layers = list()
        for n, l in enumerate(range(self._num_layers)):
            self._layers.append(tf.keras.layers.Dense(
                                        self._num_units,
                                        activation=tf.nn.relu))
            if n == 0:
                self._layers[-1].build(input_shape)
            else:
                self._layers[-1].build((num_units))
            self._layers.append(tf.keras.layers.BatchNormalization())
        self._value_output = tf.keras.layers.Dense(1,activation=None)
        self._value_output.build((num_units))
        self._action_output = tf.keras.layers.Dense(
                                        self._dim_actions,
                                        activation=tf.nn.tanh)
        self._action_output.build((num_units))
        self._action_dist_std = tf.Variable([1., 1, 1],
                                        trainable=False)
        self._action_dist =  None

    def get_params(self):
        weights = []
        for layer in self.layers:
            weights += layer.trainable_weights
        return weights+\
            self._action_output.trainable_weights + \
            self._value_output.trainable_weights + \
            [self._action_dist_std]

def call(self, inputs):
    x = self._layers[0](inputs)
    for layer in self._layers[1:self._num_layers]:
        x = layer(x)

    return self._value_output(x)

def log_prob(self, x):
    return self._action_dist.log_prob(x)
```

```python
def sample(self, inputs, output='action'):
    x = self._layers[0](inputs)
    for layer in self._layers[1:self._num_layers]:
        x = layer(x)
    self._action_dist = tfd.Normal(self._action_output(x),
                                   [1,1,1])

    if output == 'action':
        return self._action_dist.sample()
    elif output == 'entropy':
        return tf.reduce_mean(self._action_dist.entropy())
    else:
        raise ValueError("unknown sample type: {}".format(output))
```

This class initializes a network that accepts input states and action pairs and generates two outputs – one generates new actions (3D coordinates representing the next move of the hopper in the virtual space) – the Actor – and the other generates values (how successful the movement is in navigating the hopper farther in the virtual space) – the Critic. The value output is a single scalar that increases with the quality of the hopper's movement, while the action is a 3-unit vector representing a move in 3D space with a mean and standard deviation per coordinate.

Because our network has multiple outputs, we need to be careful about setting the input layers and initializing them. Notice that we explicitly call build on the two output layers, rather than letting them be automatically instantiated in the forward pass, as this will cause errors in compiling the model. We also instantiate a variable, _action_dist_std, to contain the standard deviation of the action dimensions, which we'll use to sample new coordinates in the model. We've also included BatchNormalization layers to prevent the gradients from exploding or vanishing in our network.[29]

We also need to be able to return the trainable parameters in the model for our gradient calculation, using the get_params method of the Actor-Critic network:

```python
def get_params(self):
    weights = []
    for layer in self.layers:
        weights += layer.trainable_weights
    return weights+\
        self._action_output.trainable_weights + \
        self._value_output.trainable_weights + \
        [self._action_dist_std]
```

In our forward pass, we calculate the output of the Critic:

```python
    def call(self, inputs):
        x = self._layers[0](inputs)
        for layer in self._layers[1:self._num_layers]:
            x = layer(x)

        return self._value_output(x)
```

To sample new actions (3D moves) from the Actor, we run the sample function with the argument `'action'` – if we supply `'entropy'` instead, we return the entropy of the action distribution:

```python
def sample(self, inputs, output='action'):
    x = self._layers[0](inputs)
    for layer in self._layers[1:self._num_layers]:
        x = layer(x)
    self._action_dist = tfd.Normal(self._action_output(x), [1,1,1])

    if output == 'action':
        return self._action_dist.sample()
    elif output == 'entropy':
        return tf.reduce_mean(self._action_dist.entropy())
    else:
        raise ValueError("unknown sample type: {}".format(output))
```

Finally, we need to be able to return the log probability of the action distribution (for our loss function) for the PPO network, described below:

```python
    def log_prob(self, x):
        return self._action_dist.log_prob(x)
```

Our IRL agent – for which we will use **Proximal Policy Optimization (PPO)** policy updates, an improvement on TRPO published in 2017 [29] – makes use of this Actor-Critic network as the "policy" function.

```python
class PPO(tf.keras.Model):

    def __init__(self, name='ppo', dim_actions=3, num_layers=2, num_
 units=100, eps=0.2, v_coeff=0.5, ent_coeff=0.01, lr=3e-2, **kwargs):
        super().__init__(name=name, *kwargs)
        self._dim_actions = dim_actions
        self._num_layers = num_layers
        self._num_units = num_units
        self._eps = eps
        self._v_coeff = v_coeff
```

```python
            self._ent_coeff = ent_coeff
            self._policy = ActorCritic(num_layers=self._num_layers,
                                       num_units=self._num_units,
                                       dim_actions=self._dim_actions)
            self._new_policy = ActorCritic(num_layers=self._num_layers,
                                           num_units=self._num_units,
                                           dim_actions=self._dim_actions)
            self._policy.compile(run_eagerly=True)
            self._new_policy.compile(run_eagerly=True)
            self._optimizer = tf.keras.optimizers.Adam(lr)
```

This class initializes a neural network (_policy) and provides a placeholder for updates to that network (_new_policy), so that with each step of the algorithm we can update the new policy with reference to its improvement over the last policy.

The loss function inside the train_policy loop is optimized using a gradient descent algorithm where the magnitude of the gradients is constrained to a fixed range ("clipped") so that large gradients don't lead the loss function (and weights) to change drastically between rounds of training:

```python
   def loss(self, actions, observations, advantages, returns):
         ratio = tf.exp(self._new_policy.log_prob(actions) -
                        self._policy.log_prob(actions))
         surr = ratio * advantages
         actor_loss = tf.reduce_mean(
                tf.minimum(surr, tf.clip_by_value(ratio, 1 - self._eps,
                                      1 + self._eps) * advantages))
         critic_loss = tf.reduce_mean(tf.square(returns - self._new_
policy.call(observations)))
         return -1*actor_loss - self._ent_coeff * \
     tf.reduce_mean(self._new_policy.sample(observations, 'entropy'))\
                        + self._v_coeff * critic_loss
```

In this loss function, we first take a ratio between the old policy (current parameters of the Actor-Critic network) and a potential update (new policy) – the exponential of the difference of their log probabilities (which is the likelihood of the observed actions under the action distribution of each network) gives a ratio. If the new, proposed network is an improvement (its parameters fit the observed action sequence better), the ratio is greater than 1. Otherwise, the proposal is unchanged in quality (a ratio of 1) or worse (a ratio less than 1) than the current parameters of the Actor-Critic.

We multiply this ratio by the "advantages," which are the difference between returns (the Q-function we described earlier) and the current values of the Actor-Critic's existing state. In this GAIL implementation, we compute advantages through Generalized Advantage Estimation[29], which uses an exponentially smoothed estimate of the Q-function, where gamma (coefficient) and tau (exponents) control how much the estimate of future reward decays in the future relative to no future information (tau = 0) or no decay of importance of future data versus present (tau = 1):

```
def compute_gae(next_value, rewards, masks, values, gamma=0.99,
tau=0.95):
    values = values + [next_value]
    gae = 0
    returns = []
    for step in reversed(range(len(rewards))):
        delta = rewards[step] + gamma * values[step + 1] * \
                masks[step] - values[step]
        gae = delta + gamma * tau * masks[step] * gae
        returns.insert(0, gae + values[step])
    return returns
```

The loss function above then uses the advantages multiplied by surr (the "surrogate" term) and computes two values – the first being the actor loss, which constrains the loss term given by the advantages to be within a given range, denoted by the clip_by_value function. This prevents extremes (much less than 1 or greater than 1) of the probability ratio of the new and old policy from making the loss function unstable. To this, we add the critic loss, the squared difference between the critic value and the advantage function we computed above. Taking a weighted sum of the actor and critic functions and the entropy of the action probability distribution (whether it assigns high value to a subset of positions, and thus contains "information" about the distribution of potential actions) gives the overall quality of the policy as an objective for the loss function.

Note that the actor_loss is multiplied by negative 1 (because it is the ratio between the old and new policy probability – thus if it improves it is greater than 1, but the loss function should be minimized, thus a larger negative value). Similarly, the entropy term has more information if it is larger, and we take the negative of this as well as we minimize the loss function. The critic loss becomes better the closer to 0 it is, so we leave this term as positive.

To use this loss function, we define a custom train function called `train_policy`:

```
def train_policy(self, actions, observations, advantages, returns):
    params = self._new_policy.get_params()
    with tf.GradientTape(watch_accessed_variables=False) as g:
        g.watch(params)
        def loss(actions, observations, advantages, returns):
            ...

        cost = loss(actions, observations, advantages, returns)
    grads = g.gradient(cost, params)
    grads = [grad if grad is not None else tf.zeros_like(var)
        for var, grad in zip(params, grads)]
    self._optimizer.apply_gradients(zip(grads, params),
        experimental_aggregate_gradients=False)
```

We use the get_params() function to extract the trainable parameters of the PPO policy network, "watch" them using GradientTape, and compute the loss using the loss function above. Also, since the Actor-Critic has two outputs (action and value), only one of which (value) is affected by a reward update, we could have nonexistent gradients, which is why we replace any empty gradients with a 0.

In each step of the GAIL inner loop which we described above, we also need to be able to replace the old policy with the new, using a deep copy (a copy that creates a new variable with the same values, rather than a pointer to the original variable):

```
def update_policy(self):
    self._policy = copy.deepcopy(self._new_policy)
```

Finally, we can use calls to the Actor-Critic policy network to get the value (reward) estimate and sample new actions:

```
def get_action(self, x):
    return self._new_policy.sample(x, output='action')

def get_value(self, x):
    return self._new_policy.call(x)
```

The discriminator

With our PPO algorithm, we have the "agent" which we are trying to teach to behave like an expert. We can sample from our TRPO trained examples of the hopper that we downloaded as a "generator."

So we now just need a discriminator network, which seeks to distinguish the expert behavior from the agent we are training:

```python
class Discriminator(tf.keras.Model):

    def __init__(self, name='discriminator', dim_actions=3, num_
layers=2, num_units=100, lr=3e-2, **kwargs):
        super().__init__(name=name, **kwargs)
        self._dim_actions = dim_actions
        self._num_layers = num_layers
        self._num_units = num_units
        self._layers = list()
        for l in range(self._num_layers):
            self._layers.append(tf.keras.layers.Dense(
                                            self._num_units,
                                            activation=tf.nn.relu))
            self._layers.append(tf.keras.layers.BatchNormalization())
        self._layers.append(tf.keras.layers.Dense(1,activation=None))
        self._optimizer = tf.keras.optimizers.Adam(lr)

        return self._new_policy.call(x)
```

Like the Actor-Critic, this is a 3-layer neural network with `BatchNormalization` applied between layers. Its single output indicates the quality of the input (like the value function of the Actor-Critic), and should be lower when the network is more "expert-like." Notice that to get the "reward" output to match the sign of the Actor-Critic value output, we reverse the sign of the discriminator because it predicts closer to 0 for expert observations:

```python
def get_reward(self, x):
    return -1 *tf.squeeze(tf.math.log(tf.sigmoid(self.call(x))))
```

This transformation is applied to the same `call` function we saw earlier for the Actor-Critic network.

```python
    def call(self, x):
        for layer in self._layers:
            x = layer(x)
        return x
```

Training and results

To train the network, we apply a loss function that tries to classify expert (observation, action) pairs as 0s and agent (observation, action) pairs as 1s. When the agent learns to generate high quality (observation, action) pairs that resemble the expert, the discriminator will have increasing difficulty distinguishing between samples from the agent and expert, and will assign agent samples a label of 0 as well:

```python
def loss(self, x):
    expert_out, policy_out = tf.sigmoid(tf.split(self.call(x),
                             num_or_size_splits=2, axis=0))
    return (tf.nn.sigmoid_cross_entropy_with_logits(tf.ones_like(policy_out), policy_out) + tf.nn.sigmoid_cross_entropy_with_logits(tf.zeros_like(expert_out), expert_out))
```

As before, we extract the parameters of the network through get_params():

```python
def get_params(self):
    weights = []
    for layer in self.layers:
        weights += layer.trainable_weights
    return weights
```

We then apply our loss function to these parameters using train_discriminator:

```python
def train_discriminator(self, x):
    params = self.get_params()
    with tf.GradientTape(watch_accessed_variables=False) as g:
        g.watch(params)
        cost = self.loss(x)
    grads = g.gradient(cost, params)
    grads = [grad if grad is not None else tf.zeros_like(var)
        for var, grad in zip(params, grads)]
    self._optimizer.apply_gradients(zip(grads, params),
        experimental_aggregate_gradients=False)
```

Chapter 12

Finally, we need an update function for our PPO minibatch step, where we randomly sample observations from the agent in each inner loop of the GAIL algorithm:

```python
def ppo_iteration(mini_batch_size, observations, actions, returns, advantages):
    batch_size = observations.shape[0]
    for _ in range(batch_size // mini_batch_size):
        rand_ids = np.random.randint(0, batch_size, mini_batch_size)
        yield (observations[rand_ids, :], actions[rand_ids, :],
               returns[rand_ids, :], advantages[rand_ids, :])
```

We also want to be able to plot the progress of our agent as we train it, for which we'll take samples from the environment using a model and plot the average reward and the performance of the discriminator (how closely the agent and expert discriminator reward matches):

```python
from IPython.display import clear_output
import matplotlib.pyplot as plt

def plot(frame_idx, rewards, policy_ob_ac_rew, expert_ob_ac_rew):
    clear_output(True)
    plt.figure(figsize=(20,5))
    plt.subplot(131)
    plt.title('frame %s. reward: %s' % (frame_idx, rewards[-1]))
    plt.ylabel('Agent Reward')
    plt.xlabel('Step in Training')
    plt.plot(rewards)
    plt.subplot(132)
    plt.title('frame %s.' % (frame_idx))
    plt.plot(policy_ob_ac_rew)
    plt.plot(expert_ob_ac_rew)
    plt.legend(['Agent','Expert'])
    plt.xlabel('Steps in Test Simulation')
    plt.ylabel('Discriminator Reward')
    plt.show()
```

This function makes two plots, shown in *Figure 12.10*. On the left is the reward for a set of test observations for the agent, which should increase as the agent becomes better at moving the hopper. On the right is plotted, for each of n-steps of a sample agent and expert movement of the hopper, how well the discriminator can tell the difference between the two (whether the orange and blue lines overlap, which is optimal, or are far apart, in which case the GAIL algorithm hasn't converged):

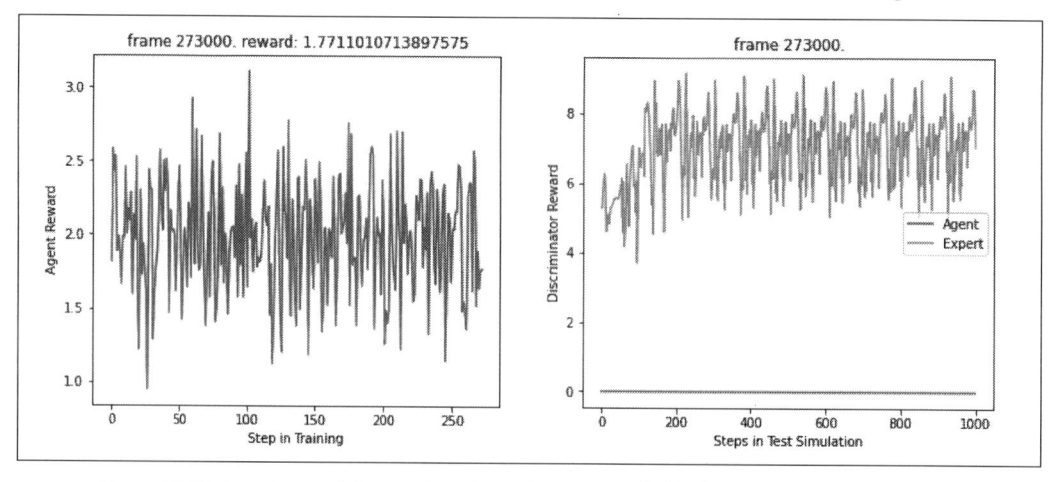

Figure 12.10: Agent reward for a series of test observations (left), discriminator reward (right). Plots generated by plot().

The test samples are generated using the test_env function, which resembles the Pybullet simulations we saw above – it uses the current agent and computes n-steps of the simulation under the current policy, returning the average reward:

```
def test_env(model, vis=False):
    ob = env.reset()
    ob = tf.reshape(tf.convert_to_tensor(ob), (1,11))
    done = False
    total_reward = 0
    while not done:
        if vis:
            env.render()
        ac = model.get_action(ob)[0]
        ac = tf.reshape(tf.convert_to_tensor(ac), (3, 1))
        next_ob, reward, done, _ = env.step(ac)
        ob = next_ob
        ob = tf.reshape(tf.convert_to_tensor(ob), (1,11))
        total_reward += reward
    return total_reward
```

For our main function, we'll set a number of maximum simulation steps and the hyperparameters of the algorithm, including the learning rate of the ADAM optimizer (lr), the number of units in the hidden layer of each network, the number of steps to run each hopper simulation for the agent (num_steps), the number of samples to choose in each Agent update (minibatch size), the number of steps to run each inner loop updating the Agent (ppo_epochs), the overall max number of steps in the algorithm (max_frames), and a container to hold the out-of-sample rewards estimates that we showed how to plot above (test_rewards):

```
ppo_hidden_size           = 32
discriminator_hidden_size = 32
lr                        = 3e-4
num_steps                 = 1000
mini_batch_size           = 50
ppo_epochs                = 5

max_frames  = 100000000
frame_idx   = 0
test_rewards = []
```

First we initialize the discriminator and PPO networks, set a counter for the inner loop for Agent update (i_update), and set up the Pybullet environment:

```
ob = env.reset()
ppo = PPO(lr=lr, num_units=ppo_hidden_size)
discriminator = Discriminator(lr=lr, num_units=discriminator_hidden_size)
i_update = 0
```

At each step, we'll compute a number of timesteps using our current policy, and create a list of these observations, actions, and rewards. At regular intervals, we will plot the results using the functions we described above:

```
while frame_idx < max_frames:
    i_update += 1

    values = []
    obs = []
    acs = []
    rewards = []
    masks = []
    entropy = 0

    for _ in range(num_steps):
```

```python
            ob = tf.reshape(tf.convert_to_tensor(ob), (1,11))
            ac = ppo.get_action(ob)
            ac = tf.reshape(tf.convert_to_tensor(ac), (3, 1))
            next_ob, _, done, _ = env.step(ac)
            reward = discriminator.get_reward(np.concatenate([ob,
                     tf.transpose(ac)], axis=1))
            value = ppo.get_value(ob)
            values.append(value)
            rewards.append(reward)
            masks.append((1-done))

            obs.append(ob)
            acs.append(np.transpose(ac))

            ob = next_ob
            frame_idx += 1

            if frame_idx % 1000 == 0 and i_update > 1:
                test_reward = np.mean([test_env(ppo) for _ in range(10)])
                test_rewards.append(test_reward)
                plot(frame_idx, test_rewards,
                    discriminator.get_reward(policy_ob_ac),
                    discriminator.get_reward(expert_ob_ac))

        next_ob = tf.reshape(tf.convert_to_tensor(next_ob), (1,11))

        next_value = ppo.get_value(next_ob)
        returns = compute_gae(next_value, rewards, masks, values)

        returns = np.concatenate(returns)
        values = np.concatenate(values)
        obs = np.concatenate(obs)
        acs = np.concatenate(acs)
        advantages = returns - values
```

Notice that if our simulation is terminated, we "mask" any observations after completion so that they don't affect our gradient calculation. Also note that we are converting the NumPy data from the sample into tensors using the `tf.convert_to_tensor` and `tf.reshape` functions. We use the `compute_gae` function described above to smooth out the estimated advantage function.

We then periodically (here, every 3 cycles) compute an update to the PPO policy using minibatch updates.

```
# Policy Update
if i_update % 3 == 0:
    ppo.update_policy()
    for _ in range(ppo_epochs):
        for ob_batch, ac_batch, return_batch, adv_batch in ppo_iteration(mini_batch_size, obs, acs, returns, advantages):
            ppo.train_policy(ac_batch, ob_batch, adv_batch,
                return_batch)
```

Finally, we sample an expert trajectory from our previously loaded data in the TRPO policy, concatenate the observations and actions from the expert and new policy, and make a gradient update of the discriminator:

```
# Discriminator Update
expert_samples = np.random.randint(0, mujoco_hopper_np['acs'].\
                                    shape[0], 1)
expert_ob_ac = np.concatenate([
mujoco_hopper_np['obs'][expert_samples,:num_steps,:].reshape(num_steps,11),
mujoco_hopper_np['acs'][expert_samples,:num_steps,:].reshape(num_steps,3)],1)
    policy_ob_ac = np.concatenate([obs, acs], 1)
    discriminator.train_discriminator(np.concatenate([expert_ob_ac,
policy_ob_ac], axis=0))
```

Note that you can observe the hopper being trained in the simulation window while the algorithm is running – the difficulty of finding a mathematical definition of "reward" is shown by the fact that during training, we can see the hopper making creative movements (such as crawling, *Figure 12.11*) that allow it to move in the simulation space (and thus receive reward) but are not like the expert "hopping" motion.

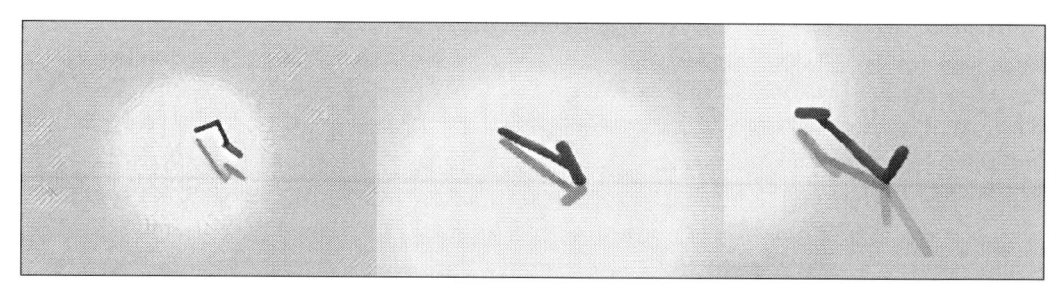

Figure 12.11: Hopper "crawling" during GAIL training

Summary

In this chapter, we explored another application of generative models in reinforcement learning. First, we described how RL allows us to learn the behavior of an agent in an environment, and how deep neural networks allowed Q-learning to scale to complex environments with extremely large observation and action spaces.

We then discussed inverse reinforcement learning, and how it varies from RL by "inverting" the problem and attempting to "learn by example." We discussed how the problem of trying to compare a proposed and expert network can be scored using entropy, and how a particular, regularized version of this entropy loss has a similar form as the GAN problem we studied in *Chapter 6*, called GAIL (Generative Adversarial Imitation Learning). We saw how GAIL is but one of many possible formulations of this general idea, using different loss functions. Finally, we implemented GAIL using the bullet-gym physics simulator and OpenAI Gym.

In the final chapter, we will conclude by exploring recent research in generative AI in diverse problem domains including bioinformatics and fluid mechanics, providing references for further reading as you continue your discovery of this developing field.

References

1. Mnih, V., Kavukcuoglu, K., Silver, D., Graves, A., Antonoglou, I., Wierstra, D., & Riedmiller, M. (2013). *Playing Atari with Deep Reinforcement Learning*. arXiv. https://arxiv.org/abs/1312.5602

2. Bareketain, P. (2019, March 10). Understanding *Stabilising Experience Replay for Deep Multi-Agent Reinforcement Learning*. Medium. https://medium.com/@parnianbrk/understanding-stabilising-experience-replay-for-deep-multi-agent-reinforcement-learning-84b4c04886b5

3. Wikipedia user waldoalverez, under a CC BY-SA 4.0 license (https://creativecommons.org/licenses/by-sa/4.0/).

4. Amit, R., Meir, R., & Ciosek, K. (2020). *Discount Factor as a Regularizer in Reinforcement Learning*. Proceedings of the 37th International Conference on Machine Learning, Vienna, Austria, PMLR 119, 2020. http://proceedings.mlr.press/v119/amit20a/amit20a.pdf

5. Matiisen, T. (2015, December 19). *Demystifying Deep Reinforcement Learning*. Computational Neuroscience Lab. https://neuro.cs.ut.ee/demystifying-deep-reinforcement-learning/

6. Bellman, R.E. (2003) [1957]. *Dynamic Programming*. Dover.

7. Watkins, C.J.C.H. (1989), *Learning from Delayed Rewards* (PDF) (Ph.D. thesis), Cambridge University, http://www.cs.rhul.ac.uk/~chrisw/new_thesis.pdf
8. Sutton, R., & Barto, A. (1998). *Reinforcement Learning: An Introduction.* MIT Press.
9. Melo, F.S. *Convergence of Q-Learning: A simple proof.* http://users.isr.ist.utl.pt/~mtjspaan/readingGroup/ProofQlearning.pdf
10. Watkins, C.J.C.H., & Dayan, P. (1992). *Q-learning.* Machine learning, 8(3-4):279-292
11. Nair, A., Dalal, M., Gupta, A., & Levine, S. (2020). *Accelerating Online Reinforcement Learning with Offline Datasets.* arXiv. https://arxiv.org/abs/2006.09359
12. Sutton, R.S. & Barto A.G. (2018). *Reinforcement Learning: An Introduction* (2nd ed.). MIT Press.
13. Rummery, G.A., & Niranjan, M. (1994). *On-line Q-learning using Connectionist Systems.* Cambridge University Engineering Department.
14. Mnih, V., Kavukcuoglu, K., Silver, D., Graves, A., Antonoglou, I., Wierstra, D., & Riedmiller, M. (2013). *Playing Atari with Deep Reinforcement Learning.* arXiv. https://arxiv.org/abs/1312.5602
15. Silver, D., Huang, A., Maddison, C.J., Guez, A., Sifre, L., van den Driessche, G., Schrittwieser, J., Antonoglou, I., Panneershelvam, V., Lanctot, M., Dieleman, S., Grewe, D., Nham, J., Kalchbrenner, N., Sutskever, I., Lillicrap, T., Leach, M., Kavukcuoglu, K., Graepel, T., & Hassabis, D. (2016). *Mastering the game of Go with deep neural networks and tree search.* Nature 529, 484–489. https://www.nature.com/articles/nature16961
16. Silver, D., Schrittwieser, J., Simonyan, K., Antonoglou, I., Huang, A., Guez, A., Hubert, T., Baker, L., Lai, M., Bolton, A., Chen, Y., Lillicrap, T., Hui, F., Sifre, L., van den Driessche, G., Graepel, T., & Hassabis, D. (2017). *Mastering the game of Go without human knowledge.* Nature 550, 354-359. https://www.nature.com/articles/nature24270
17. Silver, D., Hubert, T., Schrittwieser, J., Antonoglou, I., Lai, M., Guez, A., Lanctot, M., Sifre, L., Kumaran, D., Graepel, T., Lillicrap, T., Simonyan, K., & Hassabis, D. (2017). *Mastering Chess and Shogi by Self-Play with a General Reinforcement Learning Algorithm.* arXiv. https://arxiv.org/abs/1712.01815
18. Vinyals, O., Babuschkin, I., Silver. D. et al. (2019). *Grandmaster level in StarCraft II using multi-agent reinforcement learning.* Nature 575, 350-354. https://www.nature.com/articles/s41586-019-1724-z
19. Pomerleau, D.A. (1991). *Efficient training of artificial neural networks for autonomous navigation.* Neural Computation, 3(1):88-97.

20. Ho, J., & Ermon, S. (2016). *Generative Adversarial Imitation Learning.* arXiv. https://arxiv.org/abs/1606.03476

21. Ross, S., & Bagnell, J.A. (2010). *Efficient Reductions for Imitation Learning.* Proceedings of the Thirteenth International Conference on Artificial Intelligence and Statistics, PMLR 9:661-668

22. Based on a figure from Arora, S., & Doshi, P. (2018). *A Survey of Inverse Reinforcement Learning: Challenges, Methods and Progress.* arXiv. https://arxiv.org/abs/1806.06877

23. Based on a figure from Ziebart, B.D., Maas, A., Bagnell, J.A., & Dey, A.K. (2008). *Maximum Entropy Inverse Reinforcement Learning.* Proceedings of the Twenty-Third AAAI Conference on Artificial Intelligence (2008)

24. Abbeel, P., & Ng, A. Y. (2004). *Apprenticeship learning via inverse reinforcement learning.* In Proc. ICML, 1–8.

25. Jaynes, E. T. (1957). *Information theory and statistical mechanics.* Physical Review 106:620–630.

26. M. Bloem and N. Bambos, *Infinite time horizon maximum causal entropy inverse reinforcement learning,* 53rd IEEE Conference on Decision and Control, 2014, pp. 4911-4916, doi: 10.1109/CDC.2014.7040156. http://citeseerx.ist.psu.edu/viewdoc/download?doi=10.1.1.720.5621&rep=rep1&type=pdf

27. Kramer, G. (1998). *Directed information for channels with feedback.* PhD dissertation, Swiss Federal Institute of Technology, Zurich. http://citeseerx.ist.psu.edu/viewdoc/download;jsessionid=91AB2ACCC7B3CD1372C2BC2EA267ECEF?doi=10.1.1.728.3888&rep=rep1&type=pdf

28. Schulman, J., Levine, S., Moritz, P., Jordan, M.I., & Abbeel, P. (2015). *Trust Region Policy Optimization.* arXiv. https://arxiv.org/abs/1502.05477

29. Ioffe, S., & Szegedy, C. (2015). *Batch Normalization: Accelerating Deep Network Training by Reducing Internal Covariate Shift.* arXiv. https://arxiv.org/abs/1502.03167

30. Schulman, J., Wolski, F., Dhariwal, P., Radford, A., & Klimov, O. (2017). *Proximal Policy Optimization Algorithms.* arXiv. https://arxiv.org/abs/1707.06347

31. Schulman, J., Moritz, P., Levine, S., Jordan, M., & Abbeel, P. (2015). *High-Dimensional Continuous Control Using Generalized Advantage Estimation.* arXiv. https://arxiv.org/abs/1506.02438

13
Emerging Applications in Generative AI

In the preceding chapters, we have examined a large number of applications using generative AI, from generating pictures and text to even music. However, this is a large and ever-expanding field; the number of publications on Google Scholar matching a search for "generative adversarial networks" is 27,200, of which 16,200 were published in 2020! This is astonishing for a field that essentially started in 2014, the exponential growth of which can also be appreciated on the Google n-gram viewer (*Figure 13.1*):

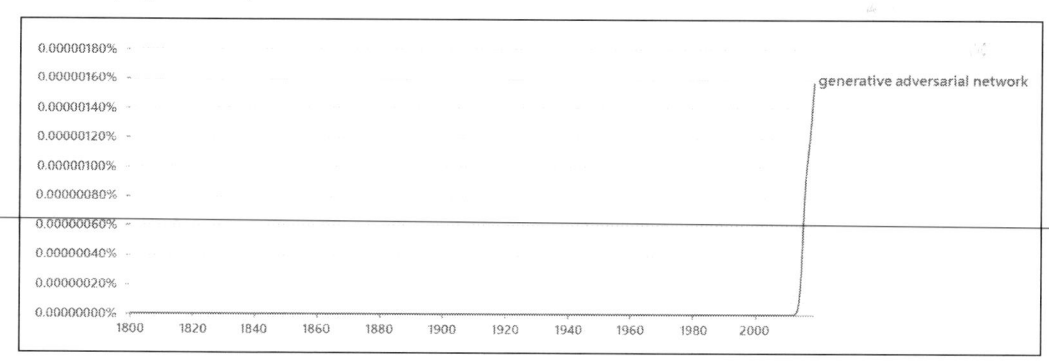

Figure 13.1: Google n-gram of "generative adversarial networks"

As we saw in this volume, generative adversarial networks are only one class of models in the broader field of generative AI, which also includes models such as variational autoencoders, BERT, and GPT-3. As a single book cannot hope to cover all of these areas, we conclude this volume with discussion of a number of emerging topics in this field: drug discovery and protein folding, solving mathematical equations, generating video from images, and generating recipes. Interested readers are encouraged to consult the referenced literature for more detailed discussion of each topic.

Finding new drugs with generative models

One field that we have not covered in this volume in which generative AI is making a large impact is biotechnology research. We discuss two areas: drug discovery and predicting the structure of proteins.

Searching chemical space with generative molecular graph networks

At its base, a medicine – be it drugstore aspirin or an antibiotic prescribed by a doctor – is a *chemical graph* consisting of nodes (atoms) and edges (bonds) (*Figure 13.2*). Like the generative models used for textual data (*Chapters 3, 9, and 10*), graphs have the special property of not being fixed length. There are many ways to encode a graph, including a binary representation based on numeric codes for the individual fragments (*Figure 13.2*) and "SMILES" strings that are linearized representations of 3D molecules (*Figure 13.3*). You can probably appreciate that the number of potential features in a chemical graph is quite large; in fact, the number of potential chemical structures that are in the same size and property range as known drugs has been estimated[1] at 10^{60} – larger even than the number of papers on generative models; for reference, the number of molecules in the observable universe[2] is around 10^{78}.

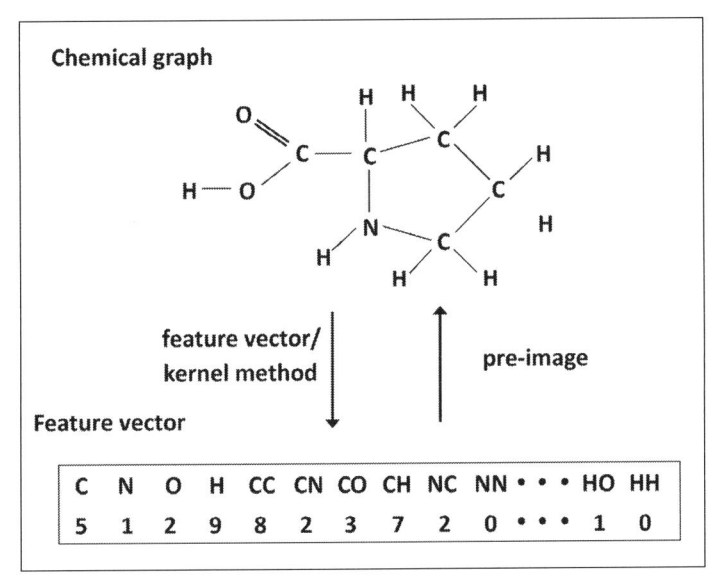

Figure 13.2: The chemical graph[3]

One can appreciate, then, that a large challenge of drug discovery – finding new drugs for existing and emerging diseases – is the sheer size of the potential space one might need to search. While experimental approaches for "drug screening" – testing thousands, millions, or even billions of compounds in high-throughput experiments to find a chemical needle in a haystack with potential therapeutic properties – have been used for decades, the development of computational methods such as machine learning has opened the door for "virtual screening" on a far larger scale. Using modern computational approaches, scientists can test huge libraries of completely virtual compounds for their ability to interact with proteins of interest for disease research. How can a large library of such virtual molecules be generated?

Emerging Applications in Generative AI

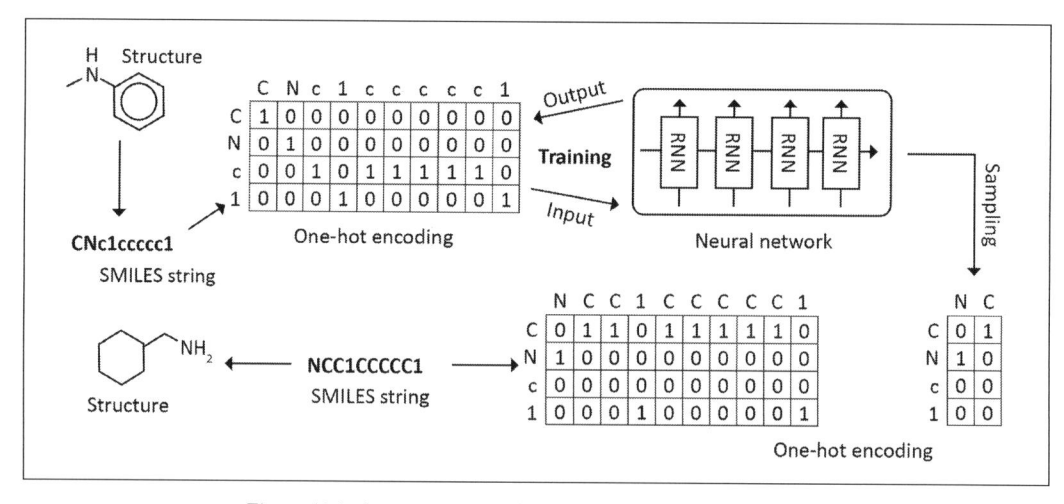

Figure 13.3: A generative model for small molecule generation[6]

Returning to our encoding of the chemical graph, it's probably not surprising that we can use a generative model based on recursive neural networks, such as LSTMs, to sample from the huge space of possible molecular graph configurations. Because molecules follow particular structural motifs, this problem is more complex than simply independently sampling sets of atoms, as they must form a coherent molecule following chemical structural constraints. *Figure 13.3* illustrates what this process might look like; taking a 2D structure, encoding it into binary feature vectors (not unlike how we've seen text represented in earlier chapters), then running these vectors through a recursive neural network to train a model that predicts the next atom or bond based on the prior atoms/bonds in the sequence. Once the model is trained on input data, it can be utilized to generate new molecules by sampling new structures, one at a time, from this generator. Variational autoencoders (*Chapter 5, Painting Pictures with Neural Networks using VAEs*) have also been used to generate molecules[4] (*Figure 13.4*), as have generative adversarial networks[5] (*Figure 13.5*), which we introduced in *Chapter 6, Image Generation with GANs*.

Chapter 13

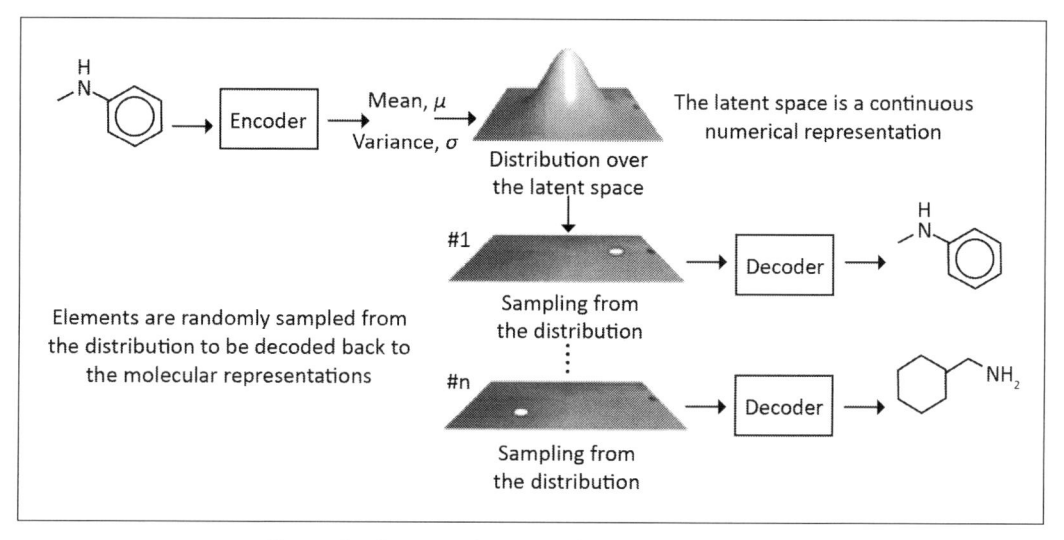

Figure 13.4: Variational autoencoders for small molecules[6]

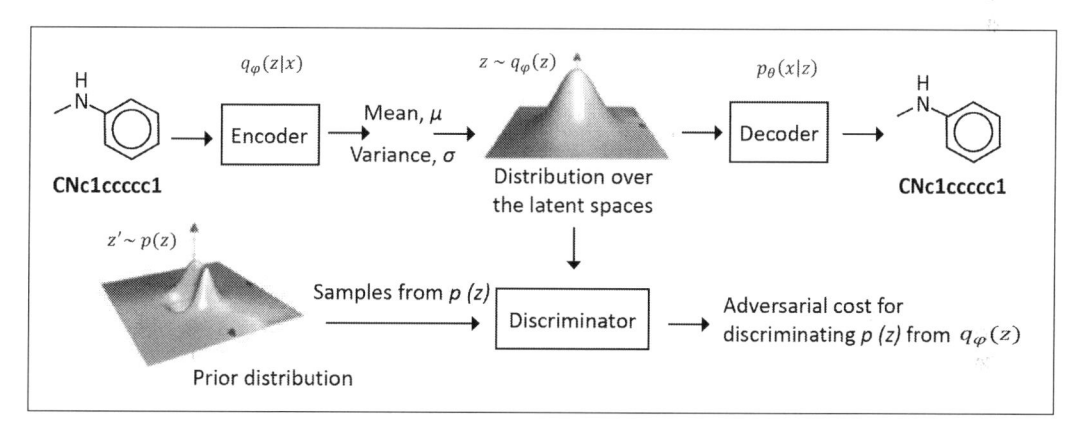

Figure 13.5: Generative adversarial models for small molecules[6]

Folding proteins with generative models

Once we have the set of virtual molecules from such a model, the next challenge is to figure out which, if any, of them have the potential to be drugs. Scientists test this through "virtual docking," in which a large library of simulated molecules are tested to see if they fit in the pockets of protein structures also represented in a computer.

Molecular dynamics simulations are used to approximate the energetic attraction/repulsion between a potential drug and a protein that might affect a disease in the body based on the relative chemical structures of the protein and chemical. A challenge is that these protein structures against which drugs are "docked" in these simulations are typically derived from X-ray crystallography experiments, a painstaking process of diffracting X-rays through a protein structure to obtain a representation of its 3D form.

Further, this process is only applicable to a subset of proteins that are stable in liquid suspension, which excludes a huge number of molecules relevant to disease that are expressed on the surface of the cell, where they are surrounded and stabilized by the fat particles in the cell membrane.

Here, too, generative AI can help: the researchers at DeepMind (a research subsidiary of Google that was also responsible for AlphaGo and other breakthroughs) recently released a program called **AlphaFold** that can solve the 3D structure of proteins directly from their genetic sequence, allowing researchers to bypass the painstaking process of experimental crystallography. *Figure 13.6* illustrates how this is done: first a network is trained to predict the 3D inter-amino acid (the building block of proteins) distances within a protein from its linear sequence code, representing the most likely angles and distances between parts in the folded structure:

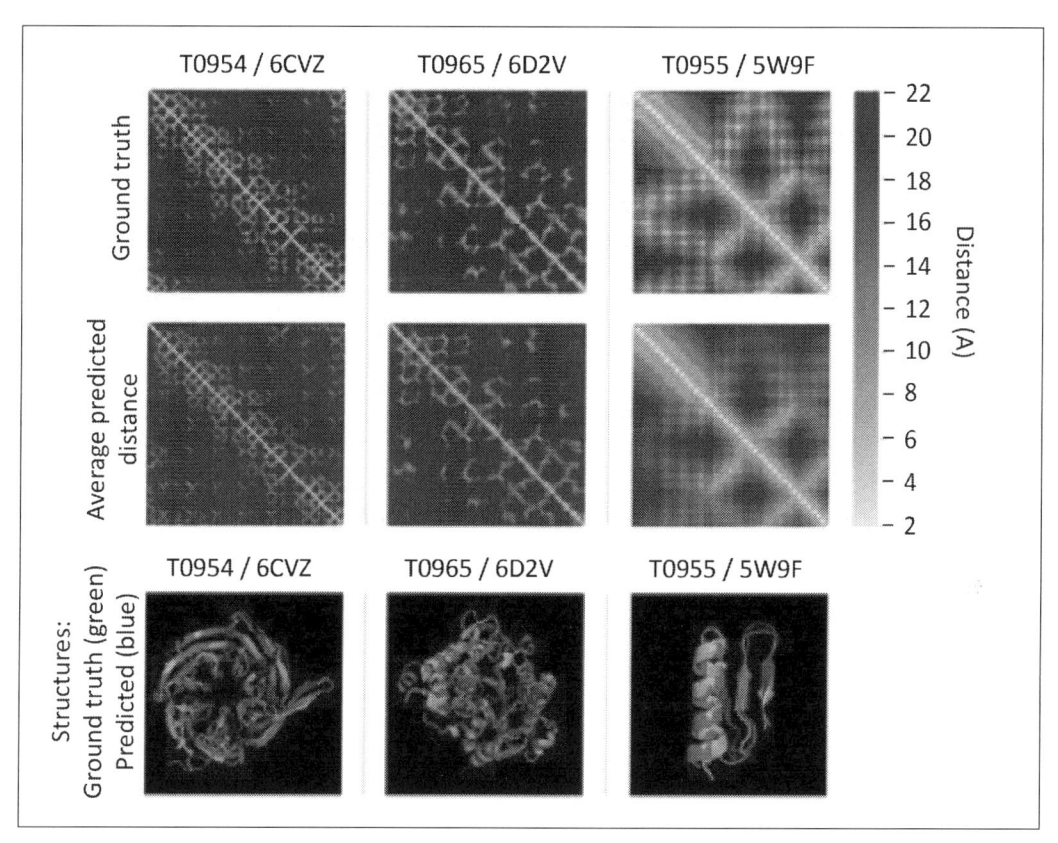

Figure 13.6: Training a neural network to predict the distance between amino acids in a protein sequence[7]

Emerging Applications in Generative AI

Then, for proteins without a structure, AlphaFold proposes new protein fragments using a generative model (*Figure 13.7*), and scores which ones have a high likelihood of forming a stable 3D structure:

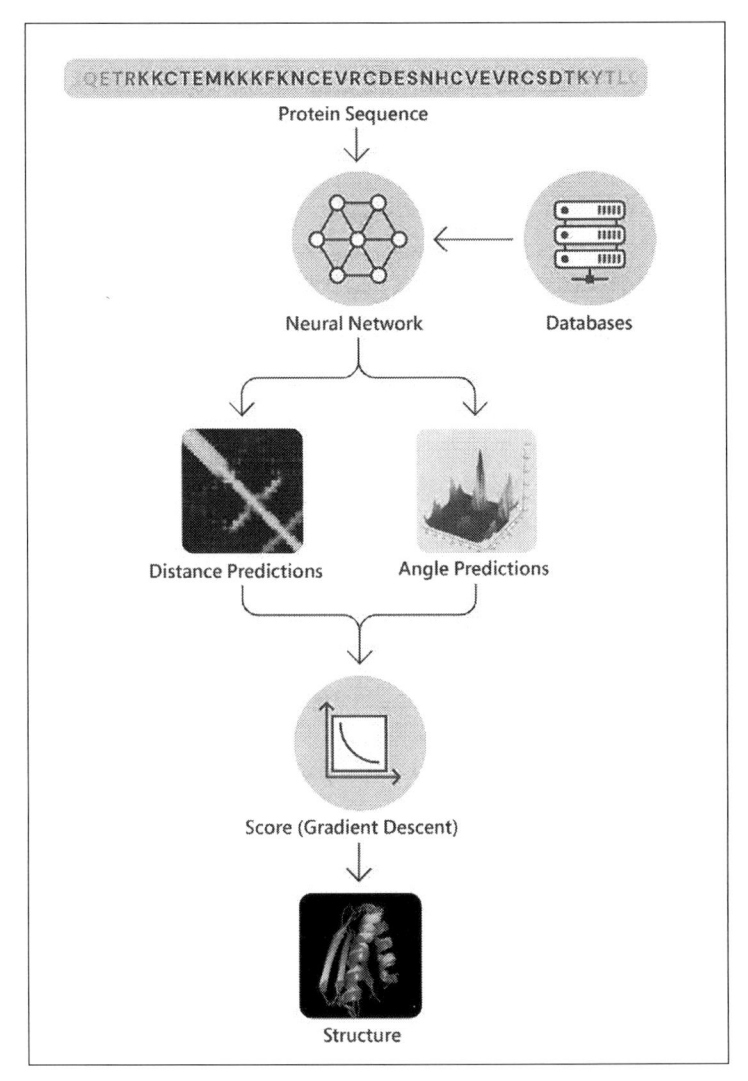

Figure 13.7: Generative model to predict protein conformation[7]

These examples show how it is possible to simulate both drugs and the structure of their potential targets in the human body using generative AI, taking what are difficult or impossible experiments in the real world and harnessing the massive computational capacity of new models to potentially discover new medicines.

Solving partial differential equations with generative modeling

Another field in which deep learning in general, and generative learning in particular, have led to recent breakthroughs is the solution of **partial differential equations** (**PDEs**), a kind of mathematical model used for diverse applications including fluid dynamics, weather prediction, and understanding the behavior of physical systems. More formally, a PDE imposes some condition on the partial derivatives of a function, and the problem is to find a function that fulfills this condition. Usually some set of initial or boundary conditions is placed on the function to limit the search space within a particular grid. As an example, consider Burger's equation,[8] which governs phenomena such as the speed of a fluid at a given position and time (*Figure 13.8*):

$$\frac{\partial u}{\partial t} + u\frac{\partial u}{\partial x} = v\frac{\partial^2 u}{\partial x^2} \quad (1)$$

Where u is speed, t is time, x is a positional coordinate, and v is the viscosity ("oiliness") of the fluid. If the viscosity is 0, this simplifies to the *inviscid* equation:

$$\frac{\partial u}{\partial t} + u\frac{\partial u}{\partial x} = 0 \quad (2)$$

The solution of this equation depends upon the form of the function u and its initial condition at $t=0$; for example, if u is a linear function, it has a closed-form analytical solution (in other words, the solution can be derived using only the manipulation of mathematical formulae and variable substitutions, rather than requiring numerical methods to minimize an error function for potential solutions selection using an algorithm)[9]. In most cases, however, one needs numerical methods, and one popular approach is using **finite element methods** (**FEMs**) to divide the output (x, t) into a "grid" and solve for u numerically within each of those grids. This is analogous to the use of a "basis" set of functions such as cosines and sines (Fourier analysis) or wavelets to decompose complex functions into a sum of simpler underlying functions.[10]

Emerging Applications in Generative AI

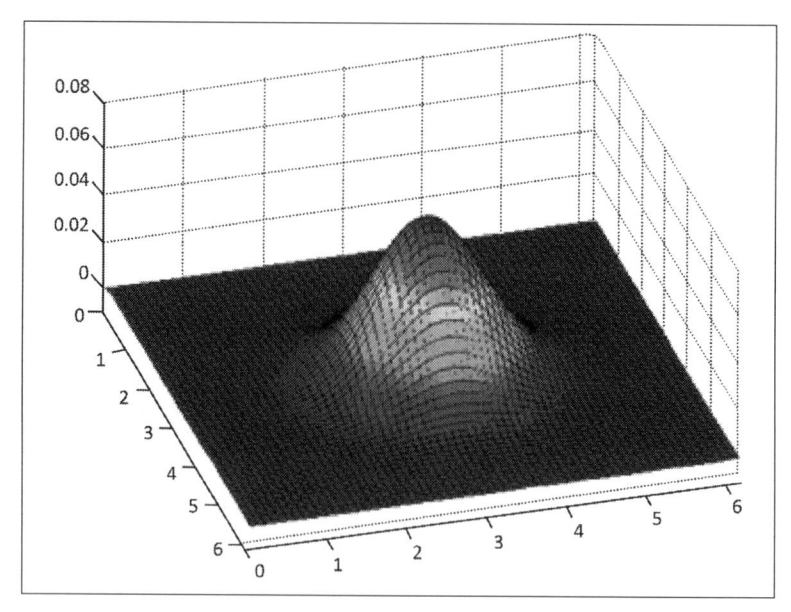

Figure 13.8: A visualization of Burger's equation in two dimensions[11]

However, consider the problem we now have: for a given set of conditions (the boundary conditions), we want to output a function value across a grid, creating a heatmap of the function value at each point in space and time, not unlike an image we've seen in prior generative applications! Indeed, convolutional generative models have been used to map boundary conditions to an output grid (*Figure 13.9*)[12]:

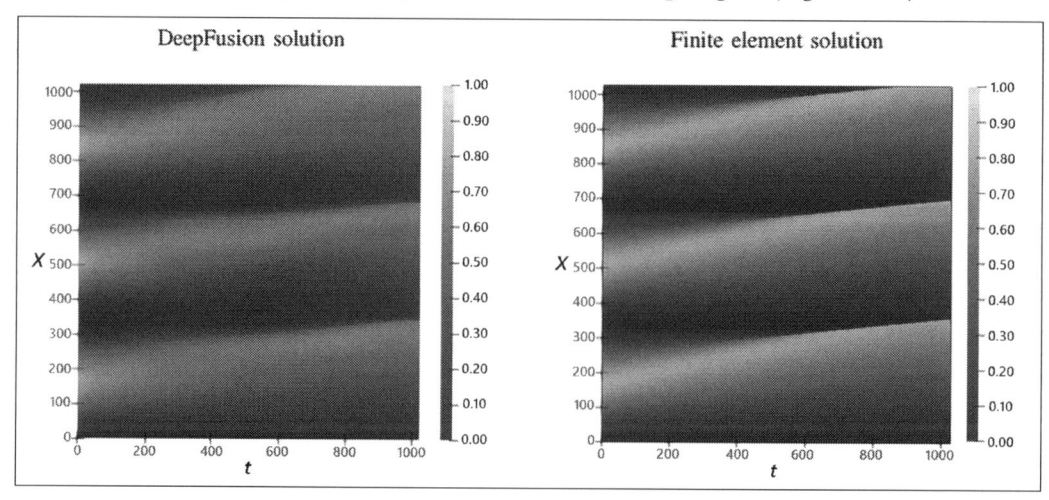

Figure 13.9: Solution of Burger's inviscid equation using FEM methods (right), and deep learning (left)[12]

As described earlier, the typical strategy of using FEM is to solve numerically for u at each element in a grid, where most of the computational burden is from repetitively computing the solution rather than checking it[12]; thus generative AI can operate more efficiently by sampling a large set of possible solutions (with that set constrained by initial conditions or the numerical range of each variable) and checking if they fulfill the conditions of the PDE, completely circumventing the need for solving for the function in each element of the grid. *Figure 13.10* shows how a set of boundary conditions (b) and viscosity variables (v) can be input into a convolutional network that then generates the solution of the PDE.

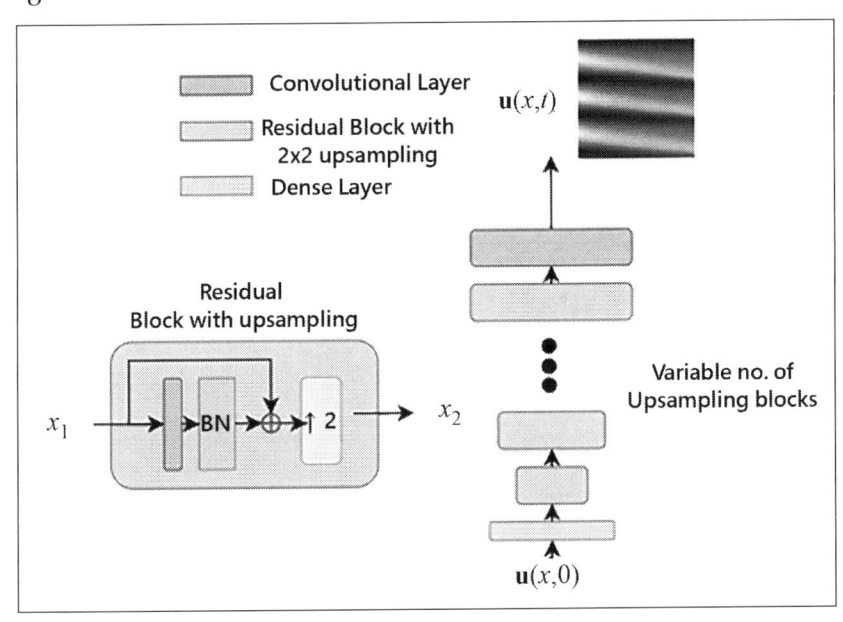

Figure 13.10: DiffNet used to sample potential solutions for Burger's Equation[12]

The network in this example is termed **DiffNet**. It has two terms in its error function; one (L_p, equation 4) encourages the generated grids to match the PDE surface (low error), while the other forces the solution to reproduce the desired boundary conditions on x and t (L_b, equation 5).

$$L = L_p + \lambda L_b, \qquad (3)$$
$$\text{where} \quad L_p(\theta) = E_{b,v}[||A_v(G_\theta(b,v)) - f||_2^2], \qquad (4)$$
$$L_b(\theta) = E_b[||B(G_\theta(b,v)) - b||_2^2]. \qquad (5)$$

Together, these two constraints resemble the other adversarial generative examples we've seen in past chapters; one term tries to minimize error (like the discriminator) while another tries to approximate a distribution (here, the boundary conditions on the variables).

Few shot learning for creating videos from images

In prior chapters, we have seen how GANs can generate novel photorealistic images after being trained on a group of example photos. This technique can also be used to create variations of an image, either applying "filters" or new poses or angles of the base image. Extending this approach to its logical limit, could we create a "talking head" out of a single or a limited set of images? This problem is quite challenging – classical (or deep learning) approaches that apply "warping" transformations to a set of images create noticeable artifacts that degrade the realism of the output [13,14]. An alternative approach is to use generative models to sample potential angular and positional variations of the input images (*Figure 13.11*), as performed by Zakharov et al. in their paper *Few Shot Adversarial Learning of Realistic Neural Talking Head Models*.[15]

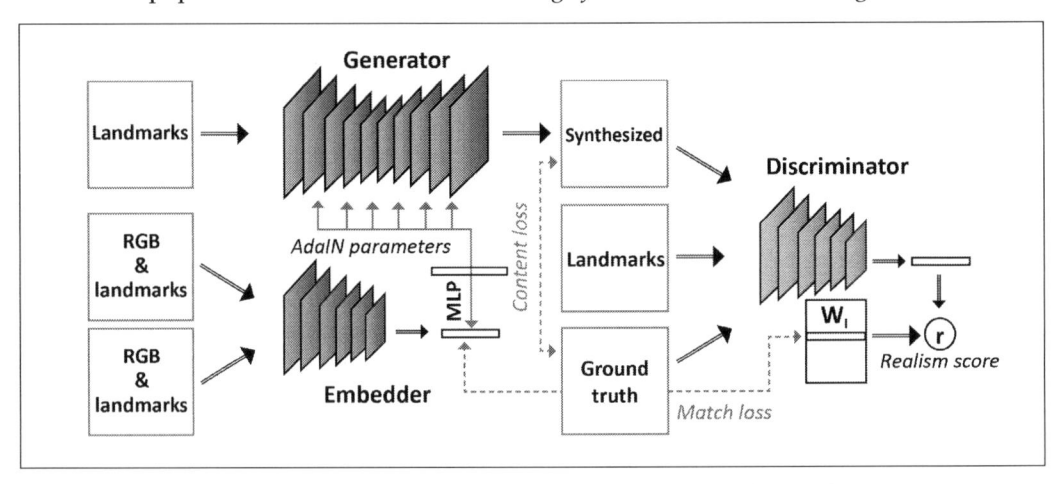

Figure 13.11: Generative architecture for creating moving frames from single images
(based on Zakharov et al., Figure 2.)

This architecture has three networks that process a set of input videos. The first generates embeddings of landmark features (a simplified representation of the face, such as its outline and the location of important features like the eyes and nose), along with the pixels of the original image, into a numerical vector. The second generates novel video frames with this embedding as an input along with the image and landmark data. Finally, the next frame in the video is compared with this generated image via a discriminator.

This is referred to as *few shot* learning because it uses only a small number of video frames to learn to generate new video sequences, which could be unbounded in length. This model can then be applied to input data with only a single example, such as still photos, generating "talking heads" from historical photos, or even paintings such as the Mona Lisa.[16] Readers may refer to the cited paper for sample output.

These "living portraits" are in some way the evolution of deepfakes – rather than copying one image of a moving face to another, lifelike motions are simulated from a picture that had no prior motion data associated with it. Like the portrait auction we discussed in *Chapter 1, An Introduction to Generative AI: "Drawing" Data from Models*, this is an example in which generative AI is truly bringing new art to life.

Generating recipes with deep learning

A final example we will discuss is related to earlier examples in this book, on generating textual descriptions of images using GANs. A more complex version of this same problem is to generate a structured description of an image that has multiple components, such as the recipe for a food depicted in an image. This description is also more complex because it relies on a *particular sequence* of these components (instructions) in order to be coherent (*Figure 13.12*):

Title: Biscuits
Ingredients:
Flour, butter, sugar, egg, milk, salt
Intructions:
- Preheat oven to 450 degrees.
- Cream butter and sugar.
- Add egg and milk.
- Sift flour and salt together.
- Add to creamed mixture.
- Roll out on floured board to 1/4 inch thickness.
- Cut with biscuit cutter.
- Place on ungreased cookie sheet.
- Bake for 10 minutes.

Figure 13.12: A recipe generated from an image of food[17]

As *Figure 13.13* demonstrates, this "inverse cooking" problem has also been studied using generative models[17] (Salvador et al.).

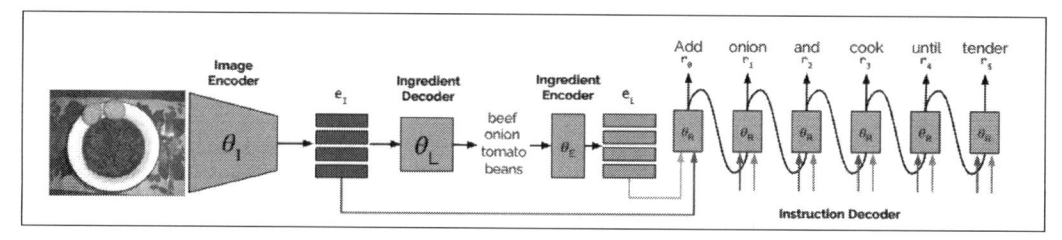

Figure 13.13: Architecture of a generative model for inverse cooking[17]

Like many of the examples we've seen in prior chapters, an "encoder" network receives an image as input, and then "decodes" using a sequence model into text representations of the food components, which are combined with the image embedding to create a set of instructions decoded by a third layer of the network. This "instruction decoder" uses the transformer architecture described in *Chapter 10, NLP 2.0: Using Transformers to Generate Text*, in our discussion of BERT, to apply weighted relevance to different portions of the image and output ingredient list.

Summary

In this chapter, we examined a number of emerging applications of generative models. One is in the field of biotechnology, where they can be used to create large collections of new potential drug structures. Also in the biotechnology field, generative models are used to create potential protein folding structures that can be used for computational drug discovery.

We explored how generative models can be used to solve mathematical problems, in particular PDEs, by mapping a set of boundary conditions of a fluid dynamics equation to a solution grid. We also examined a challenging problem of generating videos from a limited set of input images, and finally generating complex textual descriptions (components and sequences of instructions) from images of food to create recipes.

Well done for reaching the end of the book. As a final summary, let's recap everything we've learned:

- *Chapter 1, An Introduction to Generative AI: "Drawing" Data from Models*: What generative models are
- *Chapter 2, Setting Up a TensorFlow Lab*: How to set up a TensorFlow 2 environment in the cloud
- *Chapter 3, Building Blocks of Deep Neural Networks*: The building blocks of neural network models used in generative AI
- *Chapter 4, Teaching Networks to Generate Digits*: How restricted Boltzmann machines (some of the earliest generative models) can generate hand-drawn digits
- *Chapter 5, Painting Pictures with Neural Networks Using VAEs*: How variational autoencoders can generate images from random data
- *Chapter 6, Image Generation with GANs*: The building blocks of GANs and how they are used to generate high resolution images from random noise
- *Chapter 7, Style Transfer with GANs*: How GANs (CycleGAN and pix2pix) can be leveraged to transfer style from one domain to another
- *Chapter 8, Deepfakes with GANs*: Basic building blocks for deepfakes to generate fake photos and videos
- *Chapter 9, The Rise of Methods for Text Generation*: The basics of language generation using deep learning models
- *Chapter 10, NLP 2.0: Using Transformers to Generate Text*: How transformers and different state-of-the-art architectures (like GPT-x) have revolutionized the language generation and NLP domain in general
- *Chapter 11, Composing Music with Generative Models*: How generative models can be leveraged to generate music from random data
- *Chapter 12, Play Video Games with Generative AI: GAIL*: How generative models can be used to train "agents" that can navigate virtual environments through reinforcement learning
- *Chapter 13, Emerging Applications in Generative AI*: Some exciting emerging applications of generative AI

We hope this book has demonstrated the varied traditional and cutting-edge use cases to which generative modeling is being applied and that you are curious enough to learn more by reading the referenced background, or even trying to implement some of the models yourself!

References

1. Kirkpatrick, P., & Ellis, C. (2004). *Chemical space.* Nature 432, 823. https://www.nature.com/articles/432823a

2. Villanueva, J.C. (2009, July 30). *How Many Atoms Are There in the Universe?* Universe Today. https://www.universetoday.com/36302/atoms-in-the-universe/#:~:text=At%20this%20level%2C%20it%20is,hundred%20thousand%20quadrillion%20vigintillion%20atoms

3. Based on a figure from Akutsu, T., & Nagamochi, H. (2013). *Comparison and enumeration of chemical graphs.* Computational and Structural Biotechnology Journal, Vol. 5 Issue 6

4. Gómez-Bombarelli R., Wei, J. N., Duvenaud, D., Hernández-Lobato, J. M., Sánchez-Lengeling, B., Sheberla, D., Aguilera-Iparraguirre, J., Hirzel, T. D., Adams, R. P., Aspuru-Guzik, A. *Automatic chemical design using a data-driven continuous representation of molecules.* ACS central science 2018, 4, 268-276.

5. Blaschke, T., Olivecrona, M., Engkvist, O., Bajorath, J., Chen, H. *Application of generative autoencoder in de novo molecular design.* Molecular informatics 2018, 37, 1700123.

6. Bian Y., & Xie, X-Q. (2020). *Generative chemistry: drug discovery with deep learning generative models.* arXiv. https://arxiv.org/abs/2008.09000

7. Senior, A., Jumper, J., Hassabis, D., & Kohli, P. (2020, January 15). *AlphaFold: Using AI for scientific discovery.* DeepMind blog. https://deepmind.com/blog/article/AlphaFold-Using-AI-for-scientific-discovery

8. Cameron, M. *Notes on Burgers's equation.* https://www.math.umd.edu/~mariakc/burgers.pdf

9. Chandrasekhar, S. (1943). *On the decay of plane shock waves* (No. 423). Ballistic Research Laboratories.

10. COMSOL Multiphysics Encyclopedia. (2016, March 15). *The Finite Element Method (FEM).* https://www.comsol.com/multiphysics/finite-element-method

11. Wikipedia. (2021, April 14). *Burgers' equation.* https://en.wikipedia.org/wiki/Burgers%27_equation#%20Inviscid_Burgers'_%20equation

12. Botelho, S., Joshi, A., Khara, B., Sarkar, S., Hegde, C., Adavani, S., & Ganapathysubramanian, B. (2020). *Deep Generative Models that Solve PDEs: Distributed Computing for Training Large Data-Free Models.* arXiv. https://arxiv.org/abs/2007.12792

13. Averbuch-Elor, H., Cohen-Or, D., Kopf, J., & Cohen, M.F. (2017). *Bringing portraits to life.* ACM Transactions on Graphics (TOG), 36(6):196

14. Ganin, Y., Kononenko, D., Sungatullina, D., & Lempitsky, V. (2016). *DeepWarp: Photorealistic Image Resynthesis for Gaze Manipulation*. European Conference on Computer Vision, 311-326. Springer.

15. Zakharov, E., Shysheya, A., Burkov, E., & Lempitsky, V. (2019). *Few-Shot Adversarial Learning of Realistic Neural Talking Head Models*. arXiv. `https://arxiv.org/abs/1905.08233`

16. Hodge, M. (2019, May 24). *REALLY SAYING SOMETHING Samsung's 'deepfake' video of a TALKING Mona Lisa painting reveals the terrifying new frontier in fake news*. The Sun. `https://www.thesun.co.uk/news/9143575/deepfake-talking-mona-lisa-samsung/`

17. Salvador, A., Drozdzal, M., Giro-i-Nieto, X., & Romero, A. (2019). *Inverse Cooking: Recipe Generation from Food Images*. arXiv. `https://arxiv.org/abs/1812.06164`

Share your experience

Thank you for taking the time to read this book. If you enjoyed this book, help others to find it. Leave a review at `https://www.amazon.com/dp/1800200889`.

packt.com

Subscribe to our online digital library for full access to over 7,000 books and videos, as well as industry leading tools to help you plan your personal development and advance your career. For more information, please visit our website.

Why subscribe?

- Spend less time learning and more time coding with practical eBooks and Videos from over 4,000 industry professionals
- Learn better with Skill Plans built especially for you
- Get a free eBook or video every month
- Fully searchable for easy access to vital information
- Copy and paste, print, and bookmark content

At www.Packt.com, you can also read a collection of free technical articles, sign up for a range of free newsletters, and receive exclusive discounts and offers on Packt books and eBooks.

Other Books You May Enjoy

If you enjoyed this book, you may be interested in these other books by Packt:

Transformers for Natural Language Processing
Denis Rothman

ISBN: 978-1-80056-579-1

- Use the latest pretrained transformer models
- Grasp the workings of the original Transformer, GPT-2, BERT, T5, and other transformer models
- Create language understanding Python programs using concepts that outperform classical deep learning models
- Use a variety of NLP platforms, including Hugging Face, Trax, and AllenNLP
- Apply Python, TensorFlow, and Keras programs to sentiment analysis, text summarization, speech recognition, machine translations, and more
- Measure the productivity of key transformers to define their scope, potential, and limits in production

Deep Reinforcement Learning with Python – Second Edition

Sudharsan Ravichandiran

ISBN: 978-1-83921-068-6

- Understand core RL concepts including the methodologies, math, and code
- Train an agent to solve Blackjack, FrozenLake, and many other problems using OpenAI Gym
- Train an agent to play Ms Pac-Man using a Deep Q Network
- Learn policy-based, value-based, and actor-critic methods
- Master the math behind DDPG, TD3, TRPO, PPO, and many others
- Explore new avenues such as the distributional RL, meta RL, and inverse RL
- Use Stable Baselines to train an agent to walk and play Atari games

Index

Symbols

3D Guided Fine-Grained Face Manipulation
   reference link 256
3D Morphable Model (3DMM) 256
68-point system 258

A

Actor-Critic network 424-430
Adaptive Gradient (Adagrad) 94
Adaptive Momentum Estimation (ADAM) 95
adversarial imitation 417-419
adversarial learning 417-419
adversarial loss 227
AI applications 2
   discriminative models 3-6
   generative models 3-6
   generative models, implementing 6, 7
AI Winter 75
ALBERT
   reference link 359
AlexNet 87, 88
   architecture 89, 90
AlphaFold 446
Amazon Web Services (AWS) 36
   Kubeflow, installing 44-46
attention 348, 350
   calculating 349
   multi-head self-attention 356, 357
   self-attention 352
audio domain representation 376
autoencoder 265
   architecture 274-277
   dataset preparation 267-274
   face swapper, training 278-280
   results and limitations 280-285
   task definition 267
   using, for face swapping 266
automata theory 69
Azure
   Kubeflow, installing 48, 49

B

backpropagation 75
   in practice 79-81
   limitations 82-84
   with example 76-78
backpropagation through time (BPTT) 92, 323
Bag of Words (BoW) 306-309
Bayes' theorem 10, 11
beam search 330, 331
Bi-Directional Encoder Representations (BERT) model 7, 358, 359
   DistilBERT 359
bidirectional LSTMs 338, 339
blending 280
BookCorpus 360
Borg 36
bottleneck features 265
BoW model
   measure of occurrence 307
   vocabulary 307

C

Canadian Institute for Advanced Research (CIFAR)
   importing 150-153
causal convolutions 342
character-level language model 324-328
chatbot 17

CNN architectures 85, 86
CNN innovations 89
computer-assisted music generation 375
Conditional GANs (CGANs) 184-190
conditional probability 9
contextual embeddings 350, 351
Continuous Bag of Words (CBOW)
    model 311-313
contrastive divergence (CD) 113, 144
    gradient, approximating 113-117
control plane 37
causal convolutions 342
convolutional kernels 86
convolutions 340-343
CycleGAN 266
    overall setup 225-227
    unpaired style transfer 224
CycleGAN implementation 229
    discriminator setup 231, 232
    GAN setup 232, 234
    generator setup 229, 230
    training loop 234-238
cycle loss 228

D

data
    modeling, with Restricted Boltzmann
        Machines (RBM) 111-113
decoding step 329
decoding strategies 329
    beam search 330, 331
    greedy decoding 329
    overview 333-335
    sampling 331, 332
Deep Belief Network (DBN) 117
    creating, with Keras Model API 127-132
Deep Convolutional GAN (DCGAN) 181-183
    vector arithmetic 184
Deep Dream
    reference link 209
DeepFaceLab
    reference link 300
deepfake architecture, challenges 297
    ethical issues 297

deepfake architecture, technical
    challenges 298
    generalization 298
    occlusions 298
    temporal issues 299
deepfakes
    creative and productive, use cases 249, 250
    high-level workflow 263, 264
    malicious, use cases 251
    overview 249
deepfakes, architectures 264
    encoder-decoder (ED) 265
    GANs 265
deepfakes, operation modes 251
    editing techniques 254, 255
    re-enactment techniques 253, 254
    replacement techniques 252, 253
deep learning 12
    recipes, generating with 453, 454
deep models
    reviewing 84
deep music generation 375
deep neural network development 24-27
deep Q-learning 411-413
    examples 412
Deepware
    reference link 298
dependent data 8
DiffNet 451
digit classifier
    creating 13
Directed Acyclic Graph (DAG) 26
DiscoGAN 239-242
discriminative modeling 10, 11
    example 10
discriminator 7
discriminator model 170
DistBelief framework 26
DistilBERT
    reference link 359
distributed representation 310
dlib
    used, for detecting facial landmark 258-260
Docker 32, 33
    commands 33, 34

containers, connecting with
    docker-compose 35, 36
  syntax 33, 34
docker-compose
  reference link 35
  used, for connecting Docker
    containers 35, 36
Dockerfile 33
Docker installation
  reference link 33
Domain Specific Language (DSL) 56
dropout 88
DualGAN 243, 244

E

Earth Mover's (EM) 191
editing techniques 254, 255
Elastic Container Service (ECS) 35
Elastic Kubernetes Services (EKS) 38
  service 44
ELMo architecture 351
encoder-decoder (ED) 265
end-to-end machine learning lab 42
Evidence Lower Bound (ELBO) 145
experience replay technique 411

F

FaceApp 255
Facebook AI Research (FAIR) 319
FaceSwap 299
FaceSwap-GAN 300
Facial Action Coding System (FACS) 255, 256
facial landmark 257
  detecting, with dlib 258-260
  detecting, with MTCNN 260-262
  detecting, with OpenCV 257
FakeApp 297
fake content generation
  3D Morphable Model (3DMM) 256
  Facial Action Coding System (FACS) 255, 256
  facial landmarks 257
  key feature 255
fake news 17
FastText 319, 320
Field Programmable Gate Array (FPGAs) 69
finite element methods (FEM) 449

G

game rules 17
GANimation
  reference link 256
Gated Recurrent Units (GRUs) 322, 339
Gaussian Multilayer Perceptron (MLP) 157
Generative Adversarial Imitation Learning (GAIL) 417
  Actor-Critic network 424-430
  discriminator 430
  executing, on PyBullet Gym 420-424
  training and results 432-437
Generative Adversarial Networks (GANs) 162, 170, 209, 249, 265
  discriminative modeling 10, 11
  discriminator 7
  discriminator model 170
  generator 7
  generator model 171
  improving 181
  maximum likelihood game 174, 175
  non-saturating generator cost 174
  training 172, 173
  vanilla GAN 175-181
Generative Adversarial Networks (GANs), challenges
  evaluation metrics 206
  instability, training 204
  mode collapse 204, 205
  uninformative loss 206
generative models 11, 12, 209
  challenges 18
  drugs, finding with 442
  example 11
  need for 12
  partial differential equations (PDEs), solving with 449-451
  proteins, folding with 446, 448
  taxonomy 168, 169
generative molecular graph networks
  chemical space, searching with 442-444
Generative Pre-Training (GPT) 359, 360
  GPT-2 360-367
  GPT-3 367-369
generator 7
generator model 171

[465]

Gibbs sampling 116
GloVe 317, 318
GLUE
    reference link 359
Google Cloud Platform (GCP) 37, 46
    Kubeflow, installing 46, 47
Google Cloud Storage (GCS) 105
Google Kubernetes Engine (GKE) 38
gradient descent 94
    Adaptive Gradient (Adagrad) 94
    Adaptive Momentum Estimation (ADAM) 95
Graphical Processing Units (GPUs) 18, 69
greedy decoding 329

H

High-Resolution Face Swapping, for Visual Effects
    reference link 256
Hopfield network 109
hyperparameters 59

I

identity loss 228, 229
image encoding
    creating 138-143
images
    generating 13, 14
    videos, creating from 452, 453
image transformation 14-17
independent and identically distributed (IID) 321
independent data 8
Infrastructure as a Service (IaaS) 50
instance normalization 229
Integrated Development Environment (IDE) 30
interpretability 310
Inverse Autoregressive Flow (IAF) 148, 150
inverse reinforcement learning (IRL) 413-417

J

joint probability 9

K

Katib 59
Keras 26
Keras Model API
    used, for creating Deep Belief Network (DBN) 127-132
Kubeflow 39, 42
    components 53, 54
    framework 6
    installing, in AWS 44-46
    installing, in GCP 46, 47
    installing, on Azure 48, 49
    installing, with Terraform 50, 52
    locally executing, with MiniKF 43, 44
Kubeflow Katib
    using, to optimize model hyperparameters 60-62
Kubeflow notebook servers 54, 55
Kubeflow pipelines 55-59
Kubernetes 32, 36
    commands 38, 39
Kubernetes command-line tool (kubectl) 38
    reference link 38
Kubernetes components
    cloud-controller-manager 37
    etcd 37
    kube-api-server 37
    kube-controller-manager 37
    kube-scheduler 37
Kullback-Leibler divergence (KL divergence) 145, 174
Kustomize tool
    for configuration management 39-42
    reference link 40

L

language modeling 322, 323
Latent Semantic Analysis (LSA) 317
lightweight virtualization solution 32
log variance 157
Long Short-Term Memory (LSTM) 92, 93, 320, 322
    bidirectional LSTMs 338, 339
    convolutions, for text 335
    model, for music generation 383, 384
    variants, for text 335

M

Markov Chain Monte Carlo (MCMC) 115
Markov Decision Process (MDP) 407
Markov property 111
maximum entropy 416
mean absolute error (MAE) 276
microservices 35
Microsoft's deepfake detection tool
   reference link 298
MiniKF
   used, for executing Kubeflow locally 43, 44
MNIST database 104, 105
MNIST dataset
   loading, in TensorFlow 105, 106
   retrieving, in TensorFlow 105-107
model hyperparameters
   optimizing, with Kubeflow Katib 60-62
Mujoco framework
   reference link 420
multi-head self-attention 356, 357
Multi joint dynamics with contacts
   (Mujoco) 420
multi-layer perceptron (MLP) 75, 177
Multi-Task Cascaded Convolutional Networks
   (MTCNN) 260
   used, for detecting facial landmark 260-262
MuseGAN 395
   critic model 399, 401
   generators 396-398
   multi-track interdependency 391
   musical texture 391
   results 401
   temporal structure 391
   training 401
music
   representing 376-378
Musical Instrument Digital
   Interface (MIDI) 377
music generation 374-376
music generation, components
   performance generation 375
   score generation 375
music generation, GANs 385
   discriminator network 387
   generator network 386, 387
   results 388, 390
   training 388, 390
music generation,
   for LSTM model 378 383, 384
   dataset preparation 379-382

N

namespaces 39
National Institute of Standards and
   Technology (NIST) 104
network
   creating, from TensorFlow 2.0 153-164
   for sequence data 91
Neural Machine Translation (NMT) 348
neural networks 209
Neural Style Transfer
   reference link 209
Neuron Doctrine 69
nodes 37
non-saturating generator cost 174

O

object-oriented (OO) 25
OpenAI 359
OpenCV
   used, for detecting facial landmark 257
optimizer
   building 93

P

paired style transfer, with pix2pix-GAN 210
   overall loss 219
   Patch-GAN discriminator 216-219
   U-Net generator 211-216
pair-wise style transfer 211
Parameter Server 26
partial differential equations (PDEs)
   solving, with generative modeling 449-451
Patch-GAN discriminator 216-219
perceptron 68
   Gaussian Multilayer Perceptron (MLP) 157
   tuning 73, 74
Persistent Volume (PV) 55

pipelines 55
pix2pix 266
  training 219-223
pix2pix-GAN
  use cases 223
  using, for paired style transfer 210
polyphonic music generation, MuseGAN 391
  composer model 393
  hybrid model 393
  jamming model 392, 393
  temporal model 394, 395
positional encodings 357
principal component analysis (PCA) 139
probability
  rules 7-9
Probability Axioms 8
probability density function (pdf) 158
progressive GAN 196
  equalized learning rate 199
  growth-smooth fade-in 198, 199
  minibatch standard deviation 199
  overall method 196, 197, 198
  pixelwise normalization 200
  TensorFlow Hub implementation 200-203
Proximal Policy Optimization (PPO) policy 427
PyBullet Gym
  GAIL, executing on 420-424

R

recipes
  generating, with deep learning 453, 454
Rectified Linear Unit (ReLU) 79
Recurrent Neural
     Networks (RNNs) 91, 92, 321
re-enactment techniques 253, 254
  expression 253
  gaze 253
  mouth 253
  pose 253
  with pix2pix 286
re-enactment techniques, with pix2pix 286
  dataset preparation 286, 287
  pix2pix GAN, setting up 287-293
  pix2pix GAN, training 288-293
  results and limitations 293-296

REFACE 255
reinforcement learning (RL) 18
  action 406-411
  agents 406-411
  inverse reinforcement learning (IRL) 413-417
  policies 406-411
  rewards 406-411
  spaces 406-411
replacement techniques 252, 253
  swap 252
  transfer 252
replicaset 37
Restricted Boltzmann Machines (RBM)
  contrastive divergence (CD) 113-117
  creating, with TensorFlow Keras
     layers API 120-127
  data, modeling with 111-113
  Hopfield network 109-111
  neural networks, energy equations 109-111
  pixels, generating with statistical
     mechanics 109
  stacking, to generate images 117-119
reverse-mode automatic differentiation 79
RoBERTa
  reference link 359
Robust management of multi-container
     applications 36

S

sampling 331, 332
  temperature parameter 332
  Top-k sampling 333
self-attention 352
Short-Time Fourier Transformation (STFT) 377
skip-gram model 313-317
softmax function 9
sound composition 17
Stacked LSTMs 336, 337
State-Action-Reward-State-Action
     (SARSA) 411
Stochastic Gradient Descent (SGD) 26
style transfer 14-17, 211, 238
Support Vector Machines (SVMs) 104

T

TagLM architecture 351
temperature parameter 332
TensorFlow 6, 24-27
   MNIST dataset, loading 105-108
   MNIST dataset, retrieving 105-108
TensorFlow 2.0 6, 28-30
   network, creating 153-164
TensorFlow Hub
   implementing 200-203
TensorFlow Keras layers API
   used, for creating Restricted Boltzmann
      Machines (RBM) 120-127
Tensor Processing Units (TPUs) 69
Terraform
   reference link 50
   used, for installing Kubeflow 50, 52
text 306, 340-343
   Bag of Words (BoW) 306-309
   representing 306
text generation 320, 322
   character-level language model 324-328
   decoding strategies 329
   language modeling 322, 323
Threshold Logic Unit (TLU) 69-73
Top-k sampling 333
transformer 17, 353
   architectures 353
   multi-head self-attention 356, 357
   overall architecture 353-355
   positional encodings 357
Trust Region Policy Optimization (TRPO) 419

U

ULMFiT model 351
U-Net generator 211-216
unpaired style transfer, with Cycle-GAN 224
   adversarial loss 227
   cycle loss 228
   identity loss 228, 229
   overall loss 229
upsampling block 214

V

vanishing gradients 82
Variational Autoencoder (VAE) 6, 265
   reference link 153
variational inference 118
Variational Lower Bound 145
variational objective 143-147
   reparameterization trick 147, 148
videos
   creating, from images 452, 453
virtual clusters 39
Virtual Machine (VM) 32
Visual Studio Code (VSCode) 31, 32

W

wasserstein GAN 190-195
WebText dataset 361
Wengert Tape 81
Word2vec 311

X

Xavier initialization 96
XLNet
   reference link 359

Z

zero-sum game 172

Made in the USA
Middletown, DE
16 September 2022